1965

This book may be kept

FOURT~ ~~~

A fine c'
the Book

JOHNSON

JOHNSON

PROSE AND POETRY

SELECTED BY MONA WILSON

LONDON
RUPERT HART-DAVIS
1963

First Edition 1950
Second Edition 1957
Third Impression 1963

Printed in Great Britain by Butler & Tanner Ltd., Frome and London

CONTENTS

5

INDEX TO
FIRST LINES OF POEMS

CHRONOLOGICAL TABLE

1709 Born Lichfield, Sept. 18.
1716 School at Lichfield.
1725 School at Stourbridge.
1728 Pembroke College, Oxford.
1731 Leaves Oxford on death of his father.
1732 Usher at Market Bosworth school.
1735 Translation of Lobo. Marries Mrs. Elizabeth Porter. Opens school near Lichfield.
1737 Goes to London with David Garrick.
       Returns to Lichfield, finishes *Irene*. Settles in London.
1738 Writes for *Gentleman's Magazine*. *London, a Poem*.
1741 Begins to write, in *Gentleman's Magazine*, *Reports of the Debates in the Senate of Lilliput*.
1744 *Life of Mr. Richard Savage*.
1747 *Plan of a Dictionary*.
1749 *The Vanity of Human Wishes*. *Irene* produced and published.
1750 First *Rambler*, March 20.
1752 Last *Rambler*, March 14.
1753 Begins to write for *The Adventurer*, March 20.
1755 Letter to Lord Chesterfield, Feb. 7. *A Dictionary of the English Language*, April 15.
1736 *Proposals for Printing the Dramatick Works of William Shakespeare*.
1758 First *Idler*, April 15.
1759 Johnson's mother's death, January. *Rasselas*, April.
1760 Last *Idler*, April 5.
1763 Meets Boswell, May 16.
1764 The Club founded.
1765 *Plays of William Shakespeare*, October.
1770 *The False Alarm*, January.
1773 Scottish travels with Boswell, August to November.
1775 *Journey to the Western Islands of Scotland*, January. D.C.L., Oxford.
1779–81 *Prefaces . . . to the Works of the English Poets*.
1784 Johnson's death, Dec. 13.

INTRODUCTION

I SHALL say nothing of Johnson's life. No one should read even a selection from his writings who is not already familiar with the man. Boswell must come first. This is not to say that he is greater than his writings, or that they are only interesting because he wrote them, but that they are the utterance of the whole man: no one else could have written them. There is no disparity between himself and his work: he has not been mysteriously chosen as the vehicle for expressing something inexplicably greater than and different from himself. The man and his writings are one. To read them without knowing him—and, thanks to Boswell, he can be known better than any of the dead, better than most of the living —is to miss the vivifying power of his personality. He is often dull: unless you know him much of his writing is dead as well as dull. Many of his pages were written for bread, many in sorrow and despair, all of them in the torture of a melancholy, which he may hold off for a time but never dispels. It would be a weary if not an impossible task to read the whole of Johnson's writings without the support of a personal sympathy. His prejudices and limitations exasperate the stranger: he must be your friend before you can be tolerant and amused. Often—and most often when he is at ease and at his best—he leaves off writing, and begins to talk. You must hear the "slow deliberate utterance" and the puffings by which it is punctuated: you must be ready to sit at his feet: resent his didacticism and you may as well close the book.

I have tried, so far as space allows, to include in this edition the work of Johnson which his disciples and friends want to read most frequently, assuming that they are ready to meet him in all his moods, listen patiently to the moralizings with which he strengthens himself to face the excess of misery over happiness in human life, bear with his prejudices, literary and political, and enjoy his trips into fiction, records of the genuine but deliberate interest in his fellow creatures with which he sought to distract himself from his own woes. My choice is unlikely to satisfy any devotee of Johnson: let such a critic reflect that when the author and the man are one

9

it is difficult to survey his writings with complete detachment: no selection from Johnson's work could be altogether impersonal.

Lovers of Johnson will share my gratitude to Mr. John Crow for his indefatigable revision of the selected texts.

Johnson would assuredly have given his approval to *A Shropshire Lad*. I have therefore asked Mr. G. M. Young to add a note on *A Short Song of Congratulation* (p. 948).

MONA WILSON

ACKNOWLEDGMENT

I desire to record my gratitude to the Huntington Library of California and to the Oxford University Press for permission to print texts of which they own manuscript or copyright.　　　　M. W.

NOTE ON THE TEXT

THE extracts in this selection are arranged, as nearly as possible, in the order in which they were written. Parts of a series, such as the essays in *The Rambler*, have been grouped together; the *Life of Savage* was originally published in 1744; it was in 1779 included in the *Lives of the Poets*. In this selection it is not placed with the other, later-written lives.

The texts are, with three exceptions, the earliest available. Johnson altered and revised, as new editions were prepared. Whether his alterations were always improvements is a matter for argument; textual variations between edition and edition are often to be attributed rather to printing-house custom than to Johnson's second thoughts. Johnson's thoughts, second, third, and fourth, are difficult to track. The second and third editions of the Dictionary contain corrections to the preface: they are clearly author's corrections and some of them are obviously desirable. The fourth edition is the last corrected by Johnson, but it is evident that he made the corrections for this in a copy of the first edition and failed to incorporate some of the improvements of the second and third editions. This selection uses the text of the fourth edition. Editions other than the first have been used for the *Life of Savage* (second) and *Rasselas* (second).

The reproduction of the contemporary texts deprives this selection of any consistency in spelling, capitalisation, punctuation and so forth. In some pieces, the initials of substantive nouns will be found to be capitals; in others, they are lower-case letters. The present edition does not follow the eighteenth-century custom of placing quotation-marks at the beginning of every line of a quoted speech.

Patent misprints have been silently corrected. Two curious ones may here be noted, both from *The Rambler*. In number 87, the 1751 edition reads "Manners by Actions of Justice", which is corrected in 1752 to "manners by axioms of justice". Similarly the 1751 reading in number 89, "before their Approaches perceived", is corrected in 1752 to "before their approach is perceived". These errors, if they were found in an Elizabethan dramatic text, would be classified as "bad-quarto errors"; in the twentieth century they would be interpreted as evidence that the author used a dictaphone.

Omissions, in this edition, of a word or words in the early edition from which the text is taken, are indicated either by three dots in the line or a row of dots.

The fact that the beginning or ending of a selected passage is not the beginning or ending of the original entire piece of Johnson's writing is not indicated. When italic side-heads are used, they do not derive from original editions but have been inserted by the editor or the preparer of the text.

Each selected piece in this book is preceded by a textual note. The responsibility for these notes is mine.

For much assistance and many kindnesses received, I desire to give thanks. The staff of the North Library of the British Museum has displayed its customary tact, erudition and zeal. The authorities of the University of London Library have graciously borne with all my demands. Messrs. McLeish of Little Russell Street, London, lent me a copy of the first edition of *A Journey to the Western Islands*. Other loans were made to me by Mr. John Carter.

No man who labours on the text of Johnson can say how much he owes to the *Bibliography of Samuel Johnson* by W. P. Courtney and D. Nichol Smith, to the edition of Johnson's poems by Nichol Smith and E. L. McAdam, and to many of the writings of A. T. Hazen and of R. W. Chapman. Dr. Chapman has, apart from the guidance of his printed words, been a most kind and courteous replier to questions. Mr. F. S. Ferguson has never failed to give me assistance by word of mouth.

JOHN CROW

Note To Second Edition

THIS edition had already gone to press when Professor Arthur Sherbo of Illinois, in the *Johnsonian News Letter*, pointed out that the note on Edmund's speech in *King Lear*, "This is the excellent foppery of the world", pp. 589f. below, was not written by Johnson but by Warburton. He explained that owing to the omission of Warburton's name from the first three editions of Johnson's *Shakespeare*, it has always since been assumed that the note was Johnson's own.

J. C.

PREFACE

TO THE TRANSLATION OF

FATHER LOBO'S VOYAGE
TO ABYSSINIA

Johnson's translation of Lobo was published in 1735.
I have taken the text from the two British Museum
copies of the first edition (279. c. 5. and 978. k. 19.).

PREFACE

TO THE TRANSLATION OF

FATHER LOBO'S VOYAGE

TO ABYSSINIA

THE following Relation is so Curious and Entertaining, and the Dissertations that Accompany it so Judicious and Instructive, that the Translator is confident his Attempt stands in need of no Apology, whatever Censures may fall on the Performance.

The *Portuguese* Traveller, contrary to the general Vein of his Countrymen, has amused his Reader with no Romantick Absurdities or Incredible Fictions, whatever he relates, whether true or not, is at least probable, and he who tells nothing exceeding the bounds of probability, has a right to demand, that they should believe him, who cannot contradict him.

He appears by his modest and unaffecting Narration to have described Things as he saw them, to have copied Nature from the Life, and to have consulted his Senses not his Imagination; He meets with no *Basilisks* that destroy with their Eyes, his *Crocodiles* devour their Prey without Tears, and his *Cataracts* fall from the Rock without Deafening the Neighbouring Inhabitants.

The Reader will here find no Regions cursed with irremediable Barrenness, or bless'd with Spontaneous Fecundity, no perpetual Gloom or unceasing Sunshine ; nor are the Nations here described either devoid of all Sense of Humanity, or consummate in all private and social Virtues, here are no *Hottentots* without Religion, Polity, or Articulate Language, no *Chinese* perfectly Polite, and compleatly skill'd in all Sciences : He will discover, what will always be discover'd by a diligent and impartial Enquirer, that wherever Human Nature is to be found, there is a mixture of Vice and Virtue, a contest of Passion and Reason, and that the Creator doth not appear Partial in his Distributions, but has balanced

15

in most Countries their particular Inconveniences by particular Favours.

In his Account of the Mission, where his Veracity is most to be suspected, He neither exaggerates overmuch the Merits of the Jesuits, if we consider the partial Regard paid by the *Portuguese* to their Countrymen, by the *Jesuits* to their Society, and by the *Papists* to their Church, nor aggravates the Vices of the *Abyssins*; but if the Reader will not be satisfied with a Popish Account of a Popish Mission, he may have recourse to the History of the Church of *Abyssinia*, written by Dr. *Geddes*, in which he will find the Actions and Sufferings of the Missionaries placed in a different Light, though the same in which Mr. *Le Grand*, with all his Zeal for the Roman Church, appears to have seen them.

This Learned Dissertator, however valuable for his Industry and Erudition, is yet more to be esteem'd for having dared so freely in the midst of *France* to declare his Disapprobation of the Patriarch *Oviedo*'s sanguinary Zeal, who was continually importuning the *Portuguese* to beat up their Drums for Missionaries, who might preach the Gospel with Swords in their Hands, and propagate by Desolation and Slaughter the true Worship of the God of Peace.

It is not easy to forbear reflecting with how little Reason these Men profess themselves the Followers of JESUS, who left this great Characteristick to his Disciples, that they should be known *by loving one another*, by universal and unbounded Charity and Benevolence.

Let us suppose an Inhabitant of some remote and superiour Region, yet unskill'd in the Ways of Men, having read and considered the Precepts of the Gospel, and the Example of our Saviour, to come down in search of the *True Church*: If he would not enquire after it among the Cruel, the Insolent, and the Oppressive; among those who are continually grasping at Dominion over Souls as well as Bodies; among those who are employed in procuring to themselves impunity for the most enormous Villanies, and studying methods of destroying their Fellow-creatures, not for their Crimes but their Errors; if he would not expect to meet *Benevolence* engaged in Massacres, or to find *Mercy* in a Court of Inquisition, he would not look for the *True Church* in the Church of *Rome*.

Mr. *Le Grand* has given in one Dissertation an Example of great Moderation, in deviating from the Temper of his Religion, but in the others has left Proofs, that Learning and Honesty are often too

16

weak to oppose Prejudice. He has made no scruple of preferring the Testimony of Father *du Bernat*, to the Writings of all the Portuguese Jesuits, to whom he allows great Zeal, but little Learning, without giving any other Reason than that his Favourite was a Frenchman. This is writing only to Frenchmen and to Papists: A Protestant would be desirous to know why he must imagine that Father *du Bernat* had a cooler Head or more Knowledge; and why one Man whose account is singular, is not more likely to be mistaken than many agreeing in the same Account.

If the *Portuguese* were byass'd by any particular Views, another byass equally powerful may have deflected the Frenchman from the Truth, for they evidently write with contrary Designs; the *Portuguese*, to make their Mission seem more necessary, endeavour'd to place in the strongest light the Differences between the *Abyssinian* and *Roman* Church, but the Great *Ludolfus* laying hold on the Advantage, reduced these later Writers to prove their Conformity.

Upon the whole, the Controversy seems of no great Importance to those who believe the Holy Scriptures sufficient to teach the way of Salvation, but of whatever Moment it may be thought, there are not proofs sufficient to decide it.

His Discourses on indifferent Subjects, will divert as well as instruct, and if either in these or in the Relation of Father *Lobo*, any Argument shall appear unconvincing, or description obscure, they are defects incident to all Mankind, which, however, are not too rashly to be imputed to the Authors, being, sometimes, perhaps more justly chargeable on the Translator.

In this Translation (if it may be so call'd) great Liberties have been taken, which, whether justifiable or not, shall be fairly confess'd, and let the Judicious part of Mankind pardon or condemn them.

In the first part the greatest Freedom has been used, in reducing the Narration into a narrow Compass, so that it is by no Means a Translation but an Epitome, in which whether every thing either useful or entertaining be comprised, the compiler is least qualified to determine.

In the account of *Abyssinia*, and the Continuation, the Authors have been follow'd with more exactness, and as few Passages appeared either insignificant or tedious, few have been either shortened or omitted.

The Dissertations are the only part in which an exact Translation has been attempted, and even in those, Abstracts are sometimes given instead of literal Quotations, particularly in the first; and sometimes other parts have been contracted.

Several Memorials and Letters, which are printed at the end of the Dissertations to secure the credit of the foregoing Narrative, are entirely left out.

'Tis hoped, that, after this Confession, whoever shall compare this Attempt with the Original, if he shall find no Proofs of Fraud or Partiality, will candidly overlook any failure of Judgment.

SELECTIONS FROM
DEBATES IN THE SENATE
OF LILLIPUT

The text of Johnson's versions of Pitt's speeches has been taken from *The Gentleman's Magazine*, November, 1741 (vol. 11, p. 563, col. 1, and p. 569, col. 1, to p. 570, col. 2.).

SELECTIONS FROM

DEBATES IN THE SENATE OF LILLIPUT

The Urg; Ptit spoke to the following Purport. *SIR*, It is common for those to have the greatest Regard to their own Interest who discover the least for that of others. I do not, therefore, despair of recalling the Advocates of this Bill from the Prosecution of their favourite Measures by Arguments of greater Efficacy than those which are founded on Reason and Justice.

Nothing, Sir, is more evident, than that some Degree of Reputation is absolutely necessary to Men who have any Concern in the Administration of a Government like ours; they must either secure the Fidelity of their Adherents by the Assistance of Wisdom, or of Virtue; their Enemies must either be awed by their Honesty, or terrified by their Cunning. Mere artless Bribery will never gain a sufficient Majority to set them entirely free from Apprehensions of Censure. To different Tempers different Motives must be applied: Some, who place their Felicity in being accounted Wise, are in very little Care to preserve the Character of Honesty; others may be persuaded to join in Measures which they easily discover to be weak and ill-concerted, because they are convinced that the Authors of them are not corrupt but mistaken, and are unwilling that any Man should be punished for natural Defects or casual Ignorance.

I cannot say, Sir, which of these Motives influence the Advocates for the Bill before us; a Bill in which such Cruelties are proposed as are yet unknown among the most savage Nations, such as Slavery has not yet borne, or Tyranny invented, such as cannot be heard without Resentment, nor thought of without Horror.

It is, Sir, perhaps, not unfortunate, that one more Expedient has been added rather ridiculous than shocking, and that these

Tyrants of the Administration, who amuse themselves with oppressing their Fellow Subjects, who add without Reluctance one Hardship to another, invade the Liberty of those whom they have already overborn with Taxes, first plunder and then imprison, who take all Opportunities of Heightening the publick Distresses, and make the Miseries of War the Instruments of new Oppressions, are too ignorant to be formidable, and owe their Power not to their Abilities, but to casual Prosperity, or to the Influence of Money.

The other Clauses of this Bill complicated at once with Cruelty and Folly, have been treated with becoming Indignation; but this may be considered with less Ardour of Resentment, and fewer Emotions of Zeal, because, tho' perhaps equally iniquitous, it will do no Harm; for a Law that can never be executed can never be felt.

That it will consume the Manufacture of Paper and swell the Books of Statutes, is all the Good or Hurt that can be hoped or fear'd from a Law like this; a Law which fixes what is in its own Nature mutable, which prescribes Rules to the Seasons and Limits to the Wind.

I am too well acquainted, Sir, with the Disposition of its two chief Supporters, to mention the Contempt with which this Law will be treated by Posterity, for they have already shewn abundantly their Disregard of succeeding Generations; but I will remind them, that they are now venturing their whole Interest at once, and hope they will recollect before it is too late that those who believe them to intend the Happiness of their Country will never be confirmed in their Opinion by open Cruelty and notorious Oppression; and that those who have only their own Interest in View, will be afraid of adhering to those Leaders, however old and practised in Expedients, however strengthen'd by Corruption, or elated with Power, who have no reason to hope for Success from either their Virtue or Abilities.

. . . . .

The Urg; Ptit *replied. SIR*, The atrocious Crime of being a young Man, which the honourable Gentleman has with such Spirit and Decency charged upon me, I shall neither attempt to palliate, nor deny, but content myself with wishing that I may be one of those whose Follies may cease with their Youth, and not of that Number, who are ignorant in spite of Experience.

Whether Youth can be imputed to any Man as a Reproach, I will not, Sir, assume the Province of determining; but surely Age may become justly contemptible, if the Opportunities which it brings have past away without Improvement, and Vice appears to prevail when the Passions have subsided. The Wretch that, after having seen the Consequences of a thousand Errors, continues still to blunder, and whose Age has only added Obstinacy to Stupidity, is surely the Object of either Abhorrence or Contempt, and deserves not that his grey Head should secure him from Insults.

Much more, Sir, is he to be abhorr'd, who, as he has advanced in Age, has receded from Virtue, and becomes more wicked with less Temptation; who prostitutes himself for Money which he cannot enjoy, and spends the Remains of his Life in the Ruin of his Country.

But Youth, Sir, is not my only Crime; I have been accused of acting a theatrical Part—A theatrical Part may either imply some Peculiarities of Gesture, or a Dissimulation of my real Sentiments, and an Adoption of the Opinions and Language of another Man.

In the first Sense, Sir, the Charge is too trifling to be confuted, and deserves only to be mentioned, that it may be despised. I am at Liberty, like every other Man, to use my own Language; and though I may perhaps have some Ambition to please this Gentleman, I shall not lay myself under any Restraint, nor very sollicitously copy his Diction, or his Mien, however matured by Age, or modelled by Experience.

If any Man shall by charging me with theatrical Behaviour imply, that I utter any Sentiments but my own, I shall treat him as a Calumniator, and a Villian; nor shall any Protection shelter him from the Treatment which he deserves. I shall, on such an Occasion, without Scruple, trample upon all those Forms with which Wealth and Dignity intrench themselves, nor shall any Thing but Age restrain my Resentment; Age, which always brings one Privilege, that of being insolent and supercilious without Punishment.

But, with Regard, Sir, to those whom I have offended, I am of Opinion, that if I had acted a borrowed Part, I should have avoided their Censure; the Heat that offended them is the Ardour of Conviction, and that Zeal for the Service of my Country, which neither Hope nor Fear shall influence me to suppress. I will not sit unconcerned while my Liberty is invaded, nor look in Silence upon publick Robbery.—I will exert my Endeavours at whatever Hazard, to repel the Aggressor, and drag the Thief to Justice, whoever may

23

protect them in their Villany, and whoever may partake of their Plunder.—And if the Honourable Gentleman——

Here the Urg; Wintinnong call'd to Order, and Urg; Ptit sitting down, he spoke thus.

It is necessary, Sir, that the Order of this Assembly be observed, and the Debate resumed without personal Altercations. Such Expressions as have been vented on this Occasion, become not an Assembly entrusted with the Liberty and Welfare of their Country. To interrupt the Debate on a Subject so important as that before us, is, in some measure to obstruct the publick Happiness, and violate our Trust: But much more heinous is the Crime of exposing our Determinations to Contempt, and inciting the People to suspicion or Mutiny, by indecent Reflections, or unjust Insinuations.

I do not, Sir, undertake to decide the Controversy between the two Gentlemen, but must be allowed to observe, that no Diversity of Opinion can justify the Violation of Decency, and the Use of rude and virulent Expressions; Expressions dictated only by Resentment, and uttered without Regard to——

Here the Urg; Ptit called to Order, and said.

SIR,

If this be to preserve Order, there is no Danger of Indecency from the most licentious Tongue; for what Calumny can be more atrocious, or what Reproach more severe, than that of speaking with Regard to any thing but Truth. Order may sometimes be broken by Passion, or Inadvertency, but will hardly be reestablish'd by Monitors like this, who cannot govern his own Passion, whilst he is restraining the Impetuosity of others.

Happy, Sir, would it be for Mankind, if every one knew his own Province; we should not then see the same Man at once a Criminal and a Judge. Nor would this Gentleman assume the Right of dictating to others what he has not learned himself.

That I may return in some Degree the Favour which he intends me, I will advise him never hereafter to exert himself on the Subject of Order; but whenever he finds himself inclined to speak on such Occasions, to remember how he has now succeeded, and condemn in Silence what his Censures will never reform.

LONDON: A POEM

—Quis ineptæ
Tam patiens Urbis, tam ferreus ut teneat se ?
Juv.

The text is printed from the British Museum copy of the first edition, 1738 (162. n. 14.), checked by the Museum copy of the second folio edition, 1738 (11630. h. 30.). The early editions read, in line 14 of page 29, *H——y*'s Jest.

LONDON:

A POEM,

IN IMITATION OF THE

THIRD SATIRE OF JUVENAL

Tho' Grief and Fondness in my Breast rebel,
When injur'd THALES bids the Town farewell,
Yet still my calmer Thoughts his Choice commend,
I praise the Hermit, but regret the Friend,
Who now resolves, from Vice and LONDON far,
To breathe in distant Fields a purer Air,
And, fix'd on CAMBRIA's solitary Shore,
Give to St DAVID one *true Briton* more.

For who would leave, unbrib'd, *Hibernia*'s Land,
Or change the Rocks of *Scotland* for the *Strand*?
There none are swept by sudden Fate away,
But all whom Hunger spares, with Age decay:
Here Malice, Rapine, Accident, conspire,
And now a Rabble rages, now a Fire;
Their Ambush here relentless Ruffians lay,
And here the fell Attorney prowls for Prey;
Here falling Houses thunder on your Head,
And here a female Atheist talks you dead.

While THALES waits the Wherry that contains
Of dissipated Wealth the small Remains,
On *Thames*'s Banks, in silent Thought we stood,
Where GREENWICH smiles upon the silver Flood:
Struck with the Seat that gave ELIZA* Birth,

* Q. Elizabeth *born at* Greenwich.

27

We kneel, and kiss the consecrated Earth;
In pleasing Dreams the blissful Age renew,
And call BRITANNIA's Glories back to view;
Behold her Cross triumphant on the Main,
The Guard of Commerce, and the Dread of *Spain*,
Ere Masquerades debauch'd, Excise oppress'd,
Or *English* Honour grew a standing Jest.

    A transient Calm the happy Scenes bestow,
And for a Moment lull the Sense of Woe.
At length awaking, with contemptuous Frown,
Indignant THALES eyes the neighb'ring Town.

⊦ Since Worth, he cries, in these degen'rate Days,
Wants ev'n the cheap Reward of empty Praise;
In those curst Walls, devote to Vice and Gain;
Since unrewarded Science toils in vain;
Since Hope but sooths to double my Distress,
And ev'ry Moment leaves my Little less;
While yet my steady Steps no Staff sustains,
And Life still vig'rous revels in my Veins;
Grant me, kind Heaven, to find some happier Place,
Where Honesty and Sense are no Disgrace;
Some pleasing Bank where verdant Osiers play,
Some peaceful Vale with Nature's Paintings gay;
Where once the harrass'd BRITON found Repose,
And safe in Poverty defy'd his Foes;
Some secret Cell, ye Pow'rs, indulgent give,
Let —— live here, for —— has learn'd to live.
Here let those reign, whom Pensions can incite
To vote a patriot Black, a Courtier white;
Explain their Country's dear-bought Rights away,
And plead for Pirates in the Face of Day;
With slavish Tenets taint our poison'd Youth,
And lend a Lye the Confidence of Truth.

    Let such raise Palaces, and Manors buy,
Collect a Tax, or farm a Lottery;
With warbling Eunuchs fill our silenc'd Stage,
And lull to Servitude a thoughtless Age.

Heroes, proceed! What Bounds your Pride shall hold?
What Check restrain your Thirst of Pow'r and Gold?
Behold rebellious Virtue quite o'erthrown,
Behold our Fame, our Wealth, our Lives your own.

To such the Plunder of a Land is giv'n,
When publick Crimes inflame the Wrath of Heav'n:
But what, my Friend, what Hope remains for me,
Who start at Theft, and blush at Perjury?
Who scarce forbear, tho' BRITAIN's Court he sing,
To pluck a titled Poet's borrow'd Wing;
A Statesman's Logic unconvinc'd can hear,
And dare to slumber o'er the *Gazetteer*;
Despise a Fool in half his Pension drest,
And strive in vain to laugh at *Hervey*'s Jest.

Others with softer Smiles, and subtler Art,
Can sap the Principles, or taint the Heart;
With more Address a Lover's Note convey,
Or bribe a Virgin's Innocence away.
Well may they rise, while I, whose Rustic Tongue
Ne'er knew to puzzle Right, or varnish Wrong,
Spurn'd as a Beggar, dreaded as a Spy,
Live unregarded, unlamented die.

For what but social Guilt the Friend endears?
Who shares *Orgilio*'s Crimes, his Fortune shares.
But thou, should tempting Villainy present
All *Marlb'rough* hoarded, or all *Villiers* spent,
Turn from the glitt'ring Bribe thy scornful Eye,
Nor sell for Gold, what Gold could never buy,
The peaceful Slumber, self-approving Day,
Unsullied Fame, and Conscience ever gay.

The cheated Nation's happy Fav'rites see!
Mark whom the Great caress, who frown on me!
LONDON! the needy Villain's gen'ral Home,
The Common Shore of *Paris* and of *Rome*;
With eager Thirst, by Folly or by Fate,
Sucks in the Dregs of each corrupted State.
Forgive my Transports on a Theme like this,
I cannot bear a *French* Metropolis.

Illustrious EDWARD! from the Realms of Day,
The Land of Heroes and of Saints survey;
Nor hope the *British* Lineaments to trace,
The rustic Grandeur, or the surly Grace;
But lost in thoughtless Ease, and empty Show,
Behold the Warriour dwindled to a Beau;
Sense, Freedom, Piety, refin'd away,
Of FRANCE the Mimic, and of SPAIN the Prey.

All that at home no more can beg or steal,
Or like a Gibbet better than a Wheel;
Hiss'd from the Stage, or hooted from the Court,
Their Air, their Dress, their Politicks import;
Obsequious, artful, voluble and gay,
On *Britain*'s fond Credulity they prey.
No gainful Trade their Industry can 'scape,
They sing, they dance, clean Shoes, or cure a Clap;
All Sciences a fasting Monsieur knows,
And bid him go to Hell, to Hell he goes.

Ah! what avails it, that, from Slav'ry far,
I drew the Breath of Life in *English* Air;
Was early taught a *Briton*'s Right to prize,
And lisp the Tale of HENRY's Victories;
If the gull'd Conqueror receives the Chain,
And what their Armies lost, their Cringes gain?

Studious to please, and ready to submit,
The supple *Gaul* was born a Parasite:
Still to his Int'rest true, where'er he goes,
Wit, Brav'ry, Worth, his lavish Tongue bestows;
In ev'ry Face a Thousand Graces shine,
From ev'ry Tongue flows Harmony divine.
These Arts in vain our rugged Natives try,
Strain out with fault'ring Diffidence a lye,
And gain a Kick for awkward Flattery.

Besides, with Justice, this discerning Age
Admires their wond'rous Talents for the Stage:
Well may they venture on the Mimic's Art,
Who play from Morn to Night a borrow'd Part;

30

Practis'd their Master's Notions to embrace,
Repeat his Maxims, and reflect his Face;
With ev'ry wild Absurdity comply,
And view each Object with another's Eye;
To shake with Laughter ere the Jest they hear,
To pour at Will the counterfeited Tear;
And as their Patron hints the Cold or Heat,
To shake in Dog-days, in *December* sweat.

How, when Competitors like these contend,
Can surly Virtue hope to fix a Friend?
Slaves that with serious Impudence beguile,
And lye without a Blush, without a Smile;
Exalt each Trifle, ev'ry Vice adore,
Your Taste in Snuff, your Judgment in a Whore;
Can *Balbo's* Eloquence applaud, and swear
He gropes his Breeches with a Monarch's Air.

For Arts like these preferr'd, admir'd, carest,
They first invade your Table, then your Breast;
Explore your Secrets with insidious Art,
Watch the weak Hour, and ransack all the Heart;
Then soon your ill-plac'd Confidence repay,
Commence your Lords, and govern or betray.
By Numbers here from Shame or Censure free,
All Crimes are safe, but hated Poverty.
This, only this, the rigid Law persues,
This, only this, provokes the snarling Muse;
The sober Trader at a tatter'd Cloak,
Wakes from his Dream, and labours for a Joke;
With brisker Air the silken Courtiers gaze,
And turn the varied Taunt a thousand ways.
Of all the Griefs that harrass the Distrest,
Sure the most bitter is a scornful Jest;
Fate never wounds more deep the gen'rous Heart,
Than when a Blockhead's Insult points the Dart.

Has Heaven reserv'd, in Pity to the Poor,
No pathless Waste, or undiscover'd Shore?
No secret Island in the boundless Main?
No peaceful Desart yet unclaim'd by SPAIN?

Quick let us rise, the happy Seats explore,
And bear Oppression's Insolence no more.
This mournful Truth is ev'ry where confest,
SLOW RISES WORTH, BY POVERTY DEPREST:
But here more slow, where all are Slaves to Gold,
Where Looks are Merchandise, and Smiles are sold,
Where won by Bribes, by Flatteries implor'd,
The Groom retails the Favours of his Lord.

But hark! th' affrighted Crowd's tumultuous Cries
Roll thro' the Streets, and thunder to the Skies;
Rais'd from some pleasing Dream of Wealth and Pow'r,
Some pompous Palace, or some blissful Bow'r,
Aghast you start, and scarce with aking Sight,
Sustain th' approaching Fire's tremendous Light;
Swift from pursuing Horrors take your Way,
And Leave your little ALL to Flames a Prey;
Then thro' the World a wretched Vagrant roam,
For where can starving Merit find a Home?
In vain your mournful Narrative disclose,
While all neglect, and most insult your Woes.

Should Heav'n's just Bolts *Orgilio's* Wealth confound,
And spread his flaming Palace on the Ground,
Swift o'er the Land the dismal Rumour flies,
And publick Mournings pacify the Skies;
The Laureat Tribe in servile Verse relate,
How Virtue wars with persecuting Fate;
With well-feign'd Gratitude the pension'd Band
Refund the Plunder of the begger'd Land.
See! while he builds, the gaudy Vassals come,
And crowd with sudden Wealth the rising Dome;
The price of Boroughs and of Souls restore,
And raise his Treasures higher than before.
Now bless'd with all the Baubles of the Great,
The polish'd Marble, and the shining Plate.
Orgilio sees the golden Pile aspire,
And hopes from angry Heav'n another fire.

Could'st thou resign the Park and Play content,
For the fair Banks of *Severn* or of *Trent*;
There might'st thou find some elegant Retreat,
Some hireling Senator's deserted Seat;
And stretch thy Prospects o'er the smiling Land,
For less than rent the Dungeons of the *Strand*;
There prune thy Walks, support thy drooping Flow'rs,
Direct thy Rivulets, and twine thy Bow'rs;
And, while thy Beds a cheap Repast afford,
Despise the Dainties of a venal Lord:
There ev'ry Bush with Nature's Music rings,
There ev'ry Breeze bears Health upon its Wings;
On all thy Hours Security shall smile,
And bless thine Evening Walk and Morning Toil.

Prepare for Death, if here at Night you roam,
And sign your Will before you sup from Home.
Some fiery Fop, with new Commission vain,
Who sleeps on Brambles till he kills his Man;
Some frolick Drunkard, reeling from a Feast,
Provokes a Broil, and stabs you for a Jest.
Yet ev'n these Heroes, mischievously gay,
Lords of the Street, and Terrors of the Way;
Flush'd as they are with Folly, Youth and Wine,
Their prudent Insults to the Poor confine;
Afar they mark the Flambeau's bright Approach,
And shun the shining Train, and golden Coach.

In vain, these Dangers past, your Doors you close,
And hope the balmy Blessings of Repose:
Cruel with Guilt, and daring with Despair,
The midnight Murd'rer bursts the faithless Bar;
Invades the sacred Hour of silent Rest,
And plants, unseen, a Dagger in your Breast.

Scarce can our Fields, such Crowds at *Tyburn* die,
With Hemp the Gallows and the Fleet supply.
Propose your Schemes, ye Senatorian Band,
Whose *Ways and Means* support the sinking Land;
Lest Ropes be wanting in the tempting Spring,
To rig another Convoy for the K—g.

LONDON: A POEM

A single Jail, in ALFRED's golden Reign,
Could half the Nation's Criminals contain;
Fair Justice then, without Constraint ador'd,
Sustain'd the Ballance, but resign'd the Sword;
No Spies were paid, no *Special Juries* known,
Blest Age! But ah! how diff'rent from our own!

Much could I add,—but see the Boat at hand,
The Tide retiring, calls me from the Land:
Farewel!—When Youth, and Health, and Fortune spent,
Thou fly'st for Refuge to the Wilds of *Kent*;
And tir'd like me with Follies and with Crimes,
In angry Numbers warn'st succeeding Times;
Then shall thy Friend, nor thou refuse his Aid,
Still Foe to Vice forsake his *Cambrian* Shade;
In Virtue's Cause once more exert his Rage,
Thy Satire point and animate thy Page.

AN EPITAPH

UPON THE CELEBRATED

CLAUDY PHILIPS

The text of this poem is taken from *The Gentleman's Magazine*, September, 1740 (p. 464, col. 2.).

AN EPITAPH

UPON THE CELEBRATED

CLAUDY PHILIPS,

MUSICIAN,

WHO DIED VERY POOR

Philips, whose touch harmonious could remove
The pangs of guilty pow'r, and hapless love,
Rest here, distress'd by poverty no more,
Here find that calm, thou gav'st so oft before.
Sleep, undisturb'd, within this peaceful shrine,
Till angels wake thee, with a note like thine.

THE LIFE OF
MR. RICHARD SAVAGE

The text is that of the second edition, London 1748, from a copy in the possession of the preparer of the text: it has been checked throughout with the British Museum copy of the first edition, London, 1744 (1417. g. 40.). In the original, many quotations from the poems of Savage are made in footnotes. These, and some other footnotes, are omitted here. The original also contains Savage's 110-line poem, *London and Bristol delineated*, with a "Chasm" after line 96; the poem is here omitted, as are four words in the paragraph immediately after the poem. A 62-line poem in the original is omitted from p. 81. As will be seen from p. 913, the "one Gentleman" who paid twenty pounds a year (see p. 103) for Savage's subscription was Mr. Alexander Pope.

AN ACCOUNT
OF THE LIFE OF
MR. RICHARD SAVAGE,
SON OF THE EARL RIVERS

IT has been observed in all Ages, that the Advantages of Nature
or of Fortune have contributed very little to the Promotion of
Happiness; and that those whom the Splendor of their Rank, or
the Extent of their Capacity, have placed upon the Summits of
human Life, have not often given any just Occasion to Envy in
those who look up to them from a lower Station. Whether it be that
apparent Superiority incites great Designs, and great Designs are
naturally liable to fatal Miscarriages, or that the general Lot of
Mankind is Misery, and the Misfortunes of those whose Eminence
drew upon them an universal Attention, have been more carefully
recorded, because they were more generally observed, and have in
reality been only more conspicuous than those of others, not more
frequent, or more severe.

That Affluence and Power, Advantages extrinsic and adventitious, and therefore easily separable from those by whom they
are possessed, should very often flatter the Mind with Expectation of Felicity which they cannot give, raises no Astonishment;
but it seems rational to hope, that intellectual Greatness should
produce better Effects, that Minds qualified for great Attainments
should first endeavour their own Benefit, and that they who are
most able to teach others the Way to Happiness, should with most
Certainty follow it themselves.

But this Expectation, however plausible, has been very frequently disappointed. The Heroes of literary as well as civil
History have been very often no less remarkable for what they
have suffered, than for what they have atchieved; and Volumes
have been written only to enumerate the Miseries of the Learned,
and relate their unhappy Lives, and untimely Deaths.

41

To these mournful Narratives, I am about to add the Life of *Richard Savage*, a Man whose Writings entitle him to an eminent Rank in the Classes of Learning, and whose Misfortunes claim a Degree of Compassion, not always due to the Unhappy, as they were often the Consequences of the Crimes of others, rather than his own.

In the year 1697, *Anne* Countess of *Macclesfield*, having lived for some time upon very uneasy Terms with her Husband, thought a public Confession of Adultery the most obvious and expeditious Method of obtaining her Liberty, and therefore declared, that the Child, with which she was then great, was begotten by the Earl *Rivers*. Her Husband, as may be imagined, being thus made no less desirous of a Separation than herself, prosecuted his Design in the most effectual Manner; for he applied not to the Ecclesiastical Courts for a Divorce, but to the Parliament for an Act, by which his Marriage might be dissolved, the nuptial Contract totally annulled, and the Child of his Wife illegitimated. This Act, after the usual Deliberation, he obtained, tho' without the Approbation of some, who considered Marriage as an Affair only cognizable by Ecclesiastical Judges; and on *March* 3d was separated from his Wife, whose Fortune, which was very great, was repaid her; and who having as well as her Husband the Liberty of making another Choice, was in a short Time married to Colonel *Bret*.

While the Earl of *Macclesfield* was prosecuting this Affair, his Wife was, on the tenth of *January* 1697-8, delivered of a Son, and the Earl *Rivers*, by appearing to consider him as his own, left none any Reason to doubt of the Sincerity of her Declaration; for he was his Godfather, and gave him his own Name, which was by his Direction inserted in the Register of *St. Andrew*'s Parish in *Holbourn*, but unfortunately left him to the Care of his Mother, whom, as she was now set free from her Husband, he probably imagined likely to treat with great Tenderness the Child that had contributed to so pleasing an Event. It is not indeed easy to discover what Motives could be found to over-balance that natural Affection of a Parent, or what Interest could be promoted by Neglect or Cruelty. The Dread of Shame or of Poverty, by which some Wretches have been incited to abandon or to murder their Children, cannot be supposed to have affected a Woman who had proclaimed her Crimes and solicited Reproach, and on whom the Clemency of the Legislature had undeservedly bestowed a Fortune, that would have been very little diminished by the Expences which the Care of her Child could have brought upon her. It was therefore not likely that she would be wicked without Temptation, that she would look upon her Son from his Birth with a kind of Resentment and Abhorrence; and instead of supporting, assisting, and defending him, delight to see him struggling with Misery, that she would take every Opportunity of aggravating his Misfortunes, and obstructing his Resources, and with an implacable and restless Cruelty continue her Persecution from the first Hour of his Life to the last.

But whatever were her Motives, no sooner was her Son born, than she discovered a Resolution of disowning him; and in a very short Time removed him from her Sight, by committing him to the Care of a poor Woman, whom she directed to educate him as her own, and enjoined never to inform him of his true Parents.

Such was the Beginning of the Life of *Richard Savage*: Born with a legal Claim to Honour and to Riches, he was in two Months illegitimated by the Parliament, and disowned by his Mother, doomed to Poverty and Obscurity, and launched upon the Ocean of Life, only that he might be swallowed by its Quicksands, or dashed upon its Rocks.

His Mother could not indeed infect others with the same Cruelty. As it was impossible to avoid the Inquiries which the Curiosity or Tenderness of her Relations made after her Child, she was obliged to give some Account of the Measures that she had taken; and her Mother, the Lady *Mason*, whether in Approbation of her Design, or to prevent more criminal Contrivances, engaged to transact with his Nurse, pay her for her Care, and superintend his Education.

In this charitable Office she was assisted by his Godmother Mrs *Loyd*, who while she lived always looked upon him with that Tenderness, which the Barbarity of his Mother made peculiarly necessary; but her Death, which happened in his tenth Year, was another of the Misfortunes of his Childhood; for though she kindly endeavoured to alleviate his Loss by a Legacy of three hundred Pounds, yet as he had none to prosecute his Claim, to shelter him from Oppression, or call in Law to the Assistance of Justice, her Will was eluded by the Executors, and no part of the Money was ever paid.

He was however not yet wholly abandoned. The Lady *Mason* still continued her Care, and directed him to be placed at a small

43

Grammar School near St. *Alban*'s, where he was called by the Name of his Nurse, without the least Intimation that he had a Claim to any other.

Here he was initiated in Literature, and passed through several of the Classes, with what Rapidity or what Applause cannot now be known. As he always spoke with Respect of his Master, it is probable that the mean Rank, in which he then appeared, did not hinder his Genius from being distinguished, or his Industry from being rewarded, and if in so low a State he obtained Distinction and Rewards, it is not likely that they were gained but by Genius and Industry.

It is very reasonable to conjecture, that his Application was equal to his Abilities, because his Improvement was more than proportioned to the Opportunities which he enjoyed; nor can it be doubted, that if his earliest Productions had been preserved, like those of happier Students, we might in some have found vigorous Sallies of that sprightly Humour, which distinguishes the *Author to be let*, and in others, strong Touches of that ardent Imagination which painted the solemn Scenes of *the Wanderer*.

While he was thus cultivating his Genius, his Father the Earl *Rivers* was seized with a Distemper, which in a short Time put an End to his Life. He had frequently inquired after his Son, and had always been amused with fallacious and evasive Answers; but being now in his own Opinion on his Death-bed, he thought it his Duty to provide for him among his other natural Children, and therefore demanded a positive Account of him, with an Importunity not to be diverted or denied. His Mother, who could no longer refuse an Answer, determined at least to give such as should cut him off for ever from that Happiness which Competence affords, and therefore declared that he was dead; which is perhaps the first Instance of a Lye invented by a Mother to deprive her Son of a Provision which was designed him by another, and which she could not expect herself, though he should lose it.

This was therefore an Act of Wickedness which could not be defeated, because it could not be suspected; the Earl did not imagine, that there could exist in a human Form a Mother that would ruin her Son without enriching herself, and therefore bestowed upon some other Person six thousand Pounds, which he had in his Will bequeathed to *Savage*.

The same Cruelty which incited his Mother to intercept this Provision which had been intended him, prompted her in a short Time to another Project, a Project worthy of such a Disposition. She endeavoured to rid herself from the Danger of being at any Time made known to him, by sending him secretly to the *American* Plantations.

By whose Kindness this Scheme was counteracted, or by what Interposition she was induced to lay aside her Design, I know not; it is not improbable that the Lady *Mason* might persuade or compel her to desist, or perhaps she could not easily find Accomplices wicked enough to concur in so cruel an Action; for it may be conceived, that even those who had by a long Gradation of Guilt hardened their Hearts against the Sense of common Wickedness, would yet be shocked at the Design of a Mother to expose her Son to Slavery and Want, to expose him without Interest, and without Provocation; and *Savage* might on this Occasion find Protectors and Advocates among those who had long traded in Crimes, and whom Compassion had never touched before.

Being hindered, by whatever Means, from banishing him into another Country, she formed soon after a Scheme for burying him in Poverty and Obscurity in his own; and that his Station of Life, if not the Place of his Residence, might keep him for ever at a Distance from her, she ordered him to be placed with a Shoemaker in *Holbourn*, that, after the usual Time of Trial, he might become his Apprentice.

It is generally reported, that this Project was for some time successful, and that *Savage* was employed at the Awl longer than he was willing to confess; nor was it perhaps any great Advantage to him, that an unexpected Discovery determined him to quit his Occupation.

About this Time his Nurse, who had always treated him as her own Son. died, and it was natural for him to take Care of those Effects which by her Death were, as he imagined, become his own; he therefore went to her House, opened her Boxes, and examined her Papers, among which he found some Letters written to her by the Lady *Mason*, which informed him of his Birth, and the Reasons for which it was concealed.

He was no longer satisfied with the Employment which had been allotted him, but thought he had a Right to share the Affluence of his Mother, and therefore without Scruple applied to her as her

45

Son, and made use of every Art to awaken her Tenderness, and attract her Regard. But neither his Letters, nor the Interposition of those Friends which his Merit or his Distress procured him, made any Impression upon her: She still resolved to neglect, though she could no longer disown him.

It was to no Purpose that he frequently solicited her to admit him to see her; she avoided him with the most vigilant Precaution, and ordered him to be excluded from her House, by whomsoever he might be introduced, and what Reason soever he might give for entering it.

Savage was at the same Time so touched with the Discovery of his real Mother, that it was his frequent Practice to walk in the dark Evenings for several Hours before her Door, in Hopes of seeing her as she might come by Accident to the Window, or cross her Apartment with a Candle in her Hand.

But all his Assiduity and Tenderness were without Effect, for he could neither soften her Heart, nor open her Hand, and was reduced to the utmost Miseries of Want, while he was endeavouring to awaken the Affection of a Mother: He was therefore obliged to seek some other Means of Support, and having no Profession, became, by Necessity, an Author.

At this Time the Attention of all the literary World was engrossed by the *Bangorian* Controversy, which filled the Press with Pamphlets, and the Coffee-houses with Disputants. Of this Subject, as most popular, he made Choice for his first Attempt, and without any other Knowledge of the Question, than he had casually collected from Conversation, published a Poem against the Bishop.

What was the Success or Merit of this Performance I know not, it was probably lost among the innumerable Pamphlets to which that Dispute gave Occasion. Mr *Savage* was himself in a little time ashamed of it, and endeavoured to suppress it, by destroying all the Copies that he could collect.

He then attempted a more gainful Kind of Writing, and in his eighteenth Year offered to the Stage a Comedy borrowed from a *Spanish* Plot, which was refused by the Players, and was therefore given by him to Mr *Bullock*, who having more Interest, made some slight Alterations, and brought it upon the Stage, under the Title of *Woman's a Riddle*, but allowed the unhappy Author no Part of the Profit.

Not discouraged however at this Repulse, he wrote two Years afterwards *Love in a Veil*, another Comedy, borrowed likewise from the *Spanish*, but with little better Success than before; for though it was received and acted, yet it appeared so late in the Year, that the Author obtained no other Advantage from it, than the Acquaintance of Sir *Richard Steele*, and Mr *Wilks*; by whom he was pitied, caressed, and relieved.

Sir *Richard Steele* having declared in his Favour with all the Ardour of Benevolence which constituted his Character, promoted his Interest with the utmost Zeal, related his Misfortunes, applauded his Merit, took all Opportunities of recommending him, and asserted, that *the Inhumanity of his Mother had given him a Right to find every good Man his Father*.

Nor was Mr *Savage* admitted to his Acquaintance only, but to his Confidence, of which he sometimes related an Instance too extraordinary to be omitted, as it affords a very just Idea of his Patron's Character.

He was once desired by Sir *Richard*, with an Air of the utmost Importance, to come very early to his House the next Morning. Mr *Savage* came as he had promised, found the Chariot at the Door, and Sir *Richard* waiting for him, and ready to go out. What was intended, and whither they were to go, *Savage* could not conjecture, and was not willing to enquire, but immediately seated himself with his Friend, the Coachman was ordered to drive, and they hurried with the utmost Expedition to *Hyde-Park Corner*, where they stopped at a petty Tavern, and retired to a private Room. Sir *Richard* then informed him, that he intended to publish a Pamphlet, and that he had desired him to come thither that he might write for him. They soon sat down to the Work, Sir *Richard* dictated, and *Savage* wrote, till the Dinner that had been ordered was put upon the Table. *Savage* was surprised at the Meanness of the Entertainment, and after some Hesitation, ventured to ask for Wine, which Sir *Richard*, not without Reluctance, ordered to be brought. They then finished their Dinner, and proceeded in their Pamphlet, which they concluded in the Afternoon.

Mr *Savage* then imagined his Task over, and expected that Sir *Richard* would call for the Reckoning, and return home; but his Expectations deceived him, for Sir *Richard* told him, that he was without Money, and that the Pamphlet must be sold before the

Dinner could be paid for; and *Savage* was therefore obliged to go and offer their new Production to Sale for two Guineas, which with some Difficulty he obtained. Sir *Richard* then returned home, having retired that Day only to avoid his Creditors, and composed the Pamphlet only to discharge his Reckoning.

Mr *Savage* related another Fact equally uncommon, which, though it has no Relation to his Life, ought to be preserved. Sir *Richard Steele* having one Day invited to his House a great Number of Persons of the first Quality, they were surprised at the Number of Liveries which surrounded the Table; and after Dinner, when Wine and Mirth had set them free from the Observation of rigid Ceremony, one of them enquired of Sir *Richard*, how such an expensive Train of Domestics could be consistent with his Fortune. He with great Frankness confessed, that they were Fellows of whom he would very willingly be rid. And being then asked, why he did not discharge them, declared that they were Bailiffs who had introduced themselves with an Execution, and whom, since he could not send them away, he had thought it convenient to embellish with Liveries, that they might do him Credit while they staid.

His Friends were diverted with the Expedient, and by paying the Debt discharged their Attendance, having obliged Sir *Richard* to promise that they should never again find him graced with a Retinue of the same Kind.

Under such a Tutor, Mr *Savage* was not likely to learn Prudence or Frugality, and perhaps many of the Misfortunes which the Want of those Virtues brought upon him in the following Parts of his Life, might be justly imputed to so unimproving an Example.

Nor did the Kindness of Sir *Richard* end in common Favours. He proposed to have established him in some settled Scheme of Life, and to have contracted a Kind of Alliance with him by marrying him to a natural Daughter, on whom he intended to bestow a thousand Pounds. But though he was always lavish of future Bounties, he conducted his Affairs in such a Manner, that he was very seldom able to keep his Promises, or execute his own Intentions; and as he was never able to raise the Sum which he had offered, the Marriage was delayed. In the mean Time he was officiously informed that Mr *Savage* had ridiculed him; by which he was so much exasperated, that he withdrew the Allowance which he had paid him, and never afterwards admitted him to his House.

It is not indeed unlikely that *Savage* might by his Imprudence expose himself to the Malice of a Tale-bearer; for his Patron had many Follies, which as his Discernment easily discovered, his Imagination might sometimes incite him to mention too ludicrously. A little Knowledge of the World is sufficient to discover that such Weakness is very common, and that there are few who do not sometimes in the Wantonness of thoughtless Mirth, or the Heat of transient Resentment, speak of their Friends and Benefactors with Levity and Contempt, though in their cooler Moments, they want neither Sense of their Kindness, nor Reverence for their Virtue. The Fault therefore of Mr *Savage* was rather Negligence than Ingratitude; but Sir *Richard* must likewise be acquitted of Severity, for who is there that can patiently bear Contempt from one whom he has relieved and supported, whose Establishment he has laboured, and whose Interest he has promoted?

He was now again abandoned to Fortune, without any other Friend than Mr *Wilks*; a Man, who, whatever were his Abilities or Skill as an Actor, deserves at least to be remembered for his Virtues*, which are not often to be found in the World, and perhaps less often in his Profession than in others. To be humane, generous and candid, is a very high Degree of Merit in any State; but those Qualities deserve still greater Praise, when they are found in that Condition, which makes almost every other Man, for whatever Reason, contemptuous, insolent, petulant, selfish, and brutal.

As Mr *Wilks* was one of those to whom Calamity seldom complained without Relief, he naturally took an unfortunate Wit into

---

* As it is a Loss to Mankind, when any good Action is forgotten, I shall insert another Instance of Mr *Wilks*'s Generosity, very little known. Mr *Smith*, a Gentleman educated at *Dublin*, being hindred by an Impediment in his Pronunciation from engaging in Orders, for which his Friends designed him, left his own Country, and came to *London* in Quest of Employment, but found his Solicitations fruitless, and his Necessities every Day more pressing. In this Distress he wrote a Tragedy, and offered it to the Players, by whom it was rejected. Thus were his last Hopes defeated, and he had no other Prospect than of the most deplorable Poverty. But Mr *Wilks* thought his Performance, though not perfect, at least worthy of some Reward, and therefore offered him a Benefit. This Favour he improved with so much Diligence, that the House afforded him a considerable Sum, with which he went to *Leyden*, applied himself to the Study of Physic, and prosecuted his Design with so much Diligence and Success, that when Dr *Boerhaave* was desired by the Czarina to recommend proper Persons to introduce into *Russia* the Practice and Study of Physic, Dr *Smith* was one of those whom he selected. He had a considerable Pension settled on him at his Arrival, and is now one of the chief Physicians at the *Russian* court.

his Protection, and not only assisted him in any casual Distresses, but continued an equal and steady Kindness to the Time of his Death.

By his Interposition Mr *Savage* once obtained from his Mother* fifty Pounds, and a Promise of one hundred and fifty more; but it was the Fate of this unhappy Man, that few Promises of any Advantage to him were performed. His Mother was infected among others with the general Madness of the *South-Sea* Traffick, and having been disappointed in her Expectations, refused to pay what perhaps nothing but the Prospect of sudden Affluence prompted her to promise.

Being thus obliged to depend upon the Friendship of Mr *Wilks*, he was consequently an assiduous Frequenter of the Theatres, and in a short Time the Amusements of the Stage took such Possession of his Mind, that he never was absent from a Play in several Years.

This constant Attendance naturally procured him the Acquaintance of the Players, and among others, of Mrs *Oldfield*, who was so much pleased with his Conversation, and touched with his Misfortunes, that she allowed him a settled Pension of fifty Pounds a Year, which was during her Life regularly paid.

That this Act of Generosity may receive its due Praise, and that the good Actions of Mrs *Oldfield* may not be sullied by her general Character, it is proper to mention, what Mr *Savage* often declared in the strongest Terms, that he never saw her alone, or in any other Place than behind the Scenes.

At her Death, he endeavoured to shew his Gratitude in the most decent Manner, by wearing Mourning as for a Mother, but did not celebrate her in Elegies, because he knew·that too great a Profusion of Praise would only have revived those Faults which his natural Equity did not allow him to think less, because they were committed by one who favoured him; but of which, though his Virtue would not endeavour to palliate them, his Gratitude would not suffer him to prolong the Memory, or diffuse the Censure.

In his *Wanderer*, he has indeed taken an Opportunity of mentioning her, but celebrates her not for her Virtue, but her Beauty, an Excellence which none ever denied her: This is the only Encomium with which he has rewarded her Liberality, and per-

* This I write upon the Credit of the Author of his Life, which was published 1727.

haps he has even in this been too lavish of his Praise. He seems to have thought that never to mention his Benefactress, would have an Appearance of Ingratitude, though to have dedicated any particular Performance to her Memory, would have only betrayed an officious Partiality, that, without exalting her Character, would have depressed his own.

He had sometimes, by the Kindness of Mr *Wilks*, the Advantage of a Benefit, on which Occasions he often received uncommon Marks of Regard and Compassion; and was once told by the Duke of *Dorset*, that it was just to consider him as an injured Nobleman, and that in his Opinion the Nobility ought to think themselves obliged without Solicitation to take every Opportunity of supporting him by their Countenance and Patronage. But he had generally the Mortification to hear that the whole Interest of his Mother was employed to frustrate his Applications, and that she never left any Expedient untried, by which he might be cut off from the Possibility of supporting Life. The same Disposition she endeavoured to diffuse among all those over whom Nature or Fortune gave her any Influence, and indeed succeeded too well in her Design, but could not always propagate her Effrontery with her Cruelty, for some of those whom she incited against him, were ashamed of their own Conduct, and boasted of that Relief which they never gave him.

In this Censure I do not indiscriminately involve all his Relations; for he has mentioned with Gratitude the Humanity of one Lady, whose Name I am now unable to recollect, and to whom therefore I cannot pay the Praises which she deserves for having acted well in Opposition to Influence, Precept and Example.

The Punishment which our Laws inflict upon those Parents who murder their Infants, is well known, nor has its Justice ever been contested; but if they deserve Death who destroy a Child in its Birth, what Pains can be severe enough for her who forbears to destroy him only to inflict sharper Miseries upon him; who prolongs his Life only to make it miserable; and who exposes him without Care and without Pity, to the Malice of Oppression, the Caprices of Chance, and the Temptations of Poverty; who rejoices to see him overwhelmed with Calamities; and when his own Industry, or the Charity of others, has enabled him to rise for a short Time above his Miseries, plunges him again into his former Distress?

The Kindness of his Friends not affording him any constant Supply, and the Prospect of improving his Fortune, by enlarging his Acquaintance, necessarily leading him to Places of Expence, he found it necessary* to endeavour once more at dramatic Poetry, for which he was now better qualified by a more extensive Knowledge, and longer Observation. But having been unsuccessful in Comedy, though rather for Want of Opportunities than Genius, he resolved now to try whether he should not be more fortunate in exhibiting a Tragedy.

The Story which he chose for the Subject, was that of Sir *Thomas Overbury*, a Story well adapted to the Stage, though perhaps not far enough removed from the present Age, to admit properly the Fictions necessary to complete the Plan; for the Mind which naturally loves Truth is always most offended with the Violation of those Truths of which we are most certain, and we of course conceive those Facts most certain which approach nearest to our own Time.

Out of this Story he formed a Tragedy, which, if the Circumstances in which he wrote it be considered, will afford at once an uncommon Proof of Strength of Genius, and Evenness of Mind, of a Serenity not to be ruffled, and an Imagination not to be suppressed.

During a considerable Part of the Time, in which he was employed upon this Performance, he was without Lodging, and often without Meat; nor had he any other Conveniences for Study than the Fields or the Streets allowed him, there he used to walk and form his Speeches, and afterwards step into a Shop, beg for a few Moments the Use of the Pen and Ink, and write down what he had composed upon Paper which he had picked up by Accident.

If the Performance of a Writer thus distressed is not perfect, its Faults ought surely to be imputed to a Cause very different from Want of Genius, and must rather excite Pity than provoke Censure.

But when under these Discouragements the Tragedy was finished, there yet remained the Labour of introducing it on the Stage, an Undertaking which to an ingenuous Mind was in a very high Degree vexatious and disgusting; for having little Interest or Reputation, he was obliged to submit himself wholly to the Players, and admit, with whatever Reluctance, the Emendations

* In 1724.

of Mr *Cibber*, which he always considered as the Disgrace of his Performance.

He had indeed in Mr *Hill* another Critic of a very different Class, from whose Friendship he received great Assistance on many Occasions, and whom he never mentioned but with the utmost Tenderness and Regard. He had been for some Time distinguished by him with very particular Kindness, and on this Occasion it was natural to apply to him as an Author of an established Character. He therefore sent this Tragedy to him with a short Copy of Verses, in which he desired his Correction. Mr *Hill*, whose Humanity and Politeness are generally known, readily complied with his Request; but as he is remarkable for Singularity of Sentiment, and bold Experiments in Language, Mr *Savage* did not think his Play much improved by his Innovation, and had even at that Time the Courage to reject several Passages which he could not approve; and, what is still more laudable, Mr *Hill* had the Generosity not to resent the Neglect of his Alterations, but wrote the Prologue and Epilogue, in which he touches on the Circumstances of the Author with great Tenderness.

After all these Obstructions and Compliances, he was only able to bring his Play upon the Stage in the Summer, when the chief Actors had retired, and the rest were in Possession of the House for their own Advantage. Among these Mr *Savage* was admitted to play the Part of Sir *Thomas Overbury*, by which he gained no great Reputation, the Theatre being a Province for which Nature seemed not to have designed him; for neither his Voice, Look, nor Gesture, were such as are expected on the Stage, and he was himself so much ashamed of having been reduced to appear as a Player, that he always blotted out his Name from the List, when a Copy of his Tragedy was to be shown to his Friends.

In the Publication of his Performance he was more successful, for the Rays of Genius that glimmered in it, that glimmered through all the Mists which Poverty had been able to spread over it, procured him the Notice and Esteem of many Persons eminent for their Rank, their Virtue, and their Wit.

Of this Play, acted, printed, and dedicated, the accumulated Profits arose to an hundred Pounds, which he thought at that Time a very large Sum, having been never Master of so much before.

In the Dedication*, for which he received ten Guineas, there is

* To — *Tryste*, Esq; of *Herefordshire*.

53

nothing remarkable. The Preface contains a very liberal Encomium on the blooming Excellencies of Mr *Theophilus Cibber*,
which Mr *Savage* could not in the latter Part of his Life see his
Friends about to read, without snatching the Play out of their
Hands.

The Generosity of Mr *Hill* did not end on this Occasion; for
afterwards, when Mr *Savage's* Necessities returned, he encouraged
a Subscription to a Miscellany of Poems in a very extraordinary
Manner, by publishing his Story in the *Plain Dealer**, with some
affecting Lines, which he asserts to have been written by Mr
Savage upon the Treatment received by him from his Mother, but
of which he was himself the Author, as Mr *Savage* afterwards
declared. These Lines, and the Paper in which they were inserted,
had a very powerful Effect upon all but his Mother, whom, by
making her Cruelty more publick, they only hardened in her
Aversion.

Mr *Hill* not only promoted the Subscription to the Miscellany,
but furnished likewise the greatest Part of the Poems of which it is
composed, and particularly *the Happy Man*, which he published
as a Specimen.

The Subscriptions of those whom these Papers should influence
to patronise Merit in Distress, without any other Solicitation, were
directed to be left at *Button's* Coffee-house; and Mr *Savage* going
thither a few Days afterwards, without Expectation of any Effect
from his Proposal, found to his Surprise seventy Guineas†, which
had been sent him in Consequence of the Compassion excited by
Mr *Hill's* pathetic Representation.

To this Miscellany he publish'd a Preface, in which he gives an
Account of his Mother's Cruelty in a very uncommon Strain of
Humour, and with a Gaiety of Imagination, which the Success of
his Subscription probably produced.

---

* The *Plain Dealer* was a periodical Paper written by Mr *Hill* and Mr
Bond, whom Mr *Savage* called the two contending Powers of Light and Darkness. They wrote by Turns, each six Essays, and the Character of the Work
was observed regularly to rise in Mr *Hill's* Weeks, and fall in Mr *Bond's*.

† The Names of those who so generously contributed to his Relief, having
been mentioned in a former Account, ought not to be omitted here. They
were the Dutchess of *Cleveland*, Lady *Cheyney*, Lady *Castlemain*, Lady
Gower, Lady *Lechmere*, the Dutchess Dowager, and Dutchess of *Rutland*,
Lady *Strafford*, the Countess Dowager of *Warwick*, Mrs *Mary Floyer*, Mrs
Sofuel Noel, Duke of *Rutland*, Lord *Gainsborough*, Lord *Milsington*, Mr *John
Savage*.

The Dedication is addressed to the Lady *Mary Wortley Montague*, whom he flatters without Reserve, and, to confess the Truth, with very little Art. The same Observation may be extended to all his Dedications: His Compliments are constrained and violent, heaped together without the Grace of Order, or the Decency of Introduction: He seems to have written his Panegyrics for the Perusal only of his Patrons, and to have imagined that he had no other Task than to pamper them with Praises however gross, and that Flattery would make its Way to the Heart, without the Assistance of Elegance or Invention.

Soon afterwards the Death of the King furnished a general Subject for a poetical Contest, in which Mr *Savage* engaged, and is allowed to have carried the Prize of Honour from his Competitors; but I know not whether he gained by his Performance any other Advantage than the Increase of his Reputation; though it must certainly have been with farther Views that he prevailed upon himself to attempt a Species of Writing, of which all the Topics had been long before exhausted, and which was made at once difficult by the Multitudes that had failed in it, and those that had succeeded.

He was now advancing in Reputation, and though frequently involved in very distressful Perplexities, appeared however to be gaining upon Mankind, when both his Fame and his Life were endangered by an Event, of which it is not yet determined, whether it ought to be mentioned as a Crime or a Calamity.

On the 20th of *November* 1727, Mr *Savage* came from *Richmond*, where he then lodged that he might persue his Studies with less Interruption, with an Intent to discharge another Lodging which he had in *Westminster*; and accidentally meeting two Gentlemen his Acquaintances, whose Names were *Merchant* and *Gregory*, he went in with them to a neighbouring Coffee-house, and sat drinking till it was late, it being in no Time of Mr *Savage*'s Life any Part of his Character to be the first of the Company that desired to separate. He would willingly have gone to Bed in the same House, but there was not Room for the whole Company, and therefore they agreed to ramble about the Streets, and divert themselves with such Amusements as should offer themselves till Morning.

In their Walk they happened unluckily to discover Light in *Robinson*'s Coffee-house, near *Charing Cross*, and therefore went in. *Merchant*, with some Rudeness, demanded a Room, and was told that there was a good Fire in the next Parlour, which the Company were about to leave, being then paying their Reckoning. *Merchant* not satisfied with this Answer, rushed into the Room, and was followed by his Companions. He then petulantly placed himself between the Company and the Fire, and soon after kicked down the Table. This produced a Quarrel, Swords were drawn on both Sides, and one Mr *James Sinclair* was killed. *Savage* having likewise wounded a Maid that held him, forced his Way with *Merchant* out of the House; but being intimidated and confused, without Resolution either to fly or stay, they were taken in a back Court by one of the Company and some Soldiers, whom he had called to his Assistance.

Being secured and guarded that Night, they were in the Morning carried before three Justices, who committed them to the *Gatehouse*, from whence, upon the Death of Mr *Sinclair*, which happened the same Day, they were removed in the Night to *Newgate*, where they were however treated with some Distinction, exempted from the Ignominy of Chains, and confined, not among the common Criminals, but in the *Press-Yard*.

When the Day of Trial came, the Court was crouded in a very unusual Manner, and the Publick appeared to interest itself as in a Cause of general Concern. The Witnesses against Mr *Savage* and his Friends were, the Woman who kept the House, which was a House of ill Fame, and her Maid, the Men who were in the Room with Mr *Sinclair*, and a Woman of the Town, who had been drinking with them, and with whom one of them had been seen in Bed. They swore in general, that *Merchant* gave the Provocation, which *Savage* and *Gregory* drew their Swords to justify; that *Savage* drew first, and that he stabbed *Sinclair* when he was not in a Posture of Defence, or while *Gregory* commanded his Sword; that after he had given the Thrust he turned pale, and would have retired, but that the Maid clung round him, and one of the Company endeavoured to detain him, from whom he broke, by cutting the Maid on the Head, but was afterwards taken in a Court.

There was some Difference in their Depositions; one did not see *Savage* give the Wound, another saw it given when *Sinclair* held his Point towards the Ground; and the Woman of the Town asserted, that she did not see *Sinclair*'s Sword at all: This Difference however was very far from amounting to Inconsistency, but it was sufficient to shew, that the Hurry of the Quarrel was such, that it was not easy to discover the Truth with relation to particular Circumstances, and that therefore some Deductions were to be made from the Credibility of the Testimonies.

Sinclair had declared several times before his Death, that he received his Wound from *Savage*; nor did *Savage* at his Trial deny the Fact, but endeavoured partly to extenuate it by urging the Suddenness of the whole Action, and the Impossibility of any ill Design, or premeditated Malice, and partly to justify it by the Necessity of Self-Defence, and the Hazard of his own Life, if he had lost that Opportunity of giving the Thrust: He observed, that neither Reason nor Law obliged a Man to wait for the Blow which was threatned, and which, if he should suffer it, he might never be able to return; that it was allowable to prevent an Assault, and to preserve Life by taking away that of the Adversary, by whom it was endangered.

With regard to the Violence with which he endeavoured to Escape, he declared, that it was not his Design to fly from Justice, or decline a Trial, but to avoid the Expences and Severities of a Prison, and that he intended to have appeared at the Bar without Compulsion.

This Defence, which took up more than an Hour, was heard by the Multitude that thronged the Court with the most attentive and respectful Silence: Those who thought he ought not to be acquitted owned that Applause could not be refused him; and those who before pitied his Misfortunes, now reverenced his Abilities.

The Witnesses which appeared against him were proved to be Persons of Characters which did not entitle them to much Credit; a common Strumpet, a Woman by whom Strumpets were entertained, and a Man by whom they were supported; and the Character of *Savage* was by several Persons of Distinction asserted, to be that of a modest inoffensive Man, not inclined to Broils, or to Insolence, and who had, to that Time, been only known for his Misfortunes and his Wit.

Had his Audience been his Judges, he had undoubtedly been acquitted; but Mr *Page*, who was then upon the Bench, treated him with his usual Insolence and Severity, and when he had summed up the Evidence, endeavoured to exasperate the Jury, as Mr *Savage* used to relate it, with this eloquent Harangue.

"Gentlemen of the Jury, you are to consider, that Mr *Savage* is a very great Man, a much greater Man than you or I, Gentlemen of the Jury; that he wears very fine Clothes, much finer Clothes than you or I, Gentlemen of the Jury; that he has abundance of Money in his Pocket, much more Money than you or I, Gentlemen of the Jury; but, Gentlemen of the Jury, is it not a very hard Case, Gentlemen of the Jury, that Mr *Savage* should therefore kill you or me, Gentlemen of the Jury?"

Mr *Savage* hearing his Defence thus misrepresented, and the Men who were to decide his Fate incited against him by invidious Comparisons, resolutely asserted, that his Cause was not candidly explained, and began to recapitulate what he had before said with regard to his Condition, and the Necessity of endeavouring to escape the Expences of Imprisonment; but the Judge having ordered him to be silent, and repeated his Orders without Effect, commanded that he should be taken from the Bar by Force.

The Jury then heard the Opinion of the Judge, that good Characters were of no Weight against positive Evidence, though they might turn the Scale, where it was doubtful; and that though when two Men attack each other, the Death of either is only Manslaughter; but where one is the Aggressor, as in the Case before them, and in Pursuance of his first Attack, kills the other, the Law supposes the Action, however sudden, to be malicious. They then deliberated upon their Verdict, and determined that Mr *Savage* and Mr *Gregory* were guilty of Murder, and Mr *Merchant*, who had no Sword, only of Manslaughter.

Thus ended this memorable Trial, which lasted eight Hours. Mr *Savage* and Mr *Gregory* were conducted back to Prison, where they were more closely confined, and loaded with Irons of fifty Pounds Weight: Four days afterwards they were sent back to the Court to receive Sentence; on which Occasion Mr *Savage* made, as far as it could be retained in Memory, the following Speech.

"It is now, my Lord, too late to offer any Thing by way of Defence, or Vindication; nor can we expect from your Lordships, in this Court, but the Sentence which the Law requires you, as Judges, to pronounce against Men of our calamitous Condition.—But we are also persuaded, that as mere Men, and out of this Seat of rigorous Justice, you are susceptive of the tender Passions, and too humane, not to commiserate the unhappy Situation of those whom the Law sometimes perhaps—exacts—from you to pronounce upon. No doubt you distinguish between Offences, which arise out of Premeditation, and a Disposition habituated to Vice or Im-

morality, and Transgressions, which are the unhappy and unforeseen Effects of a casual Absence of Reason, and sudden Impulse of
Passion: We therefore hope you will contribute all you can to an
Extension of that Mercy, which the Gentlemen of the Jury have
been pleased to shew Mr *Merchant*, who (allowing Facts as sworn
against us by the Evidence) had led us into this our Calamity. I
hope, this will not be construed as if we meant to reflect upon that
Gentleman, or remove any Thing from us upon him, or that we repine the more at our Fate, because he has no Participation of it:
No, my Lord! For my Part, I declare nothing could more soften
my Grief, than to be without any Companion in so great a Misfortune."

Mr *Savage* had now no Hopes of Life, but from the Mercy of the
Crown, which was very earnestly solicited by his Friends, and
which, with whatever Difficulty the Story may obtain Belief, was
obstructed only by his Mother.

To prejudice the Queen against him, she made use of an Incident,
which was omitted in the order of Time, that it might be mentioned
together with the Purpose which it was made to serve. Mr *Savage*,
when he had discovered his Birth, had an incessant Desire to speak
to his Mother, who always avoided him in publick, and refused him
Admission into her House. One Evening walking, as it was his
Custom, in the Street that she inhabited, he saw the Door of her
House by Accident open; he entered it, and, finding none in the
Passage, to hinder him, went up Stairs to salute her. She discovered him before he entered her Chamber, alarmed the Family
with the most distressful Outcries, and when she had by her
Screams gathered them about her, ordered them to drive out of
the House that Villain, who had forced himself in upon her, and
endeavoured to murder her. *Savage*, who had attempted with the
most submissive Tenderness to soften her Rage, hearing her utter
so detestable an Accusation, thought it prudent to retire, and, I
believe, never attempted afterwards to speak to her.

But shocked as he was with her Falshood and her Cruelty, he
imagined that she intended no other Use of her Lye, than to set
herself free from his Embraces and Solicitations, and was very far
from suspecting that she would treasure it in her Memory, as an
Instrument of future Wickedness, or that she would endeavour for
this fictitious Assault to deprive him of his Life.

But when the Queen was solicited for his Pardon, and informed of the severe Treatment which he had suffered from his Judge, she answered, that however unjustifiable might be the Manner of his Trial, or whatever Extenuation the Action for which he was condemned might admit, she could not think that Man a proper Object of the King's Mercy, who had been capable of entering his Mother's House in the Night, with an Intent to murder her.

By whom this atrocious Calumny had been transmitted to the Queen, whether she that invented, had the Front to relate it; whether she found any one weak enough to credit it, or corrupt enough to concur with her in her hateful Design, I know not; but Methods had been taken to persuade the Queen so strongly of the Truth of it, that she for a long Time refused to hear any of those who petitioned for his Life.

Thus had *Savage* perished by the Evidence of a Bawd, a Strumpet, and his Mother, had not Justice and Compassion procured him an Advocate of Rank too great to be rejected unheard, and of Virtue too eminent to be heard without being believed. His Merit and his Calamities happened to reach the Ear of the Countess of *Hertford*, who engaged in his Support with all the Tenderness that is excited by Pity, and all the Zeal which is kindled by Generosity, and demanding an Audience of the Queen, laid before her the whole Series of his Mother's Cruelty, exposed the Improbability of an Accusation by which he was charged with an Intent to commit a Murder, that could produce no Advantage, and soon convinced her how little his former Conduct could deserve to be mentioned as a Reason for extraordinary Severity.

The Interposition of this Lady was so successful, that he was soon after admitted to Bail, and on the 9th of *March*, 1728, pleaded the King's Pardon.

It is natural to enquire upon what Motives his Mother could prosecute him in a Manner so outrageous and implacable; for what Reason she could employ all the Arts of Malice, and all the Snares of Calumny, to take away the Life of her own Son, of a Son who never injured her, who was never supported by her Expence, nor obstructed any Prospect of Pleasure or Advantage; why she should endeavour to destroy him by a Lye; a Lye which could not gain Credit, but must vanish of itself at the first Moment of Examination, and of which only this can be said to make it probable, that it may be observed from her Conduct, that the most execrable Crimes are sometimes committed without apparent Temptation.

This Mother is still alive, and may perhaps even yet, though her Malice was so often defeated, enjoy the Pleasure of reflecting, that the Life which she often endeavoured to destroy, was at least shortened by her maternal Offices; that though she could not transport her Son to the Plantations, bury him in the Shop of a Mechanick, or hasten the Hand of the publick Executioner, she has yet had the Satisfaction of imbittering all his Hours, and forcing him into Exigences, that hurried on his Death.

It is by no Means necessary to aggravate the Enormity of this Woman's Conduct, by placing it in Opposition to that of the Countess of *Hertford*; no one can fail to observe how much more amiable it is to relieve, than to oppress, and to rescue Innocence from Destruction, than to destroy without an Injury.

Mr *Savage*, during his Imprisonment, his Trial, and the Time in which he lay under Sentence of Death, behaved with great Firmness and Equality of Mind, and confirmed by his Fortitude the Esteem of those, who before admired him for his Abilities. The peculiar Circumstances of his Life were made more generally known by a short Account*, which was then published, and of which several thousands were in a few Weeks dispersed over the Nation; and the Compassion of Mankind operated so powerfully in his Favour, that he was enabled, by frequent Presents, not only to support himself, but to assist Mr *Gregory* in Prison; and when he was pardoned and released, he found the Number of his Friends not lessened.

The Nature of the Act for which he had been tried was in itself doubtful; of the Evidences which appeared against him, the Character of the Man was not unexceptionable, that of the Woman notoriously infamous; she whose Testimony chiefly influenced the Jury to condemn him, afterwards retracted her Assertions. He always himself denied that he was drunk, as had been generally reported. Mr *Gregory*, who is now Collector of *Antigua*, is said to declare him far less criminal than he was imagined even by some who favoured him: And *Page* himself afterward confessed, that he had treated him with uncommon Rigour. When all these Particulars are rated together, perhaps the Memory of *Savage* may not be much sullied by his Trial.

Some Time after he obtained his Liberty, he met in the Street the Woman that had sworn with so much Malignity against him.

* Written by Mr *Beckingham* and another Gentleman.

61

She informed him, that she was in Distress, and, with a Degree of Confidence not easily attainable, desired him to relieve her. He, instead of insulting her Misery, and taking Pleasure in the Calamities of one who had brought his Life into Danger, reproved her gently for her Perjury, and changing the only Guinea that he had, divided it equally between her and himself.

This is an Action which in some Ages would have made a Saint, and perhaps in others a Hero, and which, without any hyperbolical Encomiums, must be allowed to be an Instance of uncommon Generosity, an Act of complicated Virtue; by which he at once relieved the Poor, corrected the Vicious, and forgave an Enemy; by which he at once remitted the strongest Provocations, and exercised the most ardent Charity.

Compassion was indeed the distinguishing Quality of *Savage*; he never appeared inclined to take Advantage of Weakness, to attack the defenceless, or to press upon the falling; whoever was distressed was certain at least of his Good-Wishes; and when he could give no Assistance, to extricate them from Misfortunes, he endeavoured to sooth them by Sympathy and Tenderness.

But when his Heart was not softened by the Sight of Misery, he was sometimes obstinate in his Resentment, and did not quickly lose the Remembrance of an Injury. He always continued to speak with anger of the Insolence and Partiality of *Page*, and a short Time before his Death revenged it by a Satire.

It is natural to enquire in what Terms Mr *Savage* spoke of this fatal Action, when the Danger was over, and he was under no Necessity of using any Art to set his Conduct in the fairest Light. He was not willing to dwell upon it, and if he transiently mentioned it, appeared neither to consider himself as a Murderer, nor as a Man wholly free from the Guilt of Blood*. How much and how long he regretted it, appeared in a Poem which he published many Years afterwards. On Occasion of a Copy of Verses in which the Failings of good Men were recounted, and in which the Author had endeavoured to illustrate his Position, that *the best may sometimes deviate from Virtue*, by an Instance of Murder committed by *Savage* in the Heat of Wine, *Savage* remarked, that it was no very just Representation of a good Man, to suppose him liable to Drunkenness, and disposed in his Riots to cut Throats.

He was now indeed at Liberty, but was, as before, without any

* In one of his letters he stiles it, a *fatal Quarrel, but too well known.*

other Support than accidental Favours and uncertain Patronage afforded him; Sources by which he was sometimes very liberally supplied, and which at other Times were suddenly stopped; so that he spent his Life between Want and Plenty, or, what was yet worse, between Beggary and Extravagance; for as whatever he received was the Gift of Chance, which might as well favour him at one Time as another, he was tempted to squander what he had, because he always hoped to be immediately supplied.

Another Cause of his Profusion was the absurd Kindness of his Friends, who at once rewarded and enjoyed his Abilities, by treating him at Taverns, and habituating him to Pleasures which he could not afford to enjoy, and which he was not able to deny himself, though he purchased the Luxury of a single Night by the Anguish of Cold and Hunger for a Week.

The Experience of these Inconveniences determined him to endeavour after some settled Income, which, having long found Submission and Intreaties fruitless, he attempted to extort from his Mother by rougher Methods. He had now, as he acknowledged, lost that Tenderness for her, which the whole Series of her Cruelty had not been able wholly to repress, till he found, by the Efforts which she made for his Destruction, that she was not content with refusing to assist him, and being neutral in his Struggles with Poverty, but was as ready to snatch every Opportunity of adding to his Misfortunes, and that she was to be considered as an Enemy implacably malicious, whom nothing but his Blood could satisfy. He therefore threatned to harass her with Lampoons, and to publish a copious Narrative of her Conduct, unless she consented to purchase an Exemption from Infamy, by allowing him a Pension.

This Expedient proved successful. Whether Shame still survived, though Virtue was extinct, or whether her Relations had more delicacy than herself, and imagined that some of the Darts which Satire might point at her would glance upon them: Lord *Tyrconnel*, whatever were his Motives, upon his Promise to lay aside his Design of exposing the Cruelty of his Mother, received him into his Family, treated him as his Equal, and engaged to allow him a Pension of two hundred Pounds a Year.

This was the Golden Part of Mr *Savage*'s Life; and for some Time he had no Reason to complain of Fortune; his Appearance was splendid, his Expences large, and his Acquaintance extensive. He was courted by all who endeavoured to be thought Men of Genius, and caressed by all who valued themselves upon a refined Taste. To admire Mr *Savage*, was a Proof of Discernment, and to be acquainted with him was a Title to poetical Reputation. His Presence was sufficient to make any Place of publick Entertainment popular; and his Approbation and Example constituted the Fashion. So powerful is Genius, when it is invested with the Glitter of Affluence; Men willingly pay to Fortune that Regard which they owe to Merit, and are pleased when they have an Opportunity at once of gratifying their Vanity, and practising their Duty.

This Interval of Prosperity furnished him with Opportunities of enlarging his Knowledge of human Nature, by contemplating Life from its highest Gradations to its lowest; and had he afterwards applied to Dramatic Poetry, he would perhaps not have had many Superiors; for as he never suffered any Scene to pass before his Eyes without Notice, he had treasured in his Mind all the different Combinations of Passions, and the innumerable Mixtures of Vice and Virtue, which distinguish one Character from another; and as his Conception was strong, his Expressions were clear, he easily received Impressions from Objects, and very forcibly transmitted them to others.

Of his exact Observations on human Life he has left a Proof, which would do Honour to the greatest Names, in a small Pamphlet, called *The Author to be let*, where he introduces *Iscariot Hackney*, a prostitute Scribler, giving an Account of his Birth, his Education, his Disposition and Morals, Habits of Life, and Maxims of Conduct. In the Introduction are related many secret Histories of the petty Writers of that Time, but sometimes mixed with ungenerous Reflections on their Birth, their Circumstances, or those of their Relations; nor can it be denied, that some Passages are such as *Iscariot Hackney* might himself have produced.

He was accused likewise of living in an Appearance of Friendship with some whom he satirised, and of making use of the Confidence which he gained by a seeming Kindness to discover Failings and expose them; it must be confessed, that Mr *Savage*'s Esteem was no very certain Possession, and that he would lampoon at one Time those whom he had praised at another.

It may be alledged, that the same Man may change his Principles, and that he who was once deservedly commended, may be afterwards satirised with equal Justice; or that the Poet was dazzled with the Appearance of Virtue, and found the Man whom he had celebrated, when he had an Opportunity of examining him more nearly, unworthy of the Panegyric which he had too hastily bestowed; and that as a false Satire ought to be recanted, for the sake of him whose Reputation may be injured, false Praise ought likewise to be obviated, lest the Distinction between Vice and Virtue should be lost, lest a bad Man should be trusted upon the Credit of his Encomiast, or lest others should endeavour to obtain the like Praises by the same Means.

But though these Excuses may be often plausible, and sometimes just, they are very seldom satisfactory to Mankind; and the Writer, who is not constant to his Subject, quickly sinks into Contempt, his Satire loses its Force, and his Panegyric its Value, and he is only considered at one Time as a Flatterer, and as a Calumniator at another.

To avoid these Imputations, it is only necessary to follow the Rules of Virtue, and to preserve an unvaried Regard to Truth. For though it is undoubtedly possible, that a Man, however cautious, may be sometimes deceived by an artful Appearance of Virtue, or by false Evidences of Guilt, such Errors will not be frequent; and it will be allowed, that the Name of an Author would never have been made contemptible, had no Man ever said what he did not think, or misled others, but when he was himself deceived.

The Author to be let was first published in a single Pamphlet, and afterwards inserted in a Collection of Pieces relating to the *Dunciad*, which were addressed by Mr *Savage* to the Earl of *Middlesex*, in a Dedication, which he was prevailed upon to sign, though he did not write it, and in which there are some Positions, that the true Author would perhaps not have published under his own Name; and on which Mr *Savage* afterwards reflected with no great Satisfaction.

The Enumeration of the bad Effects of the *uncontrolled Freedom of the Press*, and the assertion that the *Liberties taken by the Writers of Journals with their Superiors were exorbitant and unjustifiable*, very ill became Men, who have themselves not always shewn the exactest Regard to the Laws of Subordination in their Writings, and who have often satirised those that at least thought themselves their Superiors, as they were eminent for their hereditary Rank, and employed in the highest Offices of the Kingdom. But this is only an Instance of that Partiality which almost every

65

Man indulges with Regard to himself; the Liberty of the Press is a Blessing when we are inclined to write against others, and a Calamity when we find ourselves overborn by the Multitude of our Assailants; as the Power of the Crown is always thought too great by those who suffer by its Influence, and too little by those in whose Favour it is exerted; and a Standing Army is generally accounted necessary by those who command, and dangerous and oppressive by those who support it.

Mr *Savage* was likewise very far from believing, that the Letters annexed to each Species of bad Poets in the *Bathos*, were, as he was directed to assert, *set down at Random*; for when he was charged by one of his Friends with putting his Name to such an Improbability, he had no other Answer to make than that *he did not think of it*, and his Friend had too much Tenderness to reply, that next to the Crime of writing contrary to what he thought, was that of writing without thinking.

After having remarked what is false in this Dedication, it is proper that I observe the Impartiality which I recommend, by declaring, what *Savage* asserted, that the Account of the Circumstances which attended the Publication of the *Dunciad*, however strange and improbable, was exactly true.

The Publication of this Piece at this Time raised Mr *Savage* a great Number of Enemies among those that were attacked by Mr *Pope*, with whom he was considered as a Kind of Confederate, and whom he was suspected of supplying with private Intelligence and secret Incidents: so that the Ignominy of an Informer was added to the Terror of a Satirist.

That he was not altogether free from literary Hypocrisy, and that he sometimes spoke one thing, and wrote another, cannot be denied, because he himself confessed, that when he lived in great Familiarity with *Dennis*, he wrote an Epigram against him.

Mr *Savage* however set all the Malice of all the pigmy Writers at Defiance, and thought the Friendship of Mr *Pope* cheaply purchased by being exposed to their Censure and their Hatred; nor had he any Reason to repent of the Preference, for he found Mr *Pope* a steady and unalienable Friend almost to the End of his Life.

About this Time, notwithstanding his avowed Neutrality with regard to Party, he published a Panegyric on Sir *Robert Walpole*, for which he was rewarded by him with twenty Guineas; a Sum not very large, if either the Excellence of the Performance, or the

Wealth of the Patron be considered; but greater than he afterwards obtained from a Person of yet higher Rank, and more desirous in Appearance of being distinguished as a Patron of Literature.

As he was very far from approving the Conduct of Sir *Robert Walpole*, and in Conversation mentioned him sometimes with Acrimony, and generally with Contempt, as he was one of those who were always zealous in their Assertions of the Justice of the late Opposition, jealous of the Rights of the People, and alarmed by the long continued Triumph of the Court; it was natural to ask him what could induce him to employ his Poetry in Praise of that Man who was, in his Opinion, an Enemy to Liberty, and an Oppressor of his Country? He alleged, that he was then dependent upon the Lord *Tyrconnel*, who was an implicit Follower of the Ministry, and that being enjoined by him, not without Menaces, to write in Praise of his Leader, he had not Resolution sufficient to sacrifice the Pleasure of Affluence to that of Integrity.

On this and on many other Occasions he was ready to lament the Misery of living at the Tables of other Men, which was his Fate from the Beginning to the End of his Life; for I know not whether he ever had, for three Months together, a settled Habitation, in which he could claim a Right of Residence.

To this unhappy State it is just to impute much of the Inconstancy of his Conduct; for though a Readiness to comply with the Inclination of others was no Part of his natural Character, yet he was sometimes obliged to relax his Obstinacy, and submit his own Judgment and even his Virtue to the Government of those by whom he was supported: So that if his Miseries were sometimes the Consequences of his Faults, he ought not yet to be wholly excluded from Compassion, because his Faults were very often the Effects of his Misfortunes.

In this gay Period* of his Life, while he was surrounded by Affluence and Pleasure, he published *the Wanderer*, a moral Poem, of which the Design is comprised in these lines:

> I fly all public Care, all venal Strife,
> To try the *still* compar'd with *active Life*;
> To prove by these, the Sons of Men may owe
> The Fruits of Bliss to bursting Clouds of Woe;
> That even Calamity, by Thought refin'd,
> Inspirits and adorns the thinking Mind.

* 1729.

And more distinctly in the following Passage:

> By Woe the Soul to daring Action swells,
> By Woe in plaintless Patience it excels;
> From Patience prudent, clear Experience springs,
> And traces Knowledge through the Course of Things.
> Thence Hope is form'd, thence Fortitude, Success,
> Renown—whate'er Men covet and caress.

This Performance was always considered by himself as his Master-piece, and Mr *Pope* when he asked his Opinion of it, told him, that he read it once over, and was not displeased with it, that it gave him more Pleasure at the second Perusal, and delighted him still more at the third.

It has been generally objected to *the Wanderer*, that the Disposition of the Parts is irregular, that the Design is obscure, and the Plan perplexed; that the Images, however beautiful, succeed each other without Order; and that the whole Performance is not so much a regular Fabric, as a Heap of shining Materials, thrown together by Accident, which strikes rather with the solemn Magnificence of a stupendous Ruin, than the elegant Grandeur of a finished Pile.

This Criticism is universal, and therefore it is reasonable to believe it at least in a great Degree just; but Mr *Savage* was always of a contrary Opinion; he thought his Drift could only be missed by Negligence or Stupidity, and that the whole Plan was regular, and the Parts distinct.

It was never denied to abound with strong Representations of Nature, and just Observations upon Life, and it may easily be observed, that most of his Pictures have an evident Tendency to illustrate his first great Position, *that Good is the Consequence of Evil.* The Sun that burns up the Mountains, fructifies the Vales; the Deluge that rushes down the broken Rocks with dreadful Impetuosity, is separated into purling Brooks; and the Rage of the Hurricane purifies the Air.

Even in this Poem he has not been able to forbear one Touch upon the Cruelty of his Mother, which, though remarkably delicate and tender, is a Proof how deep an Impression it had upon his Mind.

This must be at least acknowledged, which ought to be thought equivalent to many other Excellencies, that this Poem can promote no other Purposes than those of Virtue, and that it is written with a very strong Sense of the Efficacy of Religion.

But my Province is rather to give the History of Mr *Savage*'s Performances than to display their Beauties, or to obviate the Criticisms, which they have occasioned, and therefore I shall not dwell upon the particular Passages which deserve Applause: I shall neither show the Excellence of his Descriptions, nor expatiate on the terrific Portrait of *Suicide*, nor point out the artful Touches, by which he has distinguished the intellectual Features of the Rebels, who suffer Death in his last Canto. It is, however, proper to observe, that *Savage* always declared the Characters wholly fictitious, and without the least Allusion to any real Persons or Actions.

From a Poem so diligently laboured, and so successfully finished, it might be reasonably expected that he should have gained considerable Advantage; nor can it without some Degree of Indignation and Concern be told that he sold the Copy for ten Guineas, of which he afterwards returned two, that the two last Sheets of the Work might be reprinted, of which he had in his Absence intrusted the Correction to a Friend, who was too indolent to perform it with Accuracy.

A superstitious Regard to the Correction of his Sheets was one of Mr *Savage*'s Peculiarities; he often altered, revised, recurred to his first Reading or Punctuation, and again adopted the Alteration; he was dubious and irresolute without End, as on a Question of the last Importance, and at last was seldom satisfied; the Intrusion or Omission of a Comma was sufficient to discompose him, and he would lament an Error of a single Letter as a heavy Calamity. In one of his Letters relating to an Impression of some Verses, he remarks, that he had, with regard to the Correction of the Proof *a spell upon him*; and indeed the Anxiety, with which he dwelt upon the minutest and most trifling Niceties, deserved no other Name than that of Fascination.

That he sold so valuable a Performance for so small a Price, was not to be imputed either to Necessity, by which the Learned and Ingenious are often obliged to submit to very hard Conditions, or to Avarice, by which the Booksellers are frequently incited to oppress that Genius by which they are supported, but to that intemperate Desire of Pleasure, and habitual Slavery to his Passions, which involved him in many Perplexities; he happened at that Time to be engaged in the Pursuit of some trifling Gratification, and being without Money for the present Occasion, sold his Poem to the first Bidder, perhaps for the first Price that was proposed, and would probably have been content with less, if less had been offered him.

This Poem was addressed to the Lord *Tyrconnel* not only in the first Lines, but in a formal Dedication filled with the highest Strains of Panegyric, and the warmest Professions of Gratitude, but by no means remarkable for Delicacy of Connection, or Elegance of Stile.

These Praises in a short Time he found himself inclined to retract, being discarded by the Man on whom he had bestowed them, and whom he then immediately discovered not to have deserved them. Of this Quarrel, which every Day made more bitter, Lord *Tyrconnel* and Mr *Savage* assigned very different Reasons, which might perhaps all in Reality concur, though they were not all convenient to be alleged by either Party. Lord *Tyrconnel* affirmed, that it was the constant Practice of Mr *Savage*, to enter a Tavern with any Company that proposed it, drink the most expensive Wines, with great Profusion, and when the Reckoning was demanded, to be without Money: If, as it often happened, his Company were willing to defray his Part, the Affair ended without any ill Consequences; but if they were refractory, and expected that the Wine should be paid for by him that drank it, his Method of Composition was, to take them with him to his own Apartment, assume the Government of the House, and order the Butler in an imperious Manner to set the best Wine in the Cellar before his Company, who often drank till they forgot the Respect due to the House in which they were entertained, indulged themselves in the utmost Extravagance of Merriment, practised the most licentious Frolics, and committed all the Outrages of Drunkenness.

Nor was this the only Charge which Lord *Tyrconnel* brought against him: Having given him a Collection of valuable Books, stamped with his own Arms, he had the Mortification to see them in a short Time exposed to Sale upon the Stalls, it being usual with Mr *Savage*, when he wanted a small Sum, to take his Books to the Pawnbroker.

Whoever was acquainted with Mr *Savage*, easily credited both these Accusations; for having been obliged from his first Entrance into the World to subsist upon Expedients, Affluence was not able to exalt him above them; and so much was he delighted with Wine and Conversation, and so long had he been accustomed to live by

Chance, that he would at any time go to the Tavern, without Scruple, and trust for his Reckoning to the Liberality of his Company, and frequently of Company to whom he was very little known. This Conduct indeed very seldom drew upon him those Inconveniences that might be feared by any other Person, for his Conversation was so entertaining, and his Address so pleasing, that few thought the Pleasûre which they received from him dearly purchased by paying for his Wine. It was his peculiar Happiness, that he scarcely ever found a Stranger, whom he did not leave a Friend; but it must likewise be added, that he had not often a Friend long, without obliging him to become a Stranger.

Mr *Savage*, on the other Hand, declared, that Lord *Tyrconnel** quarrelled with him, because he would not subtract from his own Luxury and Extravagance what he had promised to allow him, and that his Resentment was only a Plea for the Violation of his Promise: He asserted that he had done nothing that ought to exclude him from that Subsistence which he thought not so much a Favour, as a Debt, since it was offered him upon Conditions, which he had never broken; and that his only Fault was, that he could not be supported with nothing.

He acknowledged, that Lord *Tyrconnel* often exhorted him to regulate his Method of Life, and not to spend all his Nights in Taverns, and that he appeared very desirous, that he would pass those Hours with him which he so freely bestowed upon others. This demand Mr *Savage* considered as a Censure of his Conduct, which he could never patiently bear; and which even in the latter and cooler Part of his Life was so offensive to him, that he declared it as his Resolution, *to spurn that Friend who should presume to dictate to him*; and it is not likely, that in his earlier Years he received Admonitions with more Calmness.

He was likewise inclined to resent such Expectations, as tending to infringe his Liberty, of which he was very jealous when it was necessary to the Gratification of his Passions, and declared, that the Request was still more unreasonable, as the Company to which he was to have been confined was insupportably disagreeable. This Assertion affords another Instance of that Inconsistency of his Writings with his Conversation, which was so often to be observed. He forgot how lavishly he had, in his Dedication to *the* WANDERER,

---

* His Expression in one of his Letters was, that Ld *T——l had involved his Estate, and therefore poorly sought an Occasion to quarrel with him.*

extolled the Delicacy and Penetration, the Humanity and Generosity, the Candour and Politeness of the Man, whom, when he no longer loved him, he declared to be a Wretch without Understanding, without Good-Nature, and without Justice; of whose Name he thought himself obliged to leave no Trace in any future Edition of his Writings; and accordingly blotted it out of that Copy of *the Wanderer* which was in his Hands.

During his Continuance with the Lord *Tyrconnel*, he wrote *The Triumph of Health and Mirth*, on the Recovery of Lady *Tyrconnel* from a languishing Illness. This Performance is remarkable, not only for the Gayety of the Ideas, and the Melody of the Numbers, but for the agreeable Fiction upon which it is formed. *Mirth* overwhelmed with Sorrow, for the Sickness of her Favourite, takes a Flight in Quest of her Sister *Health*, whom she finds reclined upon the Brow of a lofty Mountain, amidst the Fragrance of perpetual Spring, with the Breezes of the Morning sporting about her. Being solicited by her sister *Mirth*, she readily promises her Assistance, flies away in a Cloud, and impregnates the Waters of *Bath* with new Virtues, by which the Sickness of *Belinda* is relieved.

As the Reputation of his Abilities, the particular Circumstances of his Birth and Life, the Splendor of his Appearance, and the Distinction which was for some Time paid him by Lord *Tyrconnel*, intitled him to Familiarity with Persons of higher Rank, than those to whose Conversation he had been before admitted, he did not fail to gratify that Curiosity, which induced him to take a nearer View of those whom their Birth, their Employments, or their Fortunes, necessarily place at a Distance from the greatest Part of Mankind, and to examine, whether their Merit was magnified or diminished by the Medium through which it was contemplated; whether the Splendor with which they dazzled their Admirers, was inherent in themselves, or only reflected on them by the Objects that surrounded them; and whether great Men were selected for high Stations, or high Stations made great Men.

For this Purpose, he took all Opportunities of conversing familiarly with those who were most conspicuous at that Time, for their Power, or their Influence; he watched their looser Moments, and examined their domestic Behaviour, with that Acuteness which Nature had given him, and which the uncommon Variety of his Life had contributed to increase, and that Inquisitiveness which

must always be produced in a vigorous Mind by an absolute
Freedom from all pressing or domestic Engagements. His Discernment was quick, and therefore he soon found in every Person, and
in every Affair, something that deserved Attention; he was supported by others, without any Care for himself, and was therefore
at Leisure to pursue his Observations.

More Circumstances to constitute a Critic on human Life could
not easily concur, nor indeed could any Man who assumed from
accidental Advantages more Praise than he could justly claim
from his real Merit, admit any Acquaintance more dangerous than
that of *Savage*; of whom likewise it must be confessed, that Abilities really exalted above the common Level, or Virtue refined from
Passion, or proof against Corruption could not easily find an abler
Judge, or a warmer Advocate.

What was the Result of Mr *Savage*'s Enquiry, though he was
not much accustomed to conceal his Discoveries, it may not be
entirely safe to relate, because the Persons whose Characters he
criticised are powerful; and Power and Resentment are seldom
Strangers; nor would it perhaps be wholly just, because what he
asserted in Conversation might, though true in general, be heightened by some momentary Ardour of Imagination, and as it can be
delivered only from Memory, may be imperfectly represented;
so that the Picture at first aggravated, and then unskilfully copied,
may be justly suspected to retain no great Resemblance of the
Original.

It may, however, be observed, that he did not appear to have
formed very elevated Ideas of those to whom the Administration
of Affairs, or the Conduct of Parties, has been intrusted; who have
been considered as the Advocates of the Crown, or the Guardians
of the People, and who have obtained the most implicit Confidence, and the loudest Applauses. Of one particular Person, who
has been at one Time so popular as to be generally esteemed, and
at another so formidable as to be universally detested, he observed,
that his Acquisitions had been small, or that his Capacity was
narrow, and that the whole Range of his Mind was from Obscenity
to Politics, and from Politics to Obscenity.

But the Opportunity of indulging his Speculations on great
Characters was now at an End. He was banished from the Table of
Lord *Tyrconnel*, and turned again adrift upon the World, without
Prospect of finding quickly any other Harbour. As Prudence was

not one of the Virtues by which he was distinguished, he had made no Provision against a Misfortune like this. And though it is not to be imagined, but that the Separation must for some Time have been preceded by Coldness, Peevishness, or Neglect, though it was undoubtedly the Consequence of accumulated Provocations on both Sides, yet every one that knew *Savage* will readily believe, that to him it was sudden as a Stroke of Thunder; that though he might have transiently suspected it, he had never suffered any Thought so unpleasing to sink into his Mind, but that he had driven it away by Amusements, or Dreams of future Felicity and Affluence, and had never taken any Measures by which he might prevent a Precipitation from Plenty to Indigence.

This Quarrel and Separation, and the Difficulties to which Mr *Savage* was exposed by them, were soon known both to his Friends and Enemies; nor was it long before he perceived, from the Behaviour of both, how much is added to the Lustre of Genius, by the Ornaments of Wealth.

His Condition did not appear to excite much Compassion; for he had not always been careful to use the Advantages which he enjoyed with that Moderation, which ought to have been with more than usual Caution preserved by him, who knew, if he had reflected, that he was only a Dependant on the Bounty of another, whom he could expect to support him no longer than he endeavoured to preserve his Favour, by complying with his Inclinations, and whom he nevertheless set at Defiance, and was continually irritating by Negligence or Encroachments.

Examples need not be sought at any great Distance to prove that Superiority of Fortune has a natural Tendency to kindle Pride, and that Pride seldom fails to exert itself in Contempt and Insult; and if this is often the Effect of hereditary Wealth, and of Honours enjoyed only by the Merit of others, it is some Extenuation of any indecent Triumphs to which this unhappy Man may have been betrayed, that his Prosperity was heightened by the Force of Novelty, and made more intoxicating by a Sense of the Misery in which he had so long languished, and perhaps of the Insults which he had formerly borne, and which he might now think himself entitled to revenge. It is too common for those who have unjustly suffered Pain, to inflict it likewise in their Turn, with the same Injustice, and to imagine that they have a Right to treat others as they have themselves been treated.

That Mr *Savage* was too much elevated by any good Fortune is generally known; and some Passages of his Introduction to the *Author to be let* sufficiently shew, that he did not wholly refrain from such Satire as he afterwards thought very unjust, when he was exposed to it himself; for when he was afterwards ridiculed in the Character of a distressed Poet, he very easily discovered, that Distress was not a proper Subject for Merriment, or Topic of Invective. He was then able to discern that if Misery be the Effect of Virtue, it ought to be reverenced; if of Ill-Fortune, to be pitied; and if of Vice, not to be insulted, because it is perhaps itself a Punishment adequate to the Crime by which it was produced. And the Humanity of that Man can deserve no Panegyric, who is capable of reproaching a Criminal in the Hands of the Executioner.

But these Reflections, though they readily occurred to him in the first and last Parts of his Life, were, I am afraid, for a long Time forgotten; at least they were, like many other Maxims, treasured up in his Mind, rather for Show than Use, and operated very little upon his Conduct, however elegantly he might sometimes explain, or however forcibly he might inculcate them.

His Degradation therefore from the Condition which he had enjoyed with such wanton Thoughtlessness, was considered by many as an Occasion of Triumph. Those who had before paid their Court to him, without Success, soon returned the Contempt which they had suffered, and they who had received Favours from him, for of such Favours as he could bestow he was very liberal, did not always remember them. So much more certain are the Effects of Resentment than of Gratitude: It is not only to many more pleasing to recollect those Faults which place others below them, than those Virtues by which they are themselves comparatively depressed; but it is likewise more easy to neglect, than to recompense; and though there are few who will practise a laborious Virtue, there will never be wanting Multitudes that will indulge an easy Vice

Savage however was very little disturbed at the Marks of Contempt which his Ill-Fortune brought upon him, from those whom he never esteemed, and with whom he never considered himself as levelled by any Calamities; and though it was not without some Uneasiness that he saw some, whose Friendship he valued, change their Behaviour; he yet observed their Coldness without much Emotion, considered them as the Slaves of Fortune, and the Worshippers of Prosperity; and was more inclined to despise them, than to lament himself.

It does not appear that, after this Return of his Wants, he found Mankind equally favourable to him, as at his first Appearance in the World. His Story, though in Reality not less melancholy, was less affecting, because it was no longer new; it therefore procured him no new Friends, and those that had formerly relieved him thought they might now consign him to others. He was now likewise considered by many rather as criminal, than as unhappy; for the Friends of Lord *Tyrconnel* and of his Mother were sufficiently industrious to publish his Weaknesses, which were indeed very numerous, and nothing was forgotten, that might make him either hateful or ridiculous.

It cannot but be imagined, that such Representations of his Faults must make great Numbers less sensible of his Distress; many who had only an Opportunity to hear one Part made no scruple to propagate the Account which they received; many assisted their Circulation from Malice or Revenge, and perhaps many pretended to credit them, that they might with a better Grace withdraw their Regard, or withhold their Assistance.

Savage however was not one of those who suffered themselves to be injured without Resistance, nor was less diligent in exposing the Faults of Lord *Tyrconnel*, over whom he obtained at least this Advantage, that he drove him first to the Practice of Outrage and Violence; for he was so much provoked by the Wit and Virulence of *Savage*, that he came with a Number of Attendants, that did no Honour to his Courage, to beat him at a Coffee-House. But it happened that he had left the Place a few Minutes, and his Lordship had without Danger the Pleasure of boasting how he would have treated him. Mr *Savage* went next Day to repay his Visit at his own House, but was prevailed on, by his Domestics, to retire without insisting upon seeing him.

Lord *Tyrconnel* was accused by Mr *Savage* of some Actions, which scarcely any Provocations will be thought sufficient to justify; such as seizing what he had in his Lodgings, and other Instances of wanton Cruelty, by which he increased the Distress of *Savage* without any Advantage to himself.

These mutual Accusations were retorted on both Sides for many Years, with the utmost Degree of Virulence and Rage, and Time seemed rather to augment than diminish their Resentment;

that the Anger of Mr *Savage* should be kept alive is not strange, because he felt every Day the Consequences of the Quarrel; but it might reasonably have been hoped, that Lord *Tyrconnel* might have relented, and at length have forgot those Provocations, which, however they might have once inflamed him, had not in Reality much hurt him.

The Spirit of Mr *Savage* indeed never suffered him to solicit a Reconciliation; he returned Reproach for Reproach, and Insult for Insult: his Superiority of Wit supplied the Disadvantages of his Fortune, and inabled him to form a Party, and prejudice great Numbers in his Favour.

But though this might be some Gratification of his Vanity, it afforded very little Relief to his Necessities, and he was very frequently reduced to uncommon Hardships, of which, however, he never made any mean or importunate Complaints, being formed rather to bear Misery with Fortitude, than enjoy Prosperity with Moderation.

He now thought himself again at Liberty to expose the Cruelty of his Mother, and therefore, I believe, about this Time, published *The Bastard*, a Poem remarkable for the vivacious Sallies of Thought in the Beginning, where he makes a pompous Enumeration of the imaginary Advantages of base Birth, and the pathetic Sentiments at the End, where he recounts the real Calamities which he suffered by the Crime of his Parents.

The Vigour and Spirit of the Verses, the peculiar Circumstances of the Author, the Novelty of the Subject, and the Notoriety of the Story, to which the Allusions are made, procured this Performance a very favourable Reception; great Numbers were immediately dispersed, and Editions were multiplied with unusual Rapidity.

One Circumstance attended the Publication, which *Savage* used to relate with great Satisfaction. His Mother, to whom the Poem was *with due Reverence* inscribed, happened then to be at *Bath*, where she could not conveniently retire from Censure, or conceal herself from Observation; and no sooner did the Reputation of the Poem begin to spread, than she heard it repeated in all Places of Concourse, nor could she enter the Assembly Rooms, or cross the Walks, without being saluted with some Lines from *The Bastard*.

This was perhaps the first Time that she ever discovered a Sense of Shame, and on this Occasion the Power of Wit was very conspicuous; the Wretch who had, without Scruple, proclaimed herself an Adulteress, and who had first endeavoured to starve her Son, then to transport him, and afterwards to hang him, was not able to bear the Representation of her own Conduct, but fled from Reproach, though she felt no Pain from Guilt, and left *Bath* with the utmost Haste, to shelter herself among the Crouds of *London*.

Thus *Savage* had the Satisfaction of finding, that though he could not reform his Mother, he could punish her, and that he did not always suffer alone.

The Pleasure which he received from this Increase of his poetical Reputation, was sufficient for some Time to over-balance the Miseries of Want, which this Performance did not much alleviate, for it was sold for a very trivial Sum to a Bookseller, who, though the Success was so uncommon, that five Impressions were sold, of which many were undoubtedly very numerous, had not Generosity sufficient to admit the unhappy Writer to any Part of the Profit.

The Sale of this Poem was always mentioned by Mr *Savage* with the utmost Elevation of Heart, and referred to by him as an incontestible Proof of a general Acknowledgement of his Abilities. It was indeed the only Production of which he could justly boast a general Reception.

But though he did not lose the Opportunity which Success gave him of setting a high Rate on his Abilities, but paid due Deference to the Suffrages of Mankind when they were given in his Favour, he did not suffer his Esteem of himself to depend upon others, nor found any thing sacred in the Voice of the People when they were inclined to censure him; he then readily shewed the Folly of expecting that the Publick should judge right, observed how slowly poetical Merit had often forced its Way into the World, he contented himself with the Applause of Men of Judgment; and was somewhat disposed to exclude all those from the Character of Men of Judgment, who did not applaud him.

But he was at other Times more favourable to Mankind, than to think them blind to the Beauties of his Works, and imputed the Slowness of their Sale to other Causes; either they were published at a Time when the Town was empty, or when the Attention of the Public was engrossed by some Struggle in the Parliament, or some other Object of general Concern; or they were by the Neglect of the Publisher not diligently dispersed, or by his Avarice not advertised with sufficient Frequency. Address, or Industry, or Liberality, was always wanting; and the Blame was laid rather on any Person than the Author.

By Arts like these, Arts which every Man practises in some Degree, and to which too much of the little Tranquillity of Life is to be ascribed, *Savage* was always able to live at Peace with himself. Had he indeed only made use of these Expedients to alleviate the Loss or Want of Fortune or Reputation, or any other Advantage, which it is not in Man's Power to bestow upon himself, they might have been justly mentioned as Instances of a philosophical Mind, and very properly proposed to the Imitation of Multitudes, who, for want of diverting their Imaginations with the same Dexterity, languish under Afflictions which might be easily removed.

It were doubtless to be wished, that Truth and Reason were universally prevalent; that every Thing were esteemed according to its real Value; and that Men would secure themselves from being disappointed in their Endeavours after Happiness, by placing it only in Virtue, which is always to be obtained; but if adventitious and foreign Pleasures must be persued, it would be perhaps of some Benefit, since that Persuit must frequently be fruitless, if the Practice of *Savage* could be taught, that Folly might be an Antidote to Folly, and one Fallacy be obviated by another.

But the Danger of this pleasing Intoxication must not be concealed; nor indeed can any one, after having observed the Life of *Savage*, need to be cautioned against it. By imputing none of his Miseries to himself, he continued to act upon the same Principles, and to follow the same Path; was never made wiser by his Sufferings, nor preserved by one Misfortune from falling into another. He proceeded throughout his Life to tread the same Steps on the same Circle; always applauding his past Conduct, or at least forgetting it, to amuse himself with Phantoms of Happiness, which were dancing before him; and willingly turned his Eyes from the Light of Reason, when it would have discovered the Illusion, and shewn him, what he never wished to see, his real State.

He is even accused, after having lulled his Imagination with those ideal Opiates, of having tried the same Experiment upon his Conscience; and having accustomed himself to impute all Deviations from the right to foreign Causes, it is certain that he was upon every Occasion too easily reconciled to himself, and that he appeared very little to regret those Practices which had impaired his Reputation.

The reigning Error of his Life was, that he mistook the Love for the Practice of Virtue, and was indeed not so much a good Man as the Friend of Goodness.

This at least must be allowed him, that he always preserved a strong Sense of the Dignity, the Beauty, and the Necessity of Virtue, and that he never contributed deliberately to spread Corruption amongst Mankind; his Actions, which were generally precipitate, were often blameable, but his Writings, being the Productions of Study, uniformly tended to the Exaltation of the Mind, and the Propagation of Morality and Piety.

These Writings may improve Mankind, when his Failings shall be forgotten, and therefore he must be considered upon the whole as a Benefactor to the World; nor can his personal Example do any Hurt, since whoever hears of his Faults, will hear of the Miseries which they brought upon him, and which would deserve less Pity, had not his Condition been such as made his Faults pardonable. He may be considered as a Child *exposed* to all the Temptations of Indigence, at an Age when Resolution was not yet strengthened by Conviction, nor Virtue confirmed by Habit; a Circumstance which in his *Bastard* he laments in a very affecting Manner.

> ——No Mother's Care
> Shielded my Infant Innocence with Prayer:
> No Father's guardian Hand my Youth maintain'd,
> Call'd forth my Virtues, and from Vice restrain'd.

The *Bastard*, however it might provoke or mortify his Mother, could not be expected to melt her to Compassion, so that he was still under the same Want of the Necessaries of Life, and he therefore exerted all the Interest, which his Wit, or his Birth, or his Misfortunes could procure, to obtain upon the death of *Eusden* the Place of Poet Laureat, and prosecuted his Application with so much Diligence, that the King publickly declared it his Intention to bestow it upon him; but such was the Fate of *Savage*, that even the King, when he intended his Advantage, was disappointed in his Schemes; for the Lord Chamberlain, who has the Disposal of the Laurel as one of the Appendages of his Office, either did not know the King's Design, or did not approve it, or thought the Nomination of the Laureat an Encroachment upon his Rights, and therefore bestowed the Laurel upon *Colly Cibber*.

Mr *Savage* thus disappointed took a Resolution of applying to the Queen, that having once given him Life, she would enable him to support it, and therefore published a short Poem on her Birth-Day, to which he gave the odd Title of *Volunteer Laureat*. The Event of this Essay he has himself related in the following Letter, which he prefixed to the Poem, when he afterwards reprinted it in the *Gentleman's Magazine*, from whence I have copied it intire, as this was one of the few Attempts in which Mr *Savage* succeeded.

'Mr *Urban*,

In your Magazine for *February* you published the last *Volunteer Laureat*, written on a very melancholy Occasion, the Death of the Royal Patroness of Arts and Literature in general, and of the Author of that Poem in particular; I now send you the first that Mr *Savage* wrote under that Title.—This Gentleman, notwithstanding a very considerable Interest, being, on the Death of Mr *Eusden*, disappointed of the Laureat's Place, wrote the following Verses; which were no sooner published, but the late Queen sent to a Bookseller for them: The Author had not at that Time a Friend either to get him introduced, or his Poem presented at Court; yet such was the unspeakable Goodness of that Princess, that, notwithstanding this Act of Ceremony was wanting, in a few Days after Publication, Mr *Savage* received a Bank-Bill of fifty Pounds, and a gracious Message from her Majesty, by the Lord *North* and *Guilford*, to this Effect: "That her Majesty was highly pleased with the Verses; that she took particularly kind his Lines there relating to the King; that he had Permission to write annually on the same Subject; and that he should yearly receive the like Present, till something better (which was her Majesty's Intention) could be done for him." After this, he was permitted to present one of his annual Poems to her Majesty, had the Honour of kissing her Hand, and met with the most gracious Reception.

Yours, *&c.*'

Such was the Performance, and such its Reception; a Reception which, though by no means unkind, was yet not in the highest Degree generous: To chain down the Genius of a Writer to an annual Panegyric, shewed in the Queen too much Desire of hearing her own Praises, and a greater Regard to herself than to him on whom her Bounty was conferred. It was a kind of avaricious Generosity, by which Flattery was rather purchased than Genius rewarded.

Mrs *Oldfield* had formerly given him the same Allowance with much more heroic Intention; she had no other View than to enable him to prosecute his Studies, and to set himself above the Want of Assistance, and was contented with doing good without stipulating for Encomiums.

Mr *Savage* however was not at Liberty to make Exceptions, but was ravished with the Favours which he had received, and probably yet more with those which he was promised; he considered himself now as a Favourite of the Queen, and did not doubt but a few annual Poems would establish him in some profitable Employment.

He therefore assumed the Title of *Volunteer Laureat*, not without some Reprehensions from *Cibber*, who informed him, that the Title of *Laureat* was a Mark of Honour conferred by the King, from whom all Honour is derived, and which therefore no Man has a Right to bestow upon himself; and added, that he might with equal Propriety stile himself a Volunteer Lord, or Volunteer Baronet. It cannot be denied that the Remark was just, but *Savage* did not think any Title, which was conferred upon Mr *Cibber*, so honourable as that the Usurpation of it could be imputed to him as an Instance of very exorbitant Vanity, and therefore continued to write under the same Title, and received every Year the same Reward.

He did not appear to consider these Encomiums as Tests of his Abilities, or as any thing more than annual Hints to the Queen of her Promise, or Acts of Ceremony, by the Performance of which he was intitled to his Pension, and therefore did not labour them with great Diligence, or print more than fifty each Year, except that for some of the last Years he regularly inserted them in the *Gentleman's Magazine*, by which they were dispersed over the Kingdom.

Of some of them he had himself so low an Opinion, that he intended to omit them in the Collection of Poems, for which he printed Proposals, and solicited Subscriptions; nor can it seem strange, that being confined to the same Subject, he should be at some times indolent, and at others unsuccessful; that he should sometimes delay a disagreeable Task, till it was too late to perform it well; or that he should sometimes repeat the same Sentiment on the same Occasion, or at others be misled by an Attempt after Novelty to forced Conceptions, and far-fetched Images.

He wrote indeed with a double Intention, which supplied him

with some Variety; for his Business was to praise the Queen for the Favours which he had received, and to complain to her of the Delay of those which she had promised: In some of his Pieces, therefore, Gratitude is predominant, and in some Discontent; in some he represents himself as happy in her Patronage, and in others as disconsolate to find himself neglected.

Her Promise, like other Promises made to this unfortunate Man, was never performed, though he took sufficient Care that it should not be forgotten. The Publication of his *Volunteer Laureat* procured him no other Reward than a regular Remittance of fifty Pounds.

He was not so depressed by his Disappointments as to neglect any Opportunity that was offered of advancing his Interest. When the Princess *Anne* was married, he wrote a Poem upon her Departure, only, as he declared, *because it was expected from him*, and he was not willing to bar his own Prospects by any Appearance of Neglect.

He never mentioned any Advantage gain'd by this Poem, or any Regard that was paid to it, and therefore it is likely that it was considered at Court as an Act of Duty, to which he was obliged by his Dependence, and which it was therefore not necessary to reward by any new Favour: Or perhaps the Queen really intended his Advancement, and therefore thought it superfluous to lavish Presents upon a Man whom she intended to establish for Life.

About this Time not only his Hopes were in Danger of being frustrated, but his Pension likewise of being obstructed by an accidental Calumny. The writer of the *Daily Courant*, a Paper then published under the Direction of the Ministry, charged him with a Crime, which, though not very great in itself, would have been remarkably invidious in him, and might very justly have incensed the Queen against him. He was accused by Name of influencing Elections against the Court, by appearing at the Head of a Tory Mob; nor did the Accuser fail to aggravate his Crime, by representing it as the Effect of the most atrocious Ingratitude, and a kind of Rebellion against the Queen, who had first preserved him from an infamous Death, and afterwards distinguished him by her Favour, and supported him by her Charity. The Charge, as it was open and confident, was likewise by good Fortune very particular. The Place of the Transaction was mentioned, and the whole Series of the Rioter's Conduct related. This Exactness made Mr *Savage*'s

Vindication easy, for he never had in his Life seen the Place which was declared to be the Scene of his Wickedness, nor ever had been present in any Town when its Representatives were chosen. This Answer he therefore made haste to publish, with all the Circumstances necessary to make it credible, and very reasonably demanded, that the Accusation should be retracted in the same Paper, that he might no longer suffer the Imputation of Sedition and Ingratitude. This Demand was likewise pressed by him in a private Letter to the Author of the Paper, who either trusting to the Protection of those whose Defence he had undertaken, or having entertained some personal Malice against Mr *Savage*, or fearing lest by retracting so confident an Assertion, he should impair the Credit of his Paper, refused to give him that Satisfaction.

Mr *Savage* therefore thought it necessary, to his own Vindication, to prosecute him in the King's Bench; but as he did not find any ill Effects from the Accusation, having sufficiently cleared his Innocence, he thought any farther Procedure would have the Appearance of Revenge, and therefore willingly dropped it.

He saw soon afterwards a Process commenced in the same Court against himself, on an Information in which he was accused of writing and publishing an obscene Pamphlet.

It was always Mr *Savage*'s Desire to be distinguished, and when any Controversy became popular, he never wanted some Reason for engaging in it with great Ardour, and appearing at the Head of the Party which he had chosen. As he was never celebrated for his Prudence, he had no sooner taken his Side, and informed himself of the chief Topics of the Dispute, than he took all Opportunities of asserting and propagating his Principles, without much Regard to his own Interest, or any other visible Design than that of drawing upon himself the Attention of Mankind.

The Dispute between the Bishop of *London* and the Chancellor is well known to have been for some Time the chief Topic of political Conversation, and therefore Mr *Savage*, in pursuance of his Character, endeavoured to become conspicuous among the Controvertists with which every Coffee-House was filled on that Occasion. He was an indefatigable Opposer of all the Claims of Ecclesiastical Power, though he did not know on what they were founded, and was therefore no Friend to the Bishop of *London*. But he had another Reason for appearing as a warm Advocate for

Dr *Rundle*, for he was the Friend of Mr *Foster* and Mr *Thompson*, who were the Friends of Mr *Savage*.

Thus remote was his Interest in the Question, which however, as he imagined, concerned him so nearly, that it was not sufficient to harangue and dispute, but necessary likewise to write upon it.

He therefore engaged with great Ardour in a new Poem, called by him, *The Progress of a Divine*, in which he conducts a profligate Priest, by all the Gradations of Wickedness, from a poor Curacy in the Country, to the highest Preferments of the Church, and describes, with that Humour which was natural to him, and that Knowledge which was extended to all the Diversities of human Life, his Behaviour in every Station, and insinuates that this Priest thus accomplished found at last a Patron in the Bishop of *London*.

When he was asked by one of his Friends, on what Pretence he could charge the Bishop with such an Action, he had no more to say than that he had only inverted the Accusation, and that he thought it reasonable to believe, that he, who obstructed the Rise of a good Man without Reason, would for bad Reasons promote the Exaltation of a Villain.

The Clergy were universally provoked by this Satire, and *Savage*, who, as was his constant Practice, had set his Name to his Performance, was censured in the *Weekly Miscellany* with a Severity, which he did not seem inclined to forget.

But a Return of Invective was not thought a sufficient Punishment. The Court of *King's Bench* was therefore moved against him, and he was obliged to return an Answer to a Charge of Obscenity. It was urged in his Defence, that Obscenity was criminal when it was intended to promote the Practice of Vice, but that Mr *Savage* had only introduced obscene Ideas with the View of exposing them to Detestation, and of amending the Age by shewing the Deformity of Wickedness. This Plea was admitted, and Sir *Philip Yorke*, who then presided in that Court, dismissed the Information with Encomiums upon the Purity and Excellence of Mr *Savage*'s Writings.

The Prosecution however answered in some measure the Purpose of those by whom it was set on Foot, for Mr *Savage* was so far intimidated by it, that when the Edition of his Poem was sold, he did not venture to reprint it, so that it was in a short Time forgotten, or forgotten by all but those whom it offended.

It is said that some Endeavours were used to incense the Queen against him, but he found Advocates to obviate at least Part of their Effect; for though he was never advanced, he still continued to receive his Pension.

This Poem drew more Infamy upon him than any Incident of his Life, and as his Conduct cannot be vindicated, it is proper to secure his Memory from Reproach, by informing those whom he made his Enemies, that he never intended to repeat the Provocation; and that, though when ever he thought he had any Reason to complain of the Clergy, he used to threaten them with a new Edition of *The Progress of a Divine*, it was his calm and settled Resolution to suppress it for ever.

He once intended to have made a better Reparation for the Folly or Injustice with which he might be charged, by writing another Poem, called *The Progress of a Free-Thinker*, whom he intended to lead through all the Stages of Vice and Folly, to convert him from Virtue to Wickedness, and from Religion to Infidelity by all the modish Sophistry used for that Purpose; and at last to dismiss him by his own Hand into the other World.

That he did not execute this Design is a real Loss to Mankind, for he was too well acquainted with all the Scenes of Debauchery to have failed in his Representations of them, and too zealous for Virtue not to have represented them in such a Manner as should expose them either to Ridicule or Detestation.

But this Plan was, like others, formed and laid aside, till the Vigour of his Imagination was spent, and the Effervescence of Invention had subsided, but soon gave Way to some other Design, which pleased by its Novelty for a while, and then was neglected like the former.

He was still in his usual Exigencies, having no certain Support but the Pension allowed him by the Queen, which though it might have kept àn exact Oeconomist from Want, was very far from being sufficient for Mr *Savage*, who had never been accustomed to dismiss any of his Appetites without the Gratification which they solicited, and whom nothing but Want of Money withheld from partaking of every Pleasure that fell within his View.

His Conduct with regard to his Pension was very particular. No sooner had he changed the Bill, than he vanished from the Sight of all his Acquaintances, and lay for some Time out of the Reach of all the Enquiries that Friendship or Curiosity could make after him; at length he appeared again pennyless as before, but never informed even those whom he seemed to regard most, where he had been, nor was his Retreat ever discovered.

This was his constant Practice during the whole Time that he received the Pension from the Queen: He regularly disappeared and returned. He indeed affirmed, that he retired to study, and that the Money supported him in Solitude for many Months; but his Friends declared, that the short Time in which it was spent sufficiently confuted his own Account of his Conduct.

His Politeness and his Wit still raised him Friends, who were desirous of setting him at length free from that Indigence by which he had been hitherto oppressed, and therefore solicited Sir *Robert Walpole* in his Favour with so much Earnestness, that they obtained a Promise of the next Place that should become vacant, not exceeding two hundred Pounds a Year. This Promise was made with an uncommon Declaration, *that it was not the Promise of a Minister to a Petitioner, but of a Friend to his Friend.*

Mr *Savage* now concluded himself set at Ease for ever, and, as he observes in a Poem written on that Incident of his Life, *trusted* and *was trusted,* but soon found that his Confidence was ill-grounded, and this *friendly* Promise was not inviolable. He spent a long Time in Solicitations, and at last despaired and desisted.

He did not indeed deny thât he had given the Minister some Reason to believe that he should not strengthen his own Interest by advancing him; for he had taken Care to distinguish himself in Coffee-Houses as an Advocate for the Ministry of the last Years of Queen *Anne,* and was always ready to justify the Conduct, and exalt the Character of Lord *Bolingbroke,* whom he mentions with great Regard in an Epistle upon Authors, which he wrote about that Time, but was too wise to publish, and of which only some Fragments have appeared, inserted by him in the Magazine after his Retirement.

To despair was not, however, the Character of *Savage,* when one Patronage failed, he had recourse to another. The Prince was now extremely popular, and had very liberally rewarded the Merit of some Writers whom Mr *Savage* did not think superior to himself, and therefore he resolved to address a Poem to him.

For this Purpose he made Choice of a Subject, which could regard only Persons of the highest Rank and greatest Affluence, and which was therefore proper for a Poem intended to procure the Patronage of a Prince; and having retired for some Time to *Rich-*

mond, that he might prosecute his Design in full Tranquillity, without the Temptations of Pleasure, or the Solicitations of Creditors, by which his Meditations were in equal Danger of being disconcerted, he produced a Poem *On publick Spirit, with regard to public Works*.

The Plan of this Poem is very extensive, and comprises a Multitude of Topics, each of which might furnish Matter sufficient for a long Performance, and of which some have already employed more eminent Writers; but as he was perhaps not fully acquainted with the whole Extent of his own Design, and was writing to obtain a Supply of Wants too pressing to admit of long or accurate Enquiries, he passes negligently over many Public Works, which, even in his own Opinion, deserved to be more elaborately treated.

But though he may sometimes disappoint his Reader by transient Touches upon these Subjects, which have often been considered, and therefore naturally raise Expectations, he must be allowed amply to compensate his Omissions by expatiating in the Conclusion of his Work upon a Kind of Beneficence not yet celebrated by any eminent Poet, though it now appears more susceptible of Embellishments, more adapted to exalt the Ideas, and affect the Passions, than many of those which have hitherto been thought most worthy of the Ornaments of Verse. The Settlement of Colonies in uninhabited Countries, the Establishment of those in Security whose Misfortunes have made their own Country no longer pleasing or safe, the Acquisition of Property without Injury to any, the Appropriation of the waste and luxuriant Bounties of Nature, and the Enjoyment of those Gifts which Heaven has scattered upon Regions uncultivated and unoccupied, cannot be considered without giving Rise to a great Number of pleasing Ideas, and bewildering the Imagination in delightful Prospects; and, therefore, whatever Speculations they may produce in those who have confined themselves to political Studies, naturally fixed the Attention, and excited the Applause of a Poet. The Politician, when he considers Men driven into other Countries for Shelter, and obliged to retire to Forests and Deserts, and pass their Lives and fix their Posterity in the remotest Corners of the World, to avoid those Hardships which they suffer or fear in their native Place, may very properly enquire why the Legislature does not provide a Remedy for these Miseries, rather than encourage an Escape from them. He may conclude, that the Flight of every honest Man is a Loss

88

to the Community, that those who are unhappy without Guilt ought to be relieved, and the Life which is overburthened by accidental Calamities, set at Ease by the Care of the Publick, and that those, who have by Misconduct forfeited their Claim to Favour, ought rather to be made useful to the Society which they have injured, than be driven from it. But the Poet is employed in a more pleasing Undertaking than that of proposing Laws, which, however just or expedient, will never be made, or endeavouring to reduce to rational Schemes of Government Societies which were formed by Chance, and are conducted by the private Passions of those who preside in them. He guides the unhappy Fugitive from Want and Persecution, to Plenty, Quiet, and Security, and seats him in Scenes of peaceful Solitude, and undisturbed Repose.

Savage has not forgotten, amidst the pleasing Sentiments which this Prospect of Retirement suggested to him, to censure those Crimes which have been generally committed by the Discoverers of new Regions, and to expose the enormous Wickedness of making War upon barbarous Nations because they cannot resist, and of invading Countries because they are fruitful; of extending Navigation only to propagate Vice, and of visiting distant Lands only to lay them waste. He has asserted the natural Equality of Mankind, and endeavoured to suppress that Pride which inclines Men to imagine that Right is the Consequence of Power.

His Description of the various Miseries which force Men to seek for Refuge in distant Countries, affords another Instance of his Proficiency in the important and extensive Study of human Life; and the Tenderness with which he recounts them, another Proof of his Humanity and Benevolence.

It is observable, that the Close of this Poem discovers a Change which Experience had made in Mr *Savage's* Opinions. In a Poem written by him in his Youth, and published in his Miscellanies, he declares his Contempt of the contracted Views and narrow Prospects of the middle State of Life, and declares his Resolution either to tower like the Cedar, or be trampled like the Shrub; but in this Poem, though addressed to a Prince, he mentions this State of Life as comprising those who ought most to attract Reward, those who merit most the Confidence of Power, and the Familiarity of Greatness; and accidentally mentioning this Passage to one of his Friends, declared that in his Opinion all the Virtue of Mankind was comprehended in that State.

In describing Villas and Gardens, he did not omit to condemn that absurd Custom, which prevails among the *English*, of permitting Servants to receive Money from Strangers for the Entertainment that they receive; and therefore inserted in his Poem these Lines:

> But what's the flow'ring Pride of Gardens rare,
> However royal, or however fair,
> If Gates, which to Access should still give way,
> Ope but, like *Peter*'s Paradise, for Pay?
> If perquisited Varlets frequent stand,
> And each new Walk must a new Tax demand?
> What foreign Eye but with Contempt surveys?
> What Muse shall from Oblivion snatch their Praise?

But before the Publication of his Performance he recollected, that the Queen allowed her Garden and Cave at *Richmond* to be shewn for Money, and that she so openly countenanced the Practice, that she had bestowed the Privilege of shewing them as a Place of Profit on a Man whose Merit she valued herself upon rewarding, though she gave him only the Liberty of disgracing his Country.

He therefore thought, with more Prudence than was often exerted by him, that the Publication of these Lines might be officiously represented as an Insult upon the Queen to whom he owed his Life and his Subsistence, and that the Propriety of his Observation would be no Security against the Censures which the Unseasonableness of it might draw upon him; he therefore suppressed the Passage in the first Edition, but after the Queen's Death thought the same Caution no longer necessary, and restored it to the proper Place.

The Poem was therefore published without any political Faults, and inscribed to the Prince; but Mr *Savage* having no Friend upon whom he could prevail to present it to him, had no other Method of attracting his Observation than the Publication of frequent Advertisements, and therefore received no Reward from his Patron, however generous on other Occasions.

This Disappointment he never mentioned without Indignation, being by some means or other confident that the Prince was not ignorant of his Address to him, and insinuated, that if any Advances in Popularity could have been made by distinguishing him, he had not written without Notice, or without Reward.

He was once inclined to have presented his Poem in Person, and sent to the Printer for a Copy with that Design; but either his Opinion changed, or his Resolution deserted him, and he continued to resent Neglect without attempting to force himself into Regard.

Nor was the Public much more favourable than his Patron, for only seventy-two were sold, though the Performance was much commended by some whose Judgment in that Kind of Writing is generally allowed. But *Savage* easily reconciled himself to Mankind without imputing any Defect to his Work, by observing that his Poem was unluckily published two Days after the Prorogation of the Parliament, and by consequence at a Time when all those who could be expected to regard it were in the Hurry of preparing for their Departure, or engaged in taking Leave of others upon their Dismission fron Public Affairs.

It must be however allowed, in Justification of the Public, that this Performance is not the most excellent of Mr *Savage*'s Works, and that though it cannot be denied to contain many striking Sentiments, majestic Lines, and just Observations, it is in general not sufficiently polished in the Language, or enlivened in the Imagery, or digested in the Plan.

Thus his Poem contributed nothing to the Alleviation of his Poverty, which was such as very few could have supported with equal Patience, but to which it must likewise be confessed, that few would have been exposed who receive punctually fifty Pounds a Year; a Salary which, though by no means equal to the Demands of Vanity and Luxury, is yet found sufficient to support Families above Want, and was undoubtedly more than the Necessities of Life require.

But no sooner had he received his Pension, than he withdrew to his darling Privacy, from which he return'd in a short Time to his former Distress, and for some Part of the Year, generally lived by Chance, eating only when he was invited to the Tables of his Acquaintances, from which the Meanness of his Dress often excluded him, when the Politeness and Variety of his Conversation would have been thought a sufficient Recompence for his Entertainment.

He lodged as much by Accident as he dined, and passed the Night sometimes in mean Houses, which are set open at Night to any casual Wanderers, sometimes in Cellars among the Riot and Filth of the meanest and most profligate of the Rabble; and sometimes, when he had no Money to support even the Expences of these Receptacles, walked about the Streets till he was weary, and lay down in the Summer upon a Bulk, or in the Winter, with his associates in Poverty, among the Ashes of a Glass-house.

In this Manner were passed those Days and those Nights, which Nature had enabled him to have employed in elevated Speculations, useful Studies, or pleasing Conversation. On a Bulk, in a Cellar, or in a Glass-house among Thieves and Beggars, was to be found the Author of the *Wanderer*, the Man of exalted Sentiments, extensive Views, and curious Observations, the Man whose Remarks on Life might have assisted the Statesman, whose Ideas of Virtue might have enlightned the Moralist, whose Eloquence might have influenced Senates, and whose Delicacy might have polished Courts.

It cannot be imagined but that such Necessities might sometimes force him upon disreputable Practices, and it is probable that these Lines in the *Wanderer* were occasioned by his Reflections on his own Conduct.

> Though Mis'ry leads to Fortitude and Truth,
> Unequal to the Load this languid Youth,
> (O! let none censure if untry'd by Grief,
> Or amidst Woes untempted by Relief,)
> He stoop'd, reluctant, to mean Acts of Shame,
> Which then, ev'n then, he scorn'd, and blush'd to name.

Whoever was acquainted with him, was certain to be solicited for small Sums, which the Frequency of the Request made in Time considerable, and he was therefore quickly shunned by those who were become familiar enough to be trusted with his Necessities; but his rambling Manner of Life, and constant Appearance at Houses of public Resort, always procured him a new Succession of Friends, whose Kindness had not been exhausted by repeated Requests, so that he was seldom absolutely without Resources, but had in his utmost Exigences this Comfort, that he always imagined himself sure of speedy Relief.

It was observed, that he always asked Favours of this Kind without the least Submission or apparent Consciousness of Dependence, and that he did not seem to look upon a Compliance with his Request as an Obligation that deserved any extraordinary Acknowledgements, but a Refusal was resented by him as an Affront, or complained of as an Injury; nor did he readily reconcile himself to those who either denied to lend, or gave him afterwards any Intimation, that they expected to be repaid.

He was sometimes so far compassionated by those who knew both his Merit and his Distresses, that they received him into their Families, but they soon discovered him to be a very incommodious Inmate; for being always accustomed to an irregular Manner of Life, he could not confine himself to any stated Hours, or pay any Regard to the Rules of a Family, but would prolong his Conversation till Midnight, without considering that Business might require his Friend's Application in the Morning; nor when he had persuaded himself to retire to Bed, was he without equal Difficulty, called up to Dinner; it was therefore impossible to pay him any Distinction without the entire subversion of all Oeconomy, a Kind of Establishment which, wherever he went, he always appeared ambitious to overthrow.

It must therefore be acknowledged, in Justification of Mankind, that it was not always by the Negligence or Coldness of his Friends that *Savage* was distressed, but because it was in reality very difficult to preserve him long in a State of Ease. To supply him with Money was a hopeless Attempt, for no sooner did he see himself Master of a Sum sufficient to set him free from Care for a Day, than he became profuse and luxurious. When once he had entred a Tavern, or engaged in a Scheme of Pleasure, he never retired till Want of Money obliged him to some new Expedient. If he was entertained in a Family, nothing was any longer to be regarded there but Amusements and Jollity; wherever *Savage* entered he immediately expected that Order and Business should fly before him, that all should thenceforward be left to Hazard, and that no dull Principle of domestic Management should be opposed to his Inclination, or intrude upon his Gaiety.

His Distresses, however afflictive, never dejected him; in his lowest State he wanted not Spirit to assert the natural Dignity of Wit, and was always ready to repress that Insolence which the Superiority of Fortune incited, and to trample the Reputation which rose upon any other Basis than that of Merit: He never admitted any gross Familiarities, or submitted to be treated otherwise than as an Equal. Once when he was without Lodging, Meat, or Cloaths, one of his Friends, a Man not indeed remarkable for Moderation in his Prosperity, left a Message, that he desired to see him about nine in the Morning. *Savage* knew that his Intention was to assist him, but was very much disgusted, that he should presume to prescribe the Hour of his Attendance, and, I believe, refused to visit him, and rejected his Kindness.

The same invincible Temper, whether Firmness or Obstinacy, appeared in his Conduct to the Lord *Tyrconnel*, from whom he very frequently demanded that the Allowance which was once paid him should be restored, but with whom he never appeared to entertain for a Moment the Thought of soliciting a Reconciliation, and whom he treated at once with all the Haughtiness of Superiority, and all the bitterness of Resentment. He wrote to him not in a Stile of Supplication or Respect, but of Reproach, Menace, and Contempt, and appeared determined, if he ever regained his Allowance, to hold it only by the Right of Conquest.

As many more can discover, that a Man is richer than that he is wiser than themselves, Superiority of Understanding is not so readily acknowledged as that of Condition; nor is that Haughtiness, which the Consciousness of great Abilities incites, borne with the same Submission as the Tyranny of Wealth; and therefore *Savage*, by asserting his Claim to Deference and Regard, and by treating those with Contempt whom better Fortune animated to rebel against him, did not fail to raise a great Number of Enemies in the different Classes of Mankind. Those who thought themselves raised above him by the Advantages of Riches, hated him because they found no Protection from the Petulance of his Wit. Those who were esteemed for their Writings feared him as a Critic, and maligned him as a Rival, and almost all the smaller Wits were his professed Enemies.

Among these Mr *Millar* so far indulged his Resentment as to introduce him in a Farce, and direct him to be personated on the Stage in a Dress like that which he then wore; a mean Insult which only insinuated, that *Savage* had but one Coat, and which was therefore despised by him rather than resented; for though he wrote a Lampoon against *Millar*, he never printed it: and as no other Person ought to prosecute that Revenge from which the Person who was injured desisted, I shall not preserve what Mr *Savage* suppressed; of which the Publication would indeed have been a Punishment too severe for so impotent an Assault.

The great Hardships of Poverty were to *Savage* not the Want of Lodging or of Food, but the Neglect and Contempt which it drew upon him. He complained that as his Affairs grew desperate he found his Reputation for Capacity visibly decline, that his Opinion in Questions of Criticism was no longer regarded, when his Coat was out of Fashion; and that those who in the Interval of his Prosperity were always encouraging him to great Undertakings by Encomiums on his Genius and Assurances of Success, now received any Mention of his Designs with Coldness, thought that the Subjects on which he proposed to write were very difficult; and were ready to inform him, that the Event of a Poem was uncertain, that an Author ought to employ much Time in the Consideration of his Plan, and not presume to sit down to write in Confidence of a few cursory Ideas, and a superficial Knowledge; Difficulties were started on all Sides, and he was no longer qualified for any Performance but the *Volunteer Laureat.*

Yet even this Kind of Contempt never depressed him; for he always preserved a steady Confidence in his own Capacity, and believed nothing above his Reach which he should at any Time earnestly endeavour to attain. He formed Schemes of the same Kind with regard to Knowledge and to Fortune, and flattered himself with Advances to be made in Science, as with Riches to be enjoyed in some distant Period of his Life. For the Acquisition of Knowledge he was indeed far better qualified than for that of Riches; for he was naturally inquisitive and desirous of the Conversation of those from whom any Information was to be obtained, but by no Means solicitous to improve those Opportunities that were sometimes offered of raising his Fortune; and was remarkably retentive of his Ideas, which, when once he was in Possession of them, rarely forsook him; a Quality which could never be communicated to his Money.

While he was thus wearing out his Life in Expectation that the Queen would some time recollect her Promise, he had Recourse to the usual Practice of Writers, and published Proposals for printing his Works by Subscription, to which he was encouraged by the Success of many who had not a better Right to the Favour of the Public; but whatever was the Reason, he did not find the World equally inclined to favour him, and he observed with some Discontent, that, though he offered his Works at half a Guinea, he was able to procure but a small Number in Comparison with those who subscribed twice as much to *Duck.*

Nor was it without Indignation that he saw his Proposals neglected by the Queen, who patronised Mr *Duck's* with uncommon

Ardour, and incited a Competition among those who attended the Court, who should most promote his Interest, and who should first offer a Subscription. This was a Distinction to which Mr *Savage* made no Scruple of asserting, that his Birth, his Misfortunes, and his Genius gave a fairer Title, than could be pleaded by him on whom it was conferred.

Savage's Applications were however not universally unsuccessful; for some of the Nobility countenanced his Design, encouraged his Proposals, and subscribed with great Liberality. He related of the Duke of *Chandos* particularly, that, upon receiving his Proposals, he sent him ten Guineas.

But the Money which his Subscriptions afforded him was not less volatile than that which he received from his other Schemes; whenever a Subscription was paid him he went to a Tavern, and as Money so collected is necessarily received in small Sums, he never was able to send his Poems to the Press, but for many Years continued his Solicitation, and squandered whatever he obtained.

The Project of printing his Works was frequently revived, and as his Proposals grew obsolete, new ones were printed with fresher Dates. To form Schemes for the Publication was one of his favourite Amusements, nor was he ever more at Ease than when with any Friend who readily fell in with his Schemes, he was adjusting the Print, forming the Advertisements, and regulating the Dispersion of his new Edition, which he really intended some time to publish, and which, as long Experience had shewn him the Impossibility of printing the Volume together, he at last determined to divide into weekly or monthly Numbers, that the Profits of the first might supply the Expences of the next.

Thus he spent his Time in mean Expedients and tormenting Suspense, living for the greatest Part in Fear of Prosecutions from his Creditors, and consequently skulking in obscure Parts of the Town, of which he was no Stranger to the remotest Corners. But wherever he came his Address secured him Friends, whom his Necessities soon alienated, so that he had perhaps a more numerous Acquaintance than any Man ever before attained, there being scarcely any Person eminent on any Account to whom he was not known, or whose Character he was not in some Degree able to delineate.

To the Acquisition of this extensive Acquaintance every Circumstance of his Life contributed. He excelled in the Arts of Conversation, and therefore willingly practised them: He had seldom any Home, or even a Lodging in which he could be private, and therefore was driven into public Houses for the common Conveniences of Life, and Supports of Nature. He was always ready to comply with every Invitation, having no Employment to withhold him, and often no Money to provide for himself; and by dining with one Company, he never failed of obtaining an Introduction into another.

Thus dissipated was his Life, and thus casual his Subsistence; yet did not the Distraction of his Views hinder him from Reflection, nor the Uncertainty of his Condition depress his Gaiety. When he had wandered about without any fortunate Adventure, by which he was led into a Tavern, he sometimes retired into the Fields, and was able to employ his Mind in Study to amuse it with pleasing Imaginations; and seldom appeared to be melancholy, but when some sudden Misfortune had just fallen upon him, and even then in a few Moments he would disentangle himself from his Perplexity, adopt the Subject of Conversation, and apply his Mind wholly to the Objects that others presented to it.

This Life, unhappy as it may be already imagined, was yet imbitter'd in 1738, with new Calamities. The Death of the Queen deprived him of all the Prospects of Preferment with which he so long entertained his Imagination; and as Sir *Robert Walpole* had before given him Reason to believe that he never intended the Performance of his Promise, he was now abandoned again to Fortune.

He was, however, at that time, supported by a Friend; and as it was not his Custom to look out for distant Calamities, or to feel any other Pain than that which forced itself upon his Senses, he was not much afflicted at his Loss, and perhaps comforted himself that his Pension would be now continued without the annual Tribute of a Panegyric.

Another Expectation contributed likewise to support him; he had taken a Resolution to write a second Tragedy upon the Story of Sir *Thomas Overbury*, in which he preserved a few Lines of his former Play; but made a total Alteration of the Plan, added new Incidents, and introduced new Characters; so that it was a new Tragedy, not a Revival of the former.

Many of his Friends blamed him for not making Choice of another Subject; but in Vindication of himself, he asserted, that it was not easy to find a better; and that he thought it his Interest to extinguish the Memory of the first Tragedy, which he could only do by writing one less defective upon the same Story; by which he should entirely defeat the Artifice of the Booksellers, who after the Death of any Author of Reputation, are always industrious to swell his Works, by uniting his worst Productions with his best.

In the Execution of this Scheme, however, he proceeded but slowly, and probably only employed himself upon it when he could find no other Amusement; but he pleased himself with counting the Profits, and perhaps imagined, that the theatrical Reputation which he was about to acquire, would be equivalent to all that he had lost by the Death of his Patroness.

He did not, in confidence of his approaching Riches neglect the Measures proper to secure the Continuance of his Pension, though some of his Favourers thought him culpable for omitting to write on her Death; but, on her Birth-Day next Year he gave a Proof of the Solidity of his Judgment, and the Power of his Genius.

He knew that the Track of Elegy had been so long beaten, that it was impossible to travel in it without treading in the Footsteps of those who had gone before him; and that therefore it was necessary, that he might distinguish himself from the Herd of Encomiasts, to find out some new Walk of funeral Panegyric.

This difficult Task he performed in such a Manner, that his Poem may be justly ranked among the best Pieces that the Death of Princes has produced. By transferring the Mention of her Death to her Birth-Day, he has formed a happy Combination of Topics, which any other Man would have thought it very difficult to connect in one View, but which he has united in such a Manner, that the Relation between them appears natural; and it may be justly said, that what no other Man would have thought on, it now appears scarcely possible for any Man to miss.

The Beauty of this peculiar Combination of Images is so masterly, that it is sufficient to set this Poem above Censure; and therefore it is not necessary to mention many other delicate Touches which may be found in it, and which would deservedly be admired in any other Performance.

To these Proofs of his Genius may be added, from the same Poem, an Instance of his Prudence, an Excellence for which he was not so often distinguished; he does not forget to remind the king, in the most delicate and artful Manner, of continuing his Pension.

With regard to the Success of this Address he was for some Time in Suspense, but was in no great Degree sollicitous about it, and continued his Labour upon his new Tragedy with great Tranquillity, till the Friend, who had for a considerable time supported him, removing his Family to another Place, took Occasion to dismiss him. It then became necessary to enquire more diligently what was determined in his Affair, having Reason to suspect that no great Favour was intended him, because he had not received his Pension at the usual Time.

It is said, that he did not take those Methods of retrieving his Interest which were most likely to succeed; and some of those who were employed in the Exchequer, cautioned him against too much Violence in his Proceedings; but Mr *Savage*, who seldom regulated his Conduct by the Advice of others, gave way to his Passion, and demanded of Sir *Robert Walpole*, at his Levee, the Reason of the Distinction that was made between him and the other Pensioners of the Queen, with a Degree of Roughness, which perhaps determined him to withdraw what had been only delayed.

Whatever was the Crime of which he was accused or suspected, and whatever Influence was employed against him, he received soon after an Account that took from him all Hopes of regaining his Pension; and he had now no Prospect of Subsistence but from his Play, and he knew no Way of Living for the Time required to finish it.

So peculiar were the Misfortunes of this Man, deprived of an Estate and Title by a particular Law, exposed and abandoned by a Mother, defrauded by a Mother of a Fortune which his Father had allotted him, he enter'd the World without a Friend; and though his Abilities forced themselves into Esteem and Reputation, he was never able to obtain any real Advantage, and whatever Prospects arose, were always intercepted as he began to approach them. The King's Intentions in his Favour were frustrated; his Dedication to the Prince, whose Generosity on every other Occasion was eminent, procured him no Reward; Sir *Robert Walpole*, who valued himself upon keeping his Promise to others, broke it to him without Regret; and the Bounty of the Queen was, after her Death, withdrawn from him, and from him only.

Such were his Misfortunes, which yet he bore not only with Decency, but with Cheerfulness, nor was his Gaiety clouded even by his last Disappointment, though he was in a short Time reduced to the lowest Degree of Distress, and often wanted both Lodging and Food. At this Time he gave another Instance of the insurmountable Obstinacy of his Spirit; his Cloaths were worn out, and he received Notice that at a Coffee-House some Cloaths and Linen were left for him; the Person who sent them, did not, I believe, inform him to whom he was to be obliged, that he might spare the Perplexity of acknowledging the Benefit; but though the Offer was so far generous, it was made with some Neglect of Ceremonies, which Mr *Savage* so much resented, that he refused the Present, and declined to enter the House, till the Cloaths that had been designed for him were taken away.

His Distress was now publickly known, and his Friends, therefore, thought it proper to concert some Measures for his Relief; and one of them wrote a Letter to him, in which he expressed his Concern *for the miserable withdrawing of his Pension*; and gave him Hopes that, in a short Time, he should find himself supplied with a Competence, *without any Dependence on those little Creatures which we are pleased to call the Great.*

The Scheme proposed for this happy and independent Subsistence, was, that he should retire into *Wales*, and receive an Allowance of fifty Pounds a Year, to be raised by a Subscription, on which he was to live privately in a cheap Place, without aspiring any more to Affluence, or having any farther Care of Reputation.

This Offer Mr *Savage* gladly accepted, tho' with Intentions very different from those of his Friends; for they proposed, that he should continue an Exile from *London* for ever, and spend all the remaining Part of his Life at *Swansea*; but he designed only to take the Opportunity, which their Scheme offered him, of retreating for a short Time, that he might prepare his Play for the Stage, and his other Works for the Press, and then return to *London* to exhibit his Tragedy, and live upon the Profits of his own Labour.

With regard to his Works, he proposed very great Improvements, which would have required much Time, or great Application; and when he had finish'd them, he designed to do Justice to his Subscribers, by publishing them according to his Proposals.

As he was ready to entertain himself with future Pleasures, he had planned out a Scheme of Life for the Country, of which he had no Knowledge but from Pastorals and Songs. He imagined that he should be transported to Scenes of flow'ry Felicity, like those which one Poet has reflected to another, and had projected a perpetual Round of innocent Pleasures, of which he suspected no Interruption from Pride, or Ignorance, or Brutality.

With these Expectations he was so enchanted, that when he was once gently reproach'd by a Friend for submitting to live upon a Subscription, and advised rather by a resolute Exertion of his Abilities to support himself, he could not bear to debar himself from the Happiness which was to be found in the Calm of a Cottage, or lose the Opportunity of listening, without Intermission, to the Melody of the Nightingale, which he believ'd was to be heard from every Bramble, and which he did not fail to mention as a very important Part of the Happiness of a Country Life.

While this Scheme was ripening, his Friends directed him to take a Lodging in the Liberties of the Fleet, that he might be secure from his Creditors, and sent him every Monday a Guinea, which he commonly spent before the next Morning, and trusted, after his usual Manner, the remaining Part of the Week to the Bounty of Fortune.

He now began very sensibly to feel the Miseries of Dependence: Those by whom he was to be supported, began to prescribe to him with an Air of Authority, which he knew not how decently to resent, nor patiently to bear; and he soon discovered, from the Conduct of most of his Subscribers, that he was yet in the Hands of *Little Creatures*.

Of the Insolence that he was obliged to suffer, he gave many Instances, of which none appeared to raise his Indignation to a greater Height, than the Method which was taken of furnishing him with Cloaths. Instead of consulting him, and allowing him to send to a Taylor his Orders for what they thought proper to allow him, they proposed to send for a Taylor to take his Measure, and then to consult how they should equip him.

This Treatment was not very delicate, nor was it such as *Savage*'s Humanity would have suggested to him on a like Occasion; but it had scarcely deserved Mention, had it not, by affecting him in an uncommon Degree, shewn the Peculiarity of his Character. Upon hearing the Design that was formed, he came to the Lodging of a Friend with the most violent Agonies of Rage; and being asked what it could be that gave him such Disturbance, he replied, with the utmost Vehemence of Indignation, "That they had sent for a Taylor to measure him."

How the Affair ended, was never enquired, for fear of renewing

D

his Uneasiness. It is probable that, upon Recollection, he submitted with a good Grace to what he could not avoid, and that he discovered no Resentment where he had no Power.

He was, however, not humbled to implicit and universal Compliance; for when the Gentleman, who had first informed him of the Design to support him by a Subscription, attempted to procure a Reconciliation with the Lord *Tyrconnel*, he could by no means be prevailed upon to comply with the Measures that were proposed.

A Letter was written for him to Sir *William Lemon*, to prevail upon him to interpose his good Offices with Lord *Tyrconnel*, in which he solicited Sir *William*'s Assistance, *for a Man who really needed it as much as any Man could well do*; and informed him that he was retiring *for ever to a Place where he should no more trouble his Relations, Friends, or Enemies*; he confessed, that his *Passion* had *betrayed* him to some Conduct, with regard to Lord *Tyrconnel*, *for which he could not but heartily ask his Pardon*; and as he imagined Lord *Tyrconnel*'s Passion might be yet so high, that he would not *receive a Letter from him*, begg'd that Sir *William* would endeavour to soften him; and expressed his Hopes, that he would comply with his Request, and that *so small a Relation would not harden his Heart against him*.

That any Man should presume to dictate a Letter to him, was not very agreeable to Mr *Savage*; and therefore he was, before he had opened it, not much inclined to approve it. But when he read it, he found it contained Sentiments entirely opposite to his own, and, as he asserted, to the Truth, and therefore instead of copying it, wrote his Friend a Letter full of masculine Resentment, and warm Expostulations. He very justly observed that the Style was too supplicatory, and the Representation too abject, and that he ought at least to have made him complain with *the Dignity of a Gentleman in Distress*. He declared that he would not write the Paragraph in which he was to ask Lord *Tyrconnel*'s Pardon; for *he despised his Pardon, and therefore could not heartily, and would not hypocritically ask it*. He remarked, that his Friend made a very unreasonable Distinction between himself and him; for, says he, when you mention Men of high Rank *in your own Character*, they are *those little Creatures whom we are pleased to call the Great*; but when you address them *in mine*, no Servility is sufficiently humble. He then with great Propriety explained the ill Consequences which might be expected from such a Letter, which his Relations

102

would print in their own Defence, and which would for ever be produced as a full Answer to all that he should allege against them; for he always intended to publish a minute Account of the Treatment which he had received. It is to be remembered to the Honour of the Gentleman by whom this Letter was drawn up, that he yielded to Mr *Savage*'s Reasons, and agreed that it ought to be suppressed.

After many Alterations and Delays, a Subscription was at length raised, which did not amount to fifty Pounds a Year, though twenty were paid by one Gentleman; such was the Generosity of Mankind, that what had been done by a Player without Solicitation, could not now be effected by Application and Interest; and *Savage* had a great Number to court and to obey for a Pension less than that which Mrs *Oldfield* paid him without exacting any Servilities.

Mr *Savage* however was satisfied, and willing to retire, and was convinced that the Allowance, though scanty, would be more than sufficient for him, being now determined to commence a rigid Oeconomist, and to live according to the exactest Rules of Frugality; for nothing was in his Opinion more contemptible than a Man, who, when he knew his Income, exceeded it; and yet he confessed that Instances of such Folly were too common, and lamented, that some Men were not to be trusted with their own Money.

Full of these salutary Resolutions, he left *London*, in *July* 1739, having taken Leave with great Tenderness of his Friends, and parted from the Author of this Narrative with Tears in his Eyes. He was furnished with fifteen Guineas, and informed, that they would be sufficient, not only for the Expence of his Journey, but for his Support in *Wales* for some Time; and that there remained but little more of the first Collection. He promised a strict Adherence to his Maxims of Parsimony, and went away in the Stage Coach; nor did his Friends expect to hear from him, till he informed them of his Arrival at *Swansea*.

But when they least expected, arrived a Letter dated the fourteenth Day after his Departure, in which he sent them Word, that he was yet upon the Road, and without Money; and that he therefore could not proceed without a Remittance. They then sent him the Money that was in their Hands, with which he was enabled to reach *Bristol*, from whence he was to go to *Swansea* by Water.

At *Bristol* he found an Embargo laid upon the Shipping, so that

103

he could not immediately obtain a Passage; and being therefore obliged to stay there some Time, he, with his usual Felicity, ingratiated himself with many of the principal Inhabitants, was invited to their Houses, distinguished at their publick Feasts, and treated with a Regard that gratify'd his Vanity, and therefore easily engaged his Affection.

He began very early after his Retirement to complain of the Conduct of his Friends in *London*, and irritated many of them so much by his Letters, that they withdrew, however honourably, their Contributions; and it is believed, that little more was paid him than the twenty Pounds a Year, which were allowed him by the Gentleman who proposed the Subscription.

After some Stay at *Bristol*, he retired to *Swansea*, the Place *originally* proposed for his Residence, where he lived about a Year, very much dissatisfied with the Diminution of his Salary, but contracted, as in other Places, Acquaintance with those who were most distinguished in that Country, among whom he has celebrated Mr *Powel* and Mrs *Jones*, by some Verses which he inserted in the *Gentleman's Magazine*.

Here he completed his Tragedy, of which two Acts were wanting when he left *London*, and was desirous of coming to Town to bring it upon the Stage. This Design was very warmly opposed, and he was advised by his chief Benefactor to put it into the Hands of Mr *Thompson* and Mr *Mallet*, that it might be fitted for the Stage, and to allow his Friends to receive the Profits, out of which an annual Pension should be paid him.

This Proposal he rejected with the utmost Contempt. He was by no means convinced that the Judgment of those to whom he was required to submit, was superior to his own. He was now determined, as he expressed it, to be *no longer kept in Leading-strings*, and had no elevated Idea of *his Bounty*, who proposed to *pension him out of the Profits of his own Labours*.

He attempted in *Wales* to promote a Subscription for his Works, and had once Hopes of Success; but in a short Time afterwards, formed a Resolution of leaving that Part of the Country, to which he thought it not reasonable to be confined, for the Gratification of those, who having promised him a liberal Income, had no sooner banished him to a remote Corner, than they reduced his Allowance to a Salary scarcely equal to the Necessities of Life.

His Resentment of this Treatment, which, in his own Opinion, at least, he had not deserved, was such that he broke off all Correspondence with most of his Contributors, and appeared to consider them as Persecutors and Oppressors, and in the latter Part of his Life declared, that their Conduct toward him, since his Departure from *London, had been Perfidiousness improving on Perfidiousness, and Inhumanity on Inhumanity.*

It is not to be supposed, that the Necessities of Mr *Savage* did not some times incite him to satirical Exaggerations of the Behaviour of those by whom he thought himself reduced to them. But it must be granted, that the Diminution of his Allowance was a great Hardship, and, that those who withdrew their Subscription from a Man, who, upon the Faith of their Promise, had gone into a Kind of Banishment, and abandoned all those by whom he had been before relieved in his Distress, will find it no easy Task to vindicate their Conduct.

It may be alleged, and, perhaps, justly, that he was petulant and contemptuous, that he more frequently reproached his Subscribers for not giving him more, than thanked them for what he had received; but it is to be remembred, that this Conduct, and this is the worst Charge that can be drawn up against him, did them no real Injury; and that it, therefore, ought rather to have been pitied than resented, at least, the Resentment that it might provoke ought to have been generous and manly; Epithets which his Conduct will hardly deserve, that starves the Man whom he has persuaded to put himself into his Power.

It might have been reasonably demanded by *Savage*, that they should, before they had taken away what they promised, have replaced him in his former State, that they should have taken no Advantages from the Situation to which the Appearance of their Kindness had reduced him, and that he should have been re-called to *London*, before he was abandoned. He might justly represent, that he ought to have been considered as a Lion in the Toils, and demand to be released before the Dogs should be loosed upon him.

He endeavoured, indeed, to release himself, and with an Intent to return to *London*, went to *Bristol*, where a Repetition of the Kindness which he had formerly found, invited him to stay. He was not only caressed and treated, but had a Collection made for him of about thirty Pounds, with which it had been happy if he had immediately departed for *London*; but his Negligence did not suffer him to consider, that such Proofs of Kindness were not often to be expected, and that this Ardour of Benevolence was, in a great Degree, the Effect of Novelty, and might, probably, be every Day less; and therefore he took no Care to improve the happy Time, but was encouraged by one Favour to hope for another, till at length Generosity was exhausted, and Officiousness wearied.

Another Part of his Misconduct was the Practice of prolonging his Visits, to unseasonable Hours, and disconcerting all the Families into which he was admitted. This was an Error in a Place of Commerce, which all the Charms of his Conversation could not compensate; for what Trader would purchase such airy Satisfaction by the Loss of solid Gain, which must be the Consequence of Midnight Merriment, as those Hours which were gained at Night, were generally lost in the Morning?

Thus Mr *Savage*, after the Curiosity of the Inhabitants was gratified, found the Number of his Friends daily decreasing, perhaps without suspecting for what Reason their Conduct was altered, for he still continued to harass, with his nocturnal Intrusions, those that yet countenanced him, and admitted him to their Houses.

But he did not spend all the Time of his Residence at *Bristol*, in Visits or at Taverns; for he sometimes returned to his Studies, and began several considerable Designs. When he felt an Inclination to write, he always retired from the Knowledge of his Friends, and lay hid in an obscure Part of the Suburbs, till he found himself again desirous of Company, to which it is likely that Intervals of Absence made him more welcome.

He was always full of his Design of returning to *London* to bring his Tragedy upon the Stage; but having neglected to depart with the Money that was raised for him, he could not afterwards procure a Sum sufficient to defray the Expences of his Journey; nor, perhaps, would a fresh Supply have had any other Effect, than, by putting immediate Pleasures in his Power, to have driven the Thoughts of his Journey out of his Mind.

While he was thus spending the Day in contriving a Scheme for the Morrow, Distress stole upon him by imperceptible Degrees. His Conduct had already wearied some of those who were at first enamoured of his Conversation; but he might, perhaps, still have devolved to others, whom he might have entertained with equal Success, had not the Decay of his Cloaths made it no longer consistent with their Vanity to admit him to their Tables, or to associate with him in publick Places. He now began to find every Man from home at whose House he called; and was therefore no longer able to procure the Necessaries of Life, but wandered about the Town slighted and neglected, in quest of a Dinner, which he did not always obtain.

To complete his Misery, he was persued by the Officers for small Debts which he had contracted; and was, therefore, obliged to withdraw from the small Number of Friends from whom he had still Reason to hope for Favours. His Custom was to lie in Bed the greatest Part of the Day, and to go out in the Dark with the utmost Privacy, and after having paid his Visit, return again before Morning to his Lodging, which was in the Garret of an obscure Inn.

Being thus excluded on one hand, and confined on the other, he suffered the utmost Extremities of Poverty, and often fasted so long that he was seized with Faintness, and had lost his Appetite, not being able to bear the Smell of Meat, 'till the Action of his Stomach was restored by a Cordial.

In this Distress he received a Remittance of fifty Pounds from *London*, with which he provided himself a decent Coat, and determined to go to *London*, but unhappily spent his Money at a favourite Tavern. Thus was he again confined to *Bristol*, where he was every Day hunted by Bailiffs. In this Exigence he once more found a Friend, who sheltered him in his House, though at the usual Inconveniences with which his Company was attended; for he could neither be persuaded to go to bed in the Night, nor to rise in the Day.

It is observable, that in these various Scenes of Misery, he was always disengaged and cheerful; he at some Times persued his Studies, and at others continued or enlarged his epistolary Correspondence, nor was he ever so far dejected as to endeavour to procure an Encrease of his Allowance, by any other Methods than Accusations and Reproaches.

He had now no longer any Hopes of Assistance from his Friends at *Bristol*, who as Merchants, and by Consequence sufficiently studious of Profit, cannot be supposed to have look'd with much Compassion upon Negligence and Extravagance, or to think any Excellence equivalent to a Fault of such Consequence as Neglect of Oeconomy. It is natural to imagine, that many of those who would have relieved his real Wants, were discouraged from the Exertion of their Benevolence, by Observation of the Use which was made of their Favours, and Conviction that Relief would only be momentary, and that the same Necessity would quickly return.

At last he quitted the House of his Friend, and returned to his Lodging at the Inn, still intending to set out in a few Days for *London*; but on the tenth of *January* 1742–3, having been at Supper with two of his Friends, he was at his Return to his Lodgings arrested for a Debt of about eight Pounds, which he owed at a Coffee-House, and conducted to the House of a Sheriff's Officer. The Account which he gives of this Misfortune in a Letter to one of the Gentlemen with whom he had supped, is too remarkable to be omitted.

"It was not a little unfortunate for me, that I spent yesterday's Evening with you; because the Hour hindered me from entering on my new Lodging; however, I have now got one; but such an one, as I believe Nobody would chuse.

"I was arrested at the Suit of Mrs *Read*, just as I was going up Stairs to Bed, at Mr *Bowyer*'s; but taken in so private a Manner, that I believe Nobody at the *White Lyon* is apprised of it. Tho' I let the Officers know the Strength (or rather Weakness) of my pocket yet they treated me with the utmost Civility, and even when they conducted me to Confinement, 'twas in such a Manner, that I verily believe I could have escaped, which I would rather be ruined than have done; notwithstanding the whole Amount of my Finances was but three Pence halfpenny.

"In the first Place, I must insist, that you will industriously conceal this from Mrs *S——s*; because I would not have her good Nature suffer that Pain, which, I know, she would be apt to feel on this Occasion.

"Next I conjure you, dear Sir, by all the Ties of Friendship, by no means to have one uneasy Thought on my Account; but to have the same Pleasantry of Countenance, and unruffled Serenity of Mind, which (God be praised!) I have in this, and have had in a much severer Calamity. Furthermore, I charge you, if you value my Friendship as truly as I do yours, *not* to utter, or even harbour the least Resentment against Mrs *Read*. I believe she has ruin'd me, but I freely forgive her; and (tho' I will never more have any Intimacy with her) would, at a due Distance, rather do her an Act of good than ill Will. Lastly, (pardon the Expression) I *absolutely command* you not to offer me any pecuniary Assistance, nor to attempt getting me any from any one of your Friends. At another Time, or on any other Occasion, you may, dear Friend, be well assured, I would rather write to you in the submissive Stile of a Request, than that of a peremptory Command.

"However, that my truly valuable Friend may not think I am too proud to ask a Favour, let me intreat you to let me have your Boy to attend me for this Day, not only for the Sake of saving me the Expence of Porters, but for the Delivery of some Letters to People whose Names I would not have known to Strangers.

"The civil Treatment I have thus far met from those, whose Prisoner I am, makes me thankful to the Almighty, that tho' He has thought fit to visit me (on my Birth-night) with Affliction; yet (such is his great Goodness!) my Affliction is not without alleviating Circumstances. I murmur not, but am all Resignation to the *divine Will*. As to the World, I hope that I shall be endued by Heaven with that Presence of Mind, that serene Dignity in Misfortune, that constitutes the Character of a true Nobleman; a Dignity far beyond that of Coronets; a Nobility arising from the just Principles of Philosophy, refined and exalted by those of Christianity."

He continued five Days at the Officer's, in Hopes that he should be able to procure Bail, and avoid the Necessity of going to Prison. The State in which he passed his Time, and the Treatment which he received, are very justly expressed by him in a Letter which he wrote to a Friend; "The whole Day, *says he*, has been employed in various People's filling my Head with their foolish chimerical Systems, which has obliged me coolly (as far as Nature will admit) to digest, and accommodate myself to, every different Person's Way of thinking; hurried from one wild System to another, 'till it has quite made a Chaos of my Imagination, and nothing done— promised—disappointed—Order'd to send every Hour, from one part of the Town to the other."——

When his Friends, who had hitherto caressed and applauded, found that to give Bail and pay the Debt was the same, they all refused to preserve him from a Prison, at the Expence of eight Pounds; and therefore after having been for some Time at the Officer's House, *at an immense Expence*, as he observes in his Letter, he was at length removed to *Newgate*.

This Expence he was enabled to support, by the Generosity of Mr *Nash* at *Bath*, who upon receiving from him an Account of his

Condition, immediatly sent him five Guineas, and promised to promote his Subscription at *Bath*, with all his Interest.

By his Removal to *Newgate*, he obtained at least a Freedom from Suspense, and Rest from the disturbing Vicissitudes of Hope and Disappointment; he now found that his Friends were only Companions, who were willing to share his Gaiety, but not to partake of his Misfortunes; and therefore he no longer expected any Assistance from them.

It must however be observed of one Gentleman, that he offered to release him by paying the Debt, but that Mr *Savage* would not consent, I suppose, because he thought he had before been too burthensome to him.

He was offered by some of his Friends, that a Collection should be made for his Enlargement, but he *treated the Proposal*, and declared*, *that he should again treat it, with Disdain. As to writing any mendicant Letters, he had too high a Spirit, and determined only to write to some Ministers of State, to try to regain his Pension.*

He continued to complain† of those that had sent him into the Country, and objected to them that he had *lost the Profits of his Play, which had been finished three Years*; and in another Letter declares his Resolution to publish a Pamphlet, that the World might know how *he had been used.*

This Pamphlet was never written, for he in a very short Time recover'd his usual Tranquillity, and chearfully applied himself to more inoffensive Studies. He indeed steadily declared, that he was promised an yearly Allowance of fifty Pounds, and never received half the Sum; but he seemed to resign himself to that as well as to other Misfortunes, and lose the Remembrance of it in his Amusements and Employments.

The Chearfulness with which he bore his Confinement, appears from the following Letter, which he wrote, *Jan.* 30th, to one of his Friends in *London*.

I now write to you from my Confinement in *Newgate*, where I have been ever since Monday last was Sev'n-night; and where I enjoy myself with much more Tranquillity than I have known for upwards of a twelvemonth past; having a Room entirely to myself, and persuing the Amusement of my poetical Studies, unin-

* In a Letter after his Confinement.
† Letter, *Jan.* 15.

terrupted, and agreeable to my Mind. I thank the Almighty, I am now all collected in myself; and tho' my Person is in Confinement, my Mind can expatiate on ample and useful Subjects, with all the Freedom imaginable. I am now more conversant with the Nine than ever; and if, instead of a *Newgate* Bird, I may be allowed to be a Bird of the Muses, I assure you, Sir, I sing very freely in my Cage; sometimes indeed in the plaintive Notes of the Nightingale; but, at others, in the chearful Strains of the Lark—

In another Letter he observes, that he ranges from one Subject to another, without confining himself to any particular Task, and that he was employed one Week upon one Attempt, and the next upon another.

Surely the Fortitude of this Man deserves, at least, to be mentioned with Applause; and whatever Faults may be imputed to him, the Virtue of *suffering well* cannot be denied him. The two Powers which, in the Opinion of *Epictetus*, constitute a wise Man, are those of *bearing* and *forbearing*, which cannot indeed be affirmed to have been equally possessed by *Savage*, but it was too manifest that the Want of one obliged him very *frequently* to practise the other.

He was treated by Mr *Dagg*, the Keeper of the Prison, with great Humanity; was supported by him at his own Table without any Certainty of Recompence, had a Room to himself, to which he could at any Time retire from all Disturbance, was allowed to stand at the Door of the Prison, and sometimes taken out into the Fields; so that he suffered fewer Hardships in the Prison, than he had been accustomed to undergo in the greatest part of his Life.

The Keeper did not confine his Benevolence to a gentle Execution of his Office, but made some Overtures to the Creditor for his Release, tho' without Effect; and continued, during the whole Time of his Imprisonment, to treat him with the utmost Tenderness and Civility.

Virtue is undoubtedly most laudable in that State which makes it most difficult; and therefore the Humanity of a Gaoler certainly deserves this public Attestation; and the Man whose Heart has not been hardened by such an Employment, may be justly proposed as a Pattern of Benevolence. If an Inscription was once engraved to the *honest Toll-gatherer*, less Honours ought not to be paid to the *tender Gaoler*.

Mr *Savage* very frequently received Visits, and sometimes Presents from his Acquaintances, but they did not amount to a Subsistence, for the greater Part of which he was indebted to the Generosity of this Keeper; but these Favours, however they might endear to him the particular Persons from whom he received them, were very far from impressing upon his Mind any advantageous Ideas of the People of *Bristol*; and therefore he thought he could not more properly employ himself in Prison, than in writing [a Poem called *London and Bristol delineated*] . . .

When he had brought this Poem to its present State, which . . . is not perfect, he wrote to *London* an Account of his Design, and informed his Friend, that he was determined to print it with his Name; but enjoined him not to communicate his Intention to his *Bristol* Acquaintance. The Gentleman surprised at his Resolution, endeavoured to dissuade him from publishing it, at least from prefixing his Name; and declared, that he could not reconcile the Injunction of Secrecy with his Resolution to own it at its first Appearance. To this Mr *Savage* returned an Answer agreeable to his Character in the following Terms.

"I received yours this Morning, and not without a little Surprize at the Contents. To answer a Question with a Question, you ask me concerning *London* and *Bristol, Why will I add* delineated? Why did Mr *Woolaston* add the same Word to his Religion of Nature? I suppose that it was his Will and Pleasure to add it in his Case; and it is mine to do so in my Own. You are pleased to tell me, that you understand not why Secrecy is injoined, and yet I intend to set my Name to it. My Answer is—I have my private Reasons; which I am not obliged to explain to any One. You doubt, my friend Mr *S*—— would not approve of it—And what is it to me whether he does or not? Do you imagine, that Mr *S*—— is to dictate to me? If any man, who calls himself my Friend, should assume such an Air, I would spurn at his Friendship with Contempt. You say, I seem to think so by not letting him know it—And suppose I do, what then? Perhaps I can give Reasons for that Disapprobation, very foreign from what you would imagine. You go on in saying, suppose, I should not put my Name to it—My Answer is, that I will not suppose any such Thing, being determined to the contrary; neither, Sir, would I have you suppose, that I applied to you for Want of another Press: Nor would I have you imagine, that I owe Mr *S*—— obligations which I do not."

Such was his Imprudence, and such his obstinate Adherence to his own Resolutions, however absurd. A Prisoner! supported by Charity! and, whatever Insults he might have received during the latter Part of his Stay in *Bristol*, once caressed, esteemed, and presented with a liberal Collection, he could forget on a sudden his Danger, and his Obligations, to gratify the Petulance of his Wit, or the Eagerness of his Resentment, and publish a Satire by which he might reasonably expect, that he should alienate those who then supported him, and provoke those whom he could neither resist nor escape.

This Resolution, from the Execution of which, it is probable, that only his Death could have hindered him, is sufficient to shew how much he disregarded all Considerations that opposed his present Passions, and how readily he hazarded all future Advantages for any immediate Gratifications. Whatever was his predominant Inclination, neither Hope nor Fear hinder'd him from complying with it, nor had Opposition any other Effect than to heighten his Ardour, and irritate his Vehemence.

This Performance was however laid aside, while he was employed in soliciting Assistances from several great Persons; and one Interruption succeeding another hinder'd him from supplying the Chasm, and perhaps from retouching the other Parts, which he can hardly be imagined to have finished, in his own Opinion; for it is very unequal, and some of the Lines are rather inserted to rhyme to others than to support or improve the Sense; but the first and last Parts are worked up with great Spirit and Elegance.

His Time was spent in the Prison for the most part in Study, or in receiving Visits: but sometimes he descended to lower Amusements, and diverted himself in the Kitchen with the Conversation of the Criminals; for it was not pleasing to him to be much without Company, and though he was very capable of a judicious Choice, he was often contented with the first that offered; for this he was sometimes reproved by his Friends who found him surrounded with Felons; but the Reproof was on that as on other Occasions thrown away; he continued to gratify himself, and to set very little Value on the Opinion of others.

But here, as in every other Scene of his Life, he made use of such Opportunities as occurr'd of benefiting those who were more miserable than himself, and was always ready to perform any Offices of Humanity to his fellow Prisoners.

He had now ceased from corresponding with any of his Subscribers except one, who yet continued to remit him the twenty Pounds a Year which he had promised him, and by whom it was expected, that he would have been in a very short Time enlarged, because he had directed the Keeper to enquire after the State of his Debts.

However he took care to enter his Name according to the Forms of the Court, that the Creditor might be obliged to make him some Allowance, if he was continued a Prisoner, and when on that Occasion he appeared in the Hall was treated with very unusual Respect.

But the Resentment of the City was afterwards raised by some Accounts that had been spread of the Satire, and he was informed that some of the Merchants intended to pay the Allowance which the Law required, and to detain him Prisoner at their own Expence. This he treated as an empty Menace, and perhaps might have hasten'd the Publication, only to shew how much he was superior to their Insults, had not all his Schemes been suddenly destroyed.

When he had been six Months in Prison he received from one of his Friends, in whose Kindness he had the greatest Confidence, and on whose Assistance he chiefly depended, a Letter that contained a Charge of very atrocious Ingratitude, drawn up in such Terms as sudden Resentment dictated. Mr *Savage* returned a very solemn Protestation of his Innocence, but however appeared much disturbed at the Accusation. Some Days afterwards he was seized with a Pain in his Back and Side, which as it was not violent was not suspected to be dangerous; but growing daily more languid and dejected, on the 25th of *July* he confined himself to his Room, and a Fever seized his Spirits. The Symptoms grew every Day more formidable, but his Condition did not enable him to procure any Assistance. The last Time that the Keeper saw him was on *July* the 31st, when *Savage* seeing him at his Bed-side said, with an uncommon Earnestness, *I have something to say to you, Sir*; but after a Pause moved his Hand in a melancholy Manner, and finding himself unable to recollect what he was going to communicate, said *'Tis gone*. The Keeper soon after left him, and the next Morning he died. He was buried in the Church-Yard of St *Peter*, at the Expence of the Keeper.

Such were the Life and Death of *Richard Savage*, a Man equally distinguished by his Virtues and Vices, and at once remarkable for his Weaknesses and Abilities.

He was of a middle Stature, of a thin Habit of Body, a long Visage, coarse Features, and melancholy Aspect; of a grave and manly Deportment, a solemn Dignity of Mien, but which upon a nearer Acquaintance softened into an engaging Easiness of Manners. His Walk was slow, and his Voice tremulous and mournful. He was easily excited to Smiles, but very seldom provoked to Laughter.

His Mind was in an uncommon Degree vigorous and active. His Judgment was accurate, his Apprehension quick, and his Memory so tenacious, that he was frequently observed to know what he had learned from others in a short Time better than those by whom he was informed, and could frequently recollect Incidents, with all their Combination of Circumstances, which few would have regarded at the present Time; but which the Quickness of his Apprehension impressed upon him. He had the peculiar Felicity, that his Attention never deserted him; he was present to every Object, and regardful of the most trifling Occurrences. He had the Art of escaping from his own Reflections, and accommodating himself to every new Scene.

To this Quality is to be imputed the Extent of his Knowledge, compared with the small Time which he spent in visible Endeavours to acquire it. He mingled in cursory Conversation with the same Steadiness of Attention as others apply to a Lecture, and, amidst the Appearance of thoughtless Gayety, lost no new Idea that was started, nor any Hint that could be improved. He had therefore made in Coffee-Houses the same Proficiency as others in Studies; and it is remarkable, that the Writings of a Man of little Education, and little Reading, have an Air of Learning scarcely to be found in any other Performances, but which perhaps as often obscures as embellishes them.

His Judgment was eminently exact, both with regard to Writings and to Men. The Knowledge of Life was indeed his chief Attainment, and it is not without some Satisfaction, that I can produce the Suffrage of *Savage* in favour of human Nature, of which he never appeared to entertain such odious Ideas, as some, who perhaps had neither his Judgment nor Experience, have published, either in Ostentation of their Sagacity, Vindication of their Crimes, or Gratification of their Malice.

His Method of Life particularly qualified him for Conversation, of which he knew how to practice all the Graces. He was never vehement or loud, but at once modest and easy, open and respectful; his Language was vivacious and elegant, and equally happy upon grave or humorous Subjects. He was generally censured for not knowing when to retire, but that was not the Defect of his Judgment, but of his Fortune; when he left his Company, he was frequently to spend the remaining Part of the Night in the Street, or at least was abandoned to gloomy Reflections, which it is not strange that he delayed as long as he could, and sometimes forgot that he gave others Pain to avoid it himself.

It cannot be said, that he made Use of his Abilities for the Direction of his own Conduct; an irregular and dissipated Manner of Life had made him the Slave of every Passion that happened to be excited by the Presence of its Object, and that Slavery to his Passions reciprocally produced a Life irregular and dissipated. He was not Master of his own Motions, nor could promise any thing for the next Day.

With regard to his Oeconomy, nothing can be added to the Relation of his Life: he appeared to think himself born to be supported by others, and dispensed from all Necessity of providing for himself; he therefore never prosecuted any Scheme of Advantage, nor endeavoured even to secure the Profits which his Writings might have afforded him.

His Temper was, in consequence of the Dominion of his Passions, uncertain and capricious; he was easily engaged, and easily disgusted; but he is accused of retaining his Hatred more tenaciously than his Benevolence.

He was compassionate both by Nature and Principle, and always ready to perform Offices of Humanity; but when he was provoked, and very small Offences were sufficient to provoke him, he would prosecute his Revenge with the utmost Acrimony till his Passion had subsided.

His Friendship was therefore of little Value; for though he was zealous in the Support or Vindication of those whom he loved, yet it was always dangerous to trust him, because he considered himself discharged, by the first Quarrel, from all Ties of Honour or Gratitude; and would betray those Secrets which in the Warmth of Confidence had been imparted to him. This Practice drew upon him an universal Accusation of Ingratitude; nor can it be denied that he was very ready to set himself free from the Load of an Obligation; for he could not bear to conceive himself in a State of Dependence, his Pride being equally powerful with his other Passions, and appearing in the Form of Insolence at one time, and of Vanity at another. Vanity, the most innocent Species of Pride, was most frequently predominant: he could not easily leave off when he had once begun to mention himself or his Works, nor ever read his Verses without stealing his Eyes from the Page, to discover in the Faces of his Audience, how they were affected with any favourite Passage.

A kinder Name than that of Vanity ought to be given to the Delicacy with which he was always careful to separate his own Merit from every other Man's, and to reject that Praise to which he had no Claim. He did not forget, in mentioning his Performances, to mark every Line that had been suggested or amended, and was so accurate as to relate that he owed *three Words* in *THE WAN-DERER*, to the Advice of his Friends.

His Veracity was questioned, but with little Reason; his Accounts, tho' not indeed always the same, were generally consistent. When he loved any Man, he suppress'd all his Faults, and when he had been offended by him, concealed all his Virtues: but his Characters were generally true, so far as he proceeded; tho' it cannot be denied that his Partiality might have sometimes the Effect of Falsehood.

In Cases indifferent he was zealous for Virtue, Truth and Justice; he knew very well the Necessity of Goodness to the present and future Happiness of Mankind; nor is there perhaps any Writer, who has less endeavoured to please, by flattering the Appetites, or perverting the Judgment.

As an Author, therefore, and he now ceases to influence Mankind in any other Character, if one Piece, which he had resolved to suppress, be excepted, he has very little to fear from the strictest moral or religious Censure. And though he may not be altogether secure against the Objections of the Critic, it must however be acknowledged, that his Works are the Productions of a Genius truly poetical; and, what many Writers, who have been more lavishly applauded, cannot boast, that they have an original Air, which has no Resemblance of any foregoing Writer; that the Versification and Sentiments have a Cast peculiar to themselves, which no Man can imitate with Success, because what was Nature in *Savage* would in another be Affectation. It must be confessed that his Descriptions are striking, his Images animated, his Fictions justly imagin'd, and his Allegories artfully persued; that his Diction is elevated, though sometimes forced, and his Numbers sonorous and majestick, though frequently sluggish and encumbered. Of his Stile the general Fault is Harshness, and the general Excellence is Dignity; of his Sentiments the prevailing Beauty is Sublimity, and Uniformity the prevailing Defect.

For his Life, or for his Writings, none who candidly consider his Fortune, will think an Apology either necessary or difficult. If he was not always sufficiently instructed in his Subject, his Knowledge was at least greater than could have been attained by others in the same State. If his Works were sometimes unfinished, Accuracy cannot reasonably be expected from a Man oppressed with Want, which he has no Hope of relieving but by a speedy Publication. The Insolence and Resentment of which he is accused, were not easily to be avoided by a great Mind, irritated by perpetual Hardships, and constrained hourly to return the Spurns of Contempt, and repress the Insolence of Prosperity; and Vanity surely may be readily pardoned in him, to whom Life afforded no other Comforts than barren Praises, and the Consciousness of deserving them.

Those are no proper Judges of his Conduct who have slumber'd away their Time on the Down of Abundance, nor will a wise Man easily presume to say, "Had I been in *Savage*'s Condition, I should have lived, or written, better than *Savage*."

This Relation will not be wholly without its Use, if those, who languish under any Part of his Sufferings, shall be enabled to fortify their Patience by reflecting that they feel only those Afflictions from which the Abilities of *Savage* did not exempt him; or if those, who, in confidence of superior Capacities or Attainments, disregard the common Maxims of Life, shall be reminded that nothing will supply the Want of Prudence, and that Negligence and Irregularity, long continued, will make Knowledge useless, Wit ridiculous, and Genius contemptible.

THE

PLAN OF A DICTIONARY

OF THE ENGLISH LANGUAGE

The text is that of the British Museum first edition
(quarto) of 1747 (11630. e. 10(8).); it has been compared with the text of the octavo edition of the same
year (B.M.: 626. g. 11(2).).

THE

PLAN OF A DICTIONARY

Of the ENGLISH LANGUAGE

Addressed to the Right Honourable
PHILIP DORMER, Earl of CHESTERFIELD
One of His Majesty's Principal Secretaries of State

MY LORD,

WHEN first I undertook to write an English Dictionary, I had no expectation of any higher patronage than that of the proprietors of the copy, nor prospect of any other advantage than the price of my labour; I knew, that the work in which I engaged is generally considered as drudgery for the blind, as the proper toil of artless industry, a task that requires neither the light of learning, nor the activity of genius, but may be successfully performed without any higher quality than that of bearing burthens with dull patience, and beating the track of the alphabet with sluggish resolution.

Whether this opinion, so long transmitted and so widely propagated, had its beginning from truth and nature, or from accident and prejudice, whether it be decreed by the authority of reason, or the tyranny of ignorance, that of all the candidates for literary praise, the unhappy lexicographer holds the lowest place, neither vanity nor interest incited me to enquire. It appeared that the province allotted me was of all the regions of learning generally confessed to be the least delightful, that it was believed to produce neither fruits nor flowers, and that after a long and laborious cultivation, not even the barren laurel had been found upon it.

Yet on this province, my Lord, I enter'd with the pleasing hope, that as it was low, it likewise would be safe. I was drawn forward with the prospect of employment, which, tho' not splendid, would be useful, and which tho' it could not make my life envied, would keep it innocent, which would awaken no passion, engage me in no contention, nor throw in my way any temptation to disturb the quiet of others by censure, or my own by flattery.

I had read indeed of times, in which princes and statesmen thought it part of their honour to promote the improvement of their native tongues, and in which dictionaries were written under the protection of greatness. To the patrons of such undertakings, I willingly paid the homage of believing that they, who were thus solicitous for the perpetuity of their language, had reason to expect that their actions would be celebrated by posterity, and that the eloquence which they promoted would be employed in their praise. But I considered such acts of beneficence as prodigies, recorded rather to raise wonder than expectation; and content with the terms that I had stipulated, had not suffer'd my imagination to flatter me with any other encouragement, when I found that my design had been thought by your Lordship of importance sufficient to attract your favour.

How far this unexpected distinction can be rated among the happy incidents of life, I am not yet able to determine. Its first effect has been to make me anxious lest it should fix the attention of the public too much upon me, and as it once happened to an epic poet of France, by raising the reputation of the attempt, obstruct the reception of the work. I imagine what the world will expect from a scheme, prosecuted under your Lordship's influence, and I know that expectation, when her wings are once expanded, easily reaches heights which performance never will attain, and when she has mounted the summit of perfection, derides her follower, who dies in the pursuit.

Not therefore, to raise expectation, but to repress it, I here lay before your Lordship the plan of my undertaking, that more may not be demanded than I intend, and that before it is too far advanced to be thrown into a new method, I may be advertised of its defects or superfluities. Such informations I may justly hope from the emulation with which those who desire the praise of elegance or discernment must contend in the promotion of a design that you, my Lord, have not thought unworthy to share your attention with treaties and with wars.

In the first attempt to methodise my ideas, I found a difficulty which extended itself to the whole work. It was not easy to determine by what rule of distinction the words of this dictionary were to be chosen. The chief intent of it is to preserve the purity and ascertain the meaning of our English idiom; and this seems to require nothing more than that our language be considered so far as it is our own; that the words and phrases used in the general intercourse of life, or found in the works of those whom we commonly stile polite writers, be selected, without including the terms of particular professions, since, with the arts to which they relate, they are generally derived from other nations, and are very often the same in all the languages of this part of the world. This is perhaps the exact and pure idea of a grammatical dictionary; but in lexicography, as in other arts, naked science is too delicate for the purposes of life. The value of a work must be estimated by its use: It is not enough that a dictionary delights the critic, unless at the same time it instructs the learner; as it is to little purpose, that an engine amuses the philosopher by the subtilty of its mechanism, if it requires so much knowledge in its application, as to be of no advantage to the common workman.

The title which I prefix to my work has long conveyed a very miscellaneous idea, and they that take a dictionary into their hands have been accustomed to expect from it, a solution of almost every difficulty. If foreign words therefore were rejected, it could be little regarded, except by critics, or those who aspire to criticism; and however it might enlighten those that write, would be all darkness to them that only read. The unlearned much oftner consult their dictionaries, for the meaning of words, than for their structures or formations; and the words that most want explanation, are generally terms of art, which therefore experience has taught my predecessors to spread with a kind of pompous luxuriance over their productions.

The academicians of France, indeed, rejected terms of science in their first essay, but found afterwards a necessity of relaxing the rigour of their determination; and, tho' they would not naturalize them at once by a single act, permitted them by degrees to settle themselves among the natives, with little opposition, and it would surely be no proof of judgment to imitate them in an error which they have now retracted, and deprive the book of its chief use by scrupulous distinctions.

Of such words however, all are not equally to be considered as parts of our language, for some of them are naturalized and incorporated, but others still continue aliens, and are rather auxiliaries than subjects. This naturalization is produced either by an admission into common speech in some metaphorical signification, which is the acquisition of a kind of property among us, as we say the *zenith* of advancement, the *meridian* of life, the *cynosure*** of neighbouring eyes; or it is the consequence of long intermixture and frequent use, by which the ear is accustomed to the sound of words till their original is forgotten, as in *equator*, *satellites*; or of the change of a foreign to an English termination, and a conformity to the laws of the speech into which they are adopted, as in *category*, *cachexy*, *peripneumony*.

Of those which yet continue in the state of aliens, and have made no approaches toward assimilation, some seem necessary to be retained, because the purchasers of the dictionary will expect to find them. Such are many words in the common law, as *capias*, *habeas corpus*, *præmunire*, *nisi prius* : such are some terms of controversial divinity, as *hypostasis*; and of physick, as the names of diseases; and in general all terms which can be found in books not written professedly upon particular arts, or can be supposed necessary to those who do not regularly study them. Thus when a reader not skilled in physick happens in Milton upon this line,

> . . . . pining atrophy,
> *Marasmus*, and wide-wasting pestilence,

he will with equal expectation look into his dictionary for the word *marasmus*, as for *atrophy*, or *pestilence*, and will have reason to complain if he does not find it.

It seems necessary to the completion of a dictionary design'd not merely for critics but for popular use, that it should comprise, in some degree, the peculiar words of every profession; that the terms of war and navigation should be inserted so far as they can be required by readers of travels, and of history; and those of law, merchandise and mechanical trades, so far as they can be supposed useful in the occurrences of common life.

But there ought, however, to be some distinction made between the different classes of words, and therefore it will be proper to print those which are incorporated into the language in the usual character, and those which are still to be considered as foreign, in the Italick letter.

* Milton.

Another question may arise, with regard to appellatives, or the names of species. It seems of no great use to set down the words *horse, dog, cat, willow, alder, dasy, rose,* and a thousand others, of which it will be hard to give an explanation not more obscure than the word itself. Yet it is to be considered, that, if the names of animals be inserted, we must admit those which are more known, as well as those with which we are, by accident, less acquainted; and if they are all rejected how will the reader be relieved from difficulties produced by allusions to the crocodile, the camæleon, the ichneumon, and the hyæna? If no plants are to be mentioned, the most pleasing part of nature will be excluded, and many beautiful epithets be unexplained. If only those which are less known are to be mentioned, who shall fix the limits of the reader's learning? The importance of such explications appears from the mistakes which the want of them has occasioned. Had Shakspear had a dictionary of this kind he had not made the *woodbine* entwine the *honeysuckle*; nor would Milton, with such assistance, have disposed so improperly of his *ellops* and his *scorpion*.

Besides, as such words, like others, require that their accents should be settled, their sounds ascertained, and their etymologies deduced, they cannot be properly omitted in the dictionary. And though the explanations of some may be censured as trivial, because they are almost universally understood, and those of others as unnecessary, because they will seldom occur, yet it seems not proper to omit them, since it is rather to be wished that many readers should find more than they expect, than that one should miss what he might hope to find.

When all the words are selected and arranged, the first part of the work to be considered is the ORTHOGRAPHY, which was long vague and uncertain, which at last, when its fluctuation ceased, was in many cases settled but by accident, and in which, according to your Lordship's observation, there is still great uncertainty among the best critics; nor is it easy to state a rule by which we may decide between custom and reason, or between the equiponderant authorities of writers alike eminent for judgment and accuracy.

The great orthographical contest has long subsisted between etymology and pronunciation. It has been demanded, on one hand, that men should write as they speak; but as it has been shewn that this conformity never was attained in any language, and that it is not more easy to perswade men to agree exactly in speaking than in writing, it may be asked with equal propriety, why men do not rather speak as they write. In France, where this controversy was at its greatest height, neither party, however ardent, durst adhere steadily to their own rule; the etymologist was often forced to spell with the people; and the advocate for the authority of pronunciation, found it sometimes deviating so capriciously from the received use of writing, that he was constrained to comply with the rule of his adversaries, lest he should loose the end by the means, and be left alone by following the croud.

When a question of orthography is dubious, that practice has, in my opinion, a claim to preference, which preserves the greatest number of radical letters, or seems most to comply with the general custom of our language. But the chief rule which I propose to follow, is to make no innovation, without a reason sufficient to balance the inconvenience of change; and such reasons I do not expect often to find. All change is of itself an evil, which ought not to be hazarded but for evident advantage; and as inconstancy is in every case a mark of weakness, it will add nothing to the reputation of our tongue. There are, indeed, some who despise the inconveniencies of confusion, who seem to take pleasure in departing from custom, and to think alteration desirable for its own sake, and the reformation of our orthography, which these writers have attempted, should not pass without its due honours, but that I suppose they hold singularity its own reward, or may dread the fascination of lavish praise.

The present usage of spelling, where the present usage can be distinguished, will therefore in this work be generally followed, yet there will be often occasion to observe, that it is in itself inaccurate, and tolerated rather than chosen; particularly, when by a change of one letter, or more, the meaning of a word is obscured, as in *farrier*, for *ferrier*, as it was formerly written, from *ferrum*, or *fer*; in *gibberish* for *gebrish*, the jargon of Geber and his chymical followers, understood by none but their own tribe. It will be likewise sometimes proper to trace back the orthography of different ages, and shew by what gradations the word departed from its original.

Closely connected with orthography is PRONUNCIATION, the stability of which is of great importance to the duration of a language, because the first change will naturally begin by corruptions in the living speech. The want of certain rules for the pronunciation of former ages, had made us wholly ignorant of the metrical art of our ancient poets; and since those who study their sentiments regret the loss of their numbers, it is surely time to provide that the harmony of the moderns may be more permanent.

A new pronunciation will make almost a new speech, and therefore since one great end of this undertaking is to fix the English language, care will be taken to determine the accentuation of all polysyllables by proper authorities, as it is one of those capricious phænomena which cannot be easily reduced to rules. Thus there is no antecedent reason for difference of accent in the two words *dolorous* and *sonorous*, yet of the one Milton gives the sound in this line,

> He pass'd o'er many a region *dolorous*,

and that of the other in this,

> *Sonorous* metal blowing martial sounds.

It may be likewise proper to remark metrical licences, such as contractions, *generous, gen'rous, reverend, rev'rend*; and coalitions, as *region, question*.

But it is still more necessary to fix the pronunciation of monosyllables, by placing with them words of correspondent sound, that one may guard the other against the danger of that variation, which to some of the most common, has already happened, so that the words *wound*, and *wind*, as they are now frequently pronounced, will not rhyme to *sound*, and *mind*. It is to be remarked that many words written alike are differently pronounced, as *flow*, and *brow*, which may be thus registred *flow, woe, brow, now*, or of which the exemplification may be generally given by a distich. Thus the words *tear* or lacerate, and *tear* the water of the eye, have the same letters, but may be distinguished thus, *tear, dare; tear, peer*.

Some words have two sounds, which may be equally admitted, as being equally defensible by authority. Thus *great* is differently used.

> For Swift and him despis'd the farce of state,
> The sober follies of the wise and *great*.   Pope.

> As if misfortune made the throne her seat,
> And none could be unhappy but the *great*.   Rowe.

The care of such minute particulars may be censured as trifling, but these particulars have not been thought unworthy of attention in more polished languages.

The accuracy of the French, in stating the sounds of their letters, is well known; and, among the Italians, Crescembeni has not thought it unnecessary to inform his countrymen of the words, which, in compliance with different rhymes, are allowed to be differently spelt, and of which the number is now so fix'd, that no modern poet is suffered to encrease it.

When the orthography and pronunciation are adjusted, the ETYMOLOGY or DERIVATION is next to be considered, and the words are to be distinguished according to their different classes, whether simple, as *day, light,* or compound as *day-light;* whether primitive, as, to *act,* or derivative, as *action, actionable, active, activity.* This will much facilitate the attainment of our language, which now stands in our dictionaries a confused heap of words without dependence, and without relation.

When this part of the work is performed, it will be necessary to inquire how our primitives are to be deduced from foreign languages, which may be often very successfully performed by the assistance of our own etymologists. This search will give occasion to many curious disquisitions, and sometimes perhaps to conjectures, which, to readers unacquainted with this kind of study, cannot but appear improbable and capricious. But it may be reasonably imagined, that what is so much in the power of men as language, will very often be capriciously conducted. Nor are these disquisitions and conjectures to be considered altogether as wanton sports of wit, or vain shews of learning; our language is well known not to be primitive or self-originated, but to have adopted words of every generation, and either for the supply of its necessities, or the encrease of its copiousness, to have received additions from very distant regions; so that in search of the progenitors of our speech, we may wander from the tropic to the frozen zone, and find some in the valleys of Palestine, and some upon the rocks of Norway.

Beside the derivation of particular words, there is likewise an etymology of phrases. Expressions are often taken from other languages, some apparently, as to *run a risque, courir un risque;* and some even when we do not seem to borrow their words; thus, to *bring about* or accomplish, appears an English phrase, but in reality our native word *about* has no such import, and is only a French expression, of which we have an example in the common phrase, *venir à bout d'une affaire.*

In exhibiting the descent of our language, our etymologists seem to have been too lavish of their learning, having traced almost every word through various tongues, only to shew what was shewn sufficiently by the first derivation. This practice is of great use in synoptical lexicons, where mutilated and doubtful languages are explained by their affinity to others more certain and extensive, but is generally superfluous in English etymologies. When the word is easily deduced from a Saxon original, I shall not often enquire further, since we know not the parent of the Saxon dialect, but when it is borrowed from the French, I shall shew whence the French is apparently derived. Where a Saxon root cannot be found, the defect may be supplied from kindred languages, which will be generally furnished with much liberality by the writers of our glossaries; writers who deserve often the highest praise, both of judgment and industry, and may expect at least to be mentioned with honour by me, whom they have freed from the greatest part of a very laborious work, and on whom they have imposed, at worst, only the easy task of rejecting superfluities.

By tracing in this manner every word to its original, and not admitting, but with great caution, any of which no original can be found, we shall secure our language from being over-run with *cant*, from being crouded with low terms, the spawn of folly or affectation, which arise from no just principles of speech, and of which therefore no legitimate derivation can be shewn.

When the etymology is thus adjusted, the ANALOGY of our language is next to be considered; when we have discovered whence our words are derived, we are to examine by what rules they are governed, and how they are inflected through their various terminations. The terminations of the English are few, but those few have hitherto remained unregarded by the writers of our dictionaries. Our substantives are declined only by the plural termination, our adjectives admit no variation but in the degrees of comparison, and our verbs are conjugated by auxiliary words, and are only changed in the preter tense.

To our language may be with great justness applied the observation of *Quintilian*, that speech was not formed by an analogy sent from heaven. It did not descend to us in a state of uniformity and perfection, but was produced by necessity and enlarged by accident, and is therefore composed of dissimilar parts, thrown together by negligence, by affectation, by learning, or by ignorance.

Our inflections therefore are by no means constant, but admit of numberless irregularities, which in this dictionary will be diligently noted. Thus *fox* makes in the plural *foxes*, but *ox* makes *oxen*. *Sheep* is the same in both numbers. Adjectives are sometimes compared by changing the last syllable, as *proud, prouder, proudest*; and sometimes by particles prefixed, as *ambitious, more* ambitious, *most* ambitious. The forms of our verbs are subject to great variety; some end their preter tense in *ed*, as I *love*, I *loved*, I have *loved*, which may be called the regular form, and is followed by most of our verbs of southern original. But many depart from this rule, without agreeing in any other, as I *shake*, I *shook*, I have *shaken*, or *shook* as it is sometimes written in poetry; I *make*, I *made*, I have *made*; I *bring*, I *brought*; I *wring*, I *wrung*, and many others, which, as they cannot be reduced to rules, must be learned from the dictionary rather than the grammar.

The verbs are likewise to be distinguished according to their qualities, as actives from neuters; the neglect of which has already introduced some barbarities in our conversation, which, if not obviated by just animadversions, may in time creep into our writings.

Thus, my Lord, will our language be laid down, distinct in its minutest subdivisions, and resolved into its elemental principles. And who upon this survey can forbear to wish, that these fundamental atoms of our speech might obtain the firmness and immutability of the primogenial and constituent particles of matter, that they might retain their substance while they alter their appearance, and be varied and compounded, yet not destroyed.

But this is a privilege which words are scarcely to expect; for, like their author, when they are not gaining strength, they are generally losing it. Though art may sometimes prolong their duration, it will rarely give them perpetuity, and their changes will be almost always informing us, that language is the work of man, of a being from whom permanence and stability cannot be derived.

Words having been hitherto considered as separate and unconnected, are now to be likewise examined as they are ranged in their various relations to others by the rules of SYNTAX or con-

130

struction, to which I do not know that any regard has been yet shewn in English dictionaries, and in which the grammarians can give little assistance. The syntax of this language is too inconstant to be reduced to rules, and can be only learned by the distinct consideration of particular words as they are used by the best authors. Thus, we say, according to the present modes of speech, the soldier died *of* his wounds, and the sailor perished *with* hunger; and every man acquainted with our language would be offended by a change of these particles, which yet seem originally assigned by chance, there being no reason to be drawn from grammar why a man may not, with equal propriety, be said to die *with* a wound, or perish *of* hunger.

Our syntax therefore is not to be taught by general rules, but by special precedents; and in examining whether Addison has been with justice accused of a solecism in this passage,

> The poor inhabitant . . .
> Starves in the midst of nature's bounty curst,
> And in the loaden vineyard *dies for thirst,*

it is not in our power to have recourse to any established laws of speech, but we must remark how the writers of former ages have used the same word, and consider whether he can be acquitted of impropriety, upon the testimony of Davies, given in his favour by a similar passage.

> She loaths the watry glass wherein she gaz'd,
> And shuns it still, although *for thirst she dye.*

When the construction of a word is explained, it is necessary to pursue it through its train of PHRASEOLOGY, through those forms where it is used in a manner peculiar to our language, or in senses not to be comprised in the general explanations; as from the verb *make*, arise these phrases, to *make love*, to *make an end*, to *make way*, as he *made way* for his followers, the ship *made way* before the wind; to *make a bed*, to *make merry*, to *make a mock*, to *make presents*, to *make a doubt*, to *make out an assertion*, to *make good* a breach, to *make good* a cause, to *make nothing* of an attempt, to *make lamentation*, to *make a merit*, and many others which will occur in reading with that view, and which only their frequency hinders from being generally remarked.

The great labour is yet to come, the labour of interpreting these words and phrases with brevity, fulness and perspicuity; a task of

131

which the extent and intricacy is sufficiently shown by the miscarriage of those who have generally attempted it. This difficulty is encreased by the necessity of explaining the words in the same language, for there is often only one word for one idea; and though it be easy to translate the words *bright, sweet, salt, bitter*, into another language, it is not easy to explain them.

With regard to the INTERPRETATION many other questions have required consideration. It was some time doubted whether it be necessary to explain the things implied by particular words. As under the term *baronet*, whether instead of this explanation, *a title of honour next in degree to that of baron*, it would be better to mention more particularly the creation, privileges and rank of baronets; and whether under the word *barometer*, instead of being satisfied with observing that it is *an instrument to discover the weight of the air*, it would be fit to spend a few lines upon its invention, construction and principles. It is not to be expected that with the explanation of the one the herald should be satisfied, or the philosopher with that of the other; but since it will be required by common readers, that the explications should be sufficient for common use, and since without some attention to such demands the dictionary cannot become generally valuable, I have determined to consult the best writers for explanations real as well as verbal, and perhaps I may at last have reason to say, after one of the augmenters of Furetier, that my book is more learned than its author.

In explaining the general and popular language, it seems necessary to sort the several senses of each word, and to exhibit first its natural and primitive signification, as

To *arrive*, to reach the shore in a voyage. He *arrived* at a safe harbour.

Then to give its consequential meaning, *to arrive*, to reach any place whether by land or sea; as, he *arrived* at his country seat.

Then its metaphorical sense, to obtain any thing desired; as, he *arrived* at a peerage.

Then to mention any observation that arises from the comparison of one meaning with another; as, it may be remarked of the word *arrive*, that in consequence of its original and etymological sense, it cannot be properly applied but to words signifying something desirable; thus, we say a man *arrived* at happiness, but cannot say without a mixture of irony, he *arrived* at misery.

Ground, the earth, generally as opposed to the air or water. He swam till he reached *ground*. The bird fell to the *ground*.

Then follows the accidental or consequential signification, in which *ground* implies any thing that lies under another; as, he laid colours upon a rough *ground*. The silk had blue flowers on a red *ground*.

Then the remoter or metaphorical signification; as, the *ground* of his opinion was a false computation. The *ground* of his work was his father's manuscript.

After having gone through the natural and figurative senses, it will be proper to subjoin the poetical sense of each word, where it differs from that which is in common use; as, *wanton* applied to any thing of which the motion is irregular without terror, as

> In *wanton* ringlets curl'd her hair.

To the poetical sense may succeed the familiar; as of *toast*, used to imply the person whose health is drunk.

> The wise man's passion, and the vain man's *toast*.   POPE.

The familiar may be followed by the burlesque; as of *mellow*, applied to good fellowship.

> In all thy humours whether grave, or *mellow*.   ADDISON.

Or of *bite* used for *cheat*.

> . . . . More a dupe than wit,
> Sappho can tell you, how this man was *bit*.   POPE.

And lastly, may be produced the peculiar sense, in which a word is found in any great author. As *faculties* in Shakspeare signifies the powers of authority.

> . . . . This Duncan
> Has born his *faculties* so meek, has been
> So clear in his great office, that &c.

The signification of adjectives, may be often ascertained by uniting them to substantives, as *simple swain, simple sheep*; sometimes the sense of a substantive may be elucidated by the epithets annexed to it in good authors, as the *boundless ocean*, the *open lawns*, and where such advantage can be gained by a short quotation it is not to be omitted.

The difference of signification in words generally accounted

E   133

synonimous, ought to be carefully observed; as in *pride, haughtiness, arrogance*; and the strict and critical meaning ought to be distinguished from that which is loose and popular; as in the word *perfection*, which though in its philosophical and exact sense, it can be of little use among human beings, is often so much degraded from its original signification, that the academicians have inserted in their work the *perfection of a language*, and with a little more licentiousness might have prevailed on themselves to have added *the perfection of a dictionary*.

There are many other characters of words which it will be of use to mention. Some have both an active and passive signification, as *fearful*, that which gives or which feels terror, a *fearful prodigy*, a *fearful hare*. Some have a personal, some a real meaning, as in opposition to *old* we use the adjective *young* of animated beings, and *new* of other things. Some are restrained to the sense of praise, and others to that of disapprobation, so commonly, though not always, we *exhort* to good actions, we *instigate* to ill; we *animate*, *incite*, and *encourage* indifferently to good or bad. So we usually *ascribe* good, but *impute* evil; yet neither the use of these words, nor perhaps of any other in our licentious language, is so established as not to be often reversed by the correctest writers. I shall therefore, since the rules of stile, like those of law, arise from precedents often repeated, collect the testimonies on both sides, and endeavour to discover and promulgate the decrees of custom, who has so long possessed, whether by right or by usurpation, the sovereignty of words.

It is necessary likewise to explain many words by their opposition to others; for contraries are best seen when they stand together. Thus the verb *stand* has one sense as opposed to *fall*, and another as opposed to *fly*; for want of attending to which distinction, obvious as it is, the learned Dr. Bentley has squandered his criticism to no purpose, on these lines of Paradise Lost.

> . . . . In heaps
> Chariot and charioteer lay over-turn'd,
> And fiery foaming steeds. What *stood, recoil'd,*
> O'erwearied, through the faint Satanic host,
> Defensive scarce, or with pale fear surpris'd
> *Fled* ignominious. . . .

"Here," says the critic, "as the sentence is now read, we find that what *stood, fled*," and therefore he proposes an alteration, which he might have spared if he had consulted a dictionary, and found that nothing more was affirmed than that those *fled* who did *not fall*.

In explaining such meanings as seem accidental and adventitious, I shall endeavour to give an account of the means by which they were introduced. Thus to *eke out* any thing, signifies to lengthen it beyond its just dimensions by some low artifice, because the word *eke* was the usual refuge of our old writers when they wanted a syllable. And *buxom*, which means only *obedient*, is now made, in familiar phrases, to stand for *wanton*, because of an antient form of marriage, before the reformation, the bride promised complaisance and obedience in these terms: "I will be bonair and *buxom* in bed and at board."

I know well, my Lord, how trifling many of these remarks will appear separately considered, and how easily they may give occasion to the contemptuous merriment of sportive idleness, and the gloomy censures of arrogant stupidity; but dulness it is easy to despise, and laughter it is easy to repay. I shall not be solicitous what is thought of my work by such as know not the difficulty or importance of philological studies, nor shall think those that have done nothing qualified to condemn me for doing little. It may not, however, be improper to remind them, that no terrestrial greatness is more than an aggregate of little things, and to inculcate after the Arabian proverb, that drops added to drops constitute the ocean.

There remains yet to be considered the DISTRIBUTION of words into their proper classes, or that part of lexicography which is strictly critical.

The popular part of the language, which includes all words not appropriated to particular sciences, admits of many distinctions and subdivisions; as, into words of general use; words employed chiefly in poetry; words obsolete; words which are admitted only by particular writers, yet not in themselves improper; words used only in burlesque writing; and words impure and barbarous.

Words of general use will be known by having no sign of particularity, and their various senses will be supported by authorities of all ages.

The words appropriated to poetry will be distinguished by some mark prefixed, or will be known by having no authorities but those of poets.

135

Of antiquated or obsolete words, none will be inserted but such as are to be found in authors who wrote since the accession of Elizabeth, from which we date the golden age of our language; and of these many might be omitted, but that the reader may require, with an appearance of reason, that no difficulty should be left unresolved in books which he finds himself invited to read, as confessed and established models of stile. These will be likewise pointed out by some note of exclusion, but not of disgrace.

The words which are found only in particular books, will be known by the single name of him that has used them; but such will be omitted, unless either their propriety, elegance, or force, or the reputation of their authors affords some extraordinary reason for their reception.

Words used in burlesque and familiar compositions, will be likewise mentioned with their proper authorites, such as *dudgeon* from Butler, and *leasing* from Prior, and will be diligently characterized by marks of distinction.

Barbarous or impure words and expressions, may be branded with some note of infamy, as they are carefully to be eradicated wherever they are found; and they occur too frequently even in the best writers. As in Pope,

> . . . *in* endless error *hurl'd.*

> *'Tis these* that early taint the female soul.

In Addison,

> Attend to what a *lesser* muse indites.

And in Dryden,

> A dreadful quiet felt, and *worser* far
> Than arms . . .

If this part of the work can be well performed, it will be equivalent to the proposal made by Boileau to the academicians, that they should review all their polite writers, and correct such impurities as might be found in them, that their authority might not contribute, at any distant time, to the depravation of the language.

With regard to questions of purity, or propriety, I was once in doubt whether I should not attribute too much to myself in attempting to decide them, and whether my province was to extend beyond the proposition of the question, and the display of the suffrages on each side; but I have been since determined by your Lordship's opinion, to interpose my own judgment, and shall therefore endeavour to support what appears to me most consonant to grammar and reason. Ausonius thought that modesty forbad him to plead inability for a task to which Cæsar had judged him equal.

> Cur me posse negem posse quod ille putat?

And I may hope, my Lord, that since you, whose authority in our language is so generally acknowledged, have commissioned me to declare my own opinion, I shall be considered as exercising a kind of vicarious jurisdiction, and that the power which might have been denied to my own claim, will be readily allowed me as the delegate of your Lordship.

In citing authorities, on which the credit of every part of this work must depend, it will be proper to observe some obvious rules, such as of preferring writers of the first reputation to those of an inferior rank, of noting the quotations with accuracy, and of selecting, when it can be conveniently done, such sentences, as, besides their immediate use, may give pleasure or instruction by conveying some elegance of language, or some precept of prudence, or piety.

It has been asked, on some occasions, who shall judge the judges? And since with regard to this design, a question may arise by what authority the authorities are selected, it is necessary to obviate it, by declaring that many of the writers whose testimonies will be alleged, were selected by Mr. Pope, of whom I may be justified in affirming, that were he still alive, solicitous as he was for the success of this work, he would not be displeased that I have undertaken it.

It will be proper that the quotations be ranged according to the ages of their authors, and it will afford an agreeable amusement, if to the words and phrases which are not of our own growth, the name of the writer who first introduced them can be affixed, and if, to words which are now antiquated, the authority be subjoined of him who last admitted them. Thus for *scathe* and *buxom*, now obsolete, Milton may be cited.

> . . . . The mountain oak
> Stands *scath'd* to heaven . . .
> . . . He with broad sails
> Winnow'd the *buxom* air. . . .

By this method every word will have its history, and the reader will be informed of the gradual changes of the language, and have before his eyes the rise of some words, and the fall of others. But observations so minute and accurate are to be desired rather than expected, and if use be carefully supplied, curiosity must sometimes bear its disappointments.

This, my Lord, is my idea of an English Dictionary, a dictionary by which the pronunciation of our language may be fixed, and its attainment facilitated; by which its purity may be preserved, its use ascertained, and its duration lengthened. And though, perhaps, to correct the language of nations by books of grammar, and amend their manners by discourses of morality, may be tasks equally difficult; yet as it is unavoidable to wish, it is natural likewise to hope, that your Lordship's patronage may not be wholly lost; that it may contribute to the preservation of antient, and the improvement of modern writers; that it may promote the reformation of those translators, who for want of understanding the characteristical difference of tongues, have formed a chaotic dialect of heterogeneous phrases; and awaken to the care of purer diction, some men of genius, whose attention to argument makes them negligent of stile, or whose rapid imagination, like the Peruvian torrents, when it brings down gold, mingles it with sand.

When I survey the Plan which I have laid before you, I cannot, my Lord, but confess, that I am frighted at its extent, and, like the soldiers of Cæsar, look on Britain as a new world, which it is almost madness to invade. But I hope, that though I should not complete the conquest, I shall at least discover the coast, civilize part of the inhabitants, and make it easy for some other adventurer to proceed farther, to reduce them wholly to subjection, and settle them under laws.

We are taught by the great Roman orator, that every man should propose to himself the highest degree of excellence, but that he may stop with honour at the second or third: though therefore my performance should fall below the excellence of other dictionaries, I may obtain, at least, the praise of having endeavoured well, nor shall I think it any reproach to my diligence, that I have retired without a triumph from a contest with united academies and long successions of learned compilers. I cannot hope in the warmest moments, to preserve so much caution through so long a work, as not often to sink into negligence, or to obtain so much knowledge of all its parts, as not frequently to fail by ignorance. I expect that sometimes the desire of accuracy, will urge me to superfluities, and sometimes the fear of prolixity betray me to omissions; that in the extent of such variety I shall be often bewildred, and in the mazes of such intricacy, be frequently entangled; that in one part refinement will be subtilised beyond exactness, and evidence dilated in another beyond perspicuity. Yet I do not despair of approbation from those who knowing the uncertainty of conjecture, the scantiness of knowedge, the fallibility of memory, and the unsteadiness of attention, can compare the causes of error with the means of avoiding it, and the extent of art with the capacity of man; and whatever be the event of my endeavours, I shall not easily regret an attempt which has procured me the honour of appearing thus publickly,

My Lord,
Your Lordship's
Most Obedient and
Most Humble Servant,
SAM. JOHNSON

PROLOGUE

SPOKEN BY MR. GARRICK

AT THE OPENING OF

THE THEATRE IN DRURY LANE

The text of this poem has been taken from the British Museum copy of the first edition, 1747 (C. 17. ff. 5.).

PROLOGUE

SPOKEN BY MR. GARRICK,

At the Opening of the THEATRE in DRURY LANE 1747

WHEN Learning's Triumph o'er her barb'rous Foes
First rear'd the Stage, immortal SHAKSPEAR rose;
Each Change of many-colour'd Life he drew,
Exhausted Worlds, and then imagin'd new:
Existence saw him spurn her bounded Reign,
And panting Time toil'd after him in vain:
His pow'rful Strokes presiding Truth impress'd,
And unresisted Passion storm'd the Breast.

Then JOHNSON came, instructed from the School,
To please in Method, and invent by Rule;
His studious Patience, and laborious Art,
By regular Approach essay'd the Heart;
Cold Approbation gave the ling'ring Bays,
For those who durst not censure, scarce cou'd praise.
A Mortal born he met the general Doom,
But left, like *Egypt*'s Kings, a lasting Tomb.

The Wits of *Charles* found easier Ways to Fame,
Nor wish'd for JOHNSON'S Art, or SHAKSPEAR'S Flame,
Themselves they studied, as they felt, they writ,
Intrigue was Plot, Obscenity was Wit.
Vice always found a sympathetick Friend;
They pleas'd their Age, and did not aim to mend.
Yet Bards like these aspir'd to lasting Praise,
And proudly hop'd to pimp in future Day
Their Cause was gen'ral, their Supports were strong,
Their Slaves were willing, and their Reign was long;
Till Shame regain'd the Post that Sense betray'd,
And Virtue call'd Oblivion to her Aid.

Then crush'd by Rules, and weaken'd as refin'd,
For Years the Pow'r of Tragedy declin'd;
From Bard, to Bard, the frigid Caution crept,
Till Declamation roar'd, while Passion slept.
Yet still did Virtue deign the Stage to tread,
Philosophy remain'd, though Nature fled.
But forc'd at length her antient Reign to quit,
She saw great *Faustus* lay the Ghost of Wit:
Exulting Folly hail'd the joyful Day,
And Pantomime, and Song, confirm'd her Sway.

But who the coming Changes can presage,
And mark the future Periods of the Stage?——
Perhaps if Skill could distant Times explore,
New *Behns*, new *Durfeys*, yet remain in Store.
Perhaps, where *Lear* has rav'd, and *Hamlet* dy'd,
On flying Cars new Sorcerers may ride.
Perhaps, for who can guess th' Effects of Chance?
Here *Hunt* may box, or *Mahomet* may dance.

Hard is his Lot, that here by Fortune plac'd,
Must watch the wild Vicissitudes of Taste;
With ev'ry Meteor of Caprice must play,
And chase the new-blown Bubbles of the Day.
Ah! let not Censure term our Fate our Choice,
The Stage but echoes back the publick Voice.
The Drama's Laws the Drama's Patrons give,
For we that live to please, must please to live.

Then prompt no more the Follies you decry,
As Tyrants doom their Tools of Guilt to die;
'Tis yours this Night to bid the Reign commence
Of rescu'd Nature, and reviving Sense;
To chase the Charms of Sound, the Pomp of Show,
For useful Mirth, and salutary Woe;
Bid scenic Virtue form the rising Age,
And Truth diffuse her Radiance from the Stage.

THE
VISION OF THEODORE

The Vision of Theodore first appeared on pp. 516–526 of vol. 2 of *The Preceptor : . . . London : . . . R. Dodsley . . .*, 1748. The British Museum copy (1031. i. 3, 4.) has been used for the present text.

THE

VISION OF THEODORE

The HERMIT of TENERIFFE

FOUND IN HIS CELL

Son of Perseverance, whoever thou art, whose Curiosity has led thee hither, read and be wise. He that now calls upon thee is *Theodore* the Hermit of *Teneriffe*, who in the fifty-seventh Year of his Retreat left this Instruction to Mankind, lest his solitary Hours should be spent in vain.

I was once what thou art now, a Groveller on the Earth, and a Gazer at the Sky; I traffick'd and heaped Wealth together, I loved and was favoured, I wore the Robe of Honour, and heard the Musick of Adulation; I was ambitious, and rose to Greatness; I was unhappy, and retired. I sought for some time what I at length found here, a Place where all real Wants might be easily supplied, and where I might not be under the Necessity of purchasing the Assistance of Men by the Toleration of their Follies. Here I saw Fruits and Herbs and Water, and here determined to wait the Hand of Death, which I hope, when at last it comes, will fall lightly upon me.

Forty-eight Years had I now passed in Forgetfulness of all mortal Cares, and without any Inclination to wander farther than the Necessity of procuring Sustenance required; but as I stood one Day beholding the Rock that overhangs my Cell, I found in myself a Desire to climb it; and when I was on its Top, was in the same manner determined to scale the next, till by Degrees I conceived a Wish to view the Summit of the Mountain, at the Foot of which I had so long resided. This Motion of my Thoughts I endeavoured to suppress, not because it appeared criminal, but because it was new; and all Change, not evidently for the better, alarms a Mind taught by Experience to distrust itself. I was often afraid that my Heart was deceiving me, that my Impatience of Confinement arose from some earthly Passion, and that my Ardour to survey the Works of Nature, was only a hidden Longing to mingle once again in the Scenes of Life. I therefore endeavoured to settle my Thoughts into their former State, but found their Distraction every Day greater. I was always reproaching myself with the Want of Happiness within my Reach; and at last began to question whether it was not Laziness rather than Caution, that restrained me from climbing to the Summit of *Teneriffe*.

I rose therefore before the Day, and began my Journey up the Steep of the Mountain; but I had not advanced far, old as I was and burthened with Provisions, when the Day began to shine upon me; the Declivities grew more precipitous, and the Sand slided from beneath my Feet; at last, fainting with Labour, I arrived at a small Plain, almost inclosed by Rocks and open only to the East. I sat down to rest a while, in full Persuasion that when I had recovered my Strength, I should proceed on my Design; but when once I had tasted Ease, I found many Reasons against disturbing it. The Branches spread a Shade over my Head, and the Gales of Spring wafted Odours to my Bosom.

As I sat thus forming alternately Excuses for Delay, and Resolutions to go forward, an irresistible Heaviness suddenly surprized me; I laid my Head upon the Bank and resigned myself to Sleep: when methought I heard a Sound as of the Flight of Eagles, and a Being of more than human Dignity stood before me. While I was deliberating how to address him, he took me by the Hand with an Air of Kindness, and asked me solemnly, but without Severity, '*Theodore*, whither art thou going?' 'I am climbing, answered I, to the Top of the Mountain, to enjoy a more extensive Prospect of the Works of Nature.' 'Attend first (said he) to the Prospect which this Place affords, and what thou dost not understand I will explain. I am one of the benevolent Beings who watch over the Children of the Dust, to preserve them from those Evils which will not ultimately terminate in Good, and which they do not, by their own Faults, bring upon themselves. Look round therefore without Fear: observe, contemplate, and be instructed.'

Encouraged by this Assurance, I looked and beheld a Mountain higher than *Teneriffe*, to the Summit of which the Human Eye

could never reach; when I had tired myself with gazing upon its
Height, I turned my Eyes towards its Foot, which I could easily
discover, but was amazed to find it without Foundation, and
placed inconceivably in Emptiness and Darkness. Thus I stood
terrified and confused; above were Tracts inscrutable, and below
was total Vacuity. But my Protector, with a Voice of Admonition,
cried out, *Theodore*, be not affrighted, but raise thy Eyes again;
the *Mountain* of *Existence* is before thee, survey it, and be
wise.

I then looked with more deliberate Attention, and observed
the Bottom of the Mountain to be of gentle Rise, and overspread
with Flowers; the Middle to be more steep, embarrassed with
Crags, and interrupted by Precipices, over which hung Branches
loaded with Fruits, and among which were scattered Palaces and
Bowers. The Tracts which my Eye could reach nearest the Top
were generally barren; but there were among the Clefts of the
Rocks, a few hardy Evergreens, which though they did not give
much Pleasure to the Sight or Smell, yet seemed to cheer the
Labour and facilitate the Steps of those who were clambering
among them.

Then beginning to examine more minutely the different Parts,
I observed, at a great Distance, a Multitude of both Sexes issuing
into View from the Bottom of the Mountain. Their first Actions I
could not accurately discern; but as they every Moment approached nearer, I found that they amused themselves with gathering
Flowers under the Superintendance of a modest Virgin in a white
Robe, who seemed not over solicitous to confine them to any
settled Pace, or certain Track; for she knew that the whole
Ground was smooth and solid, and that they could not easily be
hurt or bewildered. When, as it often happened, they plucked a
Thistle for a Flower, *Innocence*, so was she called, would smile at
the Mistake. Happy, said I, are they who are under so gentle a
Government, and yet are safe. But I had no Opportunity to dwell
long on the Consideration of their Felicity; for I found that
Innocence continued her Attendance but a little Way, and seemed
to consider only the flowery Bottom of the Mountain as her proper
Province. Those whom she abandoned scarcely knew that they
were left, before they perceived themselves in the Hands of
Education, a Nymph more severe in her Aspect and imperious in
her Commands, who confined them to certain Paths, in their

Opinion, too narrow and too rough. These they were continually solicited to leave by *Appetite*, whom *Education* could never fright away, though she sometimes awed her to such Timidity, that the Effects of her Presence were scarcely perceptible. Some went back to the first Part of the Mountain, and seemed desirous of continuing busied in plucking Flowers, but were no longer guarded by *Innocence*; and such as *Education* could not force back, proceeded up the Mountain by some miry Road, in which they were seldom seen, and scarcely ever regarded.

As *Education* led her Troop up the Mountain, nothing was more observable than that she was frequently giving them Cautions to beware of *Habits*; and was calling out to one or another at every Step, that a *Habit* was ensnaring them; that they would be under the Dominion of *Habit* before they perceived their Danger; and that those whom a *Habit* should once subdue, had little hope of regaining their Liberty.

Of this Caution, so frequently repeated, I was very solicitous to know the Reason, when my Protector directed my Regard to a Troop of Pygmies, which appeared to walk silently before those that were climbing the Mountain, and each to smooth the Way before her Follower. I found that I had missed the Notice of them before, both because they were so minute as not easily to be discerned, and because they grew every Moment nearer in their Colour to the Objects with which they were surrounded. As the Followers of *Education* did not appear to be sensible of the Presence of these dangerous Associates, or, ridiculing their diminutive Size, did not think it possible that human Beings should ever be brought into Subjection by such feeble Enemies, they generally heard her Precepts of Vigilance with Wonder; and, when they thought her Eye withdrawn, treated them with Contempt. Nor could I myself think her Cautions so necessary as her frequent Inculcation seemed to suppose, till I observed that each of these petty Beings held secretly a Chain in her Hand, with which she prepared to bind those whom she found within her Power. Yet these *Habits* under the Eye of *Education* went quietly forward, and seemed very little to encrease in Bulk or Strength; for though they were always willing to join with *Appetite*, yet when *Education* kept them apart from her, they would very punctually obey Command, and make the narrow Roads in which they were confin'd easier and smoother.

It was observable, that their Stature was never at a Stand, but continually growing or decreasing, yet not always in the same Proportions; nor could I forbear to express my Admiration, when I saw in how much less Time they generally gained than lost Bulk. Though they grew slowly in the Road of *Education*, it might however be perceived that they grew; but if they once deviated at the Call of *Appetite*, their Stature soon became gigantic, and their Strength was such, that *Education* pointed out to her Tribe many that were led in Chains by them, whom she could never more rescue from their Slavery. She pointed them out, but with little Effect; for all her Pupils appeared confident of their own Superiority to the strongest *Habit*, and some seemed in secret to regret that they were hindered from following the Triumph of *Appetite*.

It was the peculiar Artifice of *Habit* not to suffer her Power to be felt at first. Those whom she led, she had the Address of appearing only to attend, but was continually doubling her Chains upon her Companions, which were so slender in themselves, and so silently fastened, that while the Attention was engaged by other Objects, they were not easily perceived. Each Link grew tighter as it had been longer worn, and when by continual Additions they became so heavy as to be felt, they were very frequently too strong to be broken.

When *Education* had proceeded in this Manner to the Part of the Mountain where the Declivity began to grow craggy, she resigned her Charge to two Powers of superior Aspect. The meaner of them appeared capable of presiding in Senates or governing Nations, and yet watched the Steps of the other with the most anxious Attention, and was visibly confounded and perplexed if ever she suffered her Regard to be drawn away. The other seemed to approve her Submission as pleasing, but with such a Condescension as plainly shewed that she claimed it as due; and indeed so great was her Dignity and Sweetness, that he who would not reverence, must not behold her.

'*Theodore*,' said my protector, 'be fearless, and be wise; approach these Powers, whose Dominion extends to all the remaining Part of the *Mountain* of *Existence*.' I trembled, and ventured to address the inferior Nymph, whose Eyes though piercing and awful, I was not unable to sustain. 'Bright Power,' said I, 'by whatever Name it is lawful to address thee, tell me, thou who presidest here, on what

Condition thy Protection will be granted.' 'It will be granted! said she, only to Obedience. I am *Reason*, of all subordinate Beings the noblest and the greatest; who, if thou wilt receive my Laws, will reward thee like the rest of my Votaries, by conducting thee to *Religion*.' Charmed by her Voice and Aspect, I professed my Readiness to follow her. She then presented me to her *Mistress*, who looked upon me with Tenderness. I bowed before her, and she smil'd.

When *Education* delivered up those for whose Happiness she had been so long solicitous, she seemed to expect that they should express some Gratitude for her Care, or some Regret at the Loss of that Protection which she had hitherto afforded them. But it was easy to discover, by the Alacrity which broke out at her Departure, that her Presence had been long displeasing, and that she had been teaching those who felt in themselves no want of Instruction. They all agreed in rejoicing that they should no longer be subject to her Caprices, or disturb'd by her Documents, but should be now under the Direction only of *Reason*, to whom they made no doubt of being able to recommend themselves by a steady Adherence to all her Precepts. *Reason* counselled them at their first Entrance upon her Province, to inlist themselves among the Votaries of *Religion*; and informed them, that if they trusted to her alone, they would find the same Fate with her other Admirers, whom she had not been able to secure against *Appetites* and *Passions*, and who having been seized by *Habits* in the Regions of *Desire*, had been dragged away to the Caverns of *Despair*. Her Admonition was vain, the greater Number declared against any other Direction, and doubted not but by her Superintendency they should climb with Safety up the *Mountain* of *Existence*. 'My power, said *Reason*, is to advise, not to compel; I have already told you the Danger of your Choice. The Path now seems plain and even, but there are Asperities and Pitfals, over which *Religion* only can conduct you. Look upwards, and you perceive a Mist before you settled upon the highest visible Part of the Mountain, a Mist by which my Prospect is terminated, and which is pierced only by the Eyes of *Religion*. Beyond it are the Temples of *Happiness*, in which those who climb the Precipice by her Direction, after the Toil of their Pilgrimage repose for ever. I know not the Way, and therefore can only conduct you to a better Guide. *Pride* has sometimes reproached me with the

Narrowness of my View, but when she endeavoured to extend it, could only shew me, below the Mist, the Bowers of *Content*; even they vanished as I fix'd my Eyes upon them; and those whom she persuaded to travel towards them were inchained by *Habits*, and ingulfed by *Despair*, a cruel Tyrant, whose Caverns are beyond the Darkness on the right Side and on the left, from whose Prisons none can escape, and whom I cannot teach you to avoid.'

Such was the Declaration of *Reason* to those who demanded her Protection. Some that recollected the Dictates of *Education*, finding them now seconded by another Authority, submitted with Reluctance to the strict Decree, and engaged themselves among the Followers of *Religion*, who were distinguished by the Uniformity of their March, though many of them were Women, and by their continual Endeavours to move upwards, without appearing to regard the Prospects which at every Step courted their Attention.

All those who determined to follow either *Reason* or *Religion*, were continually importuned to forsake the Road, sometimes by *Passions*, and sometimes by *Appetites*, of whom both had reason to boast the Success of their Artifices; for so many were drawn into Bypaths, that any way was more populous than the right. The Attacks of the *Appetites* were more impetuous, those of the *Passions* longer continued. The *Appetites* turned their Followers directly from the true Way, but the *Passions* marched at first in a Path nearly in the same Direction with that of *Reason* and *Religion*; but deviated by slow Degrees, till at last they entirely changed their Course. *Appetite* drew aside the Dull, and *Passion* the Sprightly. Of the *Appetites Lust* was the strongest, and of the *Passions Vanity*. The most powerful Assault was to be feared, when a *Passion* and an *Appetite* joined their Enticements; and the Path of *Reason* was best followed, when a *Passion* called to one side, and an *Appetite* to the other.

These Seducers had the greatest Success upon the Followers of *Reason*, over whom they scarcely ever failed to prevail, except when they counteracted one another. They had not the same Triumphs over the Votaries of *Religion*; for though they were often led aside for a Time, *Religion* commonly recalled them by her Emissary *Conscience*, before *Habit* had Time to enchain them. But they that professed to obey *Reason*, if once they forsook her, seldom returned; for she had no Messenger to summon them but *Pride*, who generally betrayed her Confidence, and imployed all her Skill to support *Passion*; and if ever she did her Duty, was found unable to prevail, if *Habit* had interposed.

I soon found that the great Danger to the Followers of *Religion* was only from *Habit*; every other Power was easily resisted, nor did they find any Difficulty when they inadvertently quitted her, to find her again by the Direction of *Conscience*, unless they had given Time to *Habit* to draw her Chain behind them, and bar up the Way by which they had wandered. Of some of those the Condition was justly to be pitied, who turned at every Call of *Conscience*, and tried, but without Effect, to burst the Chains of *Habit*: saw *Religion* walking forward at a Distance, saw her with Reverence, and longed to join her; but were, when ever they approached her, withheld by *Habit*, and languished in sordid Bondage which they could not escape, though they scorned and hated it.

It was evident that the *Habits* were so far from growing weaker by these repeated Contests, that if they were not totally overcome, every Struggle enlarged their Bulk and increased their Strength; and a *Habit* oppos'd and victorious was more than twice as strong as before the Contest. The Manner in which those who were weary of their Tyranny endeavoured to escape from them, appeared by the Event to be generally wrong; they tried to loose their Chains one by one, and to retreat by the same Degrees as they advanced; but before the Deliverance was completed, *Habit* always threw new Chains upon her Fugitive: nor did any escape her but those who by an Effort sudden and violent, burst their Shackles at once, and left her at a Distance ; and even of these many rushing too precipitately forward, and hindered by their Terrors from stopping where they were safe, were fatigued with their own Vehemence, and resigned themselves again to that Power from whom an Escape must be so dearly bought, and whose Tyranny was little felt, except when it was resisted.

Some however there always were, who, when they found *Habit* prevailing over them, called upon *Reason* or *Religion* for Assistance; each of them willingly came to the Succour of her Suppliant; but neither with the same Strength nor the same Success. *Habit*, insolent with her Power, would often presume to parley with *Reason*, and offer to loose some of her Chains if the rest might remain. To this *Reason*, who was never certain of Victory, frequently consented, but always found her Concession destructive, and saw the Captive led away by *Habit* to his former Slavery. *Religion* never submitted to Treaty, but held out her Hand with Certainty of Conquest; and if the Captive to whom she gave it did not quit his Hold, always led him away in Triumph, and placed him in the direct Path to the Temple of *Happiness*, where *Reason* never failed to congratulate his Deliverance, and encourage his Adherence to that Power to whose timely Succour he was indebted for it.

When the Traveller was again placed in the Road of *Happiness*, I saw *Habit* again gliding before him, but reduced to the Stature of a Dwarf, without Strength and without Activity; but when the *Passions* or *Appetites* which had before seduced him, made their Approach, *Habit* would on a sudden start into Size, and with unexpected Violence push him towards them. The Wretch thus impelled on one Side, and allured on the other, too frequently quitted the Road of *Happiness*, to which, after his second Deviation from it, he rarely returned. But if by a timely Call upon *Religion*, the Force of *Habit* was eluded, her Attacks grew fainter, and at last her Correspondence with the Enemy was entirely destroyed. She then began to employ those restless Faculties in compliance with the Power which she could not overcome; and as she grew again in Stature and in Strength, cleared away the Asperities of the Road to *Happiness*.

From this Road I could not easily withdraw my Attention, because all who travelled it appeared chearful and satisfied; and the farther they proceeded, the greater appeared their Alacrity, and the stronger their Conviction of the Wisdom of their Guide. Some who had never deviated but by short Excursions, had *Habit* in the Middle of their Passage, vigorously supporting them and driving off their *Appetites* and *Passions*, which attempted to interrupt their Progress. Others, who had entered this Road late, or had long forsaken it, were toiling on without her Help at least, and commonly against her Endeavours. But I observed, when they approached to the barren Top, that few were able to proceed without some support from *Habit*, and that those whose *Habits* were strong advanced towards the Mists with little Emotion, and entered them at last with Calmness and Confidence; after which they were seen only by the Eye of *Religion*, and though *Reason* looked after them with the most earnest Curiosity, she could only obtain a faint Glimpse, when her Mistress, to enlarge her Prospect, raised her from the Ground. *Reason* however, discerned that they were safe, but *Religion* saw that they were happy.

'Now, *Theodore*, said my Protector, withdraw thy View from the Regions of Obscurity, and see the Fate of those who, when they were dismissed by *Education*, would admit no Direction but that of *Reason*. Survey their Wanderings, and be wise.'

I looked then upon the Road of *Reason*, which was indeed, so-far as it reached, the same with that of *Religion*, nor had *Reason* discovered it but by her Instructions. Yet when she had once been taught it, she clearly saw that it was right; and *Pride* had sometimes incited her to declare that she discovered it herself, and persuaded her to offer herself as a Guide to *Religion*; whom after many vain Experiments she found it her highest Privilege to follow. *Reason* was however at last well instructed in Part of the Way, and appeared to teach it with some Success, when her Precepts were not misrepresented by *Passion*, or her Influence overborn by *Appetite*. But neither of these Enemies was she able to resist. When *Passion* seized upon her Votaries, she seldom attempted Opposition, she seemed indeed to contend with more Vigour against *Appetite*, but was generally overwearied in the Contest; and if either of her Opponents had confederated with *Habit*, her Authority was wholly at an End. When *Habit* endeavoured to captivate the Votaries of *Religion*, she grew by slow Degrees, and gave time to escape; but in seizing the unhappy Followers of *Reason*, she proceeded as one that had nothing to fear, and enlarged her Size, and doubled her Chains without Intermission, and without Reserve.

Of those who forsook the Directions of *Reason*, some were led aside by the Whispers of *Ambition*, who was perpetually pointing to stately Palaces, situated on Eminences on either side, recounting the Delights of Affluence, and boasting the Security of Power. They were easily persuaded to follow her, and *Habit* quickly threw her Chains upon them; they were soon convinced of the Folly of their Choice, but few of them attempted to return. *Ambition* led them forward from Precipice to Precipice, where many fell and were seen no more. Those that escaped, were, after a long Series of Hazards, generally delivered over to *Avarice*, and enlisted by her in the Service of *Tyranny*, where they continued to heap up Gold till their Patrons or their Heirs pushed them headlong at last into the Caverns of *Despair*.

Others were inticed by *Intemperance* to ramble in search of those Fruits that hung over the Rocks, and filled the Air with their Fragrance. I observed, that the *Habits* which hovered about these soon grew to an enormous Size, nor were there any who less attempted to return to *Reason*, or sooner sunk into the Gulphs that lay before them. When these first quitted the Road, *Reason* looked after them with a Frown of Contempt, but had little Expectations of being able to reclaim them; for the Bowl of Intoxication was of such Qualities, as to make them lose all Regard but for the present Moment; neither *Hope* nor *Fear* could enter their Retreats, and *Habit* had so absolute a Power, that even *Conscience*, if *Religion* had employed her in their Favour, would not have been able to force an Entrance.

There were others whose Crime it was rather to neglect *Reason* than to disobey her, and who retreated from the Heat and Tumult of the Way, not to the Bowers of *Intemperance*, but to the Maze of *Indolence*. They had this Peculiarity in their Condition, that they were always in sight of the Road of *Reason*, always wishing for her Presence, and always resolving to return to-morrow. In these was most eminently conspicuous the Subtlety of *Habit*, who hung imperceptible Shackles upon them, and was every Moment leading them farther from the Road, which they always imagined that they had the Power of reaching. They wandered on from one Double of the Labyrinth to another with the Chains of *Habit* hanging secretly upon them, till as they advanced, the Flowers grew paler, and the scents fainter: they proceeded in their dreary March without Pleasure in their Progress, yet without Power to return; and had this Aggravation above all others, that they were criminal but not delighted. The Drunkard for a Time laughed over his Wine; the ambitious Man triumphed in the Miscarriage of his Rival; but the Captives of *Indolence* had neither Superiority nor Merriment. *Discontent* lowered in their Looks, and *Sadness* hovered round their Shades; yet they crawled on reluctant and gloomy, till they arrived at the Depth of the Recess, varied only with Poppies and Nightshade, where the Dominion of *Indolence* terminates, and the hopeless Wanderer is delivered up to *Melancholy*: the Chains of *Habit* are rivetted for ever, and *Melancholy* having tortured her Prisoner for a Time, consigns him at last to the Cruelty of *Despair*.

While I was musing on this miserable Scene, my Protector called out to me, 'Remember, *Theodore*, and be wise, and let not HABIT prevail against thee.' I started, and beheld myself surrounded by the Rocks of *Teneriffe*; the Birds of Light were singing in the Trees, and the Glances of the Morning darted upon me.

THE
VANITY
OF HUMAN WISHES

The Vanity of Human Wishes was first published in 1749. The text here used is taken from the British Museum copy (840. k. 4(6).) of this edition. Johnson's improved version of line 20 on page 165 is to be found in later editions: it reads

Toil, envy, want, the patron, and the jail.

The 1749 edition reads *Force* for *Fear* at line 17 on page 166: as this is a misprint, the corrected reading has been printed here. It is possible that, six lines lower down, *spread* is a misprint (later editions read *spreads*), but as doubt is possible, *spread* appears in the text.

THE

VANITY OF HUMAN WISHES

THE TENTH SATIRE OF JUVENAL

IMITATED

LET Observation with extensive View,
Survey Mankind, from *China* to *Peru*;
Remark each anxious Toil, each eager Strife,
And watch the busy Scenes of crouded Life;
Then say how Hope and Fear, Desire and Hate,
O'erspread with Snares the clouded Maze of Fate,
Where wav'ring Man, betray'd by vent'rous Pride,
To tread the dreary Paths without a Guide;
As treach'rous Phantoms in the Mist delude,
Shuns fancied Ills, or chases airy Good.
How rarely Reason guides the stubborn Choice,
Rules the bold Hand, or prompts the suppliant Voice,
How Nations sink, by darling Schemes oppress'd,
When Vengeance listens to the Fool's Request.
Fate wings with ev'ry Wish th' afflictive Dart,
Each Gift of Nature, and each Grace of Art,
With fatal Heat impetuous Courage glows,
With fatal Sweetness Elocution flows,
Impeachment stops the Speaker's pow'rful Breath,
And restless Fire precipitates on Death.

But scarce observ'd the Knowing and the Bold,
Fall in the gen'ral Massacre of Gold;
Wide-wasting Pest! that rages unconfin'd,
And crouds with Crimes the Records of Mankind,
For Gold his Sword the Hireling Ruffian draws,
For Gold the hireling Judge distorts the Laws;

Wealth heap'd on Wealth, nor Truth nor Safety buys,
The Dangers gather as the Treasures rise.

Let Hist'ry tell where rival Kings command,
And dubious Title shakes the madded Land,
When Statutes glean the Refuse of the Sword,
How much more safe the Vassal than the Lord,
Low sculks the Hind beneath the Rage of Pow'r,
And leaves the *bonny Traytor* in the *Tow'r*,
Untouch'd his Cottage, and his Slumbers sound,
Tho' Confiscation's Vulturs clang around.

The needy Traveller, serene and gay,
Walks the wild Heath, and sings his Toïl away.
Does Envy seize thee? crush th' upbraiding Joy,
Encrease his Riches and his Peace destroy,
New Fears in dire Vicissitude invade,
The rustling Brake alarms, and quiv'ring Shade,
Nor Light nor Darkness bring his Pain Relief,
One shews the Plunder, and one hides the Thief.

Yet still the gen'ral Cry the Skies assails
And Gain and Grandeur load the tainted Gales;
Few know the toiling Statesman's Fear or Care,
Th' insidious Rival and the gaping Heir.

Once more, *Democritus*, arise on Earth,
With chearful Wisdom and instructive Mirth,
See motley Life in modern Trappings dress'd,
And feed with varied Fools th' eternal Jest:
Thou who couldst laugh where Want enchain'd Caprice,
Toil crush'd Conceit, and Man was of a Piece;
Where Wealth unlov'd without a Mourner dy'd;
And scarce a Sycophant was fed by Pride;
Where ne'er was known the Form of mock Debate,
Or seen a new-made Mayor's unwieldy State;
Where change of Fav'rites made no Change of Laws,
And Senates heard before they judg'd a Cause;
How wouldst thou shake at *Britain's* modish Tribe,
Dart the quick Taunt, and edge the piercing Gibe?
Attentive Truth and Nature to descry,
And pierce each Scene with Philosophic Eye.

To thee were solemn Toys or empty Shew,
The Robes of Pleasure and the Veils of Woe:
All aid the Farce, and all thy Mirth maintain,
Whose Joys are causeless, or whose Griefs are vain.

Such was the Scorn that fill'd the Sage's Mind,
Renew'd at ev'ry Glance on Humankind;
How just that Scorn ere yet thy Voice declare,
Search ev'ry State, and canvass ev'ry Pray'r.

Unnumber'd Suppliants croud Preferment's Gate,
Athirst for Wealth, and burning to be great;
Delusive Fortune hears th' incessant Call,
They mount, they shine, evaporate, and fall.
On ev'ry Stage the Foes of Peace attend,
Hate dogs their Flight, and Insult mocks their End.
Love ends with Hope, the sinking Statesman's Door
Pours in the Morning Worshiper no more;
For growing Names the weekly Scribbler lies,
To growing Wealth the Dedicator flies,
From every Room descends the painted Face,
That hung the bright *Palladium* of the Place,
And smoak'd in Kitchens, or in Auctions sold,
To better Features yields the Frame of Gold;
For now no more we trace in ev'ry Line
Heroic Worth, Benevolence Divine:
The Form distorted justifies the Fall,
And Detestation rids th' indignant Wall.

But will not *Britain* hear the last Appeal,
Sign her Foes Doom, or guard her Fav'rites Zeal;
Through Freedom's Sons no more Remonstrance rings,
Degrading Nobles and controuling Kings;
Our supple Tribes repress their Patriot Throats,
And ask no Questions but the Price of Votes;
With Weekly Libels and Septennial Ale,
Their Wish is full to riot and to rail.

In full-blown Dignity, see *Wolsey* stand,
Law in his Voice, and Fortune in his Hand:
To him the Church, the Realm, their Pow'rs consign,
Thro' him the Rays of regal Bounty shine,

Turn'd by his Nod the Stream of Honour flows,
His Smile alone Security bestows:
Still to new Heights his restless Wishes tow'r,
Claim leads to Claim, and Pow'r advances Pow'r;
Till Conquest unresisted ceas'd to please,
And Rights submitted, left him none to seize.
At length his Sov'reign frowns—the Train of State
Mark the keen Glance, and watch the Sign to hate.
Where-e'er he turns he meets a Stranger's Eye,
His suppliants scorn him, and his Followers fly;
Now drops at once the Pride of aweful State,
The golden Canopy, the glitt'ring Plate,
The regal Palace, the luxurious Board,
The liv'ried Army, and the menial Lord.
With Age, with Cares, with Maladies oppress'd,
He seeks the Refuge of Monastic Rest.
Grief aids Disease, remember'd Folly stings,
And his last Sighs reproach the Faith of Kings.

Speak thou, whose Thoughts at humble Peace repine,
Shall *Wolsey*'s Wealth, with *Wolsey*'s End, be thine?
Or liv'st thou now, with safer Pride content,
The richest Landlord on the banks of *Trent*?
For why did *Wolsey* by the Steps of Fate,
On weak Foundations raise th' enormous Weight?
Why but to sink beneath Misfortune's Blow,
With louder Ruin to the Gulphs below?

What gave great *Villiers* to th' Assassin's Knife,
And fix'd Disease on *Harley*'s closing Life?
What murder'd *Wentworth*, and what exil'd *Hyde*,
By Kings protected, and to Kings ally'd?
What but their Wish indulg'd in Courts to shine,
And Pow'r too great to keep or to resign?

When first the College Rolls receive his Name,
The young Enthusiast quits his Ease for Fame;
Resistless burns the Fever of Renown,
Caught from the strong Contagion of the Gown;
O'er *Bodley*'s Dome his future Labours spread,
And *Bacon*'s Mansion trembles o'er his Head;

Are these thy Views? proceed, illustrious Youth,
And Virtue guard thee to the Throne of Truth,
Yet should thy Soul indulge the gen'rous Heat,
Till captive Science yields her last Retreat;
Should Reason guide thee with her brightest Ray,
And pour on misty Doubt resistless Day;
Should no false Kindness lure to loose Delight,
Nor Praise relax, nor Difficulty fright;
Should tempting Novelty thy Cell refrain,
And Sloth's bland Opiates shed their Fumes in vain;
Should Beauty blunt on Fops her fatal Dart,
Nor claim the Triumph of a letter'd Heart;
Should no Disease thy torpid Veins invade,
Nor Melancholy's Phantoms haunt thy Shade;
Yet hope not Life from Grief or Danger free,
Nor think the Doom of Man revers'd for thee:
Deign on the passing World to turn thine Eyes,
And pause awhile from Learning to be wise;
There mark what Ills the Scholar's Life assail,
Toil, Envy, Want, the Garret, and the Jail.
See Nations slowly wise, and meanly just,
To buried Merit raise the tardy Bust.
If Dreams yet flatter, once again attend,
Hear *Lydiat*'s Life, and *Galileo*'s End.

Nor deem, when Learning her lost Prize bestows
The glitt'ring Eminence exempt from Foes;
See when the Vulgar 'scap'd, despis'd or aw'd,
Rebellion's vengeful Talons seize on *Laud*.
From meaner Minds, tho' smaller Fines content
The plunder'd Palace or sequester'd Rent;
Mark'd out by dangerous Parts he meets the Shock,
And fatal Learning leads him to the Block:
Around his Tomb let Art and Genius weep,
But hear his Death, ye Blockheads, hear and sleep.

The festal Blazes, the triumphal Show,
The ravish'd Standard, and the captive Foe,
The Senate's Thanks, the Gazette's pompous Tale,
With Force resistless o'er the Brave prevail.

F

Such Bribes the rapid *Greek* o'er *Asia* whirl'd,
For such the steady *Romans* shook the World;
For such in distant Lands the *Britons* shine,
And stain with Blood the *Danube* or the *Rhine*;
This Pow'r has Praise, that Virtue scarce can warm
Till Fame supplies the universal Charm.
Yet Reason frowns on War's unequal Game,
Where wasted Nations raise a single Name,
And mortgag'd States their Grandsires Wreaths regret
From Age to Age in everlasting Debt;
Wreaths which at last the dear-bought Right convey
To rust on Medals, or on Stones decay.

On what foundation stands the Warrior's Pride?
How just his Hopes let *Swedish Charles* decide;
A Frame of Adamant, a Soul of Fire,
No Dangers fright him, and no Labours tire;
O'er Love, o'er Fear, extends his wide Domain,
Unconquer'd Lord of Pleasure and of Pain;
No Joys to him pacific Scepters yield,
War sounds the Trump, he rushes to the Field;
Behold surrounding Kings their Pow'r combine,
And One capitulate, and One resign;
Peace courts his Hand, but spread her Charms in vain;
"Think Nothing gain'd, he cries, till nought remain,
On *Moscow*'s Walls till *Gothic* Standards fly,
And all is Mine beneath the Polar Sky."
The March begins in Military State,
And Nations on his Eye suspended wait;
Stern Famine guards the solitary Coast,
And Winter barricades the Realms of Frost;
He comes, nor Want nor Cold his Course delay;—
Hide, blushing Glory, hide *Pultowa*'s Day:
The vanquish'd Hero leaves his broken Bands,
And shews his Miseries in distant Lands;
Condemn'd a needy Supplicant to wait,
While Ladies interpose, and Slaves debate.
But did not Chance at length her Error mend?
Did no subverted Empire mark his End?
Did rival Monarchs give the fatal Wound?
Or hostile Millions press him to the Ground?

His Fall was destin'd to a barren Strand,
A petty Fortress, and a dubious Hand;
He left the Name, at which the World grew pale,
To point a Moral, or adorn a Tale.

All Times their Scenes of pompous Woes afford,
From *Persia*'s Tyrant to *Bavaria*'s Lord.
In gay Hostility, and barb'rous Pride,
With half Mankind embattled at his Side,
Great *Xerxes* comes to seize the certain Prey,
And starves exhausted Regions in his Way;
Attendant Flatt'ry counts his Myriads o'er,
Till counted Myriads sooth his Pride no more;
Fresh Praise is try'd till Madness fires his Mind,
The Waves he lashes, and enchains the Wind;
New Pow'rs are claim'd, new Pow'rs are still bestow'd,
Till rude Resistance lops the spreading God;
The daring *Greeks* deride the Martial Shew,
And heap their Vallies with the gaudy Foe;
Th' insulted Sea with humbler Thoughts he gains,
A single Skiff to speed his Flight remains;
Th' incumber'd Oar scarce leaves the dreaded Coast
Through purple Billows and a floating Host.

The bold *Bavarian*, in a luckless Hour,
Tries the dread Summits of *Cesarean* Pow'r,
With unexpected Legions bursts away,
And sees defenceless Realms receive his Sway;
Short Sway! fair *Austria* spreads her mournful Charms,
The Queen, the Beauty, sets the World in Arms;
From Hill to Hill the Beacons rousing blaze
Spreads wide the Hope of Plunder and of Praise;
The fierce *Croatian*, and the wild *Hussar*,
And all the Sons of Ravage croud the War;
The baffled Prince in Honour's flatt'ring Bloom
Of hasty Greatness finds the fatal Doom,
His Foes Derision, and his Subjects Blame,
And steals to Death from Anguish and from Shame.

Enlarge my Life with Multitude of Days,
In Health, in Sickness, thus the Suppliant prays;

Hides from himself his State, and shuns to know,
That Life protracted is protracted Woe.
Time hovers o'er, impatient to destroy,
And shuts up all the Passages of Joy:
In vain their Gifts the bounteous Seasons pour,
The Fruit Autumnal, and the Vernal Flow'r,
With listless Eyes the Dotard views the Store,
He views, and wonders that they please no more;
Now pall the tastless Meats, and joyless Wines,
And Luxury with Sighs her Slave resigns.
Approach, ye Minstrels, try the soothing Strain,
Diffuse the tuneful Lenitives of Pain:
No Sounds alas would touch th' impervious Ear,
Though dancing Mountains witness'd *Orpheus* near;
Nor Lute nor Lyre his feeble Pow'rs attend,
Nor sweeter Musick of a virtuous Friend,
But everlasting Dictates croud his Tongue,
Perversely grave, or positively wrong.
The still returning Tale, and ling'ring Jest,
Perplex the fawning Niece and pamper'd Guest,
While growing Hopes scarce awe the gath'ring Sneer,
And scarce a Legacy can bribe to hear;
The watchful Guests still hint the last Offence,
The Daughter's Petulance, the Son's Expence,
Improve his heady Rage with treach'rous Skill,
And mould his Passions till they make his Will.

Unnumber'd Maladies each Joint invade,
Lay Siege to Life and press the dire Blockade;
But unextinguish'd Av'rice still remains,
And dreaded Losses aggravate his Pains;
He turns, with anxious Heart and cripled Hands,
His Bonds of Debt, and Mortgages of Lands;
Or views his Coffers with suspicious Eyes,
Unlocks his Gold, and counts it till he dies.

But grant, the Virtues of a temp'rate Prime
Bless with an Age exempt from Scorn or Crime;
An Age that melts with unperceiv'd Decay,
And glides in modest Innocence away;

Whose peaceful Day Benevolence endears,
Whose Night congratulating Conscience cheers;
The gen'ral Fav'rite as the gen'ral Friend:
Such Age there is, and who could wish its End?

Yet ev'n on this her Load Misfortune flings,
To press the weary Minutes flagging Wings:
New Sorrow rises as the Day returns,
A Sister sickens, or a Daughter mourns.
Now Kindred Merit fills the sable Bier,
Now lacerated Friendship claims a Tear.
Year chases Year, Decay pursues Decay,
Still drops some Joy from with'ring Life away;
New Forms arise, and diff'rent Views engage,
Superfluous lags the Vet'ran on the Stage,
Till pitying Nature signs the last Release,
And bids afflicted Worth retire to Peace.

But few there are whom Hours like these await,
Who set unclouded in the Gulphs of Fate.
From *Lydia*'s Monarch should the Search descend,
By *Solon* caution'd to regard his End,
In Life's last Scene what Prodigies surprise,
Fears of the Brave, and Follies of the Wise?
From *Marlb'rough*'s Eyes the Streams of Dotage flow,
And *Swift* expires a Driv'ler and a Show.

The teeming Mother, anxious for her Race,
Begs for each Birth the Fortune of a Face:
Yet *Vane* could tell what Ills from Beauty spring;
And *Sedley* curs'd the Form that pleas'd a King.
Ye Nymphs of rosy Lips and radiant Eyes,
Whom Pleasure keeps too busy to be wise,
Whom Joys with soft Varieties invite
By Day the Frolick, and the Dance by Night,
Who frown with Vanity, who smile with Art,
And ask the latest Fashion of the Heart,
What Care, what Rules your heedless Charms shall save,
Each Nymph your Rival, and each Youth your Slave?
An envious Breast with certain Mischief glows,
And Slaves, the Maxim tells, are always Foes.

Against your Fame with Fondness Hate combines,
The Rival batters, and the Lover mines.
With distant Voice neglected Virtue calls,
Less heard, and less the faint Remonstrance falls;
Tir'd with Contempt, she quits the slipp'ry Reign,
And Pride and Prudence take her Seat in vain.
In croud at once, where none the Pass defend,
The harmless Freedom, and the private Friend.
The Guardians yield, by Force superior ply'd;
To Int'rest, Prudence; and to Flatt'ry, Pride.
Here Beauty falls betray'd, despis'd, distress'd,
And hissing Infamy proclaims the rest.

Where then shall Hope and Fear their Objects find?
Must dull Suspence corrupt the stagnant Mind?
Must helpless Man, in Ignorance sedate,
Swim darkling down the Current of his Fate?
Must no Dislike alarm, no Wishes rise,
No Cries attempt the Mercies of the Skies?
Enquirer, cease, Petitions yet remain,
Which Heav'n may hear, nor deem Religion vain.
Still raise for Good the supplicating Voice,
But leave to Heav'n the Measure and the Choice.
Safe in his Pow'r, whose Eyes discern afar
The secret Ambush of a specious Pray'r.
Implore his Aid, in his Decisions rest,
Secure whate'er he gives, he gives the best.
Yet with the Sense of sacred Presence prest,
When strong Devotion fills thy glowing Breast,
Pour forth thy Fervours for a healthful Mind,
Obedient Passions, and a Will resign'd;
For Love, which scarce collective Man can fill;
For Patience sov'reign o'er transmuted Ill;
For Faith, that panting for a happier Seat,
Thinks Death kind Nature's Signal of Retreat:
These Goods for Man the Laws of Heav'n ordain,
These Goods he grants, who grants the Pow'r to gain;
With these celestial Wisdom calms the Mind,
And makes the Happiness she does not find.

A
NEW PROLOGUE
SPOKEN BY MR. GARRICK

First published, 1750. The text has been taken from the British Museum copy (643. m. 14(20).) of this edition. In line 23, the misprint of *Dust* for *Bust* has been corrected in ink in the British Museum copy.

A NEW PROLOGUE

SPOKEN BY MR. GARRICK,

THURSDAY, APRIL 5, 1750.

At the Representation of COMUS, for the Benefit of Mrs ELIZABETH
FOSTER, MILTON's Grand-Daughter, and only surviving
Descendant

Ye patriot Crouds, who burn for *England*'s Fame,
Ye Nymphs, whose Bosoms beat at MILTON's Name,
Whose gen'rous Zeal, unbought by flatt'ring Rhimes,
Shames the mean Pensions of *Augustan* Times;
Immortal Patrons of succeeding Days,
Attend this Prelude of perpetual Praise!
Let Wit, condemn'd the feeble War to wage
With close Malevolence, or public Rage;
Let Study, worn with Virtue's fruitless Lore,
Behold this Theatre, and grieve no more.
This Night, distinguish'd by your Smile, shall tell,
That never BRITON can in vain excel;
The slighted Arts Futurity shall trust,
And rising Ages hasten to be just.

    At length our mighty Bard's victorious Lays
Fill the loud Voice of universal Praise,
And baffled Spite, with hopeless Anguish dumb,
Yields to Renown the Centuries to come.
With ardent Haste, each Candidate of Fame
Ambitious catches at his tow'ring Name:
He sees, and pitying sees, vain Wealth bestow
Those pageant Honours which he scorn'd below:
While Crowds aloft the laureat Bust behold,
Or trace his Form on circulating Gold,

Unknown, unheeded, long his Offspring lay,
And Want hung threat'ning o'er her slow Decay.
What tho' she shine with no MILTONIAN Fire,
No fav'ring Muse her morning Dreams inspire;
Yet softer Claims the melting Heart engage,
Her Youth laborious, and her blameless Age:
Hers the mild Merits of domestic Life,
The patient Suff'rer, and the faithful Wife.
Thus grac'd with humble Virtue's native Charms
Her Grandsire leaves her in *Britannia*'s Arms;
Secure with Peace, with Competence, to dwell,
While tutelary Nations guard her Cell.
Yours is the Charge, ye Fair, ye Wise, ye Brave!
'Tis yours to crown Desert—beyond the Grave.

SELECTIONS FROM
THE RAMBLER

The Rambler ran for two years, from March 20, 1750, to March 17, 1752. The text here used is that of the original parts (B.M.: 637. m. 12.). The six-volume second edition of 1752 (B.M.: PP. 5251. aaa.) has been consulted throughout. When, in numbers 14, 46, 87, and 89, readings from the original parts make no apparent sense, readings from the six-volume edition have been accepted. Reference has already been made (pp. 11–12) to the curious, apparently auditory, errors of numbers 87 and 89.

The translations of the classical quotations were printed for binding in at the ends of the two volumes of the original parts. These translations have been worked into the text. The unsigned translations may be regarded as Johnson's own. It has not seemed necessary to establish the text of Vida, a long quotation from whose *De Arte Poetica* (3. 365–439, with omissions) is included in number 92; however, the seventeenth line of the quoted passage,

Convulsum remis rostrisque stridentibus aequor

is one which no man could presume to scan. It is, however, the line which Johnson quoted, the line which Christopher Pitt translated, and the line which appeared in half a dozen editions of Vida which have been examined. The *editio princeps* (Rome, 1527) gave the true reading, *tridentibus*; the line will be recognised as derived from *Aeneid* 5. 143.

The tag from the Greek Anthology (Anth. P. 11. 186), which Johnson quoted in number 59, was translated into Latin by Johnson himself. His version is to be found in McAdam and Nichol Smith. Later editions of *The Rambler* contrived to work two misprints into the three Greek words.

Johnson's own misquotations have not been corrected.

SELECTIONS FROM

THE RAMBLER

9

IT is pleasing to contemplate a Manufacture rising gradually from its first mean State by the successive Labours of innumerable Minds; to consider the first hollow Trunk of an Oak, in which, perhaps, the Shepherd could scarce venture to cross a Brook swelled with a Shower, enlarged at last into a Ship of War, attacking Fortresses, terrifying Nations, setting Storms and Billows at Defiance, and visiting the remotest Parts of the Globe. And it might contribute to dispose us to a kinder Regard for the Labours of one another, if we were to consider from what unpromising Beginnings the most useful Productions of Art have probably arisen. Who, when he saw the first Sand or Ashes, by a casual Intenseness of Heat melted into a Metalline Form, rugged with Excrescences, and clouded with Impurities, would have imagined, that in this formless Lump lay concealed so many Conveniencies of Life, as would in time constitute a great Part of the Happiness of the World? Yet by some such fortuitous Liquefaction was Mankind taught to procure a Body at once in a high Degree solid and transparent, which might admit the Light of the Sun, and exclude the Violence of the Wind; which might extend the Sight of the Philosopher to new Ranges of Existence, and charm him at one Time with the unbounded Extent of the material Creation, and at another with the endless Subordination of animal Life, and, what is yet of more Importance, might supply the Decays of Nature, and succour old Age with subsidiary Sight. Thus was the first Artificer in Glass employed, though without his own Knowledge or Expectation. He was facilitating and prolonging the Enjoyment of Light, enlarging the Avenues of Science, and conferring the highest and most lasting Pleasures; he was enabling the Student to contemplate Nature, and the Beauty to behold herself.

14

There are, indeed, a far greater Number whose Curiosity to gain a more familiar Knowledge of successful Writers, is not so much prompted by an Opinion of their Power to improve as to delight, and who expect from them not Arguments against Vice, or Dissertations on Temperance or Justice, but Flights of Wit, Strains of Humour, and Sallies of Pleasantry, or, at least, acute Remarks, nice Distinctions, Justness of Sentiment, and Elegance of Diction.

This Expectation is, indeed, specious and probable, and yet, such is the Fate of all human Hopes, that it is very often frustrated, and those who raise Admiration by their Books disgust by their Company. A Man of Letters for the most part spends, in the Privacies of Study, that Season of Life in which the Manners are to be softened into Ease, and polished into Elegance, and, when he has gained Knowledge enough to be respected, has neglected the minuter Acts by which he might have pleased; and when he enters Life, if of a weak and timorous Temper, he is diffident and bashful, from the Knowledge of his Defects; or if he was born with Spirit and Resolution, he is ferocious and arrogant from the Consciousness of his Merit: he is either dissipated by the Awe of superior Company, and unable to assemble his Ideas, recollect his Reading, and arrange his Argument; or he is hot, and dogmatical, quick in Opposition, and tenacious in Defence, disabled by his own Violence, and confused by his haste to triumph.

The Graces of Writing and Conversation are of different Kinds, and though he who excels in one might have been, perhaps, equally successful in the other, with Opportunity and Application, yet as many please by extemporary Talk, who are utterly unacquainted with the more accurate Method, and more laboured Beauties, which Composition requires; so it is very possible, that Men, wholly accustomed to Works of Study, may want that Readiness of Conception, and Affluence of Language, which is always required in colloquial Entertainment. They may want Address to watch the Hints which Conversation offers for the Display of their particular Attainments, or they may be so much unfurnished with Matter on common Subjects, that Discourse not professedly literary glides over them as heterogeneous Bodies, without admitting their Conceptions to mix in the Circulation.

A Transition from an Author's Books to his Conversation, is too often like an Entrance into a large City, after a distant Prospect. Remotely, we see nothing but Spires of Temples, and Turrets of Palaces, and imagine it the Residence of Splendour, Grandeur, and Magnificence; but, when we have passed the Gates, we find it perplexed with narrow Passages, disgraced with despicable Cottages, embarrassed with Obstructions, and clouded with Smoke.

20

The Hatred, which Dissimulation always draws upon itself, is so great, that if I did not know how much Cunning differs from Wisdom, I should wonder that any Men have so little Knowledge of their own Interest, as to aspire to wear a Mask for Life, to try to impose upon the World a Character, to which they feel themselves void of any just Claim; and to hazard their Quiet, their Fame, and even their Profit, by exposing themselves to the Danger of that Reproach, Malevolence, and Neglect, which such a Discovery as they have always to fear will certainly bring upon them.

It might be imagined, that the Pleasure of Reputation should consist in the Satisfaction of having our Opinion of our own Merit confirmed by the Suffrage of the Publick; and that, to be extolled for a Quality, which a Man knows himself to want, should give him no other Happiness than to be mistaken for the Owner of an Estate, over which he chances to be travelling. But he, who subsists upon Affectation, knows nothing of this Delicacy; like a desperate Adventurer in Commerce, he takes up Reputation upon Trust, mortgages Possessions which he never had, and enjoys, to the fatal Hour of Bankruptcy, though with a thousand Terrors and Anxieties, the unnecessary Splendour of borrowed Riches.

Affectation is to be always distinguished from Hypocrisy, as being the Art of counterfeiting those Qualities which we might, with Innocence and Safety, be known to want. Thus the Man, who, to carry on any Fraud, or, to conceal any Crime, pretends to Rigours of Devotion, and Exactness of Life, is guilty of Hypocrisy; and his Guilt is greater, as the End, for which he puts on the false Appearance, is more pernicious. But he that, with an awkward Address, and unpleasing Countenance, boasts of the Conquests made by him among the Ladies, and counts over the Thousands, which he might have possessed, if he would have submitted to the Yoke of Matrimony, is chargeable only with Affectation. Hypocrisy is the necessary Burthen of Villainy, Affectation part of the chosen Trappings of Folly; the one completes a Villain, the other only finishes a Fop. Contempt is the proper Punishment of Affectation, and Detestation the just Consequence of Hypocrisy.

With the Hypocrite, it is not at present my Intention to expostulate, though even he might be taught the Excellency of Virtue, by the Necessity of seeming to be virtuous; but the Man of Affectation may, perhaps, be reclaimed, by finding how little he is likely to gain by perpetual Constraint, and incessant Vigilance, and how much more securely he might make his way to Esteem, by cultivating real, than displaying counterfeit Qualities.

Every Thing future is to be estimated by a wise Man, with regard to the Probability of attaining it, and its Value, when attained; and neither of these Considerations will much contribute to the Encouragement of Affectation. For, if the Pinnacles of Fame be, at best, slippery, how unsteady must his Footing be, who stands upon Pinnacles without Foundation! If Praise be made, by the Inconstancy and Malice of those who must confer it, a Blessing which no Man can promise himself from the most conspicuous Merit, and vigorous Industry, how faint must be the Hope of gaining it, when the Uncertainty is multiplied by the Weakness of the Pretensions! He that pursues Fame with just Claims, trusts his Happiness to the Winds; but he that endeavours after it, by false Merit, has to fear, not only the Violence of the Storm, but the Leaks of his Vessel. Though he should happen to keep above Water for a Time, by the Help of a soft Breeze, and a calm Sea, at the first Gust he must inevitably founder, with this melancholy Reflexion, that, if he would have been content with his natural Station, he might have escaped his Calamity. Affectation may possibly succeed for a Time, and a Man may, by great Attention, persuade others, that he really has the Qualities, which he presumes to boast; but the Hour will come, when he must exert them, and then whatever he enjoyed in Praise, he must suffer in Reproach.

Applause and Admiration are by no means to be counted among the Necessaries of Life, and therefore any indirect Arts to obtain them have very little Claim to Pardon or Compassion. There is scarcely any Man without some valuable or improveable Qualities, by which he might always secure himself from Contempt; and perhaps Exemption from Ignominy is the most eligible Reputation, as Freedom from Pain is, among some Philosophers, the Definition of Happiness.

If we therefore compare the Value of the Praise obtained by fictitious Excellence, even while the Cheat is yet undiscovered, with that Kindness, which every Man may win by his Virtue, and that Esteem, which most Men may gain by common Understanding, steadily and honestly applied, we shall find that when from the adscititious Happiness all the Deductions are made, by Fear and Accident, there will remain nothing equiponderant to the Security of Truth. The State of the Possessor of humble Virtues, to the Affecter of great Excellencies, is that of a small well built Cottage of Stone, to the Palace raised with Ice by the Empress of *Russia*; it was for a time splendid and luminous, but the first Sunshine melted it to nothing.

21

A succesful Author is equally in Danger of the Diminution of his Fame, whether he continues or ceases to write. The regard of the Public is not to be kept but by Tribute, and the Remembrance of past Service will quickly languish, unless some new Performance sometimes revives it. Yet in every new Attempt there is new Hazard, and there are few who do not, at some unluckly Time, injure their own Characters by attempting to enlarge them.

There are many possible Causes of the Inequality which we may so frequently observe in the Performances of the same Man, from the Influence of which no Ability or Industry is sufficiently secured, and which have so often sullied the Splendour of Genius, that the Wit, as well as the Conqueror, may be properly cautioned not to indulge his Pride with too early Triumphs, but to defer to the end of Life his Estimate of Happiness.

> ——*Ultima semper*
> *Expectanda dies homini, dicique beatus*
> *Ante obitum nemo supremaque funera debet.*
>
> But no frail man, however great or high,
> Can be concluded blest before he die.   ADDISON.

Among the Motives which urge an Author to Undertakings that injure his Reputation, one of the most frequent is scarcely to be mentioned; because it is not to be counted among his Follies, but his Miseries. It very often happens that the Works of Learning

181

or of Wit are performed at the Direction of those by whom they are to be rewarded; the Writer has not always the Choice of his Subject, but is compelled to accept any Task which is thrown before him, without much Consideration of his own Convenience, and without Time to prepare himself for the Execution by previous Studies.

But Miscarriages of this kind are likewise frequently the Consequences of that Acquaintance with the Great, which is generally considered as one of the chief Privileges of Literature and Genius. A Man, who has once learned to think himself exalted by Familiarity with those, whom nothing but their Birth, or their Fortunes, or such Stations as are seldom gained by moral Excellence, set above him, will not be long without submitting his Understanding to their Conduct, and suffering them to prescribe the Course of his Studies, and employ him for their own Purposes either of Diversion or Interest. His Desire of pleasing those whose Favour he has weakly made necessary to himself, will not suffer him always to consider how little he is qualified for the Work imposed, his Vanity will not allow him to confess his Deficiencies, or that Cowardice, which always encroaches fast upon such as spend their Lives in the Company of Persons higher than themselves, leaves them not Resolution to assert the Liberty of Choice.

But though we suppose that a Man has Fortune to avoid the Necessity of Dependance, and Spirit to repel the Usurpations of Patronage, yet he may easily, by writing long, happen to write ill. There is a general Succession of Effects, in which Contraries are produced by periodical Vicissitudes; Labour and Care are rewarded with Success, Success produces Confidence, Confidence relaxes Industry, and Negligence ruins that Reputation which Diligence had raised.

He that happens not to be lulled by Praise into Supineness, may be animated by it to Undertakings above his Strength, or incited to fancy himself alike qualified for every Kind of Composition, and able to comply with the public Taste through all its Variations. From some Opinion like this, many Men have engaged, at an advanced Age, in Attempts which they had not Time to complete, and after a few weak Efforts, sunk into the Grave with Vexation to see the rising Generation gain ground upon them. That Judgment which appears often so penetrating, when it is employed upon the Works of others, very often fails when it is applied to Performances,

where Interest or Passion can exert their Power. We are blinded
in examining our own Labours by innumerable Prejudices. Our
juvenile Compositions please us, because they bring to our Minds
the Remembrance of Youth; our later Performances we are ready
to esteem, because we are unwilling to think that we have made no
Improvement; what flows easily from the Pen charms us, because
we read with Pleasure that which flatters our Opinion of our own
Powers; what was composed with great Struggles of the Mind we
are unwilling to reject, because we cannot bear that so much
Labour should be fruitless. But the Reader has none of these
Prepossessions, and only wonders that the Author is so unlike
himself, without considering that the same Soil will, with different
Culture, afford different Products.

23

Tres mihi Convivæ prope dissentire videntur;
Poscentur vario multum diversa Palato.   Hor.

Three guests I have, dissenting at my feast,
Requiring each to gratify his taste
With different food.   Francis.

That every Man should regulate his Actions by his own Conscience, without any Regard to the Opinions of the rest of the
World, is one of the first Precepts of moral Prudence; and is not
only justified by the Suffrage of Reason, which tells that none of
the Gifts of Heaven are to lie useless, but by the Voice likewise
of Experience, which will soon inform us that, if we make the
Praise or Blame of others, the Rule or Motive of our Conduct, we
shall be distracted by a boundless Variety of irreconcilable
Judgments; be held in perpetual Suspense between contrary
Impulses, and consult for ever without Determination.

I know not whether, for the same Reason, it is not necessary for
an Author to place some Confidence in his own Skill, and to satisfy
himself in the Knowledge that he has not deviated from the
established Rules of Composition; without submitting his Works to
frequent Examinations before he gives them to the Publick, or
endeavouring to secure Success by a solicitous Conformity to
Advice and Criticism.

It is, indeed, quickly discoverable, that Consultation and Compliance can conduce very little to the Perfection of any literary
Performance; for whoever is so doubtful of his own Abilities as to

encourage the Advice and Remarks of others, will find himself
every day embarrassed with new Difficulties, and will harrass his
Mind, to no purpose, with the hopeless Labour of uniting heterogeneous Ideas, digesting independent Hints, and collecting into
one Point the several Rays of borrowed Light, emitted often with
contrary Directions.

Of all Authors, those who retail their Labours in periodical
Sheets would be most unhappy, if they were much to regard the
Censures or the Admonitions of their Readers; for, as their Works
are not sent into the World at once, but by small Parts in gradual
Succession, it is always imagined, by those who think themselves
qualified to instruct them, that they may yet redeem their former
Failings by hearkening to Information, supply by new Improvements the Deficiencies of their Plan, and make every day Advances
towards Perfection, by the Help of the Criticisms which are so
liberally afforded.

I have had occasion to observe, sometimes with Vexation, and
sometimes with Merriment, the different Temper with which the
same Man reads a printed and manuscript Performance. When a
Book is once in the Hands of the Public, it is considered as permanent and unalterable; and the Reader, if he be free from personal Prejudices, takes it up with no other Intention than of pleasing
or instructing himself: he, therefore, accommodates his Mind to
the Author's Design, and, having no Interest in refusing the
Amusement that is offered him, never interrupts his own Tranquillity by studied Cavils, or destroys his Satisfaction in that which
is not well, by an anxious Enquiry how it might be better; but is
often contented without Pleasure, and pleased without Perfection.

But if the same Man be called to consider the Merit of a Production yet unpublished, he brings an Imagination heated with
Objections to Passages, which he has yet never heard, he invokes
all the Powers of Criticism, and stores his Memory with *Taste*,
and *Grace*, and *Purity*, and *Delicacy*, and *Manners*, and *Unities*,
Sounds which, having been once uttered by those who understood them, have been since re-echoed without Meaning, and
kept up, to the Disturbance of the World, by a constant Reper-
cussion from one Coxcomb to another. He considers himself as
obliged to shew, by some Proof of his Abilities, that he is not
consulted to no Purpose, and, therefore, watches every Opening
for Objection, and looks round for every Opportunity to propose

made some Attack upon my Quiet. When we were first acquainted, his great Topick was the Misery of Youth without a Fortune; and whenever we walked out together he solaced me with a long Enumeration of Pleasures, which, as they were beyond the Reach of my Fortune, were without the Verge of my Desires, and which I should never have considered as the Objects of a Wish, had not his unseasonable Representations placed them in my Sight.

Another of his Topicks is the Neglect of Merit, with which he never fails to amuse every Man whom he sees not eminently fortunate. If he meets with a young Officer, he always informs him of Gentlemen whose personal Courage is unquestioned, and whose military Skill qualifies them to command Armies, and who have, notwithstanding all their Merit, grown old with subaltern Commissions. For a Genius in the Church, he is always provided with a Curacy for Life. The Lawyer he informs of many Men of great Parts and deep Study, who have never had an Opportunity to speak in the Courts: and meeting *Serenus* the Physician, "Ah doctor, says he, what a-foot still, when so many Blockheads are rattling their Chariots? I told you seven Years ago you would never meet with Encouragement, and I hope you will now take more Notice, when I tell you, that your *Greek*, and your Diligence, and your Honesty, will never enable you to live like yonder Apothecary, who prescribes to his own Shop, and laughs at the Physician."

Suspirius has, in his Time, intercepted fifteen Authors in their Way to the Stage; persuaded nine and thirty Merchants to retire from a prosperous Trade for fear of Bankruptcy, broke off an hundred and thirteen Matches by Prognostications of Unhappiness, and enabled the Small-Pox to kill nineteen Ladies, by perpetual Alarms for fear of their Beauty.

Whenever my evil Stars bring us together, he never fails to represent to me the Folly of my Persuits, and informs me that we are much older than when we begun our Acquaintance, that the Infirmities of Decrepitude are coming fast upon me, that whatever I now get I shall enjoy it but a little Time, that Fame is to a Man tottering on the Edge of the Grave of very little Importance, and that the Time is now at hand when I ought to look for no other Pleasures than a good Dinner and an easy Chair.

Thus he goes on in his unharmonious Strain, displaying present Miseries, and foreboding more, Νυκτικόραξ ᾄδει θανατηφόρον, every

Syllable is loaded with Misfortune, and Death is always brought nearer to the View. Yet, what always raises my Resentment and Indignation, I do not perceive that his mournful Meditations have much Effect upon himself. He talks, and has long talked of Calamities, without discovering, otherwise than by the Tone of his Voice, that he feels any of the Evils which he laments or threatens, but has the same Habit of uttering Lamentations, as others of telling Stories, and falls into Expressions of Condolence for past, or Apprehension of future Mischiefs, as all Men studious of their Ease have recourse to those Subjects upon which they can most fluently or copiously discourse.

It is reported of the *Sybarites*, that they destroyed all their Cocks, that they might dream out their Morning Dreams without Disturbance. Though I would not so far promote Effeminacy as to propose the *Sybarites* for an Example, yet since there is no Man so corrupt, or foolish, but something useful may be learned from him, I could wish that in Imitation of a People not often to be copied, some Regulations might be made to exclude Screech-Owls from all Company as the Enemies of Mankind, and confine them to some proper Receptacle, where they may mingle Sighs at leisure, and thicken the Gloom of one another.

Thou Prophet of evil, says Homer's Agamemnon, *thou never foretellest me Good, but the Joy of thy Heart is to predict Misfortunes.* Whoever is of the same Temper might there find the Means of indulging his Thoughts, and improving his Vein of Denunciation, and the Flock of Screech-Owls might hoot together without Injury to the Rest of the World.

Yet, though I have so little Kindness for this dark Generation, I am very far from intending to debar the soft and tender Mind from the Privilege of Complaining, when the Sigh rises from the Desire not of giving Pain, but of gaining Ease. To hear Complaints with Patience, even when Complaints are vain, is one of the Duties of Friendship; and though it must be allowed that he suffers most like a Hero that hides his Grief in Silence,

> *Spem Vultu simulat, premit altum Corde Dolorem,*
> His outward smiles conceal'd his inward smart.   DRYDEN,

yet, it cannot be denied that he who complains acts like a Man, like a social Being who looks for Help from his Fellow-Creatures. Pity is to many of the Unhappy a Source of Comfort in hopeless

Distresses, as it contributes to recommend them to themselves, by proving that they have not lost the Regard of others, and Heaven seems to indicate the Duty even of barren Compassion, by inclining us to weep for Evils which we cannot remedy.

60

I have often thought that there has rarely passed a Life of which a judicious and faithful Narrative would not be useful. For, not only every Man has in the mighty Mass of the World great Numbers in the same Condition with himself, to whom his Mistakes and Miscarriages, Escapes and Expedients would be of immediate and apparent Use; but there is such an Uniformity in the Life of Man, if it be considered apart from adventitious and separable Decorations and Disguises, that there is scarce any Possibility of Good or Ill, but is common to Humankind. A great Part of the Time of those who are placed at the greatest Distance by Fortune, or by Temper, must unavoidably pass in the same Manner; and though, when the Claims of Nature are satisfied, Caprice, and Vanity, and Accident, begin to produce Discriminations, and Peculiarities, yet the Eye is not very heedful, or quick, which cannot discover the same Causes still terminating their Influence in the same Effects, though sometimes accelerated, sometimes retarded, or perplexed by multiplied Combinations. We are all prompted by the same Motives, all deceived by the same Fallacies, all animated by Hope, obstructed by Danger, entangled by Desire, and seduced by Pleasure.

It is frequently objected to Relations of particular Lives, that they are not distinguished by any striking or wonderful Vicissitudes. The Scholar who passed his Life among his Books, the Merchant who conducted only his own Affairs, the Priest whose Sphere of Action was not extended beyond that of his Duty, are considered as no proper Objects of publick Regard, however they might have excelled in their several Stations, whatever might have been their Learning, Integrity, and Piety. But this Notion arises from false Measures of Excellence and Dignity, and must be eradicated by considering, that, in the Eye of uncorrupted Reason, what is of most Use is of most Value.

It is, indeed, not improper to take honest Advantages of Prejudice, and to gain Attention by a great Name; but the Business of the Biographer is often to pass slightly over those Performances and Incidents, which produce vulgar Greatness, to lead the Thoughts into domestick Privacies, and display the minute Details of daily Life, where exterior Appendages are cast aside, and Men excel each other only by Prudence, and by Virtue. The Life of *Thuanus* is, with great Propriety, said by its Author to have been written, that it might lay open to Posterity the private and familiar Character of that Man, *cujus Ingenium et Candorem ex ipsius Scriptis sunt olim semper miraturi*, whose Candour and Genius his Writings will to the End of Time preserve in Admiration.

There are many invisible Circumstances, which whether we read as Enquirers after natural or moral Knowledge, whether we intend to enlarge our Science, or encrease our Virtue, are more important than publick Occurrences. Thus *Salust*, the great Master, has not forgot, in his Account of *Catiline*, to remark that *his Walk was now quick, and again slow*, as an Indication of a Mind revolving something with violent Commotion. Thus the Story of *Melancthon* affords a striking Lecture on the Value of Time, by informing us that when he made an Appointment, he expected not only the Hour, but the Minute to be fixed, that Life might not run out in the Idleness of Suspense; and all the Plans and Enterprizes of *De Wit* are now of less Importance to the World, than that Part of his personal Character, which represents him as careful of his Health, and negligent of his Life.

But Biography has often been allotted to Writers who seem very little acquainted with the Nature of their Task, or very negligent about the Performance. They rarely afford any other Account than might be collected from publick Papers, and imagine themselves writing a Life when they exhibit a chronological Series of Actions or Preferments; and so little regard the Manners or Behaviour of their Heroes, that more Knowledge may be gained of a Man's real Character, by a short Conversation with one of his Servants, than from a formal and studied Narrative, begun with his Pedigree, and ended with his Funeral.

If now and then they condescend to inform the World of particular Facts, they are not always so happy as to select those which are of most Importance. I know not well what Advantage Posterity can receive from the only Circumstance by which *Tickell* has distinguished *Addison* from the Rest of Mankind, the Irregularity of his Pulse: nor can I think myself overpaid for the Time spent in reading the Life of *Malherb*, by being enabled to relate, after the learned Biographer, that *Malherb* had two predominant Opinions; one, that the Looseness of a single Woman might destroy all the Boast of ancient Descent; the other, that the *French* Beggers made use very improperly and barbarously of the Phrase *noble Gentleman*, because either Word included the Sense of both.

There are, indeed, some natural Reasons why these Narratives are often written by such as were not likely to give much Instruction or Delight, and why most Accounts of particular Persons are barren and useless. If a Life be delayed till all Interest and Envy are at an End, and all Motives to Calumny or Flattery are suppressed, we may hope for Impartiality, but must expect little Intelligence; for the Incidents which give Excellence to Biography are of a volatile and evanescent Kind, such as soon escape the Memory, and are rarely transmitted by Tradition. We know how few can portray a living Acquaintance, except by his most prominent and observable Particularities, and the grosser Features of his Mind; and it may be easily imagined how much of this little Knowledge may be lost in imparting it, and how soon a Succession of Copies will lose all Resemblance of the Original.

If the Biographer writes from personal Knowledge, and makes haste to gratify the publick Curiosity, there is Danger lest his Interest, his Fear, his Gratitude, or his Tenderness, overpower his Fidelity, and tempt him to conceal, if not to invent. There are many who think it an Act of Piety to hide the Faults or Failings of their Friends, even when they can no longer suffer by their Detection; we therefore see whole Ranks of Characters adorned with uniform Panegyrick, and not to be known from one another, but by extrinsick and casual Circumstances. "Let me remember, says *Hale*, when I find myself inclined to pity a Criminal, that there is likewise a Pity due to the Country." If there is a Regard due to the Memory of the Dead, there is yet more Respect to be paid to Knowledge, to Virtue, and to Truth.

61

A short Residence at *London* entitles a Man to Knowledge, to Wit, to Politeness, and to a despotick and dictatorial Power of prescribing to the rude Multitude, whom he condescends to honour with a biennial Visit; yet, I know not well upon what Motives, I have lately found myself inclined to cavil at this Prescription, and to doubt whether it be not, on some Occasions, proper to withhold our Veneration, till we are more authentically convinced of the Merits of the Claimant.

It is well remember'd here, that, about seven Years ago, one *Frolick*, a tall Boy, with lank Hair, remarkable for stealing Eggs, and sucking them, was taken from the School in this Parish, and sent up to *London* to study the Law. As he had given amongst us no Proofs of a Genius, designed by Nature, for extraordinary Performances, he was, from the Time of his Departure, totally forgotten, nor was there any Talk of his Vices or Virtues, his good or his ill Fortune, till last Summer a Report burst upon us, that Mr *Frolick* was come down in the first Post-Chaise which this Village had seen, having travelled with such Rapidity that one of his Postilions had broken his Leg, and another narrowly escaped Suffocation in a Quicksand. But that Mr *Frolick* seemed totally unconcerned, for such Things were never heeded at *London*.

Mr *Frolick* next Day appeared among the Gentlemen at their weekly Meeting on the Bowling-Green, and now were seen the Effects of a *London* Education. His Dress, his Language, his Ideas, were all new, and he did not much endeavour to conceal his Contempt of every thing that differed from the Opinions, or Practice, of the modish World. He shewed us the Deformity of our Skirts and Sleeves, informed us where Hats of the proper Size were to be sold, and recommended to us the Reformation of a thousand Absurdities in our Cloaths, our Cookery, and our Conversation. When any of his Phrases were unintelligible, he could not suppress the Joy of confessed Superiority, but frequently delayed the Explanation that he might enjoy his Triumph over our Barbarity.

When he is pleased to entertain us with a Story, he takes care to croud into it Names of Streets, Squares and Buildings, with which he knows we are unacquainted. His favourite Topicks of Discourse are the Pranks of Drunkards, and the Tricks put upon Country Gentlemen by Porters and Link-Boys. When he is with Ladies he tells them of the innumerable Pleasures to which he can introduce them, but never fails to hint, how much they will be deficient, at their first Arrival, in the Knowledge of the Town. What it is *to know the Town* he has not indeed hitherto informed us, though there is no Phrase so frequent in his Mouth, nor any Knowledge which he appears to think of so great Value, or so difficult Attainment.

But my Curiosity has been most engaged by the Recital of his own Adventures and Atchievements. I have heard of the Union of various Characters in single Persons, but never met with such a Constellation of great Qualities as this Man's Narrative affords. Whatever has distinguished the Hero; whatever has elevated the Wit; whatever has indeared the Lover, are all concentered in M1 *Frolick*, whose Life has, for seven Years, been a regular Interchange of Intrigues, Dangers, Waggeries, and who has distinguished himself in every Character that can be feared, envied, or admired.

I question whether all the Officers of the royal Navy can bring together, from all their Journals, a Collection of so many wonderful Escapes as this Man has known upon the *Thames*, on which he has been a thousand and a thousand times on the Point of perishing, sometimes by the Terrors of foolish Women in the same Boat, sometimes by his own acknowledged Imprudence in passing the River in the Dark, and sometimes by shooting the Bridge, under which he has rencountered mountainous Waves, and dreadful Cataracts.

Nor less has been his Temerity by Land, nor fewer his Hazards. He has reeled with Giddiness on the Top of the Monument; he has crossed the Street amidst the Rush of Coaches; he has been surrounded by Robbers without Number; he has headed Parties at the Play-House, he has scaled the Windows of every Toast of whatever Condition; he has been hunted for whole Winters by his Rivals; he has slept upon Bulks; he has cut Chairs, he has bilked Coachmen; he has rescued his Friends from the Bailiffs, has knocked down the Constable, has bullied the Justice, and performed many other Exploits, that have filled the Town with Wonder and with Merriment.

But yet greater is the Fame of his Understanding than his Bravery; for he informs us, that he is, at *London*, the established Arbitrator of all Points of Honour and the decisive Judge of all Performances of Genius; that no musical Performer is in Reputation till the Opinion of *Frolick* has ratified his Pretensions; that the Theatres suspend their Sentence till he begins the Clap or Hiss, in which they are all proud to concur; that no publick Entertainment has failed or succeeded, but because he opposed or favoured it; that all Controversies at the Gaming-Table are referred to his Determination; that he adjusts the Ceremonial at every Assembly, and prescribes every Fashion of Pleasure or of Dress.

With every Man, whose Name occurs in the Papers of the Day, he is intimately acquainted; and there are very few Posts, either in the State or Army, of which he has not more or less influenced the Disposal. He has been very frequently consulted both upon War and Peace; but the Time is not yet come when the Nation shall know how much it is indebted to the Genius of *Frolick*.

Yet, notwithstanding all these Declarations, I cannot hitherto persuade myself to see that Mr *Frolick* has more Wit, or Knowledge, or Courage, than the Rest of Mankind, or that any uncommon Enlargement of his Faculties has happened in the Time of his Absence. For when he talks on Subjects known to the Rest of the Company, he has no Advantage over us, but by Catches of Interruption, Briskness of Interrogation, and Pertness of Contempt; and therefore if he has stunned the World with his Name, and gained a Place in the first Ranks of Humanity, I cannot but conclude, that either a little Understanding confers Eminence at *London*, or that Mr *Frolick* thinks us unworthy of the Exertion of his Powers, or that his Faculties are benumbed by rural Stupidity, as the magnetick Needle loses its Animation in the polar Climes.

I would not, however, like many hasty Philosophers, search after the Cause till I am certain of the Effect; and, therefore, I desire to be informed, whether you have yet heard the great Name of Mr *Frolick*. If he is celebrated by other Tongues than his own, I shall willingly propagate his Praise; but if he has swelled among us with empty Boasts, and Honours conferred only by himself, I shall treat him with rustick Sincerity, and drive him as an Impostor from this Part of the Kingdom to some Region of more Credulity.

I am, &c.

RURICOLA.

68

The Main of Life is, indeed, composed of small Incidents, and petty Occurrences; of Wishes for Objects not remote, and grief for Disappointments of no fatal Consequence; of insect Vexations which sting us and fly away, Impertinences which buzz a while about us, and are heard no more; of meteorous Pleasures which dance before us and are dissipated, of Compliments which glide off the Soul like other Musick, and are forgotten by him that gave and him that received them.

Such is the general Heap out of which every Man is to cull his own Condition: for, as the Chymists tell us, that all Bodies are resolvable into the same Elements, and that the boundless Variety of Things arises from the different Proportions of very few Ingredients; so a few Pains, and a few Pleasures are all the Materials of human Life, and of these the Proportions are partly allotted by Providence, and partly left to the Arrangement of Reason and of Choice.

As these are well or ill disposed, Man is for the most part happy or miserable. For very few are involved in great Events, or have their Thread of Life entwisted with the Chain of Causes on which Armies or Nations are suspended; and even those who seem wholly busied in publick Affairs, and elevated above low Cares, or trivial Pleasures, pass the chief Part of their Time in familiar and domestick Scenes; from these they came into publick Life, to these they are every Hour recalled by Passions not to be suppressed; in these they have the Reward of their Toils, and to these at last they retire.

The great End of Prudence is to give Chearfulness to those Hours, which Splendour cannot gild, and Acclamation cannot exhilarate; those soft Intervals of unbended Amusement, in which a Man shrinks to his own natural Dimensions, and throws aside the Ornaments or Disguises, which he feels in Privacy to be useless Incumbrances, and to lose all Effect when they become familiar. To be happy at home is the ultimate Result of all Ambition, the end to which every Enterprise and Labour tends, and of which every Desire prompts the Prosecution.

It is, indeed, at home that every Man must be known, by those who would make a just Estimate either of his Virtue or Felicity; for Smiles and Embroidery are alike occasional, and the Mind is often dressed for Show in painted Honour, and fictitious Benevolence.

72

Good Humour may be defined *a Habit of being pleased,* a constant and perennial Softness of Manner, Easiness of Approach, and Suavity of Disposition; like that which every Man perceives in himself, when the first Transports of new Felicity have subsided, and his Thoughts are only kept in Motion by a slow Succession of soft Impulses. Good Humour is a State between Gayety and Unconcern; the Act or Emanation of a Mind at leisure to regard the Gratification of another.

It is imagined by many, that whenever they aspire to please, they are required to be merry, to shew the Gladness of their Souls by Flights of Pleasantry, and bursts of Laughter, and to lose all Reserve and Reflection in overflowing Jollity. But, though these Men may be courted for a Time, and heard with Applause and Admiration, they seldom delight us long. We enjoy them a little, and then retire to Easiness and Good Humour, as the Eye gazes a while on Eminences glittering with the Sun, but soon turns aking away to Verdure and to Flowers.

Gayety is to good Humour as animal Perfumes to vegetable Fragrance; the one overpowers weak Spirits, and the other recreates and revives them. Gayety seldom fails to give some Pain; the Hearers either strain their Faculties to accompany its Towerings, or are left behind in Envy and Despair. Good Humour boasts no Faculties which every one does not believe in his own Power, and pleases principally by not offending.

It is well known that the most certain way to give any Man Pleasure, is to persuade him that you receive Pleasure from him, to encourage him to Freedom and Confidence, and to avoid any such appearance of Superiority as may overbear and depress him. We see many that, by this Art only, spend their Days in the midst of Caresses, Invitations, and Civilities; and without any great Qualities or extraordinary Attainments, are the universal Favourites of both Sexes, and are certain to find a Friend in every Place, because they heighten every Man's Opinion of himself. The Darlings of Mankind will, indeed, be generally found such as excite neither Jealousy nor Fear; are not considered as Candidates for any eminent Degree of Reputation, but content themselves with common Accomplishments, and endeavour rather to sollicit Kindness than to raise Esteem; therefore in Assemblies and Places of Resort it seldom fails to happen, that though at the Entrance of some particular Person every Face brightens with Gladness, and every Hand is extended in Salutation, yet if you persue him beyond the first Exchange of Civilities, you will find him of very small Importance, and only welcome to the Company, as one by whom all conceive themselves admired, and with whom any one is at Liberty to amuse himself when he can find no other Auditor or Companion; as one with whom all are at Ease, who will hear a Jest without Criticism, and a Narrative without Contradiction, who laughs with every Wit, and yields to every Disputer.

There are many whose Vanity always inclines them to associate with those from whom they have no Reason to fear Mortification; and there are Times in which the Wise and the Knowing are willing to receive Praise without the Labour of deserving it, in which the most elevated Mind is willing to descend, and the most active to be at rest. All therefore are at some Hour or another fond of Companions whom they can entertain upon easy Terms, and who will relieve them from Solitude, without condemning them to Vigilance and Caution. We are most inclined to love when we have nothing to fear, and he that always indulges us in our present Disposition, and encourages us to please ourselves, will not be long without Preference in our Affection to those whose Learning holds us at the Distance of Pupils, or whose Wit calls all Attention from us, and leaves us without Importance and without Regard.

81

The Measure of Justice prescribed to us, in our Transactions with others, is remarkably clear and comprehensive: *whatsoever ye would that Men should do unto you, even so do unto them.* A Law by which every Claim of Right may be immediately adjusted, as far as the private Conscience requires to be informed; a Law, of which every Man may find the Exposition in his own Breast, and which may always be observed by Honesty of Intention, and Purity of Will.

Over this Law indeed some Men have been subtle enough to throw Mists, which have darkened their own Eyes, and found means of perplexing that universal Principle upon which every Question of Justice, between one Man and another, is to be decided. They have enquired whether a Man, conscious to himself of unreasonable Desires, be bound to gratify them in another. But surely it requires not long Deliberation to conclude that the Desires, which are to be considered as the Measure of Justice, must be such as we approve; that we ought to pay no Regard to those Expectations in another, which we condemn in ourselves, and which, however they may intrude upon our Imagination, we know it our Duty to resist and suppress.

One of the most celebrated Cases which have been produced as requiring some Skill in Casuistry to adapt it to this great Rule, is that of a Criminal asking Mercy of his Judge, who cannot but know that if he was in the State of the Supplicant, he should desire that Pardon which he now denies. The difficulty of this

Supposition will vanish, if we remember that the Parties are in reality, on one Side the Criminal, and on the other the Community, of which the Magistrate is only the Minister, and by which he is intrusted with the publick Safety. The Magistrate therefore, in pardoning a Man unworthy of Pardon, betrays the Trust with which he is invested, gives away what is not his own, and, without Question, does to others what he would not that others should do to him. Even the Community, whose Right is still greater to arbitrary Grants of Mercy, is yet bound by those Laws which regard the great Republick of Mankind, and cannot justify such Forbearances as may promote Wickedness, and lessen the general Confidence and Security in which all have an equal Interest, and which all are therefore bound to maintain. For this Reason no State has a Right to erect a general Sanctuary for Fugitives, or give Protection to such as have forfeited their Lives by Crimes against the Laws of common Morality, equally acknowledged by all Nations, because none can, without Infraction of the universal League of social Beings, incite, by Prospects of Impunity and Safety, those practises in another Dominion, which they would themselves punish in their own.

85

I have always admired the Wisdom of those by whom our Female Education was instituted, for having contrived, that every Woman of whatever Condition should be taught some Arts of Manufacture, by which the Vacuities of recluse and domestick Leisure may always be filled up; since the Weakness of their Sex, and the general System of Life, exclude them from many Employments which by diversifying the Circumstances of Men, preserve them from being cankered by the Rust of their own Thoughts. I know not how much of the Virtue and Happiness of the World may be the Consequence of this judicious Regulation. Perhaps, the most powerful Fancy might be unable to figure the Confusion and Slaughter that would be produced by so many piercing Eyes and vivid Understandings, turned loose at once upon Mankind, with no other Business than to sparkle and intrigue, to perplex and to destroy.

For my Part, whenever Chance brings within my Observation a Knot of Misses busy at their Needles, I consider myself as in the School of Virtue; and though I have no extraordinary Skill in

Plain-work or Embroidery, look upon their operations with, at least, as much Satisfaction as their Governess, because I regard them as providing a Security against the most dangerous Ensnarers of the Soul, by enabling themselves to exclude Idleness from their solitary Moments, and with Idleness her attendant Train of Passions, Fancies, and Chimeras, Fears, Sorrows and Desires. *Ovid* and *Cervantes* inform, that Love has no Power but over those whom he catches unemployed; and *Hector*, in the *Iliad*, when he sees *Andromache* overwhelmed with Terrors, sends her for Consolation to the Loom and the Distaff.

It is certain that any wild Wish or vain Imagination never takes such firm Possession of the Mind, as when it is found empty and unoccupied; for the old peripatetick Principle, that *Nature abhors a Vacuum*, may be properly applied to the Intellect; it will embrace any Thing however absurd or criminal rather than be wholly without an Object. Perhaps every Man may date the Predominance of those Desires that disturb his Life and contaminate his Conscience, from some unhappy Hour when too much Leisure exposed him to their Incursions, for he has lived with little Observation either on himself or others, who does not know that to be idle is to be vicious.

87

If we consider in what manner those who assume the Office of directing the Conduct of others perform what they have undertaken, it will not be very wonderful that their Labours, however zealous or affectionate, are frequently useless. For what is the Advice that is commonly given, but a few general Maxims, enforced with Vehemence and inculcated with Importunity, but failing for Want of particular Reference, and immediate Application?

It is not often that any Man can have that Knowledge of another, that is necessary to make Instruction useful. We are sometimes not ourselves conscious of the original Motives of our Actions, and when we know them, our first Care is to hide them from the sight of others, and often from those most diligently, whose Superiority either of Power or Understanding may intitle them to inspect our Conduct; it is therefore very probable that he who endeavours the Cure of our intellectual Maladies, mistakes their Cause; and that his Prescriptions avail nothing, because he knows not which of the Passions or Desires is vitiated.

Advice, as it always gives a temporary Appearance of Superiority, can never be very grateful, even when it is most necessary or most judicious. But for the same Reasons every one is eager to instruct his Neighbours. To be wise or to be virtuous, is to buy Dignity and Importance at a high Price; but when nothing is necessary to Elevation but Detection of the Follies or the Faults of others, no man is so insensible to the Voice of Fame as to linger on the Ground.

——Tentanda via est qua me quoque possim
Tollere humo, victorque virûm volitare per ora.

New ways I must attempt, my groveling name,
To raise aloft, and wing my flight to fame.   DRYDEN.

Vanity is so frequently the apparent motive of Advice, that we, for the most Part, summon our Powers to oppose it without any very accurate Enquiry whether it is right. It is sufficient that another is growing great in his own Eyes at our Expence, and that he assumes an Authority over us without our Permission, and many would be contented to suffer the Consequences of their own Mistakes, rather than the Insolence of him who triumphs as their Deliverer.

It was the Maxim, I think, of *Alphonsus* of *Arragon*, that *dead Counsellors are safest*. The Grave puts an end to Flattery and Artifice, and the Information that we receive from Books is pure from Interest, Fear, or Ambition. Dead Counsellors are likewise most instructive; because they are heard with Patience and with Reverence : We are not unwilling to believe that Man wiser than ourselves, from whose Abilities we may receive Advantage, without any Danger of Rivalry or Opposition, and who affords us the Light of his Experience, without hurting our Eyes by Flashes of Insolence.

By the Consultation of Books, whether of dead or living Authors, many Temptations to Petulence and Opposition, which occur in oral Conferences, are avoided. An Author cannot obtrude his Advice unasked, nor can be often suspected of any malignant Intention to insult his Readers with his Knowledge or his Wit. Yet so prevalent is the Habit of comparing ourselves with others, while they remain within the Reach of our Passions, that Books are seldom read impartially, but by those from whom the Writer is placed at such a Distance that his Life or Death is indifferent.

We see that Authors may be perused, and perused with Attention, to little Effect; and that Maxims of Prudence, or Principles of Virtue, may be treasured in the Memory without influencing the Conduct. Of the Numbers that pass their Lives among Books, very few read to become wiser or better, apply any general Reproof of Vice to themselves, or try their own Manners by Axioms of Justice. They purpose either to consume those Hours for which they can find no other Amusement, to gain or preserve that Respect which the Learned have always obtained, or to gratify their Curiosity with Knowledge, which, like Gold in the Chests of Misers, is of no Use to others or themselves.

89

It has been observed that the most studious are not always the most learned. There is, indeed, no great Difficulty to perceive that this Difference of Proficiency may arise from the Difference of intellectual Powers, of the Choice of Books, or the Convenience of Information. But I believe it likewise frequently happens that the most recluse are not the most vigorous Prosecutors of Study. Many impose upon the World, and many upon themselves, with an Appearance of severe and exemplary Diligence, when they, in reality, give themselves up to the Luxury of Fancy, please their Minds with regulating the past, or planning out the future; place themselves at Will in Situations of Happiness, and slumber away their Days in voluntary Visions. In the Journey of Life some are left behind, because they are naturally feeble and slow; some because they miss the Way; and many because they leave it by Choice, and instead of pressing onward with a steady Pace, delight themselves with momentary Deviations, turn aside to pluck every Flower, and repose in every Shade.

There is nothing more fatal to a Man whose Business is to think, than to have learned the Art of regaling his Mind with those airy Gratifications. Other Vices or Follies are restrained by Fear, reformed by Admonition, or rejected by the Conviction which the Comparison of our Conduct with that of others, may in Time produce. But this invisible Riot of the Mind, this secret Prodigality of Being, is secure from Detection, and fearless of Reproach. The Dreamer retires to his Apartments, shuts out the Cares and Interruptions of Mankind, and abandons himself to his own Fancy; new Worlds rise up before him, one Image is succeeded by another, and a long Succession of Delights dances round him. He is at last called back to Life by Nature, or by Custom, and enters peevish into Society, because he cannot model it to his own Will. He returns from his idle Excursions with the Peevishness, though not with the Knowledge, of a Student, and hastens again to the same Felicity with the Eagerness of a Man bent upon the Advancement of some favourite Science. The Infatuation strengthens by Degrees, and, like the Poison of Opiates, weakens his Powers, without any external Symptoms of Malignity.

It happens, indeed, that these Hypocrites of Learning are in Time detected, and convinced by Disgrace and Disappointment of the Difference between the Labour of Thought, and the Sport of Musing. But this Discovery is often not made till it is too late to recover the Time that has been fooled away. A thousand Accidents may, indeed, awaken these Drones to a more early Sense of their Danger and their Shame. But those who are convinced of the Necessity of breaking from this habitual Drowsiness, too often relapse in spite of their Resolution; for these ideal Seducers are always near, and neither any Particularity of Time nor Place is necessary to their Influence; they invade the Soul without Warning, and have often charmed down Resistance before their Approach is perceived or suspected.

There must be a Time in which every Man trifles; and the only Choice that Nature offers us, is, to trifle in Company or alone. To join Profit with Pleasure has been an old Precept among Men who have had very different Conceptions of Profit. All have agreed that our Amusements should not terminate wholly in the present Moment, but contribute more or less to future Advantages. He that amuses himself among well chosen Companions, can scarcely fail to receive from the most careless and obstreperous Merriment which Virtue can allow, some useful Hints; nor can converse on the most familiar Topics, without some casual Information. The loose Sparkles of thoughtless Wit may give new Light to the Mind, and the gay Contention for paradoxical Positions rectify the Opinions.

This is the Time in which those Friendships that give Happiness or Consolation, Relief or Security, are generally formed. A wise and good Man is never so amiable as in his unbended and familiar Intervals. Heroic Generosity, or philosophical Discoveries may compel Veneration and Respect, but Love always implies some Kind of natural or voluntary Equality, and is only to be excited by that Levity and Chearfulness which disencumbers all Minds from Awe and Solicitude, invites the Modest to Freedom, and exalts the Timorous to Confidence. This Ease and Frankness is certain to please, whatever be the Character of him that exerts it; if our Superiors descend from their Elevation, we love them for lessening the Distance at which we are placed below them; and Inferiors, from whom we can receive no other advantage, will always keep our Affections while they give us pleasure.

Every Man finds himself differently affected by the Sight of Fortresses of War, and Palaces of Pleasure; we look on the Height and Strength of the Bulwarks with a kind of gloomy Satisfaction, because we cannot think of Defence without thinking likewise of Danger; but range delighted through the gay Apartments of the Palace, because nothing is impressed by them on the Mind but Joy and Festivity. Such is the Difference between great and amiable Characters; with Protectors we are safe, with Companions we are happy.

92

*Jam nunc minaci murmure cornuum
Perstringis aures, jam litui strepunt.*   HOR.

Lo! now the clarion's voice I hear,
Its threatning murmurs pierce mine ear;
And in thy lines with brazen breath
The trumpet sounds the charge of death.   FRANCIS.

It has been long observed, that the Idea of Beauty is vague and undefined, different in different Minds, and diversified by Time or Place. It has been, indeed, a Term hitherto used to signify that which pleases us we know not why, and in our Approbation of which we can for the most Part only justify ourselves by the Concurrence of Numbers, without much Power of enforcing our Opinion upon others by any Argument, but Example and Authority. It is, indeed, so little subject to the Examinations of Reason, that *Paschal* supposed it to end where Demonstration begins, and maintains that without Incongruity and Absurdity we cannot speak of *Geometrical Beauty*.

To trace all the Sources of that various Pleasure which we ascribe to the Agency of Beauty, or to disentangle all the Perceptions involved in its Idea, would, perhaps, require a very great part of the Life of an *Aristotle* or *Plato*. It is, however, in many Cases, apparent that this Quality is relative and comparative; that we pronounce Things beautiful, because they have something which we agree, for whatever Reason, to call Beauty, in a greater Degree than we have been accustomed to find in other Things of the same Kind; and that we transfer the Epithet as our Knowledge encreases, and appropriate it to higher Excellence, when higher Excellence comes within our View.

Much of the Beauty of Writing is of this Kind, and therefore *Boileau* justly remarks, that the Works which have stood the Test of Time, and been admired through all the Changes which the Mind of Man has suffered from the various Revolutions of Knowledge, and the Prevalence of contrary Customs, have a better Claim to our Regard than any Modern can boast, because the long Continuance of their Reputation proves that they are adequate to our Faculties, and agreeable to Nature.

It is, however, the Task of Criticism to establish Principles, to exalt Opinion to Knowledge, and to distinguish those Means of pleasing which depend upon known Causes and rational Deduction, from the nameless and inexplicable Elegancies which appeal wholly to the Fancy, of which we only feel that they delight, and which may well be termed the Enchantresses of the Soul, and to reduce those Regions of Literature under the Dominion of Science, which have hitherto known only the Anarchy of Ignorance, the Caprices of Fancy, and the Tyranny of Prescription.

There is nothing in the Art of versifying so much exposed to the Power of Imagination as the Accommodation of the Sound to the Sense, or the Representation of particular Images, by the Flow of the Verse in which they are expressed. Every Reader has innumerable Passages, in which he, and perhaps he alone, discovers such Resemblances; and since the Attention of the present Race of poetical Readers seems particularly turned upon this Species of Elegance, I shall endeavour to examine how much this Conformity has been observed by the Poets, or directed by the Criticks, how far it can be established upon Nature and Reason, and on what Occasions it has been practised by *Milton*.

Homer, the Father of all poetical Beauty, has been particularly celebrated by *Dionysius*, as *he that, of all the Poets, had the greatest Variety of Sound ; for there are,* says he, *innumerable Passages, in*

218

*which Length of Time, Bulk of Body, Extremity of Passion, and
Stillness of Repose; or, in which, on the contrary, Brevity, Speed, and
Eagerness, are evidently marked out by the Sound of the Syllables.*
Thus the Anguish and slow Pace with which the blind Polypheme
groped out with his Hands the Entrance of his Cave, are perceived
in the Cadence of the Verses which describe it.

> Κύκλωψ δὲ στενάχων τε καὶ ὡδίνων ὀδύνῃσι,
> Χερσί ψηλαφόων ————

> Mean time the *Cyclop*, raging with his wound,
> Spreads his wide arms, and searches round and round. POPE.

Thus the Efforts of *Achilles* struggling in his Armour against the
Current of a River, sometimes resisting and sometimes yielding,
may be perceived in the Elisions of the Syllables, the slow Succession of the Feet, and the Strength of the Consonants.

> Δεινὸν δ' ἄμφ' 'Αχιλῆα κυκώμενον ἵστατο κῦμα,
> "Ωθει δ' ἐν σάκεϊ πίπτων ῥόος, οὐδὲ πόδεσσιν
> Εἶχε στηρίξασθαι.————

> So oft the surge, in watry mountains spread,
> Beats on his back, or bursts upon his head.
> Yet dauntless still the adverse flood he braves,
> And still indignant bounds above the waves.
> Tir'd by the tides, his knees relax with toil ;
> Wash'd from beneath him, slides the slimy soil. POPE.

When he describes the Crush of Men dashed against a Rock, he
collects the most unpleasing and harsh Sounds.

> Σὺν δὲ δύω μάρψας ὥς τε σκύλακας ποτὶ γαίῃ
> Κόπτ'. ἐκ δ' ἐγκέφαλος χαμάδις ῥέε, δεῦε δὲ γαῖαν.

> ————His bloody hand
> Snatch'd two, unhappy! of my martial band,
> And dash'd like dogs against the stony floor:
> The pavement swims with brains and mingled gore. POPE.

And when he would place before the Eyes something dreadful
and astonishing, he makes Choice of the strongest Vowels, and the
Letters of most difficult Utterance.

> Τῇ δ' ἐπὶ μὲν Γοργὼ βλοσυρῶπις ἐστεφάντο
> Δεινὸν δερκομένη, περὶ δὲ Δεῖμός τε Φόβος τε.

> Tremendous *Gorgon* frown'd upon its field,
> And circling terrors fill'd th' expressive shield. POPE.

Many other Examples *Dionysius* produces, but these will
sufficiently shew, that he was fanciful, or that we have lost the

genuine Pronunciation; for I know not whether in any one of these Instances the Similitude can be discovered. It seems, indeed, probable, that the Veneration with which *Homer* was read, produced many supposititious Beauties; for though it is certain, that the Sound of many of his Verses very justly corresponds with the Things expressed, yet when the Force of his Imagination is considered with the Flexibility of his Language, of which the Syllables might be often contracted or dilated at Pleasure, it will seem unlikely that such Conformity should happen less frequently even without Design.

It is not however to be doubted, that *Virgil* who wrote amidst the Light of Criticism, and who owed so much of his Success to Art and Labour, endeavoured among other Excellencies to exhibit this Similitude; nor has he been less happy in this than in the other Graces of Versification. This Felicity of his Numbers was at the Revival of Learning displayed with great Elegance by *Vida* in his Art of Poetry.

> *Haud satis est illis utcunque claudere versum. . . .*
> *Omnia sed numeris vocum concordibus aptant,*
> *Atque sono quæcunque canunt imitantur, & apta*
> *Verborum facie, & quæsito carminis ore.*
> *Nam diversa opus est veluti dare versibus ora, . . .*
> *Hic melior motuque pedum, & pernicibus alis,*
> *Molle viam tacito lapsu per levia radit:*
> *Ille autem membris, ac mole ignavius ingens*
> *Incedit, tardo molimine subsidendo.*
> *Ecce aliquis subit egregio pulcherrimus ore,*
> *Cui lætum membris Venus omnibus afflat honorem.*
> *Contra alius rudis, informes ostendit & artus,*
> *Hirsutumque supercilium, ac caudam sinuosam,*
> *Ingratus visu, sonitu illætabilis ipso. . . .*
> *Ergo ubi jam nautæ spumas salis ære ruentes*
> *Incubuere mari, videas spumare, reductis*
> *Convulsum remis, rostrisque stridentibus æquor.*
> *Tunc longe sale saxa sonant, tunc & freta ventis*
> *Incipiunt agitata tumescere: littore fluctus*
> *Illidunt rauco, atque refracta remurmurat unda*
> *Ad scopulos, cumulo insequitur præruptus aquæ mons. . . .*
> *Cum vero ex alto speculatus cærula Nereus*
> *Leniit in morem stagni, placidæque paludis,*
> *Labitur uncta vadis abies, natat uncta carina. . . .*
> *Verba etiam res exiguas angusta sequuntur,*
> *Ingentesque juvant ingentia: cuncta gigantem*
> *Vasta decent, vultus immanes, pectora lata,*
> *Et magni membrorum artus, magna ossa lacertique.*

Atque adeo, siquid geritur molimine magno,
Adde moram, & pariter tecum quoque verba laborent
Segnia: seu quando vi multa gleba coactis
Æternum frangenda bidentibus, æquore seu cum
Cornua velatarum obvertimus antennarum.
At mora si fuerit damno, properare jubebo.
Si se forte cava extulerit mala vipera terra,
Tolle moras, cape saxa manu, cape robora, pastor;
Ferte citi flammas, date tela, repellite pestem.
Ipse etiam versus ruat, in præcepsque feratur,
Immenso cum præcipitans ruit Oceano nox,
Aut cum perculsus graviter procumbit humi bos,
Cumque etiam requies rebus datur, ipsa quoque ultro
Carmina paulisper cursu cessare videbis
In medio interrupta: quierunt cum freta ponti,
Postquam auræ posuere, quiescere protinus ipsum
Cernere erit, mediisque incœptis sistere versum.
Quid dicam, senior cum telum imbelle sine ictu
Invalidus jacit, & defectis viribus æger?
Num quoque tum versus segni pariter pede languet:
Sanguis hebet, frigent effœtœ in corpore vires.
Fortem autem juvenem deceat prorumpere in arces,
Evertisse domos, præfractaque quadrupedantum
Pectora pectoribus perrumpere, sternere turres
Ingentes, totoque ferum dare funera campo.

'Tis not enough his verses to compleat,
In measure, number, or determin'd feet.
To all, proportion'd terms he must dispense,
And make the sound a picture of the sense;
The correspondent words exactly frame,
The look, the features, and the mien the same.
With rapid feet and wings, without delay,
This swiftly flies, and smoothly skims away:
This blooms with youth and beauty in his face,
And *Venus* breathes on ev'ry limb a grace:
That, of rude form, his uncouth members shows,
Looks horrible, and frowns with his rough brows;
His monstrous tail in many a fold and wind,
Voluminous and vast, curls up behind:
At once the image and the lines appear
Rude to the eye and frightful to the ear.
Lo! when the sailors steer the pond'rous ships,
And plough, with brazen beaks, the foamy deeps,
Incumbent on the main that roars around;
Beneath the lab'ring oars the waves resound;
The prows wide-ecchoing thro' the dark profound:
To the loud call each distant rock replies;
Tost by the storm the tow'ring surges rise;

While the hoarse ocean beats the sounding shore,
Dash'd from the strand, the flying waters roar,
Flash at the shock, and gath'ring in a heap,
The liquid mountains rise, and over-hang the deep.
But when blue *Neptune* from his car surveys,
And calms at one regard the raging seas;
Stretch'd like a peaceful lake the deep subsides,
And the pitch'd vessel o'er the surface glides.
When things are small, the terms should still be so;
For low words please us, when the theme is low.
But when some giant, horrible and grim,
Enormous in his gait, and vast in ev'ry limb,
Stalks tow'ring on; the swelling words must rise
In just proportion to the monster's size.
If some large weight his huge arms strive to shove,
The verse too labours; the throng'd words scarce move.
When each stiff clod beneath the pond'rous plough
Crumbles and breaks, th' encumber'd lines must flow.
Nor less, when pilots catch the friendly gales,
Unfurl their shrouds, and hoist the wide-stretch'd sails.
But if the poem suffers from delay,
Let the lines fly precipitate away,
And when the viper issues from the brake,
Be quick; with stones, and brands, and fire, attack }
His rising crest, and drive the serpent back.
When night descends, or stun'd by num'rous strokes,
And groaning, to the earth drops the vast ox;
The line too sinks with correspondent sound,
Flat with the steer, and headlong to the ground.
When the wild waves subside, and tempests cease,
And hush the roarings of the sea to peace;
So oft we see the interrupted strain
Stopp'd in the midst—and with the silent main }
Pause for a space—at last it glides again.
When *Priam* strains his aged arms, to throw
His unavailing jav'lin at the foe;
(His blood congeal'd, and ev'ry nerve unstrung)
Then with the theme complies the artful song;
Like him, the solitary numbers flow,
Weak, trembling, melancholy, stiff, and slow.
Not so young *Pyrrhus*, who with rapid force
Beats down embattled armies in his course.
The raging youth on trembling *Ilion* falls,
Burns her strong gates, and shakes her lofty walls;
Provokes his flying courser to the speed,
In full career to charge the warlike steed:
He piles the field with mountains of the slain;
He pours, he storms, he thunders thro' the plain.   PITT.

From *Vida*, Mr *Pope* seems to have transplanted this Flower;

which is the Growth of happier Climates, into a Soil less adapted
to its Nature, and less favourable to its Increase.

> Soft is the Strain when *Zephyr* gently blows,
> And the smooth Stream in smoother Numbers flows;
> But when loud Billows lash the sounding Shore,
> The hoarse rough Verse should like the Torrent roar.
> When *Ajax* strives, some Rock's vast Weight to throw,
> The Line too labours, and the Words move slow;
> Not so when swift *Camilla* scours the Plain,
> Flies o'er th' unbending Corn, and skims along the main.

From these Lines, laboured with great Attention, and celebrated
by a rival Wit, may be judged what can be expected from the most
diligent Endeavours after this Imagery of Sound. The Verse
intended to represent the Whisper of the Vernal Breeze, must
surely be confessed, not much to excel in Softness or Volubility;
and the smooth Stream, runs with a perpetual Clash of jarring
Consonants. The Noise and Turbulence of the Torrent, is, indeed,
distinctly imaged; for it requires very little Skill to make our
Language rough. But in the Lines, which mention the Effort of
Ajax, there is no particular Heaviness or Delay. The Swiftness of
Camilla is rather contrasted than exemplified. Why the Verse
should be lengthened to express Speed, will not easily be discovered. In the Dactyls used for that Purpose by the Ancients,
two short Syllables were pronounced with such Rapidity, as to be
equal only to one long; they, therefore, naturally exhibit the Act
of passing through a Long space in a short Time. But the *Alexan-
drine*, by its Pause in the Midst, is a tardy and stately Measure;
and the Word *unbending*, one of the most sluggish and slow which
our Language affords, cannot much accelerate its Motion.

These Rules and these Examples have taught our present
Criticks to enquire very studiously and minutely into Sounds and
Cadences. It is, therefore, useful to examine with what Skill they
have proceeded, what Discoveries they have made, and whether
any Rules can be established, which may guide us hereafter in such
Researches.

99

To love all Men is our Duty, so far as Love is opposed to Hatred,
and so far as it includes a general Habit of Benevolence, and
Readiness of occasional Kindness; but to love all equally is impossible, at least impossible without the Extinction of those Passions

which now produce all our Pains and all our Pleasures; without the Disuse, if not the Abolition, of some of our Faculties, and the Suppression of all our Hopes and Fears in Apathy and Indifference.

The Necessities of our Condition require a thousand Offices of Tenderness, which mere Regard for the Species will never dictate. Every Man has innumerable Grievances which only the Solicitude of Friendship will discover and remedy, and which would remain for ever unheeded in the mighty Heap of human Calamity, were it only surveyed by the Eye of general Benevolence equally attentive to every Misery.

106

No Place affords a more striking Conviction of the Vanity of human Hopes, than a publick Library; for who can see the Wall crouded on every Side by mighty Volumes, the Works of laborious Meditation and accurate Enquiry, now scarcely known but by the Catalogue, and preserved only to Encrease the Pomp of Learning, without considering how many Hours have been wasted in vain Endeavours, how often Imagination has anticipated the Praises of Futurity, how many Statues have risen to the Eye of Vanity, how many ideal Converts have elevated Zeal, how often Wit has exulted in the eternal Infamy of his Antagonists, and Ambition delighted in the gradual Advances of her Authority, the Immutability of his Decrees, and the Perpetuity of her Power?

> ——*Non unquam dedit*
> *Documenta Fors majora, quàm fragili loco*
> *Starent Superbi.*——

> Insulting chance ne'er call'd with louder voice,
> On swelling mortals to be proud no more.

Of the innumerable Authors whose Performances are thus treasured up in magnificent Obscurity, most are undoubtedly forgotten, because they have never deserved to be remembered, and owed the Honours which they once obtained, not to Judgment or to Genius, to Labour or to Art, but to the Prejudice of Faction, the Stratagems of Intrigue, or the Servility of Adulation.

Nothing is more common than to find Men whose Works are now totally neglected, mentioned with Praises by their Contemporaries, as the Oracles of their Age, and the Legislators of Learning. Curiosity is naturally excited, their Volumes after long

Enquiry are found, but seldom reward the Labour of the Search; every Period of Time has produced those Bubbles of artificial Fame, which are kept up a while by the Breath of Fashion, and then break at once and are forgotten. The Learned often bewail the Loss of ancient Writers whose Characters have survived their Works; but, perhaps, if we could now retrieve them, we should find them only the *Granvilles*, *Montagues*, *Stepneys*, and *Sheffeilds* of their Time, and wonder by what Infatuation or Caprice they rose to Reputation.

It cannot, however, be denied, that many have sunk into Oblivion whom it were unjust to number with this despicable Class. Various Kinds of literary Fame seem destined to various Measures of Duration. Some spread into Exuberance with a very speedy Growth, but soon wither and decay; some rise more slowly, but last long. *Parnassus* has its Flowers of transient Fragrance, as well as its Oaks of towering Height, and its Laurels of eternal Verdure.

Among those whose Reputation is exhausted in a short Time by its own Luxuriance, are the Writers who take Advantage of some present Incidents or Characters which strongly interest the Passions and engage universal Attention. It is not difficult to obtain Readers when we discuss a Question which every one is desirous to understand, which is debated in every Assembly, and which has divided the Nation into Parties; or when we display the Faults or Virtues of him whose publick Conduct has made almost every Man his Enemy or his Friend. To the quick Circulation of such Productions every Motive of Interest and Vanity concurs; the Disputant enlarges his Knowledge, the Zealot animates his Passion, and every Man is desirous to inform himself concerning Affairs so vehemently agitated and variously represented.

112

When female Minds are imbittered by Age or Solitude, their Malignity is generally exerted in a rigorous and spiteful Superintendence of domestic Trifles. *Eriphile* has employed her Eloquence for twenty Years upon the Degeneracy of Servants, the Nastiness of her House, the Ruin of her Furniture, the Difficulty of preserving Tapestry from the Moths, and the Carelesness of the Sluts whom she employs in brushing it. It is her Business every Morning to visit all the Rooms, in Hopes of finding a Chair without its Cover, a Window shut or open contrary to her Orders, a Spot on the Hearth, or a Feather on the Floor, that the rest of the Day may be justifiably spent in Taunts of Contempt and Vociferations of Anger. She lives for no other Purpose but to preserve the Neatness of a House and Gardens, and feels neither Inclination to Vice, nor Aspiration after Virtue, while she is engrossed by the great Employment of keeping Gravel from Grass, and Wainscot from Dust. Of three amiable Nieces she has declared herself an irreconcileable Enemy to one, because she broke off a Tulip with her Hoop; to another, because she spilt her Coffee on a Turkey Carpet; and to the third, because she let a wet Dog run into the Parlour. She has broken off her Intercourse of Visits because Company makes a House dirty, and resolves to confine herself more to her own Affairs, and to live no longer in Mire by foolish Lenity and Indulgence.

Peevishness is generally the Vice of narrow Minds, and, except when it is the Effect of Anguish and Disease, by which the Resolution is broken, and the Mind made too feeble to bear the lightest Addition to its Miseries, proceeds from an unreasonable Persuasion of the Importance of Trifles. The proper Remedies against it are the Consideration of the Dignity of human Nature, and of the Folly of suffering Perturbation and Uneasiness from Failures unworthy of our Notice.

He that resigns his Peace to little Casualties, and suffers the Course of his Life to be interrupted by fortuitous Inadvertencies, or trivial Offences, delivers up himself to the Direction of the Wind, and loses all **that** Constancy and Equanimity which constitute the chief Praise of a wise Man.

The Province of Prudence lies between the greatest Things and the least; some surpass our Power by their Magnitude, and some escape our Notice by their Number and their Frequency. But Life will afford sufficient Exercise to every Understanding, and such is the Limitation of the human Powers, that by Attention to Trifles we must let Things of Importance pass unobserved. When we examine a Mite with a Glass we see nothing but a Mite.

That it is every Man's Interest to be pleased will need little Proof, that it is his Interest to please others Experience will inform him. It is therefore alike necessary to Happiness and Virtue, that he rid his Mind of Passions which make him uneasy to himself and hateful to the World, which enchain his Intellects and obstruct his Improvement.

114

Death is, as one of the Ancients observes, τὸ τῶν φοβερῶν φοβερώτατον, *of dreadful Things the most dreadful*, an Evil, beyond which, nothing can be threatened by sublunary Power, or feared from human Enmity or Vengeance. This Terrour should, therefore, be reserved as the last Resort of Authority, as the strongest and most operative of prohibitory Sanctions, and placed only before the Treasure of Life, to guard from Invasion what cannot be restored. To equal Robbery with Murder is to reduce Murder to Robbery, to confound in common Minds the Gradations of Injury, and incite the Commission of a greater Crime, to prevent the Detection of a less. If only Murder were punished with Death, very few Robbers would stain their Hands in Blood; but when, by the last Act of Cruelty no new Danger is incurred, and Security may probably be obtained, upon what Principle shall we bid them forbear?

It may be urged, that the Sentence is often mitigated to simple Robbery; but surely this is to confess that our Laws are unreasonable in our own Opinion; and, indeed, it may be observed, that all but Murderers have, at their last Hour, the common Sensations of Mankind pleading in their Favour.

From this Conviction of the Inequality of the Punishment to the Offence proceeds the frequent Solicitations of Pardons. They who would rejoice at the Correction of a Thief, are yet shocked at the Thought of destroying him. His Crime is extenuated by comparing it with his Misery, and Severity defeats itself by exciting Pity.

The Gibbet, indeed, certainly disables those who dye upon it from infesting the Community, but their Death seems not to contribute more to the Reformation of their Associates than any other Method of Separation. A Thief seldom passes much of his Time in Recollection or Anticipation, but from Robbery hastens to Riot, and from Riot to Robbery; nor when the Grave has closed upon his Companion has any other Care than to find another.

The Frequency of capital Punishments rarely hinders the Commission of a Crime, but generally prevents its Detection, and is, if we reason only upon prudential Principles, chiefly for that Reason, to be avoided. Whatever may be urged by Casuists or Politicians, the greater Part of Mankind, as they can never think that to pick the Pocket and to pierce the Heart are equal, will scarcely believe, that two Malefactors so different in Guilt can be justly doomed to the same Punishment; nor is the Necessity of submitting the Conscience to human Laws so plainly evinced, or so clearly stated, but that the Pious, the Tender, and the Just, will always scruple to concur with the Community in an Act which their private Judgment cannot approve.

He who knows not how often rigorous Laws produce total Impunity, and how many Crimes are concealed and forgotten for Fear of hurrying the Offender into that State in which there is no Repentance, has conversed very little with Mankind. And whatever Epithet of Reproach or Contempt this Compassion may incur from those who confound Cruelty with Firmness, I know not whether any wise Man would wish it less powerful or less extensive.

115

Camilla professed a boundless Contempt for the Folly, Levity, Ignorance, and Impertinence of her own Sex, and very frequently expressed her Wonder that Men of Learning or Experience could submit to trifle away Life with Beings incapable of solid Thought. In mixed Companies she always associated with the Men, and declared her Satisfaction when the Ladies retired. If any short Excursion into the Country was proposed, she commonly insisted upon the Exclusion of Women from the Party; because, where they were admitted, the Time was wasted in frothy Compliments, weak Indulgencies, and idle Ceremonies. To shew the Greatness of her Mind she avoided all Compliance with the Fashion, and to boast the Profundity of her Knowledge mistook the various Textures of Silk, confounded Tabbies with Damasks, and sent for Ribbands by wrong Names. She despised the useless Commerce of Visits, a Farce of empty Form without Sincerity and without Instruction, and congratulated herself that she never learned the low Stile of Message Cards. She often applauded the noble sentiment of *Plato*, who rejoiced that he was born a Man rather than a Woman, proclaimed her Approbation of *Swift's* Opinion, that Women are only a higher Species of Monkies, and confessed, that when she considered the Behaviour, or heard the Conversation of her Sex, she could not but forgive the *Turks* for suspecting them to want Souls.

It was the Joy and Pride of *Camilla* to have provoked by this contemptuous Insolence, all the Rage of Hatred, and all the

Persecutions of Calumny; nor was she ever more elevated with her own Superiority, than when she talked of Female Anger, and Female Cunning. Well, says she, has Nature provided that such Virulence should be disabled by Folly, and such Cruelty be restrained by Impotence.

Camilla doubtless expected that what she lost on one Side she should gain on the other, and imagined that every male Heart would be open to a Lady who made such generous Advances to the Borders of Virility. But Man, ungrateful Man, instead of springing forward to meet her, shrunk back at her Approach. She was persecuted by the Ladies as a Deserter, and at best received by the Men only as a Fugitive. I, for my Part, amused myself a while with her Fopperies, but Novelty soon gave Way to Detestation, for nothing out of the common Order of Nature can be long born. I had no Inclination to a Wife who had the Ruggedness of a Man without his Force, and the Ignorance of a Woman without her Softness; nor could I think my Quiet and Honour to be entrusted to such audacious Virtue as was hourly courting Danger and soliciting Assault.

121

To imitate the Fictions and Sentiments of *Spencer* can incur no Reproach, for Allegory is perhaps one of the most pleasing Vehicles of Instruction. But I am very far from extending the same Respect to his Diction or his Stanza. His Diction was in his own Time allowed to be vicious, darkened with old Words and Peculiarities of Phrase, and so remote from common Use, that *Johnson* boldly pronounces him to have written no Language. His Stanza is at once difficult and unpleasing; tiresome to the Ear by its Uniformity, and to the Attention by its Length. It was at first formed in Imitation of the *Italian* Poets, without due Regard to the Genius of our Language. The *Italians* have so little Variety of Terminations, that they were forced to contrive a Stanza which may admit the greatest Number of similar Rhimes; but our Words end with so much Diversity, that it is seldom convenient for us to bring more than two of the same Sound together. If it be justly observed by *Milton*, that Rhime obliges Poets to express their Thoughts in improper Words, these Improprieties must always be multiplied, as the Difficulty of Rhime is encreased by long Concatenations.

The Imitators of *Spencer* are indeed not very rigid Censors of

H

themselves, for they seem to conclude that when they have dis-
figured their Lines with a few obsolete Syllables they have accomplished their Design, without considering that the Laws of Imitation are broken by every Word introduced since the Time of
Spencer, as the Character of *Hector* is violated by quoting *Aristotle*
in the Play. It would indeed be difficult to exclude from a long
Poem all modern Phrases, though it is easy to sprinkle it with
Gleanings of Antiquity. Perhaps, indeed, the Stile of *Spencer* might
by long Labour be justly copied, but Life is surely given us for
higher Purposes than to gather what our Ancestors have wisely
thrown away, and to learn what is of no Value but because it has
been forgotten.

122

Of the various Kinds of Speaking or Writing, which serve
Necessity or promote Pleasure, none appears so artless or easy as
simple Narration; for what should make him that knows the
whole Order and Progress of an Affair unable to relate it? Yet we
hourly find such as endeavour to entertain or instruct us by
Recitals, clouding the Facts which they intend to illustrate, and
losing themselves and their Auditors in the Wilds of Digression,
or the Mazes of Confusion. When we have congratulated ourselves
upon a new Opportunity of Enquiry, and new Means of Information, it often happens, that without designing either Deceit or
Concealment, without Ignorance of the Fact, or Unwillingness to
disclose it, the Relator fills the Ear with empty Sounds, harrasses
the Attention with fruitless Impatience, and disturbs the Imagination by a Tumult of Events without Order of Time or Train of
Consequence.

It is natural to imagine upon the same Principle, that no Writer
has a more easy Task than the Historian. The Philosopher has the
Works of Omniscience to examine, and is therefore engaged in
Disquisitions to which finite Intellects are utterly unequal. The
Poet trusts to his Invention, and is not only in Danger of those
Inconsistencies, to which every one is exposed by Departure from
Truth, but may be censured as well for the Deficiencies of his
Matter, as for the Irregularity of Disposition, or Impropriety of
Ornament. But the happy Historian has no other Labour than of
gathering what Tradition pours down before him, or Records
treasure for his Use. He has only the Actions and Designs of Men

like himself to conceive and to relate, and is not blamed for the Inconsistency of Statesmen, the Injustice of Tyrants, or the Cowardice of Commanders. The Difficulty of making Variety consistent, or uniting Probability with Surprize needs not disturb him; the Manners and Actions of his Personages are already fixed, his materials are provided and put into his Hands, and he is at Leisure to employ all his Powers in arranging and displaying them.

Yet even with these Advantages very few in any Age have been able to raise themselves to Reputation by writing Histories, and among the innumerable Authors who fill every Nation with Accounts of their Ancestors, or undertake to transmit to Futurity the Events of their own Time, very few, when Fashion and Novelty have ceased to recommend them, are of any other Use than chronological Memorials, which Necessity may sometimes require to be consulted, but which fright away Curiosity and disgust Criticism.

It has been observed, that this Nation, which has produced so many Authors eminent for almost every other Species of literary Excellence, has been hitherto remarkably barren of historical Genius; and so far has this Defect raised Prejudices against us, that some have doubted whether an Englishman can stop at that Mediocrity of Stile, or confine his Mind to that even Tenour of Sentiment which Narrative requires.

They who imagine that Nature has so capriciously distributed Understanding, have surely no Claim to the Honour of serious Confutation. The Inhabitants of the same Country have opposite Characters in different Ages; the Prevalence or Neglect of any particular Study can proceed only from the accidental Influence of some temporary Cause; and if we have failed in History, we can have failed only because History has not hitherto been diligently cultivated.

But how is it evident that we have not Historians among us whom we may venture to place in Comparison with any that the neighbouring Nations can produce. The Attempt of *Raleigh* is deservedly celebrated for the Labour of his Researches, and the Elegance of his Stile; but he has indeed rather endeavoured to exert his Judgment than his Genius, to select Facts rather than adorn them, and has therefore, produced an historical Dissertation, but seldom risen to the Majesty of History.

The Work of *Clarendon* deserves more Regard. His Stile is indeed neither exact in itself nor suited to the Purpose of History. It is the Effusion of a Mind crouded with Ideas, and desirous of imparting them, and therefore always accumulating Words and involving one Clause and Sentence in another. But there is always Dignity in his Negligence, a rude inartificial Majesty, which, without the Niceties of laboured Elegance, swells the Mind by its Plenitude and Diffusion. His Narration is not perhaps sufficiently rapid, but stopped too frequently by Particularities, which though they might strike the Author who was present at the Transactions, will not equally detain the Attention of Posterity. But his Ignorance or Carelesness of the Art of Writing are amply compensated by his Knowledge of Nature and of Policy, the Wisdom of his Maxims, the Justness of his Reasonings, and the Variety, Distinctness, and Strength of his Characters.

But none of our Writers can, in my Opinion, justly contest the Superiority of *Knolles*, who, in his History of the *Turks*, has displayed all the Excellencies that Narration can admit. His Stile, though somewhat obscured by Time, and sometimes vitiated by false Wit, is pure, nervous, elevated, and clear. A wonderful Multiplicity of Events is so artfully arranged and so distinctly explained, that each facilitates the Knowledge of the next. Whenever a new Personage is introduced the Reader is prepared by his Character for his Actions. When a Nation is first attacked, or City besieged, he is made acquainted with its History, or Situation, so that a great Part of the World is brought into View. His Descriptions are without Minuteness, and his Digressions without Ostentation; and collateral Events are so artfully woven into the Contexture of his principal Story, that they cannot be disjoined without leaving it lacerated and broken. There is nothing turgid in his Dignity, nor superfluous in his Copiousness. His Orations only, which he feigns, like the ancient Historians, to have been pronounced on remarkable Occasions, are tedious and languid; and since they are merely the voluntary Sports of Imagination, prove how much the most judicious and skilful may be mistaken in the Estimate of their own Powers.

Nothing could have sunk this Author in Obscurity but the Remoteness and Barbarity of the People whose Story he relates. It seldom happens that all Circumstances concur to Happiness or Fame. The Nation which produced this great Historian has the

rief of seeing his Genius employed upon a foreign and unin-
eresting Subject; and that Writer, who might have secured
'erpetuity to his Name by a History of his own Country, has
xposed himself to the Danger of Oblivion by recounting Enter-
rizes and Revolutions of which none desire to be informed.

125

here is scarce any Tragedy of the last Century which has not
ebased its most important Incidents, and polluted its most
erious Interlocutions with Buffoonery and Meanness; but though
erhaps it cannot be pretended that the present Age has added
much to the Force and Efficacy of the Drama, it has at least been
ble to escape many Faults, which either Ignorance had overlooked
r Indulgence had licensed. The later Tragedies indeed have Faults
f another Kind, perhaps more destructive to Delight, though less
pen to Censure. That perpetual Tumour of Phrase with which
very Thought is now expressed by every Personage, the Paucity
f Adventures which Regularity admits and the unvaried Equality
f flowing Dialogue, has taken away from our present Writers
lmost all that Dominion over the Passions which was the Boast of
heir Predecessors, yet they may at least claim this Commendation,
hat they avoid gross Faults, and that if they cannot often move
errour or Pity, they are always careful not to provoke Laughter.

135

hould any Man pursue his Acquaintances to their Retreats, he
ould find few of them listening to *Philomel*, loitering in Woods,
r plucking Dasies, catching the healthy Gale of the Morning, or
atching the gentle Coruscations of declining Day. Some will
e discovered at a Window, by the Road Side, rejoicing when a
ew Cloud of Dust gathers towards them, as at the Approach of a
omentary Supply of Conversation, and a short Relief from the
ediousness of unideal Vacancy. Others are placed in the adjacent
illages, where they look only upon Houses, as in the rest of the
ear, with no Change of Objects, but what a Remove to any new
treet in *London* might have given them. The same Set of Acquain-
nces still settle together, and the Form of Life is no otherwise

diversified than by doing the same Things in a different Place
They pay and receive Visits in the usual Form, they frequent the
Walks in the Morning, they deal Cards at Night, they attend to
the same Tattle, and dance with the same Partners; nor can they
at their Return to their former Habitation congratulate themselve
on any other Advantage, than that they have passed their Time
like others of the same Rank, and have the same Right to talk of
the Happiness and Beauty of the Country, of Happiness which
they never felt, and Beauty which they never regarded.

To be able to procure its own Entertainments, and to subsist
upon its own Stock, is not the Prerogative of every Mind. There are
indeed Understandings so fertile and comprehensive, that they can
always feed Reflection with new Supplies, and suffer nothing from
the Preclusion of adventitious Amusements, as some Cities have
within their own Walls enclosed Ground enough to feed their
Inhabitants in a Siege. But others live only from Day to Day, and
must be constantly enabled, by foreign Supplies to keep out the
Encroachments of Languor and Stupidity. Such could not indeed
be blamed for hovering within Reach of their usual Pleasures,
more than any other Animal for not quitting its native Element,
were not their Faculties contracted by their own Fault. But let
not those who go into the Country, merely because they dare not
be left alone at Home, boast their Love of Nature or their Qualifica
tions for Solitude, nor pretend that they receive instantaneous
Infusions of Wisdom from the Dryads, and are able when they
leave Smoke and Noise behind, to act, or think, or reason for
themselves.

139

——Sit quod vis simplex duntaxat et unum.　　　　Ho

Let ev'ry piece be simple and be one.

It is required by *Aristotle* to the Perfection of a Tragedy, and is
equally necessary to every other Species of regular Composition
that it should have a Beginning, a Middle and an End. "The
Beginning, says he, is that which hath nothing necessarily
previous, but to which that which follows is naturally consequent;
the End, on the contrary, is that which by Necessity, or at least
according to the common Course of Things, succeeds something
else, but which implies nothing consequent to itself; the Middle is

connected on one Side to something that naturally goes before, and on the other to something that naturally follows it."

Such is the Rule laid down by this great Critick for the Disposition of the different Parts of a well constituted Fable. It must begin where it may be made intelligible without Introduction, and end where the Mind is left in Repose, without Expectation of any farther Event. The intermediate Passages must join the last Effect to the first Cause, by a regular and unbroken Concatenation, nothing must be therefore inserted which does not apparently arise from something foregoing, and evidently make way for something that succeeds it.

This Precept is to be understood in its Rigour, only with Respect to great and essential Events, and cannot be extended in the same Force, to minuter Circumstances, and unessential Decorations, which yet are more happy, as they contribute more to the main Design.

It is always a Proof of extensive Thought and accurate Circumspection to promote various Purposes by the same Act, and the Idea of an Ornament admits Use, though it seems to exclude Necessity.

Whoever purposes, as it is expressed by *Milton, to build the lofty Rhyme,* must acquaint himself with the Laws of poetical Architecture, and take Care that his Edifice be solid as well as beautiful, that nothing stand single or independent so as that it may be taken away without injuring the rest, but that from the Foundation to the Pinnacles one Part rest firm upon another.

This regular and consequential Distribution, is frequently neglected, but the Failures of those, whose Example can have no Influence, may be safely overlooked; nor is it of much Use to recall obscure and unregarded Names to Memory for the sake of Sporting with their Infamy. But if there is any Writer whose Genius can embellish Impropriety, and whose Authority can make Error venerable, his Works are the proper Objects of critical Inquisition. To expunge Faults where there are no Excellencies is a Task equally vain with that of the Chemist, who employs the Arts of Separation and Refinement upon Ore which contains no precious Metal to reward his Operations.

The Tragedy of *Samson Agonistes* has been celebrated as the second Performance of the great Author of *Paradise Lost,* and opposed with all the Confidence of Triumph to the dramatick Per-

formances of other Nations. It contains indeed many noble Senti
ments, Maxims of Wisdom, and Oracles of Piety, and innumerable
Passages written with the antient Spirit of choral Poetry, in
which there is a just and pleasing Mixture of *Seneca*'s moral
Declamation, and the wild Enthusiasm of the *Greek* Writers. It is
therefore worthy of Examination whether a Performance thus
illuminated with Genius, and enriched with Learning, be composed
according to the indispensable Laws of *Aristotelian* Criticism, and
omitting at present all other Considerations, whether it contains a
Beginning, a Middle, and an End.

The Beginning is undoubtedly beautiful and proper, opening
with a graceful Abruptness, and proceeding naturally to a mournful
Recital of Facts necessary to be known.

> *Samson.* A little onward lend thy guiding Hand
> To these dark Steps, a little farther on;
> For yonder Bank hath Choice of Sun and Shade;
> There I am wont to sit, when any Chance
> Relieves me from my Task of servile Toil,
> Daily in the common Prison else enjoin'd me. . . .
> —O wherefore was my Birth from Heav'n foretold
> Twice by an Angel? . . .
> —Why was my Breeding order'd and prescrib'd
> As of a Person separate to God,
> Design'd for great Exploits; if I must die
> Betray'd, captiv'd, and both my Eyes put out? . . .
> Whom have I to complain of but myself?
> Who this high Gift of Strength committed to me,
> In what Part lodg'd, how easily bereft me,
> Under the Seat of Silence could not keep,
> But weakly to a Woman must reveal it.

His Soliloquy is interrupted by a Chorus or Company of Men of his
own Tribe, who condole his Miseries, extenuate his Fault, and
conclude with a solemn Vindication of divine Justice. So that at
the Conclusion of the first Act there is no Design laid, no Discovery
made, nor any Disposition formed towards the subsequent
Event.

In the second Act *Manoah*, the Father of *Samson*, comes to see
his Son, and, being shown him by the Chorus, breaks out into
Lamentations of his Misery, and Comparisons of his present with
his former State, and represents to him the Ignominy which his
Religion suffers, by the Festival this Day celebrated, in Honour of
Dagon to whom the Idolaters ascribed his Overthrow.

236

———Thou bear'st
Enough, and more the Burthen of that Fault;
Bitterly has thou paid, and still art paying
That rigid Score. A worse Thing yet remains,
This Day the *Philistines* a pop'lar Feast
Here celebrate in *Gaza*; and proclaim
Great Pomp and Sacrifice, and Praises loud
To *Dagon*, as their God, who hath deliver'd
Thee, *Samson*, bound and blind into their Hands,
Them out of thine, who slew'st them many a slain.

Samson, touched with this Reproach, makes a Reply equally penitential and pious, which his Father considers as the Effusion of prophetick Confidence.

    Samson.   ———He, be sure,
Will not connive or linger thus provok'd,
But will arise and his great Name assert:
Dagon must stoop, and shall e'er long receive
Such a Discomfit, as shall quite despoil him
Of all these boasted Trophies won on me.

    Manoah. With Cause this Hope relieves thee, and these Words
I as a Prophecy receive; for God,
Nothing more certain, will not long defer
To vindicate the Glory of his Name.

This Part of the Dialogue, as it might tend to animate or exasperate *Samson*, cannot, I think be censured as wholly superfluous, but the succeeding Dispute, in which *Samson* contends to die, and which his Father breaks off, that he may go to solicit his Release, is only valuable for its own Beauties, and has no Tendency to introduce any Thing that follows it.

The next Event of the Drama is the Arrival of *Dalilah*, with all her Graces, Artifices and Allurements. This produces a Dialogue, in a very high Degree, elegant and instructive, from which she retires after she has exhausted her Persuasions, and is no more seen or heard of, nor has her Visit any Effect but that of raising the Character of *Samson*.

In the fourth Act enters *Harapha*, the Giant of *Gath*, whose Name had never been mentioned before, and who has now no other Motive of coming, than to see the Man whose Strength and Actions are so loudly celebrated.

> *Harapha.*——Much I have heard
> Of thy prodigious Might, and Feats perform'd,
> Incredible to me, in this displeas'd,
> That I was never present in the Place
> Of those Encounters, where we might have tried
> Each others Force in Camp or listed Fields:
> And now am come to see of whom such Noise
> Hath walk'd about, and each Limb to survey,
> If thy Appearance answer loud Report.

Samson challenges him to the Combat, and after an Interchange of Reproaches, elevated by repeated Defiance on one Side, and imbittered by contemptuous Insults on the other, *Harapha* retires, and we hear it determined, by *Samson* and the Chorus, that no Consequence good or bad will proceed from their Interview.

> *Chorus.* He will directly to the Lords, I fear,
> And with malicious Counsel stir them up
> Some Way or other farther to afflict thee.

> *Samson.* He must allege some Cause, and offer'd Fight
> Will not dare mention, lest a Question rise,
> Whether he durst accept the Offer or not;
> And that he durst not, plain enough appear'd.

At last, in the fifth Act, appears a Messenger with a Summons from the Lords assembled at the Festival of *Dagon*, by which *Samson* is required to come and entertain them with some Proof of his Strength. *Samson*, after a short Expostulation, dismisses him with a firm and resolute Refusal, but during the Absence of the Messenger, having awhile defended the Propriety of his Conduct, he at last declares himself moved by a secret Impulse to comply, and utters some dark Presages of a great Event to be brought to pass by his Agency under the Direction of Providence.

> *Samson.* Be of good Courage; I begin to feel
> Some rousing Motions in me, which dispose
> To something extraordinary my Thoughts.
> I with this Messenger will go along,
> Nothing to do, be sure, that may dishonour
> Our law, or stain my Vow of Nazarite,
> If there be ought of Presage in the Mind,
> This Day will be remarkable in my Life
> By some great Act, or of my Days the last.

While *Samson* is conducted off by the Messenger, his Father returns with Hopes of Success in his Solicitation, upon which he confers with the Chorus till their Dialogue is interrupted, first by a Shout of Triumph, and afterwards by Screams of Horror and Agony. While they are deliberating where they shall be secure, a Man who had been present at the Shew enters and relates how *Samson* having prevailed on his Guide to suffer him to lean against the main Pillars of the theatrical Edifice, tore down the Roof upon Spectators and himself.

> ——Those two massy Pillars,
> With horrible Confusion to and fro,
> He tugg'd, he shook, till down they came and drew
> The whole Roof after them, with Burst of Thunder,
> Upon the Heads of all who sat beneath.——
> ——*Samson* with these immixt inevitably
> Pull'd down the same Destruction on himself.

This is undoubtedly a just and regular Catastrophe, and the Poem, therefore, has a Beginning and an End, which *Aristotle* himself could not have disapproved, but it must be allowed to want a Middle, since nothing passes between the first Act and the last, that either hastens or delays the Death of *Samson*. The whole Drama, if its Superfluities be cut off, would scarcely fill a single Act, yet this is the Tragedy which Ignorance has admired, and Bigotry applauded.

141

Hilarisque, tamen cum pondere virtus.　　　　STAT.

Greatness with ease, and gay severity.

To the RAMBLER.

SIR,

The Politicians have long observed that the greatest Events may be often traced back to very trivial Causes, and that a petty Competition or casual Friendship, the Prudence of a Slave, or the Garrulity of a Woman have hindered or promoted the most important Schemes, and hastened or retarded the Revolutions of Empire.

Whoever shall review his Life will generally find, that the whole Tenor of his Conduct has been determined by some Accident of no apparent Moment, or by a Combination of inconsiderable Circumstances, acting when his Imagination was unoccupied, and his Judgment unsettled; and that his Principles and Actions have taken their Colour from some secret Infusion, mingled without Design in the Current of his Ideas. The Desires that predominate in our Hearts, are instilled by imperceptible Communications at the Time when we look upon the various Scenes of the World, and the different Employments of Men, with the Neutrality of Inexperience, and we come forth from the Nursery or the School, invariably destined to the Pursuit of Riches or of Fame, of great Acquisitions or petty Accomplishments.

Such was the Impulse by which I have been kept in Motion from my earliest Years. I was born to an Inheritance which gave me a Claim in my Childhood to Distinction and Caresses, and I suppose therefore that I was accustomed to hear my own Applauses, before they had much Influence on my Thoughts. The first Praise of which I remember myself sensible was that of good Humour, which, whether I deserved it or not, when it was first bestowed, I have since made it my whole Business to propagate and maintain.

When I was sent to School, the Gaiety of my Look, and the Liveliness of my Loquacity soon gained me Admission to Hearts not yet fortified against Affection by Artifice or Interest. I was entrusted with every Stratagem, adopted into every Party, associated in every Sport; my Company gave Alacrity to a Frolick, and Gladness to a Holiday. I was indeed so much employed in adjusting or executing Schemes of Diversion that I had no Leisure for my Tasks, but was always furnished with Exercises, and instructed in my Lessons by some kind Patron of the higher Classes, and my Master either not suspecting my Deficiency, or unwilling to detect what his Kindness would not have suffered him to punish, nor his Impartiality to excuse, commonly allowed me to escape with a very slight Examination, laughed at the Pertness of my Ignorance, and the Sprightliness of my Absurdities, and could seldom forbear to show that he regarded me with such tenderness, as Parts and Learning can seldom excite.

From School I was at the usual Age dismissed to the University, where I soon drew upon me the Notice of the younger Students, and was the constant Partner of their Morning Walks and Evening Compotations. I was not indeed much celebrated for my Learning, but was looked on with Indulgence as a Man of Parts, who wanted nothing but the Dullness of a Scholar, and might become eminent, whenever I should condescend to Labour and Attention. My Tutor at first reproached me with Negligence, and attempted to repress my Sallies with the Superciliousness of lettered Gravity, yet having natural good Humour lurking in his Heart, he could not long hold out against the Power of Hilarity, but after a few Months began to relax the Muscles of disciplinarian Moroseness, received me with Smiles after an Elopement, and that he might not betray his Trust to his Fondness was content to spare my Diligence by encreasing his own.

Thus I continued to dissipate the Gloom of collegiate Austerity, to waste my own Life in thoughtless Idleness, and lure others from their Studies, till the happy Hour arrived, when in the regular Progress of Education, I was sent to *London*. I soon discovered the Town to be the proper Element of a gay Character, for here I was quickly distinguished as a Wit by the Ladies, a Species of Beings, of whom I had only heard at the University, and to whom I had no sooner the Happiness of a nearer Approach, than I devoted all my Faculties to the Ambition of pleasing them.

A wit, Mr *Rambler*, in the Ladies Dialect, is not always a Man, who by the Action of a vigorous Fancy upon comprehensive Knowledge, brings distant Ideas unexpectedly together, or, by some peculiar Acuteness discovers Resemblances in Objects dissimilar to common Eyes, and by mixing heterogeneous Notions dazzles the Attention with sudden Scintillations of Conceit. A Lady's Wit is a Man who can make Ladies laugh, to which, however easy it may seem, many Gifts of Nature, and Attainments of Art commonly concur. He that hopes to be received as a Wit in female Assemblies must have a Form neither so amiable as to strike with Admiration, nor so coarse as to raise Disgust; and an Understanding too feeble to be dreaded, too forcible to be despised. The other Parts of the Character are more subject to Variation; it was formerly essential to a Wit, that his Wig should cover half his Back with a snowy Fleece, and at a Time yet more remote no Man was a Wit without his Boots; in the Days of the Spectator a Snuff-box seems to have been indispensable, but in my Time an embroidered Coat was sufficient, without any precise Regulation of the Rest of his Dress.

But Wigs and Boots and Snuff-boxes are vain without a perpetual Resolution to be merry, and who can always find Supplies of Mirth? *Juvenal* indeed, in his Comparison of the two opposite Philosophers, wonders only whence an unexhausted Fountain of Tears could be discharged, but had *Juvenal*, with all his Spirit,

241

undertaken my Province, he would have found constant Gaiety equally difficult to be supported. Consider, Mr *Rambler*, and compassionate the Condition of a Man who has taught every Company to expect from him, a continual Feast of Laughter, an unintermitted Stream of Jocularity. The Task of every other Slave has an End. The Rower in time reaches the Port, the Lexicographer at last finds the Conclusion of his Alphabet, only the hapless Wit has his Labour always to begin, the Call for Novelty is never satisfied, and one Jest only raises Expectation of another.

I know that among Men of Learning and Asperity the Retainers to the female World are not considered with much Regard; yet I cannot but hope that if you knew at how dear a Rate our Honours are purchased, you would look with some Gratulation on our Success, and with some Pity on our Miscarriages. Consider the Misery of him who is condemned to cultivate Barrenness, and romage Vacuity; who is obliged to continue his Talk when his Meaning is spent, to raise Merriment without Images, and to harrass his Imagination in quest of Thoughts which he cannot start, and his Memory in pursuit of Narratives which he cannot overtake; consider the Effort with which he strains to conceal Despondency by a Smile, and the Distress in which he sits while the Eyes of the Company are fixed upon him as the last Refuge from Silence and Depression.

It were endless to recount the Shifts to which I have been reduced, or to enumerate the different Species of artificial Wit. Sometimes I frequented Coffee-houses, and lived a Week upon an Expression, of which he who dropped it did not know the Value, and often I gleaned Jests from obsolete Farces. To collect Wit was indeed safe, for I consorted with none that looked much into Books, but to disperse it was the Difficulty. A seeming Negligence was sometimes useful, for I made a Reply not to what the Lady had said, but to what it was convenient for me to hear, and very few were so perverse as to rectify a Mistake which had given Occasion to a Burst of Merriment; sometimes I drew the Conversation up by Degrees to a proper Point, and produced a Conceit which I had treasured up, like Sportsmen who boast of killing the Foxes which they lodge in the Covert. Eminence is however sometimes gained at less Expence; I have delighted a whole Circle at one time with a Series of Quibbles, and made myself good Company at another by scalding my Fingers, or mistaking a Lady's Lap for my own Chair.

These are artful Deceits and useful Expedients; but Expedients are at length exhausted, and Deceits detected. Time itself, among other Injuries, diminishes the Power of pleasing, and I now find in my forty fifth Year many Pranks and Pleasantries very coldly received which have formerly filled a whole Room with Jollity and Exultation. I have learned at last that Gaiety must be supported by higher Qualities, and that Mirth can only please long as the Efflorescence of an exalted Mind loved for its Luxuriance, but esteemed for its Solidity.

I am,

Yours, &c.

PAPILIUS.

146

Many are the Consolations with which the unhappy Author endeavours to allay his Vexation, and fortify his Patience. He has written with too little Indulgence to the Understanding of common Readers; he has fallen upon an Age in which false Taste universally prevails, in which all Regard to solid Knowledge, and all Sense of delicate Refinement, have given Way to low Merriment and idle Buffoonry, and in which therefore no Writer can hope for Distinction, who has any higher Purpose than to raise Laughter. He finds that his Enemies, such as apparent Superiority will always raise, have been industrious, while his Performance was yet in the Press to vilify it, and that the Bookseller, whom he had resolved to enrich, has Rivals in his own Profession, who maliciously obstruct the Circulation of his Copies. He at last reposes upon the Consideration, that the noblest Works of Learning and Genius have always made their Way slowly against Ignorance and Prejudice, and that the Reputation which is never to be lost must be gradually obtained, as the Animals of longest Life are observed not soon to attain their full Stature and Strength.

By such Arts of voluntary Delusion does every Man endeavour to conceal his own Unimportance from himself. It is always long before we are convinced of the small Proportion which every Individual bears to the collective Body of Mankind, or learn how few can be interested in the Fortune of any single Man, how little Vacancy is left in the World for any new Object of Attention, and to how small Extent the brightest Blaze of Merit can be spread amidst the Mists of Business and of Folly, and how soon it is always clouded by the Intervention of other Novelties. Not only the Writer, but the Commander of Armies, and the Deliverer of Nations will easily outlive all noisy and popular Reputation: He will indeed be celebrated for a Time by the public Voice, but his Actions and his Name will soon be considered as remote and unaffecting, and will be rarely mentioned but by those whose Alliance or Dependance, gives them some Vanity to gratify by frequent Commemoration.

156

Nunquam aliud natura, aliud sapientia dicit.　　　Juv.

For wisdom ever echoes nature's voice.

Every Government, say the Politicians, is perpetually degenerating towards Corruption, from which it must be rescued at certain Periods by the Resuscitation of its first Principles, and the Reestablishment of its original Constitution. Every animal Body, according to the methodick Physicians, is by the Predominance of some exuberant Quality continually declining towards Disease and Death, which must be obviated by a seasonable Reduction of the peccant Humour to the just Equipoise which Health requires.

In the same Manner the Studies of Mankind, all, at least, which, not being subject to rigorous Demonstration, admit the Influence of Fancy and Caprice, are perpetually tending to Error and Confusion. The great Principles of Truth which the first Speculatists discovered, have their Simplicity embarrassed by ambitious Additions, or their Evidence obscured by inaccurate Augmentation, and as they descend from one Succession of Writers to another, like Light transmitted from Room to Room, they lose by Degrees their Strength and Splendor, and fade at last into total Evanescence.

It is necessary, therefore, to review the Systems of Learning, to analise Complications into Principles, and disentangle Knowledge from Opinion. It is not always possible, without a close and diligent Inspection, to separate the genuine Shoots of consequential Reasoning, which grow out of some radical Postulate, from the Branches which Art has engrafted on it. The accidental Prescriptions of Authority, when Time has procured them Veneration, are often confounded with the Laws of Nature, and those Rules are supposed coeval with Reason, of which the first Rise cannot be discovered.

Criticism, amidst her Endeavours to restrain the Licentiousness of Imagination, and detect the Stratagems of Fallacy, has suffered her Provinces to be invaded by those restless Powers; like the antient *Scythians*, by extending her Conquests over distant Regions; she has left her Throne vacant to her Slaves, and suffered Prejudice and Error to reign unmolested in her own Dominions.

Among the innumerable Rules which the natural Desire of extending Authority, or the honest Ardour of promoting Knowledge, has from Age to Age prompted Men of very different Abilities to prescribe to Writers, all which have been received and established, have not the same original Right to our Regard. Some are indeed to be considered as fundamental and indispensable, others only as useful and convenient; some as dictated by Reason and Necessity, others as enacted by despotick Antiquity; some as invincibly supported by their Conformity to the Order of Nature, and the Operations of the Intellect, others as formed by Accident, or instituted by Example, and therefore always liable to Dispute and Alteration.

That many Rules of Composition have been advanced by Criticks without consulting Nature or Reason, we cannot but suspect, when we find it peremptorily decreed by the antient Masters, that *only three speaking Personages should appear at once upon the Stage*, a Law which the Variety and Intricacy of modern Plays has made impossible to be observed, and which, therefore, we now violate without Scruple, and as Experience proves, without Inconvenience.

The Original of this Precept was merely accidental. Tragedy was a Monody or solitary Song in Honour of *Bacchus*, which was afterwards improved into a Dialogue by the Addition of another Speaker; but remembering that the Tragedy was at first pronounced only by one, they durst not for some Time venture beyond two; at last when Custom and Impunity had made them daring, they extended their Liberty to the Admission of three, but restrained themselves by a critical Edict from further Exorbitance.

By what Accident the Number of Acts was limited to five, I know not that any Author has informed us, but certainly it is not determined by any Necessity arising either from the Nature of Action or the Propriety of Exhibition. An Act is only the Representation of such a Part of the Business of the Play as proceeds in an unbroken Tenor without any intermediate Pause. Nothing is more evident than that of every real, and, by Consequence, of every dramatick Action, the Intervals may be more or fewer than five; and indeed the Rule is upon the *English* Stage, every Day broken in Effect, without any other Mischief than that which arises from an absurd Endeavour to observe it in Appearance. For whenever the Scene is shifted the Act ceases, since some Time is necessarily supposed to elapse while the Personages of the Drama change their Place.

With no greater Right to our Obedience have the Criticks confined the dramatic Action to a certain Number of Hours. Probability indeed requires that the Time of Action should approach somewhat nearly to that of Exhibition, and those Plays will always be thought most happily conducted which croud the greatest Variety into the least Space. But since it will frequently happen that some Delusion must be admitted, I know not where the Limits of Imagination can be fixed; nor have I ever observed, that Minds, not already prepossessed by Criticism, feel any Offence from the Extension of the Intervals between the Acts, nor can I conceive it absurd or impossible, that he who can multiply three Hours into twelve or twenty-four, might image with equal Ease a greater Number.

I know not whether he that professes to regard no other Laws than those of Nature, will not be inclined to receive Tragi-comedy to his Protection, whom, however generally condemned her own Laurels have hitherto shaded from the Fulminations of Criticism. For what is there in the mingled Drama which impartial Reason can condemn? The Connexion of important with trivial Incidents, since it is not only common but perpetual in the World, may surely be allowed upon the Stage, which pretends only to be the Mirrour of Life. The Impropriety of suppressing the Passions before we have raised them to the intended Agitation, and of diverting the Expectation from an Event which we keep suspended only to raise it, may be speciously urged. But will not Experience confute this Objection? Is it not certain that the tragic and comic Affections have been moved alternately with equal Force, and that no Plays have oftner filled the Eye with Tears and the Breast with

Palpitation, than those which are variegated with Interludes of Mirth?

I do not however think it always safe to judge of Works of Genius merely by the Event. These resistless Vicissitudes of the Heart, this alternate Prevalence of Merriment and Solemnity may sometimes be more properly ascribed to the Vigour of the Writer than the Justness of the Design, and instead of vindicating Tragi-Comedy by the Success of *Shakespear*, we ought perhaps to pay new Honours to that transcendant and unbounded Genius that could preside over the Passions in Sport, who to produce or actuate the Affections, needed not the slow Gradation of common Means, but could fill the Heart with instantaneous Jollity or Sorrow, and vary our Disposition as he changed his Scenes. Perhaps the Effects even of *Shakespear*'s Poetry might have been yet greater, had he not counter-acted himself, and we might have been more interested in the Distresses of his Heroes had we not been so frequently diverted by the Jokes of his Buffoons.

There are other Rules more fixed and obligatory; it is necessary that of every Play the chief Action should be single, because a Play represents some Transaction, through its regular Maturation to its final Event, and therefore two Transactions equally impor-tant must evidently constitute two Plays.

As the Design of Tragedy is to instruct by moving the Passions, it must always have a Hero or Personage apparently and in-contestably superior to the rest, upon whom the Attention may be fixed and the Expectation suspended. Of two Persons opposing each other with equal Abilities and equal Virtue, the Auditor will indeed inevitably in Time choose his Favourite, but as that Choice must be without any Cogency of Conviction, the Hopes or Fears which it raises will be faint and languid. Of two Heroes acting in Confederacy against a common Enemy, the Virtues or Dangers will give little Emotion, because each claims our Concern with the same Right, and the Heart lies at rest between equal Motives.

It ought to be the first Endeavour of a Writer to distinguish Nature from Custom, or that which is established because it is right, from that which is right only because it is established; that he may neither violate essential Principles by a Desire of Novelty, nor debar himself from the Attainment of any Beauties within his View by a needless Fear of breaking Rules which no literary Dictator had Authority to prescribe.

161

When I first cheapened my Lodgings, the Landlady told me, that she hoped I was not an Author, for the Lodgers on the first Floor had stipulated that the upper Rooms should not be occupied by a noisy Trade. I very readily promised to give no Disturbance to her Family, and soon dispatched a Bargain on the usual Terms.

I had not slept many Nights in my new Apartment before I began to inquire after my Predecessors, and found my Landlady whose Imagination is filled only with her own Affairs, very ready to give me Information.

Curiosity, like all other Desires, produces Pain, as well as Pleasure. Before she began her Narrative, I had heated my Head with Expectations of Adventures and Discoveries, of Elegance in Disguise and Learning in Distress, and was therefore somewhat mortified when I heard, that the first Tenant was a Taylor, of whom nothing was remembered but that he complained of his Room for want of Light, and, after having lodged in it a Month, in which he paid only a Week's Rent, pawned a Piece of Cloth which he was trusted to cut out, and was forced to make a precipitate Retreat from this Quarter of the Town.

The next was a young Woman newly arrived from the Country, who lived for five Weeks with great Regularity, and became by frequent Treats very much the Favourite of the Family, but at last received Visits so frequently from a Cousin in *Cheapside*, that she brought the Reputation of the House into Danger, and was therefore dismissed with good Advice.

The Room then stood empty for a Fortnight, so that my Landlady began to think that she had judged hardly, and often wished for such another Lodger. At last an elderly Man of a very grave Aspect, read the Bill, and bargained for the Room at the very first Price that was asked. He lived in very close Retirement, seldom went out till Evening, and then returned early, sometimes chearful, and at other Times dejected. It was remarkable, that whatever he purchased, he never had small Money in his Pocket, and though cool and temperate on other Occasions, was always vehement and stormy till he received his Change: He paid his Rent with great Exactness, and seldom failed once a Week to requite my Landlady's Civility with a Supper. At last, such is the Fate of human Felicity! the House was alarmed at Midnight by the

Constable, who demanded to search the Garrets. My Landlady assuring him that he had mistaken the Door, conducted him up Stairs, where he found the Tools of a Coiner; but the Tenant had crawled along the Roof to an empty House, and escaped; very much to the Joy of my Landlady, who declares him a very honest Man, and wonders why any Body should be hanged for making Money when such Numbers are in Want of it. She however confesses that she shall for the future always question the Character of those who take her Garret without beating down the Price.

The Bill was then placed again in the Window, and the poor Woman was teazed for seven Weeks by innumerable Passengers, who obliged her to climb with them every Hour up five Stories, and then disliked the Prospect, hated the Noise of a publick Street, thought the Stairs narrow, objected to a low Ceiling, required the Walls to be hung with fresher Paper, asked Questions about the Neighbourhood, could not think of living so far from their Acquaintance, wished the Window had looked to the South rather than the West, told how the Door and the Chimney might have been better disposed, bid her half the Price that she asked, or promised to give her Earnest the next Day, and came no more.

At last, a short meagre Man, in a tarnished Waistcoat, desired to see the Garret, and when he had stipulated for two long Shelves and a larger Table, hired it at a low price. When the Affair was completed, he looked round him with great Satisfaction, and repeated some Words which the Woman did not understand. In two Days he brought a great Box of Books, took Possession of his Room, and lived very inoffensively, except that he frequently disturbed the Inhabitants of the next Floor by unseasonable Noises. He was generally in Bed at Noon, but from Evening to Midnight he sometimes talked aloud with great Vehemence, sometimes stamped as in Rage, sometimes threw down his Poker, then clattered his Chairs, then sat down in deep Thought, and again burst out into loud Vociferations; sometimes he would sigh as oppressed with Misery, and sometimes shake with convulsive Laughter. When he encountered any of the Family he gave way or bowed, but rarely spoke, except that as he went up Stairs he often repeated,

——Ὅς ὑπέρτατα δώματα νάιει,

This habitant, th' aerial regions boast,

249

hard Words, to which his Neighbours listened so often, that the
learned them without understanding them. What was his Employ
ment she did not venture to ask him, but at last heard a Printer'
Boy enquire for the Author.

My Landlady was very often advised to beware of this strang
Man, who, though he was quiet for the present, might perhap
become outrageous in the hot Months, but as she was punctuall
paid, she could not find any sufficient Reason for dismissing him
till one Night he convinced her by setting Fire to his Curtain
that it was not safe to have an Author for her Inmate.

She had then for six Weeks a Succession of Tenants, who left th
House on Saturday, and instead of paying their Rent, rated thei
Landlady: At last she took in two Sisters, one of whom had spen
her little Fortune in procuring Remedies for a lingering Diseas
and was now supported and attended by the other; she climbe
with Difficulty to the Apartment, where she languished for eigh
Weeks without Impatience or Lamentation, except for the Ex
pence and Fatigue which her Sister suffered, and then calmly an
contentedly expired. The Sister followed her to the Grave, paid th
few Debts which they had contracted, wiped away the Tears
useless Sorrow, and returning to the Business of common Lif
resigned to me the vacant Habitation.

Such, Mr. *Rambler*, are the Changes which have happened in th
narrow Space where my present Fortune has fixed my Residenc
so true it is that Amusement and Instruction are always at Han
to those who have Skill and Willingness to find them, and so ju
is the observation of *Juvenal*, that a single House will shew wha
ever is done or suffered in the World.

I am, SIR, &c.

168

------*Decipit*
Frons prima multos, rara mens intelligit
Quod interiore condidit cura angulo.   PHÆDRU

The tinsel glitter, and the specious mein,
Delude the most; few pry behind the scene.

It has been observed by *Boileau*, that "a mean or common Thoug
expressed in pompous Diction, generally pleases more than a ne
or noble Sentiment delivered in low and vulgar Language; becau
the Number is much greater of those whom Custom has enabled

judge of Words, than of those whom Study has qualified to examine Things."

This Solution would be sufficient, if only those were offended with Meanness of Expression who are unable to distinguish Propriety of Thought, and to separate Propositions or Images from the Vehicles by which they are conveyed to the Understanding. But it is found that this Kind of Disgust is by no means confined to the ignorant or superficial; it operates uniformly and universally upon Readers of all Classes; every Man, however profound or abstracted, perceives himself irresistibly alienated by low Terms, and they who profess the most zealous Adherence to Truth are forced to admit that she owes Part of her Charms to her Ornaments, and loses much of her Power over the Soul, when she appears disgraced by a Dress uncouth or ill-adjusted.

We are all offended by low Terms, but we are not pleased or disgusted alike by the same Compositions, because we do not all agree to censure the same Terms as low. No Word is naturally or intrinsically meaner than another, and, therefore, our Notions of Words, as of other Things arbitrarily and capriciously established, depend wholly upon Accident and Custom. The Cottager thinks those Apartments splendid and spacious, which an Inhabitant of Palaces will despise for their Inelegance; and to him who has passed most of his Hours with the delicate and polite, many Expressions will seem despicable and sordid, which another, equally acute and judicious may hear without Offence; but a mean Term never fails to displease him who considers it as mean, as Poverty is certainly and invariably despised, though he who is poor in the Opinion of some, may by others be envied for his Wealth.

Words become low by the Occasions to which they are applied, or by the general Character of them who use them, and the Disgust which they produce, arises from the Revival of those Ideas with which they are commonly united. Thus if, in the most serious Discourse, a Phrase happens to occur which has before been successfully employed in some ludicrous Narrative, the most grave and serious Auditor finds it difficult to refrain from Laughter, when those whose Imagination is not prepossessed by the same accidental Association of Ideas, are utterly unable to guess the Reason of his Merriment. Words which convey Ideas of Dignity in one Age, are banished from elegant Writing or Conversation in another, because they are in time debased by vulgar Mouths, and can be no longer heard without the involuntary Recollection of unpleasing Images.

When *Macbeth* is confirming himself in his horrid Purpose, he breaks into the Violence of his Emotions into a Wish natural to a Murderer,

> —— Come, thick Night!
> And pall thee in the dunnest Smoke of Hell,
> That my keen Knife see not the Wound it makes;
> Nor Heav'n peep through the Blanket of the dark,
> To cry, hold, hold! ——

In this Passage is exerted all the Force of Poetry, that Force which calls new Powers into Being, which embodies Sentiment and animates lifeless Matter; yet perhaps scarce any Man ever perused it without some Disturbance of his Attention from the Counteraction of the Words to the Ideas. What can be more dreadful than to implore the Presence of Night, invested not in common Obscurity, but in the Smoke of Hell? Yet the Force of this Invocation is destroyed by the Insertion of an Epithet now seldom heard but in the Stable, and *dun* Night may come or go without any other Notice than Contempt.

If we start into Raptures when some Hero of the Iliad tells us that δόρυ μαίνεται, his Lance rages with Eagerness to destroy; if we are alarmed at the Terror of the Soldiers commanded by *Cæsar* to hew down the sacred Grove, who dreaded, says *Lucan*, that the Axe aimed at the Oak would fly back upon them,

> ——*Si robora sacra ferirent,*
> *In sua credebant redituras membra secures,*
>
> None dares with impious steel the grove to rend,
> Lest on himself the destin'd stroke descend.

we cannot surely but sympathise with the Horrors of a Wretch about to murder his Master, his Friend, his Benefactor, who suspects that the Weapon will refuse its Office, and start back from the Breast which he is preparing to violate. Yet this Sentiment is weakened by the Name of an Instrument used by Butchers and by Cooks in the meanest Employments; we do not immediately believe that any Crime of Importance is to be committed with a *Knife*, and at last from the long Habit of connecting a Knife with sordid Offices, feel Aversion rather than Terror.

Macbeth proceeds to wish, in the Madness of Guilt, that the Inspection of Heaven may be intercepted, and that he may in the

Involutions of infernal Darkness, escape the Eye of Providence. This is the utmost Extravagance of determined Wickedness; yet this is so much debased by two unfortunate Words, that, in this Instant while I am endeavouring to impress on my Reader the Energy of the Sentiment, I can scarce check my Risibility, when the Expression forces itself upon my Mind; for who can, without some Relaxation of his Gravity, hear of *Divinities peeping thro' a Blanket*.

These Imperfections of Diction are less obvious to the Reader, as he is less acquainted with the common Usages of the Age; they are therefore wholly imperceptible to a Foreigner, who learns our Language from Books, and will not so forcibly strike a solitary Academick as a modish Lady.

Among the numerous Requisites that must always concur to complete an Author, few are of more Importance than an early Entrance into the living World. The Seeds of Knowledge may be planted in Solitude, but must be cultivated in publick. Argumentation may be taught in Colleges, and Theories may be formed in Retirement, but the Artifice of Embellishment, and the Power of securing Attention must be gained by general Converse.

An Acquaintance with the prevailing Customs and fashionable Elegance is necessary likewise for other Purposes. The same Injury that noble Sentiments suffer from disagreeable Language, personal Merit may justly fear from Rudeness and Indelicacy. When the Success of *Æneas* depended on the Favour of the Queen upon whose Coasts he was driven, the Divinity that protected him thought him not sufficiently secured against Rejection by his Reputation for Bravery, but decorated him for the Interview with preternatural Beauty. Whoever desires, what none can reasonably contemn, the Favour of Mankind, must endeavour to add Grace to Strength, to make his Conversation agreeable as well as useful, and to accomplish himself with those petty Qualifications which are necessary to make the first Impressions in his Favour. Many complain of Neglect who never used any Efforts to attract Regard. It is not to be expected that the Patrons of Science, or of Virtue, should be solicitous to discover Excellencies which they who possess them never display. Few Men have Abilities so much needed by the rest of the World as to be caressed on their own Terms, and he that will not condescend to recommend himself by external Embellishments, must submit to the Fate of just Sentiments meanly expressed, and be ridiculed and forgotten before he is understood.

173

Pedantry is the unseasonable Ostentation of Learning, which may be discovered either in the Choice of a Subject, or in the Manner of treating it. He is undoubtedly guilty of Pedantry, who, when he has made himself Master of some abstruse and uncultivated Part of Learning, obtrudes his Remarks and Discoveries upon those whom he believes unable to judge of his Proficiency, and from whom as he cannot fear Contradiction, he cannot properly expect Applause.

To this Error the Student is sometimes betrayed, by the natural Recurrence of the Mind to its common Employment, by the Pleasure which every Man receives from the Recollection of pleasing Images, and the Desire of dwelling upon Topicks, on which he knows himself able to speak with Justness. But, because we are seldom so far prejudiced in Favour of each other, as to search out for Palliations of Failings, this Deviation from Politeness, is usually imputed only to Vanity, and the harmless Academick who, perhaps, intended Entertainment and Instruction, or at worst only spoke without sufficient Reflection upon the Character of his Hearers, is commonly censured as arrogant or overbearing, and eager to extend the Reputation of his own Accomplishments, without Regard to the Convenience of Society, or the Laws of Conversation.

All Discourse, of which others cannot partake, is not only an irksome Usurpation of the Time devoted to Pleasure and Entertainment, but, what never fails to excite very keen Resentment, an insolent Assertion of Superiority, and a Triumph over less enlightened Understandings. The Pedant is, therefore, not only heard with Weariness, but Malignity, and those who conceive themselves insulted by his Knowledge, never fail to tell with Acrimony how injudiciously it was exerted.

To avoid this dangerous Imputation, and recommend themselves more effectually to the gay World, Scholars sometimes divest themselves with too much Haste of their academical Formality, and in their Endeavours to accommodate their Notions and their Stile to common Conceptions, talk rather of any Thing than of that which they understand, and sink into Insipidity of Sentiment and Meanness of Expression.

There prevails among Men of Letters, an Opinion, that all

Appearance of Science is particularly hateful to Women, and that therefore, whoever desires to be well received in female Assemblies, must qualify himself by a total Rejection of all that is serious, rational, or important, must consider Argument or Criticism as perpetually interdicted, and devote all his Attention to Trifles, and all his Eloquence to Compliment.

Students often form their Notions of the present Generation, from the Writings of the last, and are not very early informed of those Changes which the gradual Diffusion of Knowledge, or the sudden Caprice of Fashion produces in the World. Whatever might be the State of female Literature in the last Century, there is now no longer any Danger lest the Scholar should want an adequate Audience at the Tea-Table, and whoever thinks it necessary to regulate his Conversation by antiquated Rules, will be rather despised for his Futility than caressed for his Politeness.

To talk intentionally in a Manner above the Comprehension of those whom we address, is unquestionable Pedantry; but surely Complaisance requires, that no Man should, without Proof, conclude his Company incapable of following him to the highest Elevation of his Fancy, or the utmost Extent of his Knowledge. It is always safer to err in Favour of others than of ourselves, and therefore we seldom hazard much by endeavouring to excel.

It ought at least to be the Care of Learning when she quits her Exaltation to descend with Dignity. Nothing is more despicable than the Airiness and Jocularity of a Man bred to severe Science, and solitary Meditation. To trifle agreeably is a Secret which Schools cannot impart; that gay Negligence and Vivacious Levity which charm down Resistance wherever they appear, are never attainable by him who has spent his first Years among the Dust of Libraries, and enters late into the living World with an unpliant Attention and established Habits.

185

At vindicta, bonum vita jucundius ipsa,
Nempe hoc indocti.——
Chrysippus *non dicit idem, nec mite* Thaletis
Ingenium, dulcique senex vicinus Hymetto,
Qui partem acceptæ sæva inter vincla Cicutæ
Accusatori nollet dare.——Quippe minuti
Semper, & infirmi est Animi, exiguique Voluptas
Ultio.   Juv.

But O ! revenge is sweet.
Thus think the crowd; who, eager to engage,
Take quickly fire, and kindle into rage.
Not so mild *Thales*, nor *Chrysippus* thought,
Nor that good man, who drank the pois'nous draught
With mind serene; and could not wish to see
His vile accuser drink as deep as he ;
Exalted *Socrates* ! divinely brave!
Injur'd he fell, and dying he forgave,
Too noble for revenge ! which still we find
The weakest frailty of a feeble mind.   DRYDEN.

No vitious Dispositions of the Mind more obstinately resist, not only the Counsels of Philosophy, but the Injunctions of Religion, than those which are complicated with an Opinion of Dignity, and which we cannot dismiss, without leaving in the Hands of Opposition some Advantage iniquitously obtained, or suffering from our own Prejudices some Imputation of Pusillanimity.

For this Reason no Law of our Redeemer is more openly transgressed, or more industriously evaded, than that by which he commands his Followers to forgive Injuries, and prohibits, under the Sanction of eternal Misery, the Gratification of that Desire which every Man feels of returning any Pain that he suffers upon him that inflicts it. Many who could have conquered their Anger, are unable to combat against Pride, and pursue Offences to extremity of Vengeance, only lest they should be insulted by the Triumph of an Enemy.

But certainly no Precept could better become him, at whose Birth *Peace* was proclaimed *to the Earth.* For what would so soon destroy all the Order of Society, and deform Life with Violence and Ravage, as a Permission to every Man to judge his own Cause, and to Apportion his own Recompence for imagined Injuries?

It is difficult for a Man of the strictest Justice not to favour himself too much in his calmest Moments, or his solitary Meditations. Every one wishes for Distinctions and Superiority, for which Thousands are wishing at the same Time, in their own Opinion, with better Claims. He that, when his Reason operates in its full Force, can thus, by the mere Prevalence of Self-love, prefer himself to his fellow Beings, is not likely to judge Equitably when his Passions are agitated by a Sense of Wrong, and his Attention wholly engrossed by his Pain, his Interest, or his Danger. Whoever claims to himself the Right of Vengeance, shows how little he is qualified to judge his own Cause, since he certainly demands what he would think unfit to be granted to another.

Nothing is more apparent than that, however injured or however provoked, some must at last be contented to forgive; for it can never be hoped, that he who commits an Injury, will contentedly acquiesce in the Penalty required. The same Haughtiness of Contempt, and Vehemence of Desire, that prompts the Act of Injustice, will more strongly incite its Justification; and Resentment can seldom so exactly balance the Punishment with the Fault, but there will remain an Overplus of Vengeance which even he who condemns his first Action will think himself entitled to retaliate. What then can ensue but a continual Exacerbation of Hatred, an unextinguishable Feud, an incessant Reciprocation of Mischief, a mutual Vigilance to entrap, and Effort to destroy.

Since the imaginary Right of Vengeance must be at last remitted, because it is impossible to live in perpetual Hostility, and equally impossible that of two Enemies, either should think himself obliged by Justice to Submission, it is surely eligible to forgive early. Every Passion is more easily subdued before it has been accustomed to long Possession of the Heart; every Idea is obliterated with less Difficulty as it has been more slightly impressed, and less frequently renewed. He who has long brooded over his Wrongs, pleased himself with Schemes of Malignity, and glutted his Imagination with the Joys of Triumph, and Supplications of humbled Enmity, will not easily open his Bosom to Amity and Reconciliation, or indulge the gentle Sentiments of Benevolence and Peace.

It is easiest to forgive, while there is yet little to be forgiven. A single Injury may be soon dismissed from the Memory, but a long Succession of ill Offices by Degrees associates itself with every Idea, and a long Contest will involve so many Circumstances, that every Place and every Action will recal it to the Mind, and fresh Remembrance of Vexation must still enkindle Rage, and irritate Revenge.

A wise Man will make Haste to forgive, because he who knows the true Value of Time will not suffer it to pass away in unnecessary Pain. He that willingly suffers the Corrosions of inveterate Hatred, and gives up his Days and Nights to the Gloom of Malice and Perturbations of Stratagem, cannot surely be said to consult his Ease. Resentment is Union of Sorrow with Malignity, a Combination of a Passion which all endeavour to avoid, with a Passion which all concur to detest. The Man who retires to meditate Mischief, and to exasperate his own Rage, whose Thoughts are employed only on Scenes of Distress and Contrivances of Ruin, whose Mind never pauses from the Remembrance of his own Sufferings, but to indulge some Hope of enjoying the Miseries of another, may justly be numbered among the most miserable of human Beings, among those who are guilty without Reward, who have neither the Gladness of Prosperity, nor the Calm of Innocence.

He that considers the Weakness both of himself and others will not long want Persuasives to Forgiveness. We cannot know to what Degree of Malignity any Injury is to be imputed, or how much its Guilt, if we were to inspect the Mind of him that committed it, would be extenuated by Mistake, Precipitance, or Negligence; nor can we be always certain how much more we feel than was intended to be inflicted, or how much we encrease the Mischief to ourselves by voluntary Aggravations. We may charge to Design the Effects of Accidents, we may think the Blow violent only because we have made ourselves delicate and tender, we are on every Side in danger of Error and of Guilt, which we are certain to avoid only by speedy Forgiveness.

From this pacifick and harmless Temper, thus propitious to others and ourselves, to domestick Tranquility and to social Happiness, no Man is withheld but by Pride, by the Fear of being insulted by his Adversary or despised by the World.

It may be laid down as an unfailing and universal Axiom, that, "all Pride is abject and mean." It is always an ignorant, lazy, or cowardly Acquiescence, in a false Appearance of Excellence, and proceeds not from Consciousness of our Attainments but Insensibility of our Wants.

Nothing can be great which is not right. Nothing which Reason condemns can be suitable to the Dignity of the human Mind. To permit ourselves to be driven by external Motives from the Way which our own Heart approves, to give Way to any Thing but Conviction, to suffer the Opinion of others to overrule our Choice, or overpower our Resolves, is to submit tamely to the lowest and most ignominious Slavery, and to resign the Right of directing our own Lives.

The utmost Excellence at which Humanity can arrive, is a constant and determinate Pursuit of Virtue, without Regard to present Dangers or Advantage; a continual Reference of every Action to the divine Will; an habitual Appeal to everlasting Justice; and an unvaried Elevation of the intellectual Eye to the Reward which Perseverance only can obtain. But that Pride which many who yet presume to boast of enlarged and generous Sentiments, allow to regulate their Measures, has nothing higher or nobler in View than the Favour and Approbation of Men, of Beings whose Superiority we are under no Obligation to acknowledge, and who, when we have courted them with the utmost Assiduity, can confer no valuable and permanent Reward; of Beings who ignorantly judge of what they do not understand, or partially determine what they never have examined; and whose Sentence is therefore of no Weight till it has received the Ratification of our own Conscience.

He that can descend to bribe Suffrages like these at the Price of his Innocence; he that can suffer the Delight of such Acclamations to suspend his Attention to the Commands of the universal Sovereign; he that suffers himself to be lulled by such Flattery into Negligence of his Duty, has very little Reason to congratulate himself upon the Greatness of his Mind: But whenever he awakes to Seriousness and Reflection, must become despicable in his own Eyes, and shrink with Shame, from the Contemplation of his Cowardice and Folly.

Of him that hopes to be forgiven it is indispensibly required, that he forgive; it is therefore superfluous to urge any other Motive; on this great Duty Eternity is suspended; and to him that refuses to practise it, the Throne of Mercy is inaccessible, and the Saviour of the World has been born in vain.

186

In one of the large Caves to which the Families of *Greenland* retire together to pass the cold Months, and which may be called their Villages or Cities, a Youth and Maid who had come from different Parts of the Country, were so much distinguished for their Beauty, that they were called by the rest of the inhabitants *Anningait* and *Ajut*, from their supposed Resemblance to their Ancestors of the same Names, who were transformed of old into the Sun and Moon.

Anningait had for some Time heard the Praises of *Ajut* with little Emotion, but, at last, by frequent Interviews became sensible of her Charms, and first made a Discovery of his Affection, by inviting her with her Parents to a Feast, where he placed before *Ajut* the Tail of a Whale. *Ajut* seemed not much delighted by this Gallantry, but, however, from that Time, was observed rarely to appear, but in a Vest made of the Skin of a white Deer; she used frequently to renew the black Dye upon her Hands and Forehead, to adorn her Sleeves with Coral and Shells, and to braid her Hair with great Exactness.

The Elegance of her Dress, and the judicious Disposition of her Ornaments, had such an Effect upon *Anningait*, that he could no longer be restrained from a Declaration of his Love. He therefore composed a Poem in her Praise, in which, among other heroick and tender Sentiments he declared, that "She was beautiful as the vernal Willow, fragrant as Thyme on the Mountains; that her Fingers were white as the Teeth of the Morse, and her Smile grateful as the Dissolution of the Ice; that he would pursue her, though she should pass the Snows of the midland Mountains, or seek shelter in the Caves of eastern Canibals; that he would tear her from the Embraces of the Genius of the Rocks, snatch her from the paws of *Ameros*, and rescue her from the Ravine of *Hufcufa*;" he concluded with a Wish, that, "whoever shall attempt to hinder his Union with *Ajut*, might be buried without his Bow, and that in the Land of Souls his Skull might serve for no other Use than to catch the Droppings of the starry Lamps."

This Ode was universally applauded, and it was expected that *Ajut* would soon yield to such Fervour and Accomplishments; but *Ajut*, with the natural Haughtiness of Beauty, expected the usual Forms of Courtship, and before she would confess herself conquered, the Sun returned, the Ice broke, and the Season of Labour called all to their Employments.

Anningait and *Ajut* for a Time always went out in the same Boat, and divided whatever was caught. *Anningait*, in the Sight of his Mistress, lost no Opportunity of signalizing his Courage; he attacked the Sea-Horses on the Ice; he pursued the Seals into the Water; and leaped upon the Back of the Whale, while he was yet struggling with the Remains of Life. Nor was his Diligence less to accumulate all that was necessary to make his Winter comfortable; he dried the Roe of Fishes, and the Flesh of Seals; he entrapped Deer and Foxes, and dressed their Skins to adorn his Bride; he feasted her with Eggs from the Rocks; and strewed her Tent with Flowers.

It happened that a Tempest drove the Fish to a distant Part of the Coast before *Anningait* had compleated his Store; he therefore entreated *Ajut*, that she would at last grant him her Hand, and accompany him to that Part of the Country, to which he was now summoned by Necessity. *Ajut* thought him not yet entitled to such Condescension, and therefore proposed, as a Trial of his Constancy, that he should return at the End of Summer to the Cavern where their Acquaintance commenced, and there expect the Reward of his Assiduities. "O Virgin, beautiful as the Sun shining on the Water, consider," said *Anningait*, "what thou hast required, how easily may my Return be precluded by a sudden Frost or unexpected Fogs; then must the Night be past without my *Ajut*. We live not, my Fair, in those fabled Countries, which lying Strangers so wantonly describe, where the whole Year is divided into short Days and Nights; where the same Habitation serves for Summer and Winter; where they raise Houses in Rows above the Ground, dwell together from Year to Year, with Flocks of tame Animals grazing in the Fields about them, and can pass at any Time, from one Place to another through Ways enclosed with Trees, or over Walls raised upon the inland Waters; and direct their Course thro' wide Countries by the Sight of green Hills or scattered Buildings. Even in Summer we have no Means of passing the Mountains, whose Snows are never dissolved, nor can remove to any distant Residence, but by our Boats coasting the Bays: Consider, *Ajut*, a few Summer Days, and a few Winter Nights, and the Life of Man is at an End. Night is the Time of Ease, and Festivity, of Revels and Gaiety; but what will be the flaming Lamp, the delicious Seal, or the soft Oil, without the Smile of *Ajut*?"

The Eloquence of *Anningait* was in vain; the Maid continued inexorable, and they parted with ardent Promises to meet again before the Night of Winter.

187

Non illum nostri possunt mutare Labores,
Non si Frigoribus mediis Hebrumque bibamus,
Sithoniasque *Nives Hiemis subeamus aquosæ——*
Omnia vincit Amor.　　　　　　　　　　VIRG.

Love alters not for us his hard decrees;
Not tho' beneath the *Thracian* clime we freeze,
Or the mild bliss of temperate skies forego,
And in mid winter tread *Sithonian* snow:
Love conquers all.——　　　　　　　　　DRYDEN.

I　　　　　　　　　　　　261

Anningait, however discomposed by the dilatory Coyness of *Ajut*, was yet resolved to omit no Tokens of amorous Respect, and therefore, presented her at his Departure with the Skins of seven white Fawns, of five Swans and eleven Seals, with a large Kettle of Brass, which he had purchased from a Ship at the Price of half a Whale, and two Horns of Sea Unicorns, with three marble Lamps, and ten Vessels of Seal-Oil.

Ajut was so much affected by the Fondness of her Lover, or so much overpowered by his Magnificence, that she followed him to the Seaside, and, when she saw him enter the Boat, she wished aloud, that he might return with Plenty of Skins and Oil; that neither the Mermaids might snatch him into the Deeps, nor the Spirits of the Rocks confine him in their Caves.

She stood a while to gaze upon the departing Vessel, and then returned to her Hut, silent and dejected. She laid aside, from that Hour, her white Deer Skin, suffered her Hair to spread unbraided on her Shoulders, and forbore to mix in the Dances of the Maidens. She endeavoured to divert her Thoughts by continual Application to feminine Employments, gathered Moss for their Winter Lamps, and dried Grass to line the Boots of *Anningait*. Of the Skins which he had bestowed upon her she made a fishing Coat, a small Boat, and Tent, all of exquisite Manufacture, and while she was thus busied, solaced her Labours with a Song, in which she prayed, "that her Lover might have Hands stronger than the Paws of the Bear, and Feet swifter than the Feet of the Raindeer; that his Dart might never err, and that his Boat might never leak; that he might never stumble on the Ice, nor faint in the Water; that the Seal might rush on his Harpoon, and the wounded Whale might dash the Waves in vain."

The large Boats in which *Greenlanders* transport their Families are always rowed by Women, for no Man will debase himself by Work, which requires neither Skill nor Courage. *Anningait* was therefore exposed by Idleness to the Ravages of Passion. He went thrice to the Stern of the Boat, with an Intent to leap into the Water, and swim back to his Mistress; but recollecting the Misery which they must endure in the Winter without Oil for the Lamp, or Skins for the Bed, he resolved to employ the Weeks of Absence in Provision for a Night of Plenty and Felicity. He then composed his Emotions as he could, and expressed in wild Numbers and uncouth Images, his Hopes, his Sorrows, and his Fears. "O Life," says he, "frail and uncertain! where shall wretched Man find thy Resemblance but in Ice floating on the Ocean? It towers on high, it sparkles at a Distance, while the Storms drive and the Waters beat it, the Sun melts it above, and the Rocks shatter it below. What is Pleasure, but a sudden Blaze streaming from the North. which plays a Moment on the Eye, mocks the Traveller with the Hopes of Light, and then vanishes forever? What is Love but a Whirlpool, which we approach without Knowledge of our Danger, and which draws us on by imperceptible Degrees, till we have lost all Power of Resistance and Escape? Till I fixed my Eyes on the Graces of *Ajut*, before I called her to the Banquet, I was careless as the sleeping Morse, I was merry as the Singers in the Stars. Why, *Ajut*, did I gaze upon thy Graces? why, my Fair, did I call thee to the Banquet? Yet, be faithful, my fair, remember *Anningait*, and meet my Return with the Smile of Virginity. I will chase the Deer, I will subdue the Whale, resistless as the Frost of Darkness, and unwearied as the Summer Sun. In a few Weeks, I shall return prosperous and wealthy; then shall the Roefish and the Porpoise, feast thy Kindred; the Fox and Hare shall cover thy Couch; the tough Hide of the Seal shall shelter thee from Cold; and the Fat of the Whale illuminate thy Dwelling."

Anningait having with these Sentiments consoled his Grief, and animated his Industry, found that they had now coasted the Headland, and saw the Whales spouting at a Distance. He therefore placed himself in his fishing Boat, called his Associates to their several Employments, plied his Oar and Harpoon with incredible Courage and Dexterity, and, by dividing his Time between the Chace and Fishery, suspended the Miseries of Absence and Suspicion.

Ajut, in the mean time, notwithstanding her neglected Dress, as she was drying some Skins in the Sun, happened to catch the eye of *Norngsuk*, when he returned from Hunting. *Norngsuk* was of Birth truly illustrious. His mother had died in Childbirth, and his Father, the most expert Fisher of *Greenland*, had perished by too close Pursuit of the Whale. His Dignity was equalled by his Riches; he was master of four Mens and two Womens Boats, had ninety Tubs of Oil in his Winter Habitation, and five and twenty Seals, buried in the Snow against the Season of Darkness. When he saw the Beauty of *Ajut*, he immediately threw over her the Skin of a Deer that he had taken, and soon after presented her with a

Branch of Coral. *Ajut* refused his Gifts, and determined to admit no Lover in the Place of *Anningait*.

Norngsuk, thus rejected, had recourse to Stratagem. He knew that *Ajut* would consult an *Angekkok*, or Diviner, concerning the Fate of her Lover, and the Felicity of her future Life. He therefore applied himself to the most celebrated *Angekkok* of that Part of the Country, and by a Present of two Seals and a marble Kettle, obtained a Promise that when *Ajut* should consult him, he would declare that her Lover was in the Land of Souls. *Ajut*, in a short Time, brought him a Coat made by herself, and enquired what Events were to befal her, with Assurances of a much larger Reward at the Return of *Anningait* if the Prediction should flatter her Desires. The *Angekkok* knew the Way to Riches, and therefore declared that *Anningait*, having already caught two Whales, would soon return Home with a large Boat laden with Provisions.

This Prognostication she was ordered to keep secret, and therefore *Norngsuk* depending upon his Artifice renewed his Addresses with greater Confidence, but finding himself still unsuccessful, applied himself to her Parents with Gifts and Promises. The Wealth of *Greenland* is too powerful for the Virtue of a *Greenlander*; they forgot the Merit and the Presents of *Anningait*, and decreed *Ajut* to the Embrace of *Norngsuk*. She entreated; she remonstrated; she wept, and raved; but finding Riches irresistible, she fled away into the Uplands, and lived in a Cave upon Berries, and Birds or Hares which she had the Fortune to ensnare; taking Care at an Hour when she was not likely to be found to view the Sea every Day, that her Lover might not miss her at his Return.

At last she saw the great Boat in which *Anningait* had departed, stealing slow and heavy laden along the Coast. She ran with all the Impatience of Affection to catch her Lover in her Arms, and to tell him her Constancy and Sufferings. When the Company reached the Land they informed her, that *Anningait*, when the Fishery was ended, being unable to support the slow Passage of the Vessel of Carriage, had set out before them in his fishing Boat, and they expected at their Arrival to find him on Shore.

Ajut, distracted at this Intelligence, was about to fly again into the Hills without knowing why; but she was now in the Hands of her Parents, who forced her back to their own Hut, and endeavoured to comfort her. They at last retired to rest, and *Ajut*

went down to the Beach, where finding a fishing Boat she entered
it without Hesitation, and telling those who wondered at her Rashness, that she was going in search of *Anningait*, rowed away with
great Swiftness, and was seen no more.

The Fate of these Lovers gave Occasion to various Fictions and
Conjectures. Some were of Opinion that they were changed into
Stars; others imagined that *Anningait* was seized in his Passage
by the Genius of the Rocks, and that *Ajut* was transformed into a
Mermaid, and still continues to seek her Lover in the Desarts of
the Sea. But the general Persuasion is, that they are both in that
Part of the Land of Souls where the Sun never sets, where Oil is
always fresh, and Provisions are always warm. The Virgins some-
times throw a Thimble, and a Needle into the Bay, from which the
hapless Maid departed; and when a *Greenlander* would praise any
Couple for virtuous Affection, he declares, that they love like
Anningait and *Ajut*.

188

——Si te colo, Sexte, non amabo.　　　MART.

The more I honour thee, the less I love.

None of the Desires dictated by Vanity is more general or more
reasonable than that of being distinguished for the Arts of Conversation. Other Accomplishments may be possessed without
Opportunity of exerting them, or wanted without Danger that the
Defect can often be remarked; but no Man can live, otherwise than
in an Hermitage, without hourly Pleasure or Vexation from the
Fondness or Neglect of those about him. There are few more
frequently envied than those who have the Power of forcing
Attention wherever they come, whose Entrance is considered as a
Promise of Felicity, and whose Departure is always lamented,
like the Recess of the Sun from northern Climates, as a Privation
of all that enlivens Fancy or inspirits Gaiety.

It is apparent, that to excel in this valuable Art, some peculiar
Qualifications are necessary; for every one's Experience will inform
him, that the Pleasure which Men are able to give in Conversation,
holds no stated Proportion to their Knowledge or their Virtue.
Many find their Way to the Tables, and the Parties of those who
never consider them as of the least Importance in any other Place;
we have all, at one Time or other, been content to love those whom

we could not esteem, and been persuaded to try the dangerous Experiment of admitting him for a Companion, whom we knew to be too ignorant for a Counsellor, and too treacherous for a Friend.

I know not, indeed, whether some Abatement of Character is not almost necessary to general Acceptance. Few can spend their Time with much Satisfaction under the Eye of uncontested Superiority, and therefore, among those who are received with universal Welcome, and whose Presence is courted at every Assembly of Jollity, there are seldom to be found Men eminently distinguished for Powers of Nature or Acquisitions of Study. The Wit whose Vivacity condemns slower Tongues to Silence, the Scholar whose Knowledge allows no Man to fansy that he instructs him, the Reasoner who suffers no Sophism to pass undetected, who condemns Negligence to Thought, and Idleness to Attention, are generally praised and feared, reverenced and avoided.

He that would please must rarely aim at such Excellence as depresses his Hearers in their own Opinion, or debars them from the Hope of contributing reciprocally to the Entertainment of the Company. That Merriment which is extorted by Sallies of the Imagination, Sprightliness of Remark, or Quickness of Reply, is too often what the *Latins* call, the *Sardinian Laughter*, a Distortion of the Face without Gladness of Heart.

For this Reason, no Stile of Conversation is more extensively acceptable than the Narrative. He who has stored his Memory with slight Anecdotes, private Incidents, and personal Particularities, seldom fails to find his Audience favourable. Almost every Man listens with Eagerness to contemporary History; perhaps, almost every Man has some real or imaginary Connection with a celebrated Character, some desire to advance, or oppose a rising Name. Vanity often co-operates with Curiosity. He that is a Hearer in one Place, qualifies himself to become a Speaker in another; for though he cannot comprehend a Series of Argument, or transport the volatile Spirit of Wit without Evaporation, yet he thinks himself able to treasure up the various Incidents of a Story, and pleases his Hopes with the Information which he shall give to some inferior Society.

Narratives are for the most Part heard without Envy, because they are not supposed to imply any intellectual Qualities above the common Rate. To be acquainted with Facts not yet ecchoed by plebeian Mouths, may happen to one Man as well as to another, and to relate them when they are known, has so little Difficulty, that every one concludes himself equal to the Task.

But it is not easy, and in some Situations not possible to accumulate such a Stock of Materials, as may support the Expence of continual Narrative; and it frequently happens, that they who attempt this Method of ingratiating themselves, please only at the first Interview, and, for want of new Supplies of Intelligence, wear out their Stories with continual Repetition.

There would be, therefore, little Hope of obtaining the Praise of a good Companion, were it not to be gained by more compendious Methods; but such is the Kindness of Mankind to all but those who aspire to real Merit, and rational Dignity, that every Understanding may find some Way to Regard, and all who are not envied, may learn the Art of procuring Love. We are willing to be pleased, but we are not willing to admire: we favour the Mirth or Officiousness that solicits our Regard, but oppose the Worth or Spirit that enforces it.

The first Place among those that please, because they desire only to please, is due to the *Merry Fellow*, whose Laugh is loud, and whose Voice is strong; who is ready to eccho every Jest with obstreperous Approbation, and countenance every Frolick with Vociferations of Applause. It is not necessary to a merry Fellow to have in himself any Fund of Jocularity, or Force of Conception; it is sufficient that he always appears in the highest Exaltation of Gladness, for the greater Part of Mankind are gay or serious by Infection, and follow, without Resistance, the Attraction of Example.

Next to the merry Fellow is the *good-natured Man*, a Being generally without Benevolence or any other Virtues than such as Indolence and Insensibility confer. The Characteristick of a *good-natured Man* is to bear a Joke; to sit unmoved and unaffected amidst Noise and Turbulence, Profaneness and Obscenity; to hear every Tale without Contradiction; to endure every Insult without reply; and to follow the Stream of Folly whatever Course it shall happen to take. The good-natured Man is commonly the Darling of the petty Wits, with whom they exercise themselves in the Rudiments of Raillery, for he never takes Advantage of Failings, nor disconcerts a puny Satirist with unexpected Sarcasms, but, while the Glass continues to circulate, contentedly bears the

Expence of uninterrupted Laughter, and retires rejoicing at his own Importance.

The *modest Man* is a Companion of a yet lower Rank, whose only Power of giving Pleasure is not to interrupt it. The modest Man satisfies himself with peaceful Silence, which all his Companions are candid enough to consider as proceeding not from Inability to speak, but Willingness to hear.

There are many who, without being able to attain any general Character of Excellence, have some single Art of Entertainment which serves them as a Passport through the World. One I have known who has been for fifteen Years the Darling of a weekly Club, because every Night precisely at Eleven, he begins his favourite Song, and during the vocal Performance by corresponding Motions of his Hand chalks out a Giant upon the Wall. Another has endeared himself to a long Succession of Acquaintances by sitting among them with his Wig reversed; another by contriving to smut the Nose of any Stranger who was to be initiated in the Club; another by purring like a Cat, and pretending to be frighted; and another by yelping like a Hound, and calling to the Drawers to drive out the Dog.

Such are the Arts by which Cheerfulness is promoted, and sometimes Friendship established, Arts, which those who despise them, should not rigorously blame, except when they are practised at the Expence of Innocence; for it is always necessary to be loved, but not always necessary to be reverenced.

208

Ἡράκλειτῳ’ ἐγώ· τί με ὦ κάτω ἕλκετ’ ἄμασοι;
Οὐχ’ ὑμῖν ἐπόναν, τοις δέ μ’ ἐπισαμένοις·
Εἷς ἐμοὶ ἄνθρωπῳ’ τρισμύριοι· οἱ δ’ ἀναριθμοι
Οὐδείς· ταῦτ’ αὐδῶ καὶ παρὰ Περσεφόνη·　　DIOG. LAERT.

Be gone ye blockheads, *Heraclitus* cries,
And leave my labours to the learn’d and wise :
By wit, by knowledge, studious to be read,
I scorn the multitude, alive and dead.

Time, which puts an End to all human Pleasures and Sorrows, has likewise concluded the Labours of the RAMBLER. Having supported for two Years the anxious Employment of a periodical Writer, and multiplied my Essays to six Volumes, I have now determined to desist.

What are the Reasons of this Resolution, it is of little Importance to declare, since no Justification is necessary when no
Objection is made. I am far from supposing, that the Cessation
of my Performances will raise any Inquiry; for I have never been
much a Favourite of the Publick, nor can boast that, in the
Progress of my Undertaking, I have been animated by the Rewards
of the Liberal, the Caresses of the Great, or the Praises of the
Eminent.

I have, however, no Intention to gratify Pride by Submission,
or Malice by Lamentation, nor think it reasonable to complain of
Neglect from those whose Attention I never solicited. If I have
not been distinguished by the Distributers of literary Honours,
I have seldom descended to any of the Arts by which Favour is
obtained. I have seen the Meteors of Fashion rise and fall, without
any Attempt to add a Moment to their Duration; I have never
complied with temporary Curiosity, nor furnished my Readers
with Abilities to discuss the Topic of the Day; I have seldom
exemplified my Assertions by living Characters from my Papers;
therefore no Man could hope either Censures of his Enemies, or
Praises of himself, and they only could be expected to peruse
them, whose Passions left them Leisure for the Contemplation of
abstracted Truth, and whom Virtue could please by her native
Dignity, without the Assistance of modish Ornaments ?

To some, however, I am indebted for Encouragement, and to
others for Assistance; the Number of my Friends was never great,
but they have been such as would not suffer me to think I was
writing in vain, and I therefore felt very little Uneasiness at the
Want of Popularity.

As my Obligations have not been frequent, my Acknowledg-
ments may be soon dispatched. I can restore to all my Correspondents their Productions, with very little Diminution of the
Bulk of my Volumes, tho' not without the Loss of some Pieces
to which particular Honours have been paid.

The Parts, from which I claim no other Praise than that of
having given them an Opportunity of appearing, are the four
Billets in the tenth Paper, the second Letter in the fifteenth; the
thirtieth, the forty-fourth, the ninety-seventh, and the hundredth
Papers; and the second Letter in the hundred and seventh.

Having thus deprived myself of many Excuses, which Candor
might have admitted for the Inequality of my Compositions, being

no longer able to allege the Necessity of gratifying my Correspondents, the Importunity with which Publication was solicited, or the Obstinacy with which Correction was rejected, I must remain accountable for all my Faults, and submit without Subterfuge to the Censures of Criticism; which, however, I shall not endeavour to soften by a formal Deprecation, or to overbear by the Influence of a Patron; for the Supplications of an Author never yet reprieved him a Moment from Oblivion; and, though Greatness has sometimes sheltered Guilt, it can afford no Protection to Ignorance or Dulness. Having hitherto attempted only the Propagation of Truth, I will not at last violate it by the Confession of Terrors which I do not feel: Having laboured to maintain the Dignity of Virtue, I will not now degrade it by the Meanness of Dedication.

The seeming Vanity with which I have sometimes spoken of myself, would perhaps require an Apology, were it not extenuated by the Example of all those who have published Essays before me, and by the Privilege which a nameless Writer has been hitherto allowed. "A mask, says *Castiglione*, confers a Right of acting and speaking with less Restraint, even when the Wearer is known to the whole Company." He that is discovered without his own Consent, may claim some Indulgence, and cannot be rigorously called to justify those Sallies or Frolicks which his Disguise is a Proof that he wishes to conceal.

But I have been cautious lest this Offence should be frequently or grossly committed; for as one of the Philosophers directs us to live with a Friend, as with one that is some time to become an Enemy, I have always thought it the Duty of an anonymous Author to write, as if he expected to be hereafter known.

I am willing to flatter my self with Hopes, that, by collecting these Papers, I am not preparing for my future Life either Shame or Repentance. That they are all happily imagined, or accurately polished; that the same Sentiment will not sometimes recur, or the same Form of Expression be too frequently repeated, I have not Confidence in my Abilities sufficient to promise. He that condemns himself to compose on a stated Day, will often bring to his Task, an Attention dissipated, a Memory overwhelmed, an Imagination embarrassed, a Mind distracted with Anxieties, and a Body languishing with Disease: He will sometimes labour on a barren Topic, till it is too late to change it; and sometimes, in the

Ardour of Invention, diffuse his Thoughts into wild Exuberance, which the pressing Hour of Publication will not suffer Judgment to examine or reduce.

Whatever shall be the final Sentence of Mankind, I have at least endeavoured to deserve their Kindness; I have laboured to refine our Language to grammatical Purity, and to clear it from colloquial Barbarisms, licentious Idioms, and irregular Combinations. Something, perhaps, I have added to the Elegance of its Construction, and something to the Harmony of its Cadence. When common Words were less pleasing to the Ear, or less distinct in their Signification, I have familiarized the Terms of Philosophy, by applying them to known Objects and popular Ideas, but have rarely admitted any Word, not authorized by former Writers; for I believe, that whoever knows the *English* Tongue in its present Extent, will be able to express all his Thoughts without farther Help from other Nations.

As it has been always my principal Design to inculcate Wisdom or Piety, I have allotted few Papers to the idle Sports of wild Imagination; and though some, perhaps, may be found, of which the highest Excellence is harmless Merriment, yet scarcely any Man is so steadily serious, as not rather to complain, that the Severity of dictatorial Instruction is too seldom relieved, and that he is driven by the sternness of Philosophy to more chearful and airy Companions.

Next to the Excursions of Fancy are the Disquisitions of Criticism, which, in my Opinion, is to be ranked only among the subordinate and instrumental Arts. The common Practice of arbitrary Decision and general Exclamation, I have carefully avoided. I have asserted nothing without a Reason; and have established all my Principles of Judgment on unalterable and evident Truth.

In the Pictures of Life I have never been so studious of Novelty or Surprize, as to depart wholly from all Resemblance; a Fault which some Writers, deservedly celebrated, frequently commit, only that they may raise, as the Occasion requires, either Mirth or Abhorrence. Some Enlargement may be allowed to Declamation, and some Exaggeration to Burlesque; but as they deviate farther from Life, they are less useful, because their Lessons will fail of Application. The Mind of the Reader is carried away from the Contemplation of his own Manners; he finds in himself no

271

Likeness to the Phantom before him, and though he laughs or rages, is not reformed.

The Essays professedly serious, if I have been able to execute my own Intentions, will be found exactly conformable to the Precepts of Christianity, without any Accommodation to the Licentiousness and Levity of the present Age. I therefore look back on this Part of my Work with Pleasure, which no Blame or Praise of Man shall diminish or augment; I shall never envy the Honours which Wit and Learning obtain in any other Cause, if I can be numbered among the Writers, who have given Ardour to Virtue, and Confidence to Truth.

Αὐτῶν ἐκ μακάρων ἀνταξιος εἴη ἀμοιβη.

Celestial pow'rs! that piety regard,
From you my labours wait their last reward.

SELECTIONS FROM
THE ADVENTURER

More than 200 of the 208 numbers of *The Rambler* are entirely by Johnson. His part in *The Adventurer* is much smaller and he is not considered to have had a hand in more than about 30 of the essays. The magazine ran from November 7, 1752 to March 9, 1754. The text has been taken from the British Museum run (637. m. 13.). Translations of classical quotations—as with *The Rambler*—were provided for binding with the original numbers: these translations have here been worked into the text.

THE ADVENTURER

69

OF every great and complicated event, part depends upon causes out of our power, and part must be effected by vigour and perseverance: with regard to that which is stiled in common language the work of chance, men will always find reasons for confidence or distrust, according to their different tempers or inclinations; and he that has been long accustomed to please himself with possibilities of fortuitous happiness, will not easily or willingly be reclaimed from his mistake: but the effects of human industry and skill are more easily subjected to calculation; whatever can be completed in a year, is divisible into parts, of which each may be performed in the compass of a day; he, therefore, that has passed the day without attention to the task assigned him, may be certain that the lapse of life has brought him no nearer to his object; for whatever idleness may expect from time, its produce will be only in proportion to the diligence with which it has been used. He that floats lazily down the stream, in persuit of something borne along by the same current, will find himself indeed move forward; but unless he lays his hand to the oar, and increases his speed by his own labour, must be always at the same distance from that which he is following.

There is, indeed, so little certainty in human affairs, that the most cautious and severe examiner may be allowed to indulge some hopes, which he cannot prove to be much favoured by probability; since after his utmost endeavours to ascertain events, he must often leave the issue in the hands of chance: and so scanty is our present allowance of happiness, that in many situations life could scarcely be supported, if hope were not allowed to relieve the present hour by pleasures borrowed from futurity; and reanimate the languor of dejection to new efforts, by pointing to distant regions of felicity, which yet no resolution or perseverance shall ever reach.

But these, like all other cordials, though they may invigorate in a small quantity, intoxicate in a greater; these pleasures, like the rest, are lawful only in certain circumstances, and to certain degrees; they may be useful in a due subserviency to nobler purposes, but become dangerous and destructive, when once they gain the ascendant in the heart: to sooth the mind to tranquillity by hope, even when that hope is likely to deceive us, may be sometimes useful; but to lull our faculties in a lethargy, is poor and despicable.

Vices and errors are differently modified, according to the state of the minds to which they are incident: to indulge hope beyond the warrant of reason, is the failure alike of mean and elevated understandings; but its foundation and its effects are totally different: the man of high courage and great abilities, is apt to place too much confidence in himself, and to expect from a vigorous exertion of his powers more than spirit or diligence can attain; between him and his wish he sees obstacles indeed, but he expects to overleap or break them; his mistaken ardour hurries him forward; and though perhaps he misses his end, he nevertheless obtains some collateral good, and performs something useful to mankind and honourable to himself.

The drone of timidity presumes likewise to hope, but without ground and without consequence; the bliss with which he solaces his hours, he always expects from others, though very often he knows not from whom; he folds his arms about him, and sits in expectation of some revolution in the state that shall raise him to greatness, or some golden shower that shall load him with wealth; he dozes away the day in musing upon the morrow; and at the end of life is roused from his dream only to discover, that the time of action is past, and that he can now shew his wisdom only by repentance.

84

———Tolle periclum,
Jam vaga prosiliet frœnis natura remotis.   Hor.

But take the danger and the shame away,
And vagrant nature bounds upon her prey.   Francis.

To the ADVENTURER.

Sir,

It has been observed, I think, by Sir WILLIAM TEMPLE, and after him by almost every other writer, that England affords a greater variety of characters, than the rest of the world. This is ascribed to the liberty prevailing amongst us, which gives every man the privilege of being wise or foolish his own way, and preserves him from the necessity of hypocrisy, or the servility of imitation.

That the position itself is true, I am not completely satisfied. To be nearly acquainted with the people of different countries can happen to very few; and in life, as in every thing else beheld at a distance, there appears an even uniformity; the petty discriminations which diversify the natural character, are not discoverable but by a close inspection; we therefore find them most at home, because there we have most opportunities of remarking them. Much less am I convinced, that this peculiar diversification, if it be real, is the consequence of peculiar liberty: for where is the government to be found, that superintends individuals with so much vigilance, as not to leave their private conduct without restraint? Can it enter into a reasonable mind to imagine, that men of every other nation are not equally masters of their own time or houses with ourselves, and equally at liberty to be parsimonious or profuse, frolic or sullen, abstinent or luxurious? Liberty is certainly necessary to the full play of predominant humours; but such liberty is to be found alike under the government of the many or the few; in monarchies or in commonwealths.

How readily the predominant passion snatches an interval of liberty, and how fast it expands itself when the weight of restraint is taken away, I had lately an opportunity to discover, as I took a short journey into the country in a stage coach; which, as every journey is a kind of adventure, may be very properly related to you, though I can display no such extraordinary assembly as CERVANTES has collected at DON QUIXOTE's inn.

In a stage coach the passengers are for the most part wholly unknown to one another, and without expectation of ever meeting again when their journey is at an end; one should therefore imagine, that it was of little importance to any of them, what conjectures the rest should form concerning him. Yet so it is, that as all think themselves secure from detection, all assume that character of which they are most desirous, and on no occasion is the general ambition of superiority more apparently indulged.

On the day of our departure, in the twilight of the morning, I ascended the vehicle, with three men and two women my fellow travellers. It was easy to observe the affected elevation of mien with which every one entered, and the supercilious civility with which they paid their compliments to each other. When the first ceremony was dispatched, we sat silent for a long time, all employed in collecting importance into our faces, and endeavouring to strike reverence and submission into our companions.

It is always observable that silence propagates itself, and that the longer talk has been suspended, the more difficult it is to find any thing to say. We began now to wish for conversation; but no one seemed inclined to descend from his dignity, or first to propose a topic of discourse. At last a corpulent gentleman, who had equipped himself for this expedition with a scarlet surtout, and a large hat with a broad lace, drew out his watch, looked on it in silence, and then held it dangling at his finger. This was, I suppose, understood by all the company as an invitation to ask the time of the day; but no body appeared to heed his overture: and his desire to be talking so far overcame his resentment, that he let us know of his own accord that it was past five, and that in two hours we should be at breakfast.

His condescension was thrown away, we continued all obdurate: the ladies held up their heads: I amused myself with watching their behaviour; and of the other two, one seemed to employ himself in counting the trees as we drove by them, the other drew his hat over his eyes, and counterfeited a slumber. The man of benevolence, to shew that he was not depressed by our neglect, hummed a tune and beat time upon his snuff-box.

Thus universally displeased with one another, and not much delighted with ourselves, we came at last to the little inn appointed for our repast, and all began at once to recompense themselves for the constraint of silence by innumerable questions and orders to the people that attended us. At last, what every one had called for was got, or declared impossible to be got at that time, and we were persuaded to sit round the same table; when the gentleman in the red surtout looked again upon his watch, told us that we had half an hour to spare, but he was sorry to see so little merriment among us; that all fellow travellers were for the time upon the level, and that it was always his way to make himself one of the company. I remember, says he, it was on just such a morning as this that I and my lord Mumble and the duke of Tenterden were out upon a ramble; we called at a little house as it might be this; and my landlady, I warrant you, not suspecting to whom she was talking, was so jocular and facetious, and made so many merry answers to our questions, that we were all ready to burst with laughter. At last the good woman happening to overhear me whispering to the duke and calling him by his title, was so surprised and confounded that we could scarcely get a word from her: and the duke never met me from that day to this, but he talks of the little house, and quarrels with me for terrifying the woman.

He had scarcely had time to congratulate himself on the veneration which this narrative must have procured him from the company, when one of the ladies having reached out for a plate on a distant part of the table, began to remark the inconveniences of travelling, and the difficulty which they who never sat at home without a great number of attendants found in performing for themselves such offices as the road required; but that people of quality often travelled in disguise, and might be generally known from the vulgar by their condescension to poor inn-keepers, and the allowance which they made for any defect in their entertainment: that for her part, while people were civil and meant well, it was never her custom to find fault; for one was not to expect upon a journey all that one enjoyed at one's own house.

A general emulation seemed now to be excited. One of the men, who had hitherto said nothing, called for the last news paper; and having perused it a while with deep pensiveness, It is impossible, says he, for any man to guess how to act with regard to the stocks; last week it was the general opinion that they would fall; and I sold out twenty thousand pound in order to a purchase: they have now risen unexpectedly; and I make no doubt but at my return to London I shall risk thirty thousand pound among them again.

A young man, who had hitherto distinguished himself only by the vivacity of his look, and a frequent diversion of his eyes from one object to another, upon this closed his snuff-box, and told us that he had a hundred times talked with the chancellor and the judges on the subject of the stocks; that for his part he did not pretend to be well acquainted with the principles on which they were established, but had always heard them reckoned pernicious to

279

trade, uncertain in their produce, and unsolid in their foundation; and that he had been advised by three judges, his most intimate friends, never to venture his money in the funds, but to put it out upon land security, till he could light upon an estate in his own country.

It might be expected, that upon these glimpses of latent dignity, we should all have began to look round us with veneration, and have behaved like the princes of romance, when the enchantment that disguises them is dissolved, and they discover the dignity of each other: yet it happened, that none of these hints made much impression on the company; every one was apparently suspected of endeavouring to impose false appearances upon the rest; all continued their haughtiness, in hopes to enforce their claims; and all grew every hour more sullen, because they found their representations of themselves without effect.

Thus we travelled on four days with malevolence perpetually increasing, and without any endeavour but to outvie each other in superciliousness and neglect; and when any two of us could separate ourselves for a moment, we vented our indignation at the sauciness of the rest.

At length the journey was at an end, and time and chance, that strip off all disguises, have discovered that the intimate of lords and dukes is a nobleman's butler, who has furnished a shop with the money he has saved; the man who deals so largely in the funds, is a clerk of a broker in Change-alley; the lady who so carefully concealed her quality, keeps a cook-shop behind the Exchange; and the young man, who is so happy in the friendship of the judges, engrosses and transcribes for bread in a garret of the Temple. Of one of the women only I could make no disadvantageous detection, because she had assumed no character, but accommodated herself to the scene before her, without any struggle for distinction or superiority.

I could not forbear to reflect on the folly of practising a fraud, which as the event shewed, had been already practised too often to suceed, and by the success of which no advantage could have been obtained; of assuming a character, which was to end with the day; and of claiming upon false pretences honours which must perish with the breath that paid them.

But Mr. Adventurer, let not those who laugh at me and my companions, think this folly confined to a stage coach. Every man in the journey of life takes the same advantage of the ignorance of his fellow travellers, disguises himself in counterfeited merit, and hears those praises with complacency which his conscience reproaches him for accepting. Every man deceives himself while he thinks he is deceiving others; and forgets that the time is at hand when every illusion shall cease; when fictitious excellence shall be torn away; and ALL must be shown to ALL in their real state.

I am, SIR,

Your humble Servant,

VIATOR.

85

A ready man is made by conversation. He that buries himself among his manuscripts, "besprent," as POPE expresses it, "with learned dust," and wears out his days and nights in perpetual research and solitary meditation, is too apt to lose in his elocution what he adds to his wisdom, and when he comes into the world, to appear overloaded with his own notions, like a man armed with weapons which he cannot wield. He has no facility of inculcating his speculations, of adapting himself to the various degrees of intellect which the accidents of conversation will present; but will talk to most unintelligibly, and to all unpleasantly.

I was once present at the lectures of a profound philosopher, a man really skilled in the science which he professed, who having occasion to explain the terms *opacum* and *pellucidum*, told us, after some hesitation, that *opacum* was as one might say *opake*, and that *pellucidum* signified *pellucid*. Such was the dexterity, with which this learned reader facilitated to his auditors the intricacies of science; and so true is it, that a man may know what he cannot teach.

BOERHAAVE complains, that the writers who have treated of chemistry before him, are useless to the greater part of students; because they presuppose their readers to have such degrees of skill as are not often to be found. Into the same error are all men apt to fall, who have familiarized any subject to themselves in solitude: they discourse, as if they thought every other man had been employed in the same inquiries; and expect that short hints and obscure allusions will produce in others the same train of ideas which they excite in themselves.

Nor is this the only inconvenience, which the man of study suffers from a recluse life. When he meets with an opinion that pleases him, he catches it up with eagerness; looks only after such arguments as tend to his confirmation; or spares himself the trouble of discussion, and adopts it with very little proof; indulges it long without suspicion, and in time unites it to the general body of his knowledge, and treasures it up among incontestible truths: but when he comes into the world among men who, arguing upon dissimilar principles, have been led to different conclusions, and being placed in various situations view the same object on many sides; he finds his darling position attacked, and himself in no condition to defend it: having thought always in one train, he is in the state of a man who having fenced always with the same master, is perplexed and amazed by a new posture of his antagonist; he is entangled in unexpected difficulties, he is harrassed by sudden objections, he is unprovided with solutions or replies, his surprize impedes his natural powers of reasoning, his thoughts are scattered and confounded, and he gratifies the pride of airy petulance with an easy victory

It is difficult to imagine, with what obstinacy truths which one mind perceives almost by intuition, will be rejected by another; and how many artifices must be practised, to procure admission for the most evident propositions into understandings frighted by their novelty, or hardened against them by accidental prejudice: it can scarcely be conceived, how frequently in these extemporaneous controversies, the dull will be subtle, and the acute absurd; how often stupidity will elude the force of argument, by involving itself in its own gloom; and mistaken ingenuity will weave artful fallacies, which reason can scarcely find means to disentangle.

In these encounters the learning of the recluse usually fails him: nothing but long habit and frequent experiments, can confer the power of changing a position into various forms, presenting it in different points of view, connecting it with known and granted truths, fortifying it with intelligible arguments, and illustrating it by apt similitudes; and he, therefore, that has collected his knowledge in solitude, must learn its application by mixing with mankind.

But while the various opportunities of conversation invite us to try every mode of argument, and every art of recommending our sentiments, we are frequently betrayed to the use of such as are not in themselves strictly defensible: a man heated in talk, and eager of victory, takes advantage of the mistakes or ignorance of his adversary, lays hold of concessions to which he knows he has no right, and urges proofs likely to prevail in his opponent, though he knows himself that they have no force: thus the severity of reason is relaxed; many topics are accumulated, but without just arrangement or distinction; we learn to satisfy ourselves with such ratiocination as silences others; and seldom recall to a close examination, that discourse which has gratified our vanity with victory and applause.

Some caution, therefore, must be used, lest copiousness and facility be made less valuable by inaccuracy and confusion: to fix the thoughts by writing, and subject them to frequent examinations and reviews, is the best method of enabling the mind to detect its own sophisms, and keep it on guard against the fallacies which it practises on others: in conversation we naturally diffuse our thoughts, and in writing we contract them; method is the excellence of writing, and unconstraint the grace of conversation.

To read, write, and converse in due proportions, is, therefore, the business of a man of letters. For all these there is not often equal opportunity; excellence, therefore, is not often attainable: and most men fail in one or other of the ends proposed, and are full without readiness, or ready without exactness. Some deficiency must be forgiven all, because all are men; and more must be allowed to pass uncensured in the greater part of the world, because none can confer upon himself abilities, and few have the choice of situations proper for the improvement of those which nature has bestowed: it is, however, reasonable, to have PERFECTION in our eye; that we may always advance towards it, though we know it never can be reached.

115

The present age, if we consider chiefly the state of our own country, may be stiled with great propriety THE AGE OF AUTHORS; for, perhaps, there never was a time, in which men of all degrees of ability, of every kind of education, of every profession and employment, were posting with ardour so general to the press. The province of writing was formerly left to those, who by study, or appearance of study, were supposed to have gained knowledge unattainable by the busy part of mankind; but in these enlightened days, every man is qualified to instruct every other man, and he that beats the anvil, or guides the plough, not contented with supplying corporal necessities, amuses himself in the hours of leisure with providing intellectual pleasures for his countrymen.

It may be observed, that of this, as of other evils, complaints have been made by every generation: but though it may, perhaps, be true, that at all times more have been willing than have been able to write, yet there is no reason for believing, that the dogmatical legions of the present race, were ever equalled in number by any former period; for so widely is spread the itch of literary praise, that almost every man is an author, either in act or in purpose; has either bestowed his favours on the public, or with-holds them, that they may be more seasonably offered, or made more worthy of acceptance.

In former times, the pen, like the sword, was considered as consigned by nature to the hands of men; the ladies contented themselves with private virtues and domestic excellence, and a female writer, like a female warrior, was considered as a kind of excentric being, that deviated, however illustriously, from her due sphere of motion, and was, therefore, rather to be gazed at with wonder, than countenanced by imitation. But as the times past are said to have been a nation of Amazons, who drew the bow and wielded the battle-axe, formed encampments, and wasted nations; the revolution of years has now produced a generation of Amazons of the pen, who with the spirit of their predecessors have set masculine tyranny at defiance, asserted their claim to the regions of sciences, and seem resolved to contest the usurpations of virility.

Some, indeed, there are of both sexes, who are authors only in desire, but have not yet attained the power of executing their intentions; whose performances have not arrived at bulk sufficient to form a volume, or who have not the confidence, however impatient of nameless obscurity, to sollicit openly the assistance of the printer. Among these are the innumerable correspondents of public papers, who are always offering assistance which no man will receive, and suggesting hints that are never taken, and who complain loudly of the perverseness and arrogance of authors, lament their insensibility of their own interest, and fill the coffeehouses with dark stories of performances by eminent hands, which have been offered and rejected.

To what cause this universal eagerness of writing can be properly ascribed, I have not yet been able to discover. It is said, that every art is propagated in proportion to the rewards conferred upon it; a position from which a stranger would naturally infer, that literature was now blessed with patronage far transcending the candour or munificence of the Augustan age, that the road to greatness was open to none but authors, and that by writing alone riches and honour were to be obtained.

But since it is true, that writers, like other competitors, are very little disposed to favour one another, it is not to be expected, that at a time, when every man writes, any man will patronize; and accordingly, there is not one that I can recollect at present, who professes the least regard for the votaries of science, invites the addresses of learned men, or seems to hope for reputation from any pen but his own.

The cause, therefore, of this epidemical conspiracy for the destruction of paper, must remain a secret; nor can I discover whether we owe it to the influences of the constellations, or the intemperature of seasons: whether the long continuance of the wind at any single point, or intoxicating vapours exhaled from the earth, have turned our nobles and our peasants, our soldiers and traders, our men and women, all into wits philosophers and writers.

It is, indeed, of more importance to search out the cure, than the cause of this intellectual malady; and he would deserve well of his country, who, instead of amusing himself with conjectural speculations, should find means of persuading the peer to inspect his steward's accounts, or repair the rural mansion of his ancestors, who could replace the tradesman behind his counter, and send back the farmer to the mattock and the flail.

131

Singularity is, I think, in its own nature universally and invariably displeasing: in whatever respect a man differs from others, he must be considered by them as either worse or better. By being better, it is well known that a man gains admiration oftener than love, since all approbation of his practice must necessarily condemn him that gives it; and though a man often pleases by inferiority, there are few who desire to give such pleasure. Yet the truth is, that singularity is almost always regarded as a brand of slight reproach; and where it is associated with acknowledged merit, serves as an abatement or an allay of excellence, by which weak eyes are reconciled to its lustre and by which though kindness is not gained, at least envy is averted.

But let no man be in haste to conclude his own merit so great or conspicuous, as to require or justify singularity: it is as hazardous for a moderate understanding to usurp the prerogatives of genius, as for a common form to play over the airs of uncontested beauty. The pride of men will not patiently endure to see one, whose understanding or attainments are but level with their own, break the rules by which they have consented to be bound, or forsake the direction which they submissively follow: all violation of established practice, implies in its own nature a rejection of the common opinion, a defiance of common censure, and an appeal from general laws to private judgment: he, therefore, who differs from others without apparent advantage, ought not to be angry if his arrogance is punished with ridicule; if those, whose example he superciliously overlooks, point him out to derision, and hoot him back again into the common road.

The pride of singularity is often exerted in little things, where right and wrong are indeterminable, and where, therefore, vanity is without excuse. But there are occasions on which it is noble to dare to stand alone. To be pious among infidels, to be disinterested in a time of general venality, to lead a life of virtue and reason in the midst of sensualists, is a proof of a mind intent on nobler things than the praise or blame of men, of a soul fixed in the contemplation of the highest good, and superior to the tyranny of custom and example.

In moral and religious questions only, a wise man will hold no consultations with fashions, because these duties are constant and immutable, and depend not on the notions of men, but the commands of HEAVEN: yet even of these, the external mode is to be in some measure regulated by the prevailing taste of the age in which we live; for he is certainly no friend to virtue, who neglects to give it any lawful attraction, or suffers it to displease the eye or alienate the affections for want of innocent compliance with fashionable decoration.

137

Τι θ' ἔρεξα.   PYTH

What have I been doing ?

As man is a being very sparingly furnished with the power of prescience, he can provide for the future only by considering the past; and as futurity is all in which he has any real interest, he ought very diligently to use the only means by which he can be enabled to enjoy it, and frequently to revolve the experiments which he has hitherto made upon life, that he may gain wisdom from his mistakes and caution from his miscarriages.

Though I do not so exactly conform to the precepts of PYTHA-GORAS, as to practise every night this solemn recollection, yet I am not so lost in dissipation as wholly to omit it; nor can I forbear sometimes to enquire of myself, in what employments my life has passed away. Much of my time has sunk into nothing, and left no trace by which it can be distinguished, and of this I now only know, that it was once in my power and might once have been improved.

Of other parts of life memory can give some account: at some hours I have been gay, and at others serious; I have sometimes mingled in conversation, and sometimes meditated in solitude; one day has ben spent in consulting the ancient sages, and another in writing ADVENTURERS.

At the conclusion of any undertaking, it is usual to compute the loss and profit. As I shall soon cease to write ADVENTURERS, I could not forbear lately to consider what has been the consequence of my labours; and whether I am to reckon the hours laid out in these compositions, as applied to a good and laudable purpose, or suffered to fume away in useless evaporations.

That I have intended well, I have the attestation of my own heart; but good intentions may be frustrated, when they are executed without suitable skill, or directed to an end unattainable in itself.

Some there are, who leave writers very little room for self congratulation; some who affirm, that books have no influence upon the public, that no age was ever made better by its authors, and that to call upon mankind to correct their manners, is like XERXES, to scourge the wind or shackle the torrent.

This opinion they pretend to support by unfailing experience. The world is full of fraud and corruption, rapine and malignity; interest is the ruling motive of mankind, and every one is endeavouring to increase his own stores of happiness by perpetual accumulation, without reflecting upon the numbers whom his superfluity condemns to want: in this state of things a book of morality is published, in which charity and benevolence are strongly enforced; and it is proved beyond opposition, that men are happy in proportion as they are virtuous, and rich as they are liberal. The book is applauded, and the author is preferred; he imagines his applause deserved, and receives less pleasure from the acquisition of reward, than the consciousness of merit. Let us look again upon mankind: interest is still the ruling motive, and the world is yet full of fraud and corruption, malevolence and rapine.

The difficulty of confuting this assertion, arises merely from its generality and comprehension: to overthrow it by a detail of distinct facts, requires a wider survey of the world than human eyes can take; the progress of reformation is gradual and silent, as the extension of evening shadows; we know that they were short at noon, and are long at sun-set, but our senses were not able to discern their increase: we know of every civil nation that it was once savage, and how was it reclaimed but by precept and admonition?

Mankind are universally corrupt, but corrupt in different degrees; as they are universally ignorant, yet with greater or less irradiations of knowledge. How has knowledge or virtue been increased and preserved in one place beyond another, but by diligent inculcation and rational inforcement.

Books of morality are daily written, yet its influence is still little in the world; so the ground is annually ploughed, and yet multitudes are in want of bread. But, surely, neither the labours of the moralist nor of the husbandman are vain: let them for a while neglect their tasks, and their usefulness will be known; the wickedness that is now frequent would become universal, the bread that is now scarce would wholly fail.

The power, indeed, of every individual is small, and the consequence of his endeavours imperceptible in a general prospect of the world. PROVIDENCE has given no man ability to do much, that something might be left for every man to do. The business of life is carried on by a general co-operation; in which the part of any single man can be no more distinguished, than the effect of a particular drop when the meadows are floated by a summer shower: yet every drop increases the inundation, and every hand adds to the happiness or misery of mankind.

That a writer, however zealous or eloquent, seldom works a visible effect upon cities or nations, will readily be granted. The book which is read most, is read by few, compared with those that read it not; and of those few, the greater part peruse it with dispositions that very little favour their own improvement.

It is difficult to enumerate the several motives, which procure to books the honour of perusal: spite, vanity, and curiosity, hope and fear, love and hatred, every passion which incites to any other action, serves at one time or other to stimulate a reader.

Some are fond to take a celebrated volume into their hands, because they hope to distinguish their penetration, by finding faults which have escaped the public; others eagerly buy it in the first bloom of reputation, that they may join the chorus of praise, and not lag, as FALSTAFF terms it, in "the rearward of the fashion."

Some read for stile, and some for argument: one has little care about the sentiment, he observes only how it is expressed; another regards not the conclusion, but is diligent to mark how it is inferred: they read for other purposes, than the attainment of practical knowledge; and are no more likely to grow wise by an examination of a treatise of moral prudence, than an architect to inflame his devotion by considering attentively the proportions of a temple.

Some read that they may embellish their conversation, or shine in dispute; some that they may not be detected in ignorance, or want the reputation of literary accomplishments: but the most general and prevalent reason of study, is the impossibility of finding another amusement equally cheap or constant, equally independent on the hour or the weather. He that wants money to follow the chace of pleasure through her yearly circuit, and is left at home when the gay world rolls to Bath or Tunbridge; he whose gout compells him to hear from his chamber, the rattle of chariots transporting happier beings to plays and assemblies, will be forced to seek in books a refuge from himself.

The author is not wholly useless, who provides innocent amusements for minds like these. There are in the present state of things so many more instigations to evil, than incitements to good, that he who keeps men in a neutral state, may be justly considered as a benefactor to life.

But, perhaps, it seldom happens, that study terminates in mere pastime. Books have always a secret influence on the understanding; we cannot at pleasure obliterate ideas: he that reads books of science, though without any fixed desire of improvement, will grow more knowing; he that entertains himself with moral or religious treatises, will imperceptibly advance in goodness; the ideas which are often offered to the mind, will at last find a lucky moment when it is disposed to receive them.

It is, therefore, urged without reason, as a discouragement to writers, that there are already books sufficient in the world; that all the topics of persuasion have been discussed, and every important question clearly stated and justly decided; and that, therefore, there is no room to hope, that pigmies should conquer where heroes have been defeated, or that the petty copiers of the present time should advance the great work of reformation, which their predecessors were forced to leave unfinished.

Whatever be the present extent of human knowledge, it is not only finite, and therefore in its own nature capable of increase; but so narrow, that almost every understanding may by a diligent application of its powers hope to enlarge it. It is, however, not necessary, that a man should forbear to write, till he has discovered some truth unknown before; he may be sufficiently useful, by only diversifying the surface of knowledge, and luring the mind by a new appearance to a second view of those beauties which it had passed over inattentively before. Every writer may find intellects correspondent to his own, to whom his expressions are familiar, and his thoughts congenial; and, perhaps, truth is often more successfully propagated by men of moderate abilities, who, adopting the opinions of others, have no care but to explain them clearly, than by subtile speculatists and curious searchers, who exact from their readers powers equal to their own, and if their fabrics of science be strong take no care to render them accessible.

For my part, I do not regret the hours which I have laid out in these little compositions. That the world has grown apparently better, since the publication of the ADVENTURER, I have not observed; but am willing to think, that many have been affected by single sentiments, of which it is their business to renew the impression; that many have caught hints of truth, which it is now their duty to persue; and that those who have received no improvement, have wanted not opportunity but intention to improve.

138

Quid purè tranquillet? honos, an dulce lucellum,
An secretum iter, et fallentis semita vitæ?   HOR.

Whether the tranquil mind and pure,
Honours or wealth our bliss insure;
Or down through life unknown to stray,
Where lonely leads the silent way?   FRANCIS.

Having considered the importance of authors to the welfare of the public, I am led by a natural train of thought, to reflect on their condition with regard to themselves; and to enquire, what degree of happiness or vexation is annexed to the difficult and laborious employment, of providing instruction or entertainment for mankind.

In estimating the pain or pleasure of any particular state, every man, indeed, draws his decisions from his own breast, and cannot with certainty determine, whether other minds are affected by the same causes in the same manner. Yet by this criterion we must be content to judge, because no other can be obtained; and, indeed, we have no reason to think it very fallacious, for excepting here and there an anomalous mind, which either does not feel like others, or dissembles its sensibility, we find men unanimously concur in attributing happiness or misery to particular conditions, as they agree in acknowledging the cold of winter and the heat of autumn.

If we apply to authors themselves for an account of their state, it will appear very little to deserve envy; for they have in all ages been addicted to complaint. The neglect of learning, the ingratitude of the present age, and the absurd preference by which ignorance and dulness often obtain favour and rewards, have been from age to age topics of invective; and few have left their names to posterity, without some appeal to future candour from the perverseness and malice of their own times.

I have, nevertheless, been often inclined to doubt, whether the authors, however querulous, are in reality more miserable than their fellow mortals. The present life is to all a state of infelicity;

every man, like an author, believes himself to merit more than he obtains, and solaces the present with the prospect of the future: others, indeed, suffer those disappointments in silence, of which the writer complains, to shew how well he has learnt the art of lamentation.

There is at least one gleam of felicity, of which few writers have missed the enjoyment: he whose hopes have so far overpowered his fears, as that he has resolved to stand forth a candidate for fame, seldom fails to amuse himself, before his appearance, with pleasing scenes of affluence or honour; while his fortune is yet under the regulation of fancy, he easily models it to his wish, suffers no thoughts of critics or rivals to intrude upon his mind, but counts over the bounties of patronage or listens to the voice of praise.

Some there are, that talk very luxuriously of the second period of an author's happiness, and tell of the tumultuous raptures of invention, when the mind riots in imagery, and the choice stands suspended between different sentiments.

These pleasures, I believe, may sometimes be indulged to those, who come to a subject of disquisition with minds full of ideas, and with fancies so vigorous, as easily to excite, select, and arrange them. To write, is, indeed, no unpleasing employment, when one sentiment readily produces another, and both ideas and expressions present themselves at the first summons: but such happiness, the greatest genius does not always obtain; and common writers know it only to such a degree, as to credit its possibility. Composition is, for the most part, an effort of slow diligence and steady perseverence, to which the mind is dragged by necessity or resolution, and from which the attention is every moment starting to more delightful amusements.

It frequently happens, that a design which, when considered at a distance, gave flattering hopes of facility, mocks us in the execution with unexpected difficulties; the mind which, while it considered it in the gross, imagined itself amply furnished with materials, finds sometimes an unexpected barrenness and vacuity, and wonders whither all those ideas are vanished, which a little before seemed struggling for emission.

Sometimes many thoughts present themselves; but so confused and unconnected, that they are not without difficulty reduced to method, or concatenated in a regular and dependent series: the mind falls at once into a labyrinth, of which neither the beginning nor end can be discovered, and toils and struggles without progress or extrication.

It is asserted by HORACE, that "if matter be once got together, words will be found with very little difficulty; " a position which, though sufficiently plausible to be inserted in poetical precepts, is by no means strictly and philosophically true. If words were naturally and necessarily consequential to sentiments, it would always follow, that he who has most knowledge must have most eloquence, and that every man would clearly express what he fully understood: yet we find, that to think, and discourse, are often the qualities of different persons; and many books might surely be produced, where just and noble sentiments are degraded and obscured by unsuitable diction.

Words, therefore, as well as things, claim the care of an author. Indeed, of many authors, and those not useless or contemptible, words are almost the only care: many make it their study, not so much to strike out new sentiments, as to recommend those which are already known to more favourable notice by fairer decorations; but every man, whether he copies or invents, whether he delivers his own thoughts or those of another, has often found himself deficient in the power of expression, big with ideas which he could not utter, obliged to ransack his memory for terms adequate to his conceptions, and at last unable to impress upon his reader the image existing in his own mind.

It is one of the common distresses of a writer, to be within a word of a happy period, to want only a single epithet to give amplification its full force, to require only a correspondent term in order to finish a paragraph with elegance and make one of its members answer to the other: but these deficiencies cannot always be supplied; and after a long study and vexation, the passage is turned anew, and the web unwoven that was so nearly finished.

But when thoughts and words are collected and adjusted, and the whole composition at last concluded, it seldom gratifies the author, when he comes coolly and deliberately to review it, with the hopes which had been excited in the fury of the performance: novelty always captivates the mind; as our thoughts rise fresh upon us, we readily believe them just and original, which, when the pleasure of production is over, we find to be mean and common, or borrowed from the works of others, and supplied by memory rather than invention.

K

But though it should happen, that the writer finds no such faults in his performance, he is still to remember, that he looks upon it with partial eyes; and when he considers, how much men who could judge of others with great exactness, have often failed of judging of themselves, he will be afraid of deciding too hastily in his own favour, or of allowing himself to contemplate with too much complacence, treasure that has not yet been brought to the test, nor passed the only trial that can stamp its value.

From the public, and only from the public, is he to await a confirmation of his claim, and a final justification of self esteem; but the public is not easily persuaded to favour an author. If mankind were left to judge for themselves, it is reasonable to imagine, that of such writings, at least, as describe the movements of the human passions, and of which every man carries the archetype within him, a just opinion would be formed; but whoever has remarked the fate of books, must have found it governed by other causes, than general consent arising from general conviction. If a new performance happens not to fall into the hands of some, who have courage to tell, and authority to propagate their opinion, it often remains long in obscurity, and perhaps perishes unknown and unexamined. A few, a very few, commonly constitute the taste of the time; the judgment which they have once pronounced, some are too lazy to discuss, and some too timorous to contradict: it may, however, be I think observed, that their power is greater to depress than exalt, as mankind are more credulous of censure than of praise.

This perversion of the public judgment, is not to be rashly numbered amongst the miseries of an author; since it commonly serves, after miscarriage, to reconcile him to himself. Because the world has sometimes passed an unjust sentence, he readily concludes the sentence unjust by which his performance is condemned; because some have been exalted above their merits by partiality, he is sure to ascribe the success of a rival, not to the merit of his work, but the zeal of his patrons. Upon the whole, as the author seems to share all the common miseries of life, he appears to partake likewise of its lenitives and abatements.

LETTER TO
LORD CHESTERFIELD

"The celebrated Letter from Samuel Johnson, LL.D., to Philip Dormer Stanhope, Earl of Chesterfield" was written on February 7, 1755: it was not printed until 1790. The present text is from the manuscript (not autograph, but corrected by Johnson) in the British Museum (Add. MS. 5713.); it has been checked with the text of Boswell's 1790 edition, from which it differs only in spelling, punctuation and capitalisation.

LORD CHESTERFIELD

TO THE RIGHT HONOURABLE THE EARL OF CHESTERFIELD.

February 1755.

My lord.

I have been lately informed by the Proprietor of the World that two Papers in which my Dictionary is recommended to the Public were written by your Lordship. To be so distinguished is an honour which, being very little accustomed to favours from the Great, I know not well how to receive, or in what terms to acknowledge.

When upon some slight encouragment I first visited your Lordship I was overpowered like the rest of Mankind by the enchantment of your adress, and could not forbear to wish that I might boast myself Le Vainqueur du Vainqueur de la Terre, that I might obtain that regard for which I saw the World contending, but I found my attendance so little incouraged, that neither pride nor modesty would suffer me to continue it. When I had once adressed your Lordship in public, I had exhausted all the art of pleasing which a retired and uncourtly Scholar can possess. I had done all that I could, and no Man is well pleased to have his all neglected, be it ever so little.

Seven years, My lord have now past since I waited in your outward Rooms or was repulsed from your Door, during which time I have been pushing on my work through difficulties of which it is useless to complain, and have brought it at last to the verge of Publication without one Act of assistance, one word of encouragement, or one smile of favour. Such treatment I did not expect, for I never had a Patron before.

The Shepherd in Virgil grew at last acquainted with Love, and found him a Native of the Rocks.

Is not a Patron, My Lord, one who looks with unconcern on a Man struggling for Life in the Water and when he has reached ground encumbers him with help. The notice which you have been pleased to take of my Labours, had it been early, had been kind; but it has been delayed till I am indifferent and cannot enjoy it, till I am solitary and cannot impart it, till I am known and do not want it.

I hope it is no very cinical asperity not to confess obligation where no benefit has been received, or to be unwilling that the Public should consider me as owing that to a Patron, which Providence has enabled me to do for myself.

Having carried on my work thus far with so little obligation to any Favourer of Learning I shall not be disappointed though I should conclude it, if less be possible, with less, for I have been long wakened from that Dream of hope, in which I once boasted myself with so much exultation,

My lord,

Your Lordship's Most humble

Most Obedient Servant

S. J.

PREFACE TO THE
ENGLISH DICTIONARY

The text here printed of the preface to Johnson's dictionary is his corrected version for the fourth (1773) edition. The British Museum copy (69. i. 11.) has been used. Earlier editions (1755, 1755–1756 and 1765) have been consulted. A footnote has been omitted.

PREFACE TO THE
ENGLISH DICTIONARY

I⊤ is the fate of those who toil at the lower employments of life, to be rather driven by the fear of evil, than attracted by the prospect of good; to be exposed to censure, without hope of praise; to be disgraced by miscarriage, or punished for neglect, where success would have been without applause, and diligence without reward.

Among these unhappy mortals is the writer of dictionaries; whom mankind have considered, not as the pupil, but the slave of science, the pionier of literature, doomed only to remove rubbish and clear obstructions from the paths through which Learning and Genius press forward to conquest and glory, without bestowing a smile on the humble drudge that facilitates their progress. Every other authour may aspire to praise; the lexicographer can only hope to escape reproach, and even this negative recompense has been yet granted to very few.

I have, notwithstanding this discouragement, attempted a dictionary of the *English* language, which, while it was employed in the cultivation of every species of literature, has itself been hitherto neglected; suffered to spread, under the direction of chance, into wild exuberance; resigned to the tyranny of time and fashion; and exposed to the corruptions of ignorance, and caprices of innovation.

When I took the first survey of my undertaking, I found our speech copious without order, and energetick without rules: wherever I turned my view, there was perplexity to be disentangled, and confusion to be regulated; choice was to be made out of boundless variety, without any established principle of selection; adulterations were to be detected, without a settled test of purity; and modes of expression to be rejected or received, without the suffrages of any writers of classical reputation or acknowledged authority.

Having therefore no assistance but from general grammar, I applied myself to the perusal of our writers; and noting whatever might be of use to ascertain or illustrate any word or phrase, accumulated in time the materials of a dictionary, which, by degrees, I reduced to method, establishing to myself, in the progress of the work, such rules as experience and analogy suggested to me; experience, which practice and observation were continually increasing; and analogy, which, though in some words obscure, was evident in others.

In adjusting the ORTHOGRAPHY, which has been to this time unsettled and fortuitous, I found it necessary to distinguish those irregularities that are inherent in our tongue, and perhaps coeval with it, from others which the ignorance or negligence of later writers has produced. Every language has its anomalies, which, though inconvenient, and in themselves once unnecessary, must be tolerated among the imperfections of human things, and which require only to be registered, that they may not be increased, and ascertained, that they may not be confounded: but every language has likewise its improprieties and absurdities, which it is the duty of the lexicographer to correct or proscribe.

As language was at its beginning merely oral, all words of necessary or common use were spoken before they were written; and while they were unfixed by any visible signs, must have been spoken with great diversity, as we now observe those who cannot read to catch sounds imperfectly, and utter them negligently. When this wild and barbarous jargon was first reduced to an alphabet, every penman endeavoured to express, as he could, the sounds which he was accustomed to pronounce or to receive, and vitiated in writing such words as were already vitiated in speech. The powers of the letters, when they were applied to a new language, must have been vague and unsettled, and therefore different hands would exhibit the same sound by different combinations.

From this uncertain pronunciation arise in a great part the various dialects of the same country, which will always be observed to grow fewer, and less different, as books are multiplied; and from this arbitrary representation of sounds by letters, proceeds that diversity of spelling observable in the *Saxon* remains, and I suppose in the first books of every nation, which perplexes or destroys analogy, and produces anomalous formations, that, being once incorporated, can never be afterward dismissed or reformed.

Of this kind are the derivatives *length* from *long*, *strength* from *strong*, *darling* from *dear*, *breadth* from *broad*, from *dry*, *drought*, and from *high*, *height*, which *Milton*, in zeal for analogy, writes *highth*; *Quid te exempta juvat spinis de pluribus una*; to change all would be too much, and to change one is nothing.

This uncertainty is most frequent in the vowels, which are so capriciously pronounced, and so differently modified, by accident or affectation, not only in every province, but in every mouth, that to them, as is well known to etymologists, little regard is to be shewn in the deduction of one language from another.

Such defects are not errours in orthography, but spots of barbarity impressed so deep in the *English* language, that criticism can never wash them away; these, therefore, must be permitted to remain untouched; but many words have likewise been altered by accident, or depraved by ignorance, as the pronunciation of the vulgar has been weakly followed; and some still continue to be variously written, as authours differ in their care or skill: of these it was proper to enquire the true orthography, which I have always considered as depending on their derivation, and have therefore referred them to their original languages: thus I write *enchant*, *enchantment*, *enchanter*, after the *French*, and *incantation* after the *Latin*; thus *entire* is chosen rather than *intire*, because it passed to us not from the *Latin integer*, but from the *French entier*.

Of many words it is difficult to say whether they were immediately received from the *Latin* or the *French*, since at the time when we had dominions in *France*, we had *Latin* service in our churches. It is, however, my opinion, that the *French* generally supplied us; for we have few *Latin* words, among the terms of domestick use, which are not *French*; but many *French*, which are very remote from *Latin*.

Even in words of which the derivation is apparent, I have been often obliged to sacrifice uniformity to custom; thus I write, in compliance with a numberless majority, *convey* and *inveigh*, *deceit* and *receipt*, *fancy* and *phantom*; sometimes the derivative varies from the primitive, as *explain* and *explanation*, *repeat* and *repetition*.

Some combinations of letters having the same power are used indifferently without any discoverable reason of choice, as in *choak*, *choke*; *soap*, *sope*; *fewel*, *fuel*, and many others; which I have sometimes inserted twice, that those who search for them under either form, may not search in vain.

In examining the orthography of any doubtful word, the mode of spelling by which it is inserted in the series of the dictionary, is to be considered as that to which I give, perhaps not often rashly, the preference. I have left, in the examples, to every authour his own practice unmolested, that the reader may balance suffrages, and judge between us: but this question is not always to be determined by reputed or by real learning; some men, intent upon greater things, have thought little on sounds and derivations; some, knowing in the ancient tongues, have neglected those in which our words are commonly to be sought. Thus *Hammond* writes *fecibleness* for *feasibleness*, because I suppose he imagined it derived immediately from the *Latin*; and some words, such as *dependant, dependent*; *dependance, dependence*, vary their final syllable, as one or another language is present to the writer.

In this part of the work, where caprice has long wantoned without controul, and vanity sought praise by petty reformation, I have endeavoured to proceed with a scholar's reverence for antiquity, and a grammarian's regard to the genius of our tongue. I have attempted few alterations, and among those few, perhaps the greater part is from the modern to the ancient practice; and I hope I may be allowed to recommend to those, whose thoughts have been perhaps employed too anxiously on verbal singularities, not to disturb, upon narrow views, or for minute propriety, the orthography of their fathers. It has been asserted, that for the law to be *known*, is of more importance than to be *right*. Change, says *Hooker*, is not made without inconvenience, even from worse to better. There is in constancy and stability a general and lasting advantage, which will always overbalance the slow improvements of gradual correction. Much less ought our written language to comply with the corruptions of oral utterance, or copy that which every variation of time or place makes different from itself, and imitate those changes, which will again be changed, while imitation is employed in observing them.

This recommendation of steadiness and uniformity does not proceed from an opinion, that particular combinations of letters have much influence on human happiness; or that truth may not be successfully taught by modes of spelling fanciful and erroneous: I am not yet so lost in lexicography, as to forget that *words are the daughters of earth, and that things are the sons of heaven.* Language is only the instrument of science, and words are but the signs of ideas: I wish, however, that the instrument might be less apt to decay, and that signs might be permanent, like the things which they denote.

In settling the orthography, I have not wholly neglected the pronunciation, which I have directed, by printing an accent upon the acute or elevated syllable. It will sometimes be found, that the accent is placed by the authour quoted, on a different syllable from that marked in the alphabetical series; it is then to be understood, that custom has varied, or that the authour has, in my opinion, pronounced wrong. Short directions are sometimes given where the sound of letters is irregular; and if they are sometimes omitted, defect in such minute observations will be more easily excused, than superfluity.

In the investigation both of the orthography and signification of words, their ETYMOLOGY was necessarily to be considered, and they were therefore to be divided into primitives and derivatives. A primitive word, is that which can be traced no further to any *English* root; thus *circumspect, circumvent, circumstance, delude, concave,* and *complicate,* though compounds in the *Latin,* are to us primitives. Derivatives, are all those that can be referred to any word in *English* of greater simplicity.

The derivatives I have referred to their primitives, with an accuracy sometimes needless; for who does not see that *remoteness* comes from *remote, lovely* from *love, concavity* from *concave,* and *demonstrative* from *demonstrate*? but this grammatical exuberance the scheme of my work did not allow me to repress. It is of great importance in examining the general fabrick of a language, to trace one word from another, by noting the usual modes of derivation and inflection; and uniformity must be preserved in systematical works, though sometimes at the expence of particular propriety.

Among other derivatives I have been careful to insert and elucidate the anomalous plurals of nouns and preterites of verbs, which in the *Teutonick* dialects are very frequent, and though familiar to those who have always used them, interrupt and embarrass the learners of our language.

The two languages from which our primitives have been derived are the *Roman* and *Teutonick:* under the *Roman* I comprehend the *French* and provincial tongues; and under the *Teutonick* range the *Saxon, German,* and all their kindred dialects. Most of our polysyllables are *Roman*, and our words of one syllable are very often *Teutonick*.

In assigning the *Roman* original, it has perhaps sometimes happened that I have mentioned only the *Latin*, when the word was borrowed from the *French*; and considering myself as employed only in the illustration of my own language, I have not been very careful to observe whether the *Latin* word be pure or barbarous, or the *French* elegant or obsolete.

For the *Teutonick* etymologies I am commonly indebted to *Junius* and *Skinner*, the only names which I have forborn to quote when I copied their books; not that I might appropriate their labours or usurp their honours, but that I might spare a perpetual repetition by one general acknowledgment. Of these, whom I ought not to mention but with the reverence due to instructors and benefactors, *Junius* appears to have excelled in extent of learning, and *Skinner* in rectitude of understanding. *Junius* was accurately skilled in all the northern languages, *Skinner* probably examined the ancient and remoter dialects only by occasional inspection into dictionaries; but the learning of *Junius* is often of no other use than to show him a track by which he may deviate from his purpose, to which *Skinner* always presses forward by the shortest way. *Skinner* is often ignorant, but never ridiculous: *Junius* is always full of knowledge; but his variety distracts his judgment, and his learning is very frequently disgraced by his absurdities.

The votaries of the northern muses will not perhaps easily restrain their indignation, when they find the name of *Junius* thus degraded by a disadvantageous comparison; but whatever reverence is due to his diligence, or his attainments, it can be no criminal degree of censoriousness to charge that etymologist with want of judgment, who can seriously derive *dream* from *drama*, because *life is a drama, and a drama is a dream*; and who declares with a tone of defiance, that no man can fail to derive *moan* from μόνος, *monos*, *single* or *solitary*, who considers that grief naturally loves to be *alone*.

Our knowledge of the northern literature is so scanty, that of words undoubtedly *Teutonick* the original is not always to be found in any ancient language; and I have therefore inserted *Dutch* or *German* substitutes, which I consider not as radical but parallel, not as the parents, but sisters of the *English*.

The words which are represented as thus related by descent or

306

cognation, do not always agree in sense; for it is incident to words, as to their authours, to degenerate from their ancestors, and to change their manners when they change their country. It is sufficient, in etymological enquiries, if the senses of kindred words be found such as may easily pass into each other, or such as may both be referred to one general idea.

The etymology, so far as it is yet known, was easily found in the volumes where it is particularly and professedly delivered; and, by proper attention to the rules of derivation, the orthography was soon adjusted. But to COLLECT the WORDS of our language was a task of greater difficulty: the deficiency of dictionaries was immediately apparent; and when they were exhausted, what was yet wanting must be sought by fortuitous and unguided excursions into books, and gleaned as industry should find, or chance should offer it, in the boundless chaos of a living speech. My search, however, has been either skilful or lucky; for I have much augmented the vocabulary.

As my design was a dictionary, common or appellative, I have omitted all words which have relation to proper names; such as *Arian, Socinian, Calvinist, Benedictine, Mahometan*; but have retained those of a more general nature, as *Heathen, Pagan*.

Of the terms of art I have received such as could be found either in books of science or technical dictionaries; and have often inserted, from philosophical writers, words which are supported perhaps only by a single authority, and which being not admitted into general use, stand yet as candidates or probationers, and must depend for their adoption on the suffrage of futurity.

The words which our authours have introduced by their knowledge of foreign languages, or ignorance of their own, by vanity or wantonness, by compliance with fashion or lust of innovation, I have registred as they occurred, though commonly only to censure them, and warn others against the folly of naturalizing useless foreigners to the injury of the natives.

I have not rejected any by design, merely because they were unnecessary or exuberant; but have received those which by different writers have been differently formed, as *viscid*, and *viscidity*, *viscous*, and *viscosity*.

Compounded or double words I have seldom noted, except when they obtain a signification different from that which the components have in their simple state. Thus *highwayman, woodman*, and *horsecourser*, require an explication; but of *thieflike* or *coach-driver* no notice was needed, because the primitives contain the meaning of the compounds.

Words arbitrarily formed by a constant and settled analogy, like diminutive adjectives in *ish*, as *greenish*, *bluish*, adverbs in *ly*, as *dully*, *openly*, substantives in *ness*, as *vileness*, *faultiness*, were less diligently sought, and sometimes have been omitted, when I had no authority that invited me to insert them; not that they are not genuine and regular offsprings of *English* roots, but because their relation to the primitive being always the same, their signification cannot be mistaken.

The verbal nouns in *ing*, such as the *keeping* of the *castle*, the *leading* of the *army*, are always neglected, or placed only to illustrate the sense of the verb, except when they signify things as well as actions, and have therefore a plural number, as *dwelling*, *living*; or have an absolute and abstract signification, as *colouring*, *painting*, *learning*.

The participles are likewise omitted, unless, by signifying rather habit or quality than action, they take the nature of adjectives; as a *thinking* man, a man of prudence; a *pacing* horse, a horse that can pace: these I have ventured to call *participial adjectives*. But neither are these always inserted, because they are commonly to be understood, without any danger of mistake, by consulting the verb.

Obsolete words are admitted, when they are found in authours not obsolete, or when they have any force or beauty that may deserve revival.

As composition is one of the chief characteristicks of a language, I have endeavoured to make some reparation for the universal negligence of my predecessors, by inserting great numbers of compounded words, as may be found under *after*, *fore*, *new*, *night*, *fair*, and many more. These, numerous as they are, might be multiplied, but that use and curiosity are here satisfied, and the frame of our language and modes of our combination amply discovered.

Of some forms of composition, such as that by which *re* is prefixed to note *repetition*, and *un* to signify *contrariety* or *privation*, all the examples cannot be accumulated, because the use of these particles, if not wholly arbitrary, is so little limited, that they are hourly affixed to new words as occasion requires, or is imagined to require them.

There is another kind of composition more frequent in our language than perhaps in any other, from which arises to foreigners the greatest difficulty. We modify the signification of many verbs by a particle subjoined; as to *come off*, to escape by a fetch; to *fall on*, to attack; to *fall off*, to apostatize; to *break off*, to stop abruptly; to *bear out*, to justify; to *fall in*, to comply; to *give over*, to cease; to *set off*, to embellish; to *set in*, to begin a continual tenour; to *set out*, to begin a course or journey; to *take off*, to copy; with innumerable expressions of the same kind, of which some appear wildly irregular, being so far distant from the sense of the simple words, that no sagacity will be able to trace the steps by which they arrived at the present use. These I have noted with great care; and though I cannot flatter myself that the collection is complete, I believe I have so far assisted the students of our language, that this kind of phraseology will be no longer insuperable; and the combinations of verbs and particles, by chance omitted, will be easily explained by comparison with those that may be found.

Many words yet stand supported only by the name of *Bailey, Ainsworth, Philips*, or the contracted *Dict.* for *Dictionaries* subjoined; of these I am not always certain that they are read in any book but the works of lexicographers. Of such I have omitted many, because I had never read them; and many I have inserted, because they may perhaps exist, though they have escaped my notice: they are, however, to be yet considered as resting only upon the credit of former dictionaries. Others, which I considered as useful, or know to be proper, though I could not at present support them by authorities, I have suffered to stand upon my own attestation, claiming the same privilege with my predecessors of being sometimes credited without proof.

The words, thus selected and disposed, are grammatically considered; they are referred to the different parts of speech; traced, when they are irregularly inflected, through their various terminations; and illustrated by observations, not indeed of great or striking importance, separately considered, but necessary to the elucidation of our language, and hitherto neglected or forgotten by *English* grammarians.

That part of my work on which I expect malignity most frequently to fasten, is the *Explanation*; in which I cannot hope to satisfy those, who are perhaps not inclined to be pleased, since I have not always been able to satisfy myself. To interpret a language by itself is very difficult; many words cannot be explained by synonimes, because the idea signified by them has not more than one appellation; nor by paraphrase, because simple ideas cannot be described. When the nature of things is unknown, or the notion unsettled and indefinite, and various in various minds, the words by which such notions are conveyed, or such things denoted, will be ambiguous and perplexed. And such is the fate of hapless lexicography, that not only darkness, but light, impedes and distresses it; things may be not only too little, but too much known, to be happily illustrated. To explain, requires the use of terms less abstruse than that which is to be explained, and such terms cannot always be found; for as nothing can be proved but by supposing something intuitively known, and evident without proof, so nothing can be defined but by the use of words too plain to admit a definition.

Other words there are, of which the sense is too subtle and evanescent to be fixed in a paraphrase; such are all those which are by the grammarians termed *expletives*, and, in dead languages, are suffered to pass for empty sounds, of no other use than to fill a verse, or to modulate a period, but which are easily perceived in living tongues to have power and emphasis, though it be sometimes such as no other form of expression can convey.

My labour has likewise been much increased by a class of verbs too frequent in the *English* language, of which the signification is so loose and general, the use so vague and indeterminate, and the senses detorted so widely from the first idea, that it is hard to trace them through the maze of variation, to catch them on the brink of utter inanity, to circumscribe them by any limitations, or interpret them by any words of distinct and settled meaning; such are *bear, break, come, cast, fall, get, give, do, put, set, go, run, make, take, turn, throw.* If of these the whole power is not accurately delivered, it must be remembered, that while our language is yet living, and variable by the caprice of every one that speaks it, these words are hourly shifting their relations, and can no more be ascertained in a dictionary, than a grove, in the agitation of a storm, can be accurately delineated from its picture in the water.

The particles are among all nations applied with so great latitude, that they are not easily reducible under any regular scheme of explication: this difficulty is not less, nor perhaps greater, in *English*, than in other languages. I have laboured them with diligence, I hope with success; such at least as can be expected in a task, which no man, however learned or sagacious, has yet been able to perform.

Some words there are which I cannot explain, because I do not understand them; these might have been omitted very often with little inconvenience, but I would not so far indulge my vanity as to decline this confession: for when *Tully* owns himself ignorant whether *lessus*, in the twelve tables, means a *funeral song*, or *mourning garment;* and *Aristotle* doubts whether οὐρεύς, in the Iliad, signifies a *mule*, or *muleteer*, I may surely, without shame, leave some obscurities to happier industry, or future information.

The rigour of interpretative lexicography requires that *the explanation, and the word explained, should be always reciprocal*; this I have always endeavoured, but could not always attain. Words are seldom exactly synonimous; a new term was not introduced, but because the former was thought inadequate: names, therefore, have often many ideas, but few ideas have many names. It was then necessary to use the proximate word, for the deficiency of single terms can very seldom be supplied by circumlocution; nor is the inconvenience great of such mutilated interpretations, because the sense may easily be collected entire from the examples.

In every word of extensive use, it was requisite to mark the progress of its meaning, and show by what gradations of intermediate sense it has passed from its primitive to its remote and accidental signification; so that every foregoing explanation should tend to that which follows, and the series be regularly concatenated from the first notion to the last.

This is specious, but not always practicable; kindred senses may be so interwoven, that the perplexity cannot be disentangled, nor any reason be assigned why one should be ranged before the other. When the radical idea branches out into parallel ramifications, how can a consecutive series be formed of senses in their nature collateral? The shades of meaning sometimes pass imperceptibly into each other; so that though on one side they apparently differ, yet it is impossible to mark the point of contact. Ideas of the same race, though not exactly alike, are sometimes so little different, that no words can express the dissimilitude, though the mind easily perceives it, when they are exhibited together; and sometimes there is such a confusion of acceptations, that discernment is wearied, and distinction puzzled, and perseverance herself hurries to an end, by crouding together what she cannot separate.

These complaints of difficulty will, by those that have never considered words beyond their popular use, be thought only the jargon of a man willing to magnify his labours, and procure veneration to his studies by involution and obscurity. But every art is obscure to those that have not learned it: this uncertainty of terms, and commixture of ideas, is well known to those who have joined philosophy with grammar; and if I have not expressed them very clearly, it must be remembered that I am speaking of that which words are insufficient to explain.

The original sense of words is often driven out of use by their metaphorical acceptations, yet must be inserted for the sake of a regular origination. Thus I know not whether *ardour* is used for *material heat*, or whether *flagrant*, in *English*, ever signifies the same with *burning*; yet such are the primitive ideas of these words, which are therefore set first, though without examples, that the figurative senses may be commodiously deduced.

Such is the exuberance of signification which many words have obtained, that it was scarcely possible to collect all their senses; sometimes the meaning of derivatives must be sought in the mother term, and sometimes deficient explanations of the primitive may be supplied in the train of derivation. In any case of doubt or difficulty, it will be always proper to examine all the words of the same race; for some words are slightly passed over to avoid repetition, some admitted easier and clearer explanation than others, and all will be better understood, as they are considered in greater variety of structures and relations.

All the interpretations of words are not written with the same skill, or the same happiness: things equally easy in themselves, are not all equally easy to any single mind. Every writer of a long work commits errours, where there appears neither ambiguity to mislead, nor obscurity to confound him; and in a search like this, many felicities of expression will be casually overlooked, many convenient parallels will be forgotten, and many particulars will admit improvement from a mind utterly unequal to the whole performance.

But many seeming faults are to be imputed rather to the nature of the undertaking, than the negligence of the performer. Thus some explanations are unavoidably reciprocal or circular, as *hind*, *the female of the stag*; *stag*, *the male of the hind*: sometimes easier words are changed into harder, as *burial* into *sepulture* or *inter-*

312

ment, drier into *desiccative, dryness* into *siccity* or *aridity, fit* into *paroxysm*; for the easiest word, whatever it be, can never be translated into one more easy. But easiness and difficulty are merely relative, and if the present prevalence of our language should invite foreigners to this dictionary, many will be assisted by those words which now seem only to increase or produce obscurity. For this reason I have endeavoured frequently to join a *Teutonick* and *Roman* interpretation, as to CHEER, to *gladden,* or *exhilarate,* that every learner of *English* may be assisted by his own tongue.

The solution of all difficulties, and the supply of all defects, must be sought in the examples, subjoined to the various senses of each word, and ranged according to the time of their authours.

When I first collected these authorities, I was desirous that every quotation should be useful to some other end than the illustration of a word; I therefore extracted from philosophers principles of science; from historians remarkable facts; from chymists complete processes; from divines striking exhortations; and from poets beautiful descriptions. Such is design, while it is yet at a distance from execution. When the time called upon me to range this accumulation of elegance and wisdom into an alphabetical series, I soon discovered that the bulk of my volumes would fright away the student, and was forced to depart from my scheme of including all that was pleasing or useful in *English* literature, and reduce my transcripts very often to clusters of words, in which scarcely any meaning is retained; thus to the weariness of copying, I was condemned to add the vexation of expunging. Some passages I have yet spared, which may relieve the labour of verbal searches, and intersperse with verdure and flowers the dusty desarts of barren philology.

The examples, thus mutilated, are no longer to be considered as conveying the sentiments or doctrine of their authours; the word for the sake of which they are inserted, with all its appendant clauses, has been carefully preserved; but it may sometimes happen, by hasty detruncation, that the general tendency of the sentence may be changed: the divine may desert his tenets, or the philosopher his system.

Some of the examples have been taken from writers who were never mentioned as masters of elegance or models of stile; but words must be sought where they are used; and in what pages, eminent for purity, can terms of manufacture or agriculture be found? Many quotations serve no other purpose, than that of proving the bare existence of words, and are therefore selected with less scrupulousness than those which are to teach their structures and relations.

My purpose was to admit no testimony of living authours, that I might not be misled by partiality, and that none of my cotemporaries might have reason to complain; nor have I departed from this resolution, but when some performance of uncommon excellence excited my veneration, when my memory supplied me, from late books, with an example that was wanting, or when my heart, in the tenderness of friendship, solicited admission for a favourite name.

So far have I been from any care to grace my pages with modern decorations, that I have studiously endeavoured to collect examples and authorities from the writers before the restoration, whose works I regard as *the wells of English undefiled,* as the pure sources of genuine diction. Our language, for almost a century, has, by the concurrence of many causes, been gradually departing from its original *Teutonick* character, and deviating towards a *Gallick* structure and phraseology, from which it ought to be our endeavour to recal it, by making our ancient volumes the groundwork of stile, admitting among the additions of later times, only such as may supply real deficiencies, such as are readily adopted by the genius of our tongue, and incorporate easily with our native idioms.

But as every language has a time of rudeness antecedent to perfection, as well as of false refinement and declension, I have been cautious lest my zeal for antiquity might drive me into times too remote, and croud my book with words now no longer understood. I have fixed *Sidney's* work for the boundary, beyond which I make few excursions. From the authours which rose in the time of *Elizabeth,* a speech might be formed adequate to all the purposes of use and elegance. If the language of theology were extracted from *Hooker* and the translation of the Bible; the terms of natural knowledge from *Bacon*; the phrases of policy, war, and navigation from *Raleigh*; the dialect of poetry and fiction from *Spenser* and *Sidney*; and the diction of common life from *Shakespeare*, few ideas would be lost to mankind, for want of *English* words, in which they might be expressed.

It is not sufficient that a word is found, unless it be so combined as that its meaning is apparently determined by the tract and tenour of the sentence; such passages I have therefore chosen, and when it happened that any authour gave a definition of a term, or such an explanation as is equivalent to a definition, I have placed his authority as a supplement to my own, without regard to the chronological order, that is otherwise observed.

Some words, indeed, stand unsupported by any authority, but they are commonly derivative nouns or adverbs, formed from their primitives by regular and constant analogy, or names of things seldom occurring in books, or words of which I have reason to doubt the existence.

There is more danger of censure from the multiplicity than paucity of examples; authorities will sometimes seem to have been accumulated without necessity or use, and perhaps some will be found, which might, without loss, have been omitted. But a work of this kind is not hastily to be charged with superfluities: those quotations, which to careless or unskilful perusers appear only to repeat the same sense, will often exhibit, to a more accurate examiner, diversities of signification, or, at least, afford different shades of the same meaning: one will shew the word applied to persons, another to things; one will express an ill, another a good, and a third a neutral sense; one will prove the expression genuine from an ancient authour; another will shew it elegant from a modern: a doubtful authority is corroborated by another of more credit; an ambiguous sentence is ascertained by a passage clear and determinate; the word, how often soever repeated, appears with new associates and in different combinations, and every quotation contributes something to the stability or enlargement of the language.

When words are used equivocally, I receive them in either sense; when they are metaphorical, I adopt them in their primitive acceptation.

I have sometimes, though rarely, yielded to the temptation of exhibiting a genealogy of sentiments, by shewing how one authour copied the thoughts and diction of another: such quotations are indeed little more than repetitions, which might justly be censured, did they not gratify the mind, by affording a kind of intellectual history.

The various syntactical structures occurring in the examples have been carefully noted; the licence or negligence with which many

315

words have been hitherto used, has made our stile capricious and indeterminate; when the different combinations of the same word are exhibited together, the preference is readily given to propriety, and I have often endeavoured to direct the choice.

Thus have I laboured by settling the orthography, displaying the analogy, regulating the structures, and ascertaining the signification of *English* words, to perform all the parts of a faithful lexicographer: but I have not always executed my own scheme, or satisfied my own expectations. The work, whatever proofs of diligence and attention it may exhibit, is yet capable of many improvements: the orthography which I recommend is still controvertible, the etymology which I adopt is uncertain, and perhaps frequently erroneous; the explanations are sometimes too much contracted, and sometimes too much diffused, the significations are distinguished rather with subtilty than skill, and the attention is harrassed with unnecessary minuteness.

The examples are too often injudiciously truncated, and perhaps sometimes, I hope very rarely, alleged in a mistaken sense; for in making this collection I trusted more to memory, than, in a state of disquiet and embarrassment, memory can contain, and purposed to supply at the review what was left incomplete in the first transcription.

Many terms appropriated to particular occupations, though necessary and significant, are undoubtedly omitted; and of the words most studiously considered and exemplified, many senses have escaped observation.

Yet these failures, however frequent, may admit extenuation and apology. To have attempted much is always laudable, even when the enterprize is above the strength that undertakes it: To rest below his own aim is incident to every one whose fancy is active, and whose views are comprehensive; nor is any man satisfied with himself because he has done much, but because he can conceive little. When first I engaged in this work, I resolved to leave neither words nor things unexamined, and pleased myself with a prospect of the hours which I should revel away in feasts of literature, with the obscure recesses of northern learning, which I should enter and ransack; the treasures with which I expected every search into those neglected mines to reward my labour, and the triumph with which I should display my acquisitions to mankind. When I had thus enquired into the original of words, I resolved to show likewise my attention to things; to pierce deep into every science, to enquire the nature of every substance of which I inserted the name, to limit every idea by a definition strictly logical, and exhibit every production of art or nature in an accurate description, that my book might be in place of all other dictionaries whether appellative or technical. But these were the dreams of a poet doomed at last to wake a lexicographer. I soon found that it is too late to look for instruments, when the work calls for execution, and that whatever abilities I had brought to my task, with those I must finally perform it. To deliberate whenever I doubted, to enquire whenever I was ignorant, would have protracted the undertaking without end, and, perhaps, without much improvement; for I did not find by my first experiments, that what I had not of my own was easily to be obtained: I saw that one enquiry only gave occasion to another, that book referred to book, that to search was not always to find, and to find was not always to be informed; and that thus to persue perfection, was, like the first inhabitants of Arcadia, to chace the sun, which, when they had reached the hill where he seemed to rest, was still beheld at the same distance from them.

I then contracted my design, determining to confide in myself, and no longer to solicit auxiliaries, which produced more incumbrance than assistance: by this I obtained at least one advantage, that I set limits to my work, which would in time be ended, though not completed.

Despondency has never so far prevailed as to depress me to negligence; some faults will at last appear to be the effects of anxious diligence and persevering activity. The nice and subtle ramifications of meaning were not easily avoided by a mind intent upon accuracy, and convinced of the necessity of disentangling combinations, and separating similitudes. Many of the distinctions which to common readers appear useless and idle, will be found real and important by men versed in the school philosophy, without which no dictionary ever shall be accurately compiled, or skilfully examined.

Some senses however there are, which, though not the same, are yet so nearly allied, that they are often confounded. Most men think indistinctly, and therefore cannot speak with exactness; and consequently some examples might be indifferently put to either signification: this uncertainty is not to be imputed to me, who do not form, but register the language; who do not teach men how they should think, but relate how they have hitherto expressed their thoughts.

The imperfect sense of some examples I lamented, but could not remedy, and hope they will be compensated by innumerable passages selected with propriety, and preserved with exactness; some shining with sparks of imagination, and some replete with treasures of wisdom.

The orthography and etymology, though imperfect, are not imperfect for want of care, but because care will not always be successful, and recollection or information come too late for use.

That many terms of art and manufacture are omitted, must be frankly acknowledged; but for this defect I may boldly allege that it was unavoidable: I could not visit caverns to learn the miner's language, nor take a voyage to perfect my skill in the dialect of navigation, nor visit the warehouses of merchants, and shops of artificers, to gain the names of wares, tools and operations, of which no mention is found in books; what favourable accident, or easy enquiry brought within my reach, has not been neglected; but it had been a hopeless labour to glean up words, by courting living information, and contesting with the sullenness of one, and the roughness of another.

To furnish the academicians *della Crusca* with words of this kind, a series of comedies called *la Fiera,* or *the Fair,* was professedly written by *Buonaroti*; but I had no such assistant, and therefore was content to want what they must have wanted likewise, had they not luckily been so supplied.

Nor are all words which are not found in the vocabulary, to be lamented as omissions. Of the laborious and mercantile part of the people, the diction is in a great measure casual and mutable; many of their terms are formed for some temporary or local convenience, and though current at certain times and places, are in others utterly unknown. This fugitive cant, which is always in a state of increase or decay, cannot be regarded as any part of the durable materials of a language, and therefore must be suffered to perish with other things unworthy of preservation.

Care will sometimes betray to the appearance of negligence. He that is catching opportunities which seldom occur, will suffer those to pass by unregarded, which he expects hourly to return; he that is searching for rare and remote things, will neglect those that are obvious and familiar: thus many of the most common and cursory words have been inserted with little illustration, because in gathering the authorities, I forbore to copy those which I thought likely to occur whenever they were wanted. It is remarkable that, in reviewing my collection, I found the word Sea unexemplified.

Thus it happens, that in things difficult there is danger from ignorance, and in things easy from confidence; the mind, afraid of greatness, and disdainful of littleness, hastily withdraws herself from painful searches, and passes with scornful rapidity over tasks not adequate to her powers, sometimes too secure for caution, and again too anxious for vigorous effort; sometimes idle in a plain path, and sometimes distracted in labyrinths, and dissipated by different intentions.

A large work is difficult because it is large, even though all its parts might singly be performed with facility; where there are many things to be done, each must be allowed its share of time and labour, in the proportion only which it bears to the whole; nor can it be expected, that the stones which form the dome of a temple, should be squared and polished like the diamond of a ring.

Of the event of this work, for which, having laboured it with so much application, I cannot but have some degree of parental fondness, it is natural to form conjectures. Those who have been persuaded to think well of my design, will require that it should fix our language, and put a stop to those alterations which time and chance have hitherto been suffered to make in it without opposition. With this consequence I will confess that I flattered myself for a while; but now begin to fear that I have indulged expectation which neither reason nor experience can justify. When we see men grow old and die at a certain time one after another, from century to century, we laugh at the elixir that promises to prolong life to a thousand years; and with equal justice may the lexicographer be derided, who being able to produce no example of a nation that has preserved their words and phrases from mutability, shall imagine that his dictionary can embalm his language, and secure it from corruption and decay, that it is in his power to change sublunary nature, and clear the world at once from folly, vanity, and affectation.

With this hope, however, academies have been instituted, to guard the avenues of their languages, to retain fugitives, and repulse intruders; but their vigilance and activity have hitherto been vain; sounds are too volatile and subtile for legal restraints;

to enchain syllables, and to lash the wind, are equally the undertakings of pride, unwilling to measure its desires by its strength. The *French* language has visibly changed under the inspection of the academy; the stile of *Amelot*'s translation of father *Paul* is observed by *Le Courayer* to be *un peu passé*; and no *Italian* will maintain, that the diction of any modern writer is not perceptibly different from that of *Boccace, Machiavel*, or *Caro*.

Total and sudden transformations of a language seldom happen; conquests and migrations are now very rare: but there are other causes of change, which, though slow in their operation, and invisible in their progress, are perhaps as much superiour to human resistance, as the revolutions of the sky, or intumescence of the tide. Commerce, however necessary, however lucrative, as it depraves the manners, corrupts the language; they that have frequent intercourse with strangers, to whom they endeavour to accommodate themselves, must in time learn a mingled dialect, like the jargon which serves the traffickers on the *Mediterranean* and *Indian* coasts. This will not always be confined to the exchange, the warehouse, or the port, but will be communicated by degrees to other ranks of the people, and be at last incorporated with the current speech.

There are likewise internal causes equally forcible. The language most likely to continue long without alteration, would be that of a nation raised a little, and but a little above barbarity, secluded from strangers, and totally employed in procuring the conveniencies of life; either without books, or, like some of the *Mahometan* countries, with very few: men thus busied and unlearned, having only such words as common use requires, would perhaps long continue to express the same notions by the same signs. But no such constancy can be expected in a people polished by arts, and classed by subordination, where one part of the community is sustained and accommodated by the labour of the other. Those who have much leisure to think, will always be enlarging the stock of ideas, and every increase of knowledge, whether real or fancied, will produce new words, or combinations of words. When the mind is unchained from necessity, it will range after convenience; when it is left at large in the fields of speculation, it will shift opinions; as any custom is disused, the words that expressed it must perish with it; as any opinion grows popular, it will innovate speech in the same proportion as it alters practice.

As by the cultivation of various sciences, a language is amplified, it will be more furnished with words deflected from their original sense; the geometrician will talk of a courtier's zenith, or the excentrick virtue of a wild hero, and the physician of sanguine expectations and phlegmatick delays. Copiousness of speech will give opportunities to capricious choice, by which some words will be preferred, and others degraded; vicissitudes of fashion will enforce the use of new, or extend the signification of known terms. The tropes of poetry will make hourly encroachments, and the metaphorical will become the current sense: pronunciation will be varied by levity or ignorance, and the pen must at length comply with the tongue; illiterate writers will at one time or other, by publick infatuation, rise into renown, who, not knowing the original import of words, will use them with colloquial licentiousness, confound distinction, and forget propriety. As politeness increases, some expressions will be considered as too gross and vulgar for the delicate, others as too formal and ceremonious for the gay and airy; new phrases are therefore adopted, which must, for the same reasons, be in time dismissed. *Swift*, in his petty treatise on the *English* language, allows that new words must sometimes be introduced, but proposes that none should be suffered to become obsolete. But what makes a word obsolete, more than general agreement to forbear it? and how shall it be continued, when it conveys an offensive idea, or recalled again to the mouths of mankind, when it has once become unfamiliar by disuse, and unpleasing by unfamiliarity.

There is another cause of alteration more prevalent than any other, which yet in the present state of the world cannot be obviated. A mixture of two languages will produce a third distinct from both, and they will always be mixed, where the chief part of education, and the most conspicuous accomplishment, is skill in ancient or in foreign tongues. He that has long cultivated another language, will find its words and combinations croud upon his memory; and haste and negligence, refinement and affectation, will obtrude borrowed terms and exotick expressions.

The great pest of speech is frequency of translation. No book was ever turned from one language into another, without imparting something of its native idiom; this is the most mischievous and comprehensive innovation; single words may enter by thousands, and the fabrick of the tongue continue the same, but new phraseology changes much at once; it alters not the single stones of the building, but the order of the columns. If an academy should be established for the cultivation of our stile, which I, who can never wish to see dependance multiplied, hope the spirit of *English* liberty will hinder or destroy, let them, instead of compiling grammars and dictionaries, endeavour, with all their influence, to stop the licence of translatours, whose idleness and ignorance, if it be suffered to proceed, will reduce us to babble a dialect of *France*.

If the changes that we fear be thus irresistible, what remains but to acquiesce with silence, as in the other insurmountable distresses of humanity? It remains that we retard what we cannot repel, that we palliate what we cannot cure. Life may be lengthened by care, though death cannot be ultimately defeated: tongues, like governments, have a natural tendency to degeneration; we have long preserved our constitution, let us make some struggles for our language.

In hope of giving longevity to that which its own nature forbids to be immortal, I have devoted this book, the labour of years, to the honour of my country, that we may no longer yield the palm of philology, without a contest, to the nations of the continent. The chief glory of every people arises from its authours: whether I shall add any thing by my own writings to the reputation of *English* literature, must be left to time: much of my life has been lost under the pressures of disease; much has been trifled away; and much has always been spent in provision for the day that was passing over me; but I shall not think my employment useless or ignoble, if by my assistance foreign nations, and distant ages, gain access to the propagators of knowledge, and understand the teachers of truth; if my labours afford light to the repositories of science, and add celebrity to *Bacon*, to *Hooker*, to *Milton*, and to *Boyle*.

When I am animated by this wish, I look with pleasure on my book, however defective, and deliver it to the world with the spirit of a man that has endeavoured well. That it will immediately become popular I have not promised to myself: a few wild blunders, and risible absurdities, from which no work of such multiplicity was ever free, may for a time furnish folly with laughter, and harden ignorance in contempt; but useful diligence will at last prevail, and there never can be wanting some who distinguish desert; who will consider that no dictionary of a living tongue ever can be perfect, since while it is hastening to publication, some words are budding, and some falling away; that a whole life cannot be spent upon syntax and etymology, and that even a whole life would not be sufficient; that he, whose design includes whatever language can express, must often speak of what he does not understand; that a writer will sometimes be hurried by eagerness to the end, and sometimes faint with weariness under a task, which *Scaliger* compares to the labours of the anvil and the mine; that what is obvious is not always known, and what is known is not always present; that sudden fits of inadvertency will surprize vigilance, slight avocations will seduce attention, and casual eclipses of the mind will darken learning; and that the writer shall often in vain trace his memory at the moment of need, for that which yesterday he knew with intuitive readiness, and which will come uncalled into his thoughts to-morrow.

In this work, when it shall be found that much is omitted, let it not be forgotten that much likewise is performed; and though no book was ever spared out of tenderness to the authour, and the world is little solicitous to know whence proceeded the faults of that which it condemns; yet it may gratify curiosity to inform it, that the *English Dictionary* was written with little assistance of the learned, and without any patronage of the great; not in the soft obscurities of retirement, or under the shelter of academick bowers, but amidst inconvenience and distraction, in sickness and in sorrow. It may repress the triumph of malignant criticism to observe, that if our language is not here fully displayed, I have only failed in an attempt which no human powers have hitherto completed. If the lexicons of ancient tongues, now immutably fixed, and comprised in a few volumes, be yet, after the toil of successive ages, inadequate and delusive; if the aggregated knowledge, and co-operating diligence of the *Italian* academicians, did not secure them from the censure of *Beni*; if the embodied criticks of *France*, when fifty years had been spent upon their work, were obliged to change its oeconomy, and give their second edition another form, I may surely be contented without the praise of perfection, which, if I could obtain, in this gloom of solitude, what would it avail me? I have protracted my work till most of those whom I wished to please have sunk into the grave, and success and miscarriage are empty sounds: I therefore dismiss it with frigid tranquillity, having little to fear or hope from censure or from praise.

PRELIMINARY DISCOURSE TO THE LONDON CHRONICLE

The preliminary discourse to the *London Chronicle* (January 1, 1757) has been taken from the British Museum copy of the *London Chronicle* (PP. London. 213. g. 1, page 1).

PRELIMINARY DISCOURSE

TO THE

LONDON CHRONICLE

I⊤ has been always lamented, that of the little Time allotted to Man, much must be spent upon Superfluities. Every Prospect has its Obstructions, which we must break to enlarge our View: Every Step of our Progress finds Impediments, which, however eager to go forward, we must stop to remove. Even those who profess to teach the Way to Happiness have multiplied our Incumbrances, and the Author of almost every Book retards his Instructions by a Preface.

The Writers of the *Chronicle* hope to be easily forgiven, though they should not be free from an Infection that has seized the whole Fraternity; and, instead of falling immediately to their Subjects, should detain the Reader for a Time with an Account of the Importance of their Design, the Extent of their Plan, and the Accuracy of the Method which they intend to prosecute. Such Premonitions, though not always necessary when the Reader has the Book complete in his Hand, and may find by his own Eyes whatever can be found in it, yet may be more easily allowed to Works published gradually in successive Parts; of which the Scheme can only be so far known as the Author shall think fit to discover it.

The Paper which we now invite the Publick to add to the Papers with which it is already rather wearied than satisfied, consists of many Parts; some of which it has in common with other periodical Sheets, and some peculiar to itself.

The first Demand made by the Reader of a Journal is, that he should find an accurate Account of foreign Transactions and domestick Incidents. This is always expected; but this is very rarely performed. Of those writers who have taken upon themselves the Task of Intelligence, some have given, and others have sold their Abilities, whether small or great, to one or other of the Parties that divide us; and without a Wish for Truth, or Thought of Decency, without Care of any other Reputation than that of a stubborn Adherence to their Abettors, carry on the same Tenour of Representation through all the Vicissitudes of Right and Wrong, neither depressed by Detection, nor abashed by Confutation; proud of the hourly Encrease of Infamy, and ready to boast of all the Contumelies that Falsehood and Slander may bring upon them, as new Proofs of their Zeal and Fidelity.

With these Heroes we have no Ambition to be numbered; we leave to the Confessors of Faction the Merit of their Sufferings, and are desirous to shelter ourselves under the Protection of Truth. That all our Facts will be authentick, or all our Remarks just, we dare not venture to promise: We can relate but what we hear, we can point out but what we see. Of remote Transactions the first Accounts are always confused, and commonly exaggerated; and in domestick Affairs, if the Power to conceal is less, the Interest to misrepresent is often greater; and what is sufficiently vexatious, Truth seems to fly from Curiosity; and as many Enquirers produce many Narratives, whatever engages the public Attention is immediately disguised by the Embellishments of Fiction. We pretend to no peculiar Power of disentangling Contradiction, or denuding Forgery. We have no settled Correspondence with the Antipodes, nor maintain any Spies in the Cabinets of Princes. But as we shall always be conscious that our Mistakes are involuntary, we shall watch the gradual Discoveries of Time, and retract whatever we have hastily and erroneously advanced.

In the Narratives of the daily Writers every Reader perceives somewhat of Neatness and Purity wanting, which at the first View it seems easy to supply: But it must be considered, that those Passages must be written in Haste, and that there is often no other Choice, but that they must want either Novelty or Accuracy; and that as Life is very uniform, the Affairs of one Week are so like those of another, that by any Attempt after Variety of Expression, Invention would soon be wearied, and Language exhausted. Some Improvements however we hope to make; and for the rest we think, that when we commit only common Faults, we shall not be excluded from common Indulgence.

The Accounts of Prices of Corn and Stocks, are to most of our Readers of more Importance than narratives of greater Sound, and as Exactness is here within the Reach of Diligence, our Readers may justly require it from us.

Memorials of a private and personal Kind, which relate Deaths, Marriages, and Preferments, must always be imperfect by Omission, and often erroneous by Misinformation; but, even in these, there shall not be wanting Care to avoid Mistakes, or to rectify them whenever they shall be found.

That Part of our Work by which it is distinguished from all others, is the *Literary Journal*, or Account of the Labours and Productions of the *Learned*. This was, for a long Time, among the Deficiencies of English Literature, but as the Caprice of Man is always starting from too little to too much, we have now, amongst other Disturbers of human Quiet, a numerous Body of *Reviewers* and *Remarkers*.

Every Art is improved by the Emulation of Competitors; those who make no Advances towards Excellence, may stand as Warnings against Faults. We shall endeavour to avoid that Petulance which treats with Contempt whatever has hitherto been reputed sacred. We shall repress that Elation of Malignity, which wantons in the Cruelties of Criticism, and not only murders Reputation, but murders it by Torture. Whenever we feel ourselves ignorant, we shall, at least, be modest. Our Intention is not to preoccupy Judgment by Praise or Censure, but to gratify Curiosity by early Intelligence, and to tell rather what our Authors have attempted, than what they have performed. The Titles of Books are necessarily short, and therefore disclose but imperfectly the Contents; they are sometimes fraudulent, and intended to raise false Expectations. In our Account this Brevity will be extended, and these Frauds, whenever they are detected, will be exposed; for though we write without Intention to injure, we shall not suffer ourselves to be made Parties to Deceit.

If any Author shall transmit a Summary of his Work, we shall willingly receive it; if any literary Anecdote, or curious Observation, shall be communicated to us, we will carefully insert it. Many Facts are known and forgotten; many Observations are made and suppressed; and Entertainment and Instruction are frequently lost, for Want of a Repository in which they may be conveniently preserved.

No Man can modestly promise what he cannot ascertain. We hope for the Praise of Knowledge and Discernment, but we claim only that of Diligence and Candour.

REVIEW

OF 'A JOURNAL OF EIGHT DAYS JOURNEY &c.'

AND

REPLY TO A PAPER

IN THE 'GAZETTEER'

The two articles on Jonas Hanway come from the *Literary Magazine* (1757), number 13, pp. "161" [162]–167 and number 14, pp. 253–6. The British Museum copies (PP. 5438.) were used for the text.

REVIEW

OF

'A Journal of Eight Days Journey

from Portsmouth to Kingston upon Thames; through Southampton, Wiltshire, &c. With Miscellaneous Thoughts, Moral and Religious; in Sixty-four Letters: Addressed to two Ladies of the Partie. To which is added An Essay on Tea, considered as pernicious to Health, obstructing Industry, and impoverishing the Nation: with an Account of its Growth, and great Consumption in these Kingdoms, with several Political Reflections; and Thoughts on Public Love: In thirty-two Letters to two Ladies. By Mr. H——y.'

Our readers may perhaps remember, that we gave them a short account of this book, with a letter extracted from it in *Novem.* 1756. The author then sent us an injunction to forbear his work till a second edition should appear: this prohibition was rather too magisterial; for an author is no longer the sole master of a book which he has given to the public; yet he has been punctually obeyed; we had no desire to offend him, and if his character may be estimated by his book, he is a man whose failings may well be pardoned for his virtues.

The second edition is now sent into the world, *corrected and enlarged*, and yielded up by the author to the attacks of criticism. But he shall find in us no malignity of censure. We wish indeed, that among other corrections he had submitted his pages to the inspection of a grammarian, that the elegancies of one line might not have been disgraced by the improprieties of another; but with us to mean well is a degree of merit which over-balances much greater errors than impurity of stile.

We have already given in our collections, one of the letters, in which Mr. *Hanway* endeavours to show, that the consumption of Tea, is injurious to the interest of our country. We shall now en-

333

deavour to follow him regularly through all his observations on this modern luxury; but it can scarcely be candid, not to make a previous declaration, that he is to expect little justice from the author of this extract, a hardened and shameless tea-drinker, who has for twenty years diluted his meals with only the infusion of this fascinating plant, whose kettle has scarcely time to cool, who with Tea amuses the evening, with Tea solaces the midnights, and with Tea welcomes the morning.

He begins by refuting a popular notion, that *Bohea* and *Green Tea* are leaves of the same shrub, gathered at different times of the year. He is of opinion, that they are produced by different shrubs. The leaves of Tea are gathered in dry weather; then dried and curled over the fire in copper pans. The *Chinese* use little green tea, imagining that it hinders digestion and excites fevers. How it should have either effect is not easily discovered, and if we consider the innumerable prejudices which prevail concerning our own plants, we shall very little regard these opinions of the *Chinese* vulgar, which experience does not confirm.

When the *Chinese* drink tea, they infuse it slightly, and extract only the more volatile parts, but though this seems to require great quantities at a time, yet the author believes, perhaps only because he has an inclination to believe it, that the *English* and *Dutch* use more than all the inhabitants of that extensive empire. The *Chinese* drink it sometimes with acids, seldom with sugar; and this practice, our author, who has no intention to find any thing right at home, recommends to his countrymen.

The history of the rise and progress of tea-drinking is truly curious. Tea was first imported from *Holland* by the earls of *Arlington* and *Ossory*, in 1666: from their ladies the women of quality learned its use. Its price was then three pounds a pound, and continued the same to 1707. In 1715, we began to use green tea, and the practice of drinking it descended to the lower class of the people. In 1720, the *French* began to send it hither by a clandestine commerce. From 1717 to 1726, we imported annually seven hundred thousand pounds. From 1732 to 1742, a million and two hundred thousand pounds were every year brought to *London*; in some years afterwards three millions, and in 1755, near four millions of pounds, or two thousand tuns, in which we are not to reckon that which is surreptitiously introduced, which perhaps is nearly as much. Such quantities are indeed sufficient to alarm us; it is at least worth enquiry, to know what are the qualities of such a plant, and what the consequences of such a trade.

He then proceeds to enumerate the mischiefs of tea, and seems willing to charge upon it every mischief that he can find. He begins however, by questioning the virtues ascribed to it, and denies that the crews of the *Chinese* ships are preserved in their voyage homewards from the scurvy by tea. About this report I have made some enquiry, and though I cannot find that these crews are wholly exempt from scorbutic maladies; they seem to suffer them less than other mariners in any course of equal length. This I ascribe to the tea, not as possessing any medicinal qualities, but as tempting them to drink more water, to dilute their salt food more copiously, and perhaps to forbear punch, or other strong liquors.

He then proceeds in the pathetic strain, to tell the ladies how, by drinking tea they injure their health, and, what is yet more dear, their beauty.

"To what can we ascribe the numerous complaints which prevail? how many *sweet creatures* of your sex, languish with a *weak digestion, low spirits, lassitudes, melancholy,* and twenty disorders, which in spite of the *faculty* have yet no names, except the general one of *nervous complaints*? let them change their diet, and among other articles leave off drinking tea, it is more than probable the greatest part of them will be restored to health.

" Hot water is also very hurtful to the teeth. The *Chinese* do not drink their tea so hot as we do, and yet they have bad teeth. This cannot be ascribed entirely to *sugar*, for they use very little, as already observed: but we all know that *hot* or *cold* things which *pain* the teeth, destroy them also. If we drank less tea, and used gentle *acids* for the gums and teeth, particularly *sour oranges,* though we had a less number of *French dentists,* I fancy this *essential* part of beauty would be much *better* preserved.

" The women in the united provinces who *sip tea* from morning till night, are also as remarkable for *bad teeth.* They also look pallid, and many are troubled with certain feminine disorders arising from a relaxed habit. The *Portuguese* ladies, on the other hand, entertain with *sweet-meats,* and yet they have very good *teeth*: but their food in general is more of the farinaceous and vegetable kind than ours. They also *drink cold water* instead of *sipping hot,* and never taste any fermented liquors; for these reasons the use of *sugar,* does not seem to be at all pernicious to them.

"Men seem to have lost their stature, and comeliness; and women their beauty. I am not *young*, but methinks there is not quite so much *beauty* in this land as there was. Your very *chambermaids* have lost their bloom, I suppose by *sipping tea*. Even the agitations of the passions at *cards* are not so great enemies to female charms. What *Shakespeare* ascribes to the concealment of love, is *in this age* more frequently occasioned by the use of *tea*."

To raise the fright still higher, he quotes an account of a pig's tail scalded with tea, on which however he does not much insist.

Of these dreadful effects, some are perhaps imaginary, and some may have another cause. That there is less beauty in the present race of females, than in those who entered the world with us, all of us are inclined to think on whom beauty has ceased to smile; but our fathers and grand-fathers made the same complaint before us, and our posterity will still find beauties irresistibly powerful.

That the diseases commonly called nervous, tremours, fits, habitual depression, and all the maladies which proceed from laxity and debility, are more frequent than in any former time, is, I believe, true, however deplorable. But this new race of evils, will not be expelled by the prohibition of tea. This general languour is the effect of general luxury, of general idleness. If it be most to be found among tea-drinkers, the reason is, that tea is one of the stated amusements of the idle and luxurious. The whole mode of life is changed, every kind of voluntary labour, every exercise that strengthened the nerves, and hardened the muscles, is fallen into disuse. The inhabitants are crowded together in populous cities, so that no occasion of life requires much motion; every one is near to all that he wants; and the rich and delicate seldom pass from one street to another, but in carriages of pleasure. Yet we eat and drink, or strive to eat and drink like the hunters and huntresses, the farmers and the housewives of the former generation, and they that pass ten hours in bed, and eight at cards, and the greater part of the other six at the table, are taught to impute to tea, all the diseases which a life unnatural in all its parts, may chance to bring upon them.

Tea, among the greater part of those who use it most, is drunk in no great quantity. As it neither exhilerates the heart, nor stimulates the palate; it is commonly an entertainment merely nominal, a pretence for assembling to prattle, for interrupting business or diversifying idleness. They who drink one cup, and who drink twenty, are equally punctual in preparing or partaking it; and indeed, there are few but discover by their indifference about it, that they are brought together not by the tea, but the tea table. Three cups make the common quantity, so slightly impregnated, that perhaps they might be tinged with the *Athenian* cicuta, and produce less effects than those letters charge upon tea.

Our author proceeds to shew yet other bad qualities of this hated leaf.

"Green tea, when made strong even by infusion, is an *emetic*, nay, I am told it is used as such in *China*, a decoction of it certainly performs this operation; yet by long use it is drunk by many without such an effect. The infusion also, when it is made strong, and stands long to draw the grosser particles, will *convulse* the bowels: even in the manner *commonly* used it has this effect on some constitutions, as I have already remarked to you from my *own experience*.

"You see I confess my *weakness* without reserve, but those who are very fond of tea, if their digestion is weak, and they find themselves disordered, they generally ascribe it to any *cause* except the *true* one. I am aware that the effect just mentioned is imputed to the hot water; let it be so, and my argument is still good: but who pretends to say it is not *partly* owing to particular kinds of tea; perhaps such as partake of *copperas*, which there is cause to apprehend is sometimes the case: if we judge from the manner in which it is said to be cured, together with its ordinary effects, there is some foundation for this opinion. Put a drop of strong tea, either *green* or *bohea*, but chiefly the former, on the blade of a knife, though it is not corrosive in the same manner as vitriol, yet there appears to be a corrosive quality in it, very different from that of fruit which stain the knife."

He afterwards quotes *Paulli* to prove, that tea is a *desiccative, and ought not to be used after the fortieth year*. I have then long exceeded the limits of permission, but I comfort myself, that all the enemies of tea cannot be in the right. If tea be desiccative according to *Paulli*, it cannot weaken the fibres, as our author imagines; if it be emetic, it must constringe the stomach, rather than relax it.

The formidable quality of tinging the knife, it has in common with acorns, the bark, and leaves of oak, and every astringent bark or leaf, the copperas which is given to the tea, is really in the knife. Ink may be made of any ferrugineous matter and astringent vegetable, as it is generally made of galls and copperas.

From tea the writer digresses to spirituous liquors, about which he will have no controversy with the *Literary Magazine*, we shall therefore insert almost his whole letter, and add to it one testimony, that the mischiefs arising on every side from this compendious mode of drunkenness, are enormous and insupportable; equally to be found among the great and the mean; filling palaces with disquiet and distraction, harder to be born, as it cannot be mentioned; and overwhelming multitudes with incurable diseases and unpitied poverty.

"Though *tea* and *gin* have spread their baneful influence over this island, and his majesty's other dominions, yet you may be well assured, that the governors of the foundling-hospital will exert their utmost skill and vigilance, to prevent the children under their care from being poisoned, or enervated by one or the other. This, however, is not the case of *workhouses*: it is well known, to the shame of those who are charged with the care of them, that *gin* has been too often permitted to enter their gates; and the debauched appetites of the people who inhabit these houses, has been urged as a reason for it.

"*Desperate* diseases require *desperate* remedies: if laws are rigidly executed against murderers in the highway, those who provide a draught of gin, which we see is *murderous*, ought not to be *countenanced*. I am now informed, that in certain hospitals, where the number of the *sick* used to be about 5600 in 14 years.

From 1704, to 1718, they increased to 8189;
From 1718, to 1734, still augmented to 12710;
And from 1734, to 1749, *multiplied* to 38147.

"What a dreadful *spectre* does this exhibit! nor must we wonder when satisfactory evidence was given before the great council of the nation, that near eight millions of gallons of distilled spirits, at the standard it is commonly reduced to for drinking, was actually consumed annually in drams! the shocking difference in the numbers of the *sick*, and we may presume of the *dead* also, was supposed to keep pace with *gin*; and the most ingenious and unprejudiced physicians ascribed it to this cause. What is to be done under these melancholy circumstances? shall we still countenance the *distillery*, for the sake of the *revenue*; out of tenderness to the *few* who will suffer by its being abolished; for fear of the madness of the people; or that foreigners will run it in upon us? there can be no *evil* so great as that we now suffer, except the making the same consumption, and paying for it to foreigners in *money*, which I hope never will be the case.

As to the *revenue*, it certainly may be replaced by taxes upon the *necessaries* of life, even upon the *bread we eat*, or in other words, upon the *land*, which is the great source of supply to the *public*, and to *individuals*. Nor can I persuade myself, but that the people may be *weaned* from the habit of poisoning themselves. The difficulty of *smugling* a bulky *liquid*, joined to the severity which *ought* to be exercised towards smuglers, whose *illegal* commerce is of so *infernal* a nature, must, in time, produce the effect desired. Spirituous liquors being abolished, instead of having the most undisciplined and abandoned poor, we might soon boast a race of men, temperate, religious, and industrious even to a *proverb*. We should soon see the *ponderous* burden of the *poors-rate* decrease, and the *beauty* and *strength* of the land rejuvinate. Schools, workhouses and hospitals, might then be sufficient to clear our streets of distress and misery, which never will be the case whilst the love of poison prevails, and the means of ruin, is sold in above one thousand houses in the *city of London,* in two thousand two hundred in *Westminster*, and one thousand nine hundred and thirty in *Holborn* and St. *Giles's.*

"But if other uses still demand *liquid fire*, I would really propose, that it should be sold only in quart bottles, sealed up with the king's seal, with a very high duty, and none sold without being mixed with a *strong emetic.*

"Many become objects of charity by their *intemperance*, and this excludes others who are such by the unavoidable accidents of life; or who cannot by any means support themselves. Hence it appears, that the introducing *new habits* of life, is the most substantial charity: and that the *regulation* of charity-schools, hospitals and workhouses, not the augmentation of their number, can make them answer the wise ends for which they were instituted.

"The children of beggars should be also taken from them, and bred up to labour, as children of the public. Thus the *distressed* might be relieved, at a sixth part of the present expence; the idle be compelled to *work*, or *starve*; and the *mad* be sent to *Bedlam*. We should not see human nature disgraced by the aged, the

339

maimed, the sickly, and young children, begging their bread, nor would compassion be abused by those who have reduced it to an *art* to catch the unwary. Nothing is wanting but common sense and *honesty* in the execution of *laws*.

"To prevent such abuse in the *streets*, seems more practicable than to abolish *bad habits within doors*, where *greater* numbers perish. We see in many familiar instances the fatal effects of example. The careless spending of time among *servants*, who are charged with the care of infants, is often fatal: the nurse frequently destroys the child! the poor infant being left neglected, expires whilst she is sipping her tea! this may appear to you as *rank prejudice*, or *jest*; but I am assured, from the most *indubitable* evidence, that many very extraordinary cases of this kind, have *really* happened among those whose *duty* does not permit of such kind of habits.

"It is partly from such causes, that nurses of the children of the *public* often *forget* themselves, and become *impatient* when infants cry: the next step to this, is using extraordinary means to quiet them. I have already mentioned the term *killing nurse*, as known in some workhouses: *Venice treacle*, *Poppey water*, and *Godfrey's cordial*, have been the *kind* instruments of lulling the child to his *everlasting* rest. If these *pious* women could send up an ejaculation when the child expired, all was *well*, and no questions *asked* by the *superiors*. A ingenious friend of mine informs me that this has been so often the case, in some workhouses, that *Venice* treacle has acquired the appellation of *the Lord have mercy upon me*, in allusion to the nurses *hackneyed* expression of *pretended* grief when infants expire! *Farewel!*"

I know not upon what observation Mr. *Hanway* founds his confidence in the governors of the *Foundling Hospital*, men of whom I have not any knowledge, but whom I intreat to consider a little the minds as well as bodies of the children. I am inclined to believe irreligion equally pernicious with gin and tea, and therefore think it not unseasonable to mention, that when a few months ago I wandered through the hospital, I found not a child that seemed to have heard of his creed or the commandments. To breed up children in this manner, is to rescue them from an early grave, that they may find employment for the gibbet; from dying in innocence, that they may perish by their crimes.

Having considered the effects of tea upon the health of the

drinker, which, I think, he has aggravated in the vehemence of his zeal, and which, after soliciting them by this watery luxury, year after year, I have not yet felt; he proceeds to examine how it may be shewn to affect our interest; and first calculates the national loss by the time spent in drinking tea. I have no desire to appear captious, and shall therefore readily admit, that tea is a liquor not proper for the lower classes of the people, as it supplies no strength to labour, or relief to disease, but gratifies the taste without nourishing the body. It is a barren superfluity, to which those who can hardly procure what nature requires, cannot prudently habituate themselves. Its proper use is to amuse the idle, and relax the studious, and dilute the full meals of those who cannot use exercise, and will not use abstinence. That time is lost in this insipid entertainment, cannot be denied; many trifle away at the tea-table, those moments which would be better spent; but that any national detriment can be inferred from this waste of time, does not evidently appear, because I know not that any work remains undone for want of hands. Our manufactures seem to be limited, not by the possibility of work, but by the possibility of sale.

His next argument is more clear. He affirms, that one hundred and fifty thousand pounds in silver are paid to the *Chinese* annually, for three millions of pounds of tea, and that for two millions more brought clandestinely from the neighbouring coasts, we pay at twenty-pence a pound, one hundred sixty-six thousand six hundred and sixty-six pounds. The author justly conceives, that this computation will waken us; for, says he, "The loss of health, the loss of time, the injury of morals, are not very sensibly felt by some, who are alarmed when you talk of the loss of money." But he excuses the *East-India* company, as men not obliged to be political arithmeticians, or to enquire so much what the nation loses, as how themselves may grow rich. It is certain, that they who drink tea have no right to complain of those that import it, but if Mr. *Hanway*'s computation be just, the importation and the use of it ought at once to be stopped by a penal law.

The author allows one slight argument in favour of tea, which, in my opinion, might be with far greater justice urged, both against that, and many other parts of our naval trade. "The tea trade employs, he tells us, six ships, and five or six hundred seamen, sent annually to *China*. It likewise brings in a revenue of three hundred and sixty thousand pounds, which, as a tax on luxury, may be considered as of great utility to the state." The utility of this tax I cannot find; a tax on luxury is no better than another tax, unless it hinders luxury, which cannot be said of the impost upon tea, while it is thus used by the great and the mean, the rich and the poor. The truth is, that by the loss of one hundred and fifty thousand pounds, we procure the means of shifting three hundred and sixty thousand at best, only from one hand to another; but perhaps, sometimes into hands, by which it is not very honestly employed. Of the five or six hundred seamen sent to *China*, I am told, that sometimes half, commonly a third part perish in the voyage; so that instead of setting this navigation against the inconveniencies already alleged, we may add to them, the yearly loss of two hundred men in the prime of life, and reckon, that the trade of *China* has destroyed ten thousand men since the beginning of this century.

If tea be thus pernicious, if it impoverishes our country, if it raises temptation, and gives opportunity to illicit commerce, which I have always looked on as one of the strongest evidences of the inefficacy of our law, the weakness of our government, and the corruption of our people, let us at once resolve to prohibit it for ever.

"If the *question* was how to promote industry, most *advantageously*, in lieu of our tea-trade, supposing every branch of our commerce to be already fully supplied with men and money? if a *quarter* the sum now spent in tea, were laid out annually in plantations, in making public gardens, in paving and widening streets, in making *roads*, in rendering *rivers* navigable, erecting *palaces*, building *bridges*, or neat and convenient *houses*, where are now only *huts*; *draining* lands, or rendering those which are now *barren* of some *use*; should we not be gainers, and provide more for health, pleasure, and long life, compared with the consequences of the *tea-trade*?"

Our riches would be much better employed to these purposes, but if this project does not please, let us first resolve to save our money, and we shall afterwards very easily find ways to spend it.

REPLY TO A PAPER

In the GAZETTEER of *May* 26, 1757.

IT is observed in the sage *Gil Blas*, that an exasperated author is not easily pacified. I have, therefore, very little hope of making my peace with the writer of the Eight days journey. Indeed so little, that I have long deliberated whether I should not rather sit silently down under his displeasure than aggravate my misfortune by a defence of which my heart forebodes the ill success. Deliberation is often useless. I am afraid that I have at last made the wrong choice, and that I might better have resigned my cause without a struggle to time and fortune, since I shall run the hazard of a new offence by the necessity of asking him *why he is angry?*

Distress and terror often discover to us those faults with which we should never have reproached ourselves in a happy state. Yet, dejected as I am, when I review the transaction between me and this writer, I cannot find that I have been deficient in reverence. When his book was first printed, he hints that I procured a sight of it before it was published. How the sight of it was procured I do not very exactly remember, but if my curiosity was greater than my prudence, if I laid rash hands on the fatal volume, I have surely suffered like him who burst the box, from which evil rushed into the world.

I took it, however, and inspected it as the work of an author not higher than myself, and was confirmed in my opinion when I found that these letters were *not written to be printed*. I concluded, however, that though not *written* to be *printed*, they were *printed* to be *read*, and inserted one of them in the collection of *November* last. Not many days after I received a note, informing me that I ought to have waited for a more correct edition. This injunction was obey'd. The edition appear'd, and I supposed myself at liberty to tell my thoughts upon it, as upon any other book, upon a royal manifesto, or an act of parliament. But see the fate of ignorant temerity! I now find, but find too late, that instead of a writer whose only power is in his pen, I have irritated an important member of an important corporation; a man who, as he tells us in his letters, puts horses to his chariot.

It was allowed to the disputant of old to yield up the controversy with little resistance to the master of forty legions. Those who know how weakly naked truth can defend her advocates, would forgive me if I should pay the same respect to a governor of the foundlings. Yet the consciousness of my own rectitude of intention incites me to ask once again, how I have offended?

There are only three subjects upon which my unlucky pen has happened to venture. Tea; the Author of the journal; and the Foundling hospital.

Of Tea, what have I said? that I have drank it twenty years without hurt, and therefore believe it not to be poison. That if it dries the fibres, it cannot soften them, that if it constringes, it cannot relax. I have modestly doubted whether it has diminished the strength of our men, or the beauty of our women, and whether it much hinders the progress of our woollen or iron manufactures; but I allowed it to be a barren superfluity, neither medicinal nor nutritious, that neither supplied strength nor chearfulness, neither relieved weariness nor exhilarated sorrow: I inserted, without charge or suspicion of falshood, the sums exported to purchase it; and proposed a law to prohibit it for ever.

Of the author, I unfortunately said, that his injunction was somewhat too magisterial. This I said before I knew that he was a governor of the foundlings; but he seems inclined to punish this failure of respect, as the Czar of *Muscovy* made war upon *Sweden*, because he was not treated with sufficient honours when he passed through the country in disguise. Yet was not this irreverence without extenuation. Something was said of the merit of *meaning well*, and the journalist was declared to be a man *whose failings might well be pardoned for his virtues*. This is the highest praise which human gratitude can confer upon human merit, praise that would have more than satisfied *Titus* or *Augustus*, but which I must own to be inadequate and penurious when offered to the member of an important corporation.

I am asked whether I meant to *satirize* the man or *criticise* the writer, when I say that *he believes, only perhaps, because he has inclination to believe it, that the* English *and* Dutch *consume more tea*

than the vast empire of China. Between the writer and the man I did
not at that time consider the distinction. The writer I found not of
more than mortal might, and I did not immediately recollect that
the man put horses to his chariot. But I did not write wholly without consideration. I knew but two causes of belief, evidence and
inclination. What evidence the journalist could have of the *Chinese*
consumption of tea, I was not able to discover. The officers of the
East India company are excluded, they best know why, from the
towns and the country of *China*; they are treated as we treat
gypsies and vagrants, and obliged to retire every night to their
own hovel. What intelligence such travellers may bring is of no
great importance. And tho' the missionaries boast of having once
penetrated further, I think they have never calculated the tea
drank by the *Chinese*. There being thus no evidence for his opinion,
to what could I ascribe it but to inclination?

I am yet charged more heavily for having said, that *he has no
intention to find any thing right at home.* I believe every reader restrained this imputation to the subject which produced it, and supposed me to insinuate only that he meant to spare no part of the
tea-table, whether essence or circumstance. But this line he has
selected as an instance of virulence and acrimony, and confutes it by
a lofty and splendid panegyric on himself. He asserts, that he finds
many things right at home, and that he loves his country almost
to enthusiasm.

I had not the least doubt that he found in his country many
things to please him, nor did I suppose that he desired the same
inversion of every part of life, as of the use of tea. The proposal of
drinking tea sour showed indeed such a disposition to practical
paradoxes, that there was reason to fear lest some succeeding
letter should recommend the dress of the *Picts*, or the cookery of
the *Eskimaux*. However I met with no other innovations, and
therefore was willing to hope that he found something right at
home.

But his love of his country seemed not to rise quite to enthusiasm, when amidst his rage against tea, he made a smooth apology
for the *East India* company, as men who might not think themselves obliged to be political arithmeticians. I hold, though no enthusiastic patriot, that every man who lives and trades under the
protection of a community, is obliged to consider whether he hurts
or benefits those who protect him, and that the most which can be

indulged to private interest is a neutral traffic, if any such can be, by which our country is not injured, tho' it may not be benefited.

But he now renews his declamation against Tea, notwithstanding the greatness or power of those that have interest or inclination to support it. I know not of what power or greatness he may dream. The importers only have an interest in defending it. I am sure they are not great, and I hope they are not powerful. Those whose inclination leads them to continue this practice, are too numerous, but I believe their power is such, as the journalist may defy without enthusiasm. The love of our country, when it rises to enthusiasm is an ambiguous and uncertain virtue: When a man is enthusiastic he ceases to be reasonable, and when he once departs from reason, what will he do but drink sour tea? As the journalist, tho' enthusiastically zealous for his country, has with regard to smaller things the placid happiness of philosophical indifference, I can give him no disturbance by advising him to restrain even the love of his country within due limits, lest it should sometimes swell too high, fill the whole capacity of his soul, and leave less room for the love of truth.

Nothing now remains but that I review my positions concerning the Foundling hospital. What I declared last month, I declare now once more, that I found none of the children, that appeared to have heard of the catechism. It is enquired how I wandered, and how I examined? There is doubtless subtilty in the question; I know not well how to answer it. Happily I did not wander alone, I attended some ladies with another gentleman, who all heard and assisted the enquiry with equal grief and indignation. I did not conceal my observations. Notice was given of this shameful defect soon after, at my request, to one of the highest names of the society. This I am now told is incredible; but since it is true, and the past is out of human power, the most important corporation cannot make it false. But why is it incredible? Because in the rules of the hospital the children are ordered to learn the rudiments of religion. Orders are easily made, but they do not execute themselves. They say their catechism, at stated times, under an able master. But this able master was, I think, not elected before last *February*, and my visit happened, if I mistake not, in *November*. The children were shy, when interrogated by a stranger. This may be true, but the same shyness I do not remember to have hindered them from

346

answering other questions, and I wonder why children so much accustomed to new spectators should be eminently shy.

My opponent in the first paragraph, calls the inference that I made from this negligence, a hasty conclusion: to the decency of this expression I had nothing to object. But as he grew hot in his career, his enthusiasm began to sparkle, and in the vehemence of his postscript he charges my assertions, and my reasons for advancing them, with folly and malice. His argumentation being somewhat enthusiastical, I cannot fully comprehend, but it seems to stand thus. My insinuations are foolish or malicious, since I know not one of the governors of the hospital; for he that knows not the governors of the hospital must be very foolish or malicious.

He has, however, so much kindness for me, that he advises me to consult my safety when I talk of corporations. I know not what the most important corporation can do, becoming manhood, by which my safety is endangered. My reputation is safe, for I can prove the fact; my quiet is safe, for I meant well; and for any other safety I am not used to be very sollicitous.

I am always sorry when I see any being labouring in vain; and in return for the Journalists attention to my safety, I will confess some compassion for his tumultuous resentment, since all his invectives fume into the air, with so little effect upon me, that I still esteem him as one that has the *merit of meaning well,* and still believe him to be *a man whose failings may be justly pardoned for his virtues.*

347

REVIEW

OF 'A FREE ENQUIRY INTO THE
NATURE AND ORIGIN OF EVIL'

The Soame Jenyns review appeared in three consecutive numbers of the *Literary Magazine*, all in the year 1757—number 13, pp. 171–5; number 14, pp. 251–3; number 15, pp. 301–6. This text has been taken from the British Museum copies of this magazine (PP. 5438.).

REVIEW

OF

A FREE ENQUIRY

INTO THE

NATURE AND ORIGIN OF EVIL

THIS is a treatise consisting of six letters upon a very difficult and important question, which I am afraid this author's endeavours will not free from the perplexity, which has intangled the speculatists of all ages, and which must always continue while *we see* but *in part*. He calls it a *Free* enquiry, and indeed his *freedom* is, I think, greater than his modesty. Though he is far from the contemptible arrogance, or the impious licentiousness of *Bolingbroke*, yet he decides too easily upon questions out of the reach of human determination, with too little consideration of mortal weakness, and with too much vivacity for the necessary caution.

In the first letter *on evil in general*, he observes, that, 'it is the solution of this important question, *whence came evil*, alone, that can ascertain the moral characteristic of God, without which there is an end of all distinction between good and evil.' Yet he begins this enquiry by this declaration. 'That there is a supreme being, infinitely powerful, wise and benevolent, the great creator and preserver of all things, is a truth so clearly demonstrated, that it shall be here taken for granted.' What is this but to say, that we have already reason to grant the existence of those attributes of God, which the present enquiry is designed to prove? The present enquiry is then surely made to no purpose. The attributes to the demonstration of which the solution of this great question is necessary, have been demonstrated without any solution, or by means of the solution of some former writer.

He rejects the *Manichean* system, but imputes to it an absurdity, from which, amidst all its absurdities it seems to be free, and adopts the system of Mr. *Pope*. 'That pain is no evil, if asserted with

351

regard to the individuals who suffer it, is downright nonsense; but if considered as it affects the universal system, is an undoubted truth, and means only that there is no more pain in it than what is necessary to the production of happiness. How many soever of these evils then force themselves into the creation, so long as the good preponderates, it is a work well worthy of infinite wisdom and benevolence; and, notwithstanding the imperfections of its parts, the whole is most undoubtedly perfect.' And in the former part of the letter, he gives the principle of his system in these words. 'Omnipotence cannot work contradictions, it can only effect all possible things. But so little are we acquainted with the whole system of nature, that we know not what are possible, and what are not: but if we may judge from that constant mixture of pain with pleasure, and inconveniency with advantage, which we must observe in every thing around us, we have reason to conclude, that to endue created beings with perfection, that is, to produce good exclusive of evil, is one of those impossibilities which even infinite power cannot accomplish.'

This is elegant and acute, but will by no means calm discontent or silence curiosity; for whether evil can be wholly separated from good or not, it is plain that they may be mixed in various degrees, and as far as human eyes can judge, the degree of evil might have been less without any impediment to good.

The second Letter *on the Evils of Imperfection*, is little more than a paraphrase of *Pope's* epistles, or yet less than a paraphrase, a mere translation of poetry into prose. This is surely to attack difficulty with very disproportionate abilities, to cut the *Gordian* knot with very blunt instruments. When we are told of the insufficiency of former solutions, why is one of the latest, which no man can have forgotten, given us again? I am told, that this pamphlet is not the effort of hunger; What can it be then but the product of vanity? and yet how can vanity be gratified by plagiarism, or transcription? When this speculatist finds himself prompted to another performance, let him consider whether he is about to disburthen his mind or employ his fingers; and if I might venture to offer him a subject, I should wish that he would solve this question, Why he that has nothing to write, should desire to be a writer?

Yet is not this letter without some sentiments, which though not new, are of great importance, and may be read with pleasure in the thousandth repetition.

'Whatever we enjoy is purely a free gift from our Creator; but that we enjoy no more, can never sure be deemed an injury, or a just reason to question his infinite benevolence. All our happiness is owing to his goodness; but that it is no greater, is owing only to ourselves, that is, to our not having any inherent right to any happiness, or even to any existence at all. This is no more to be imputed to God, than the wants of a beggar to the person who has relieved him: that he had something was owing to his benefactor: but that he had no more, only to his own original poverty.'

Thus far he speaks what every man must approve, and what every wise man has said before him. He then gives us the system of subordination, not invented, for it was known I think to the *Arabian* metaphysicians, but adopted by *Pope*; and from him borrowed by the diligent researches of this great investigator.

'No system can possibly be formed, even in imagination, without a subordination of parts. Every animal body must have different members, subservient to each other; every picture must be composed of various colours, and of light and shade; all harmony must be formed of trebles, tenors, and basses; every beautiful and useful edifice must consist of higher and lower, more and less magnificent apartments. This is in the very essence of all created things, and therefore cannot be prevented by any means whatever, unless by not creating them at all.'

These instances are used instead of *Pope's Oak* and *weeds*, or *Jupiter* and his *satellites*; but neither *Pope*, nor this writer have much contributed to solve the difficulty. Perfection or imperfection of unconscious beings has no meaning as referred to themselves; the *bass* and the *treble* are equally perfect; the mean and magnificent apartments feel no pleasure or pain from the comparison. *Pope* might ask the *weed*, why it was less than the *Oak*, but the *weed* would never ask the question for itself. The *bass* and *treble* differ only to the hearer, meanness and magnificence only to the inhabitant. There is no evil but must inhere in a conscious being, or be referred to it; that is, evil must be felt before it is evil. Yet even on this subject many questions might be offered which human understanding has not yet answered, and which the present haste of this extract will not suffer me to dilate.

He proceeds to a humble detail of *Pope's* opinion: 'The universe is a system whose very essence consists in subordination; a scale of beings descending by insensible degrees from infinite perfection to

353

absolute nothing; in which, tho' we may justly expect to find perfection in the whole, could we possibly comprehend it; yet would it be the highest absurdity to hope for it in all its parts, because the beauty and happiness of the whole depend altogether on the just inferiority of its parts, that is, on the comparative imperfections of the several beings of which it is composed.

'It would have been no more an instance of God's wisdom to have created no beings but of the highest and most perfect order, than it would be of a painter's art, to cover his whole piece with one single colour the most beautiful he could compose. Had he confined himself to such, nothing could have existed but demigods, or archangels, and then all inferior orders must have been void and uninhabited: but as it is surely more agreeable to infinite benevolence, that all these should be filled up with beings capable of enjoying happiness themselves, and contributing to that of others, they must necessarily be filled with inferior beings, that is, with such as are less perfect, but from whose existence, notwithstanding that less perfection, more felicity upon the whole accrues to the universe, than if no such had been created. It is moreover highly probable, that there is such a connection between all ranks and orders by subordinate degrees, that they mutually support each others existence, and every one in its place is absolutely necessary towards sustaining the whole vast and magnificent fabrick.

'Our pretences for complaint could be of this only, that we are not so high in the scale of existence as our ignorant ambition may desire: a pretence which must eternally subsist; because, were we ever so much higher, there would be still room for infinite power to exalt us; and since no link in the chain can be broke, the same reason for disquiet must remain to those who succeed to that chasm, which must be occasioned by our preferment. A man can have no reason to repine, that he is not an angel; nor a horse, that he is not a man; much less, that in their several stations they possess not the faculties of another; for this would be an insufferable misfortune.'

This doctrine of the regular subordination of beings, the scale of existence, and the chain of nature, I have often considered, but always left the Inquiry in doubt and uncertainty.

That every being not infinite, compared with infinity, must be imperfect, is evident to intuition; that whatever is imperfect must have a certain line which it cannot pass, is equally certain. But the reason which determined this limit, and for which such being was suffered to advance thus far and no further, we shall never be able to discern. Our discoveries tell us, the Creator has made beings of all orders, and that therefore one of them must be such as man. But this system seems to be established on a concession which if it be refused cannot be extorted.

Every reason which can be brought to prove, that there are beings of every possible sort, will prove that there is the greatest number possible of every sort of beings; but this with respect to man we know, if we known any thing, not to be true.

It does not appear even to the imagination, that of three orders of being, the first and the third receive any advantage from the imperfection of the second, or that indeed they may not equally exist, though the second had never been, or should cease to be, and why should that be concluded necessary, which cannot be proved even to be useful?

The scale of existence from infinity to nothing, cannot possibly have being. The highest being not infinite must be, as has been often observed, at an infinite distance below infinity. *Cheyne*, who, with the desire inherent in mathematicians to reduce every thing to mathematical images, considers all existence as a *cone*, allows that the basis is at an infinite distance from the body. And in this distance between finite and infinite, there will be room for ever for an infinite series of indefinable existence.

Between the lowest positive existence and nothing, wherever we suppose positive existence to cease, is another chasm infinitely deep; where there is room again for endless orders of subordinate nature, continued for ever and for ever, and yet infinitely superior to non-existence.

To these meditations humanity is unequal. But yet we may ask, not of our maker, but of each other, since on the one side creation, wherever it stops, must stop infinitely below infinity, and on the other infinitely above nothing, what necessity there is that it should proceed so far either way, that beings so high or so low should ever have existed. We may ask; but I believe no created wisdom can give an adequate answer.

Nor is this all. In the scale, wherever it begins or ends, are infinite vacuities. At whatever distance we suppose the next order of beings to be above man, there is room for an intermediate order of beings between them; and if for one order then for infinite orders;

since every thing that admits of more or less, and consequently all the parts of that which admits them, may be infinitely divided. So that, as far as we can judge, there may be room in the vacuity between any two steps of the scale, or between any two points of the cone of being for infinite exertion of infinite power.

Thus it appears how little reason those who repose their reason upon the scale of being have to triumph over them who recur to any other expedient of solution, and what difficulties arise on every side to repress the rebellions of presumptuous decision. *Qui pauca considerat, facile pronunciat.* In our passage through the boundless ocean of disquisition we often take fogs for land, and after having long toiled to approach them find, instead of repose and harbours, new storms of objection and fluctuations of uncer-tainty.

We are next entertained with *Pope's* alleviations of those evils which we are doomed to suffer.

'Poverty, or the want of riches, is generally compensated by having more hopes and fewer fears, by a greater share of health, and a more exquisite relish of the smallest enjoyments, than those who possess them are usually bless'd with. The want of taste and genius, with all the pleasures that arise from them, are commonly recompensed by a more useful kind of common sense, together with a wonderful delight, as well as success, in the busy pursuits of a scrambling world. The sufferings of the sick are greatly relieved by many trifling gratifications imperceptible to others, and sometimes almost repaid by the inconceivable transports occasioned by the return of health and vigour. Folly cannot be very grievous, be-cause imperceptible; and I doubt not but there is some truth in that rant of a mad poet, that there is a pleasure in being mad, which none but madmen know. Ignorance, or the want of know-ledge and literature, the appointed lot of all born to poverty, and the drudgeries of life, is the only opiate capable of infusing that insensibility which can enable them to endure the miseries of the one, and the fatigues of the other. It is a cordial administered by the gracious hand of providence; of which they ought never to be deprived by an ill-judged and improper education. It is the basis of all subordination, the support of society, and the privilege of individuals: and I have ever thought it a most remarkable in-stance of the divine wisdom, that whereas in all animals, whose individuals rise little above the rest of their species, knowledge is instinctive; in man, whose individuals are so widely different, it is acquired by education; by which means the prince and the labourer, the philosopher and the peasant, are in some measure fitted for their respective situations.'

Much of these positions is perhaps true, and the whole paragraph might well pass without censure, were not objections necessary to the establishment of knowledge. *Poverty* is very gently paraphrased by *want of riches*. In that sense almost every man may in his own opinion be poor. But there is another poverty which is *want of competence*, of all that can soften the miseries of life, of all that can diversify attention, or delight imagination. There is yet another poverty which is want *of necessaries*, a species of poverty which no care of the publick, no charity of particulars, can preserve many from feeling openly, and many secretly.

That hope and fear are inseparably or very frequently connected with poverty, and riches, my surveys of life have not informed me. The milder degrees of poverty are sometimes supported by hope, but the more severe often sink down in motionless despondence. Life must be seen before it can be known. This author and *Pope* perhaps never saw the miseries which they imagine thus easy to be born. The poor indeed are insensible of many little vexations which sometimes imbitter the possessions and pollute the enjoyments of the rich. They are not pained by casual incivility, or mortified by the mutilation of a compliment; but this happiness is like that of a malefactor who ceases to feel the cords that bind him when the pincers are tearing his flesh.

That want of taste for one enjoyment is supplied by the pleasures of some other, may be fairly allowed. But the compensations of sickness I have never found near to equivalence, and the transports of recovery only prove the intenseness of the pain.

With folly no man is willing to confess himself very intimately acquainted, and therefore its pains and pleasures are kept secret. But what the author says of its happiness seems applicable only to fatuity, or gross dulness, for that inferiority of understanding which makes one man without any other reason the slave, or tool, or property of another, which makes him sometimes useless, and sometimes ridiculous, is often felt with very quick sensibility. On the happiness of madmen, as the case is not very frequent, it is not necessary to raise a disquisition, but I cannot forbear to observe, that I never yet knew disorders of mind encrease felicity:

357

M

every madman is either arrogant and irascible, or gloomy and suspicious, or possessed by some passion or notion destructive to his quiet. He has always discontent in his look, and malignity in his bosom. And, if we had the power of choice, he would soon repent who should resign his reason to secure his peace.

Concerning the portion of ignorance necessary to make the condition of the lower classes of mankind safe to the public and tolerable to themselves, both morals and policy exact a nicer enquiry than will be very soon or very easily made. There is undoubtedly a degree of knowledge which will direct a man to refer all to providence, and to acquiesce in the condition which omniscient goodness has determined to allot him; to consider this world as a phantom that must soon glide from before his eyes, and the distresses and vexations that encompass him, as dust scattered in his path, as a blast that chills him for a moment, and passes off for ever.

Such wisdom, arising from the comparison of a part with the whole of our existence, those that want it most cannot possibly obtain from philosophy, nor unless the method of education, and the general tenour of life are changed, will very easily receive it from religion. The bulk of mankind is not likely to be very wise or very good: and I know not whether there are not many states of life, in which all knowledge less than the highest wisdom, will produce discontent and danger. I believe it may be sometimes found, that a *little learning* is to a poor man a *dangerous thing*. But such is the condition of humanity, that we easily see, or quickly feel the wrong, but cannot always distinguish the right. Whatever knowledge is superfluous, in irremediable poverty, is hurtful, but the difficulty is to determine when poverty is irremediable, and at what point superfluity begins. Gross ignorance every man has found equally dangerous with perverted knowledge. Men left wholly to their appetites and their instincts, with little sense of moral or religious obligation, and with very faint distinctions of right and wrong, can never be safely employed, or confidently trusted: they can be honest only by obstinacy, and diligent only by compulsion or caprice. Some instruction, therefore, is necessary, and much perhaps may be dangerous.

Though it should be granted that those who are *born to poverty and drudgery* should not be *deprived* by an *improper education* of the *opiate* of *ignorance*; even this concession will not be of much use

358

to direct our practice, unless it be determined who are those that are *born to poverty*. To entail irreversible poverty upon generation after generation only because the ancestor happened to be poor, is in itself cruel, if not unjust, and is wholly contrary to the maxims of a commercial nation, which always suppose and promote a rotation of property, and offer every individual a chance of mending his condition by his diligence. Those who communicate literature to the son of a poor man, consider him as one not born to poverty, but to the necessity of deriving a better fortune from himself. In this attempt, as in others, many fail, and many succeed. Those that fail will feel their misery more acutely; but since poverty is now confessed to be such a calamity as cannot be born without the opiate of insensibility, I hope the happiness of those whom education enables to escape from it, may turn the ballance against that exacerbation which the others suffer.

I am always afraid of determining on the side of envy or cruelty. The privileges of education may sometimes be improperly bestowed, but I shall always fear to with-hold them, lest I should be yielding to the suggestions of pride, while I persuade myself that I am following the maxims of policy; and under the appearance of salutary restraints, should be indulging the last of dominion, and that malevolence which delights in seeing others depressed.

Pope's doctrine is at last exhibited in a comparison, which, like other proofs of the same kind, is better adapted to delight the fancy than convince the reason.

'Thus the universe resembles a large and well-regulated family, in which all the officers and servants, and even the domestic animals, are subservient to each other in a proper subordination: each enjoys the privileges and perquisites peculiar to his place, and at the same time contributes by that just subordination to the magnificence and happiness of the whole.'

The magnificence of a house is of use or pleasure always to the master, and sometimes to the domestics. But the magnificence of the universe adds nothing to the supreme Being; for any part of its inhabitants with which human knowledge is acquainted, an universe much less spacious or splendid would have been sufficient; and of happiness it does not appear that any is communicated from the Beings of a lower world to those of a higher.

The enquiry after the cause of *natural evil* is continued in the third letter, in which, as in the former, there is mixture of borrowed truth, and native folly, of some notions just and trite, with others uncommon and ridiculous.

His opinion of the value and importance of happiness is certainly just, and I shall insert it, not that it will give any information to any reader, but it may serve to shew how the most common notion may be swelled in sound, and diffused in bulk, till it shall perhaps astonish the author himself.

'Happiness is the only thing of real value in existence; neither riches, nor power, nor wisdom, nor learning, nor strength, nor beauty, nor virtue, nor religion, nor even life itself, being of any importance, but as they contribute to its production. All these are in themselves neither good nor evil; happiness alone is their great end, and they are desireable only as they tend to promote it.'

Success produces confidence. After this discovery of the value of happiness, he proceeds without any distrust of himself to tell us what has been hid from all former enquirers.

'The true solution of this important question, so long and so vainly searched for by the philosophers of all ages and all countries, I take to be at last no more than this, that these real evils proceed from the same sourse as those imaginary ones of imperfection before treated of, namely, from that subordination, without which no created system can subsist; all subordination implying imperfection, all imperfection evil, and all evil some kind of inconveniency or suffering: so that there must be particular inconveniencies and sufferings annexed to every particular rank of created beings by the circumstances of things, and their modes of existence.

'God indeed might have made us quite other creatures, and placed us in a world quite differently constituted; but then we had been no longer men, and whatever beings had occupied our stations in the universal system, they must have been liable to the same inconveniences.'

In all this there is nothing that can silence the enquiries of curiosity, or calm the perturbations of doubt. Whether subordination implies imperfection may be disputed. The means respecting themselves, may be as perfect as the end. The weed as a weed is no less perfect than the oak as an oak. That *imperfection implies evil, and evil suffering*, is by no means evident. Imperfection may imply privative evil, or the absence of some good, but this privation produces no suffering, but by the help of knowledge. An infant at the breast is yet an imperfect man, but there is no reason for belief that he is unhappy by his immaturity, unless some positive pain be superadded.

When this author presumes to speak of the universe, I would advise him a little to distrust his own faculties, however large and comprehensive. Many words easily understood on common occasion, become uncertain and figurative when applied to the works of Omnipotence. Subordination in human affairs is well understood, but when it is attributed to the universal system, its meaning grows less certain, like the petty distinctions of locality, which are of good use upon our own globe, but have no meaning with regard to infinite space, in which nothing is *high* or *low*.

That if a man, by exaltation to a higher nature were exempted from the evils which he now suffers, some other being must suffer them; that if man were not man, some other being must be man, is a position arising from his established notion of the scale of being. A notion to which *Pope* has given some importance by adopting it, and of which I have therefore endeavoured to show the uncertainty and inconsistency. This scale of being I have demonstrated to be raised by presumptuous imagination, to rest on nothing at the bottom, to lean on nothing at the top, and to have vacuities from step to step through which any order of being may sink into nihility without any inconvenience, so far as we can judge to the next rank above or below it. We are therefore little enlightned by a writer who tells us that any being in the state of man must suffer what man suffers, when the only question, that requires to be resolved is, Why any being is in this state?

Of poverty and labour he gives just and elegant representations, which yet do not remove the difficulty of the first and fundamental question, though supposing the present state of man necessary, they may supply some motives to content.

'Poverty is what all could not possibly have been exempted from, not only by reason of the fluctuating nature of human possessions, but because the world could not subsist without it; for had all been rich, none could have submitted to the commands of another, or the necessary drudgeries of life; thence all governments must have been dissolved, arts neglected, and lands uncultivated, and so an universal penury have overwhelmed all, instead of now and then pinching a few. Hence, by the by, appears the great excellence of charity, by which men are enabled by a particular distribution of the blessings and enjoyments of life, on proper occasions, to prevent that poverty which by a general one omnipotence itself could never have prevented: so that, by inforcing this duty, God as it were demands our assistance to promote universal happiness, and to shut out misery at every door, where it strives to intrude itself.

'Labour, indeed, God might easily have excused us from, since at his command, the earth would readily have poured forth all her treasures without our inconsiderable assistance: but if the severest labour cannot sufficiently subdue the malignity of human nature, what plots and machinations, what wars, rapine and devastation, what profligacy and licentiousness must have been the consequences of universal idleness! so that labour ought only to be looked upon as a task kindly imposed upon us by our indulgent creator, necessary to preserve our health, our safety, and our innocence.'

I am afraid that *the latter end of his commonwealth forgets the beginning.* If God *could easily have excused us from labour,* I do not comprehend why *he could not possibly have exempted all from poverty.* For poverty, in its easier and more tolerable degree, is little more than necessity of labour, and, in its more severe and deplorable state, little more than inability for labour. To be poor is to work for others, or to want the succour of others without work. And the same exuberant fertility which would make work unnecessary might make poverty impossible.

Surely a man who seems not completely master of his own opinion, should have spoken more cautiously of omnipotence, nor have presumed to say what it could perform, or what it could prevent. I am in doubt whether those who stand highest in *the scale of being* speak thus confidently of the dispensations of their maker.

For fools rush in, where angels fear to tread.

Of our inquietudes of mind his account is still less reasonable. 'Whilst men are injured, they must be inflamed with anger; and whilst they see cruelties, they must be melted with pity; whilst they perceive danger, they must be sensible of fear.' This is to give a reason for all evil, by shewing that one evil produces another. If there is danger there ought to be fear; but if fear is an evil, why should there be danger? His vindication of pain is of the same kind; pain is useful to alarm us, that we may shun greater evils, but those greater evils must be presupposed that the fitness of pain may appear.

Treating on death, he has expressed the known and true doctrine with spriteliness of fancy and neatness of diction. I shall therefore insert it. There are truths which, as they are always necessary, do not grow stale by repetition.

'Death, the last and most dreadful of all evils, is so far from being one, that it is the infallible cure for all others.

> To die, is landing on some silent shore,
> Where billows never beat, nor tempests roar.
> Eere well we feel the friendly stroke, 'tis o'er.   GARTH.

For, abstracted from the sickness and sufferings usually attending it, it is no more than the expiration of that term of life God was pleased to bestow on us, without any claim or merit on our part. But was it an evil ever so great, it could not be remedied but by one much greater, which is by living for ever; by which means our wickedness, unrestrained by the prospect of a future state, would grow so insupportable, our sufferings so intolerable by perseverance, and our pleasures so tiresome by repetition, that no being in the universe could be so compleatly miserable as a species of immortal men. We have no reason, therefore, to look upon death as an evil, or to fear it as a punishment, even without any supposition of a future life: but if we consider it as a passage to a more perfect state, or a remove only in an eternal succession of still improving states (for which we have the strongest reasons) it will then appear a new favour from the divine munificence; and a man must be as absurd to repine at dying, as a traveller would be, who proposed to himself a delightful tour through various unknown countries, to lament that he cannot take up his residence at the first dirty inn which he baits at on the road.

'The instability of human life, or the changes of its successive periods, of which we so frequently complain, are no more than the necessary progress of it to this necessary conclusion; and are so far from being evils deserving these complaints, that they are the source of our greatest pleasures as they are the source of all novelty, from which our greatest pleasures are ever derived. The continual succession of seasons in the human life, by daily presenting to us new scenes, render it agreeable, and like those of the year, afford us delights by their change, which the choicest of them could not give us by their continuance. In the spring of life, the

gilding of the sun-shine, the verdure of the fields, and the variegated paintings of the sky, are so exquisite in the eyes of infants
at their first looking abroad into a new world, as nothing perhaps
afterwards can equal. The heat and vigour of the succeeding summer of youth ripens for us new pleasures, the blooming maid, the
nightly revel, and the jovial chace: the serene autumn of complete
manhood feasts us with the golden harvests of our worldly pursuits: nor is the hoary winter of old age destitute of its peculiar
comforts and enjoyments, of which the recollection and relation
of those past are perhaps none of the least; and at last death opens
to us a new prospect, from whence we shall probably look back
upon the diversions and occupations of this world with the same
contempt we do now on our tops and hobby-horses, and with the
same surprize, that they could ever so much entertain or engage
us.'

I would not willingly detract from the beauty of this paragraph, and in gratitude to him who has so well inculcated such
important truths, I will venture to admonish him, since the chief
comfort of the old is the recollection of the past, so to employ his
time and his thoughts, that when the imbecillity of age shall come
upon him, he may be able to recreate its languors by the remembrance of hours spent, not in presumptuous decisions, but modest
inquiries, not in dogmatical limitations of omnipotence, but in
humble acquiescence and fervent adoration. Old age will shew
him that much of the book now before us has no other use than to
perplex the scrupulous, and to shake the weak, to encourage impious presumption, or stimulate idle curiosity.

Having thus dispatched the consideration of particular evils, he
comes at last to a general reason for which *evil* may be said to be
our good. He is of opinion that there is some inconceivable benefit
in pain abstractedly considered; that pain however inflicted, or
wherever felt, communicates some good to the general system of
being, and that every animal is some way or other the better for
the pain of every other animal. This opinion he carries so far as to
suppose that there passes some principle of union through all
animal life, as attraction is communicated to all corporeal nature,
and that the evils suffered on this globe, may by some inconceivable means contribute to the felicity of the inhabitants of the remotest planet.

How the origin of evil is brought nearer to human conception by any *inconceivable* means, I am not able to discover. We believed that the present system of creation was right, though we could not explain the adaptation of one part to the other, or for the whole succession of causes and consequences. Where has this enquirer added to the little knowledge that we had before. He has told us of the benefits of evil, which no man feels, and relations between distant parts of the universe, which he cannot himself conceive. There was enough in this question inconceivable before, and we have little advantage from a new inconceivable solution.

I do not mean to reproach this author for not knowing what is equally hidden from learning and from ignorance. The shame is to impose words for ideas upon ourselves or others. To imagine that we are going forward when we are only turning round. To think that there is any difference between him that gives no reason, and him that gives a reason, which by his own confession cannot be conceived.

But that he may not be thought to conceive nothing but things inconceivable, he has at last thought on a way by which human sufferings may produce good effects. He imagines that as we have not only animals for food, but choose some for our diversion, the same privilege may be allowed to some beings above us, *who may deceive, torment, or destroy us for the ends only of their own pleasure or utility.* This he again finds impossible to be conceived, *but that impossibility lessens not the probability of the conjecture, which by analogy is so strongly confirmed.*

I cannot resist the temptation of contemplating this analogy, which I think he might have carried further very much to the advantage of his argument. He might have shewn that these *hunters whose game is man* have many sports analogous to our own. As we drown whelps and kittens, they amuse themselves now and then with sinking a ship, and stand round the fields of *Blenheim* or the walls of *Prague,* as we encircle a cock-pit. As we shoot a bird flying, they take a man in the midst of his business or pleasure, and knock him down with an apoplexy. Some of them, perhaps, are virtuosi, and delight in the operations of an asthma, as a human philosopher in the effects of the air pump. To swell a man with a tympany is as good sport as to blow a frog. Many a merry bout have these frolic beings at the vicissitudes of an ague, and good sport it is to see a man tumble with an epilepsy, and revive and tumble again, and all this he knows not why. As they are wiser and more powerful than we, they have more exquisite diversions, for we have no way of procuring any sport so brisk and so lasting as the paroxysms of the gout and stone which undoubtedly must make high mirth, especially if the play be a little diversified with the blunders and puzzles of the blind and deaf. We know not how far their sphere of observation may extend. Perhaps now and then a merry being may place himself in such a situation as to enjoy at once all the varieties of an epidemical disease, or amuse his leisure with the tossings and contortions of every possible pain exhibited together.

One sport the merry malice of these beings has found means of enjoying to which we have nothing equal or similar. They now and then catch a mortal proud of his parts, and flattered either by the submission of those who court his kindness, or the notice of those who suffer him to court theirs. A head thus prepared for the reception of false opinions, and the projection of vain designs, they easily fill with idle notions, till in time they make their plaything an author: their first diversion commonly begins with an Ode or an epistle, then rises perhaps to a political irony, and is at last brought to its height, by a treatise of philosophy. Then begins the poor animal to entangle himself in sophisms, and flounder in absurdity, to talk confidently of the scale of being, and to give solutions which himself confesses impossible to be understood. Sometimes, however, it happens that their pleasure is without much mischief. The author feels no pain, but while they are wondering at the extravagance of his opinion, and pointing him out to one another as a new example of human folly, he is enjoying his own applause, and that of his companions, and perhaps is elevated with the hope of standing at the head of a new sect.

Many of the books which now croud the world, may be justly suspected to be written for the sake of some invisible order of beings, for surely they are of no use to any of the corporeal inhabitants of the world. Of the productions of the last bounteous year, how many can be said to serve any purpose of use or pleasure. The only end of writing is to enable the readers better to enjoy life, or better to endure it: and how will either of those be put more in our power by him who tells us, that we are puppets, of which some creature not much wiser than ourselves manages the wires. That a set of beings unseen and unheard, are hovering about us, trying experiments upon our sensibility, putting us in agonies to see our limbs quiver, torturing us to madness, that they may laugh at our vagaries, sometimes obstructing the bile, that they may see how a man looks when he is yellow: sometimes breaking a traveller's bones to try how he will get home; sometimes wasting a man to a skeleton, and sometimes killing him fat for the greater elegance of his hide.

This is an account of natural evil, which though, like the rest, not quite new is very entertaining, though I know not how much it may contribute to patience. The only reason why we should contemplate evil is, that we may bear it better, and I am afraid nothing is much more placidly endured, for the sake of making others sport.

The first pages of the fourth letter are such as incline me both to hope and wish that I shall find nothing to blame in the succeeding part. He offers a criterion of action, on account of virtue and vice, for which I have often contended, and which must be embraced by all who are willing to know why they act, or why they forbear, to give any reason of their conduct to themselves or others.

'In order to find out the true origin of moral evil, it will be necessary, in the first place, to enquire into its nature and essence; or what it is that constitutes one action evil, and another good. Various have been the opinions of various authors on this criterion of virtue; and this variety has rendered that doubtful, which must otherwise have been clear and manifest to the meanest capacity. Some indeed have denied that there is any such thing, because different ages and nations have entertained different sentiments concerning it: but this is just as reasonable as to assert, that there are neither sun, moon, nor stars, because astronomers have supported different systems of the motions and magnitudes of these celestial bodies. Some have placed it in conformity to truth, some to the fitness of things, and others to the will of God. But all this is merely superficial: they resolve us not why truth, or the fitness of things, are either eligible or obligatory, or why God should require us to act in one manner rather than another. The true reason of which can possibly be no other than this, because some actions produce happiness, and others misery: so that all moral good and evil are nothing more than the production of natural. This alone it is that makes truth preferable to falshood, this that determines the fitness of things, and this that induces God to command some actions, and forbid others. They who extol the truth, beauty, and harmony of virtue, exclusive of its consequences, deal but in pompous nonsense; and they who would persuade us, that good and evil are things indifferent, depending wholly on the will of God, do but confound the nature of things, as well as all our notions of God himself, by representing him capable of willing contradictions; that is, that we should be, and be happy, and at the same time that we should torment and destroy each other; for injuries cannot be made benefits, pain cannot be made pleasure, and consequently vice cannot be made virtue by any power whatever. It is the consequences, therefore, of all human actions that must stamp their value. So far as the general practice of any action tends to produce good, and introduce happiness into the world, so far we may pronounce it virtuous; so much evil as it occasions, such is the degree of vice it contains. I say the general practice, because we must always remember, in judging by this rule, to apply it only to the general species of actions, and not to particular actions; for the infinite wisdom of God, desirous to set bounds to the destructive consequences which must otherwise have followed from the universal depravity of mankind, has so wonderfully contrived the nature of things, that our most vitious actions may sometimes accidentally and collaterally produce good. Thus, for instance, robbery may disperse useless hoards to the benefit of the public; adultery may bring heirs and good humour too into many families, where they would otherwise have been wanting; and murder free the world from tyrants and oppressors. Luxury maintains its thousands, and vanity its ten thousands. Superstition and arbitrary power contribute to the grandeur of many nations, and the liberties of others are preserved by the perpetual contentions of avarice, knavery, selfishness, and ambition: and thus the worst of vices, and the worst of men are often compelled by providence to serve the most beneficial purposes, contrary to their own malevolent tendencies and inclinations; and thus private vices become public benefits by the force only of accidental circumstances. But this impeaches not the truth of the criterion of virtue before mentioned, the only solid foundation on which any true system of ethicks can be built, the only plain, simple, and uniform rule by which we can pass any judgment on our actions; but by this we may be enabled, not only to determine which are good, and which are evil, but almost mathematically to demonstrate the proportion of virtue, or vice which belongs to each, by comparing them with the degrees of happiness or misery which they occasion. But tho' the production of happiness is the essence of virtue, it is by no means the end: the great end is the probation of mankind, or the giving them an opportunity of exalting or degrading themselves in another state by their behaviour in the present. And thus indeed it answers two most important purposes; those are, the conservation of our happiness, and the test of our obedience; for had not such a test seemed necessary to God's infinite wisdom, and productive of universal good, he would never have permitted the happiness of men, even in this life, to have depended on so precarious a tenure, as their mutual good behaviour to each other. For it is observable, that he who best knows our formation, has trusted no one thing of importance to our reason or virtue: he trusts only to our appetites for the support of the individual, and the continuance of our species; to our vanity or compassion, for our bounty to others; and to our fears, for the preservation of ourselves; often to our vices for the support of government, and sometimes to our follies for the preservation of our religion. But since some test of our obedience was necessary, nothing sure could have been commanded for that end so fit and proper, and at the same time so useful, as the practice of virtue: nothing have been so justly rewarded with happiness, as the production of happiness in conformity to the will of God. It is this conformity alone which adds merit to virtue, and constitutes the essential difference between morality and religion. Morality obliges men to live honestly and soberly, because such behaviour is most conducive to publick happiness, and consequently to their own; religion, to pursue the same course, because conformable to the will of their creator. Morality induces them to embrace virtue from prudential considerations; religion from those of gratitude and obedience. Morality therefore, entirely abstracted from religion, can have nothing meritorious in it; it being wisdom, prudence, or good œconomy, which, like health, beauty, or riches, are rather obligations conferred upon us by God, than merits in us towards him; for tho' we may be justly punished for injuring ourselves, we can claim no reward for self-preservation; as suicide deserves punishment and infamy, but a man deserves no reward or honours for not being guilty of it. This I take to be the meaning of all those passages in our scriptures in which works are represented to have no merit without faith; that is, not without believing in historical

REVIEW OF A FREE ENQUIRY

facts, in creeds, and articles; but without being done in pursuance of our belief in God, and in obedience to his commands. And now, having mentioned scripture, I cannot omit observing that the christian is the only religious or moral institution in the world, that ever set in a right light these two material points, the essence and the end of virtue; that ever founded the one in the production of happiness, that is, in universal benevolence, or, in their language, charity to all men; the other, in the probation of man, and his obedience to his creator. Sublime and magnificent as was the philosophy of the ancients, all their moral systems were deficient in these two important articles. They were all built on the sandy foundations of the innate beauty of virtue, or enthusiastick patriotism; and their great point in view was the contemptible reward of human glory; foundations which were by no means able to support the magnificent structures which they erected upon them; for the beauty of virtue independent of its effects, is unmeaning nonsense; patriotism which injures mankind in general for the sake of a particular country, is but a more extended selfishness, and really criminal; and all human glory but a mean and ridiculous delusion. The whole affair then of religion and morality, the subject of so many thousand volumes, is, in short, no more than this: The supreme being, infinitely good, as well as powerful, desirous to diffuse happiness by all possible means, has created innumerable ranks and orders of Beings, all subservient to each other by proper subordination. One of these is occupied by Man, a creature endued with such a certain degree of knowledge, reason, and free-will, as is suitable to his situation, and placed for a time on this globe as in a school of probation and education. Here he has an opportunity given him of improving or debasing his nature, in such a manner as to render himself fit for a rank of higher perfection and happiness, or to degrade himself to a state of greater imperfection and misery; necessary indeed towards carrying on the business of the universe, but very grievous and burthensome to those individuals, who, by their own misconduct, are obliged to submit to it. The test of this his behaviour, is doing good, that is, co-operating with his creator, as far as his narrow sphere of action will permit, in the production of happiness. And thus the happiness and misery of a future state will be the just reward or punishment of promoting or preventing happiness in this. So artificially by this means is the nature of all human virtue and vice contrived, that their rewards and punishments are woven as it were in their very essence; their immediate effects give us a foretaste of their future, and their fruits in the present life are the proper samples of what they must unavoidably produce in another. We have reason given us to distinguish these consequences, and regulate our conduct; and, lest that should neglect its post, Conscience also is appointed as an instinctive kind of monitor, perpetually to remind us both of our interest and our duty.'

Si sic omnia dixisset! To this account of the essence of vice and virtue, it is only necessary to add, that the consequences of human actions being sometimes uncertain and sometimes remote, it is not possible in many cases for most men, nor in all cases for any man to determine what actions will ultimately produce happiness, and therefore it was proper that *Revelation* should lay down a rule to be followed invariably in opposition to appearances, and in every change of circumstances, by which we may be certain to promote the general felicity, and be set free from the dangerous temptation of *doing evil that good may come*.

Because it may easily happen, and in effect will happen very frequently, that our own private happiness may be promoted by an act injurious to others, when yet no man can be obliged by nature to prefer ultimately the happiness of others to his own. Therefore, to the instructions of infinite wisdom it was necessary that infinite power should add penal sanctions. That every man to whom those instructions shall be imparted may know, that he can never ultimately injure himself by benefiting others, or ultimately by injuring others benefit himself; but that however the lot of the good and bad may be huddled together in the seeming confusion of our present state, the time shall undoubtedly come, when the most virtuous will be most happy.

I am sorry that the remaining part of this letter is not equal to the first. The author has indeed engaged in a disquisition in which we need not wonder if he fails, in the solution of questions on which philosophers have employed their abilities from the earliest times,

> And found no end, in wand'ring mazes lost.

He denies that man was created *perfect*, because the system requires subordination, and because the power of losing his perfection of *rendering himself wicked and miserable is the highest imperfection imaginable.* Besides the regular gradations of the scale of being required somewhere *such a creature as man with all his infirmities about him, and the total removal of those would be altering his nature, and when he became perfect he must cease to be man.*

I have already spent some considerations on the *scale of being,* of which yet I am obliged to renew the mention whenever a new argument is made to rest upon it, and I must therefore again remark, that consequences cannot have greater certainty than the postulate from which they are drawn, and that no system can be more hypothetical than this, and perhaps no hypothesis more absurd.

He again deceives himself with respect to the perfection with which *man* is held to be originally vested. *That man came perfect, that is indued with all possible perfection, out of the hands of his creator, is a false notion, derived from the philosophers.—The universal system required subordination, and consequently comparative imperfection.* That *man was ever indued with all possible perfection,* that is with all perfection of which the idea is not contradictory or destructive of itself, is undoubtedly *false.* But it can hardly be called *a false notion,* because no man ever thought it, nor can it be derived from the *philosophers;* for without pretending to guess what philosophers he may mean, it is very safe to affirm, that no philosopher ever said it. Of those who now maintain that *man* was once perfect, who may very easily be found, let the author enquire whether *man* was ever omniscient, whether he was ever omnipotent, whether he ever had even the lower power of Archangels or Angels. Their answers will soon inform him, that the supposed perfection of *man* was not absolute, but respective, that he was perfect in a sense consistent enough with subordination, perfect not as compared with different beings, but with himself in his present degeneracy, not perfect as an angel, but perfect as man.

From this perfection, whatever it was, he thinks it necessary that man should be debarred, because pain is necessary to the good of the universe; and the pain of one order of beings extending its salutary influence to innumerable orders above and below, it was necessary that man should suffer; but because it is not suitable to justice that pain should be inflicted on innocence, it was necessary that man should be criminal.

This is given as a satisfactory account of the original of moral evil, which amounts only to this, that God created beings whose

372

guilt he foreknew, in order that he might have proper objects of pain, because the pain of part is no man knows how or why, necessary to the felicity of the whole.

The perfection which man once had, may be so easily conceived, that without any unusual strain of imagination we can figure its revival. All the duties to God or man that we neglected we may fancy performed, all the crimes that are committed we may conceive forborn. Man will then be restored to his moral perfections, and into what head can it enter, that by this change the universal system would be shaken, or the condition of any order of beings altered for the worse.

He comes in the fifth letter to political, and in the sixth to religious evils. Of political evil, if we suppose the origin of moral evil discovered the account is by no means difficult: polity being only the conduct of immoral men in publick affairs. The evils of each particular kind of government are very clearly and elegantly displayed, and from their secondary causes very rationally deduced, but the first cause lies still in its antient obscurity. There is in this letter nothing new, nor any thing eminently instructive; one of his practical deductions, that *from government evils cannot be eradicated, and their excess can only be prevented,* has been always allowed; the question upon which all dissension arises, is when that excess begins, at what point men shall cease to bear, and attempt to remedy.

Another of his precepts, though not new, well deserves to be transcribed, because it cannot be too frequently impressed.

'What has here been said of their imperfections and abuses, is by no means intended as a defence of them: every wise man ought to redress them to the utmost of his power; which can be effected by one method only: that is, by a reformation of Manners: for as all political evils derive their original from moral, these can never be remov'd, until those are first amended. He, therefore, who strictly adheres to virtue and sobriety in his conduct, and inforces them by his example, does more real service to a state, than he who displaces a minister, or dethrones a tyrant; this gives but a temporary relief, but that exterminates the cause of the disease. No immoral man then can possibly be a true patriot; and all those who profess outrageous zeal for the liberty and prosperity of their country, and at the same time infringe her laws, affront her religion, and debauch her people, are but despicable quacks, by fraud or ignorance increasing the disorders they pretend to remedy.'

Of religion he has said nothing but what he has learned, or might have learned from the divines, that it is not universal, because it must be received upon conviction, and successively received by those whom conviction reached; that its evidences and sanctions are not irresistible, because it was intended to induce, not to compel, and that it is obscure, because we want faculties to comprehend it. What he means by his assertion that it wants policy I do not well understand, he does not mean to deny that a good christian will be a good governor or a good subject, and he has before justly observed that the good man only is a patriot.

Religion has been, he says, corrupted by the wickedness of those to whom it was communicated, and has lost part of its efficacy by its connection with temporal interest and human passion.

He justly observes, that from all this, no conclusion can be drawn against the divine original of christianity, since the objections arise not from the nature of the revelation, but of him to whom it is communicated.

All this is known, and all this is true, but why, we have not yet discovered. Our author, if I understand him right, pursues the argument thus: The religion of man produces evils, because the morality of man is imperfect; his morality is imperfect, that he may be justly a subject of punishment: he is made subject to punishment because the pain of part is necessary to the happiness of the whole; pain is necessary to happiness no mortal can tell why or how.

Thus, after having clambered with great labour from one step of argumentation to another, instead of rising into the light of knowledge, we are devolved back into dark ignorance, and all our effort ends in belief that for the evils of life there is some good reason, and in confession, that the reason cannot be found. This is all that has been produced by the revival of *Chrysippus*'s untractableness of matter, and the *Arabian* scale of existence. A system has been raised, which is so ready to fall to pieces of itself, that no great praise can be derived from its destruction. To object is always easy, and it has been well observed by a late writer, that *the hand which cannot built a hovel, may demolish a temple.**

* New Practice of Physic.

374

SELECTIONS FROM
THE IDLER

The *Idler* essays appeared first in the *Universal Chronicle* from April 15, 1758 to April 5, 1760. The text is taken from the British Museum copies of this periodical (N.R. Burney, 60b.). A collected edition (B.M.: 629. b. 34.) was published in 1761. It may be found that the numeration of the essays from which these selections are taken differs from that in some of the collected editions—it is that of *The Idler* in the *Universal Chronicle*.

On p. 383, the reading *insiduous* has been used. Later editions have *insidious*; the spelling *insiduous* is found also, as the New English Dictionary points out, in the *Lives of the Poets*.

8

To learn of an enemy has always been accounted politick and
honourable, and therefore I hope it will raise no prejudices against
my project, to confess that I borrowed it from a Frenchman.

When the Isle of Rhodes was, many centuries ago, in the hands
of that Military Order now called the Knights of Malta, it was
ravaged by a Dragon, who inhabited a den under a rock, from
which he issued forth when he was hungry or wanton, and without
fear or mercy devoured men and beasts as they came in his way.
Many Councils were held, and many devices offered, for his destruction; but as his back was armed with impenetrable scales,
none would venture to attack him. At last Dudon, a French Knight,
undertook the deliverance of the Island. From some place of security he took a view of the Dragon, or, as a modern Soldier would say,
reconnoitred him, and observed that his belly was naked and vul-
nerable. He then returned home to take his *arrangements*; and,
by a very exact imitation of Nature, made a Dragon of pasteboard,
in the belly of which he put beef and mutton, and accustomed two
sturdy mastiffs to feed themselves, by tearing their way to the
concealed flesh. When his dogs were well practised in this method
of plunder, he marched out with them at his heels, and shewed
them the Dragon; they rushed upon him in quest of their dinner;
Dudon battered his scull while they lacerated his belly; and neither
his sting nor claws were able to defend him.

Something like this might be practised in our present state. Let
a fortification be raised on Salisbury-Plain, resembling *Brest*, or
Toulon, or *Paris* itself, with all the usual preparations for defence:
Let the inclosure be filled with Beef and Ale: Let the soldiers,
from some proper eminence, see Shirts waving upon lines, and
here and there a plump Landlady hurrying about with pots in

her hands. When they are sufficiently animated to advance, lead them in exact order, with fife and drum, to that side whence the wind blows, till they come within the scent of roast-meat and tobacco. Contrive that they may approach the place about an hour after dinner-time, assure them that there is no danger, and command an attack.

If nobody within either moves or speaks, it is not unlikely that they may carry the place by storm; but if a panic should seize them, it will be proper to defer the enterprize to a more hungry hour. When they have entered, let them fill their bellies and return to the camp.

On the next day let the same place be shewn them again, but with some additions of strength or terror. I cannot pretend to inform our Generals thro' what gradations of danger they should train their men to fortitude. They best know what the soldiers and what themselves can bear. It will be proper that the war should every day vary its appearance. Sometimes, as they mount the rampart, a Cook may throw fat upon the fire, to accustom them to a sudden blaze; and sometimes, by the clatter of empty pots, they may be inured to formidable noises. But let it never be forgotten, that Victory must always repose with a full Belly.

In time it will be proper to bring our prisoners from the coast, and place them upon the walls in martial order. At their first appearance their hands must be tied, but they may be allowed to grin. In a month they may guard the place with their hands loosed, provided that on pain of death they be forbidden to strike.

By this method our army will soon be brought to look an enemy in the face. But it has been lately observed, that fear is received by the ear as well as the eyes, and the Indian War-cry is represented as too dreadful to be endured, as a sound that will force the bravest Veteran to drop his weapon, and desert his rank; that will deafen his ear, and chill his breast; that will neither suffer him to hear orders or to feel shame, or retain any sensibility but the dread of death.

That the savage clamours of naked Barbarians should thus terrify troops disciplined to war, and ranged in array with arms in their hands, is surely strange. But this is no time to reason. I am of opinion, that, by a proper mixture of Asses, Bulls, Turkeys, Geese and Tragedians, a noise might be procured equally horrid with the

War-cry. When our men have been encouraged by frequent victories, nothing will remain but to qualify them for extreme danger, by a sudden concert of terrific vociferation. When they have endured this last trial, let them be led to action, as men who are no longer to be frightened; as men, who can bear at once the grimaces of the Continent, and the howl of America.

18

The publick pleasures of far the greater part of mankind are counterfeit. Very few carry their philosophy to places of diversion, or are very careful to analyse their enjoyments. The general condition of life is so full of misery, that we are glad to catch delight without inquiring whence it comes, or by what power it is bestowed.

The mind is seldom quickened to very vigorous operations but by pain, or the dread of pain. We do not disturb ourselves with the detection of fallacies which do us no harm, nor willingly decline a pleasing effect to investigate its cause. He that is happy, by whatever means, desires nothing but the continuance of happiness, and is no more sollicitous to distribute his sensations into their proper species than the common gazer on the beauties of the spring to separate light into its original rays.

Pleasure is therefore seldom such as it appears to others, nor often such as we represent it to ourselves. Of the Ladies that sparkle at a musical performance, a very small number has any quick sensibility of harmonious sounds. But every one that goes has her pleasure. She has the pleasure of wearing fine cloaths, and of shewing them, of outshining those whom she suspects to envy her; she has the pleasure of appearing among other Ladies in a place whither the race of meaner mortals seldom intrudes, and of reflecting that, in the conversations of the next morning, her name will be mentioned among those that sat in the first row; she has the pleasure of returning courtesies, or refusing to return them, of receiving compliments with civility, or rejecting them with disdain. She has the pleasure of meeting some of her acquaintance, of guessing why the rest are absent, and of telling them that she saw the opera, on pretence of inquiring why they would miss it. She has the pleasure of being supposed to be pleased with a refined amusement, and of hoping to be numbered among the votresses of harmony. She has the pleasure of escaping for two hours the superiority of a sister, or the controul of a husband; and from all these pleasures she concludes that heavenly musick is the balm of life.

All assemblies of gaiety are brought together by motives of the same kind. The theatre is not filled with those that know or regard the skill of the Actor, nor the Ball room, by those who dance, or attend to the dancers. To all places of general resort, where the standard of pleasure is erected, we run with equal eagerness, or appearance of eagerness, for very different reasons. One goes that he may say he has been there, another because he never misses. This man goes to try what he can find, and that to discover what others find. Whatever diversion is costly will be frequented by those who desire to be thought rich; and whatever has, by any accident, become fashionable, easily continues its reputation, because every one is ashamed of not partaking it.

To every place of entertainment we go with expectation, and desire of being pleased; we meet others who are brought by the same motives; no one will be the first to own the disappointment; one face reflects the smile of another, till each believes the rest delighted, and endeavours to catch and transmit the circulating rapture. In time, all are deceived by the cheat to which all contribute. The fiction of happiness is propagated by every tongue, and confirmed by every look, till at last all profess the joy which they do not feel, consent to yield to the general delusion; and when the voluntary dream is at an end, lament that bliss is of so short a duration.

If *Druggett* pretended to pleasures, of which he had no perception, or boasted of one amusement where he was indulging another, what did he which is not done by all those who read his story? of whom some pretend delight in conversation, only because they dare not be alone, some praise the quiet of solitude; because they are envious of sense, and impatient of folly; and some gratify their pride, by writing characters which expose the vanity of life.

I am, Sir,

Your humble Servant.

23

To the IDLER.

Sir,

As I was passing lately under one of the gates of this city, I was struck with horror by a rueful cry, which summoned me *to remember the poor Debtors.*

The wisdom and justice of the English laws are, by Englishmen at least, loudly celebrated; but scarcely the most zealous admirers of our Institutions can think that law wise, which, when men are capable of work, obliges them to beg; or just, which exposes the liberty of one to the passions of another.

The prosperity of a people is proportionate to the number of hands and minds usefully employed. To the community sedition is a fever, corruption is a gangrene, and idleness an atrophy. Whatever body, and whatever society, wastes more than it acquires, must gradually decay; and every being that continues to be fed, and ceases to labour, takes away something from the publick stock.

The confinement, therefore, of any man in the sloth and darkness of a prison, is a loss to the nation, and no gain to the Creditor. For of the multitudes who are pining in those cells of misery, a very small part is suspected of any fraudulent act by which they retain what belongs to others. The rest are imprisoned by the wantonness of pride, the malignity of revenge, or the acrimony of disappointed expectation.

If those who thus rigorously exercise the power, which the law has put into their hands, be asked, why they continue to imprison those whom they know to be unable to pay them: One will answer, that his Debtor once lived better than himself; another, that his wife looked above her neighbours, and his children went in silk cloaths to the dancing school; and another, that he pretended to be a joker and a wit. Some will reply, that if they were in debt they should meet with the same treatment; some, that they owe no more than they can pay, and need therefore give no account of their actions. Some will confess their resolution, that their Debtors shall rot in jail; and some will discover, that they hope, by cruelty, to wring the payment from their friends.

The end of all civil regulations is to secure private happiness from private malignity; to keep individuals from the power of one another; but this end is apparently neglected, when a man, irritated with loss, is allowed to be the judge of his own cause, and to assign the punishment of his own pain; when the distinction between guilt and unhappiness, between casualty and design, is intrusted to eyes blind with interest, to understandings depraved by resentment.

Since poverty is punished among us as a crime, it ought at least to be treated with the same lenity as other crimes; the offender ought not to languish, at the will of him whom he has offended, but to be allowed some appeal to the justice of his country. There can be no reason, why any Debtor should be imprisoned, but that he may be compelled to payment; and a term should therefore be fixed, in which the Creditor should exhibit his accusation of concealed property. If such property can be discovered, let it be given to the Creditor; if the charge is not offered, or cannot be proved, let the prisoner be dismissed.

Those who made the laws have apparently supposed, that every deficiency of payment is the crime of the Debtor. But the truth is, that the Creditor always shares the act, and often more than shares the guilt of improper trust. It seldom happens that any man imprisons another but for debts which he suffered to be contracted, in hope of advantage to himself, and for bargains in which he proportioned his profit to his own opinion of the hazard; and there is no reason, why one should punish the other, for a contract in which both concurred.

Many of the inhabitants of prisons may justly complain of harder treatment. He that once owes more than he can pay, is often obliged to bribe his Creditor to patience, by encreasing his debt. Worse and worse commodities, at a higher and higher price, are forced upon him; he is impoverished by compulsive traffick, and at last overwhelmed, in the common receptacles of misery, by debts, which, without his own consent, were accumulated on his head. To the relief of such distress, and to the redress of such misery, no other objection can be made, but that by such easy dissolution of debts, fraud will be left without punishment, and imprudence without awe, and that when insolvency shall become no longer punishable, credit will cease.

The motive to credit, is the hope of advantage. Commerce can never be at a stop, while one man wants what another can supply; and credit will never be denied, while it is likely to be repaid with profit. He that trusts one whom he designs to sue, is criminal by the act of Trust; the cessation of such insiduous traffick is to be desired, and no reason can be given, why a change of the law should impair any other.

We see nation trade with nation, where no payment can be compelled. Mutual convenience produces mutual confidence, and the Merchants continue to satisfy the demands of each other, though they have nothing to dread but the loss of trade.

It is vain to continue an institution, which experience shews to be ineffectual. We have now imprisoned one generation of Debtors after another, but we do not find that their numbers lessen. We have now learned, that rashness and imprudence will not be deterred from taking credit; let us try whether fraud and avarice may be more easily restrained from giving it.

I am, Sir, &c.

26

To the IDLER.

Sir,

I am a very constant frequenter of the Playhouse, a place to which I suppose the Idler not much a stranger, since he can have no where else so much entertainment, with so little concurrence of his own endeavour. At all other assemblies, he that comes to receive delight, will be expected to give it; but in the Theatre, nothing is necessary to the amusement of two hours, but to sit down and be willing to be pleased.

The last week has offered two new Actors to the town. The appearance and retirement of Actors, are the great events of the theatrical world; and their first performances fill the pit with conjecture and prognostication, as the first actions of a new Monarch fill nations with hope or fear.

What opinion I have formed of the future character of these candidates for dramatic glory, it is not necessary to declare. Their entrance gave me a higher and nobler pleasure than any borrowed character can afford. I saw the ranks of the Theatre emulating each other, in candour and humanity, and contending, who should most effectually assist the struggles of endeavour, dissipate the blush of diffidence, and still the flutter of timidity.

This behaviour is such as becomes a people, too tender to repress those who wish to please, too generous to insult those who can make no resistance. A publick Performer is so much in the power

383

of spectators, that all unnecessary severity is prohibited by that general law of humanity which forbids us to be cruel where there is nothing to be feared.

In every new Performer something must be pardoned. No man can by any force of resolution, secure to himself the full possession of his own powers, under the eye of a large assembly. Variation of gesture, and flexion of voice, are to obtained only by experience.

There is nothing for which such numbers think themselves qualified as for theatrical exhibition. Every human being has an action graceful to his own eye, a voice musical to his own ear, and a sensibility which Nature forbids him to know that any other bosom can excel. An act in which such numbers fancy themselves excellent, and which the Publick liberally rewards, will excite many competitors, and in many attempts there must be many miscarriages.

The care of the Critic should be to distinguish error from inability, faults of inexperience from defects of Nature. Action irregular and turbulent may be reclaimed; vociferation vehement and confused may be restrained and modulated; the stalk of the tyrant may become the gait of a man; the yell of inarticulate distress may be reduced to human lamentation. All these faults should be for a time overlooked, and afterwards censured with gentleness and candour. But if in an Actor there appears an utter vacancy of meaning, a frigid equality, a stupid languor, a torpid apathy, the greatest kindness that can be shewn him, is a speedy sentence of expulsion.

I am, Sir, &c.

The plea which my Correspondent has offered for young Actors, I am very far from wishing to invalidate. I always considered those combinations which are sometimes formed in the Playhouse as acts of fraud or of cruelty; he that applauds him who does not deserve praise is endeavouring to deceive the publick; he that hisses in malice or sport, is an oppressor and a robber.

But surely this laudable forbearance might be justly extended to young Poets. The art of the Writer, like that of the Player, is attained by slow degrees. The power of distinguishing and discriminating comic characters, or of filling Tragedy with poetical images, must be the gift of Nature, which no instruction nor labour can supply; but the art of dramatic disposition, the contexture of the scenes, the opposition of characters, the involution of the plot, the expedients of suspension, and the stratagems of surprize, are to be learned by practice; and it is cruel to discourage a Poet for ever, because he has not from genius what only experience can bestow.

Life is a stage. Let me likewise sollicit candour for the young Actor on the stage of life. They that enter into the world are too often treated with unreasonable rigour by those that were once as ignorant and heady as themselves, and distinction is not always made between the faults which require speedy and violent eradication, and those that will gradually drop away in the progression of life. Vicious sollicitations of appetite, if not checked, will grow more importunate, and mean arts of profit or ambition will gather strength in the mind if they are not early suppressed. But mistaken notions of superiority, desires of useless show, pride of little accomplishments, and all the train of vanity will be brushed away by the wing of time.

Reproof should not exhaust its power upon petty failings, let it watch diligently against the incursion of vice, and leave foppery and futility to die of themselves.

31

One of the amusements of idleness is reading, without the fatigue of close attention, and the world therefore swarms with writers, whose only wish is to be read.

No species of literary men has lately been so much multiplied as the writers of news. Not many years ago the nation was content with one Gazette, but now we have not only in the metropolis papers for every morning, and every evening, but almost every large town has its weekly historian, who regularly circulates his periodical intelligence, and fills the villages of his district with conjectures on the events of war, and with debates on the true interest of Europe.

To write news in its perfection requires such a combination of qualities, that a man completely fitted for the task is not always to be found. In Sir Henry Wotton's jocular definition, *An Ambassador* is said to be *a man of virtue sent abroad to tell lies for the advantage his country*; a News-writer is *a man without virtue, who writes lies ai home for his own profit*. To these compositions is required neither genius nor knowledge, neither industry nor spriteliness, but contempt of shame, and indifference to truth are absolutely necessary. He who by a long familiarity with infamy has obtained these qualities may confidently tell to-day what he intends to contradict to-morrow; he may affirm fearlessly what he knows that he shall be obliged to recant, and may write letters from Amsterdam or Dresden to himself.

In a time of war the nation is always of one mind, eager to hear something good of themselves and ill of the enemy. At this time the task of News-writers is easy, they have nothing to do but to tell that a battle is expected, and afterwards that a battle has been fought, in which we and our friends, whether conquering or conquered, did all, and our enemies did nothing.

Scarcely any thing awakens attention like a tale of cruelty. The Writer of news never fails in the intermission of action to tell how the enemies murdered children and ravished virgins; and if the scene of action be somewhat distant, scalps half the inhabitants of a province.

Among the calamities of War may be justly numbered the diminution of the love of truth, by the falshoods which interest dictates and credulity encourages. A Peace will equally leave the Warrior and Relator of Wars destitute of employment; and I know not whether more is to be dreaded from streets filled with Soldiers accustomed to plunder, or from garrets filled with Scribblers accustomed to lie.

35

He only can please long, who by tempering the acid of satire with the sugar of civility, and allaying the heat of wit with the frigidity of humble chat, can make the true punch of conversation; and as that punch can be drank in the greatest quantity which has the largest proportion of water, so that companion will be oftenest welcome, whose talk flows out with inoffensive copiousness, and unenvied insipidity.

46

Genius is chiefly exerted in historical pictures, and the art of the Painter of Portraits is often lost in the obscurity of his subject. But it is in Painting as in Life; what is greatest is not always best. I should grieve to see Reynolds transfer to Heroes and to Goddesses, to empty Splendor and to airy fiction, that art which is now employed in diffusing friendship, in reviving tenderness, in quickening the affections of the absent, and continuing the presence of the dead.

70

In the general emulation of wit and genius which the festivity of the Restoration produced, the Poets shook off their constraint, and considered Translation as no longer confined to servile closeness. But reformation is seldom the work of pure virtue or unassisted reason. Translation was improved more by accident than conviction. The Writers of the foregoing age had at least learning equal to their genius, and being often more able to explain the sentiments or illustrate the allusions of the Ancients, than to exhibit their graces and transfuse their spirit, were perhaps willing sometimes to conceal their want of Poetry by profusion of Literature, and therefore translated literally, that their fidelity might shelter their insipidity or harshness. The Wits of Charles's time had seldom more than slight and superficial views, and their care was to hide their want of learning behind the colours of a gay imagination, they therefore translated always with freedom, sometimes with licentiousness, and perhaps expected that their Readers should accept sprightliness for knowledge, and consider ignorance and mistake as the impatience and negligence of a mind too rapid to stop at difficulties, and too elevated to descend to minuteness.

Thus was Translation made more easy to the Writer, and more delightful to the Reader, and there is no wonder if ease and pleasure have found their advocates. The paraphrastic liberties have been almost universally admitted, and Sherbourn, whose learning was eminent and who had no need of any excuse to pass slightly over obscurities, is the only Writer who in later times has attempted to justify or revive the ancient severity.

There is undoubtedly a mean to be observed. Dryden saw very early that closeness best preserved an Author's sense, and that freedom best exhibited his spirit, he therefore will deserve the highest prase who can give a representation at once faithful and pleasing, who can convey the same thoughts with the same graces, and who when he translates changes nothing but the language.

73

It would add much to human happiness, if an art could be taught of forgetting all of which the remembrance is at once useless and afflictive, if that pain which never can end in pleasure could be driven totally away, that the mind might perform its functions without incumbrance, and the past might no longer encroach upon the present.

Little can be done well to which the whole mind is not applied; the business of every day calls for the day to which it is assigned, and he will have little leisure to regret yesterday's vexations who resolves not to have a new subject of regret to-morrow.

But to forget or to remember at pleasure, are equally beyond the power of man. Yet as memory may be assisted by method, and the decays of knowledge repaired by stated times of recollection, so the power of forgetting is capable of improvement. Reason will, by a resolute contest, prevail over imagination, and the power may be obtained of transferring the attention as judgment shall direct.

The incursions of troublesome thoughts are often violent and importunate; and it is not easy to a mind accustomed to their inroads to expel them immediately by putting better images into motion; but this enemy of quiet is above all others weakened by every defeat; the reflection which has been once overpowered and ejected, seldom returns with any formidable power.

Employment is the great instrument of intellectual dominion. The mind cannot retire from its enemy into total vacancy, or turn aside from one object but by passing to another. The gloomy and the resentful are always found among those who have nothing to do, or that do nothing. We must be busy about good or evil, and he to whom the present offers nothing will be looking backward on the past.

THE HISTORY OF

RASSELAS

PRINCE OF ABISSINIA

Rasselas was published first in 1759. A second edition followed later in the same year. The text here used is that of the second edition (B.M.: 12611. de. 3.) except that the title of the book has been changed from *The Prince of Abissinia, A Tale* to its later and more accustomed form. Reference was made throughout to the first edition (B.M.: C. 71. h. 18.).

HISTORY OF RASSELAS

PRINCE OF ABISSINIA

CHAPTER I

Description of a palace in a valley.

YE who listen with credulity to the whispers of fancy, and persue with eagerness the phantoms of hope; who expect that age will perform the promises of youth, and that the deficiencies of the present day will be supplied by the morrow; attend to the history of Rasselas prince of Abissinia.

Rasselas was the fourth son of the mighty emperour, in whose dominions the Father of waters begins his course; whose bounty pours down the streams of plenty, and scatters over half the world the harvests of Egypt.

According to the custom which has descended from age to age among the monarchs of the torrid zone, Rasselas was confined in a private palace, with the other sons and daughters of Abissinian royalty, till the order of succession should call him to the throne.

The place, which the wisdom or policy of antiquity had destined for the residence of the Abissinian princes, was a spacious valley in the kingdom of Amhara, surrounded on every side by mountains, of which the summits overhang the middle part. The only passage, by which it could be entered, was a cavern that passed under a rock, of which it has long been disputed whether it was the work of nature or of human industry. The outlet of the cavern was concealed by a thick wood, and the mouth which opened into the valley was closed with gates of iron, forged by the artificers of ancient days, so massy that no man could without the help of engines open or shut them.

From the mountains on every side, rivulets descended that filled all the valley with verdure and fertility, and formed a lake in the

391

middle inhabited by fish of every species, and frequented by every fowl whom nature has taught to dip the wing in water. This lake discharged its superfluities by a stream which entered a dark cleft of the mountain on the northern side, and fell with dreadful noise from precipice to precipice till it was heard no more.

The sides of the mountains were covered with trees, the banks of the brooks were diversified with flowers; every blast shook spices from the rocks, and every month dropped fruits upon the ground. All animals that bite the grass, or brouse the shrub, whether wild or tame, wandered in this extensive circuit, secured from beasts of prey by the mountains which confined them. On one part were flocks and herds feeding in the pastures, on another all the beasts of chase frisking in the lawns; the sprightly kid was bounding on the rocks, the subtle monkey frolicking in the trees, and the solemn elephant reposing in the shade. All the diversities of the world were brought together, the blessings of nature were collected, and its evils extracted and excluded.

The valley, wide and fruitful, supplied its inhabitants with the necessaries of life, and all delights and superfluities were added at the annual visit which the emperour paid his children, when the iron gate was opened to the sound of musick; and during eight days every one that resided in the valley was required to propose whatever might contribute to make seclusion pleasant, to fill up the vacancies of attention, and lessen the tediousness of time. Every desire was immediately granted. All the artificers of pleasure were called to gladden the festivity; the musicians exerted the power of harmony, and the dancers shewed their activity before the princes, in hope that they should pass their lives in this blissful captivity, to which those only were admitted whose performance was thought able to add novelty to luxury. Such was the appearance of security and delight which this retirement afforded, that they to whom it was new always desired that it might be perpetual; and as those, on whom the iron gate had once closed, were never suffered to return, the effect of longer experience could not be known. Thus every year produced new schemes of delight, and new competitors for imprisonment.

The palace stood on an eminence raised about thirty paces above the surface of the lake. It was divided into many squares or courts, built with greater or less magnificence according to the rank of those for whom they were designed. The roofs were turned into arches of massy stone joined by a cement that grew harder by time, and the building stood from century to century, deriding the solstitial rains and equinoctial hurricanes, without need of reparation.

This house, which was so large as to be fully known to none but some ancient officers who successively inherited the secrets of the place, was built as if suspicion herself had dictated the plan. To every room there was an open and secret passage, every square had a communication with the rest, either from the upper stories by private galleries, or by subterranean passages from the lower apartments. Many of the columns had unsuspected cavities, in which a long race of monarchs had reposited their treasures. They then closed up the opening with marble, which was never to be removed but in the utmost exigencies of the kingdom; and recorded their accumulations in a book which was itself concealed in a tower not entered but by the emperour, attended by the prince who stood next in succession.

CHAPTER II

The discontent of Rasselas in the happy valley.

HERE the sons and daughters of Abissinia lived only to know the soft vicissitudes of pleasure and repose, attended by all that were skilful to delight, and gratified with whatever the senses can enjoy. They wandered in gardens of fragrance, and slept in the fortresses of security. Every art was practised to make them pleased with their own condition. The sages who instructed them, told them of nothing but the miseries of publick life, and described all beyond the mountains as regions of calamity, where discord was always raging, and where man preyed upon man.

To heighten their opinion of their own felicity, they were daily entertained with songs, the subject of which was the *happy valley*. Their appetites were excited by frequent enumerations of different enjoyments, and revelry and merriment was the business of every hour from the dawn of morning to the close of even.

These methods were generally successful; few of the Princes had ever wished to enlarge their bounds, but passed their lives in full conviction that they had all within their reach that art or nature could bestow, and pitied those whom fate had excluded from this seat of tranquility, as the sport of chance, and the slaves of misery.

393

Thus they rose in the morning and lay down at night, pleased with each other and with themselves, all but Rasselas, who, in the twenty-sixth year of his age, began to withdraw himself from their pastimes and assemblies, and to delight in solitary walks and silent meditation. He often sat before tables covered with luxury, and forgot to taste the dainties that were placed before him: he rose abruptly in the midst of the song, and hastily retired beyond the sound of musick. His attendants observed the change and endeavoured to renew his love of pleasure: he neglected their officiousness, repulsed their invitations, and spent day after day on the banks of rivulets sheltered with trees, where he sometimes listened to the birds in the branches, sometimes observed the fish playing in the stream, and anon cast his eyes upon the pastures and mountains filled with animals, of which some were biting the herbage, and some sleeping among the bushes.

This singularity of his humour made him much observed. One of the Sages, in whose conversation he had formerly delighted, followed him secretly, in hope of discovering the cause of his disquiet. Rasselas, who knew not that any one was near him, having for some time fixed his eyes upon the goats that were brousing among the rocks, began to compare their condition with his own.

"What," said he, "makes the difference between man and all the rest of the animal creation? Every beast that strays beside me has the same corporal necessities with myself; he is hungry and crops the grass, he is thirsty and drinks the stream, his thirst and hunger are appeased, he is satisfied and sleeps; he rises again and is hungry, he is again fed and is at rest. I am hungry and thirsty like him, but when thirst and hunger cease I am not at rest; I am, like him, pained with want, but am not, like him, satisfied with fulness. The intermediate hours are tedious and gloomy; I long again to be hungry that I may again quicken my attention. The birds peck the berries or the corn, and fly away to the groves where they sit in seeming happiness on the branches, and waste their lives in tuning one unvaried series of sounds. I likewise can call the lutanist and the singer, but the sounds that pleased me yesterday weary me to day, and will grow yet more wearisome to morrow. I can discover within me no power of perception which is not glutted with its proper pleasure, yet I do not feel myself delighted. Man has surely some latent sense for which this place affords no gratification, or he has some desires distinct from sense which must be satisfied before he can be happy."

After this he lifted up his head, and seeing the moon rising, walked towards the palace. As he passed through the fields, and saw the animals around him, "Ye, said he, are happy, and need not envy me that walk thus among you, burthened with myself; nor do I, ye gentle beings, envy your felicity; for it is not the felicity of man. I have many distresses from which ye are free; I fear pain when I do not feel it; I sometimes shrink at evils recollected, and sometimes start at evils anticipated: surely the equity of providence has ballanced peculiar sufferings with peculiar enjoyments."

With observations like these the prince amused himself as he returned, uttering them with a plaintive voice, yet with a look that discovered him to feel some complacence in his own perspicacity, and to receive some solace of the miseries of life, from consciousness of the delicacy with which he felt, and the eloquence with which he bewailed them. He mingled cheerfully in the diversions of the evening, and all rejoiced to find that his heart was lightened.

CHAPTER III

The wants of him that wants nothing.

On the next day his old instructor, imagining that he had now made himself acquainted with his disease of mind, was in hope of curing it by counsel, and officiously sought an opportunity of conference, which the prince, having long considered him as one whose intellects were exhausted, was not very willing to afford: "Why, said he, does this man thus intrude upon me; shall I be never suffered to forget those lectures which pleased only while they were new, and to become new again must be forgotten?" He then walked into the wood, and composed himself to his usual meditations; when before his thoughts had taken any settled form, he perceived his persuer at his side, and was at first prompted by his impatience to go hastily away; but, being unwilling to offend a man whom he he had once reverenced and still loved, he invited him to sit down with him on the bank.

The old man, thus encouraged, began to lament the change which had been lately observed in the prince, and to enquire why he so often retired from the pleasures of the palace, to loneliness and silence. "I fly from pleasure, said the prince, because pleasure has ceased to please; I am lonely because I am miserable, and am unwilling to cloud with my presence the happiness of others." "You, Sir, said the sage, are the first who has complained of misery in the *happy valley*. I hope to convince you that your complaints have no real cause. You are here in full possession of all that the emperour of Abissinia can bestow; here is neither labour to be endured nor danger to be dreaded, yet here is all that labour or danger can procure or purchase. Look round and tell me which of your wants is without supply: if you want nothing, how are you unhappy?"

"That I want nothing, said the prince, or that I know not what I want, is the cause of my complaint; if I had any known want, I should have a certain wish; that wish would excite endeavour, and I should not then repine to see the sun move so slowly towards the western mountain, or lament when the day breaks and sleep will no longer hide me from myself. When I see the kids and the lambs chasing one another, I fancy that I should be happy if I had something to persue. But, possessing all that I can want, I find one day and one hour exactly like another, except that the latter is still more tedious than the former. Let your experience inform me how the day may now seem as short as in my childhood, while nature was yet fresh, and every moment shewed me what I never had observed before. I have already enjoyed too much; give me something to desire."

The old man was surprized at this new species of affliction, and knew not what to reply, yet was unwilling to be silent. "Sir, said he, if you had seen the miseries of the world, you would know how to value your present state." "Now, said the prince, you have given me something to desire; I shall long to see the miseries of the world, since the sight of them is necessary to happiness."

CHAPTER IV

The prince continues to grieve and muse.

AT this time the sound of musick proclaimed the hour of repast, and the conversation was concluded. The old man went away sufficiently discontented to find that his reasonings had produced the only conclusion which they were intended to prevent. But in the decline of life shame and grief are of short duration; whether it be that we bear easily what we have born long, or that, finding ourselves in age less regarded, we less regard others; or, that we look with slight regard upon afflictions, to which we know that the hand of death is about to put an end.

The prince, whose views were extended to a wider space, could not speedily quiet his emotions. He had been before terrified at the length of life which nature promised him, because he considered that in a long time much must be endured; he now rejoiced in his youth, because in many years much might be done.

This first beam of hope, that had been ever darted into his mind, rekindled youth in his cheeks, and doubled the lustre of his eyes. He was fired with the desire of doing something, though he knew not yet with distinctness, either end or means.

He was now no longer gloomy and unsocial; but, considering himself as master of a secret stock of happiness, which he could enjoy only by concealing it, he affected to be busy in all schemes of diversion, and endeavoured to make others pleased with the state of which he himself was weary. But pleasures never can be so multiplied or continued, as not to leave much of life unemployed; there were many hours, both of the night and day, which he could spend without suspicion in solitary thought. The load of life was much lightened: he went eagerly into the assemblies, because he supposed the frequency of his presence necessary to the success of his purposes; he retired gladly to privacy, because he had now a subject of thought.

His chief amusement was to picture to himself that world which he had never seen; to place himself in various conditions; to be entangled in imaginary difficulties, and to be engaged in wild adventures: but his benevolence always terminated his projects in the relief of distress, the detection of fraud, the defeat of oppression, and the diffusion of happiness.

Thus passed twenty months of the life of Rasselas. He busied himself so intensely in visionary bustle, that he forgot his real solitude; and, amidst hourly preparations for the various incidents of human affairs, neglected to consider by what means he should mingle with mankind.

One day, as he was sitting on a bank, he feigned to himself an orphan virgin robbed of her little portion by a treacherous lover, and crying after him for restitution and redress. So strongly was the image impressed upon his mind, that he started up in the maid's defence, and ran forward to seize the plunderer with all the eagerness of real pursuit. Fear naturally quickens the flight of guilt. Rasselas could not catch the fugitive with his utmost efforts; but, resolving to weary, by perseverance, him whom he could not surpass in speed, he pressed on till the foot of the mountain stopped his course.

Here he recollected himself, and smiled at his own useless impetuosity. Then raising his eyes to the mountain, "This, said he, is the fatal obstacle that hinders at once the enjoyment of pleasure, and the exercise of virtue. How long is it that my hopes and wishes have flown beyond this boundary of my life, which yet I never have attempted to surmount!"

Struck with this reflection, he sat down to muse and remembered that since he first resolved to escape from his confinement, the sun had passed twice over him in his annual course. He now felt a degree of regret with which he had never been before acquainted. He considered how much might have been done, in the time which had passed, and left nothing real behind it. He compared twenty months with the life of man. "In life, said he, is not to be counted the ignorance of infancy, or imbecility of age. We are long before we are able to think, and we soon cease from the power of acting. The true period of human existence may be reasonably estimated at forty years, of which I have mused away the four and twentieth part. What I have lost was certain, for I have certainly possessed it; but of twenty months to come who can assure me?"

The consciousness of his own folly pierced him deeply, and he was long before he could be reconciled to himself. "The rest of my time, said he, has been lost by the crime or folly of my ancestors, and the absurd institutions of my country; I remember it with disgust, yet without remorse: but the months that have passed since new light darted into my soul, since I formed a scheme of reasonable felicity, have been squandered by my own fault. I have lost that which can never be restored: I have seen the sun rise and set for twenty months, an idle gazer on the light of heaven: In this time the birds have left the nest of their mother, and committed themselves to the woods and to the skies: the kid has forsaken the teat, and learned by degrees to climb the rocks in quest of independant sustenance. I only have made no advances, but am still helpless and ignorant. The moon by more than twenty changes, admonished me of the flux of life; the stream that rolled before my feet upbraided my inactivity. I sat feasting on intellectual luxury, regardless alike of the examples of the earth, and the instructions of the planets. Twenty months are past, who shall restore them!"

These sorrowful meditations fastened upon his mind; he past four months in resolving to lose no more time in idle resolves, and was awakened to more vigorous exertion by hearing a maid, who had broken a porcelain cup, remark, that what cannot be repaired is not to be regretted.

This was obvious; and Rasselas reproached himself that he had not discovered it, having not known, or not considered, how many useful hints are obtained by chance, and how often the mind, hurried by her own ardour to distant views, neglects the truths that lie open before her. He, for a few hours, regretted his regret, and from that time bent his whole mind upon the means of escaping from the valley of happiness.

CHAPTER V

The prince meditates his escape.

HE now found that it would be very difficult to effect that which it was very easy to suppose effected. When he looked round about him, he saw himself confined by the bars of nature which had never yet been broken, and by the gate, through which none that once had passed it were ever able to return. He was now impatient as an eagle in a grate. He passed week after week in clambering the mountains, to see if there was any aperture which the bushes might conceal, but found all the summits inaccessible by their prominence. The iron gate he despaired to open; for it was not only secured with all the power of art, but was always watched by successive sentinels, and was by its position exposed to the perpetual observation of all the inhabitants.

He then examined the cavern through which the waters of the lake were discharged; and, looking down at a time when the sun shone strongly upon its mouth, he discovered it to be full of broken rocks, which, though they permitted the stream to flow through many narrow passages, would stop anybody of solid bulk. He returned discouraged and dejected; but, having now known the blessing of hope, resolved never to despair.

In these fruitless searches he spent ten months. The time, however, passed chearfully away: in the morning he rose with new hope, in the evening applauded his own diligence, and in the night slept sound after his fatigue. He met a thousand amusements which beguiled his labour, and diversified his thoughts. He discerned the various instincts of animals, and properties of plants, and found the place replete with wonders, of which he purposed to solace himself with the contemplation, if he should never be able to accomplish his flight; rejoicing that his endeavours, though yet unsuccessful, had supplied him with a source of inexhaustible enquiry.

But his original curiosity was not yet abated; he resolved to obtain some knowledge of the ways of men. His wish still continued, but his hope grew less. He ceased to survey any longer the walls of his prison, and spared to search by new toils for interstices which he knew could not be found, yet determined to keep his design always in view, and lay hold on any expedient that time should offer.

CHAPTER VI

A dissertation on the art of flying.

AMONG the artists that had been allured into the happy valley, to labour for the accommodation and pleasure of its inhabitants, was a man eminent for his knowledge of the mechanick powers, who had contrived many engines both of use and recreation. By a wheel, which the stream turned, he forced the water into a tower, whence it was distributed to all the apartments of the palace. He erected a pavillion in the garden, around which he kept the air always cool by artificial showers. One of the groves, appropriated to the ladies, was ventilated by fans, to which the rivulets that ran through it gave a constant motion; and instruments of soft musick were placed at proper distances, of which some played by the impulse of the wind, and some by the power of the stream.

This artist was sometimes visited by Rasselas, who was pleased with every kind of knowledge, imagining that the time would come when all his acquisitions should be of use to him in the open world. He came one day to amuse himself in his usual manner, and found the master busy in building a sailing chariot: he saw that the design was practicable upon a level surface, and with expressions of great esteem solicited its completion. The workman was pleased to find himself so much regarded by the prince, and resolved to gain yet higher honours. "Sir, said he, you have seen but a small part of what the mechanick sciences can perform. I have been long of opinion, that, instead of the tardy conveyance of ships and chariots, man might use the swifter migration of wings; that the fields of air are open to knowledge, and that only ignorance and idleness need crawl upon the ground."

This hint rekindled the prince's desire of passing the mountains; having seen what the mechanist had already performed, he was willing to fancy that he could do more; yet resolved to enquire further before he suffered hope to afflict him by disappointment. "I am afraid, said he to the artist, that your imagination prevails over your skill, and that you now tell me rather what you wish than what you know. Every animal has his element assigned him; the birds have the air, and man and beasts the earth." "So, replied the mechanist, fishes have the water, in which yet beasts can swim by nature, and men by art. He that can swim needs not despair to fly: to swim is to fly in a grosser fluid, and to fly is to swim in a subtler. We are only to proportion our power of resistance to the different density of the matter through which we are to pass. You will be necessarily upborn by the air, if you can renew any impulse upon it, faster than the air can recede from the pressure."

"But the exercise of swimming, said the prince, is very laborious; the strongest limbs are soon wearied; I am afraid the act of flying will be yet more violent, and wings will be of no great use, unless we can fly further than we can swim."

"The labour of rising from the ground, said the artist, will be great, as we see it in the heavier domestick fowls; but, as we mount higher, the earth's attraction, and the body's gravity, will be gradually diminished, till we shall arrive at a region where the man will float in the air without any tendency to fall: no care will then be necessary, but to move forwards, which the gentlest impulse will effect. You, Sir, whose curiosity is so extensive, will easily conceive with what pleasure a philosopher, furnished with wings, and hovering in the sky, would see the earth, and all it's inhabitants, rolling beneath him, and presenting to him successively, by it's diurnal motion, all the countries within the same parallel. How must it amuse the pendent spectator to see the moving scene of land and ocean, cities, and desarts! To survey with equal security the marts of trade, and the fields of battle; mountains infested by barbarians, and fruitful regions gladdened by plenty, and lulled by peace! How easily shall we then trace the Nile through all his passage; pass over to distant regions, and examine the face of nature from one extremity of the earth to the other!"

"All this, said the prince, is much to be desired, but I am afraid that no man will be able to breathe in these regions of speculation and tranquility. I have been told, that respiration is difficult upon lofty mountains, yet from these precipices, though so high as to produce great tenuity of the air, it is very easy to fall : therefore I suspect, that from any height, where life can be supported, there may be danger of too quick descent."

"Nothing, replied the artist, will ever be attempted, if all possible objections must be first overcome. If you will favour my project I will try the first flight at my own hazard. I have considered the structure of all volant animals, and find the folding continuity of the bat's wings most easily accomodated to the human form. Upon this model I shall begin my task to morrow, and in a year expect to tower into the air beyond the malice or persuit of man. But I will work only on this condition, that the art shall not be divulged, and that you shall not require me to make wings for any but ourselves."

"Why, said Rasselas, should you envy others so great an advantage? All skill ought to be exerted for universal good; every man has owed much to others, and ought to repay the kindness that he has received."

"If men were all virtuous, returned the artist, I should with great alacrity teach them all to fly. But what would be the security of the good, if the bad could at pleasure invade them from the sky? Against an army sailing through the clouds neither walls, nor mountains, nor seas, could afford any security. A flight of northern savages might hover in the wind, and light at once with irresistible violence upon the capital of a fruitful region that was rolling under them. Even this valley, the retreat of princes, the abode of happiness, might be violated by the sudden descent of some of the naked nations that swarm on the coast of the southern sea."

The prince promised secrecy, and waited for the performance, not wholly hopeless of success. He visited the work from time to time, observed its progress, and remarked many ingenious contrivances to facilitate motion, and unite levity with strength. The artist was every day more certain that he should leave vultures and eagles behind him, and the contagion of his confidence seized upon the prince.

In a year the wings were finished; and, on a morning appointed, the maker appeared furnished for flight on a little promontory: he waved his pinions a while to gather air, then leaped from his stand, and in an instant dropped into the lake. His wings, which were of no use in the air, sustained him in the water, and the prince drew him to land, half dead with terrour and vexation.

CHAPTER VII

The prince finds a man of learning.

THE prince was not much afflicted by this disaster, having suffered himself to hope for a happier event, only because he had no other means of escape in view. He still persisted in his design to leave the happy valley by the first opportunity.

His imagination was now at a stand; he had no prospect of entering into the world; and, notwithstanding all his endeavours to support himself, discontent by degrees preyed upon him, and he began again to lose his thoughts in sadness, when the rainy season, which in these countries is periodical, made it inconvenient to wander in the woods.

The rain continued longer and with more violence than had been ever known: the clouds broke on the surrounding mountains, and the torrents streamed into the plain on every side, till the cavern was too narrow to discharge the water. The lake overflowed its banks, and all the level of the valley was covered with the inundation. The eminence, on which the palace was built, and some other spots of rising ground, were all that the eye could now discover. The herds and flocks left the pastures, and both the wild beasts and the tame retreated to the mountains.

This inundation confined all the princes to domestick amusements, and the attention of Rasselas was particularly seized by a poem, which Imlac rehearsed upon the various conditions of humanity. He commanded the poet to attend him in his apartment, and recite his verses a second time; then entering into familiar talk, he thought himself happy in having found a man who knew the world so well, and could so skilfully paint the scenes of life. He asked a thousand questions about things, to which, though common to all other mortals, his confinement from childhood had kept him a stranger. The poet pitied his ignorance, and loved his curiosity, and entertained him from day to day with novelty and instruction, so that the prince regretted the necessity of sleep, and longed till the morning should renew his pleasure.

As they were sitting together, the prince commanded Imlac to relate his history, and to tell by what accident he was forced, or by what motive induced, to close his life in the happy valley. As he was going to begin his narrative, Rasselas was called to a concert and obliged to restrain his curiosity till the evening.

CHAPTER VIII

The history of Imlac.

THE close of the day is, in the regions of the torrid zone, the only season of diversion and entertainment, and it was therefore mid-night before the musick ceased, and the princesses retired. Rasselas then called for his companion and required him to begin the story of his life.

"Sir, said Imlac, my history will not be long: the life that is devoted to knowledge passes silently away, and is very little diversified by events. To talk in publick, to think in solitude, to read and to hear, to inquire, and answer inquiries, is the business of a scholar. He wanders about the world without pomp or terrour, and is neither known nor valued but by men like himself.

"I was born in the kingdom of Goiama, at no great distance from the fountain of the Nile. My father was a wealthy merchant, who traded between the inland countries of Africk and the ports of the red sea. He was honest, frugal, and diligent, but of mean sentiments and narrow comprehension: he desired only to be rich, and to conceal his riches, lest he should be spoiled by the governours of the province."

"Surely, said the prince, my father must be negligent of his charge, if any man in his dominions dares take that which belongs to another. Does he not know that kings are accountable for injustice permitted as well as done? If I were emperour, not the meanest of my subjects should be oppressed with impunity. My blood boils when I am told that a merchant durst not enjoy his honest gains for fear of losing them by the rapacity of power. Name the governour who robbed the people, that I may declare his crimes to the emperour."

"Sir, said Imlac, your ardour is the natural effect of virtue animated by youth: the time will come when you will acquit your father, and perhaps hear with less impatience of the governour. Oppression, is, in the Abissinian dominions, neither frequent nor tolerated; but no form of government has been yet discovered, by which cruelty can be wholly prevented. Subordination supposes power on one part and subjection on the other; and if power be in the hands of men, it will sometimes be abused. The vigilance of the supreme magistrate may do much, but much will still remain undone. He can never know all the crimes that are committed, and can seldom punish all that he knows."

"This, said the prince, I do not understand, but I had rather hear thee than dispute. Continue thy narration."

"My father, proceeded Imlac, originally intended that I should have no other education, than such as might qualify me for commerce; and discovering in me great strength of memory, and quickness of apprehension, often declared his hope that I should be some time the richest man in Abissinia."

"Why, said the prince, did thy father desire the increase of his wealth, when it was already greater than he durst discover or enjoy? I am unwilling to doubt thy veracity, yet inconsistencies cannot both be true."

"Inconsistencies, answered Imlac, cannot both be right, but, imputed to man, they may both be true. Yet diversity is not inconsistency. My father might expect a time of greater security. However, some desire is necessary to keep life in motion, and he whose real wants are supplied, must admit those of fancy."

"This, said the prince, I can in some measure conceive. I repent that I interrupted thee."

"With this hope, proceeded Imlac, he sent me to school; but when I had once found the delight of knowledge, and felt the pleasure of intelligence and the pride of invention, I began silently to despise riches, and determined to disappoint the purpose of my father, whose grossness of conception raised my pity. I was twenty years old before his tenderness would expose me to the fatigue of travel, in which time I had been instructed, by successive masters, in all the literature of my native country. As every hour taught me something new, I lived in a continual course of gratifications; but, as I advanced towards manhood, I lost much of the reverence with which I had been used to look on my instructors; because, when the lesson was ended, I did not find them wiser or better than common men.

"At length my father resolved to initiate me in commerce, and, opening one of his subterranean treasuries, counted out ten thousand pieces of gold. This, young man, said he, is the stock with which you must negociate. I began with less than the fifth part, and you see how diligence and parsimony have increased it. This is your own to waste or to improve. If you squander it by negligence or caprice, you must wait for my death before you will be rich: if, in four years, you double your stock, we will thenceforward let subordination cease, and live together as friends and partners; for he shall always be equal with me, who is equally skilled in the art of growing rich.

"We laid our money upon camels, concealed in bales of cheap goods, and travelled to the shore of the red sea. When I cast my eye on the expanse of waters my heart bounded like that of a prisoner escaped. I felt an unextinguishable curiosity kindle in my mind, and resolved to snatch this opportunity of seeing the manners of other nations, and of learning sciences unknown in Abissinia.

"I remembered that my father had obliged me to the improvement of my stock, not by a promise which I ought not to violate, but by a penalty which I was at liberty to incur; and therefore determined to gratify my predominant desire, and by drinking at the fountains of knowledge, to quench the thirst of curiosity.

"As I was supposed to trade without connexion with my father, it was easy for me to become acquainted with the master of a ship, and procure a passage to some other country. I had no motives of choice to regulate my voyage; it was sufficient for me that, whereever I wandered, I should see a country which I had not seen before. I therefore entered a ship bound for Surat, having left a letter for my father declaring my intention.

CHAPTER IX

The history of Imlac continued.

"When I first entered upon the world of waters, and lost sight of land, I looked round about me with pleasing terrour, and thinking my soul enlarged by the boundless prospect, imagined that I could gaze round for ever without satiety; but, in a short time, I grew weary of looking on barren uniformity, where I could only see again what I had already seen. I then descended into the ship, and doubted for a while whether all my future pleasures would not end like this in disgust and disappointment. Yet, surely, said I, the ocean and the land are very different; the only variety of water is rest and motion, but the earth has mountains and vallies, desarts and cities: it is inhabited by men of different customs and contrary opinions; and I may hope to find variety in life, though I should miss it in nature.

"With this thought I quieted my mind; and amused myself during the voyage, sometimes by learning from the sailors the art of navigation, which I have never practised, and sometimes by forming schemes for my conduct in different situations, in not one of which I have been ever placed.

"I was almost weary of my naval amusements when we landed safely at Surat. I secured my money, and purchasing some commodities for show, joined myself to a caravan that was passing into the inland country. My companions, for some reason or other, conjecturing that I was rich, and, by my inquiries and admiration, finding that I was ignorant, considered me as a novice whom they had a right to cheat, and who was to learn at the usual expence the art of fraud. They exposed me to the theft of servants, and the exaction of officers, and saw me plundered upon false pretences, without any advantage to themselves, but that of rejoicing in the superiority of their own knowledge."

"Stop a moment, said the prince. Is there such depravity in man, as that he should injure another without benefit to himself? I can easily conceive that all are pleased with superiority; but your ignorance was merely accidental, which, being neither your crime nor your folly, could afford them no reason to applaud themselves; and the knowledge which they had, and which you wanted, they might as effectually have shewn by warning, as betraying you."

"Pride, said Imlac, is seldom delicate, it will please itself with very mean advantages; and envy feels not its own happiness, but when it may be compared with the misery of others. They were my enemies because they grieved to think me rich, and my oppressors because they delighted to find me weak."

"Proceed, said the prince: I doubt not of the facts which you relate, but imagine that you impute them to mistaken motives."

"In this company, said Imlac, I arrived at Agra, the capital of Indostan, the city in which the great Mogul commonly resides. I applied myself to the language of the country, and in a few months was able to converse with the learned men; some of whom I found morose and reserved, and others easy and communicative; some were unwilling to teach another what they had with difficulty learned themselves; and some shewed that the end of their studies was to gain the dignity of instructing.

"To the tutor of the young princes I recommended myself so much, that I was presented to the emperour as a man of uncommon knowledge. The emperour asked me many questions concerning my country and my travels; and though I cannot now recollect any thing that he uttered above the power of a common man, he dismissed me astonished at his wisdom, and enamoured of his goodness.

"My credit was now so high, that the merchants, with whom I had travelled, applied to me for recommendations to the ladies of the court. I was surprised at their confidence of solicitation, and gently reproached them with their practices on the road. They heard me with cold indifference, and shewed no tokens of shame or sorrow.

"They then urged their request with the offer of a bribe; but what I would not do for kindness I would not do for money; and refused them, not because they had injured me, but because I would not enable them to injure others; for I knew they would have made use of my credit to cheat those who should buy their wares.

"Having resided at Agra till there was no more to be learned, I travelled into Persia, where I saw many remains of ancient magnificence, and observed many new accommodations of life. The Persians are a nation eminently social, and their assemblies afforded me daily opportunities of remarking characters and manners, and of tracing human nature through all its variations.

"From Persia I passed into Arabia, where I saw a nation at once pastoral and warlike; who live without any settled habitation; whose only wealth is their flocks and herds; and who have yet carried on, through all ages, an hereditary war with all mankind, though they neither covet nor envy their possessions.

CHAPTER X

Imlac's history continued.   A dissertation upon poetry.

"WHEREVER I went, I found that Poetry was considered as the highest learning, and regarded with a veneration somewhat approaching to that which men would pay to the Angelick Nature. And it yet fills me with wonder, that, in almost all countries, the most ancient poets are considered as the best: whether it be that every other kind of knowledge is an acquisition gradually attained, and poetry is a gift conferred at once; or that the first poetry of every nation surprised them as a novelty, and retained the credit by consent which it received by accident at first: or whether, as the province of poetry is to describe Nature and Passion, which are always the same, the first writers took possession of the most striking objects for description, and the most probable occurrences for fiction, and left nothing to those that followed them, but transscription of the same events, and new combinations of the same images. Whatever be the reason, it is commonly observed that the early writers are in possession of nature, and their followers of art: that the first excel in strength and invention, and the latter in elegance and refinement.

"I was desirous to add my name to this illustrious fraternity. I read all the poets of Persia and Arabia, and was able to repeat by memory the volumes that are suspended in the mosque of Mecca. But I soon found that no man was ever great by imitation. My desire of excellence impelled me to transfer my attention to nature and to life. Nature was to be my subject, and men to be my auditors: I could never describe what I had not seen: I could not hope to move those with delight or terrour, whose interests and opinions I did not understand.

"Being now resolved to be a poet, I saw every thing with a new purpose; my sphere of attention was suddenly magnified: no kind of knowledge was to be overlooked. I ranged mountains and deserts for images and resemblances, and pictured upon my mind every tree of the forest and flower of the valley. I observed with equal care the crags of the rock and the pinnacles of the palace. Sometimes I wandered along the mazes of the rivulet, and sometimes watched the changes of the summer clouds. To a poet nothing can be useless. Whatever is beautiful, and whatever is dreadful, must be familiar to his imagination: he must be conversant with all that is awfully vast or elegantly little. The plants of the garden, the animals of the wood, the minerals of the earth, and meteors of the sky, must all concur to store his mind with inexhaustible variety: for every idea is useful for the inforcement or decoration of moral or religious truth; and he, who knows most, will have most power of diversifying his scenes, and of gratifying his reader with remote alusions and unexpected instruction.

"All the appearances of nature I was therefore careful to study, and every country which I have surveyed has contributed something to my poetical powers."

"In so wide a survey, said the prince, you must surely have left much unobserved. I have lived, till now, within the circuit of these mountains, and yet cannot walk abroad without the sight of something which I had never beheld before, or never heeded."

"The business of a poet, said Imlac, is to examine, not the individual, but the species; to remark general properties and large appearances: he does not number the streaks of the tulip, or describe the different shades in the verdure of the forest. He is to exhibit in his portraits of nature such prominent and striking features, as recal the original to every mind; and must neglect the minuter discriminations, which one may have remarked, and another have neglected, for those characteristicks which are alike obvious to vigilance and carelessness.

"But the knowledge of nature is only half the task of a poet; he must be acquainted likewise with all the modes of life. His character requires that he estimate the happiness and misery of every condition; observe the power of all the passions in all their combinations, and trace the changes of the human mind as they are modified by various institutions and accidental influences of climate or custom, from the spriteliness of infancy to the desponddence of decrepitude. He must divest himself of the prejudices of his age and country; he must consider right and wrong in their abstracted and invariable state; he must disregard present laws and opinions, and rise to general and transcendental truths, which will always be the same: he must therefore content himself with the slow progress of his name; contemn the applause of his own time, and commit his claims to the justice of posterity. He must write as the interpreter of nature, and the legislator of mankind, and consider himself as presiding over the thoughts and manners of future generations; as a being superiour to time and place.

"His labour is not yet at an end: he must know many languages and many sciences; and, that his stile may be worthy of his thoughts, must by incessant practice, familiarize to himself every delicacy of speech and grace of harmony."

CHAPTER XI

Imlac's narrative continued. A hint on pilgrimage.

IMLAC now felt the enthusiastic fit, and was proceeding to aggrandize his own profession, when the prince cried out, "Enough! Thou hast convinced me, that no human being can ever be a poet. Proceed with thy narration."

"To be a poet, said Imlac, is indeed very difficult." "So difficult, returned the prince, that I will at present hear no more of his labours. Tell me whither you went when you had seen Persia."

"From Persia, said the poet, I travelled through Syria, and for three years resided in Palestine, where I conversed with great numbers of the northern and western nations of Europe; the nations which are now in possession of all power and all knowledge; whose armies are irresistible, and whose fleets command the remotest parts of the globe. When I compared these men with the natives of our own kingdom, and those that surround us, they appeared almost another order of beings. In their countries it is difficult to wish for any thing that may not be obtained: a thousand arts, of which we never heard, are continually labouring for their convenience and pleasure; and whatever their own climate has denied them is supplied by their commerce."

"By what means, said the prince, are the Europeans thus powerful? or why, since they can so easily visit Asia and Africa for trade or conquest, cannot the Asiastics and Africans invade their coasts, plant colonies in their ports, and give laws to their natural princes? The same wind that carries them back would bring us thither."

"They are more powerful, Sir, than we, answered Imlac, because they are wiser; knowledge will always predominate over ignorance, as man governs the other animals. But why their knowledge is more than ours, I know not what reason can be given, but the unsearchable will of the Supreme Being."

"When, said the prince with a sigh, shall I be able to visit Palestine, and mingle with this mighty confluence of nations? Till that happy moment shall arrive, let me fill up the time with such representations as thou canst give me. I am not ignorant of the motive that assembles such numbers in that place, and cannot but consider it as the centre of wisdom and piety, to which the best and wisest men of every land must be continually resorting."

"There are some nations, said Imlac, that send few visitants to Palestine; for many numerous and learned sects in Europe, concur to censure pilgrimage as superstitious, or deride it as ridiculous."

"You know, said the prince, how little my life has made me acquainted with diversity of opinions: it will be too long to hear the arguments on both sides; you, that have considered them, tell me the result."

"Pilgrimage, said Imlac, like many other acts of piety, may be reasonable or superstitious, according to the principles upon which it is performed. Long journies in search of truth are not commanded. Truth, such as is necessary to the regulation of life, is always found where it is honestly sought. Change of place is no natural cause of the increase of piety, for it inevitably produces dissipation of mind. Yet, since men go every day to view the fields where great actions have been performed, and return with stronger impressions of the event, curiosity of the same kind may naturally dispose us to view that country whence our religion had its beginning; and I believe no man surveys those awful scenes without some confirmation of holy resolutions. That the Supreme Being may be more easily propitiated in one place than in another, is the dream of idle superstition; but that some places may operate upon our own minds in an uncommon manner, is an opinion which hourly experience will justify. He who supposes that his vices may be more successfully combated in Palestine, will, perhaps, find himself mistaken, yet he may go thither without folly: he who thinks they will be more freely pardoned, dishonours at once his reason and religion."

"These, said the prince, are European distinctions. I will consider them another time. What have you found to be the effect of knowledge? Are those nations happier than we?"

"There is so much infelicity, said the poet, in the world, that scarce any man has leisure from his own distresses to estimate the comparative happiness of others. Knowledge is certainly one of the means of pleasure, as is confessed by the natural desire which every mind feels of increasing its ideas. Ignorance is mere privation, by which nothing can be produced: it is a vacuity in which the soul sits motionless and torpid for want of attraction; and, without knowing why, we always rejoice when we learn, and grieve when we forget. I am therefore inclined to conclude, that, if nothing counteracts the natural consequence of learning, we grow more happy as our minds take a wider range.

"In enumerating the particular comforts of life we shall find many advantages on the side of the Europeans. They cure wounds and diseases with which we languish and perish. We suffer inclemencies of weather which they can obviate. They have engines for the despatch of many laborious works, which we must perform by manual industry. There is such communication between distant places, that one friend can hardly be said to be absent from another. Their policy removes all publick inconveniencies: they have roads cut through their mountains, and bridges laid upon their rivers. And, if we descend to the privacies of life, their habitations are more commodious, and their possessions are more secure."

"They are surely happy, said the prince, who have all these conveniencies, of which I envy none so much as the facility with which separated friends interchange their thoughts."

"The Europeans, answered Imlac, are less unhappy than we, but they are not happy. Human life is every where a state in which much is to be endured, and little to be enjoyed."

CHAPTER XII

The story of Imlac continued.

"I AM not yet willing, said the prince, to suppose that happiness is so parsimoniously distributed to mortals; nor can believe but that, if I had the choice of life, I should be able to fill every day with pleasure. I would injure no man, and should provoke no resentment: I would relieve every distress, and should enjoy the

413

benedictions of gratitude. I would choose my friends among the wise, and my wife among the virtuous; and therefore should be in no danger from treachery, or unkindness. My children should, by my care, be learned and pious, and would repay to my age what their childhood had received. What would dare to molest him who might call on every side to thousands enriched by his bounty, or assisted by his power? And why should not life glide quietly away in the soft reciprocation of protection and reverence? All this may be done without the help of European refinements, which appear by their effects to be rather specious than useful. Let us leave them and persue our journey."

"From Palestine, said Imlac, I passed through many regions of Asia; in the more civilized kingdoms as a trader, and among the Barbarians of the mountains as a pilgrim. At last I began to long for my native country, that I might repose after my travels, and fatigues, in the places where I had spent my earliest years, and gladden my old companions with the recital of my adventures. Often did I figure to myself those, with whom I had sported away the gay hours of dawning life, sitting round me in its evening, wondering at my tales, and listening to my counsels.

"When this thought had taken possession of my mind, I considered every moment as wasted which did not bring me nearer to Abissinia. I hastened into Egypt, and, notwithstanding my impatience, was detained ten months in the contemplation of its ancient magnificence, and in enquiries after the remains of its ancient learning. I found in Cairo a mixture of all nations; some brought thither by the love of knowledge, some by the hope of gain, and many by the desire of living after their own manner without observation, and of lying hid in the obscurity of multitudes: for, in a city, populous as Cairo, it is possible to obtain at the same time the gratifications of society, and the secrecy of solitude.

"From Cairo I travelled to Suez, and embarked on the Red sea, passing along the coast till I arrived at the port from which I had departed twenty years before. Here I joined myself to a caravan and re-entered my native country.

"I now expected the caresses of my kinsmen, and the congratulations of my friends, and was not without hope that my father, whatever value he had set upon riches, would own with gladness and pride a son who was able to add to the felicity and honour of the nation. But I was soon convinced that my thoughts

were vain. My father had been dead fourteen years, having divided
his wealth among my brothers, who were removed to some other
provinces. Of my companions the greater part was in the grave,
of the rest some could with difficulty remember me, and some considered me as one corrupted by foreign manners.

"A man used to vicissitudes is not easily dejected. I forgot, after
a time, my disappointment, and endeavoured to recommend myself
to the nobles of the kingdom: they admitted me to their tables,
heard my story, and dismissed me. I opened a school, and was prohibited to teach. I then resolved to sit down in the quiet of domestick life, and addressed a lady that was fond of my conversation,
but rejected my suit, because my father was a merchant.

"Wearied at last with solicitation and repulses, I resolved to
hide myself for ever from the world, and depend no longer on the
opinion or caprice of others. I waited for the time when the gate
of the *happy valley* should open that I might bid farewell to hope
and fear: the day came; my performance was distinguished with
favour, and I resigned myself with joy to perpetual confinement."

"Hast thou here found happiness at last? said Rasselas. Tell me
without reserve; art thou content with thy condition? or, dost
thou wish to be again wandering and inquiring? All the inhabitants
of this valley celebrate their lot, and, at the annual visit of the
emperour, invite others to partake of their felicity."

"Great prince, said Imlac, I shall speak the truth: I know not
one of all your attendants who does not lament the hour when he
entered this retreat. I am less unhappy than the rest, because I
have a mind replete with images, which I can vary and combine at
pleasure. I can amuse my solitude by the renovation of the knowledge which begins to fade from my memory, and by recollection
of the incidents of my past life. Yet all this ends in the sorrowful
consideration, that my acquirements are now useless, and that
none of my pleasures can be again enjoyed. The rest, whose minds
have no impression but of the present moment, are either corroded
by malignant passions, or sit stupid in the gloom of perpetual
vacancy."

"What passions can infest those, said the prince, who have no
rivals? We are in a place where impotence precludes malice, and
where all envy is repressed by community of enjoyments."

"There may be community, said Imlac, of material possessions,
but there can never be community of love or of esteem. It must

415

happen that one will please more than another; he that knows himself despised will always be envious; and still more envious and malevolent, if he is condemned to live in the presence of those who despise him. The invitations, by which they allure others to a state which they feel to be wretched, proceed from the natural malignity of hopeless misery. They are weary of themselves, and of each other, and expect to find relief in new companions. They envy the liberty which their folly has forfeited, and would gladly see all mankind imprisoned like themselves.

"From this crime, however, I am wholly free. No man can say that he is wretched by my persuasion. I look with pity on the crowds who are annually soliciting admission to captivity, and wish that it were lawful for me to warn them of their danger."

"My dear Imlac, said the prince, I will open to thee my whole heart. I have long meditated an escape from the happy valley. I have examined the mountains on every side, but find myself insuperably barred: teach me the way to break my prison; thou shalt be the companion of my flight, the guide of my rambles, the partner of my fortune, and my sole director in the *choice of life.*"

"Sir, answered the poet, your escape will be difficult, and, perhaps, you may soon repent your curiosity. The world, which you figure to yourself smooth and quiet as the lake in the valley, you will find a sea foaming with tempests, and boiling with whirlpools: you will be sometimes overwhelmed by the waves of violence, and sometimes dashed against the rocks of treachery. Amidst wrongs and frauds, competitions and anxieties, you will wish a thousand times for these seats of quiet, and willingly quit hope to be free from fear."

"Do not seek to deter me from my purpose, said the prince: I am impatient to see what thou hast seen; and, since thou art thyself weary of the valley, it is evident, that thy former state was better than this. Whatever be the consequence of my experiment, I am resolved to judge with my own eyes of the various conditions of men, and then to make deliberately my *choice of life.*"

"I am afraid, said Imlac, you are hindered by stronger restraints than my persuasions; yet, if your determination is fixed, I do not counsel you to despair. Few things are impossible to diligence and skill."

CHAPTER XIII

Rasselas discovers the means of escape.

THE prince now dismissed his favourite to rest, but the narrative of wonders and novelties filled his mind with perturbation. He revolved all that he had heard, and prepared innumerable questions for the morning.

Much of his uneasiness was now removed. He had a friend to whom he could impart his thoughts, and whose experience could assist in him his designs. His heart was no longer condemned to swell with silent vexation. He thought that even the *happy valley* might be endured with such a companion, and that, if they could range the world together, he should have nothing further to desire.

In a few days the water was discharged, and the ground dried. The prince and Imlac then walked out together to converse without the notice of the rest. The prince, whose thoughts were always on the wing, as he passed by the gate, said, with a countenance of sorrow, "Why art thou so strong, and why is man so weak?"

"Man is not weak, answered his companion; knowledge is more than equivalent to force. The master of mechanicks laughs at strength. I can burst the gate, but cannot do it secretly. Some other expedient must be tried."

As they were walking on the side of the mountain, they observed that the conies, which the rain had driven from their burrows, had taken shelter among the bushes, and formed holes behind them, tending upwards in an oblique line. "It has been the opinion of antiquity, said Imlac, that human reason borrowed many arts from the instinct of animals; let us, therefore, not think ourselves degraded by learning from the coney. We may escape by piercing the mountain in the same direction. We will begin where the summit hangs over the middle part, and labour upward till we shall issue out beyond the prominence."

The eyes of the prince, when he heard this proposal, sparkled with joy. The execution was easy, and the success certain.

No time was now lost. They hastened early in the morning to chuse a place proper for their mine. They clambered with great fatigue among crags and brambles, and returned without having discovered any part that favoured their design. The second and the third day were spent in the same manner, and with the same frustration. But, on the fourth, they found a small cavern, concealed by a thicket, where they resolved to make their experiment.

Imlac procured instruments proper to hew stone and remove earth, and they fell to their work on the next day with more eagerness than vigour. They were presently exhausted by their efforts, and sat down to pant upon the grass. The prince, for a moment, appeared to be discouraged. "Sir, said his companion, practice will enable us to continue our labour for a longer time; mark, however, how far we have advanced, and you will find that our toil will some time have an end. Great works are performed, not by strength, but perseverance: yonder palace was raised by single stones, yet you see its height and spaciousness. He that shall walk with vigour three hours a day will pass in seven years a space equal to the circumference of the globe."

They returned to their work day after day, and, in a short time, found a fissure in the rock, which enabled them to pass far with very little obstruction. This Rasselas considered as a good omen. "Do not disturb your mind, said Imlac, with other hopes or fears than reason may suggest: if you are pleased with prognosticks of good, you will be terrified likewise with tokens of evil, and your whole life will be a prey to superstition. Whatever facilitates our work is more than an omen, it is a cause of success. This is one of those pleasing surprises which often happen to active resolution. Many things difficult to design prove easy to performance."

CHAPTER XIV

Rasselas and Imlac receive an unexpected visit.

THEY had now wrought their way to the middle, and solaced their toil with the approach of liberty, when the prince, coming down to refresh himself with air, found his sister Nekayah standing before the mouth of the cavity. He started and stood confused, afraid to tell his design, and yet hopeless to conceal it. A few moments determined him to repose on her fidelity, and secure her secrecy by a declaration without reserve.

"Do not imagine, said the princess, that I came hither as a spy: I had long observed from my window, that you and Imlac directed your walk every day towards the same point, but I did not suppose that you had any better reason for the preference than a cooler shade, or more fragrant bank; nor followed you with any other design than to partake of your conversation. Since then not suspicion but fondness has detected you, let me not lose the advantage of my discovery. I am equally weary of confinement with yourself, and not less desirous of knowing what is done or suffered in the world. Permit me to fly with you from this tasteless tranquility, which will yet grow more loathsome when you have left me. You may deny me to accompany you, but cannot hinder me from following."

The prince, who loved Nekayah above his other sisters, had no inclination to refuse her request, and grieved that he had lost an opportunity of shewing his confidence by a voluntary communication. It was therefore agreed that she should leave the valley with them; and that, in the mean time, she should watch, lest any other straggler, should by chance or curiosity, follow them to the mountain.

At length their labour was at an end; they saw light beyond the prominence, and, issuing to the top of the mountain, beheld the Nile, yet a narrow current, wandering beneath them.

The prince looked round with rapture, anticipated all the pleasure of travel, and in thought was already transported beyond his father's dominions. Imlac, though very joyful at his escape, had less expectation of pleasure in the world, which he had before tried, and of which he had been weary.

Rasselas was so much delighted with a wider horizon, that he could not soon be persuaded to return into the valley. He informed his sister that the way was open, and that nothing now remained but to prepare for their departure.

CHAPTER XV

The prince and princess leave the valley, and see many wonders.

THE prince and princess had jewels sufficient to make them rich whenever they came into a place of commerce, which, by Imlac's direction, they hid in their cloaths, and, on the night of the next full moon, all left the valley. The princess was followed only by a single favourite, who did not know whither she was going.

They clambered through the cavity, and began to go down on the other side. The princess and her maid turned their eyes towards every part, and, seeing nothing to bound their prospect, considered themselves as in danger of being lost in a dreary vacuity. They stopped and trembled. "I am almost afraid, said the princess, to begin a journey of which I cannot perceive an end, and to venture into this immense plain where I may be approached on every side by men whom I never saw." The prince felt nearly the same emotions, though he thought it more manly to conceal them.

Imlac smiled at their terrours, and encouraged them to proceed; but the princess continued irresolute till she had been imperceptibly drawn forward too far to return.

In the morning they found some shepherds in the field, who set milk and fruits before them. The princess wondered that she did not see a palace ready for her reception, and a table spread with delicacies; but being faint and hungry, she drank the milk and eat the fruits, and thought them of a higher flavour than the products of the valley.

They travelled forward by easy journeys, being all unaccustomed to toil or difficulty, and knowing, that though they might be missed, they could not be persued. In a few days they came into a more populous region, where Imlac was diverted with the admiration which his companions expressed at the diversity of manners, stations and employments.

Their dress was such as might not bring upon them the suspicion of having any thing to conceal, yet the prince, wherever he came, expected to be obeyed, and the princess was frighted, because those that came into her presence did not prostrate themselves before her. Imlac was forced to observe them with great vigilance, lest they should betray their rank by their unusual behaviour, and detained them several weeks in the first village to accustom them to the sight of common mortals.

By degrees the royal wanderers were taught to understand that they had for a time laid aside their dignity, and were to expect only such regard as liberality and courtesy could procure. And Imlac, having, by many admonitions, prepared them to endure the tumults of a port, and the ruggedness of the commercial race, brought them down to the sea-coast.

The prince and his sister, to whom every thing was new, were gratified equally at all places, and therefore remained for some months at the port without any inclination to pass further. Imlac was content with their stay, because he did not think it safe to expose them, unpractised in the world, to the hazards of a foreign country.

At last he began to fear lest they should be discovered, and proposed to fix a day for their departure. They had no pretensions to judge for themselves, and referred the whole scheme to his direction. He therefore took passage in a ship to Suez; and, when the time came, with great difficulty prevailed on the princess to enter the vessel. They had a quick and prosperous voyage, and from Suez travelled by land to Cairo.

CHAPTER XVI

They enter Cairo, and find every man happy.

As they approached the city, which filled the strangers with astonishment, "This, said Imlac to the prince, is the place where travellers and merchants assemble from all the corners of the earth. You will here find men of every character, and every occupation. Commerce is here honourable: I will act as a merchant, and you shall live as strangers, who have no other end of travel than curiosity; it will soon be observed that we are rich; our reputation will procure us acess to all whom we shall desire to know; you will see all the conditions of humanity, and enable yourself at leisure to make your *choice of life*."

They now entered the town, stunned by the noise, and offended by the crowds. Instruction had not yet so prevailed over habit, but that they wondered to see themselves pass undistinguished along the street, and met by the lowest of the people without reverence or notice. The princess could not at first bear the thought of being levelled with the vulgar, and, for some days, continued in her chamber, where she was served by her favourite Pekuah as in the palace of the valley.

Imlac, who understood traffick, sold part of the jewels the next day, and hired a house, which he adorned with such magnificence, that he was immediately considered as a merchant of great wealth. His politeness attracted many acquaintance, and his generosity made him courted by many dependants. His table was crowded by men of every nation, who all admired his knowledge, and solicited his favour. His companions, not being able to mix in the conversation, could make no discovery of their ignorance or surprise, and

O 421

were gradually initiated in the world as they gained knowledge of the language.

The prince had, by frequent lectures, been taught the use and nature of money; but the ladies could not, for a long time, comprehend what the merchants did with small pieces of gold and silver, or why things of so little use should be received as equivalent to the necessaries of life.

They studied the language two years, while Imlac was preparing to set before them the various ranks and conditions of mankind. He grew acquainted with all who had any thing uncommon in their fortune or conduct. He frequented the voluptuous and the frugal, the idle and the busy, the merchants and the men of learning.

The prince, being now able to converse with fluency, and having learned the caution necessary to be observed in his intercourse with strangers, began to accompany Imlac to places of resort, and to enter into all assemblies, that he might make his *choice of life*.

For some time he thought choice needless, because all appeared to him equally happy. Wherever he went he met gayety and kindness, and heard the song of joy, or the laugh of carelessness. He began to believe that the world overflowed with universal plenty, and that nothing was withheld either from want or merit; that every hand showered liberality, and every heart melted with benevolence: "and who then, says he, will be suffered to be wretched?"

Imlac permitted the pleasing delusion, and was unwilling to crush the hope of inexperience; till one day, having sat a while silent, "I know not, said the prince, what can be the reason that I am more unhappy than any of our friends. I see them perpetually and unalterably chearful, but feel my own mind restless and uneasy. I am unsatisfied with those pleasures which I seem most to court; I live in the crowds of jollity, not so much to enjoy company as to shun myself, and am only loud and merry to conceal my sadness."

"Every man, said Imlac, may, by examining his own mind, guess what passes in the minds of others: when you feel that your own gaiety is counterfeit, it may justly lead you to suspect that of your companions not to be sincere. Envy is commonly reciprocal. We are long before we are convinced that happiness is never to be found, and each believes it possessed by others, to keep alive the hope of obtaining it for himself. In the assembly, where you passed the last night, there appeared such spriteliness of air, and volatility of fancy, as might have suited beings of an higher order, formed to inhabit serener regions inaccessible to care or sorrow: yet, believe me, prince, there was not one who did not dread the moment when solitude should deliver him to the tyranny of reflection."

"This, said the prince, may be true of others, since it is true of me; yet, whatever be the general infelicity of man, one condition is more happy than another, and wisdom surely directs us to take the least evil in the *choice of life.*"

"The causes of good and evil, answered Imlac, are so various and uncertain, so often entangled with each other, so diversified by various relations, and so much subject to accidents which cannot be foreseen, that he who would fix his condition upon incontestable reasons of preference, must live and die inquiring and deliberating."

"But surely, said Rasselas, the wise men, to whom we listen with reverence and wonder, chose that mode of life for themselves which they thought most likely to make them happy."

"Very few, said the poet, live by choice. Every man is placed in his present condition by causes which acted without his foresight, and with which he did not always willingly co-operate; and therefore you will rarely meet one who does not think the lot of his neighbour better than his own."

"I am pleased to think, said the prince, that my birth has given me at least one advantage over others, by enabling me to determine for myself. I have here the world before me; I will review it at leisure: surely happiness is somewhere to be found."

CHAPTER XVII

The prince associates with young men of spirit and gaiety.

RASSELAS rose next day, and resolved to begin his experiments upon life. "Youth, cried he, is the time of gladness: I will join myself to the young men, whose only business is to gratify their desires, and whose time is all spent in a succession of enjoyments."

To such societies he was readily admitted, but a few days brought him back weary and disgusted. Their mirth was without images, their laughter without motive; their pleasures were gross and sensual, in which the mind had no part; their conduct was at once wild and mean; they laughed at order and at law, but the frown of power dejected, and the eye of wisdom abashed them.

The prince soon concluded, that he should never be happy in a course of life of which he was ashamed. He thought it unsuitable to a reasonable being to act without a plan, and to be sad or chearful only by chance. "Happiness, said he, must be something solid and permanent, without fear and without uncertainty."

But his young companions had gained so much of his regard by their frankness and courtesy, that he could not leave them without warning and remonstrance. "My friends, said he, I have seriously considered our manners and our prospects, and find that we have mistaken our own interest. The first years of man must make provision for the last. He that never thinks never can be wise. Perpetual levity must end in ignorance; and intemperance, though it may fire the spirits for an hour, will make life short or miserable. Let us consider that youth is of no long duration, and that in maturer age, when the enchantments of fancy shall cease, and phantoms of delight dance no more about us, we shall have no comforts but the esteem of wise men, and the means of doing good. Let us, therefore, stop, while to stop is in our power; let us live as men who are sometime to grow old, and to whom it will be the most dreadful of all evils not to count their past years but by follies, and to be reminded of their former luxuriance of health only by the maladies which riot has produced."

They stared a while in silence one upon another, and, at last, drove him away by a general chorus of continued laughter.

The consciousness that his sentiments were just, and his intentions kind, was scarcely sufficient to support him against the horrour of derision. But he recovered his tranquility, and persued his search.

CHAPTER XVIII

The prince finds a wise and happy man.

As he was one day walking in the street, he saw a spacious building which all were, by the open doors, invited to enter: he followed the stream of people, and found it a hall or school of declamation, in which professors read lectures to their auditory. He fixed his eye upon a sage raised above the rest, who discoursed with great energy on the government of the passions. His look was venerable, his action graceful, his pronunciation clear, and his diction elegant. He shewed, with great strength of sentiment, and variety of illustration, that human nature is degraded and debased, when the lower faculties predominate over the higher; that when fancy, the parent of passion, usurps the dominion of the mind, nothing ensues but the natural effect of unlawful government, perturbation and confusion; that she betrays the fortresses of the intellect to rebels, and excites her children to sedition against reason their lawful sovereign. He compared reason to the sun, of which the light is constant, uniform, and lasting; and fancy to a meteor, of bright but transitory lustre, irregular in its motion, and delusive in its direction.

He then communicated the various precepts given from time to time for the conquest of passion, and displayed the happiness of those who had obtained the important victory, after which man is no longer the slave of fear, nor the fool of hope; is no more emaciated by envy, inflamed by anger, emasculated by tenderness, or depressed by grief; but walks on calmly through the tumults or privacies of life, as the sun persues alike his course through the calm or the stormy sky.

He enumerated many examples of heroes immovable by pain or pleasure, who looked with indifference on those modes or accidents to which the vulgar give the names of good and evil. He exhorted his hearers to lay aside their prejudices, and arm themselves against the shafts of malice or misfortune, by invulnerable patience; concluding, that this state only was happiness, and that this happiness was in every one's power.

Rasselas listened to him with the veneration due to the instructions of a superiour being, and, waiting for him at the door, humbly implored the liberty of visiting so great a master of true wisdom. The lecturer hesitated a moment, when Rasselas put a purse of gold into his hand, which he received with a mixture of joy and wonder.

"I have found, said the prince, at his return to Imlac, a man who can teach all that is necessary to be known, who, from the unshaken throne of rational fortitude, looks down on the scenes of life changing beneath him. He speaks, and attention watches his lips. He reasons, and conviction closes his periods. This man shall be my future guide: I will learn his doctrines, and imitate his life."

"Be not too hasty, said Imlac, to trust, or to admire, the teachers of morality: they discourse like angels, but they live like men."

Rasselas, who could not conceive how any man could reason so forcibly without feeling the cogency of his own arguments, paid his visit in a few days, and was denied admission. He had now learned the power of money, and made his way by a piece of gold to the inner apartment, where he found the philosopher in a room half darkened, with his eyes misty, and his face pale. "Sir, said he, you are come at a time when all human friendship is useless; what I suffer cannot be remedied, what I have lost cannot be supplied. My daughter, my only daughter, from whose tenderness I expected all the comforts of my age, died last night of a fever. My views, my purposes, my hopes are at an end: I am now a lonely being disunited from society."

"Sir, said the prince, mortality is an event by which a wise man can never be surprised: we know that death is always near, and it should therefore always be expected." "Young man, answered the philosopher, you speak like one that has never felt the pangs of separation." "Have you then forgot the precepts, said Rasselas, which you so powerfully enforced? Has wisdom no strength to arm the heart against calamity? Consider, that external things are naturally variable, but truth and reason are always the same." "What comfort, said the mourner, can truth and reason afford me? of what effect are they now, but to tell me, that my daughter will not be restored?"

The prince, whose humanity would not suffer him to insult misery with reproof, went away convinced of the emptiness of rhetorical sound, and the inefficacy of polished periods and studied sentences.

CHAPTER XIX

A glimpse of pastoral life.

HE was still eager upon the same inquiry; and, having heard of a hermit, that lived near the lowest cataract of the Nile, and filled the whole country with the fame of his sanctity, resolved to visit his retreat, and enquire whether that felicity, which publick life could not afford, was to be found in solitude; and whether a man, whose age and virtue made him venerable, could teach any peculiar art of shunning evils, or enduring them.

Imlac and the princess agreed to accompany him, and, after the necessary preparation, they began their journey. Their way lay through fields, where shepherds tended their flocks, and the lambs were playing upon the pasture. "This, said the poet, is the life which has been often celebrated for its innocence and quiet: let us pass the heat of the day among the shepherds tents, and know whether all our searches are not to terminate in pastoral simplicity."

The proposal pleased them, and they induced the shepherds, by small presents and familiar questions, to tell their opinion of their own state: they were so rude and ignorant, so little able to compare the good with the evil of the occupation, and so indistinct in their narratives and descriptions, that very little could be learned from them. But it was evident that their hearts were cankered with discontent; that they considered themselves as condemned to labour for the luxury of the rich, and looked up with stupid malevolence toward those that were placed above them.

The princess pronounced with vehemence, that she would never suffer these envious savages to be her companions, and that she should not soon be desirous of seeing any more specimens of rustick happiness; but could not believe that all the accounts of primeval pleasures were fabulous, and was yet in doubt whether life had any thing that could be justly preferred to the placid gratifications of fields and woods. She hoped that the time would come, when with a few virtuous and elegant companions, she should gather flowers planted by her own hand, fondle the lambs of her own ewe, and listen, without care, among brooks and breezes, to one of her maidens reading in the shade.

CHAPTER XX

The danger of prosperity.

On the next day they continued their journey, till the heat compelled them to look round for shelter. At a small distance they saw a thick wood, which they no sooner entered than they perceived that they were approaching the habitations of men. The shrubs were diligently cut away to open walks where the shades were darkest; the boughs of opposite trees were artificially interwoven; seats of flowery turf were raised in vacant spaces, and a rivulet, that

427

wantoned along the side of a winding path, had its banks sometimes opened into small basons, and its stream sometimes obstructed by little mounds of stone heaped together to increase its
murmurs.

They passed slowly through the wood, delighted with such unexpected accommodations, and entertained each other with conjecturing what, or who, he could be, that in those rude and
unfrequented regions, had leisure and art for such harmless
luxury.

As they advanced, they heard the sound of musick, and saw
youths and virgins dancing in the grove; and, going still further,
beheld a stately palace built upon a hill surrounded with woods.
The laws of eastern hospitality allowed them to enter, and the
master welcomed them like a man liberal and wealthy.

He was skilful enough in appearances soon to discern that they
were no common guests, and spread his table with magnificence.
The eloquence of Imlac caught his attention, and the lofty courtesy
of the princess excited his respect. When they offered to depart he
entreated their stay, and was the next day still more unwilling to
dismiss them than before. They were easily persuaded to stop, and
civility grew up in time to freedom and confidence.

The prince now saw all the domesticks chearful, and all the face
of nature smiling round the place, and could not forbear to hope
that he should find here what he was seeking; but when he was
congratulating the master upon his possessions, he answered with a
sigh, "My condition has indeed the appearance of happiness, but
appearances are delusive. My prosperity puts my life in danger;
the Bassa of Egypt is my enemy, incensed only by my wealth and
popularity. I have been hitherto protected against him by the
princes of the country; but, as the favour of the great is uncertain,
I know not how soon my defenders may be persuaded to share the
plunder with the Bassa. I have sent my treasures into a distant
country, and, upon the first alarm, am prepared to follow them.
Then will my enemies riot in my mansion, and enjoy the gardens
which I have planted."

They all joined in lamenting his danger, and deprecating his
exile; and the princess was so much disturbed with the tumult of
grief and indignation, that she retired to her apartment. They continued with their kind inviter a few days longer, and then went
forward to find the hermit.

CHAPTER XXI

The happiness of solitude.   The hermit's history

THEY came on the third day, by the direction of the peasants, to the hermit's cell: it was a cavern in the side of a mountain, over-shadowed with palm-trees; at such a distance from the cataract, that nothing more was heard than a gentle uniform murmur, such as composed the mind to pensive meditation, especially when it was assisted by the wind whistling among the branches. The first rude essay of nature had been so much improved by human labour, that the cave contained several apartments, appropriated to different uses, and often afforded lodging to travellers, whom darkness or tempests happened to overtake.

The hermit sat on a bench at the door, to enjoy the coolness of the evening. On one side lay a book with pens and papers, on the other mechanical instruments of various kinds. As they approached him unregarded, the princess observed that he had not the countenance of a man that had found, or could teach, the way to happiness.

They saluted him with great respect, which he repaid like a man not unaccustomed to the forms of courts. "My children, said he, if you have lost your way, you shall be willingly supplied with such conveniencies for the night as this cavern will afford. I have all that nature requires, and you will not expect delicacies in a hermit's cell."

They thanked him, and, entering, were pleased with the neatness and regularity of the place. The hermit set flesh and wine before them, though he fed only upon fruits and water. His discourse was chearful without levity, and pious without enthusiasm. He soon gained the esteem of his guests, and the princess repented of her hasty censure.

At last Imlac began thus: "I do not now wonder that your reputation is so far extended; we have heard at Cairo of your wisdom, and came hither to implore your direction for this young man and maiden in the *choice of life.*"

"To him that lives well, answered the hermit, every form of life is good; nor can I give any other rule for choice, than to remove from all apparent evil."

"He will remove most certainly from evil, said the prince, who shall devote himself to that solitude which you have recommended by your example."

"I have indeed lived fifteen years in solitude, said the hermit, but have no desire that my example should gain any imitators. In my youth I professed arms, and was raised by degrees to the highest military rank. I have traversed wide countries at the head of my troops, and seen many battles and sieges. At last, being disgusted by the preferments of a younger officer, and feeling that my vigour was beginning to decay, I was resolved to close my life in peace, having found the world full of snares, discord and misery. I had once escaped from the persuit of the enemy by the shelter of this cavern, and therefore chose it for my final residence. I employed artificers to form it into chambers, and stored it with all that I was likely to want.

"For some time after my retreat, I rejoiced like a tempest-beaten sailor at his entrance into the harbour, being delighted with the sudden change of the noise and hurry of war, to stillness and repose. When the pleasure of novelty went away, I employed my hours in examining the plants which grow in the valley, and the minerals which I collected from the rocks. But that enquiry is now grown tasteless and irksome. I have been for some time unsettled and distracted: my mind is disturbed with a thousand perplexities of doubt, and vanities of imagination, which hourly prevail upon me, because I have no opportunities of relaxation or diversion. I am sometimes ashamed to think that I could not secure myself from vice, but by retiring from the exercise of virtue, and begin to suspect that I was rather impelled by resentment, than led by devotion, into solitude. My fancy riots in scenes of folly, and I lament that I have lost so much, and have gained so little. In solitude, if I escape the example of bad men, I want likewise the counsel and conversation of the good. I have been long comparing the evils with the advantages of society, and resolve to return into the world to morrow. The life of a solitary man will be certainly miserable, but not certainly devout."

They heard his resolution with surprise, but, after a short pause, offered to conduct him to Cairo. He dug up a considerable treasure which he had hid among the rocks, and accompanied them to the city, on which, as he approached it, he gazed with rapture.

CHAPTER XXII

The happiness of a life led according to nature.

RASSELAS went often to an assembly of learned men, who met at stated times to unbend their minds, and compare their opinions. Their manners were somewhat coarse, but their conversation was instructive, and their disputations acute, though sometimes too violent, and often continued till neither controvertist remembered upon what question they began. Some faults were almost general among them: every one was desirous to dictate to the rest, and every one was pleased to hear the genius or knowledge of another depreciated.

In this assembly Rasselas was relating his interview with the hermit, and the wonder with which he heard him censure a course of life which he had so deliberately chosen, and so laudably followed. The sentiments of the hearers were various. Some were of opinion, that the folly of his choice had been justly punished by condemnation to perpetual perseverance. One of the youngest among them, with great vehemence, pronounced him an hypocrite. Some talked of the right of society to the labour of individuals, and considered retirement as a desertion of duty. Others readily allowed, that there was a time when the claims of the publick were satisfied, and when a man might properly sequester himself, to review his life, and purify his heart.

One, who appeared more affected with the narrative than the rest, thought it likely, that the hermit would, in a few years, go back to his retreat, and, perhaps, if shame did not restrain, or death intercept him, return once more from his retreat into the world: "For the hope of happiness, said he, is so strongly impressed, that the longest experience is not able to efface it. Of the present state, whatever it be, we feel, and are forced to confess, the misery, yet, when the same state is again at a distance, imagination paints it as desirable. But the time will surely come, when desire will be no longer our torment, and no man shall be wretched but by his own fault."

"This, said a philosopher, who had heard him with tokens of great impatience, is the present condition of a wise man. The time is already come, when none are wretched but by their own fault. Nothing is more idle, than to enquire after happiness, which nature

431

has kindly placed within our reach. The way to be happy is to live according to nature, in obedience to that universal and unalterable law with which every heart is originally impressed; which is not written on it by precept, but engraven by destiny, not instilled by education, but infused at our nativity. He that lives according to nature will suffer nothing from the delusions of hope, or importunities of desire: he will receive and reject with equability of temper; and act or suffer as the reason of things shall alternately prescribe. Other men may amuse themselves with subtle definitions, or intricate ratiocination. Let them learn to be wise by easier means: let them observe the hind of the forest, and the linnet of the grove: let them consider the life of animals, whose motions are regulated by instinct; they obey their guide and are happy. Let us therefore, at length, cease to dispute, and learn to live; throw away the incumbrance of precepts, which they who utter them with so much pride and pomp do not understand, and carry with us this simple and intelligible maxim, That deviation from nature is deviation from happiness."

When he had spoken, he looked round him with a placid air, and enjoyed the consciousness of his own beneficence. "Sir, said the prince, with great modesty, as I, like all the rest of mankind, am desirous of felicity, my closest attention has been fixed upon your discourse: I doubt not the truth of a position which a man so learned has so confidently advanced. Let me only know what it is to live according to nature."

"When I find young men so humble and so docile, said the philosopher, I can deny them no information which my studies have enabled me to afford. To live according to nature, is to act always with due regard to the fitness arising from the relations and qualities of causes and effects; to concur with the great and unchangeable scheme of universal felicity; to co-operate with the general disposition and tendency of the present system of things."

The prince soon found that this was one of the sages whom he should understand less as he heard him longer. He therefore bowed and was silent, and the philosopher, supposing him satisfied, and the rest vanquished, rose up and departed with the air of a man that had co-operated with the present system.

CHAPTER XXIII

The prince and his sister divide between them the work of observation.

RASSELAS returned home full of reflexions, doubtful how to direct his future steps. Of the way to happiness he found the learned and simple equally ignorant; but, as he was yet young, he flattered himself that he had time remaining for more experiments and further enquiries. He communicated to Imlac his observations and his doubts, but was answered by him with new doubts, and remarks that gave him no comfort. He therefore discoursed more frequently and freely with his sister, who had yet the same hope with himself, and always assisted him to give some reason why, though he had been hitherto frustrated, he might succeed at last.

"We have hitherto, said she, known but little of the world: we have never yet been either great or mean. In our own country, though we had royalty, we had no power, and in this we have not yet seen the private recesses of domestick peace. Imlac favours not our search, lest we should in time find him mistaken. We will divide the task between us: you shall try what is to be found in the splendour of courts, and I will range the shades of humbler life. Perhaps command and authority may be the supreme blessings, as they afford most opportunities of doing good: or, perhaps, what this world can give may be found in the modest habitations of middle fortune; too low for great designs, and too high for penury and distress."

CHAPTER XXIV

The prince examines the happiness of high stations.

RASSELAS applauded the design, and appeared next day with a splendid retinue at the court of the Bassa. He was soon distinguished for his magnificence, and admitted, as a prince whose curiosity had brought him from distant countries, to an intimacy with the great officers, and frequent conversation with the Bassa himself.

He was at first inclined to believe, that the man must be pleased with his own condition, whom all approached with reverence, and heard with obedience, and who had the power to extend his edicts to a whole kingdom. "There can be no pleasure, said he, equal to that of feeling at once the joy of thousands all made happy by wise administration. Yet, since, by the law of subordination, this sublime delight can be in one nation but the lot of one, it is surely reasonable to think that there is some satisfaction more popular and accessible, and that millions can hardly be subjected to the will of a single man, only to fill his particular breast with incommunicable content."

These thoughts were often in his mind, and he found no solution of the difficulty. But as presents and civilities gained him more familiarity, he found that almost every man who stood high in employment hated all the rest, and was hated by them, and that their lives were a continual succession of plots and detections, stratagems and escapes, faction and treachery. Many of those, who surrounded the Bassa, were sent only to watch and report his conduct; every tongue was muttering censure, and every eye was searching for a fault.

At last the letters of revocation arrived, the Bassa was carried in chains to Constantinople, and his name was mentioned no more.

"What are we now to think of the prerogatives of power, said Rasselas to his sister; is it without any efficacy to good? or, is the subordinate degree only dangerous, and the supreme safe and glorious? Is the Sultan the only happy man in his dominions? or, is the Sultan himself subject to the torments of suspicion, and the dread of enemies?"

In a short time the second Bassa was deposed. The Sultan, that had advanced him, was murdered by the Janisaries, and his successor had other views and different favourites.

CHAPTER XXV

The princess persues her enquiry with more diligence than success.

THE princess, in the mean time, insinuated herself into many families; for there are few doors, through which liberality, joined with good humour, cannot find its way. The daughters of many houses were airy and chearful, but Nekayah had been too long accustomed to the conversation of Imlac and her brother to be much pleased with childish levity and prattle which had no meaning. She found their thoughts narrow, their wishes low, and their merriment often artificial. Their pleasures, poor as they were, could not be preserved pure, but were embittered by petty competitions and worthless emulation. They were always jealous of the beauty of each other; of a quality to which solicitude can add nothing, and from which detraction can take nothing away. Many were in love with triflers like themselves, and many fancied that they were in love when in truth they were only idle. Their affection was seldom fixed on sense or virtue, and therefore seldom ended but in vexation. Their grief, however, like their joy, was transient; every thing floated in their mind unconnected with the past or future, so that one desire easily gave way to another, as a second stone cast into the water effaces and confounds the circles of the first.

With these girls she played as with inoffensive animals, and found them proud of her countenance, and weary of her company.

But her purpose was to examine more deeply, and her affability easily persuaded the hearts that were swelling with sorrow to discharge their secrets in her ear: and those whom hope flattered, or prosperity delighted, often courted her to partake their pleasures.

The princess and her brother commonly met in the evening in a private summer-house on the bank of the Nile, and related to each other the occurrences of the day. As they were sitting together, the princess cast her eyes upon the river that flowed before her. "Answer, said she, great father of waters, thou that rollest thy floods through eighty nations, to the invocations of the daughter of thy native king, Tell me if thou waterest, through all thy course, a single habitation from which thou dost not hear the murmurs of complaint?"

"You are, then, said Rasselas, not more successful in private houses, than I have been in courts." "I have, since the last partition of our provinces, said the princess, enabled myself to enter familiarly into many families, where there was the fairest show of prosperity and peace, and know not one house that is not haunted by some fury that destroys its quiet.

"I did not seek ease among the poor, because I concluded that there it could not be found. But I saw many poor whom I had supposed to live in affluence. Poverty has, in large cities, very different appearances: it is often concealed in splendour, and often in extravagance. It is the care of a very great part of mankind to conceal their indigence from the rest: they support themselves by temporary expedients, and every day is lost in contriving for the morrow.

"This, however, was an evil, which, though frequent, I saw with less pain, because I could relieve it. Yet some have refused my bounties; more offended with my quickness to detect their wants, than pleased with my readiness to succour them: and others, whose exigencies compelled them to admit my kindness, have never been able to forgive their benefactress. Many however, have been sincerely grateful without the ostentation of gratitude, or the hope of other favours."

CHAPTER XXVI

The princess continues her remarks upon private life.

NEKAYAH perceiving her brother's attention fixed, proceeded in her narrative.

"In families, where there is or is not poverty, there is commonly discord: if a kingdom be, as Imlac tells us, a great family, a family likewise is a little kingdom, torn with factions and exposed to revolutions. An unpractised observer expects the love of parents and children to be constant and equal; but this kindness seldom continues beyond the years of infancy: in a short time the children become rivals to their parents. Benefits are allayed by reproaches, and gratitude debased by envy.

"Parents and children seldom act in concert: each child endeavours to appropriate the esteem or fondness of the parents, and the parents, with yet less temptation, betray each other to their children; thus some place their confidence in the father, and some in the mother, and, by degrees, the house is filled with artifices and feuds.

"The opinions of children and parents, of the young and the old, are naturally opposite, by the contrary effects of hope and despondence, of expectation and experience, without crime or folly on either side. The colours of life in youth and age appear different, as the face of nature in spring and winter. And how can children credit the assertions of parents, which their own eyes show them to be false?

"Few parents act in such a manner as much to enforce their maxims by the credit of their lives. The old man trusts wholly to slow contrivance and gradual progression: the youth expects to force his way by genius, vigour, and precipitance. The old man pays regard to riches, and the youth reverences virtue. The old man deifies prudence: the youth commits himself to magnanimity and chance. The young man, who intends no ill, believes that none is intended, and therefore acts with openness and candour: but his father, having suffered the injuries of fraud, is impelled to suspect, and too often allured to practice it. Age looks with anger on the temerity of youth, and youth with contempt on the scrupulosity of age. Thus parents and children, for the greatest part, live on to love less and less: and, if those whom nature has thus closely united are the torments of each other, where shall we look for tenderness and consolation?"

"Surely, said the prince, you must have been unfortunate in your choice of acquaintance: I am unwilling to believe, that the most tender of all relations is thus impeded in its effects by natural necessity."

"Domestick discord, answered she, is not inevitably and fatally necessary; but yet it is not easily avoided. We seldom see that a whole family is virtuous: the good and evil cannot well agree; and the evil can yet less agree with one another: even the virtuous fall sometimes to variance, when their virtues are of different kinds, and tending to extremes. In general, those parents have most reverence who most deserve it: for he that lives well cannot be despised.

"Many other evils infest private life. Some are the slaves of servants whom they have trusted with their affairs. Some are kept in continual anxiety to the caprice of rich relations, whom they cannot please, and dare not offend. Some husbands are imperious, and some wives perverse: and, as it is always more easy to do evil than good, though the wisdom or virtue of one can very rarely make many happy, the folly or vice of one may often make many miserable."

"If such be the general effect of marriage, said the prince, I shall, for the future, think it dangerous to connect my interest with that of another, lest I should be unhappy by my partner's fault."

"I have met, said the princess, with many who live single for that reason; but I never found that their prudence ought to raise envy. They dream away their time without friendship, without fondness, and are driven to rid themselves of the day, for which they have no use, by childish amusements, or vicious delights. They act as beings under the constant sense of some known inferiority, that fills their minds with rancour, and their tongues with censure. They are peevish at home, and malevolent abroad; and, as the out-laws of human nature, make it their business and their pleasure to disturb that society which debars them from its privileges. To live without feeling or exciting sympathy, to be fortunate without adding to the felicity of others, or afflicted without tasting the balm of pity, is a state more gloomy than solitude: it is not retreat but exclusion from mankind. Marriage has many pains, but celibacy has no pleasures."

"What then is to be done? said Rasselas; the more we enquire, the less we can resolve. Surely he is most likely to please himself that has no other inclination to regard."

CHAPTER XXVII

Disquisition upon greatness.

THE conversation had a short pause. The prince, having considered his sister's observations, told her, that she had surveyed life with prejudice, and supposed misery where she did not find it. "Your narrative, says he, throws yet a darker gloom upon the prospects of futurity: the predictions of Imlac were but faint sketches of the evils painted by Nekayah. I have been lately convinced that quiet is not the daughter of grandeur, or of power: that her presence is not to be bought by wealth, nor enforced by conquest. It is evident, that as any man acts in a wider compass, he must be more exposed to opposition from enmity or miscarriage from chance; whoever has many to please or to govern, must use the ministry of many agents, some of whom will be wicked, and some ignorant; by some he will be misled, and by others betrayed. If he gratifies one he will offend another: those that are not favoured will think themselves injured; and, since favours can be conferred but upon few, the greater number will be always discontented."

"The discontent, said the princess, which is thus unreasonable, I hope that I shall always have spirit to despise, and you, power to repress."

"Discontent, answered Rasselas, will not always be without reason under the most just and vigilant administration of publick affairs. None, however attentive, can always discover that merit which indigence or faction may happen to obscure; and none, however powerful, can always reward it. Yet, he that sees inferiour desert advanced above him, will naturally impute that preference to partiality or caprice; and, indeed, it can scarcely be hoped that any man, however magnanimous by nature, or exalted by condition will be able to persist for ever in the fixed and inexorable justice of distribution: he will sometimes indulge his own affections, and sometimes those of his favourites; he will permit some to please him who can never serve him; he will discover in those whom he loves qualities which in reality they do not possess; and to those, from whom he receives pleasure, he will in his turn endeavour to give it. Thus will recommendations sometimes prevail which were purchased by money, or by the more destructive bribery of flattery and servility.

"He that has much to do will do something wrong, and of that wrong must suffer the consequences; and, if it were possible that he should always act rightly, yet when such numbers are to judge of his conduct, the bad will censure and obstruct him by malevolence, and the good sometimes by mistake

"The highest stations cannot therefore hope to be the abodes of happiness, which I would willingly believe to have fled from thrones and palaces to seats of humble privacy and placid obscurity. For what can hinder the satisfaction, or intercept the expectations, of him whose abilities are adequate to his employments, who sees with his own eyes the whole circuit of his influence, who chooses by his own knowledge all whom he trusts, and whom none are tempted to deceive by hope or fear? Surely he has nothing to do but to love and to be loved, to be virtuous and to be happy."

"Whether perfect happiness would be procured by perfect goodness, said Nekayah, this world will never afford an opportunity of deciding. But this, at least, may be maintained, that we do not always find visible happiness in proportion to visible virtue. All natural and almost all political evils, are incident alike to the bad and good: they are confounded in the misery of a famine, and not much distinguished in the fury of a faction; they sink together in a tempest, and are driven together from their country by invaders. All that virtue can afford is quietness of conscience, a steady prospect of a happier state; this may enable us to endure calamity with patience; but remember that patience must suppose pain."

CHAPTER XXVIII

Rasselas and Nekayah continue their conversation.

"Dear princess, said Rasselas, you fall into the common errours of exaggeratory declamation, by producing, in a familiar disquisition, examples of national calamities, and scenes of extensive misery, which are found in books rather than in the world, and which, as they are horrid, are ordained to be rare. Let us not imagine evils which we do not feel, nor injure life by misrepresentations. I cannot bear that querulous eloquence which threatens every city with a siege like that of Jerusalem, that makes famine attend on every flight of locusts, and suspends pestilence on the wing of every blast that issues from the south.

"On necessary and inevitable evils, which overwhelm kingdoms at once, all disputation is vain: when they happen they must be endured. But it is evident, that these bursts of universal distress are more dreaded than felt: thousands and ten thousands flourish in youth, and wither in age, without the knowledge of any other than domestick evils, and share the same pleasures and vexations whether their kings are mild or cruel, whether the armies of their country persue their enemies, or retreat before them. While courts are disturbed with intestine competitions, and ambassadours are negotiating in foreign countries, the smith still plies his anvil, and the husbandman drives his plow forward; the necessaries of life are required and obtained, and the successive business of the seasons continues to make its wonted revolutions.

"Let us cease to consider what, perhaps, may never happen, and what, when it shall happen, will laugh at human speculation. We will not endeavour to modify the motions of the elements, or to fix the destiny of kingdoms. It is our business to consider what beings like us may perform; each labouring for his own happiness, by promoting within his circle, however narrow, the happiness of others.

"Marriage is evidently the dictate of nature; men and women are made to be companions of each other, and therefore I cannot be persuaded but that marriage is one of the means of happiness."

"I know not, said the princess, whether marriage be more than one of the innumerable modes of human misery. When I see and reckon the various forms of connubial infelicity, the unexpected causes of lasting discord, the diversities of temper, the oppositions of opinion, the rude collisions of contrary desire where both are urged by violent impulses, the obstinate contests of disagreeing virtues, where both are supported by consciousness of good intention, I am sometimes disposed to think with the severer casuists of most nations, that marriage is rather permitted than approved, and that none, but by the instigation of a passion too much indulged, entangle themselves with indissoluble compacts."

"You seem to forget, replied Rasselas, that you have, even now, represented celibacy as less happy than marriage. Both conditions may be bad, but they cannot both be worst. Thus it happens when wrong opinions are entertained, that they mutually destroy each other, and leave the mind open to truth."

"I did not expect, answered the princess, to hear that imputed to falshood which is the consequence only of frailty. To the mind, as to the eye, it is difficult to compare with exactness objects vast in their extent, and various in their parts. Where we see or conceive the whole at once we readily note the discriminations and decide the preference: but of two systems, of which neither can be surveyed by any human being in its full compass of magnitude and multiplicity of complication, where is the wonder, that judging of the whole by parts, I am alternately affected by one and the other as either presses on my memory or fancy? We differ from ourselves just as we differ from each other, when we see only part of the question, as in the multifarious relations of politicks and morality: but when we perceive the whole at once, as in numerical computations, all agree in one judgment, and none ever varies his opinion."

"Let us not add, said the prince, to the other evils of life, the bitterness of controversy, nor endeavour to vie with each other in subtilties of argument. We are employed in a search, of which both are equally to enjoy the success, or suffer by the miscarriage. It is therefore fit that we assist each other. You surely conclude too hastily from the infelicity of marriage against its institution; will not the misery of life prove equally that life cannot be the gift of heaven? The world must be peopled by marriage, or peopled without it."

"How the world is to be peopled, returned Nekayah, is not my care, and needs not be yours. I see no danger that the present generation should omit to leave successors behind them: we are not now enquiring for the world but for ourselves."

CHAPTER XXIX

The debate of marriage continued.

"THE good of the whole, says Rasselas, is the same with the good of all its parts. If marriage be best for mankind it must be evidently best for individuals, or a permanent and necessary duty must be the cause of evil, and some must be inevitably sacrificed to the convenience of others. In the estimate which you have made of the two states, it appears that the incommodities of a single life are, in a great measure, necessary and certain, but those of the conjugal state accidental and avoidable.

"I cannot forbear to flatter myself that prudence and benevolence will make marriage happy. The general folly of mankind is the cause of general complaint. What can be expected but disappointment and repentance from a choice made in the immaturity of youth, in the ardour of desire, without judgment, without foresight, without enquiry after conformity of opinions, similarity of manners, rectitude of judgment, or purity of sentiment.

"Such is the common process of marriage. A youth and maiden meeting by chance, or brought together by artifice, exchange glances, reciprocate civilities, go home, and dream of one another. Having little to divert attention, or diversify thought, they find themselves uneasy when they are apart, and therefore conclude that they shall be happy together. They marry, and discover what nothing but voluntary blindness before had concealed; they wear out life in altercations, and charge nature with cruelty.

"From those early marriages proceeds likewise the rivalry of parents and children: the son is eager to enjoy the world before the father is willing to forsake it, and there is hardly room at once for two generations. The daughter begins to bloom before the mother can be content to fade, and neither can forbear to wish for the absence of the other.

"Surely all these evils may be avoided by that deliberation and delay which prudence prescribes to irrevocable choice. In the variety and jollity of youthful pleasures life may be well enough supported without the help of a partner. Longer time will increase experience, and wider views will allow better opportunities of enquiry and selection: one advantage, at least, will be certain; the parents will be visibly older than their children."

"What reason cannot collect, said Nekayah, and what experiment has not yet taught, can be known only from the report of others. I have been told that late marriages are not eminently happy. This is a question too important to be neglected, and I have often proposed it to those, whose accuracy of remark, and comprehensiveness of knowledge, made their suffrages worthy of regard. They have generally determined, that it is dangerous for a man and woman to suspend their fate upon each other, at a time when opinions are fixed, and habits are established; when friendships have been contracted on both sides, when life has been planned into method, and the mind has long enjoyed the contemplation of its own prospects.

"It is scarcely possible that two travelling through the world under the conduct of chance, should have been both directed to the same path, and it will not often happen that either will quit the track which custom has made pleasing. When the desultory levity of youth has settled into regularity, it is soon succeeded by pride ashamed to yield, or obstinacy delighting to contend. And even though mutual esteem produces mutual desire to please, time itself, as it modifies unchangeably the external mien, determines likewise the direction of the passions, and gives an inflexible rigidity to the manners. Long customs are not easily broken: he that attempts to change the course of his own life, very often labours in vain; and how shall we do that for others which we are seldom able to do for ourselves?"

"But surely, interposed the prince, you suppose the chief motive of choice forgotten or neglected. Whenever I shall seek a wife, it shall be my first question, whether she be willing to be led by reason?"

"Thus it is, said Nekayah, that philosophers are deceived. There are a thousand familiar disputes which reason never can decide; questions that elude investigation, and make logick ridiculous; cases where something must be done, and where little can be said. Consider the state of mankind, and enquire how few can be supposed to act upon any occasions, whether small or great, with all the reasons of action present to their minds. Wretched would be the pair above all names of wretchedness, who should be doomed to adjust by reason every morning all the minute detail of a domestick day.

"Those who marry at an advanced age, will probably escape the

443

encroachments of their children; but, in diminution of this advantage, they will be likely to leave them, ignorant and helpless, to a guardian's mercy; or, if that should not happen, they must at least go out of the world before they see those whom they love best either wise or great.

"From their children, if they have less to fear, they have less also to hope, and they lose, without equivalent, the joys of early love, and the convenience of uniting with manners pliant, and minds susceptible of new impressions, which might wear away their dissimilitudes by long cohabitation, as soft bodies, by continual attrition, conform their surfaces to each other.

"I believe it will be found that those who marry late are best pleased with their children, and those who marry early with their partners."

"The union of these two affections, said Rasselas, would produce all that could be wished. Perhaps there is a time when marriage might unite them, a time neither too early for the father, nor too late for the husband."

"Every hour, answered the princess, confirms my prejudice in favour of the position so often uttered by the mouth of Imlac, 'That nature sets her gifts on the right hand and on the left.' Those conditions, which flatter hope and attract desire, are so constituted, that, as we approach one, we recede from another. There are goods so opposed that we cannot seize both, but, by too much prudence may pass between them at too great a distance to reach either. This is often the fate of long consideration; he does nothing who endeavours to do more than is allowed to humanity. Flatter not yourself with contrarieties of pleasure. Of the blessings set before you make your choice, and be content. No man can taste the fruits of autumn while he is delighting his scent with the flowers of the spring: no man can, at the same time, fill his cup from the source and from the mouth of the Nile."

CHAPTER XXX

Imlac enters, and changes the conversation.

HERE Imlac entered, and interrupted them. "Imlac, said Rasselas, I have been taking from the princess the dismal history of private life, and am almost discouraged from further search."

"It seems to me, said Imlac, that while you are making the

444

choice of life, you neglect to live. You wander about a single city, which, however large and diversified, can now afford few novelties, and forget that you are in a country, famous among the earliest monarchies for the power and wisdom of its inhabitants; a country where the sciences first dawned that illuminate the world, and beyond which the arts cannot be traced of civil society or domestick life.

"The old Egyptians have left behind them monuments of industry and power before which all European magnificence is confessed to fade away. The ruins of their architecture áre the schools of modern builders, and from the wonders which time has spared we may conjecture, though uncertainly, what it has destroyed."

"My curiosity, said Rasselas, does not very strongly lead me to survey piles of stone, or mounds of earth; my business is with man. I came hither not to measure fragments of temples, or trace choaked aqueducts, but to look upon the various scenes of the present world."

"The things that are now before us, said the princess, require attention, and deserve it. What have I to do with the heroes or the monuments of ancient times? with times which never can return, and heroes, whose form of life was different from all that the present condition of mankind requires or allows."

"To know any thing, returned the poet, we must know its effects; to see men we must see their works, that we may learn what reason has dictated, or passion has incited, and find what are the most powerful motives of action. To judge rightly of the present, we must oppose it to the past; for all judgment is comparative, and of the future nothing can be known. The truth is, that no mind is much employed upon the present: recollection and anticipation fill up almost all our moments. Our passions are joy and grief, love and hatred, hope and fear. Of joy and grief the past is the object, and the future of hope and fear; even love and hatred respect the past, for the cause must have been before the effect.

"The present state of things is the consequence of the former, and it is natural to inquire what were the sources of the good that we enjoy, or the evil that we suffer. If we act only for ourselves, to neglect the study of history is not prudent: if we are entrusted with the care of others, it is not just. Ignorance, when it is voluntary, is criminal; and he may properly be charged with evil who refused to learn how he might prevent it.

"There is no part of history so generally useful as that which relates the progress of the human mind, the gradual improvement of reason, the successive advances of science, the vicissitudes of learning and ignorance which are the light and darkness of thinking beings, the extinction and resuscitation of arts, and the revolutions of the intellectual world. If accounts of battles and invasions are peculiarly the business of princes, the useful or elegant arts are not to be neglected; those who have kingdoms to govern, have understandings to cultivate.

"Example is always more efficacious than precept. A soldier is formed in war, and a painter must copy pictures. In this, contemplative life has the advantage: great actions are seldom seen, but the labours of art are always at hand for those who desire to know what art has been able to perform.

"When the eye or the imagination is struck with any uncommon work the next transition of an active mind is to the means by which it was performed. Here begins the true use of such contemplation; we enlarge our comprehension by new ideas, and perhaps recover some art lost to mankind, or learn what is less perfectly known in our own country. At least we compare our own with former times, and either rejoice at our improvements, or, what is the first motion towards good, discover our defects."

"I am willing, said the prince, to see all that can deserve my search." "And I, said the princess, shall rejoice to learn something of the manners of antiquity."

"The most pompous monument of Egyptian greatness, and one of the most bulky works of manual industry, said Imlac, are the pyramids; fabricks raised before the time of history, and of which the earliest narratives afford us only uncertain traditions. Of these the greatest is still standing very little injured by time."

"Let us visit them to morrow, said Nekayah. I have often heard of the Pyramids, and shall not rest, till I have seen them within and without with my own eyes."

CHAPTER XXXI

They visit the Pyramids.

THE resolution being thus taken, they set out the next day. They laid tents upon their camels, being resolved to stay among the pyramids till their curiosity was fully satisfied. They travelled gently, turned aside to every thing remarkable, stopped from time to time and conversed with the inhabitants, and observed the various appearances of towns ruined and inhabited, of wild and cultivated nature.

When they came to the great pyramid they were astonished at the extent of the base, and the height of the top. Imlac explained to them the principles upon which the pyramidal form was chosen for a fabrick intended to co-extend its duration with that of the world: he showed that its gradual diminution gave it such stability, as defeated all the common attacks of the elements, and could scarcely be overthrown by earthquakes themselves, the least resistible of natural violence. A concussion that should shatter the pyramid would threaten the dissolution of the continent.

They measured all its dimensions, and pitched their tents at its foot. Next day they prepared to enter its interiour apartments, and having hired the common guides climbed up to the first passage, when the favourite of the princess, looking into the cavity, stepped back and trembled. "Pekuah, said the princess, of what art thou afraid?" "Of the narrow entrance, answered the lady, and of the dreadful gloom. I dare not enter a place which must surely be inhabited by unquiet souls. The original possessors of these dreadful vaults will start up before us, and, perhaps, shut us in for ever." She spoke, and threw her arms round the neck of her mistress.

"If all your fear be of apparitions, said the prince, I will promise you safety: there is no danger from the dead; he that is once buried will be seen no more."

"That the dead are seen no more, said Imlac, I will not undertake to maintain against the concurrent and unvaried testimony of all ages, and of all nations. There is no people, rude or learned, among whom apparitions of the dead are not related and believed. This opinion, which, perhaps, prevails as far as human nature is diffused, could become universal only by its truth: those, that never heard of one another, would not have agreed in a tale which nothing but experience can make credible. That it is doubted by single cavillers can very little weaken the general evidence, and some who deny it with their tongues confess it by their fears.

"Yet I do not mean to add new terrours to those which have already seized upon Pekuah. There can be no reason why spectres should haunt the pyramid more than other places, or why they should have power or will to hurt innocence and purity. Our entrance is no violation of their priviledges; we can take nothing from them, how then can we offend them?"

"My dear Pekuah, said the princess, I will always go before you, and Imlac shall follow you. Remember that you are the companion of the princess of Abissinia."

"If the princess is pleased that her servant should die, returned the lady, let her command some death less dreadful than enclosure in this horrid cavern. You know I dare not disobey you: I must go if you command me; but, if I once enter, I never shall come back."

The princess saw that her fear was too strong for expostulation or reproof, and embracing her, told her that she should stay in the tent till their return. Pekuah was yet not satisfied, but entreated the princess not to persue so dreadful a purpose as that of entering the recesses of the pyramid. "Though I cannot teach courage, said Nekayah, I must not learn cowardise; nor leave at last undone what I came hither only to do."

CHAPTER XXXII

They enter the Pyramid.

PEKUAH descended to the tents, and the rest entered the pyramid: they passed through the galleries, surveyed the vaults of marble, and examined the chest in which the body of the founder is supposed to have been reposited. They then sat down in one of the most spacious chambers to rest a while before they attempted to return.

"We have now, said Imlac, gratified our minds with an exact view of the greatest work of man, except the wall of China.

"Of the wall it is very easy to assign the motives. It secured a wealthy and timorous nation from the incursions of Barbarians, whose unskilfulness in arts made it easier for them to supply their wants by rapine than by industry, and who from time to time poured in upon the habitations of peaceful commerce, as vultures descend upon domestick fowl. Their celerity and fierceness made the wall necessary, and their ignorance made it efficacious.

"But for the pyramids no reason has ever been given adequate to the cost and labour of the work. The narrowness of the chambers proves that it could afford no retreat from enemies, and treasures might have been reposited at far less expense with equal security. It seems to have been erected only in compliance with that hunger of imagination which preys incessantly upon life, and must be always appeased by some employment. Those who have already all that they can enjoy, must enlarge their desires. He that has built for use, till use is supplied, must begin to build for vanity, and extend his plan to the utmost power of human performance, that he may not be soon reduced to form another wish.

"I consider this mighty structure as a monument of the insufficiency of human enjoyments. A king, whose power is unlimited and whose treasures surmount all real and imaginary wants, is compelled to solace, by the erection of a pyramid, the satiety of dominion and tastelessness of pleasures, and to amuse the tediousness of declining life, by seeing thousands labouring without end, and one stone, for no purpose, laid upon another. Whoever thou art, that, not content with a moderate condition, imaginest happiness in royal magnificence, and dreamest that command or riches can feed the appetite of novelty with perpetual gratifications, survey the pyramids, and confess thy folly!"

CHAPTER XXXIII

The princess meets with an unexpected misfortune.

THEY rose up, and returned through the cavity at which they had entered, and the princess prepared for her favourite a long narrative of dark labyrinths, and costly rooms, and of the different impressions which the varieties of the way had made upon her. But, when they came to their train, they found every one silent and dejected: the men discovered shame and fear in their countenances, and the women were weeping in the tents.

What had happened they did not try to conjecture, but immediately enquired. "You had scarcely entered into the pyramid, said one of the attendants, when a troop of Arabs rushed upon us: we were too few to resist them, and too slow to escape. They were about to search the tents, set us on our camels, and drive us along before them, when the approach of some Turkish horsemen put them to flight; but they seized the lady Pekuah with her two maids, and carried them away: the Turks are now persuing them by our instigation, but I fear they will not be able to overtake them."

The princess was overpowered with surprise and grief. Rasselas, in the first heat of his resentment, ordered his servants to follow him, and prepared to persue the robbers with his sabre in his hand. "Sir, said Imlac, what can you hope from violence or valour? the Arabs are mounted on horses trained to battle and retreat; we have only beasts of burden. By leaving our present station we may lose the princess, but cannot hope to regain Pekuah."

In a short time the Turks returned, having not been able to reach the enemy. The princess burst out into new lamentations, and Rasselas could scarcely forbear to reproach them with cowardice; but Imlac was of opinion, that the escape of the Arabs was no addition to their misfortune, for, perhaps, they would have killed their captives rather than have resigned them.

CHAPTER XXXIV

They return to Cairo without Pekuah.

THERE was nothing to be hoped from longer stay. They returned to Cairo repenting of their curiosity, censuring the negligence of the government, lamenting their own rashness which had neglected to procure a guard, imagining many expedients by which the loss of Pekuah might have been prevented, and resolving to do something for her recovery, though none could find any thing proper to be done.

Nekayah retired to her chamber, where her women attempted to comfort her, by telling her that all had their troubles, and that lady Pekuah had enjoyed much happiness in the world for a long time, and might reasonably expect a change of fortune. They hoped that some good would befal her wheresoever she was, and that their mistress would find another friend who might supply her place.

The princess made them no answer, and they continued the form of condolence, not much grieved in their hearts that the favourite was lost.

Next day the prince presented to the Bassa a memorial of the wrong which he had suffered, and a petition for redress. The Bassa threatened to punish the robbers, but did not attempt to catch them, nor, indeed, could any account or description be given by which he might direct the persuit.

It soon appeared that nothing would be done by authority. Governors, being accustomed to hear of more crimes than they can punish, and more wrongs than they can redress, set themselves at ease by indiscriminate negligence, and presently forget the request when they lose sight of the petitioner.

Imlac then endeavoured to gain some intelligence by private agents. He found many who pretended to an exact knowledge of all the haunts of the Arabs, and to regular correspondence with their chiefs, and who readily undertook the recovery of Pekuah. Of these, some were furnished with money for their journey, and came back no more; some were liberally paid for accounts which a few days discovered to be false. But the princess would not suffer any means, however improbable, to be left untried. While she was doing something she kept her hope alive. As one expedient failed, another was suggested; when one messenger returned unsuccessful, another was despatched to a different quarter.

Two months had now passed, and of Pekuah nothing had been heard; the hopes which they had endeavoured to raise in each other grew more languid, and the princess, when she saw nothing more to be tried, sunk down inconsolable in hopeless dejection. A thousand times she reproached herself with the easy compliance by which she permitted her favourite to stay behind her. "Had not my fondness, said she, lessened my authority, Pekuah had not dared to talk of her terrours. She ought to have feared me more than spectres. A severe look would have overpowered her; a peremptory command would have compelled obedience. Why did foolish indulgence prevail upon me? Why did I not speak, and refuse to hear?"

"Great princess, said Imlac, do not reproach yourself for your virtue, or consider that as blameable by which evil has accidentally been caused. Your tenderness for the timidity of Pekuah was generous and kind. When we act according to our duty, we commit the event to him by whose laws our actions are governed, and who will suffer none to be finally punished for obedience. When, in prospect of some good, whether natural or moral, we break the rules prescribed us, we withdraw from the direction of superiour wisdom, and take all consequences upon ourselves. Man cannot so far know the connexion of causes and events, as that he may venture to do wrong in order to do right. When we persue our end by lawful means, we may always console our miscarriage by the hope of future recompense. When we consult only our own policy, and attempt to find a nearer way to good, by overleaping the settled

451

boundaries of right and wrong, we cannot be happy even by success, because we cannot escape the consciousness of our fault; but, if we miscarry, the disappointment is irremediably embittered. How comfortless is the sorrow of him, who feels at once the pangs of guilt, and the vexation of calamity which guilt has brought upon him?

"Consider, princess, what would have been your condition, if the lady Pekuah had entreated to accompany you, and, being compelled to stay in the tents, had been carried away; or how would you have born the thought, if you had forced her into the pyramid, and she had died before you in agonies of terrour."

"Had either happened, said Nekayah, I could not have endured life till now: I should have been tortured to madness by the remembrance of such cruelty, or must have pined away in abhorrence of myself."

"This at least, said Imlac, is the present reward of virtuous conduct, that no unlucky consequence can oblige us to repent it."

CHAPTER XXXV

The princess languishes for want of Pekuah.

NEKAYAH, being thus reconciled to herself, found that no evil is insupportable but that which is accompanied with consciousness of wrong. She was, from that time, delivered from the violence of tempestuous sorrow, and sunk into silent pensiveness and gloomy tranquillity. She sat from morning to evening recollecting all that had been done or said by her Pekuah, treasured up with care every trifle on which Pekuah had set an accidental value, and which might recal to mind any little incident or careless conversation. The sentiments of her, whom she now expected to see no more, were treasured in her memory as rules of life, and she deliberated to no other end than to conjecture on any occasion what would have been the opinion and counsel of Pekuah.

The women, by whom she was attended, knew nothing of her real condition, and therefore she could not talk to them but with caution and reserve. She began to remit her curiosity, having no great care to collect notions which she had no convenience of uttering. Rasselas endeavoured first to comfort and afterwards to divert her; he hired musicians, to whom she seemed to listen, but did not hear them, and procured masters to instruct her in various arts, whose lectures, when they visited her again, were again to be repeated. She had lost her taste of pleasure and her ambition of excellence. And her mind, though forced into short excursions, always recurred to the image of her friend.

Imlac was every morning earnestly enjoined to renew his enquiries, and was asked every night whether he had yet heard of Pekuah, till not being able to return the princess the answer that she desired, he was less and less willing to come into her presence. She observed his backwardness, and commanded him to attend her. "You are not, said she, to confound impatience with resentment, or to suppose that I charge you with negligence, because I repine at your unsuccessfulness. I do not much wonder at your absence; I know that the unhappy are never pleasing, and that all naturally avoid the contagion of misery. To hear complaints is wearisome alike to the wretched and the happy; for who would cloud by adventitious grief the short gleams of gaiety which life allows us? or who, that is struggling under his own evils, will add to them the miseries of another?

"The time is at hand, when none shall be disturbed any longer by the sighs of Nekayah: my search after happiness is now at an end. I am resolved to retire from the world with all its flatteries and deceits, and will hide myself in solitude, without any other care than to compose my thoughts, and regulate my hours by a constant succession of innocent occupations, till, with a mind purified from all earthly desires, I shall enter into that state, to which all are hastening, and in which I hope again to enjoy the friendship of Pekuah."

"Do not entangle your mind, said Imlac, by irrevocable determinations, nor increase the burthen of life by a voluntary accumulation of misery: the weariness of retirement will continue or increase when the loss of Pekuah is forgotten. That you have been deprived of one pleasure is no very good reason for rejection of the rest."

"Since Pekuah was taken from me, said the princess, I have no pleasure to reject or to retain. She that has no one to love or trust has little to hope. She wants the radical principle of happiness. We may, perhaps, allow that what satisfaction this world can afford, must arise from the conjunction of wealth, knowledge and goodness: wealth is nothing but as it is bestowed, and knowledge nothing but as it is communicated: they must therefore be imparted

P   453

to others, and to whom could I now delight to impart them? Goodness affords the only comfort which can be enjoyed without a partner, and goodness may be practised in retirement."

"How far solitude may admit goodness, or advance it, I shall not, replied Imlac, dispute at present. Remember the confession of the pious hermit. You will wish to return into the world, when the image of your companion has left your thoughts." "That time, said Nekayah, will never come. The generous frankness, the modest obsequiousness, and the faithful secrecy of my dear Pekuah, will always be more missed, as I shall live longer to see vice and folly."

"The state of a mind oppressed with a sudden calamity, said Imlac, is like that of the fabulous inhabitants of the new created earth, who, when the first night came upon them, supposed that day would never return. When the clouds of sorrow gather over us, we see nothing beyond them, nor can imagine how they will be dispelled: yet a new day succeeded to the night, and sorrow is never long without a dawn of ease. But they who restrain themselves from receiving comfort, do as the savages would have done, had they put out their eyes when it was dark. Our minds, like our bodies, are in continual flux; something is hourly lost, and something acquired. To lose much at once is inconvenient to either, but while the vital powers remain uninjured, nature will find the means of reparation. Distance has the same effect on the mind as on the eye, and while we glide along the stream of time, whatever we leave behind us is always lessening, and that which we approach increasing in magnitude. Do not suffer life to stagnate; it will grow muddy for want of motion: commit yourself again to the current of the world; Pekuah will vanish by degrees; you will meet in your way some other favourite, or learn to diffuse yourself in general conversation."

"At least, said the prince, do not despair before all remedies have been tried: the enquiry after the unfortunate lady is still continued, and shall be carried on with yet greater diligence, on condition that you will promise to wait a year for the event, without any unalterable resolution."

Nekayah thought this a reasonable demand, and made the promise to her brother, who had been advised by Imlac to require it. Imlac had, indeed, no great hope of regaining Pekuah, but he supposed, that if he could secure the interval of a year, the princess would be then in no danger of a cloister.

CHAPTER XXXVI

Pekuah is still remembered.   The progress of sorrow.

NEKAYAH, seeing that nothing was omitted for the recovery of her favourite, and having, by her promise, set her intention of retirement at a distance, began imperceptibly to return to common cares and common pleasures. She rejoiced without her own consent at the suspension of her sorrows, and sometimes caught herself with indignation in the act of turning away her mind from the remembrance of her, whom yet she resolved never to forget.

She then appointed a certain hour of the day for meditation on the merits and fondness of Pekuah, and for some weeks retired constantly at the time fixed, and returned with her eyes swollen and her countenance clouded. By degrees she grew less scrupulous, and suffered any important and pressing avocation to delay the tribute of daily tears. She then yielded to less occasions; sometimes forgot what she was indeed afraid to remember, and, at last, wholly released herself from the duty of periodical affliction.

Her real love of Pekuah was yet not diminished. A thousand occurrences brought her back to memory, and a thousand wants, which nothing but the confidence of friendship can supply, made her frequently regretted. She, therefore, solicited Imlac never to desist from enquiry, and to leave no art of intelligence untried, that, at least, she might have the comfort of knowing that she did not suffer by negligence or sluggishness. "Yet what, said she, is to be expected from our persuit of happiness, when we find the state of life to be such, that happiness itself is the cause of misery? Why should we endeavour to attain that, of which the possession cannot be secured? I shall henceforward fear to yield my heart to excellence, however bright, or to fondness, however tender, lest I should lose again what I have lost in Pekuah."

CHAPTER XXXVII

The princess hears news of Pekuah.

IN seven months, one of the messengers, who had been sent away upon the day when the promise was drawn from the princess, returned, after many unsuccessful rambles, from the borders of

Nubia, with an account that Pekuah was in the hands of an Arab chief, who possessed a castle or fortress on the extremity of Egypt. The Arab, whose revenue was plunder, was willing to restore her, with her two attendants, for two hundred ounces of gold.

The price was no subject of debate. The princess was in extasies when she heard that her favourite was alive, and might so cheaply be ransomed. She could not think of delaying for a moment Pekuah's happiness or her own, but entreated her brother to send back the messenger with the sum required. Imlac, being consulted, was not very confident of the veracity of the relator, and was still more doubtful of the Arab's faith, who might, if he were too liberally trusted, detain at once the money and the captives. He thought it dangerous to put themselves in the power of the Arab, by going into his district, and could not expect that the Rover would so much expose himself as to come into the lower country, where he might be seized by the forces of the Bassa.

It is difficult to negotiate where neither will trust. But Imlac, after some deliberation, directed the messenger to propose that Pekuah should be conducted by ten horsemen to the monastry of St. Anthony, which is situated in the deserts of Upper Egypt, where she should be met by the same number, and her ransome should be paid.

That no time might be lost, as they expected that the proposal would not be refused, they immediately began their journey to the monastry; and, when they arrived, Imlac went forward with the former messenger to the Arab's fortress. Rasselas was desirous to go with them, but neither his sister nor Imlac would consent. The Arab, according to the custom of his nation, observed the laws of hospitality with great exactness to those who put themselves into his power, and, in a few days, brought Pekuah with her maids, by easy journeys, to the place appointed, where receiving the stipulated price, he restored her with great respect to liberty and her friends, and undertook to conduct them back towards Cairo beyond all danger of robbery or violence.

The princess and her favourite embraced each other with transport too violent to be expressed, and went out together to pour the tears of tenderness in secret, and exchange professions of kindness and gratitude. After a few hours they returned into the refectory of the convent, where, in the presence of the prior and his brethren, the prince required of Pekuah the history of her adventures.

CHAPTER XXXVIII

The adventures of the lady Pekuah.

"At what time, and in what manner, I was forced away, said Pekuah, your servants have told you. The suddenness of the event struck me with surprise, and I was at first rather stupified than agitated with any passion of either fear or sorrow. My confusion was encreased by the speed and tumult of our flight while we were followed by the Turks, who, as it seemed, soon despaired to overtake us, or were afraid of those whom they made a shew of menacing.

"When the Arabs saw themselves out of danger they slackened their course, and as I was less harassed by external violence, I began to feel more uneasiness in my mind. After some time we stopped near a spring shaded with trees in a pleasant meadow, where we were set upon the ground, and offered such refreshments as our masters were partaking. I was suffered to sit with my maids apart from the rest, and none attempted to comfort or insult us. Here I first began to feel the full weight of my misery. The girls sat weeping in silence, and from time to time looked on me for succour. I knew not to what condition we were doomed, nor could conjecture where would be the place of our captivity, or whence to draw any hope of deliverance. I was in the hands of robbers and savages, and had no reason to suppose that their pity was more than their justice, or that they would forbear the gratification of any ardour of desire, or caprice of cruelty. I, however, kissed my maids, and endeavoured to pacify them by remarking, that we were yet treated with decency, and that, since we were now carried beyond persuit, there was no danger of violence to our lives.

"When we were to be set again on horseback, my maids clung round me, and refused to be parted, but I commanded them not to irritate those who had us in their power. We travelled the remaining part of the day through an unfrequented and pathless country, and came by moonlight to the side of a hill, where the rest of the troop was stationed. Their tents were pitched, and their fires kindled, and our chief was welcomed as a man much beloved by his dependants.

"We were received into a large tent, where we found women who
457

had attended their husbands in the expedition. They set before us the supper which they had provided, and I eat it rather to encourage my maids than to comply with any appetite of my own. When the meat was taken away they spread the carpets for repose. I was weary, and hoped to find in sleep that remission of distress which nature seldom denies. Ordering myself therefore to be undrest, I observed that the women looked very earnestly upon me, not expecting, I suppose, to see me so submissively attended. When my upper vest was taken off, they were apparently struck with the splendour of my cloaths, and one of them timorously laid her hand upon the embroidery. She then went out, and, in a short time, came back with another woman, who seemed to be of higher rank, and greater authority. She did, at her entrance, the usual act of reverence, and, taking me by the hand, placed me in a smaller tent, spread with finer carpets, where I spent the night quietly with my maids.

"In the morning, as I was sitting on the grass, the chief of the troop came towards me. I rose up to receive him, and he bowed with great respect. "Illustrious lady, said he, my fortune is better than I had presumed to hope; I am told by my women, that I have a princess in my camp." Sir, answered I, your women, have deceived themselves and you; I am not a princess, but an unhappy stranger who intended soon to have left this country, in which I am now to be imprisoned for ever. "Whoever, or whencesoever, you are, returned the Arab, your dress, and that of your servants, show your rank to be high, and your wealth to be great. Why should you, who can so easily procure your ransome, think yourself in danger of perpetual captivity? The purpose of my incursions is to encrease my riches, or more properly to gather tribute. The sons of Ishmael are the natural and hereditary lords of this part of the continent, which is usurped by late invaders, and low-born tyrants, from whom we are compelled to take by the sword what is denied to justice. The violence of war admits no distinction; the lance that is lifted at guilt and power will sometimes fall on innocence and gentleness."

"How little, said I, did I expect that yesterday it should have fallen upon me."

"Misfortunes, answered the Arab, should always be expected. If the eye of hostility could learn reverence or pity, excellence like yours had been exempt from injury. But the angels of affliction spread their toils alike for the virtuous and the wicked, for the mighty and the mean. Do not be disconsolate; I am not one of the lawless and cruel rovers of the desart; I know the rules of civil life: I will fix your ransome, give a pasport to your messenger, and perform my stipulation with nice punctuality."

"You will easily believe that I was pleased with his courtesy; and finding that his predominant passion was desire of money, I began now to think my danger less, for I knew that no sum would be thought too great for the release of Pekuah. I told him that he should have no reason to charge me with ingratitude, if I was used with kindness, and that any ransome, which could be expected for a maid of common rank, would be paid, but that he must not persist to rate me as a princess. He said, he would consider what he should demand, and then, smiling, bowed and retired.

"Soon after the women came about me, each contending to be more officious than the other, and my maids themselves were served with reverence. We travelled onward by short journeys. On the fourth day the chief told me, that my ransome must be two hundred ounces of gold, which I not only promised him, but told him, that I would add fifty more, if I and my maids were honourably treated.

"I never knew the power of gold before. From that time I was the leader of the troop. The march of every day was longer or shorter as I commanded, and the tents were pitched where I chose to rest. We now had camels and other conveniencies for travel, my own women were always at my side, and I amused myself with observing the manners of the vagrant nations, and with viewing remains of ancient edifices with which these deserted countries appear to have been, in some distant age, lavishly embellished.

"The chief of the band was a man far from illiterate: he was able to travel by the stars or the compass, and had marked in his erratick expeditions such places as are most worthy the notice of a passenger. He observed to me, that buildings are always best preserved in places little frequented, and difficult of access: for, when once a country declines from its primitive splendour, the more inhabitants are left, the quicker ruin will be made. Walls supply stones more easily than quarries, and palaces and temples will be demolished to make stables of granate, and cottages of porphyry.

CHAPTER XXXIX

The adventures of Pekuah continued.

"WE wandered about in this manner for some weeks, whether, as our chief pretended, for my gratification, or, as I rather suspected, for some convenience of his own. I endeavoured to appear contented where sullenness and resentment would have been of no use, and that endeavour conduced much to the calmness of my mind; but my heart was always with Nekayah, and the troubles of the night much overbalanced the amusements of the day. My women, who threw all their cares upon their mistress, set their minds at ease from the time when they saw me treated with respect, and gave themselves up to the incidental alleviations of our fatigue without solicitude or sorrow. I was pleased with their pleasure, and animated with their confidence. My condition had lost much of its terrour, since I found that the Arab ranged the country merely to get riches. Avarice is an uniform and tractable vice: other intellectual distempers are different in different constitutions of mind; that which sooths the pride of one will offend the pride of another; but to the favour of the covetous there is a ready way, bring money and nothing is denied.

"At last we came to the dwelling of our chief, a strong and spacious house built with stone in an island of the Nile, which lies, as I was told under the tropick. "Lady, said the Arab, you shall rest after your journey a few weeks in this place, where you are to consider yourself as sovereign. My occupation is war: I have therefore chosen this obscure residence, from which I can issue unexpected, and to which I can retire unpersued. You may now repose in security: here are few pleasures, but here is no danger." He then led me into the inner apartments, and seating me on the richest couch, bowed to the ground. His women, who considered me as a rival, looked at me with malignity; but being soon informed that I was a great lady detained only for my ransome, they began to vie with each other in obsequiousness and reverence.

"Being again comforted with new assurances of speedy liberty, I was for some days diverted from patience by the novelty of the place. The turrets overlooked the country to a great distance, and afforded a view of many windings of the stream. In the day I wandered from one place to another as the course of the sun varied the

460

splendour of the prospect, and saw many things which I had never seen before. The crocodiles and river-horses are common in this unpeopled region, and I often looked upon them with terrour, though I knew that they could not hurt me. For some time I expected to see mermaids and tritons, which, as Imlac has told me, the European travellers have stationed in the Nile, but no such beings ever appeared, and the Arab, when I enquired after them, laughed at my credulity.

"At night the Arab always attended me to a tower set apart for celestial observations, where he endeavoured to teach me the names and courses of the stars. I had no great inclination to this study, but an appearance of attention was necessary to please my instructor, who valued himself for his skill, and, in a little while, I found some employment requisite to beguile the tediousness of time, which was to be passed always amidst the same objects. I was weary of looking in the morning on things from which I had turned away weary in the evening: I therefore was at last willing to observe the stars rather than do nothing, but could not always compose my thoughts, and was very often thinking on Nekayah when others imagined me contemplating the sky. Soon after the Arab went upon another expedition, and then my only pleasure was to talk with my maids about the accident by which we were carried away, and the happiness that we should all enjoy at the end of our captivity."

"There were women in your Arab's fortress, said the princess, why did you not make them your companions, enjoy their conversation, and partake their diversions? In a place where they found business or amusement why should you alone sit corroded with idle melancholy? or why could not you bear for a few months that condition to which they were condemned for life?"

"The diversions of the women, answered Pekuah, were only childish play, by which the mind accustomed to stronger operations could not be kept busy. I could do all which they delighted in doing by powers merely sensitive, while my intellectual faculties were flown to Cairo. They ran from room to room as a bird hops from wire to wire in his cage. They danced for the sake of motion, as lambs frisk in a meadow. One sometimes pretended to be hurt that the rest might be alarmed, or hid herself that another might seek her. Part of their time passed in watching the progress of light bodies that floated on the river, and part in marking the various forms into which clouds broke in the sky.

"Their business was only needlework, in which I and my maids sometimes helped them; but you know that the mind will easily straggle from the fingers, nor will you suspect that captivity and absence from Nekayah could receive solace from silken flowers.

"Nor was much satisfaction to be hoped from their conversation: for of what could they be expected to talk? They had seen nothing; for they had lived from early youth in that narrow spot: of what they had not seen they could have no knowledge, for they could not read. They had no ideas but of the few things that were within their view, and had hardly names for any thing but their cloaths and their food. As I bore a superiour character, I was often called to terminate their quarrels, which I decided as equitably as I could. If it could have amused me to hear the complaints of each against the rest, I might have been often detained by long stories, but the motives of their animosity were so small that I could not listen without intercepting the tale."

"How, said Rasselas, can the Arab, whom you represented as a man of more than common accomplishments, take any pleasure in his seraglio when it is filled only with women like these? Are they exquisitely beautiful?"

"They do not, said Pekuah, want that unaffecting and ignoble beauty which may subsist without spriteliness or sublimity, without energy of thought or dignity of virtue. But to a man like the Arab such beauty was only a flower casually plucked and carelessly thrown away. Whatever pleasures he might find among them, they were not those of friendship or society. When they were playing about him he looked on them with inattentive superiority: when they vied for his regard he sometimes turned away disgusted. As they had no knowledge, their talk could take nothing from the tediousness of life: as they had no choice, their fondness, or appearance of fondness, excited in him neither pride nor gratitude; he was not exalted in his own esteem by the smiles of a woman who saw no other man, nor was much obliged by that regard, of which he could never know the sincerity, and which he might often perceive to be exerted not so much to delight him as to pain a rival. That which he gave, and they received, as love, was only a careless distribution of superfluous time, such love as man can bestow upon

462

that which he despises, such as has neither hope or fear, neither joy nor sorrow."

"You have reason, lady, to think yourself happy, said Imlac. that you have been thus easily dismissed. How could a mind, hungry for knowledge, be willing, in an intellectual famine, to lose such a banquet as Pekuah's conversation?"

"I am inclined to believe, answered Pekuah, that he was for some time in suspense; for, notwithstanding his promise, whenever I proposed to dispatch a messenger to Cairo, he found some excuse for delay. While I was detained in his house he made many incursions into the neighbouring countries, and, perhaps, he would have refused to discharge me, had his plunder been equal to his wishes. He returned always courteous, related his adventures, delighted to hear my observations, and endeavoured to advance my acquaintance with the stars. When I importuned him to send away my letters, he soothed me with professions of honour and sincerity; and, when I could be no longer decently denied, put his troop again in motion, and left me to govern in his absence. I was much afflicted by this studied procrastination, and was sometimes afraid that I should be forgotten; that you would leave Cairo, and I must end my days in an island of the Nile.

"I grew at last hopeless and dejected, and cared so little to entertain him, that he for a while more frequently talked with my maids. That he should fall in love with them, or with me, might have been equally fatal, and I was not much pleased with the growing friendship. My anxiety was not long; for, as I recovered some degree of chearfulness, he returned to me, and I could not forbear to despise my former uneasiness.

"He still delayed to send for my ransome, and would, perhaps, never have determined, had not your agent found his way to him. The gold, which he would not fetch, he could not reject when it was offered. He hastened to prepare for our journey hither, like a man delivered from the pain of an intestine conflict. I took leave of my companions in the house, who dismissed me with cold indifference."

Nekayah, having heard her favourite's relation, rose and embraced her, and Rasselas gave her an hundred ounces of gold, which she presented to the Arab for the fifty that were promised.

CHAPTER XL

The history of a man of learning.

THEY returned to Cairo, and were so well pleased at finding themselves together, that none of them went much abroad. The prince began to love learning, and one day declared to Imlac, that he intended to devote himself to science, and pass the rest of his days in literary solitude.

"Before you make your final choice, answered Imlac, you ought to examine its hazards, and converse with some of those who are grown old in the company of themselves. I have just left the observatory of one of the most learned astronomers in the world, who has spent forty years in unwearied attention to the motions and appearances of the celestial bodies, and has drawn out his soul in endless calculations. He admits a few friends once a month to hear his deductions and enjoy his discoveries. I was introduced as a man of knowledge worthy of his notice. Men of various ideas and fluent conversation are commonly welcome to those whose thoughts have been long fixed upon a single point, and who find the images of other things stealing away. I delighted him with my remarks, he smiled at the narrative of my travels, and was glad to forget the constellations, and descend for a moment into the lower world.

"On the next day of vacation I renewed my visit, and was so fortunate as to please him again. He relaxed from that time the severity of his rule, and permitted me to enter at my own choice. I found him always busy, and always glad to be relieved. As each knew much which the other was desirous of learning, we exchanged our notions with great delight. I perceived that I had every day more of his confidence, and always found new cause of admiration in the profundity of his mind. His comprehension is vast, his memory capacious and retentive, his discourse is methodical, and his expression clear.

"His integrity and benevolence are equal to his learning. His deepest researches and most favourite studies are willingly interrupted for any opportunity of doing good by his counsel or his riches. To his closest retreat, at his most busy moments, all are admitted that want his assistance: "For though I exclude idleness and pleasure, I will never, says he, bar my doors against charity.

To man is permitted the contemplation of the skies, but the practice of virtue is commanded."

"Surely, said the princess, this man is happy."

"I visited him, said Imlac, with more and more frequency, and was every time more enamoured of his conversation: he was sublime without haughtiness, courteous without formality, and communicative without ostentation. I was at first, great princess, of your opinion, thought him the happiest of mankind, and often congratulated him on the blessing that he enjoyed. He seemed to hear nothing with indifference but the praises of his condition, to which he always returned a general answer, and diverted the conversation to some other topic.

"Amidst this willingness to be pleased, and labour to please, I had quickly reason to imagine that some painful sentiment pressed upon his mind. He often looked up earnestly towards the sun, and let his voice fall in the midst of his discourse. He would sometimes, when we were alone, gaze upon me in silence with the air of a man who longed to speak what he was yet resolved to suppress. He would often send for me with vehement injunctions of haste, though, when I came to him, he had nothing extraordinary to say. And sometimes, when I was leaving him, would call me back, pause a few moments and then dismiss me.

CHAPTER XLI

The astronomer discovers the cause of his uneasiness.

"At last the time came when the secret burst his reserve. We were sitting together last night in the turret of his house, watching the emersion of a satellite of Jupiter. A sudden tempest clouded the sky, and disappointed our observation. We sat a while silent in the dark, and then he addressed himself to me in these words: "Imlac, I have long considered thy friendship as the greatest blessing of my life. Integrity without knowledge is weak and useless, and knowledge without integrity is dangerous and dreadful. I have found in thee all the qualities requisite for trust, benevolence, experience, and fortitude. I have long discharged an office which I must soon quit at the call of nature, and shall rejoice in the hour of imbecility and pain to devolve it upon thee."

"I thought myself honoured by this testimony, and protested

that whatever could conduce to his happiness would add likewise to mine."

"Hear, Imlac, what thou wilt not without difficulty credit. I have possessed for five years the regulation of the weather, and the distribution of the seasons: the sun has listened to my dictates, and passed from tropick to tropick by my direction; the clouds, at my call, have poured their waters, and the Nile has overflowed at my command; I have restrained the rage of the dog-star, and mitigated the fervours of the crab. The winds alone, of all the elemental powers, have hitherto refused my authority, and multitudes have perished by equinoctial tempests which I found myself unable to prohibit or restrain. I have administered this great office with exact justice, and made to the different nations of the earth an impartial dividend of rain and sunshine. What must have been the misery of half the globe, if I had limited the clouds to particular regions, or confined the sun to either side of the equator?"

CHAPTER XLII

The opinion of the astronomer is explained and justified.

"I SUPPOSE he discovered in me, through the obscurity of the room, some tokens of amazement and doubt, for, after a short pause, he proceeded thus:

"Not to be easily credited will neither surprise nor offend me; for I am, probably, the first of human beings to whom this trust has been imparted. Nor do I know whether to deem this distinction a reward or punishment; since I have possessed it I have been far less happy than before, and nothing but the consciousness of good intention could have enabled me to support the weariness of unremitted vigilance."

"How long, sir, said I, has this great office been in your hands?"

"About ten years ago, said he, my daily observations of the changes of the sky led me to consider, whether, if I had the power of the seasons, I could confer greater plenty upon the inhabitants of the earth. This contemplation fastened on my mind, and I sat days and nights in imaginary dominion, pouring upon this country and that the showers of fertility, and seconding every fall of rain with a due proportion of sunshine. I had yet only the will to do good, and did not imagine that I should ever have the power.

"One day as I was looking on the fields withering with heat, I felt in my mind a sudden wish that I could send rain on the southern mountains, and raise the Nile to an inundation. In the hurry of my imagination I commanded rain to fall, and, by comparing the time of my command, with that of the inundation, I found that the clouds had listned to my lips."

"Might not some other cause, said I, produce this concurrence? the Nile does not always rise on the same day."

"Do not believe, said he with impatience, that such objections could escape me: I reasoned long against my own conviction, and laboured against truth with the utmost obstinacy. I sometimes suspected myself of madness, and should not have dared to impart this secret but to a man like you, capable of distinguishing the wonderful from the impossible, and the incredible from the false."

"Why, sir, said I, do you call that incredible, which you know, or think you know, to be true?"

"Because, said he, I cannot prove it by any external evidence; and I know too well the laws of demonstration to think that my conviction ought to influence another, who cannot, like me, be conscious of its force. I, therefore, shall not attempt to gain credit by disputation. It is sufficient that I feel this power, that I have long possessed, and every day exerted it. But the life of man is short, the infirmities of age increase upon me, and the time will soon come when the regulator of the year must mingle with the dust. The care of appointing a successor has long disturbed me; the night and the day have been spent in comparisons of all the characters which have come to my knowledge, and I have yet found none so worthy as thyself.

CHAPTER XLIII

The astronomer leaves Imlac his directions.

"Hear therefore, what I shall impart, with attention, such as the welfare of a world requires. If the task of a king be considered as difficult, who has the care only of a few millions, to whom he cannot do much good or harm, what must be the anxiety of him, on whom depends the action of the elements, and the great gifts of light and heat!—Hear me therefore with attention.

"I have diligently considered the position of the earth and sun, and formed innumerable schemes in which I changed their situation. I have sometimes turned aside the axis of the earth, and sometimes varied the ecliptick of the sun: but I have found it impossible to make a disposition by which the world may be advantaged; what one region gains, another loses by any imaginable alteration, even without considering the distant parts of the solar system with which we are unacquainted. Do not, therefore, in thy administration of the year, indulge thy pride by innovation; do not please thyself with thinking that thou canst make thyself renowned to all future ages, by disordering the seasons. The memory of mischief is no desirable fame. Much less will it become thee to let kindness, or interest prevail. Never rob other countries of rain to pour it on thine own. For us the Nile is sufficient."

"I promised that when I possessed the power, I would use it with inflexible integrity, and he dismissed me, pressing my hand."

"My heart, said he, will be now at rest, and my benevolence will no more destroy my quiet: I have found a man of wisdom and virtue, to whom I can chearfully bequeath the inheritance of the sun."

The prince heard this narration with very serious regard, but the princess smiled, and Pekuah convulsed herself with laughter. "Ladies, said Imlac, to mock the heaviest of human affliction is neither charitable nor wise. Few can attain this man's knowledge, and few practise his virtues; but all may suffer his calamity. Of the uncertainties of our present state, the most dreadful and alarming is the uncertain continuance of reason."

The princess was recollected, and the favourite was abashed. Rasselas, more deeply affected, inquired of Imlac, whether he thought such maladies of the mind frequent, and how they were contracted.

CHAPTER XLIV

The dangerous prevalence of imagination.

"DISORDERS of intellect, answered Imlac, happen much more often than superficial observers will easily believe. Perhaps, if we speak with rigorous exactness, no human mind is in its right state. There is no man whose imagination does not sometimes predominate over his reason, who can regulate his attention wholly by his will, and whose ideas will come and go at his command. No man will be found in whose mind airy notions do not sometimes tyrannise, and force him to hope or fear beyond the limits of sober probability. All power of fancy over reason is a degree of insanity; but while this power is such as we can controul and repress, it is not visible to others, nor considered as any depravation of the mental faculties: it is not pronounced madness but when it becomes ungovernable, and apparently influences speech or action.

"To indulge the power of fiction, and send imagination out upon the wing, is often the sport of those who delight too much in silent speculation. When we are alone we are not always busy; the labour of excogitation is too violent to last long; the ardour of enquiry will sometimes give way to idleness or satiety. He who has nothing external that can divert him, must find pleasure in his own thoughts, and must conceive himself what he is not; for who is pleased with what he is? He then expatiates in boundless futurity, and culls from all imaginable conditions that which for the present moment he should most desire, amuses his desires with impossible enjoyments, and confers upon his pride unattainable dominion. The mind dances from scene to scene, unites all pleasures in all combinations, and riots in delights which nature and fortune, with all their bounty cannot bestow.

"In time some particular train of ideas fixes the attention, all other intellectual gratifications are rejected, the mind, in weariness or leisure, recurs constantly to the favourite conception, and feasts on the luscious falsehood whenever she is offended with the bitterness of truth. By degrees the reign of fancy is confirmed; she grows first imperious, and in time despotick. Then fictions begin to operate as realities, false opinions fasten upon the mind, and life passes in dreams of rapture or of anguish.

"This, Sir, is one of the dangers of solitude, which the hermit has confessed not always to promote goodness, and the astronomer's misery has proved to be not always propitious to wisdom."

"I will no more, said the favourite, imagine myself the queen of Abissinia. I have often spent the hours, which the princess gave to my own disposal, in adjusting ceremonies and regulating the court; I have repressed the pride of the powerful, and granted the petitions of the poor; I have built new palaces in more happy situations, planted groves upon the tops of mountains, and have exulted in the beneficence of royalty, till, when the princess entered, I had almost forgotten to bow down before her."

"And I, said the princess, will not allow myself any more to play the shepherdess in my waking dreams. I have often soothed my thoughts with the quiet and innocence of pastoral employments, till I have in my chamber heard the winds whistle, and the sheep bleat; sometimes freed the lamb entangled in the thicket, and sometimes with my crook encountered the wolf. I have a dress like that of the village maids, which I put on to help my imagination, and a pipe on which I play softly, and suppose myself followed by my flocks."

"I will confess, said the prince, an indulgence of fantastick delight more dangerous than yours. I have frequently endeavoured to image the possibility of a perfect government, by which all wrong should be restrained, all vice reformed, and all the subjects preserved in tranquility and innocence. This thought produced innumerable schemes of reformation, and dictated many useful regulations and salutary edicts. This has been the sport and sometimes the labour of my solitude; and I start, when I think with how little anguish I once supposed the death of my father and my brothers."

"Such, says Imlac, are the effects of visionary schemes: when we first form them we know them to be absurd, but familiarise them by degrees, and in time lose sight of their folly."

CHAPTER XLV

They discourse with an old man.

THE evening was now far past, and they rose to return home. As they walked along the bank of the Nile, delighted with the beams of the moon quivering on the water, they saw at a small distance an old man, whom the prince had often heard in the assembly of the sages. "Yonder, said he, is one whose years have calmed his passions, but not clouded his reason: let us close the disquisitions of the night, by enquiring what are his sentiments of his own state, that we may know whether youth alone is to struggle with vexation, and whether any better hope remains for the latter part of life."

Here the sage approached and saluted them. They invited him to join their walk, and prattled a while as acquaintance that had unexpectedly met one another. The old man was chearful and talkative, and the way seemed short in his company. He was pleased to find himself not disregarded, accompanied them to their house, and, at the prince's request, entered with them. They placed him in the seat of honour, and set wine and conserves before him.

"Sir, said the princess, an evening walk must give to a man of learning, like you, pleasures which ignorance and youth can hardly conceive. You know the qualities and the causes of all that you behold, the laws by which the river flows, the periods in which the planets perform their revolutions. Every thing must supply you with contemplation, and renew the consciousness of your own dignity."

"Lady, answered he, let the gay and the vigorous expect pleasure in their excursions, it is enough that age can obtain ease. To me the world has lost its novelty: I look round, and see what I remember to have seen in happier days. I rest against a tree, and consider, that in the same shade I once disputed upon the annual overflow of the Nile with a friend who is now silent in the grave. I cast my eyes upwards, fix them on the changing moon, and think with pain on the vicissitudes of life. I have ceased to take much delight in physical truth; for what have I to do with those things which I am soon to leave?"

"You may at least recreate yourself, said Imlac, with the recollection of an honourable and useful life, and enjoy the praise which all agree to give you."

"Praise, said the sage, with a sigh, is to an old man an empty sound. I have neither mother to be delighted with the reputation of her son, nor wife to partake the honours of her husband. I have outlived my friends and my rivals. Nothing is now of much importance; for I cannot extend my interest beyond myself. Youth is delighted with applause, because it is considered as the earnest of some future good, and because the prospect of life is far extended: but to me, who am now declining to decrepitude, there is little to be feared from the malevolence of men, and yet less to be hoped from their affection or esteem. Something they may yet take away, but they can give me nothing. Riches would now be useless, and high employment would be pain. My retrospect of life recalls to my view many opportunities of good neglected, much time squandered upon trifles, and more lost in idleness and vacancy. I leave many great designs unattempted, and many great attempts unfinished. My mind is burthened with no heavy crime, and therefore

I compose myself to tranquility; endeavour to abstract my thoughts from hopes and cares, which, though reason knows them to be vain, still try to keep their old possession of the heart; expect, with serene humility, that hour which nature cannot long delay; and hope to possess in a better state that happiness which here I could not find, and that virtue which here I have not attained."

He rose and went away, leaving his audience not much elated with the hope of long life. The prince consoled himself with remarking, that it was not reasonable to be disappointed by this account; for age had never been considered as the season of felicity, and, if it was possible to be easy in decline and weakness, it was likely that the days of vigour and alacrity might be happy: that the noon of life might be bright, if the evening could be calm.

The princess suspected that age was querulous and malignant, and delighted to repress the expectations of those who had newly entered the world. She had seen the possessors of estates look with envy on their heirs, and known many who enjoyed pleasure no longer than they can confine it to themselves.

Pekuah conjectured, that the man was older than he appeared, and was willing to impute his complaints to delirious dejection; or else supposed that he had been unfortunate, and was therefore discontented: "For nothing, said she, is more common than to call our own condition, the condition of life."

Imlac, who had no desire to see them depressed, smiled at the comforts which they could so readily procure to themselves, and remembered, that at the same age, he was equally confident of unmingled prosperity, and equally fertile of consolatory expedients. He forbore to force upon them unwelcome knowledge, which time itself would soon impress. The princess and her lady retired; the madness of the astronomer hung upon their minds, and they desired Imlac to enter upon his office, and delay next morning the rising of the sun.

CHAPTER XLVI

The princess and Pekuah visit the astronomer.

THE princess and Pekuah having talked in private of Imlac's astronomer, thought his character at once so amiable and so strange, that they could not be satisfied without a nearer knowledge, and Imlac was requested to find the means of bringing them together.

This was somewhat difficult; the philosopher had never received any visits from women, though he lived in a city that had in it many Europeans who followed the manners of their own countries, and many from other parts of the world that lived there with European liberty. The ladies would not be refused, and several schemes were proposed for the accomplishment of their design. It was proposed to introduce them as strangers in distress, to whom the sage was always accessible; but, after some deliberation, it appeared, that by this artifice no acquaintance could be formed, for their conversation would be short, and they could not decently importune him often. "This, said Rasselas, is true; but I have yet a stronger objection against the misrepresentation of your state. I have always considered it as treason against the great republick of human nature, to make any man's virtues the means of deceiving him, whether on great or little occasions. All imposture weakens confidence and chills benevolence. When the sage finds that you are not what you seemed, he will feel the resentment natural to a man who, conscious of great abilities, discovers that he has been tricked by understandings meaner than his own, and, perhaps, the distrust, which he can never afterwards wholly lay aside, may stop the voice of counsel, and close the hand of charity; and where will you find the power of restoring his benefactions to mankind, or his peace to himself?"

To this no reply was attempted, and Imlac began to hope that their curiosity would subside; but, next day, Pekuah told him, she had now found an honest pretence for a visit to the astronomer, for she would solicite permission to continue under him the studies in which she had been initiated by the Arab, and the princess might go with her either as a fellow-student, or because a woman could not decently come alone. "I am afraid, said Imlac, that he will soon be weary of your company: men advanced far in knowledge do not love to repeat the elements of their art, and I am not certain that even of the elements, as he will deliver them connected with inferences, and mingled with reflections, you are a very capable auditress." "That, said Pekuah, must be my care: I ask of you only to take me thither. My knowledge is, perhaps, more than you imagine it, and by concurring always with his opinions I shall make him think it greater than it is."

The astronomer, in pursuance of this resolution, was told, that a foreign lady, travelling in search of knowledge, had heard of his reputation, and was desirous to become his scholar. The uncommonness of the proposal raised at once his surprize and curiosity, and when, after a short deliberation, he consented to admit her, he could not stay without impatience till the next day.

The ladies dressed themselves magnificently, and were attended by Imlac to the astronomer, who was pleased to see himself approached with respect by persons of so splendid an appearance. In the exchange of the first civilities he was timorous and bashful; but when the talk became regular, he recollected his powers, and justified the character which Imlac had given. Enquiring of Pekuah what could have turned her inclination towards astronomy, he received from her a history of her adventure at the pyramid, and of the time passed in the Arab's island. She told her tale with ease and elegance, and her conversation took possession of his heart. The discourse was then turned to astronomy: Pekuah displayed what she knew: he looked upon her as a prodigy of genius, and intreated her not to desist from a study which she had so happily begun.

They came again and again, and were every time more welcome than before. The sage endeavoured to amuse them, that they might prolong their visits, for he found his thoughts grow brighter in their company; the clouds of solicitude vanished by degrees, as he forced himself to entertain them, and he grieved when he was left at their departure to his old employment of regulating the seasons.

The princess and her favourite had now watched his lips for several months, and could not catch a single word from which they could judge whether he continued, or not, in the opinion of his preternatural commission. They often contrived to bring him to an open declaration, but he easily eluded all their attacks, and on which side soever they pressed him escaped from them to some other topick.

As their familiarity increased they invited him often to the house of Imlac, where they distinguished him by extraordinary respect. He began gradually to delight in sublunary pleasures. He came early and departed late; laboured to recommend himself by assiduity and compliance; excited their curiosity after new arts, that they might still want his assistance; and when they made any excursion of pleasure or enquiry, entreated to attend them.

By long experience of his integrity and wisdom, the prince and his sister were convinced that he might be trusted without danger; and lest he should draw any false hopes from the civilities which he received, discovered to him their condition, with the motives of their journey, and required his opinion on the choice of life.

"Of the various conditions which the world spreads before you, which you shall prefer, said the sage, I am not able to instruct you. I can only tell that I have chosen wrong. I have passed my time in study without experience; in the attainment of sciences which can, for the most part, be but remotely useful to mankind. I have purchased knowledge at the expence of all the common comforts of life: I have missed the endearing elegance of female friendship, and the happy commerce of domestick tenderness. If I have obtained any prerogatives above other students, they have been accompanied with fear, disquiet, and scrupulosity; but even of these prerogatives, whatever they were, I have, since my thoughts have been diversified by more intercourse with the world, begun to question the reality. When I have been for a few days lost in pleasing dissipation, I am always tempted to think that my enquiries have ended in errour, and that I have suffered much, and suffered it in vain."

Imlac was delighted to find that the sage's understanding was breaking through its mists, and resolved to detain him from the planets till he should forget his task of ruling them, and reason should recover its original influence.

From this time the astronomer was received into familiar friendship, and partook of all their projects and pleasures: his respect kept him attentive, and the activity of Rasselas did not leave much time unengaged. Something was always to be done; the day was spent in making observations which furnished talk for the evening, and the evening was closed with a scheme for the morrow.

The sage confessed to Imlac that since he had mingled in the gay tumults of life, and divided his hours by a succession of amusements, he found the conviction of his authority over the skies fade gradually from his mind, and began to trust less to an opinion which he never could prove to others, and which he now found subject to variation from causes in which reason had no part. "If I am accidentally left alone for a few hours, said he, my inveterate persuasion rushes upon my soul, and my thoughts are chained down by some irresistible violence, but they are soon disentangled by the prince's conversation, and instantaneously released at the entrance of Pekuah. I am like a man habitually afraid of spectres, who is set at ease by a lamp, and wonders at the dread which harassed him in the dark, yet, if his lamp be extinguished, feels again the terrours which he knows that when it is light he shall feel no more. But I am sometimes afraid lest I indulge my quiet by criminal negligence, and voluntarily forget the great charge with which I am instructed. If I favour myself in a known errour, or am determined by my own ease in a doubtful question of this importance, how dreadful is my crime!"

"No disease of the imagination, answered Imlac, is so difficult of cure, as that which is complicated with the dread of guilt: fancy and conscience then act interchangeably upon us, and so often shift their places, that the illusions of one are not distinguished from the dictates of the other. If fancy presents images not moral or religious, the mind drives them away when they give it pain, but when melancholick notions take the form of duty, they lay hold on the faculties without opposition, because we are afraid to exclude or banish them. For this reason the superstitious are often melancholy, and the melancholy almost always superstitious.

"But do not let the suggestions of timidity overpower your better reason: the danger of neglect can be but as the probability of the obligation, which when you consider it with freedom, you find very little, and that little growing every day less. Open your heart to the influence of the light, which, from time to time, breaks in upon you: when scruples importune you, which you in your lucid moments know to be vain, do not stand to parley, but fly to business or to Pekuah, and keep this thought always prevalent, that you are only one atom of the mass of humanity, and have neither such virtue nor vice, as that you should be singled out for supernatural favours or afflictions."

CHAPTER XLVII
The prince enters and brings a new topick.

"ALL this, said the astronomer, I have often thought, but my reason has been so long subjugated by an uncontrolable and overwhelming idea, that it durst not confide in its own decisions. I now see how fatally I betrayed my quiet, by suffering chimeras to prey upon me in secret; but melancholy shrinks from communication, and I never found a man before, to whom I could impart my troubles, though I had been certain of relief. I rejoice to find my own sentiments confirmed by yours, who are not easily deceived, and can have no motive or purpose to deceive. I hope that time and variety will dissipate the gloom that has so long surrounded me, and the latter part of my days will be spent in peace."

"Your learning and virtue, said Imlac, may justly give you hopes."

Rasselas then entered with the princess and Pekuah, and enquired whether they had contrived any new diversion for the next day. "Such, said Nekayah, is the state of life, that none are happy but by the anticipation of change: the change itself is nothing; when we have made it, the next wish is to change again. The world is not yet exhausted; let me see something to morrow which I never saw before."

"Variety, said Rasselas, is so necessary to content, that even the happy valley disgusted me by the recurrence of its luxuries; yet I could not forbear to reproach myself with impatience, when I saw the monks of St. Anthony support, without complaint, a life, not of uniform delight, but uniform hardship."

"Those men, answered Imlac, are less wretched in their silent convent than the Abissinian princes in their prison of pleasure. Whatever is done by the monks is incited by an adequate and reasonable motive. Their labour supplies them with necessaries; it therefore cannot be omitted and is certainly rewarded. Their devotion prepares them for another state, and reminds them of its approach, while it fits them for it. Their time is regularly distributed; one duty succeeds another, so that they are not left open to the distraction of unguided choice, nor lost in the shades of listless inactivity. There is a certain task to be performed at an appropriated hour; and their toils are cheerful, because they consider them as acts of piety, by which they are always advancing towards endless felicity."

"Do you think, said Nekayah, that the monastick rule is a more holy and less imperfect state than any other? May not he equally hope for future happiness who converses openly with mankind, who succours the distressed by his charity, instructs the ignorant by his learning, and contributes by his industry to the general system of life; even though he should omit some of the mortifications which are practised in the cloister, and allow himself such harmless delights as his condition may place within his reach?"

"This, said Imlac, is a question which has long divided the wise, and perplexed the good. I am afraid to decide on either part. He that lives well in the world is better than he that lives well in a monastery. But, perhaps, every one is not able to stem the temptations of publick life; and, if he cannot conquer, he may properly retreat. Some have little power to do good, and have likewise little strength to resist evil. Many are weary of their conflicts with adversity, and are willing to eject those passions which have long busied them in vain. And many are dismissed by age and diseases from the more laborious duties of society. In monasteries the weak and timorous may be happily sheltered, the weary may repose, and the penitent may meditate. Those retreats of prayer and contemplation have something so congenial to the mind of man, that, perhaps, there is scarcely one that does not purpose to close his life in pious abstraction with a few associates serious as himself."

"Such, said Pekuah, has often been my wish, and I have heard the princess declare, that she would not willingly die in a croud."

"The liberty of using harmless pleasures, proceeded Imlac, will not be disputed; but it is still to be examined what pleasures are harmless. The evil of any pleasure that Nekayah can image is not in the act itself, but in its consequences. Pleasure, in itself harmless, may become mischievous, by endearing to us a state which we know to be transient and probatory, and withdrawing our thoughts from that, of which every hour brings us nearer to the beginning, and of which no length of time will bring us to the end. Mortification is not virtuous in itself, nor has any other use, but that it disengages us from the allurements of sense. In the state of future perfection to which we all aspire, there will be pleasure without danger, and security without restraint."

The princess was silent, and Rasselas, turning to the astronomer, asked him, whether he could not delay her retreat, by shewing her something which she had not seen before.

"Your curiosity, said the sage, has been so general, and your pursuit of knowledge so vigorous, that novelties are not now very easily to be found; but what you can no longer procure from the living may be given by the dead. Among the wonders of this country are the catacombs, or the ancient repositories, in which the bodies of the earliest generations were lodged, and where, by the virtue of the gums which embalmed them, they yet remain without corruption."

"I know not, said Rasselas, what pleasure the sight of the catacombs can afford; but, since nothing else offered, I am resolved to view them, and shall place this with many other things which I have done, because I would do something."

They hired a guard of horsemen, and the next day visited the catacombs. When they were about to descend into the sepulchral caves, "Pekuah, said the princess, we are now again invading the habitations of the dead; I know that you will stay behind; let me find you safe when I return." "No, I will not be left, answered Pekuah; I will go down between you and the prince."

They then all descended, and roved with wonder through the labyrinth of subterraneous passages, where the bodies were laid in rows on either side.

CHAPTER XLVIII

Imlac discourses on the nature of the soul.

"WHAT reason, said the prince, can be given, why the Egyptians should thus expensively preserve those carcasses which some nations consume with fire, others lay to mingle with the earth, and all agree to remove from their sight, as soon as decent rites can be performed?"

"The original of ancient customs, said Imlac, is commonly unknown; for the practice often continues when the cause has ceased; and concerning superstitious ceremonies it is vain to conjecture; for what reason did not dictate reason cannot explain. I have long believed that the practice of embalming arose only from tenderness to the remains of relations or friends, and to this opinion I am more inclined, because it seems impossible that this care should have been general: had all the dead been embalmed, their respositories must in time have been more spacious than the dwellings of the living. I suppose only the rich or honourable were secured from corruption, and the rest left to the course of nature.

"But it is commonly supposed that the Egyptians believed the soul to live as long as the body continued undissolved, and therefore tried this method of eluding death."

"Could the wise Egyptians, said Nekayah, think so grosly of the soul? If the soul could once survive its separation, what could it afterwards receive or suffer from the body?"

"The Egyptians would doubtless think erroneously, said the astronomer, in the darkness of heathenism, and the first dawn of philosophy. The nature of the soul is still disputed amidst all our opportunities of clearer knowledge: some yet say, that it may be material, who, nevertheless, believe it to be immortal."

"Some, answered Imlac, have indeed said that the soul is material, but I can scarcely believe that any man has thought it, who knew how to think; for all the conclusions of reason enforce the immateriality of mind, and all the notices of sense and investigations of science concur to prove the unconsciousness of matter.

"It was never supposed that cogitation is inherent in matter, or that every particle is a thinking being. Yet, if any part of matter be devoid of thought, what part can we suppose to think? Matter can differ from matter only in form, density, bulk, motion, and direction of motion: to which of these, however varied or combined, can consciousness be annexed? To be round or square, to be solid or fluid, to be great or little, to be moved slowly or swiftly one way or another, are modes of material existence, all equally alien from the nature of cogitation. If matter be once without thought, it can only be made to think by some new modification, but all the modifications which it can admit are equally unconnected with cogitative powers."

"But the materialists, said the astronomer, urge that matter may have qualities with which we are unacquainted."

"He who will determine, returned Imlac, against that which he knows, because there may be something which he knows not: he that can set hypothetical possibility against acknowledged certainty, is not to be admitted among reasonable beings. All that we know of matter is, that matter is inert, senseless and lifeless; and if this conviction cannot be opposed but by referring us to something that we know not, we have all the evidence that human intellect can admit. If that which is known may be over ruled by that which is unknown, no being, not omniscient, can arrive at certainty."

"Yet let us not, said the astronomer, too arrogantly limit the Creator's power."

"It is no limitation of omnipotence, replied the poet, to suppose that one thing is not consistent with another, that the same proposition cannot be at once true and false, that the same number cannot be even and odd, that cogitation cannot be conferred on that which is created incapable of cogitation."

"I know not, said Nekayah, any great use of this question. Does that immateriality, which, in my opinion, you have sufficiently proved, necessarily include eternal duration?"

"Of immateriality, said Imlac, our ideas are negative, and therefore obscure. Immateriality seems to imply a natural power of perpetual duration as a consequence of exemption from all causes of decay: whatever perishes is destroyed by the solution of its contexture, and separation of its parts; nor can we conceive how that which has no parts, and therefore admits no solution, can be naturally corrupted or impaired."

"I know not, said Rasselas, how to conceive any thing without extension: what is extended must have parts, and you allow, that whatever has parts may be destroyed."

"Consider your own conceptions, replied Imlac, and the difficulty will be less. You will find substance without extension. An ideal form is no less real than material bulk: yet an ideal form has no extension. It is no less certain, when you think on a pyramid, that your mind possesses the idea of a pyramid, than that the pyramid itself is standing. What space does the idea of a pyramid occupy more than the idea of a grain of corn? or how can either idea suffer laceration? As is the effect such is the cause; as thought is, such is the power that thinks; a power impassive and indiscerpible."

"But the Being, said Nekayah, whom I fear to name, the Being which made the soul, can destroy it."

"He, surely, can destroy it, answered Imlac, since, however unperishable, it receives from a superior nature its power of duration. That it will not perish by any inherent cause of decay, or principle of corruption, may be shown by philosophy; but philosophy can tell no more. That it will not be annihilated by him that made it, we must humbly learn from higher authority."

The whole assembly stood awhile silent and collected. "Let us return, said Rasselas, from this scene of mortality. How gloomy would be these mansions of the dead to him who did not know that he shall never die; that what now acts shall continue its agency, and what now thinks shall think on for ever. Those that lie here stretched before us, the wise and the powerful of antient times, warn us to remember the shortness of our present state: they were, perhaps, snatched away while they were busy, like us, in the choice of life."

"To me, said the princess, the choice of life is become less important; I hope hereafter to think only on the choice of eternity."

They then hastened out of the caverns, and, under the protection of their guard, returned to Cairo.

CHAPTER XLIX

The conclusion, in which nothing is concluded.

It was now the time of the inundation of the Nile: a few days after their visit to the catacombs, the river began to rise.

They were confined to their house. The whole region being under water gave them no invitation to any excursions, and, being well supplied with materials for talk, they diverted themselves with comparisons of the different forms of life which they had observed, and with various schemes of happiness which each of them had formed.

Pekuah was never so much charmed with any place as the convent of St Anthony, where the Arab restored her to the princess, and wished only to fill it with pious maidens, and to be made prioress of the order: she was weary of expectation and disgust, and would gladly be fixed in some unvariable state.

The princess thought, that of all sublunary things, knowledge was the best: She desired first to learn all sciences, and then purposed to found a college of learned women, in which she would preside. that, by conversing with the old, and educating the young, she might divide her time between the acquisition and communication of wisdom, and raise up for the next age models of prudence, and patterns of piety.

The prince desired a little kingdom, in which he might administer justice in his own person, and see all the parts of government with his own eyes; but he could never fix the limits of his dominion, and was always adding to the number of his subjects.

Imlac and the astronomer were contented to be driven along the stream of life without directing their course to any particular port.

Of these wishes that they had formed they well knew that none could be obtained. They deliberated a while what was to be done, and resolved, when the inundation should cease, to return to Abissinia.

FRENCH
PRISONERS OF WAR

The text of the "French Prisoners" introduction (1760)
is taken from the British Museum copy (C. 59. i. 6(2).).

INTRODUCTION

TO THE

PROCEEDINGS OF THE COMMITTEE

APPOINTED TO MANAGE THE

Contributions begun at *London, Dec. XVIII MDCCLVIIII*
for cloathing *French* Prisoners of War

THE Committee intrusted with the money contributed to the relief of the subjects of France, now prisoners in the British Dominions, here lay before the public an exact account of all the sums received and expended; that the donors may judge how properly their benefactions have been applied.

Charity would lose its name, were it influenced by so mean a motive as human praise: it is, therefore, not intended to celebrate, by any particular memorial, the liberality of single persons, or distinct societies; it is sufficient, that their works praise them.

Yet he who is far from seeking honour, may very justly obviate censure. If a good example has been set, it may lose its influence by misrepresentation; and to free charity from reproach, is itself a charitable action.

Against the relief of the French, only one argument has been brought; but that one is so popular and specious, that if it were to remain unexamined, it would by many be thought irrefragable. It has been urged, that charity, like other virtues, may be improperly and unseasonably exerted; that while we are relieving Frenchmen, there remain many Englishmen unrelieved; that while we lavish pity on our enemies, we forget the misery of our friends.

Grant this argument all it can prove, and what is the conclusion? —that to relieve the French is a good action, but that a better may be conceived. This is all the result, and this all is very little.

To do the best, can seldom be the lot of man: it is sufficient if, when opportunities are presented, he is ready to do good. How little virtue could be practised, if beneficence were to wait always for the most proper objects, and the noblest occasions; occasions that may never happen, and objects that never may be found?

It is far from certain that a single Englishman will suffer by the charity to the French. New scenes of misery make new impressions; and much of the charity which produced these donations, may be supposed to have been generated by a species of calamity never known among us before. Some imagine that the laws have provided all necessary relief in common cases, and remit the poor to the care of the public; some have been deceived by fictitious misery, and are afraid of encouraging imposture; many have observed want to be the effect of vice, and consider casual almsgivers as patrons of idleness. But all these difficulties vanish in the present case: we know that for the prisoners of war there is no legal provision; we see their distress, and are certain of its cause; we know that they are poor and naked, and poor and naked without a crime.

But it is not necessary to make any concessions. The opponents of this charity must allow it to be good, and will not easily prove it not to be the best. That charity is best, of which the consequences are most extensive: the relief of enemies has a tendency to unite mankind in fraternal affection; to soften the acrimony of adverse nations, and dispose them to peace and amity: in the mean time, it alleviates captivity, and takes away something from the miseries of war. The rage of war, however mitigated, will always fill the world with calamity and horror: let it not then be unnecessarily extended; let animosity and hostility cease together; and no man be longer deemed an enemy, than while his sword is drawn against us.

The effects of these contributions may, perhaps, reach still further. Truth is best supported by virtue: we may hope from those who feel or who see our charity, that they shall no longer detest as heresy that religion, which makes its professors the followers of HIM, who has commanded us to "do good to them that hate us."

PREFACE
TO SHAKESPEARE

AND

SELECTIONS FROM THE
NOTES ON THE PLAYS

The text of the preface and (selected) notes to Johnson's *Shakespeare* have been taken from the London University Library copy of the first edition of 1765. Some use has also been made of the British Museum copy.

The preface presents few problems. It will be seen that on p. 519 Johnson misquotes *Coriolanus* and *Macbeth*.

The preparation of a pleasant-looking text of the selection from the notes has been a more difficult task. Johnson's notes were printed in the lower parts of the page, underneath the text. He, therefore, had no need to key the notes with long quotations from the text. The quotations here have often been expanded so that the reader should be spared the labour of consulting a Shakespeare. The expansions will occasionally be found to be the same as those of Sir Walter Raleigh in his *Johnson on Shakespeare*: this is no coincidence, for his selection has often been consulted. Shakespeare references here are to the *Globe* Shakespeare (1924).

The reading "lenity" in line 3 of p. 558 is that of the first edition; later editions read "levity".

PREFACE TO SHAKESPEARE

THAT praises are without reason lavished on the dead, and that the honours due only to excellence are paid to antiquity, is a complaint likely to be always continued by those, who, being able to add nothing to truth, hope for eminence from the heresies of paradox; or those, who, being forced by disappointment upon consolatory expedients, are willing to hope from posterity what the present age refuses, and flatter themselves that the regard which is yet denied by envy, will be at last bestowed by time.

Antiquity, like every other quality that attracts the notice of mankind, has undoubtedly votaries that reverence it, not from reason, but from prejudice. Some seem to admire indiscriminately whatever has been long preserved, without considering that time has sometimes co-operated with chance; all perhaps are more willing to honour past than present excellence; and the mind contemplates genius through the shades of age, as the eye surveys the sun through artificial opacity. The great contention of criticism is to find the faults of the moderns, and the beauties of the ancients. While an authour is yet living we estimate his powers by his worst performance, and when he is dead we rate them by his best.

To works, however, of which the excellence is not absolute and definite, but gradual and comparative; to works not raised upon principles demonstrative and scientifick, but appealing wholly to observation and experience, no other test can be applied than length of duration and continuance of esteem. What mankind have long possessed they have often examined and compared, and if they persist to value the possession, it is because frequent comparisons have confirmed opinion in its favour. As among the works of nature no man can properly call a river deep or a mountain high, without the knowledge of many mountains and many rivers; so in the productions of genius, nothing can be stiled excellent till it has been compared with other works of the same kind. Demonstration immediately displays its power, and has nothing to hope or fear from the flux of years; but works tentative and experimental must be estimated by their proportion to the general and collective ability of man, as it is discovered in a long succession of endeavours. Of the first building that was raised, it might be with certainty determined that it was round or square, but whether it was spacious or lofty must have been referred to time. The Pythagorean scale of numbers was at once discovered to be perfect; but the poems of *Homer* we yet know not to transcend the common limits of human intelligence, but by remarking, that nation after nation, and century after century, has been able to do little more than transpose his incidents, new name his characters, and paraphrase his sentiments.

The reverence due to writings that have long subsisted arises therefore not from any credulous confidence in the superior wisdom of past ages, or gloomy persuasion of the degeneracy of mankind, but is the consequence of acknowledged and indubitable positions, that what has been longest known has been most considered, and what is most considered is best understood.

The Poet, of whose works I have undertaken the revision, may now begin to assume the dignity of an ancient, and claim the privilege of established fame and prescriptive veneration. He has long outlived his century, the term commonly fixed as the test of literary merit. Whatever advantages he might once derive from personal allusions, local customs, or temporary opinions, have for many years been lost; and every topick of merriment or motive of sorrow, which the modes of artificial life afforded him, now only obscure the scenes which they once illuminated. The effects of favour and competition are at an end; the tradition of his friendships and his enmities has perished; his works support no opinion with arguments, nor supply any faction with invectives; they can neither indulge vanity nor gratify malignity, but are read without any other reason than the desire of pleasure, and are therefore praised only as pleasure is obtained; yet, thus unassisted by interest or passion, they have past through variations of taste and changes of manners, and, as they devolved from one generation to another, have received new honours at every transmission.

But because human judgment, though it be gradually gaining upon certainty, never becomes infallible; and approbation, though long continued, may yet be only the approbation of prejudice or fashion; it is proper to inquire, by what peculiarities of excellence *Shakespeare* has gained and kept the favour of his countrymen.

Nothing can please many, and please long, but just representations of general nature. Particular manners can be known to few, and therefore few only can judge how nearly they are copied. The irregular combinations of fanciful invention may delight a-while, by that novelty of which the common satiety of life sends us all in quest; but the pleasures of sudden wonder are soon exhausted, and the mind can only repose on the stability of truth.

Shakespeare is above all writers, at least above all modern writers, the poet of nature; the poet that holds up to his readers a faithful mirrour of manners and of life. His characters are not modified by the customs of particular places, unpractised by the rest of the world; by the peculiarities of studies or professions, which can operate but upon small numbers; or by the accidents of transient fashions or temporary opinions: they are the genuine progeny of common humanity, such as the world will always supply, and observation will always find. His persons act and speak by the influence of those general passions and principles by which all minds are agitated, and the whole system of life is continued in motion. In the writings of other poets a character is too often an individual; in those of *Shakespeare* it is commonly a species.

It is from this wide extension of design that so much instruction is derived. It is this which fills the plays of *Shakespeare* with practical axioms and domestick wisdom. It was said of *Euripides*, that every verse was a precept; and it may be said of *Shakespeare*, that from his works may be collected a system of civil and oeconomical prudence. Yet his real power is not shewn in the splendour of particular passages, but by the progress of his fable, and the tenour of his dialogue; and he that tries to recommend him by select quotations, will succeed like the pedant in *Hierocles*, who, when he offered his house to sale, carried a brick in his pocket as a specimen.

It will not easily be imagined how much *Shakespeare* excells in accommodating his sentiments to real life, but by comparing him with other authours. It was observed of the ancient schools of declamation, that the more diligently they were frequented, the more was the student disqualified for the world, because he found nothing there which he should ever meet in any other place. The same remark may be applied to every stage but that of *Shake-*

speare. The theatre, when it is under any other direction, is peopled by such characters as were never seen, conversing in a language which was never heard, upon topicks which will never arise in the commerce of mankind. But the dialogue of this authour is often so evidently determined by the incident which produces it, and is pursued with so much ease and simplicity, that it seems scarcely to claim the merit of fiction, but to have been gleaned by diligent selection out of common conversation, and common occurrences.

Upon every other stage the universal agent is love, by whose power all good and evil is distributed, and every action quickened or retarded. To bring a lover, a lady and a rival into the fable; to entangle them in contradictory obligations, perplex them with oppositions of interest, and harrass them with violence of desires inconsistent with each other; to make them meet in rapture and part in agony; to fill their mouths with hyperbolical joy and outrageous sorrow; to distress them as nothing human ever was distressed; to deliver them as nothing human ever was delivered, is the business of a modern dramatist. For this probability is violated, life is misrepresented, and language is depraved. But love is only one of many passions, and as it has no great influence upon the sum of life, it has little operation in the dramas of a poet, who caught his ideas from the living world, and exhibited only what he saw before him. He knew, that any other passion, as it was regular or exorbitant, was a cause of happiness or calamity.

Characters thus ample and general were not easily discriminated and preserved, yet perhaps no poet ever kept his personages more distinct from each other. I will not say with *Pope* that every speech may be assigned to the proper speaker, because many speeches there are which have nothing characteristical; but perhaps, though some may be equally adapted to every person, it will be difficult to find, any that can be properly transferred from the present possessor to another claimant. The choice is right, when there is reason for choice.

Other dramatists can only gain attention by hyperbolical or aggravated characters, by fabulous and unexampled excellence or depravity, as the writers of barbarous romances invigorated the reader by a giant and a dwarf; and he that should form his expectations of human affairs from the play, or from the tale, would be equally deceived. *Shakespeare* has no heroes; his scenes are occupied only by men, who act and speak as the reader thinks that he should himself have spoken or acted on the same occasion: Even where the agency is supernatural the dialogue is level with life. Other writers disguise the most natural passions and most frequent incidents; so that he who contemplates them in the book will not know them in the world: *Shakespeare* approximates the remote, and familiarizes the wonderful; the event which he represents will not happen, but if it were possible, its effects would probably be such as he has assigned; and it may be said, that he has not only shewn human nature as it acts in real exigences, but as it would be found in trials, to which it cannot be exposed.

This therefore is the praise of *Shakespeare*, that his drama is the mirrour of life; that he who has mazed his imagination, in following the phantoms which other writers raise up before him, may here be cured of his delirious extasies, by reading human sentiments in human language; by scenes from which a hermit may estimate the transactions of the world, and a confessor predict the progress of the passions.

His adherence to general nature has exposed him to the censure of criticks, who form their judgments upon narrower principles. *Dennis* and *Rhymer* think his *Romans* not sufficiently Roman; and *Voltaire* censures his kings as not completely royal. *Dennis* is offended, that *Menenius*, a senator of *Rome*, should play the buffoon; and *Voltaire* perhaps thinks decency violated when the *Danish* Usurper is represented as a drunkard. But *Shakespeare* always makes nature predominate over accident; and if he preserves the essential character, is not very careful of distinctions superinduced and adventitious. His story requires Romans or kings, but he thinks only on men. He knew that *Rome*, like every other city, had men of all dispositions; and wanting a buffoon, he went into the senate-house for that which the senate-house would certainly have afforded him. He was inclined to shew an usurper and a murderer not only odious but despicable, he therefore added drunkenness to his other qualities, knowing that kings love wine like other men, and that wine exerts its natural power upon kings. These are the petty cavils of petty minds; a poet overlooks the casual distinction of country and condition, as a painter, satisfied with the figure, neglects the drapery.

The censure which he has incurred by mixing comick and tragick scenes, as it extends to all his works, deserves more consideration. Let the fact be first stated, and then examined.

Shakespeare's plays are not in the rigorous and critical sense either tragedies or comedies, but compositions of a distinct kind; exhibiting the real state of sublunary nature, which partakes of good and evil, joy and sorrow, mingled with endless variety of proportion and innumerable modes of combination; and expressing the course of the world, in which the loss of one is the gain of another; in which, at the same time, the reveller is hasting to his wine, and the mourner burying his friend; in which the malignity of one is sometimes defeated by the frolick of another; and many mischiefs and many benefits are done and hindered without design.

Out of this chaos of mingled purposes and casualties the ancient poets, according to the laws which custom had prescribed, selected some the crimes of men, and some their absurdities; some the momentous vicissitudes of life, and some the lighter occurrences; some the terrours of distress, and some the gayeties of prosperity. Thus rose the two modes of imitation, known by the names of *tragedy* and *comedy*, compositions intended to promote different ends by contrary means, and considered as so little allied, that I do not recollect among the *Greeks* or *Romans* a single writer who attempted both.

Shakespeare has united the powers of exciting laughter and sorrow not only in one mind but in one composition. Almost all his plays are divided between serious and ludicrous characters, and, in the successive evolutions of the design, sometimes produce seriousness and sorrow, and sometimes levity and laughter.

That this is a practice contrary to the rules of criticism will be readily allowed; but there is always an appeal open from criticism to nature. The end of writing is to instruct; the end of poetry is to instruct by pleasing. That the mingled drama may convey all the instruction of tragedy or comedy cannot be denied, because it includes both in its alternations of exhibition, and approaches nearer than either to the appearance of life, by shewing how great machinations and slender designs may promote or obviate one another, and the high and the low co-operate in the general system by unavoidable concatenation.

It is objected, that by this change of scenes the passions are interrupted in their progression, and that the principal event, being not advanced by a due gradation of preparatory incidents, wants at last the power to move, which constitutes the perfection of dramatick poetry. This reasoning is so specious, that it is received as true even by those who in daily experience feel it to be false. The interchanges of mingled scenes seldom fail to produce the intended vicissitudes of passion. Fiction cannot move so much, but that the attention may be easily transferred; and though it must be allowed that pleasing melancholy be sometimes interrupted by unwelcome levity, yet let it be considered likewise, that melancholy is often not pleasing, and that the disturbance of one man may be the relief of another; that different auditors have different habitudes; and that, upon the whole, all pleasure consists in variety.

The players, who in their edition divided our authour's works into comedies, histories, and tragedies, seem not to have distinguished the three kinds, by any very exact or definite ideas.

An action which ended happily to the principal persons, however serious or distressful through its intermediate incidents, in their opinion constituted a comedy. This idea of a comedy continued long amongst us, and plays were written, which, by changing the catastrophe, were tragedies to-day and comedies to-morrow.

Tragedy was not in those times a poem of more general dignity or elevation than comedy; it required only a calamitous conclusion, with which the common criticism of that age was satisfied, whatever lighter pleasure it afforded in its progress.

History was a series of actions, with no other than chronological succession, independent on each other, and without any tendency to introduce or regulate the conclusion. It is not always very nicely distinguished from tragedy. There is not much nearer approach to unity of action in the tragedy of *Antony and Cleopatra*, than in the history of *Richard the Second*. But a history might be continued through many plays; as it had no plan, it had no limits.

Through all these denominations of the drama, *Shakespeare*'s mode of composition is the same; an interchange of seriousness and merriment, by which the mind is softened at one time, and exhilarated at another. But whatever be his purpose, whether to gladden or depress, or to conduct the story, without vehemence or emotion, through tracts of easy and familiar dialogue, he never fails to attain his purpose; as he commands us, we laugh or mourn, or sit silent with quiet expectation, in tranquillity without indifference.

When *Shakespeare*'s plan is understood, most of the criticisms of *Rhymer* and *Voltaire* vanish away. The play of *Hamlet* is opened, without impropriety, by two sentinels; *Iago* bellows at *Brabantio's* window, without injury to the scheme of the play, though in terms which a modern audience would not easily endure; the character of *Polonius* is seasonable and useful; and the Grave-diggers themselves may be heard with applause.

Shakespeare engaged in dramatick poetry with the world open before him; the rules of the ancients were yet known to few; the publick judgment was unformed; he had no example of such fame as might force him upon imitation, nor criticks of such authority as might restrain his extravagance: He therefore indulged his natural disposition, and his disposition, as *Rhymer* has remarked, led him to comedy. In tragedy he often writes with great appearance of toil and study, what is written at last with little felicity; but in his comick scenes, he seems to produce without labour, what no labour can improve. In tragedy he is always struggling after some occasion to be comick, but in comedy he seems to repose, or to luxuriate, as in a mode of thinking congenial to his nature. In his tragick scenes there is always something wanting, but his comedy often surpasses expectation or desire. His comedy pleases by the thoughts and the language, and his tragedy for the greater part by incident and action. His tragedy seems to be skill, his comedy to be instinct.

The force of his comick scenes has suffered little diminution from the changes made by a century and a half, in manners or in words. As his personages act upon principles arising from genuine passion, very little modified by particular forms, their pleasures and vexations are communicable to all times and to all places; they are natural, and therefore durable; the adventitious peculiarities of personal habits, are only superficial dies, bright and pleasing for a little while, yet soon fading to a dim tinct, without any remains of former lustre; but the discriminations of true passion are the colours of nature; they pervade the whole mass, and can only perish with the body that exhibits them. The accidental compositions of heterogeneous modes are dissolved by the chance which combined them; but the uniform simplicity of primitive qualities neither admits increase, nor suffers decay. The sand heaped by one flood is scattered by another, but the rock always continues in its place. The stream of time, which is continually washing the dissoluble fabricks of other poets, passes without injury by the adamant of *Shakespeare*.

496

If there be, what I believe there is, in every nation, a stile which never becomes obsolete, a certain mode of phraseology so consonant and congenial to the analogy and principles of its respective language as to remain settled and unaltered; this stile is probably to be sought in the common intercourse of life, among those who speak only to be understood, without ambition of elegance. The polite are always catching modish innovations, and the learned depart from established forms of speech, in hope of finding or making better; those who wish for distinction forsake the vulgar, when the vulgar is right; but there is a conversation above grossness and below refinement, where propriety resides, and where this poet seems to have gathered his comick dialogue. He is therefore more agreeable to the ears of the present age than any other authour equally remote, and among his other excellencies deserves to be studied as one of the original masters of our language.

These observations are to be considered not as unexceptionably constant, but as containing general and predominant truth. *Shakespeare*'s familiar dialogue is affirmed to be smooth and clear, yet not wholly without ruggedness or difficulty; as a country may be eminently fruitful, though it has spots unfit for cultivation: His characters are praised as natural, though their sentiments are sometimes forced, and their actions improbable; as the earth upon the whole is spherical, though its surface is varied with protuberances and cavities.

Shakespeare with his excellencies has likewise faults, and faults sufficient to obscure and overwhelm any other merit. I shall shew them in the proportion in which they appear to me, without envious malignity or superstitious veneration. No question can be more innocently discussed than a dead poet's pretensions to renown; and little regard is due to that bigotry which sets candour higher than truth.

His first defect is that to which may be imputed most of the evil in books or in men. He sacrifices virtue to convenience, and is so much more careful to please than to instruct, that he seems to write without any moral purpose. From his writings indeed a system of social duty may be selected, for he that thinks reasonably must think morally; but his precepts and axioms drop casually from him; he makes no just distribution of good or evil, nor is always careful to shew in the virtuous a disapprobation of the wicked; he carries his persons indifferently through right and wrong, and at the close dismisses them without further care, and leaves their examples to operate by chance. This fault the barbarity of his age cannot extenuate; for it is always a writer's duty to make the world better, and justice is a virtue independant on time or place.

The plots are often so loosely formed, that a very slight consideration may improve them, and so carelessly pursued, that he seems not always fully to comprehend his own design. He omits opportunities of instructing or delighting which the train of his story seems to force upon him, and apparently rejects those exhibitions which would be more affecting, for the sake of those which are more easy.

It may be observed, that in many of his plays the latter part is evidently neglected. When he found himself near the end of his work, and, in view of his reward, he shortened the labour to snatch the profit. He therefore remits his efforts where he should most vigorously exert them, and his catastrophe is improbably produced or imperfectly represented.

He had no regard to distinction of time or place, but gives to one age or nation, without scruple, the customs, institutions, and opinions of another, at the expence not only of likelihood, but of possibility. These faults *Pope* has endeavoured, with more zeal than judgment, to transfer to his imagined interpolators. We need not wonder to find *Hector* quoting *Aristotle*, when we see the loves of *Theseus* and *Hippolyta* combined with the *Gothick* mythology of fairies. *Shakespeare*, indeed, was not the only violator of chronology, for in the same age *Sidney*, who wanted not the advantages of learning, has, in his *Arcadia*, confounded the pastoral with the feudal times, the days of innocence, quiet and security, with those of turbulence, violence, and adventure.

In his comick scenes he is seldom very successful, when he engages his characters in reciprocations of smartness and contests of sarcasm; their jests are commonly gross, and their pleasantry licentious; neither his gentlemen nor his ladies have much delicacy, nor are sufficiently distinguished from his clowns by any appearance of refined manners. Whether he represented the real conversation of his time is not easy to determine; the reign of *Elizabeth* is commonly supposed to have been a time of stateliness, formality and reserve; yet perhaps the relaxations of that severity were not very elegant. There must, however, have been always some modes of gayety preferable to others, and a writer ought to chuse the best.

In tragedy his performance seems constantly to be worse, as his labour is more. The effusions of passion which exigence forces out are for the most part striking and energetick; but whenever he solicits his invention, or strains his faculties, the offspring of his throes is tumour, meanness, tediousness, and obscurity.

In narration he affects a disproportionate pomp of diction, and a wearisome train of circumlocution, and tells the incident imperfectly in many words, which might have been more plainly delivered in few. Narration in dramatick poetry is naturally tedious, as it is unanimated and inactive, and obstructs the progress of the action; it should therefore always be rapid, and enlivened by frequent interruption. *Shakespeare* found it an encumbrance, and instead of lightening it by brevity, endeavoured to recommend it by dignity and splendour.

His declamations or set speeches are commonly cold and weak, for his power was the power of nature; when he endeavoured, like other tragick writers, to catch opportunities of amplification, and instead of inquiring what the occasion demanded, to show how much his stores of knowledge could supply, he seldom escapes without the pity or resentment of his reader.

It is incident to him to be now and then entangled with an unwieldy sentiment, which he cannot well express, and will not reject; he struggles with it a while, and if it continues stubborn, comprises it in words such as occur, and leaves it to be disentangled and evolved by those who have more leisure to bestow upon it.

Not that always where the language is intricate the thought is subtle, or the image always great where the line is bulky; the equality of words to things is very often neglected, and trivial sentiments and vulgar ideas disappoint the attention, to which they are recommended by sonorous epithets and swelling figures.

But the admirers of this great poet have never less reason to indulge their hopes of supreme excellence, than when he seems fully resolved to sink them in dejection, and mollify them with tender emotions by the fall of greatness, the danger of innocence, or the crosses of love. He is not long soft and pathetick without some idle conceit, or contemptible equivocation. He no sooner begins to move, than he counteracts himself; and terrour and pity, as they are rising in the mind, are checked and blasted by sudden frigidity.

A quibble is to *Shakespeare,* what luminous vapours are to the traveller; he follows it at all adventures, it is sure to lead him out of his way, and sure to engulf him in the mire. It has some malignant power over his mind, and its fascinations are irresistible. Whatever be the dignity or profundity of his disquisition, whether he be enlarging knowledge or exalting affection, whether he be amusing attention with incidents, or enchaining it in suspense, let but a quibble spring up before him, and he leaves his work unfinished. A quibble is the golden apple for which he will always turn aside from his career, or stoop from his elevation. A quibble, poor and barren as it is, gave him such delight, that he was content to purchase it, by the sacrifice of reason, propriety and truth. A quibble was to him the fatal *Cleopatra* for which he lost the world, and was content to lose it.

It will be thought strange, that, in enumerating the defects of this writer, I have not yet mentioned his neglect of the unities; his violation of those laws which have been instituted and established by the joint authority of poets and of criticks.

For his other deviations from the art of writing, I resign him to critical justice, without making any other demand in his favour, than that which must be indulged to all human excellence; that his virtues be rated with his failings: But, from the censure which this irregularity may bring upon him, I shall, with due reverence to thát learning which I must oppose, adventure to try how I can defend him.

His histories, being neither tragedies nor comedies, are not subject to any of their laws; nothing more is necessary to all the praise which they expect, than that the changes of action be so prepared as to be understood, that the incidents be various and affecting, and the characters consistent, natural and distinct. No other unity is intended, and therefore none is to be sought.

In his other works he has well enough preserved the unity of action. He has not, indeed, an intrigue regularly perplexed and regularly unravelled; he does not endeavour to hide his design only to discover it, for this is seldom the order of real events, and *Shakespeare* is the poet of nature: But his plan has commonly what *Aristotle* requires, a beginning, a middle, and an end; one event is concatenated with another, and the conclusion follows by easy consequence. There are perhaps some incidents that might be spared, as in other poets there is much talk that only fills up time

500

A contradicts what he said on p. 498

upon the stage; but the general system makes gradual advances, and the end of the play is the end of expectation.

To the unities of time and place he has shewn no regard, and perhaps a nearer view of the principles on which they stand will diminish their value, and withdraw from them the veneration which, from the time of *Corneille*, they have very generally received, by discovering that they have given more trouble to the poet, than pleasure to the auditor.

The necessity of observing the unities of time and place arises from the supposed necessity of making the drama credible. The criticks hold it impossible, that an action of months or years can be possibly believed to pass in three hours; or that the spectator can suppose himself to sit in the theatre, while ambassadors go and return between distant kings, while armies are levied and towns besieged, while an exile wanders and returns, or till he whom they saw courting his mistress, shall lament the untimely fall of his son. The mind revolts from evident falsehood, and fiction loses its force when it departs from the resemblance of reality.

From the narrow limitation of time necessarily arises the contraction of place. The spectator, who knows that he saw the first act at *Alexandria*, cannot suppose that he sees the next at *Rome*, at a distance to which not the dragons of *Medea* could, in so short a time, have transported him; he knows with certainty that he has not changed his place; and he knows that place cannot change itself; that what was a house cannot become a plain; that what was *Thebes* can never be *Persepolis*.

Such is the triumphant language with which a critick exults over the misery of an irregular poet, and exults commonly without resistance or reply. It is time therefore to tell him, by the authority of *Shakespeare*, that he assumes, as an unquestionable principle, a position, which, while his breath is forming it into words, his understanding pronounces to be false. It is false, that any representation is mistaken for reality; that any dramatick fable in its materiality was ever credible, or, for a single moment, was ever credited.

The objection arising from the impossibility of passing the first hour at *Alexandria*, and the next at *Rome*, supposes, that when the play opens, the spectator really imagines himself at *Alexandria*, and believes that his walk to the theatre has been a voyage to *Egypt*, and that he lives in the days of *Antony* and *Cleopatra*.

Surely he that imagines this may imagine more. He that can take the stage at one time for the palace of the *Ptolemies*, may take it in half an hour for the promontory of *Actium*. Delusion, if delusion be admitted, has no certain limitation; if the spectator can be once persuaded, that his old acquaintance are *Alexander* and *Cæsar*, that a room illuminated with candles is the plain of *Pharsalia*, or the bank of *Granicus*, he is in a state of elevation above the reach of reason, or of truth, and from the heights of empyrean poetry, may despise the circumscriptions of terrestrial nature. There is no reason why a mind thus wandering in extasy should count the clock, or why an hour should not be a century in that calenture of the brains that can make the stage a field.

The truth is, that the spectators are always in their senses, and know, from the first act to the last, that the stage is only a stage, and that the players are only players. They came to hear a certain number of lines recited with just gesture and elegant modulation. The lines relate to some action, and an action must be in some place; but the different actions that compleat a story may be in places very remote from each other; and where is the absurdity of allowing that space to represent first *Athens*, and then *Sicily*, which was always known to be neither *Sicily* nor *Athens*, but a modern theatre.

By supposition, as place is introduced, time may be extended; the time required by the fable elapses for the most part between the acts; for, of so much of the action as is represented, the real and poetical duration is the same. If, in the first act, preparations for war against *Mithridates* are represented to be made in *Rome*, the event of the war may, without absurdity, be represented, in the catastrophe, as happening in *Pontus*; we know that there is neither war, nor preparation for war; we know that we are neither in *Rome* nor *Pontus*; that neither *Mithridates* nor *Lucullus* are before us. The drama exhibits successive imitations of successive actions, and why may not the second imitation represent an action that happened years after the first; if it be so connected with it, that nothing but time can be supposed to intervene. Time is, of all modes of existence, most obsequious to the imagination; a lapse of years is as easily conceived as a passage of hours. In contemplation we easily contract the time of real actions, and therefore willingly permit it to be contracted when we only see their imitation.

It will be asked, how the drama moves, if it is not credited. It is credited with all the credit due to a drama. It is credited, whenever it moves, as a just picture of a real original; as representing to the auditor what he would himself feel, if he were to do or suffer what is there feigned to be suffered or to be done. The reflection that strikes the heart is not, that the evils before us are real evils, but that they are evils to which we ourselves may be exposed. If there be any fallacy, it is not that we fancy the players, but that we fancy ourselves unhappy for a moment; but we rather lament the possibility than suppose the presence of misery, as a mother weeps over her babe, when she remembers that death may take it from her. The delight of tragedy proceeds from our consciousness of fiction; if we thought murders and treasons real, they would please no more.

Imitations produce pain or pleasure, not because they are mistaken for realities, but because they bring realities to mind. When the imagination is recreated by a painted landscape, the trees are not supposed capable to give us shade, or the fountains coolness; but we consider, how we should be pleased with such fountains playing beside us, and such woods waving over us. We are agitated in reading the history of *Henry* the Fifth, yet no man takes his book for the field of *Agencourt*. A dramatick exhibition is a book recited with concomitants that encrease or diminish its effect. Familiar comedy is often more powerful on the theatre, than in the page; imperial tragedy is always less. The humour of *Petruchio* may be heightened by grimace; but what voice or what gesture can hope to add dignity or force to the soliloquy of *Cato*.

A play read, affects the mind like a play acted. It is therefore evident, that the action is not supposed to be real, and it follows that between the acts a longer or shorter time may be allowed to pass, and that no more account of space or duration is to be taken by the auditor of a drama, than by the reader of a narrative, before whom may pass in an hour the life of a hero, or the revolutions of an empire.

Whether *Shakespeare* knew the unities, and rejected them by design, or deviated from them by happy ignorance, it is, I think, impossible to decide, and useless to enquire. We may reasonably suppose, that, when he rose to notice, he did not want the counsels and admonitions of scholars and criticks, and that he at last deliberately persisted in a practice, which he might have begun by chance. As nothing is essential to the fable, but unity of action, and as the unities of time and place arise evidently from false assumptions, and, by circumscribing the extent of the drama, lessen its variety, I cannot think it much to be lamented, that they were not known by him, or not observed: Nor, if such another poet could arise, should I very vehemently reproach him, that his first act passed at *Venice*, and his next in *Cyprus*. Such violations of rules merely positive, become the comprehensive genius of *Shakespeare*, and such censures are suitable to the minute and slender criticism of *Voltaire:*

> *Non usque adeo permiscuit imis*
> *Longus summa dies, ut non, si voce Metelli*
> *Serventur leges, malint a Cœsare tolli.*

Yet when I speak thus slightly of dramatick rules, I cannot but recollect how much wit and learning may be produced against me; before such authorities I am afraid to stand, not that I think the present question one of those that are to be decided by mere authority, but because it is to be suspected, that these precepts have not been so easily received but for better reasons than I have yet been able to find. The result of my enquiries, in which it would be ludicrous to boast of impartiality, is, that the unities of time and place are not essential to a just drama, that though they may sometimes conduce to pleasure, they are always to be sacrificed to the nobler beauties of variety and instruction; and that a play, written with nice observation of critical rules, is to be contemplated as an elaborate curiosity, as the product of superfluous and ostentatious art, by which is shewn, rather what is possible, than what is necessary.

He that, without diminution of any other excellence, shall preserve all the unities unbroken, deserves the like applause with the architect, who shall display all the orders of architecture in a citadel, without any deduction from its strength; but the principal beauty of a citadel is to exclude the enemy; and the greatest graces of a play, are to copy nature and instruct life.

Perhaps, what I have here not dogmatically but deliberatively written, may recal the principles of the drama to a new examination. I am almost frighted at my own temerity; and when I estimate the fame and the strength of those that maintain the contrary opinion, am ready to sink down in reverential silence; as *Æneas* withdrew from the defence of *Troy*, when he saw *Neptune* shaking the wall, and *Juno* heading the besiegers.

Those whom my arguments cannot persuade to give their approbation to the judgment of *Shakespeare*, will easily, if they consider
the condition of his life, make some allowance for his ignorance.

Every man's performances, to be rightly estimated, must be
compared with the state of the age in which he lived, and with his
own particular opportunities; and though to the reader a book be
not worse or better for the circumstances of the authour, yet as
there is always a silent reference of human works to human
abilities, and as the enquiry, how far man may extend his designs,
or how high he may rate his native force, is of far greater dignity
than in what rank we shall place any particular performance,
curiosity is always busy to discover the instruments, as well as to
survey the workmanship, to know how much is to be ascribed to
original powers, and how much to casual and adventitious help.
The palaces of *Peru* or *Mexico* were certainly mean and incommodious habitations, if compared to the houses of *European*
monarchs; yet who could forbear to view them with astonishment,
who remembered that they were built without the use of iron?

The *English* nation, in the time of *Shakespeare*, was yet struggling to emerge from barbarity. The philology of *Italy* had been
transplanted hither in the reign of *Henry* the Eighth; and the
learned languages had been successfully cultivated by *Lilly*,
Linacer, and *More*; by *Pole*, *Cheke*, and *Gardiner*; and afterwards
by *Smith*, *Clerk*, *Haddon*, and *Ascham*. Greek was now taught to
boys in the principal schools; and those who united elegance with
learning, read, with great diligence, the *Italian* and *Spanish* poets.
But literature was yet confined to professed scholars, or to men
and women of high rank. The publick was gross and dark; and to
be able to read and write, was an accomplishment still valued for
its rarity.

Nations, like individuals, have their infancy. A people newly
awakened to literary curiosity, being yet unacquainted with the
true state of things, knows not how to judge of that which is proposed as its resemblance. Whatever is remote from common
appearance is always welcome to vulgar, as to childish credulity;
and of a country unenlightened by learning, the whole people is the
vulgar. The study of those who then aspired to plebeian learning
was laid out upon adventures, giants, dragons, and enchantments.
The Death of Arthur was the favourite volume.

The mind, which has feasted on the luxurious wonders of fiction,
505

has no taste of the insipidity of truth. A play which imitated only the common occurrences of the world, would, upon the admirers of *Palmerin* and *Guy* of *Warwick*, have made little impression; he that wrote for such an audience was under the necessity of looking round for strange events and fabulous transactions, and that incredibility, by which maturer knowledge is offended, was the chief recommendation of writings, to unskilful curiosity.

Our authour's plots are generally borrowed from novels, and it is reasonable to suppose, that he chose the most popular, such as were read by many, and related by more; for his audience could not have followed him through the intricacies of the drama, had they not held the thread of the story in their hands.

The stories, which we now find only in remoter authours, were in his time accessible and familiar. The fable of *As you like it*, which is supposed to be copied from *Chaucer*'s Gamelyn, was a little pamphlet of those times; and old Mr. *Cibber* remembered the tale of *Hamlet* in plain *English* prose, which the criticks have now to seek in *Saxo Grammaticus*.

His *English* histories he took from *English* chronicles and *English* ballads; and as the ancient writers were made known to his countrymen by versions, they supplied him with new subjects; he dilated some of *Plutarch*'s lives into plays, when they had been translated by *North*.

His plots, whether historical or fabulous, are always crouded with incidents, by which the attention of a rude people was more easily caught than by sentiment or argumentation; and such is the power of the marvellous even over those who despise it, that every man finds his mind more strongly seized by the tragedies of *Shakespeare* than of any other writer; others please us by particular speeches, but he always makes us anxious for the event, and has perhaps excelled all but *Homer* in securing the first purpose of a writer, by exciting restless and unquenchable curiosity, and compelling him that reads his work to read it through.

The shows and bustle with which his plays abound, have the same original. As knowledge advances, pleasure passes from the eye to the ear, but returns, as it declines, from the ear to the eye. Those to whom our authour's labours were exhibited had more skill in pomps or processions than in poetical language, and perhaps wanted some visible and discriminated events, as comments on the dialogue. He knew how he should most please; and whether his practice is more agreeable to nature, or whether his example has prejudiced the nation, we still find that on our stage something must be done as well as said, and inactive declamation is very coldly heard, however musical or elegant, passionate or sublime.

Voltaire expresses his wonder, that our authour's extravagances are endured by a nation, which has seen the tragedy of *Cato*. Let him be answered, that *Addison* speaks the language of poets, and *Shakespeare*, of men. We find in *Cato* innumerable beauties which enamour us of its authour, but we see nothing that acquaints us with human sentiments or human actions; we place it with the fairest and the noblest progeny which judgment propagates by conjunction with learning, but *Othello* is the vigorous and vivacious offspring of observation impregnated by genius. *Cato* affords a splendid exhibition of artificial and fictitious manners, and delivers just and noble sentiments, in diction easy, elevated and harmonious, but its hopes and fears communicate no vibration to the heart; the composition refers us only to the writer; we pronounce the name of *Cato*, but we think on *Addison*.

The work of a correct and regular writer is a garden accurately formed and diligently planted, varied with shades, and scented with flowers; the composition of *Shakespeare* is a forest, in which oaks extend their branches, and pines tower in the air, interspersed sometimes with weeds and brambles, and sometimes giving shelter to myrtles and to roses; filling the eye with awful pomp, and gratifying the mind with endless diversity. Other poets display cabinets of precious rarities, minutely finished, wrought into shape, and polished unto brightness. *Shakespeare* opens a mine which contains gold and diamonds in unexhaustible plenty, though clouded by incrustations, debased by impurities, and mingled with a mass of meaner minerals.

It has been much disputed, whether *Shakespeare* owed his excellence to his own native force, or whether he had the common helps of scholastick education, the precepts of critical science, and the examples of ancient authours.

There has always prevailed a tradition, that *Shakespeare* wanted learning, that he had no regular education, nor much skill in the dead languages. *Johnson*, his friend, affirms, that *he had small Latin, and no Greek*; who, besides that he had no imaginable temptation to falsehood, wrote at a time when the character and acquisitions of *Shakespeare* were known to multitudes. His evidence ought therefore to decide the controversy, unless some testimony of equal force could be opposed.

Some have imagined, that they have discovered deep learning in many imitations of old writers; but the examples which I have known urged, were drawn from books translated in his time; or were such easy coincidences of thought, as will happen to all who consider the same subjects; or such remarks on life or axioms of morality as float in conversation, and are transmitted through the world in proverbial sentences.

I have found it remarked, that, in this important sentence, *Go before, I'll follow*, we read a translation of, *I prae, sequar*. I have been told, that when *Caliban*, after a pleasing dream, says, *I cry'd to sleep again*, the authour imitates *Anacreon*, who had, like every other man, the same wish on the same occasion.

There are a few passages which may pass for imitations, but so few, that the exception only confirms the rule; he obtained them from accidental quotations, or by oral communication, and as he used what he had, would have used more if he had obtained it.

The *Comedy of Errors* is confessedly taken from the *Menæchmi* of *Plautus*; from the only play of *Plautus* which was then in *English*. What can be more probable, than that he who copied that, would have copied more; but that those which were not translated were inaccessible?

Whether he knew the modern languages is uncertain. That his plays have some *French* scenes proves but little; he might easily procure them to be written, and probably, even though he had known the language in the common degree, he could not have written it without assistance. In the story of *Romeo* and *Juliet* he is observed to have followed the *English* translation, where it deviates from the *Italian*; but this on the other part proves nothing against his knowledge of the original. He was to copy, not what he knew himself, but what was known to his audience.

It is most likely that he had learned *Latin* sufficiently to make him acquainted with construction, but that he never advanced to an easy perusal of the *Roman* authours. Concerning his skill in modern languages, I can find no sufficient ground of determination; but as no imitations of *French* or *Italian* authours have been discovered, though the *Italian* poetry was then high in esteem, I am inclined to believe, that he read little more than *English*, and chose for his fables only such tales as he found translated.

That much knowledge is scattered over his works is very justly observed by *Pope*, but it is often such knowledge as books did not supply. He that will understand *Shakespeare*, must not be content to study him in the closet, he must look for his meaning sometimes among the sports of the field, and sometimes among the manufactures of the shop.

There is however proof enough that he was a very diligent reader, nor was our language then so indigent of books, but that he might very liberally indulge his curiosity without excursion into foreign literature. Many of the *Roman* authours were translated, and some of the *Greek*; the reformation had filled the kingdom with theological learning; most of the topicks of human disquisition had found *English* writers; and poetry had been cultivated, not only with diligence, but success. This was a stock of knowledge sufficient for a mind so capable of appropriating and improving it.

But the greater part of his excellence was the product of his own genius. He found the *English* stage in a state of the utmost rudeness; no essays either in tragedy or comedy had appeared, from which it could be discovered to what degree of delight either one or other might be carried. Neither character nor dialogue were yet understood. *Shakespeare* may be truly said to have introduced them both amongst us, and in some of his happier scenes to have carried them both to the utmost height.

By what gradations of improvement he proceeded, is not easily known; for the chronology of his works is yet unsettled. *Rowe* is of opinion, that *perhaps we are not to look for his beginning, like those of other writers, in his least perfect works; art had so little, and nature so large a share in what he did, that for ought I know,* says he, *the performances of his youth, as they were the most vigorous, were the best.* But the power of nature is only the power of using to any certain purpose the materials which diligence procures, or opportunity supplies. Nature gives no man knowledge, and when images are collected by study and experience, can only assist in combining or applying them. *Shakespeare,* however favoured by nature, could impart only what he had learned; and as he must increase his ideas, like other mortals, by gradual acquisition, he, like them, grew wiser as he grew older, could display life better, as he knew it more, and instruct with more efficacy, as he was himself more amply instructed.

There is a vigilance of observation and accuracy of distinction

509

which books and precepts cannot confer; from this almost all original and native excellence proceeds. *Shakespeare* must have looked upon mankind with perspicacity, in the highest degree curious and attentive. Other writers borrow their characters from preceding writers, and diversify them only by the accidental appendages of present manners; the dress is a little varied, but the body is the same. Our authour had both matter and form to provide; for except the characters of *Chaucer*, to whom I think he is not much indebted, there were no writers in *English*, and perhaps not many in other modern languages, which shewed life in its native colours.

The contest about the original benevolence or malignity of man had not yet commenced. Speculation had not yet attempted to analyse the mind, to trace the passions to their sources, to unfold the seminal principles of vice and virtue, or sound the depths of the heart for the motives of action. All those enquiries, which from that time that human nature became the fashionable study, have been made sometimes with nice discernment, but often with idle subtility, were yet unattempted. The tales, with which the infancy of learning was satisfied, exhibited only the superficial appearances of action, related the events but omitted the causes, and were formed for such as delighted in wonders rather than in truth. Mankind was not then to be studied in the closet; he that would know the world, was under the necessity of gleaning his own remarks, by mingling as he could in its business and amusements.

Boyle congratulated himself upon his high birth, because it favoured his curiosity, by facilitating his access. *Shakespeare* had no such advantage; he came to *London* a needy adventurer, and lived for a time by very mean employments. Many works of genius and learning have been performed in states of life, that appear very little favourable to thought or to enquiry; so many, that he who considers them is inclined to think that he sees enterprise and perseverance predominating over all external agency, and bidding help and hindrance vanish before them. The genius of *Shakespeare* was not to be depressed by the weight of poverty, not limited by the narrow conversation to which men in want are inevitably condemned; the incumbrances of his fortune were shaken from his mind, *as dewdrops from a lion's mane.*

Though he had so many difficulties to encounter, and so little assistance to surmount them, he has been able to obtain an exact knowledge of many modes of life, and many casts of native dispositions; to vary them with great multiplicity; to mark them by nice distinctions; and to shew them in full view by proper combinations. In this part of his performances he had none to imitate, but has himself been imitated by all succeeding writers; and it may be doubted, whether from all his successors more maxims of theoretical knowledge, or more rules of practical prudence, can be collected, than he alone has given to his country.

Nor was his attention confined to the actions of men; he was an exact surveyor of the inanimate world; his descriptions have always some peculiarities, gathered by contemplating things as they really exist. It may be observed, that the oldest poets of many nations preserve their reputation, and that the following generations of wit, after a short celebrity, sink into oblivion. The first, whoever they be, must take their sentiments and descriptions immediately from knowledge; the resemblance is therefore just, their descriptions are verified by every eye, and their sentiments acknowledged by every breast. Those whom their fame invites to the same studies, copy partly them, and partly nature, till the books of one age gain such authority, as to stand in the place of nature to another, and imitation, always deviating a little, becomes at last capricious and casual. *Shakespeare*, whether life or nature be his subject, shews plainly, that he has seen with his own eyes; he gives the image which he receives, not weakened or distorted by the intervention of any other mind; the ignorant feel his representations to be just, and the learned see that they are compleat.

Perhaps it would not be easy to find any authour, except *Homer*, who invented so much as *Shakespeare*, who so much advanced the studies which he cultivated, or effused so much novelty upon his age or country. The form, the characters, the language, and the shows of the *English* drama are his. *He seems*, says *Dennis*, *to have been the very original of our* English *tragical harmony, that is, the harmony of blank verse, diversified often by dissyllable and trissyllable terminations. For the diversity distinguishes it from heroick harmony, and by bringing it nearer to common use makes it more proper to gain attention, and more fit for action and dialogue. Such verse we make when we are writing prose; we make such verse in common conversation.*

I know not whether this praise is rigorously just. The dissyllable

511

termination, which the critick rightly appropriates to the drama, is to be found, though, I think, not in *Gorboduc* which is confessedly before our authour; yet in *Hieronnymo*, of which the date is not certain, but which there is reason to believe at least as old as his earliest plays. This however is certain, that he is the first who taught either tragedy or comedy to please, there being no theatrical piece of any older writer, of which the name is known, except to antiquaries and collectors of books, which are sought because they are scarce, and would not have been scarce, had they been much esteemed.

To him we must ascribe the praise, unless *Spenser* may divide it with him, of having first discovered to how much smoothness and harmony the *English* language could be softened. He has speeches, perhaps sometimes scenes, which have all the delicacy of *Rowe*, without his effeminacy. He endeavours indeed commonly to strike by the force and vigour of his dialogue, but he never executes his purpose better, than when he tries to sooth by softness.

Yet it must be at last confessed that as we owe every thing to him, he owes something to us; that, if much of his praise is paid by perception and judgement, much is likewise given by custom and veneration. We fix our eyes upon his graces, and turn them from his deformities, and endure in him what we should in another loath or despise. If we endured without praising, respect for the father of our drama might excuse us; but I have seen, in the book of some modern critick, a collection of anomalies, which shew that he has corrupted language by every mode of depravation, but which his admirer has accumulated as a monument of honour.

He has scenes of undoubted and perpetual excellence, but perhaps not one play, which, if it were now exhibited as the work of a contemporary writer, would be heard to the conclusion. I am indeed far from thinking, that his works were wrought to his own ideas of perfection; when they were such as would satisfy the audience, they satisfied the writer. It is seldom that authours, though more studious of fame than *Shakespeare*, rise much above the standard of their own age; to add a little to what is best will always be sufficient for present praise, and those who find themselves exalted into fame, are willing to credit their encomiasts, and to spare the labour of contending with themselves.

It does not appear, that *Shakespeare* thought his works worthy of posterity, that he levied any ideal tribute upon future times, or had any further prospect, than of present popularity and present profit. When his plays had been acted, his hope was at an end; he solicited no addition of honour from the reader. He therefore made no scruple to repeat the same jests in many dialogues, or to entangle different plots by the same knot of perplexity, which may be at least forgiven him, by those who recollect, that of *Congreve*'s four comedies, two are concluded by a marriage in a mask, by a deception, which perhaps never happened, and which, whether likely or not, he did not invent.

So careless was this great poet of future fame, that, though he retired to ease and plenty, while he was yet little *declined into the vale of years*, before he could be disgusted with fatigue, or disabled by infirmity, he made no collection of his works, nor desired to rescue those that had been already published from the depravations that obscured them, or secure to the rest a better destiny, by giving them to the world in their genuine state.

Of the plays which bear the name of *Shakespeare* in the late editions, the greater part were not published till about seven years after his death, and the few which appeared in his life are apparently thrust into the world without the care of the authour, and therefore probably without his knowledge.

Of all the publishers, clandestine or professed, their negligence and unskilfulness has by the late revisers been sufficiently shown. The faults of all are indeed numerous and gross, and have not only corrupted many passages perhaps beyond recovery, but have brought others into suspicion, which are only obscured by obsolete phraseology, or by the writer's unskilfulness and affectation. To alter is more easy than to explain, and temerity is a more common quality than diligence. Those who saw that they must employ conjecture to a certain degree, were willing to indulge it a little further. Had the authour published his own works, we should have sat quietly down to disentangle his intricacies, and clear his obscurities; but now we tear what we cannot loose, and eject what we happen not to understand.

The faults are more than could have happened without the concurrence of many causes. The stile of *Shakespeare* was in itself ungrammatical, perplexed and obscure; his works were transcribed for the players by those who may be supposed to have seldom understood them; they were transmitted by copiers equally unskilful, who still multiplied errours; they were perhaps sometimes mutilated by the actors, for the sake of shortening the speeches; and were at last printed without correction of the press.

In this state they remained, not as Dr. *Warburton* supposes, because they were unregarded, but because the editor's art was not yet applied to modern languages, and our ancestors were accustomed to so much negligence of *English* printers, that they could very patiently endure it. At last an edition was undertaken by *Rowe*; not because a poet was to be published by a poet, for *Rowe* seems to have thought very little on correction or explanation, but that our authour's works might appear like those of his fraternity, with the appendages of a life and recommendatory preface. *Rowe* has been clamorously blamed for not performing what he did not undertake, and it is time that justice be done him, by confessing, that though he seems to have had no thought of corruption beyond the printer's errours, yet he has made many emendations, if they were not made before, which his successors have received without acknowledgement, and which, if they had produced them, would have filled pages and pages with censures of the stupidity by which the faults were committed, with displays of the absurdities which they involved, with ostentatious expositions of the new reading, and self congratulations on the happiness of discovering it.

Of *Rowe*, as of all the editors, I have preserved the preface, and have likewise retained the authour's life, though not written with much elegance or spirit; it relates however what is now to be known, and therefore serves to pass through all succeeding publications.

The nation had been for many years content enough with Mr. *Rowe*'s performance, when Mr. *Pope* made them acquainted with the true state of *Shakespeare*'s text, showed that it was extremely corrupt, and gave reason to hope that there were means of reforming it. He collated the old copies, which none had thought to examine before, and restored many lines to their integrity; but, by a very compendious criticism, he rejected whatever he disliked, and thought more of amputation than of cure.

I know not why he is commended by Dr. *Warburton* for distinguishing the genuine from the spurious plays. In this choice he exerted no judgement of his own; the plays which he received, were given by *Hemings* and *Condel*, the first editors; and those which he rejected, though, according to the licentiousness of the press in those times, they were printed during *Shakespeare*'s life, with his name, had been omitted by his friends, and were never added to his works before the edition of 1664, from which they were copied by the later printers.

This was a work which *Pope* seems to have thought unworthy of his abilities, being not able to suppress his contempt of *the dull duty of an editor*. He understood but half his undertaking. The duty of a collator is indeed dull, yet, like other tedious tasks, is very necessary; but an emendatory critick would ill discharge his duty, without qualities very different from dulness. In perusing a corrupted piece, he must have before him all possibilities of meaning, with all possibilities of expression. Such must be his comprehension of thought, and such his copiousness of language. Out of many readings possible, he must be able to select that which best suits with the state of opinions, and modes of language prevailing in every age, and with his authour's particular cast of thought, and turn of expression. Such must be his knowledge, and such his taste. Conjectural criticism demands more than humanity possesses, and he that exercises it with most praise has very frequent need of indulgence. Let us now be told no more of the dull duty of an editor.

Confidence is the common consequence of success. They whose excellence of any kind has been loudly celebrated, are ready to conclude, that their powers are universal. *Pope*'s edition fell below his own expectations, and he was so much offended, when he was found to have left any thing for others to do, that he past the latter part of his life in a state of hostility with verbal criticism.

I have retained all his notes, that no fragment of so great a writer may be lost; his preface, valuable alike for elegance of composition and justness of remark, and containing a general criticism on his authour, so extensive that little can be added, and so exact, that little can be disputed, every editor has an interest to suppress, but that every reader would demand its insertion.

Pope was succeeded by *Theobald*, a man of narrow comprehension and small acquisitions, with no native and intrinsick splendour of genius, with little of the artificial light of learning, but zealous for minute accuracy, and not negligent in pursuing it. He collated the ancient copies, and rectified many errors. A man so anxiously scrupulous might have been expected to do more, but what little he was did was commonly right.

In his report of copies and editions he is not to be trusted, with-

515

out examination. He speaks sometimes indefinitely of copies, when he has only one. In his enumeration of editions, he mentions the two first folios as of high, and the third folio as of middle authority; but the truth is, that the first is equivalent to all others, and that the rest only deviate from it by the printer's negligence. Whoever has any of the folios has all, excepting those diversities which mere reiteration of editions will produce. I collated them all at the beginning, but afterwards used only the first.

Of his notes I have generally retained those which he retained himself in his second edition, except when they were confuted by subsequent annotators, or were too minute to merit preservation. I have sometimes adopted his restoration of a comma, without inserting the panegyrick in which he celebrated himself for his atchievement. The exuberant excrescence of his diction I have often lopped, his triumphant exultations over *Pope* and *Rowe* I have sometimes suppressed, and his contemptible ostentation I have frequently concealed; but I have in some places shewn him, as he would have shewn himself, for the reader's diversion, that the inflated emptiness of some notes may justify or excuse the contraction of the rest.

Theobald, thus weak and ignorant, thus mean and faithless, thus petulant and ostentatious, by the good luck of having *Pope* for his enemy, has escaped, and escaped alone, with reputation, from this undertaking. So willingly does the world support those who solicite favour, against those who command reverence; and so easily is he praised, whom no man can envy.

Our authour fell then into the hands of Sir *Thomas Hanmer*, the *Oxford* editor, a man, in my opinion, eminently qualified by nature for such studies. He had, what is the first requisite to emendatory criticism, that intuition by which the poet's intention is immediately discovered, and that dexterity of intellect which despatches its work by the easiest means. He had undoubtedly read much; his acquaintance with customs, opinions, and traditions, seems to have been large; and he is often learned without shew. He seldom passes what he does not understand, without an attempt to find or to make a meaning, and sometimes hastily makes what a little more attention would have found. He is solicitous to reduce to grammar, what he could not be sure that his authour intended to be grammatical. *Shakespeare* regarded more the series of ideas, than of words; and his language, not being designed for the reader's desk, was all that he desired it to be, if it conveyed his meaning to the audience.

Hanmer's care of the metre has been too violently censured. He found the measures reformed in so many passages, by the silent labours of some editors, with the silent acquiescence of the rest, that he thought himself allowed to extend a little further the license, which had already been carried so far without reprehension; and of his corrections in general, it must be confessed, that they are often just, and made commonly with the least possible violation of the text.

But, by inserting his emendations, whether invented or borrowed, into the page, without any notice of varying copies, he has appropriated the labour of his predecessors, and made his own edition of little authority. His confidence indeed, both in himself and others, was too great; he supposes all to be right that was done by *Pope* and *Theobald*; he seems not to suspect a critick of fallibility, and it was but reasonable that he should claim what he so liberally granted.

As he never writes without careful enquiry and diligent consideration, I have received all his notes, and believe that every reader will wish for more.

Of the last editor it is more difficult to speak. Respect is due to high place, tenderness to living reputation, and veneration to genius and learning; but he cannot be justly offended at that liberty of which he has himself so frequently given an example, nor very solicitous of what is thought of notes, which he ought never to have considered as part of his serious employments, and which, I suppose, since the ardour of composition is remitted, he no longer numbers among his happy effusions.

The original and predominant errour of his commentary, is acquiescence in his first thoughts; that precipitation which is produced by consciousness of quick discernment; and that confidence which presumes to do, by surveying the surface, what labour only can perform, by penetrating to bottom. His notes exhibit sometimes perverse interpretations, and sometimes improbable conjectures; he at one time gives the authour more profundity of meaning, than the sentence admits, and at another discovers absurdities, where the sense is plain to every other reader. But his emendations are likewise often happy and just; and his interpretation of obscure passages learned and sagacious.

R   517

Of his notes, I have commonly rejected those, against which the general voice of the publick has exclaimed, or which their own incongruity immediately condemns, and which, I suppose, the authour himself would desire to be forgotten. Of the rest, to part I have given the highest approbation, by inserting the offered reading in the text; part I have left to the judgment of the reader, as doubtful, though specious; and part I have censured without reserve, but I am sure without bitterness of malice, and, I hope, without wantonness of insult.

It is no pleasure to me, in revising my volumes, to observe how much paper is wasted in confutation. Whoever considers the revolutions of learning, and the various questions of greater or less importance, upon which wit and reason have exercised their powers, must lament the unsuccessfulness of enquiry, and the slow advances of truth, when he reflects, that great part of the labour of every writer is only the destruction of those that went before him. The first care of the builder of a new system, is to demolish the fabricks which are standing. The chief desire of him that comments an authour, is to shew how much other commentators have corrupted and obscured him. The opinions prevalent in one age, as truths above the reach of controversy, are confuted and rejected in another, and rise again to reception in remoter times. Thus the human mind is kept in motion without progress. Thus sometimes truth and errour, and sometimes contrarieties of errour, take each others place by reciprocal invasion. The tide of seeming knowledge which is poured over one generation, retires and leaves another naked and barren; the sudden meteors of intelligence which for a while appear to shoot their beams into the regions of obscurity, on a sudden withdraw their lustre, and leave mortals again to grope their way.

These elevations and depressions of renown, and the contradictions to which all improvers of knowledge must for ever be exposed, since they are not escaped by the highest and brightest of mankind, may surely be endured with patience by criticks and annotators, who can rank themselves but as the satellites of their authours. How canst thou beg for life, says *Achilles* to his captive, when thou knowest that thou are now to suffer only what must another day be suffered by *Achilles* ?

Dr. *Warburton* had a name sufficient to confer celebrity on those who could exalt themselves into antagonists, and his notes have raised a clamour too loud to be distinct. His chief assailants are the authours of *the Canons of criticism* and of the *Review of* Shakespeare'*s text*; of whom one ridicules his errours with airy petulance, suitable enough to the levity of the controversy; the other attacks them with gloomy malignity, as if he were dragging to justice an assassin or incendiary. The one stings like a fly, sucks a little blood, takes a gay flutter, and returns for more; the other bites like a viper, and would be glad to leave inflammations and gangrene behind him. When I think on one, with his confederates, I remember the danger of *Coriolanus*, who was afraid that *girls with spits, and boys with stones, should slay him in puny battle*; when the other crosses my imagination, I remember the prodigy in *Macbeth*,

> *An eagle tow'ring in his pride of place,*
> *Was by a mousing owl hawk'd at and kill'd.*

Let me however do them justice. One is a wit, and one a scholar. They have both shewn acuteness sufficient in the discovery of faults, and have both advanced some probable interpretations of obscure passages; but when they aspire to conjecture and emendation, it appears how falsely we all estimate our own abilities, and the little which they have been able to perform might have taught them more candour to the endeavours of others.

Before Dr. *Warburton*'s edition, *Critical observations on* Shakespeare had been published by Mr. *Upton*, a man skilled in languages, and acquainted with books, but who seems to have had no great vigour of genius or nicety of taste. Many of his explanations are curious and useful, but he likewise, though he professed to oppose the licentious confidence of editors, and adhere to the old copies, is unable to restrain the rage of emendation, though his ardour is ill seconded by his skill. Every cold empirick, when his heart is expanded by a successful experiment, swells into a theorist, and the laborious collator at some unlucky moment frolicks in conjecture.

Critical, historical and explanatory notes have been likewise published upon *Shakespeare* by Dr. *Grey*, whose diligent perusal of the old *English* writers has enabled him to make some useful observations. What he undertook he has well enough performed, but as he neither attempts judicial nor emendatory criticism, he employs rather his memory than his sagacity. It were to be wished that all would endeavour to imitate his modesty who have not been able to surpass his knowledge.

I can say with great sincerity of all my predecessors, what I hope will hereafter be said of me, that not one has left *Shakespeare* without improvement, nor is there one to whom I have not been indebted for assistance and information. Whatever I have taken from them it was my intention to refer to its original authour, and it is certain, that what I have not given to another, I believed when I wrote it to be my own. In some perhaps I have been anticipated; but if I am ever found to encroach upon the remarks of any other commentator, I am willing that the honour, be it more or less, should be transferred to the first claimant, for his right, and his alone, stands above dispute; the second can prove his pretensions only to himself, nor can himself always distinguish invention, with sufficient certainty, from recollection.

They have all been treated by me with candour, which they have not been careful of observing to one another. It is not easy to discover from what cause the acrimony of a scholiast can naturally proceed. The subjects to be discussed by him are of very small importance; they involve neither property nor liberty; nor favour the interest of sect or party. The various readings of copies, and different interpretations of a passage, seem to be questions that might exercise the wit, without engaging the passions. But, whether it be, that *small things make mean men proud*, and vanity catches small occasions; or that all contrariety of opinion, even in those that can defend it no longer, makes proud men angry; there is often found in commentaries a spontaneous strain of invective and contempt, more eager and venomous than is vented by the most furious controvertist in politicks against those whom he is hired to defame.

Perhaps the lightness of the matter may conduce to the vehemence of the agency; when the truth to be investigated is so near to inexistence, as to escape attention, its bulk is to be enlarged by rage and exclamation: That to which all would be indifferent in its original state, may attract notice when the fate of a name is appended to it. A commentator has indeed great temptations to supply by turbulence what he wants of dignity, to beat his little gold to a spacious surface, to work that to foam which no art or diligence can exalt to spirit.

The notes which I have borrowed or written are either illustrative, by which difficulties are explained; or judicial, by which faults and beauties are remarked; or emendatory, by which depravations are corrected.

The explanations transcribed from others, if I do not subjoin any other interpretation, I suppose commonly to be right, at least I intend by acquiescence to confess, that I have nothing better to propose.

After the labours of all the editors, I found many passages which appeared to me likely to obstruct the greater number of readers, and thought it my duty to facilitate their passage. It is impossible for an expositor not to write too little for some, and too much for others. He can only judge what is necessary by his own experience; and how long soever he may deliberate, will at last explain many lines which the learned will think impossible to be mistaken, and omit many for which the ignorant will want his help. These are censures merely relative, and must be quietly endured. I have endeavoured to be neither superfluously copious, nor scrupulously reserved, and hope that I have made my authour's meaning accessible to many who before were frighted from perusing him, and contributed something to the publick, by diffusing innocent and rational pleasure.

The compleat explanation of an authour not systematick and consequential, but desultory and vagrant, abounding in casual allusions and light hints, is not to be expected from any single scholiast. All personal reflections, when names are suppressed, must be in a few years irrecoverably obliterated; and customs, too minute to attract the notice of law, such as modes of dress, formalities of conversation, rules of visits, disposition of furniture, and practices of ceremony, which naturally find places in familiar dialogue, are so fugitive and unsubstantial, that they are not easily retained or recovered. What can be known, will be collected by chance, from the recesses of obscure and obsolete papers, perused commonly with some other view. Of this knowledge every man has some, and none has much; but when an authour has engaged the publick attention, those who can add any thing to his illustration, communicate their discoveries, and time produces what had eluded diligence.

To time I have been obliged to resign many passages, which, though I did not understand them, will perhaps hereafter be explained, having, I hope, illustrated some, which others have neglected, or mistaken, sometimes by short remarks, or marginal directions, such as every editor has added at his will, and often by comments more laborious than the matter will seem to deserve; but that which is most difficult is not always most important, and to an editor nothing is a trifle by which his authour is obscured.

The poetical beauties or defects I have not been very diligent to observe. Some plays have more, and some fewer judicial observations, not in proportion to their difference of merit, but because I gave this part of my design to chance and to caprice. The reader, I believe, is seldom pleased to find his opinion anticipated; it is natural to delight more in what we find or make, than in what we receive. Judgement, like other faculties, is improved by practice, and its advancement is hindered by submission to dictatorial decisions, as the memory grows torpid by the use of a table book. Some initiation is however necessary; of all skill, part is infused by precept, and part is obtained by habit; I have therefore shewn so much as may enable the candidate of criticism to discover the rest.

To the end of most plays, I have added short strictures, containing a general censure of faults, or praise of excellence; in which I know not how much I have concurred with the current opinion; but I have not, by any affectation of singularity, deviated from it. Nothing is minutely and particularly examined, and therefore it is to be supposed, that in the plays which are condemned there is much to be praised, and in these which are praised much to be condemned.

The part of criticism in which the whole succession of editors has laboured with the greatest diligence, which has occasioned the most arrogant ostentation, and excited the keenest acrimony, is the emendation of corrupted passages, to which the publick attention having been first drawn by the violence of contention between *Pope* and *Theobald*, has been continued by the persecution, which, with a kind of conspiracy, has been since raised against all the publishers of *Shakespeare*.

That many passages have passed in a state of depravation through all the editions is indubitably certain; of these the restoration is only to be attempted by collation of copies or sagacity of conjecture. The collator's province is safe and easy, the conjecturer's perilous and difficult. Yet as the greater part of the plays are extant only in one copy, the peril must not be avoided, nor the difficulty refused.

Of the readings which this emulation of amendment has hitherto produced, some from the labours of every publisher I have advanced into the text; those are to be considered as in my opinion sufficiently supported; some I have rejected without mention, as evidently erroneous; some I have left in the notes without censure or approbation, as resting in equipoise between objection and defence; and some, which seemed specious but not right, I have inserted with a subsequent animadversion.

Having classed the observations of others, I was at last to try what I could substitute for their mistakes, and how I could supply their omissions. I collated such copies as I could procure, and wished for more, but have not found the collectors of these rarities very communicative. Of the editions which chance or kindness put into my hands I have given an enumeration, that I may not be blamed for neglecting what I had not the power to do.

By examining the old copies, I soon found that the later publishers, with all their boasts of diligence, suffered many passages to stand unauthorised, and contented themselves with *Rowe*'s regulation of the text, even where they knew it to be arbitrary, and with a little consideration might have found it to be wrong. Some of these alterations are only the ejection of a word for one that appeared to him more elegant or more intelligible. These corruptions I have often silently rectified; for the history of our language, and the true force of our words, can only be preserved, by keeping the text of authours free from adulteration. Others, and those very frequent, smoothed the cadence, or regulated the measure; on these I have not exercised the same rigour; if only a word was transposed, or a particle inserted or omitted, I have sometimes suffered the line to stand; for the inconstancy of the copies is such, as that some liberties may be easily permitted. But this practice I have not suffered to proceed far, having restored the primitive diction wherever it could for any reason be preferred.

The emendations, which comparison of copies supplied, I have inserted in the text; sometimes where the improvement was slight, without notice, and sometimes with an account of the reasons of the change.

Conjecture, though it be sometimes unavoidable, I have not wantonly nor licentiously indulged. It has been my settled principle, that the reading of the ancient books is probably true, and therefore is not to be disturbed for the sake of elegance, perspicuity, or mere improvement of the sense. For though much credit is not due to the fidelity, nor any to the judgement of the first publishers, yet they who had the copy before their eyes were more likely to read it right, that we who read it only by imagination. But it is evident that they have often made strange mistakes by ignorance or negligence, and that therefore something may be properly attempted by criticism, keeping the middle way between presumption and timidity.

Such criticism I have attempted to practise, and where any passage appeared inextricably perplexed, have endeavoured to discover how it may be recalled to sense, with least violence. But my first labour is, always to turn the old text on every side, and try if there be any interstice, through which light can find its way; nor would *Huetius* himself condemn me, as refusing the trouble of research, for the ambition of alteration. In this modest industry I have not been unsuccessful. I have rescued many lines from the violations of temerity, and secured many scenes from the inroads of correction. I have adopted the *Roman* sentiment, that it is more honourable to save a citizen, than to kill an enemy, and have been more careful to protect than to attack.

I have preserved the common distribution of the plays into acts, though I believe it to be in almost all the plays void of authority. Some of those which are divided in the later editions have no division in the first folio, and some that are divided in the folio have no division in the preceding copies. The settled mode of the theatre requires four intervals in the play, but few, if any, of our authour's compositions can be properly distributed in that manner. An act is so much of the drama as passes without intervention of time or change of place. A pause makes a new act. In every real, and therefore in every imitative action, the intervals may be more or fewer, the restriction of five acts being accidental and arbitrary. This *Shakespeare* knew, and this he practised; his plays were written, and at first printed in one unbroken continuity, and ought now to be exhibited with short pauses, interposed as often as the scene is changed, or any considerable time is required to pass. This method would at once quell a thousand absurdities.

In restoring the authour's works to their integrity, I have considered the punctuation as wholly in my power; for what could be their care of colons and commas, who corrupted words and sentences. Whatever could be done by adjusting points is therefore silently performed, in some plays with much diligence, in others with less; it is hard to keep a busy eye steadily fixed upon evanescent atoms, or a discursive mind upon evanescent truth.

The same liberty has been taken with a few particles, or other words of slight effect. I have sometimes inserted or omitted them without notice. I have done that sometimes, which the other editors have done always, and which indeed the state of the text may sufficiently justify.

The greater part of readers, instead of blaming us for passing trifles, will wonder that on mere trifles so much labour is expended, with such importance of debate, and such solemnity of diction. To these I answer with confidence, that they are judging of an art which they do not understand; yet cannot much reproach them with their ignorance, nor promise that they would become in general, by learning criticism, more useful, happier or wiser.

As I practised conjecture more, I learned to trust it less; and after I had printed a few plays, resolved to insert none of my own readings in the text. Upon this caution I now congratulate myself, for every day encreases my doubt of my emendations.

Since I have confined my imaginations to the margin, it must not be considered as very reprehensible, if I have suffered it to play some freaks in its own dominion. There is no danger in conjecture, if it be proposed as conjecture; and while the text remains uninjured, those changes may be safely offered, which are not considered even by him that offers them as necessary or safe.

If my readings are of little value, they have not been ostentatiously displayed or importunately obtruded. I could have written longer notes, for the art of writing notes is not of difficult attainment. The work is performed, first by railing at the stupidity, negligence, ignorance, and asinine tastelessness of the former editors, and shewing, from all that goes before and all that follows, the inelegance and absurdity of the old reading; then by proposing something, which to superficial readers would seem specious, but which the editor rejects with indignation; then by producing the true reading, with a long paraphrase, and concluding with loud acclamations on the discovery, and a sober wish for the advancement and prosperity of genuine criticism.

All this may be done, and perhaps done sometimes without impropriety. But I have always suspected that the reading is right, which requires many words to prove it wrong; and the emendation wrong, that cannot without so much labour appear to be right. The justness of a happy restoration strikes at once, and the moral precept may be well applied to criticism, *quod dubitas ne feceris*.

To dread the shore which he sees spread with wrecks, is natural to the sailor. I had before my eye, so many critical adventures ended in miscarriage, that caution was forced upon me. I encountered in every page Wit struggling with its own sophistry, and Learning confused by the multiplicity of its views. I was forced to censure those whom I admired, and could not but reflect, while I was dispossessing their emendations, how soon the same fate might happen to my own, and how many of the readings which I have corrected may be by some other editor defended and established.

> *Criticks, I saw, that other's names efface,*
> *And fix their own, with labour, in the place;*
> *Their own, like others, soon their place resign'd,*
> *Or disappear'd, and left the first behind.*   POPE.

That a conjectural critick should often be mistaken, cannot be wonderful, either to others or himself, if it be considered, that in his art there is no system, no principal and axiomatical truth that regulates subordinate positions. His chance of errour is renewed at every attempt; an oblique view of the passage, a slight misapprehension of a phrase, a casual inattention to the parts connected, is sufficient to make him not only fail, but fail ridiculously; and when he succeeds best, he produces perhaps but one reading of many probable, and he that suggests another will always be able to dispute his claims.

It is an unhappy state, in which danger is hid under pleasure. The allurements of emendation are scarcely resistible. Conjecture has all the joy and all the pride of invention, and he that has once started a happy change, is too much delighted to consider what objections may rise against it.

Yet conjectural criticism has been of great use in the learned world; nor is it my intention to depreciate a study, that has exercised so many mighty minds, from the revival of learning to our own age, from the Bishop of *Aleria* to English *Bentley*. The criticks on ancient authours have, in the exercise of their sagacity, many assistances, which the editor of *Shakespeare* is condemned to want. They are employed upon grammatical and settled languages, whose construction contributes so much to perspicuity, that *Homer* has fewer passages unintelligible than *Chaucer*. The words have not only a known regimen, but invariable quantities, which direct and confine the choice. There are commonly more manuscripts than one; and they do not often conspire in the same mistakes. Yet *Scaliger* could confess to *Salmasius* how little satisfaction his emendations gave him. *Illudunt nobis conjecturæ nostræ, quarum nos pudet, posteaquam in meliores codices incidimus.* And *Lipsius* could complain, that criticks were making faults, by trying to remove them, *Ut olim vitiis, ita nunc remediis laboratur.* And indeed, where mere conjecture is to be used, the emendations of *Scaliger* and *Lipsius*, notwithstanding their wonderful sagacity and erudition, are often vague and disputable, like mine or *Theobald's*.

Perhaps I may not be more censured for doing wrong, than for doing little; for raising in the publick expectations, which at last I have not answered. The expectation of ignorance is indefinite, and that of knowledge is often tyrannical. It is hard to satisfy those who know not what to demand, or those who demand by design what they think impossible to be done. I have indeed disappointed no opinion more than my own; yet I have endeavoured to perform my task with no slight solicitude. Not a single passage in the whole work has appeared to me corrupt, which I have not attempted to restore; or obscure, which I have not endeavoured to illustrate. In many I have failed like others; and from many, after all my efforts, I have retreated, and confessed the repulse. I have not passed over, with affected superiority, what is equally difficult to the reader and to myself, but where I could not instruct him, have owned my ignorance. I might easily have accumulated a mass of seeming learning upon easy scenes; but it ought not to be imputed to negligence, that, where nothing was necessary, nothing has been done, or that, where others have said enough, I have said no more.

Notes are often necessary, but they are necessary evils. Let him, that is yet unacquainted with the powers of *Shakespeare*, and who desires to feel the highest pleasure that the drama can give, read every play from the first scene to the last, with utter negligence of all his commentators. When his fancy is once on the wing, let it not stoop at correction or explanation. When his attention is strongly engaged, let it disdain alike to turn aside to the name of *Theobald* and of *Pope*. Let him read on through brightness and obscurity, through integrity and corruption; let him preserve his comprehension of the dialogue and his interest in the fable. And when the pleasures of novelty have ceased, let him attempt exactness, and read the commentators.

Particular passages are cleared by notes, but the general effect of the work is weakened. The mind is refrigerated by interruption; the thoughts are diverted from the principal subject; the reader is weary, he suspects not why; and at last throws away the book, which he has too diligently studied.

Parts are not to be examined till the whole has been surveyed; there is a kind of intellectual remoteness necessary for the comprehension of any great work in its full design and its true proportions; a close approach shews the smaller niceties, but the beauty of the whole is discerned no longer.

It is not very grateful to consider how little the succession of editors has added to this authour's power of pleasing. He was read, admired, studied, and imitated, while he was yet deformed with all the improprieties which ignorance and neglect could accumulate upon him; while the reading was yet not rectified, nor his allusions understood; yet then did *Dryden* pronounce "that *Shakespeare* was the man, who, of all modern and perhaps ancient poets, had the largest and most comprehensive soul. All the images of nature were still present to him, and he drew them not laboriously, but luckily: When he describes any thing, you more than see it, you feel it too. Those who accuse him to have wanted learning, give him the greater commendation: he was naturally learned: he needed not the spectacles of books to read nature; he looked inwards, and found her there. I cannot say he is every where alike; were he so, I should do him injury to compare him with the greatest of mankind. He is many times flat and insipid; his comick wit degenerating into clenches, his serious swelling into bombast. But he is always great, when some great occasion is presented to him: No man can say, he ever had a fit subject for his wit, and did not then raise himself as high above the rest of poets,

Quantum lenta solent inter viburna cupressi."

It is to be lamented, that such a writer should want a commentary; that his language should become obsolete, or his sentiments obscure. But it is vain to carry wishes beyond the condition of human things; that which must happen to all, has happened to *Shakespeare,* by accident and time; and more than has been suffered by any other writer since the use of types, has been suffered by him through his own negligence of fame, or perhaps by that superiority of mind, which despised its own performances, when it compared them with its powers, and judged those works unworthy to be preserved, which the criticks of following ages were to contend for the fame of restoring and explaining.

Among these candidates of inferiour fame, I am now to stand the judgment of the publick; and wish that I could confidently produce my commentary as equal to the encouragement which I have had the honour of receiving. Every work of this kind is by its nature deficient, and I should feel little solicitude about the sentence, were it to be pronounced only by the skilful and the learned.

NOTES on the PLAYS

THE TEMPEST
1.2.250

THAT the Character and Conduct of *Prospero* may be understood, something must be known of the System of Enchantment, which supplied all the Marvellous found in the Romances of the middle Ages. This System seems to be founded on the Opinion that the fallen Spirits, having different Degrees of Guilt, had different Habitations alloted them at their Expulsion, some being confined in Hell, *some, as Hooker,* who delivers the Opinion of our Poet's Age, expresses it, *dispersed in Air, some on Earth, some in Water, others in Caves, Dens or Minerals under the Earth.* Of these some were more malignant and mischievous than others. The earthy Spirits seem to have been thought the most depraved, and the aerial the least vitiated. Thus *Prospero* observes of *Ariel,*

> ——*Thou wast a Spirit too delicate*
> *To act her* earthy *and abhorred Commands.*

Over these Spirits a Power might be obtained by certain Rites performed or Charms learned. This Power was called the *Black Art*, or *Knowledge of Enchantment.* The Enchanter being, as King *James* observes in his *Demonology,* one *who commands the Devil, whereas the Witch serves him.* Those who thought best of this Art, the Existence of which was, I am afraid, believed very seriously, held that certain Sounds and Characters had a physical Power over Spirits, and compelled their Agency; others who condemned the Practice, which in reality was surely never practised, were of Opinion, with more Reason, that the Power of Charms arose *only* from compact, and was no more than the Spirits voluntary allowed them for the Seduction of Man. The Art was held by all, though not equally criminal yet unlawful, and therefore *Casaubon,* speaking of one who had Commerce with Spirits, blames him, though he imagines him *one of the best Kind who dealt with them by Way of Command*. Thus *Prospero* repents of his Art in the last Scene. The Spirits were always considered as in some Measure enslaved to the Enchanter, at least for a Time, and as serving with Unwillingness, therefore *Ariel* so often begs for Liberty; and *Caliban* observes that the Spirits serve *Prospero* with no good Will, but *hate him rootedly*.—Of these Trifles enough.

Ariel's lays, however seasonable and efficacious, must be allowed to be of no supernatural dignity or elegance, they express nothing great, nor reveal any thing above mortal discovery.

The reason for which *Ariel* is introduced thus trifling is, that he and his companions are evidently of the fairy kind, an order of Beings to which tradition has always ascribed a sort of diminutive agency, powerful but ludicrous, a humorous and frolick controlment of nature, well expressed by the Songs of *Ariel*.

A MIDSUMMER-NIGHT'S DREAM
3.1

In the time of *Shakespear* there were many companies of players, sometimes five at the same time, contending for the favour of the publick. Of these some were undoubtedly very unskilful and very poor, and it is probable that the design of this Scene was to ridicule their ignorance, and the odd expedients to which they might be driven by the want of proper decorations. *Bottom* was perhaps the head of a rival house, and is therefore honoured with an Ass's head.

3.1.173
the fiery glow-worm's eyes.

I know not how *Shakespeare*, who commonly derived his knowledge of nature from his own observation, happened to place the glow-worm's light in his eyes, which is only in his tail.

3.2.367
——this virtuous property.

Salutiferous. So he calls, in The Tempest, *Poisonous dew*, wicked dew.

4.1.108

I know not why *Shakespear* calls this play a *Midsummer-Night's Dream*, when he so carefully informs us that it happened on the night preceding *May* day.

THE TWO GENTLEMEN OF VERONA

It is observable (I know not for what cause) that the stile of this comedy is less figurative, and more natural and unaffected than the greater part of this Author's, tho' supposed to be one of the first he wrote.

POPE.

To this observation of Mr. *Pope*, which is very just, Mr. *Theobald* has added, that this is one of *Shakespear's worst plays, and is less corrupted than any other.* Mr. *Upton* peremptorily determines, *that if any proof can be drawn from manner and style, this play must be sent packing and seek for its parent elsewhere. How otherwise*, says he, *do painters distinguish copies from originals, and have not authours their peculiar style and manner from which a true critick can form as unerring a judgment as a Painter?* I am afraid this illustration of a critick's science will not prove what is desired. A Painter knows a copy from an original by rules somewhat resembling these by which criticks know a translation, which if it be literal, and literal it must be to resemble the copy of a picture, will be easily distinguished. Copies are known from originals even when the painter copies his own picture; so if an authour should literally translate his work he would lose the manner of an original.

Mr. *Upton* confounds the copy of a picture with the imitation of a painter's manner. Copies are easily known, but good imitations are not detected with equal certainty, and are, by the best judges, often mistaken. Nor is it true that the writer has always peculiarities equally distinguishable with those of the painter. The peculiar manner of each arises from the desire, natural to every performer, of facilitating his subsequent works by recurrence to his former ideas; this recurrence produces that repetition which is called habit. The painter, whose work is partly intellectual and partly manual, has habits of the mind, the eye and the hand, the writer has only habits of the mind. Yet, some painters have differed as much from themselves as from any other; and I have been told, that there is little resemblance between the first works of *Raphael* and the last. The same variation may be expected in writers; and if it be true, as it seems, that they are less subject to habit, the difference between their works may be yet greater.

But by the internal marks of a composition we may discover the authour with probability, though seldom with certainty. When I read this play I cannot but think that I discover both in the serious

532

and ludicrous scenes, the language and sentiments of *Shakespear*. It is not indeed one of his most powerful effusions, it has neither many diversities of character, nor striking delineations of life, but it abounds in γνῶμαι beyond most of his plays, and few have more lines or passages which, singly considered, are eminently beautiful. I am yet inclined to believe that it was not very successful, and suspect that it has escaped corruption, only because being seldom played it was less exposed to the hazards of transcription.

1.1.70

That this, like many other Scenes, is mean and vulgar, will be universally allowed; but that it was interpolated by the players seems advanced without any proof, only to give a greater licence to criticism.

In this play there is a strange mixture of knowledge and ignorance, of care and negligence. The versification is often excellent, the allusions are learned and just; but the authour conveys his heroes by sea from one inland town to another in the same country; he places the Emperour at *Milan* and sends his young men to attend him, but never mentions him more; he makes *Protheus*, after an interview with *Silvia*, say he has only seen her picture, and, if we may credit the old copies, he has by mistaking places, left his scenery inextricable. The reason of all this confusion seems to be, that he took his story from a novel which he sometimes followed, and sometimes forsook, sometimes remembered, and sometimes forgot.

MEASURE FOR MEASURE

There is perhaps not one of *Shakespear*'s plays more darkened than this by the peculiarities of its Authour, and the unskilfulness of its Editors, by distortions of phrase, or negligence of transcription.

1.1.52

We have with a leaven'd *and prepared choice.*

Leaven'd has no sense in this place: we should read LEVEL'D *choice.* The allusion is to archery, when a man has fixed upon his object, after taking good aim.—WARBURTON.

No emendation is necessary. *Leaven'd choice* is one of *Shakespear*'s harsh metaphors. His train of ideas seems to be this. *I have proceeded to you with choice* mature, concocted, fermented, *leavened.* When Bread is *leavened,* it is left to ferment: a *leavened* choice is therefore a choice not hasty, but considerate, not declared as soon as it fell into the imagination, but suffered to work long in the mind. Thus explained it suits better with *prepared* than *levelled.*

2.2.142

That my sense breeds with it.

Thus all the folios. Some later Editor has changed *breeds* to *bleeds,* and Dr. *Warburton* blames poor Mr. *Theobald* for recalling the old word, which yet is certainly right. *My sense* breeds *with her sense,* that is, new thoughts are stirring in my mind, new conceptions are *hatched* in my imagination. So we say to *brood* over thought.

2.3.11

Who falling in the flaws *of her own youth,*
Hath blister'd *her report :*

Who doth not see that the integrity of the metaphor requires we should read FLAMES *of her own youth.*—WARBURTON.

Who does not see that upon such principles there is no end of correction.

3.1.14

Thou art not noble:
For all th' accommodations, that thou bear'st,
Are nurs'd by baseness.

Dr. *Warburton* is undoubtedly mistaken in supposing that by *baseness* is meant *self-love* here assigned as the motive of all human actions. *Shakespear* meant only to observe, that a minute analysis of life at once destroys that splendour which dazzles the imagination. Whatever grandeur can display, or luxury enjoy, is procured by *baseness,* by offices of which the mind shrinks from the contemplation. All the delicacies of the table may be traced back to the shambles and the dunghill, all magnificence of building was hewn from the quarry, and all the pomp of ornaments, dug from among the damps and darkness of the mine.

3.1.16

The soft and tender fork
Of a poor worm.

Worm is put for any creeping thing or *serpent*. *Shakespear* supposes falsely, but according to the vulgar notion, that a serpent wounds with his tongue, and that his tongue is *forked*. He confounds reality and fiction, a serpent's tongue is *soft* but not *forked* nor hurtful. If it could hurt, it could not be soft. In *Midsummer-Night's Dream* he has the same notion.

⸺*With* doubler *tongue*
Than thine, O serpent, never adder stung.

3.1.17

Thy best of rest is sleep,
And that thou oft provok'st; yet grosly fear'st
Thy death which is no more.

Evidently from the following passage of *Cicero; Habes somnum imaginem Mortis, eamque quotidie induis, & dubitas quin sensus in morte nullus sit, cum in ejus simulacro videas esse nullum sensum.* But the Epicurean insinuation is, with great judgment, omitted in this imitation. —WARBURTON.

Here Dr. *Warburton* might have found a sentiment worthy of his animadversion. I cannot without indignation find *Shakespear* saying, that *death is only sleep*, lengthening out his exhortation by by a sentence which in the *Friar* is impious, in the reasoner is foolish, and in the poet trite and vulgar.

3.1.32

Thou hast nor youth, nor age;
But as it were an after-dinner's sleep,
Dreaming on both.

This is exquisitely imagined. When we are young we busy ourselves in forming schemes for succeeding time, and miss the gratifications that are before us; when we are old we amuse the languour of age with the recollection of youthful pleasures or performances; so that our life, of which no part is filled with the business of the present time, resembles our dreams after dinner, when the events of the morning are mingled with the designs of the evening.

3.1.36

When thou'rt old and rich,
Thou hast neither heat, affection, limb, nor beauty
To make thy riches pleasant.

But how does beauty make *riches pleasant?* We should read BOUNTY, which compleats the sense, and is this; Thou hast neither the pleasure of enjoying riches thy self, for thou wantest vigour: nor of seeing it enjoyed by others, for thou wantest *bounty.* Where the making the want of *bounty* as inseparable from old age as the want of *health*, is extremely satyrical tho' not altogether just.—WARBURTON.

I am inclined to believe that neither man nor woman will have much difficulty to tell how *beauty makes riches pleasant*. Surely this emendation, though it is elegant and ingenious, is not such as that an opportunity of inserting it should be purchased by declaring ignorance of what every one knows, by confessing insensibility of what every one feels.

3.1.139

Is't not kind of incest, to take life
From thine own sister's shame?

In *Isabella's* declamation there is something harsh, and something forced and far-fetched. But her indignation cannot be thought violent when we consider her not only as a virgin but as a nun.

4.3.4

First here's young Mr. Rash, &c.

This enumeration of the inhabitants of the prison affords a very striking view of the practices predominant in *Shakespear's* age. Besides those whose follies are common to all times, we have four fighting men and a traveller. It is not unlikely that the originals of these pictures were then known.

4.5.1

These letters at fit time deliver me.

Peter never delivers the letters, but tells his story without any credentials. The poet forgot the plot which he had formed.

5.1.452

'Till he did look on me.

The *Duke* has justly observed that *Isabel* is *importuned against all sense* to solicit for *Angelo*, yet here *against all sense* she solicits for him. Her argument is extraordinary.

> *A due sincerity govern'd his deeds,*
> *'Till he did look on me; since it is so,*
> *Let him not die.*

That *Angelo* had committed all the crimes charged against him, as far as he could commit them, is evident. The only *intent* which *his act did not overtake*, was the defilement of *Isabel*. Of this *Angelo* was only intentionally guilty.

Angelo's crimes were such, as must sufficiently justify punishment, whether its end be to secure the innocent from wrong, or to deter guilt by example; and I believe every reader feels some indignation when he finds him spared. From what extenuation of his crime can *Isabel*, who yet supposes her brother dead, form any plea in his favour. *Since he was good 'till he looked on me, let him not die.* I am afraid our Varlet Poet intended to inculcate, that women think ill of nothing that raises the credit of their beauty, and are ready, however virtuous, to pardon any act which they think incited by their own charms.

5.1.483

It is somewhat strange, that *Isabel* is not made to express either gratitude, wonder or joy at the sight of her brother.

After the pardon of two murderers *Lucio* might be treated by the good *Duke* with less harshness; but perhaps the Poet intended to show, what is too often seen, *that men easily forgive wrongs which are not committed against themselves.*

The novel of *Cynthio Giraldi*, from which *Shakespear* is supposed to have borrowed this fable, may be read in *Shakespear illustrated*, elegantly translated, with remarks which will assist the enquirer to discover how much absurdity *Shakespear* has admitted or avoided.

I cannot but suspect that some other had new modelled the novel of *Cynthio*, or written a story which in some particulars resembled it, and that *Cinthio* was not the authour whom *Shakespear* immediately followed. The Emperour in *Cinthio* is named *Maximine*, the Duke, in *Shakespear*'s enumeration of the persons of the drama, is called *Vincentio*. This appears a very slight remark; but since the Duke has no name in the play, nor is ever mentioned but by his title, why should he be called *Vincentio* among the *Persons*, but because the name was copied from the story, and placed superfluously at the head of the list by the mere habit of transcription? It is therefore likely that there was then a story of *Vincentio* Duke of *Vienna*, different from that of *Maximine* Emperour of the *Romans*.

Of this play the light or comick part is very natural and pleasing, but the grave scenes, if a few passages be excepted, have more labour than elegance. The plot is rather intricate than artful. The time of the action is indefinite; some time, we know not how much, must have elapsed between the recess of the *Duke* and the imprisonment of *Claudio*; for he must have learned the story of *Mariana* in his disguise, or he delegated his power to a man already known to be corrupted. The unities of action and place are sufficiently preserved.

THE MERCHANT OF VENICE
1.2.49
There is the Count Palatine.

I am always inclined to believe, that *Shakespear* has more allusions to particular facts and persons than his readers commonly suppose. The Count here mentioned was, perhaps, *Albertus a Lasco*, a *Polish Palatine*, who visited *England* in our Authour's time, was eagerly caressed, and splendidly entertained, but running in debt, at last stole away, and endeavoured to repair his fortune by enchantment.

2.1.7
To prove whose blood is reddest, his or mine.

To understand how the tawney Prince, whose savage dignity is very well supported, means to recommend himself by this challenge, it must be remembered that *red* blood is a traditionary sign of courage: Thus *Macbeth* calls one of his frighted soldiers, a *lily liver'd* Lown; again in this play, Cowards are said to *have livers white as milk*; and an effeminate and timorous man is termed a *milk-sop*.

2.1.25
That slew the Sophy *and a* Persian *Prince,*

Shakespear seldom escapes well when he is entangled with Geography. The Prince of *Morocco* must have travelled far to kill the *Sophy* of *Persia*.

2.7. end

A gentle riddance—draw the curtains; go—
Let all of his complexion chuse me so.

The old quarto Edition of 1600 has no distribution of acts, but proceeds from the beginning to the end in an unbroken tenour. This play therefore having been probably divided without authority by the publishers of the first folio, lies open to a new regulation if any more commodious division can be proposed. The story is itself so wildly incredible, and the changes of the scene so frequent and capricious, that the probability of action does not deserve much care; yet it may be proper to observe, that, by concluding the second act here, time is given for *Bassanio's* passage to *Belmont*.

5.1.33

None, but a holy hermit, and her maid.

I do not perceive the use of this hermit, of whom nothing is seen or heard afterwards. The Poet had first planned his fable some other way, and inadvertently, when he changed his scheme, retained something of the original design.

5.1.129

Let me give light, but let me not be light;

There is scarcely any word with which *Shakespear* so much delights to trifle as with *light*, in its various significations.

Of *The* MERCHANT *of* VENICE the stile is even and easy, with few peculiarities of diction, or anomalies of construction. The comick part raises laughter, and the serious fixes expectation. The probability of either one or the other story cannot be maintained. The union of two actions in one event is in this drama eminently happy. *Dryden* was much pleased with his own address in connecting the two plots of his *Spanish Friar*, which yet, I believe, the critick will find excelled by this play.

AS YOU LIKE IT
2.1.13

It was the current opinion in *Shakespeare's* time, that in the head of an old toad was to be found a stone, or pearl, to which great virtues were ascribed. This stone has been often sought, but nothing has been found more than accidental or perhaps morbid indurations of the skull.

2.7.94

The thorny point
Of sharp distress has ta'en *from me the shew*
Of smooth civility.

We might read *torn* with more elegance, but elegance alone will not justify alteration.

3.2.155

Atalanta's *better part.*

I know not well what could be the better part of *Atalanta* here ascribed to *Rosalind.* Of the *Atalanta* most celebrated, and who therefore must be intended here where she has no epithet of discrimination, the *better part* seems to have been her heels, and the worse part was so bad that *Rosalind* would not thank her lover for the comparison. There is a more obscure *Atalanta,* a Huntress and a Heroine, but of her nothing bad is recorded, and therefore I know not which was the better part. *Shakespeare* was no despicable Mythologist, yet he seems here to have mistaken some other character for that of *Atalanta.*

3.2.186

I was never so be-rhymed since Pythagoras *time, that I was an* Irish *rat.*

Rosalind is a very learned Lady. She alludes to the *Pythagorean* doctrine which teaches that souls transmigrate from one animal to another, and relates that in his time she was an *Irish rat,* and by some metrical charm was rhymed to death. The power of killing rats with rhymes *Donne* mentions in his satires, and *Temple* in his treatises. Dr. *Gray* has produced a similar passage from *Randolph.*

> ——*My Poets*
> *Shall with a saytire steeped in vinegar*
> *Rhyme them to death, as they do rats in* Ireland.

3.4

There is much of nature in this petty perverseness of *Rosalind*: she finds faults in her lover, in hope to be contradicted, and when

Celia in sportive malice too readily seconds her accusations, she contradicts herself, rather than suffer her favourite to want a vindication.

4.1.38

I will scarce think you have swam in a Gondola.

That is, *been at* Venice, the seat at that time of all licentiousness, where the young *English* gentlemen wasted their fortunes, debased their morals, and sometimes lost their religion.

The fashion of travelling which prevailed very much in our author's time, was considered by the wiser men as one of the principal causes of corrupt manners. It was therefore gravely censured by *Ascham* in his *Schoolmaster*, and by Bishop *Hall* in his *Quo Vadis*, and is here, and in other passages ridiculed by *Shakespeare*.

Of this play the fable is wild and pleasing. I know not how the ladies will approve the facility with which both *Rosalind* and *Celia* give away their hearts. To *Celia* much may be forgiven for the heroism of her friendship. The character of *Jaques* is natural and well preserved. The comick dialogue is very sprightly, with less mixture of low buffoonery than in some other plays; and the graver part is elegant and harmonious. By hastening to the end of his work *Shakespeare* suppressed the dialogue between the usurper and the hermit, and lost an opportunity of exhibiting a moral lesson in which he might have found matter worthy of his highest powers.

LOVE'S LABOUR'S LOST

The stile of the rhyming scenes in this play is often entangled and obscure.

1.1.77

——while truth the while
Doth falsly blind the eye-sight of his look:
Light, seeking light, doth light of light beguile;

Falsly is here, and in many other places, the same as *dishonestly* or *treacherously*. The whole sense of this gingling declamation is only this, that *a man by too close study may read himself blind*, which might have been told with less obscurity in fewer words.

1.1.149

Necessity will make us all forsworn.

Biron amidst his extravagancies, speaks with great justness against the folly of vows. They are made without sufficient regard to the variations of life, and are therefore broken by some unforeseen necessity. They proceed commonly from a presumptuous confidence, and a false estimate of human power.

4.2

Holofernes.

I am not of the learned commentator's opinion, that the satire of *Shakespeare* is so seldom personal. It is of the nature of personal invectives to be soon unintelligible; and the authour that gratifies private malice, *animam in volnere ponit*, destroys the future efficacy of his own writings, and sacrifices the esteem of succeeding times to the laughter of a day. It is no wonder, therefore, that the sarcasms which, perhaps, in the authour's time *set the* playhouse *in a roar*, are now lost among general reflections. Yet whether the character of *Holofernes* was pointed at any particular man, I am, notwithstanding the plausibility of Dr. *Warburton*'s conjecture, inclined to doubt. Every man adheres as long as he can to his own pre-conceptions. Before I read this note I considered the character of *Holofernes* as borrowed from the *Rhombus* of Sir *Philip Sidney*, who, in a kind of pastoral entertainment exhibited to Queen *Elizabeth*, has introduced a schoolmaster so called, speaking *a leash of languages at once*, and puzzling himself and his auditors with a jargon like that of *Holofernes* in the present play. *Sidney* himself might bring the character from *Italy*; for as *Peacham* observes, the Schoolmaster has long been one of the ridiculous personages in the farces of that country.

5.1.2

Your reasons at dinner have been sharp and sententious; pleasant without scurrility, witty without affectation, audacious without impudency, learned without opinion, and strange without heresy.

I know not well what degree of respect *Shakespeare* intends to obtain for this vicar, but he has here put into his mouth a finished representation of colloquial excellence. It is very difficult to add any thing to this character of the schoolmaster's table-talk, and perhaps all the precepts of *Castiglione* will scarcely be found to comprehend a rule for conversation so justly delineated, so widely dilated, and so nicely limited.

It may be proper just to note, that *reason* here, and in many other places, signifies *discourse*, and that *audacious* is used in a good sense for *spirited, animated, confident. Opinion* is the same with *obstinacy* or *opiniatreté.*

5.2.69

PRINCESS. *None are so surely caught, when they are catch'd,*
    As wit turn'd fool: folly, in wisdom hatch'd,
    Hath wisdom's warrant, and the help of school;
    And wit's own grace to grace a learned fool.

These are observations worthy of a man who has surveyed human nature with the closest attention.

5.2.205

Vouchsafe, bright moon, and these thy stars, to shine.

When Queen *Elizabeth* asked an ambassadour how he liked her Ladies, *It is hard,* said he, *to judge of stars in the presence of the sun.*

In this play, which all the editors have concurred to censure, and some have rejected as unworthy of our Poet, it must be confessed that there are many passages mean, childish, and vulgar; and some which ought not to have been exhibited, as we are told they were, to a maiden queen. But there are scattered, through the whole, many sparks of genius; nor is there any play that has more evident marks of the hand of *Shakespeare.*

THE WINTER'S TALE
1.2.260

Whereof the execution did cry out
    Against the non-performance,——

This is one of the expressions by which *Shakespeare* too frequently clouds his meaning. This sounding phrase means, I think, no more than *a thing necessary to be done.*

3.2.55

I ne'er heard yet,
That any of those bolder vices wanted
Less *impudence to gainsay what they did,*
Than to perform it first.

It is apparent that according to the proper, at least according to the present, use of words, *less* should be *more*, or *wanted* should be *had*. But *Shakespeare* is very uncertain in his use of negatives. It may be necessary once to observe, that in our language two negatives did not originally affirm, but strengthen the negation. This mode of speech was in time changed, but as the change was made in opposition to long custom, it proceeded gradually, and uniformity was not obtained but through an intermediate confusion.

3.2.152

This vehement retractation of *Leontes*, accompanied with the confession of more crimes than he was suspected of, is agreeable to our daily experience of the vicissitudes of violent tempers, and the eruptions of minds oppressed with guilt.

4.4.21

How would he look, to see his work, so noble,
Vilely bound up!

It is impossible for any man to rid his mind of his profession. The authourship of *Shakespeare* has supplied him with a metaphor, which rather than he would lose it, he has put with no great propriety into the mouth of a country maid. Thinking of his own works his mind passed naturally to the Binder. I am glad that he has no hint at an Editor.

5.2.45

Did you see the meeting of the two Kings?

It was, I suppose, only to spare his own labour that the poet put this whole scene into narrative, for though part of the transaction was already known to the audience, and therefore could not properly be shewn again, yet the two kings might have met upon the stage, and after the examination of the old shepherd, the young Lady might have been recognized in sight of the spectators.

This play, as Dr. *Warburton* justly observes, is, with all its absurdities, very entertaining. The character of *Autolycus* is very naturally conceived, and strongly represented.

TWELFTH NIGHT
1.1.21

That instant I was turn'd into a hart,

This image evidently alludes to the story of *Acteon*, by which *Shakespeare* seems to think men cautioned against too great familiarity with forbidden beauty. *Acteon*, who saw *Diana* naked, and was torn in pieces by his hounds, represents a man, who indulging his eyes, or his imagination, with the view of a woman that he cannot gain, has his heart torn with incessant longing. An interpretation far more elegant and natural than that of Sir *Francis Bacon*, who, in his *Wisdom of the Antients*, supposes this story to warn us against enquiring into the secrets of princes, by showing, that those who know that which for reasons of state is to be concealed, will be detected and destroyed by their own servants.

1.2.41

O, that I serv'd that lady . . .

Viola seems to have formed a very deep design with very little premeditation: she is thrown by shipwreck on an unknown coast, hears that the prince is a batchelor, and resolves to supplant the lady whom he courts.

1.2.55

I'll serve this Duke.

Viola is an excellent schemer, never at a loss; if she cannot serve the lady, she will serve the Duke.

2.3.81

Malvolio's *a* Peg-a-Ramsey . . . *Tilly valley, Lady!*

Peg-a-Ramsey I do not understand. *Tilly valley* was an interjection of contempt, which Sir *Thomas More*'s lady is recorded to have had very often in her mouth.

2.5.66

wind up my watch,

In our authour's time watches were very uncommon. When *Guy Faux* was taken, it was urged as a circumstance of suspicion that a watch was found upon him.

3.4.183

Fare thee well, and God have mercy upon one of our souls: he may have mercy upon mine, but my hope is better.

It were much to be wished, that *Shakespeare* in this and some other passages, had not ventured so near profaneness.

3.4.257

He is Knight, dubb'd with unhack'd rapier, and on carpet consideration;——

That is, he is no soldier by profession, not a Knight Banneret, dubbed in the field of battle, but, *on carpet consideration*, at a festivity, or on some peaceable occasion, when knights receive their dignity kneeling not on the ground, as in war, but on a *carpet*. This is, I believe, the original of the contemptuous term a *carpet knight*, who was naturally held in scorn by the men of war.

5.1.42

Bells of St. Bennet.

When in this play he mentioned the *bed of* Ware, he recollected that the scene was in *Illyria*, and added *in England*; but his sense of the same impropriety could not restrain him from the bells of St. *Bennet*.

This play is in the graver part elegant and easy, and in some of the lighter scenes exquisitely humorous. *Ague-cheek* is drawn with great propriety, but his character is, in a great measure, that of natural fatuity, and is therefore not the proper prey of a satirist. The soliloquy of *Malvolio* is truly comick; he is betrayed to ridicule merely by his pride. The marriage of *Olivia*, and the succeeding perplexity, though well enough contrived to divert on the stage, wants credibility, and fails to produce the proper instruction required in the drama, as it exhibits no just picture of life.

THE MERRY WIVES OF WINDSOR
3.4.13

Thy father's wealth
Was the first motive that I woo'd thee.

Some light may be given to those who shall endeavour to calculate the encrease of *English* wealth, by observing, that *Latymer* in the time of *Edward* VI. mentions it as a proof of his father's prosperity, *That though but a yeoman, he gave his daughters five pounds each for her portion.* At the latter end of *Elizabeth*, seven hundred pounds were such a temptation to courtship, as make all other motives suspected. *Congreve* makes twelve thousand pounds more than a counterballance to the affectation of *Belinda.* No poet would now fly his favourite character at less than fifty thousand.

3.5.156

I'll be horn-mad.

There is no image which our authour appears so fond of as that of a cuckold's horns. Scarcely a light character is introduced that does not endeavour to produce merriment by some allusion to horned husbands. As he wrote his plays for the stage rather than the press, he perhaps reviewed them seldom, and did not observe this repetition, or finding the jest, however frequent, still successful, did not think correction necessary.

4.2.204

I spy a great peard under her muffler.

As the second stratagem, by which *Falstaff* escapes, is much the grosser of the two, I wish it had been practised first. It is very unlikely that *Ford* having been so deceived before, and knowing that he had been deceived, would suffer him to escape in so slight a disguise.

4.3.13

They must come *off.*

To come off, signifies in our authour, sometimes *to be uttered with spirit and volubility.* In this place it seems to mean what is in our time expressed by *to come down*, to pay liberally and readily. These accidental and colloquial senses are the disgrace of language, and the plague of commentators.

547

4.5.128
Good hearts.

The great fault of this play is the frequency of expressions so profane, that no necessity of preserving character can justify them. There are laws of higher authority than those of criticism.

THE TAMING OF THE SHREW
4.3.91
Like to a censer in a barber's shop:

Censers, in barber's shops, are now disused, but they may easily be imagined to have been vessels which, for the emission of the smoke, were cut with great number and varieties of interstices.

From this play the Tatler formed a story, Vol. 4. No. 131. . . .

It cannot but seem strange that *Shakespeare* should be so little known to the authour of the Tatler, that he should suffer this Story to be obtruded upon him, or so little known to the Publick, that he could hope to make it pass upon his readers as a novel narrative of a transaction in *Lincolnshire*; yet it is apparent, that he was deceived, or intended to deceive, that he knew not himself whence the story was taken, or hoped that he might rob so obscure a writer without detection.

Of this play the two plots are so well united, that they can hardly be called two without injury to the art with which they are interwoven. The attention is entertained with all the variety of a double plot, yet is not distracted by unconnected incidents.

The part between *Catharine* and *Petruchio* is eminently spritely and diverting. At the marriage of *Bianca* the arrival of the real father, perhaps, produces more perplexity than pleasure. The whole play is very popular and diverting.

THE COMEDY OF ERRORS
3.2.63
My food, my fortune, and my sweet hope's aim,
My sole earth's heaven, and my heaven's claim.

When he calls the girl his *only heaven on earth,* he utters the common cant of lovers. When he calls her *his heaven's claim,* I cannot understand him. Perhaps he means that which he asks of heaven.

MUCH ADO ABOUT NOTHING

1.1.66

Four of his five wits.

In our authour's time *wit* was the general term for intellectual powers. So *Davies* on the Soul,

> Wit, *seeking truth from cause to cause ascends,*
> *And never rests till it the first attain;*
> Will, *seeking good, finds many middle ends,*
> *But never stays till it the last do gain.*

And in another part,

> *But if a phrenzy do possess the brain,*
> *It so disturbs and blots the form of things,*
> *As fantasy proves altogether vain,*
> *And to the* wit *no true relation brings.*
> *Then doth the* wit, *admitting all for true,*
> *Build fond conclusions on those idle grounds;——*

The *wits* seem to have reckoned five, by analogy to the five senses, or the five inlets of ideas.

1.1.243

——a recheate winded in my forehead,

That is, *I will wear a horn on my forehead which the huntsman may blow.* A *recheate* is the sound by which dogs are called back. *Shakespeare* had no mercy upon the poor cockold, his *horn* is an inexhaustible subject of merriment.

1.3.14

I cannot hide what I am.

This is one of our authour's natural touches. An envious and unsocial mind, too proud to give pleasure, and too sullen to receive it, always endeavours to hide its malignity from the world and from itself, under the plainness of simple honesty, or the dignity of haughty independence.

2.1.330

Thus goes every one to the world but I, and I am sunburnt.

What is it, *to go to the world*? perhaps, to enter by marriage into a settled state: but why is the unmarried Lady *sunburnt*? I believe

S   549

we should read, *thus goes every one to the* wood *but I, and I am sun-burnt.* Thus does every one but I find a shelter, and I am left exposed to wind and *sun.* *The nearest way to the* wood, is a phrase for the readiest means to any end. It is said of a woman, who accepts a worse match than those which she had refused, that she has passed through the *wood,* and at last taken a crooked stick. But conjectural criticism has always something to abate its confidence. *Shakespeare,* in *All's well that ends well,* uses the phrase, *to go to the world,* for *marriage.* So that my emendation depends only on the opposition of *wood* to *sun-burnt.*

3.3.43

DOGBERRY. *Have a care that your Bills be not stolen.*

A *bill* is still carried by the watchmen at *Lichfield.* It was the old weapon of the *English* infantry, which, says *Temple, gave the most ghastly and deplorable wounds.* It may be called *securis falcata.*

4.1.251

LEONATO. *Being that I flow in grief,*
The smallest twine may lead me.

This is one of our authour's observations upon life. Men overpowered with distress eagerly listen to the first offers of relief, close with every scheme, and believe every promise. He that has no longer any confidence in himself, is glad to repose his trust in any other that will undertake to guide him.

ALL'S WELL THAT ENDS WELL
1.1.48

Where an unclean mind carries virtuous qualities, there commendations go with pity, they are virtues and traitors too; in her they are the better for their simpleness.

Estimable and useful qualities, joined with evil disposition, give that evil disposition power over others, who, by admiring the virtue, are betrayed to the malevolence. The *Tatler,* mentioning the sharpers of his time, observes, that some of them are men of such elegance and knowledge, that *a young man who falls into their way is* betrayed *as much by his judgment as his passions.*

1.2.36

So like a Courtier, no Contempt or Bitterness
Were in his *Pride or Sharpness; or if* they *were,*
His Equal had awak'd them.

The old text needs to be explained. He was so like a courtier,
that there was in *his dignity of manner nothing contemptuous*, and
in his keenness of wit nothing bitter. If *bitterness*, or *contemptuousness*
ever *appeared*, they had been *awakened* by some injury, not of a
man below him, but of his *Equal*. This is the complete image of a
well bred man, and somewhat like this *Voltaire* has exhibited his
hero *Lewis* XIV.

1.2.41

Who were below him
He us'd as creatures of another place,
And bow'd his eminent top to their low ranks;
Making them proud of his humility,
In their poor praise he humbled——

Every man has seen the *mean* too often *proud of* the *humility* of
the great, and perhaps the great may sometimes be *humbled in the*
praises of the mean, of those who commend them without conviction or discernment: this, however, is not so common; the *mean*
are found more frequently than the *great*.

1.3

Steward and Clown.

A· *Clown* in *Shakespeare* is commonly taken for a *licensed jester*,
or domestick *fool*. We are not to wonder that we find this character
often in his plays, since fools were, at that time, maintained in all
great families, to keep up merriment in the house. In the picture
of Sir *Thomas Moore*'s family, by *Hans Holbein*, the only servant
represented is *Patison* the *fool*. This is a proof of the familiarity to
which they were admitted, not by the great only, but the wise.

In some plays, a servant, or rustic, of remarkable petulance and
freedom of speech, is likewise called a *Clown*.

1.3.97

Tho' honesty be no puritan, yet it will do no hurt; it will wear the
surplice of humility over the black gown of a big heart.

Here is an allusion, violently enough forced in, to satirise the obstinacy with which the *Puritans* refused the use of the ecclesiastical habits, which was, at that time, one principal cause of the breach of union, and, perhaps, to insinuate, that the modest purity of the surplice was sometimes a cover for pride.

4.2.73

——Since Frenchmen *are so braid,*
Marry that will, I'll live and die a Maid.

Nothing is more common than for girls, on such occasions, to say in a pett what they do not think, or to think for a time what they do not finally resolve.

4.3.1

1 Lord.

The later Editors have with great liberality bestowed lordship upon these interlocutors, who, in the original edition, are called, with more propriety, *capt.* E. and *capt.* G. It is true that *captain* E. is in a former scene called *Lord E.* but the subordination in which they seem to act, and the timorous manner in which they converse, determines them to be only captains. Yet as the later readers of *Shakespeare* have been used to find them lords, I have not thought it worth while to degrade them in the margin.

4.3.280

He will steal, Sir, an egg out of a cloister.

I know not that *cloister*, though it may etymologically signify *any thing shut* is used by our authour, otherwise than for a *monastery*, and therefore I cannot guess whence this hyberbole could take its original: perhaps it means only this: *He will steal any thing, however trifling, from any place, however holy.*

4.3.317

Why does he ask him of me?

This is nature. Every man is on such occasions more willing to hear his neighbour's character than his own.

5.2.57

Tho' you are a fool and a knave, you shall eat;

Parolles has many of the lineaments of *Falstaff*, and seems to be the character which *Shakespeare* delighted to draw, a fellow that had more wit than virtue. Though justice required that he should be detected and exposed, yet his *vices sit so fit in him* that he is not at last suffered to starve.

5.3.21

We're reconcil'd, and the first view shall kill
All repetition:——

The first interview shall put an end to all recollection of the past. *Shakespeare* is now hastening to the end of the play, finds his matter sufficient to fill up his remaining scenes, and therefore, as on other such occasions, contracts his dialogue and precipitates his action. Decency required that *Bertram's* double crime of cruelty and disobedience, joined likewise with some hypocrisy, should raise more resentment; and that though his mother might easily forgive him, his king should more pertinaciously vindicate his own authority and *Helen's* merit: of all this *Shakespeare* could not be ignorant, but *Shakespeare* wanted to conclude his play.

5.3.231

This dialogue is too long, since the audience already knew the whole transaction; nor is there any reason for puzzling the king and playing with his passions; but it was much easier than to make a pathetical interview between *Helen* and her husband, her mother, and the king.

This play has many delightful scenes, though not sufficiently probable, and some happy characters, though not new, nor produced by any deep knowledge of human nature. *Parolles* is a boaster and a coward, such as has always been the sport of the stage, but perhaps never raised more laughter or contempt than in the hands of *Shakespeare*.

I cannot reconcile my heart to *Bertram*; a man noble without generosity, and young without truth; who marries *Helen* as a coward, and leaves her as a profligate: when she is dead by his unkindness, sneaks home to a second marriage, is accused by a woman whom he has wronged, defends himself by falshood, and is dismissed to happiness.

The story of *Bertram* and *Diana* had been told before of *Mariana* and *Angelo*, and, to confess the truth, scarcely merited to be heard a second time.

The story is copied from a novel of *Boccace*, which may be read in *Shakespear Illustrated,* with remarks not more favourable to *Bertram* than my own.

KING JOHN
1.1.24

Be thou as lightning in the eyes of France,
For ere thou canst report I will be there,
The thunder of my cannon shall be heard.

The simile does not suit well: the lightning indeed appears before the thunder is heard, but the lightning is destructive, and the thunder innocent.

1.1.27

Be thou the trumpet of our wrath,
And sullen presage of your own decay.

By the epithet *sullen,* which cannot be applied to a trumpet, it is plain, that our authour's imagination had now suggested a new idea. It is as if he had said, be a *trumpet* to alarm with our invasion, be a *bird* of *ill omen* to croak out the prognostick of your own ruin.

2.1.300

Ye men of Angiers, ——

This speech is very poetical and smooth, and except the conceit of the *widow's husband* embracing *the earth,* is just and beautiful.

2.1.477

Lest zeal now melted by the windy breath
Of soft petitions, pity and remorse,
Cool and congeal again to what it was.

We have here a very unusual, and, I think, not very just image of *zeal,* which in its highest degree is represented by others as a flame, but by *Shakespeare* as a frost. To *repress zeal,* in the language of others, is to *cool,* in *Shakespeare's* to *melt* it; when it exerts its utmost power it is commonly said to *flame,* but by *Shakespeare* to be *congealed.*

3.1.70

To me, and to the State of my great Grief,
Let Kings assemble:——

In *Much ado about nothing*, the father of *Hero*, depressed by her disgrace, declares himself so subdued by grief that *a thread may lead him*. How is it that grief in *Leonato* and lady *Constance*, produces effects directly opposite, and yet both agreeable to nature. Sorrow softens the mind while it is yet warmed by hope, but hardens it when it is congealed by despair. Distress, while there remains any prospect of relief, is weak and flexible, but when no succour remains, is fearless and stubborn; angry alike at those that injure, and at those that do not help; careless to please where nothing can be gained, and fearless to offend when there is nothing further to be dreaded. Such was this writer's knowledge of the passions.

3.1.147

Thou canst not, Cardinal, devise a name
So slight, unworthy, and ridiculous.
To charge me to an answer, as the Pope.

This must have been at the time when it was written, in our struggles with popery, a very captivating scene.

So many passages remain in which *Shakespeare* evidently takes his advantage of the facts then recent, and of the passions then in motion, that I cannot but suspect that time has obscured much of his art, and that many allusions yet remain undiscovered which perhaps may be gradually retrieved by succeeding commentators.

3.1.280

But thou hast sworn against religion,——

In this long speech, the Legate is made to shew his skill in casuistry; and the strange heap of quibble and nonsense of which it consists, was intended to ridicule that of the schools. . . .—WARBURTON.

I am not able to discover here any thing inconsequent or ridiculously subtle. The propositions, that the *voice of the church is the voice of heaven*, and that *the Pope utters the voice of the church*, neither of which *Pandulph's* auditors would deny, being once granted, the argument here used is irresistible; nor is it easy, notwithstanding the gingle, to enforce it with greater brevity or propriety. . . .

The sense, after I had considered it, appeared to me only this.

In swearing by religion against religion, to which thou hast already sworn, thou makest an oath the security for thy faith against an oath already taken. I will give, *says he*, a rule for conscience in these cases. Thou mayst be in doubt about the matter of an oath; *when thou swearest thou mayst* not *be always* sure *to swear rightly*, but let this by thy settled principle, *swear only not to be forsworn*; let not thy latter oaths be at variance with thy former.

Truth, through this whole speech, means *rectitude* of conduct.

3.2.1

Now, by my life, this day grows wond'rous hot;
Some airy devil hovers in the sky,
And pours down mischief.

We must read, *Some* fiery *devil*, if we will have the *cause* equal to the *effect*.—WARBURTON.

There is no end of such alterations; every page of a vehement and negligent writer will afford opportunities for changes of terms, if mere propriety will justify them. Not that of this change the propriety is out of controversy. Dr. *Warburton* will have the devil *fiery*, because he makes the day *hot*; the authour makes him *airy*, because *he hovers in the sky*, and the *heat* and *mischief* are natural consequences of his malignity.

3.4.61

Bind up those tresses.

It was necessary that *Constance* should be interrupted, because a passion so violent cannot be born long. I wish the following speeches had been equally happy; but they only serve to shew, how difficult it is to maintain the pathetick long.

3.4.99

Had you such a loss as I,
I could give better comfort——

This is a sentiment which great sorrow always dictates. Whoever cannot help himself casts his eyes on others for assistance, and often mistakes their inability for coldness.

3.4.107

There's nothing in this world can make me joy.

The young Prince feels his defeat with more sensibility than his father. Shame operates most strongly in the earlier years, and when can disgrace be less welcome than when a man is going to his bride?

4.1.101

Or, Hubert, *if you will, cut out my tongue,*
So I may keep mine eyes.

This is according to nature. We imagine no evil so great as that which is near us.

4.2.197

——slippers, which his nimble haste
Had falsely thrust upon contrary feet.

I know not how the commentators understand this important passage, which, in Dr. *Warburton*'s edition, is marked as eminently beautiful, and, in the whole, not without justice. But *Shakespeare* seems to have confounded a man's shoes with his gloves. He that is frighted or hurried may put his hand into the wrong glove, but either shoe will equally admit either foot. The authour seems to be disturbed by the disorder which he describes.

4.2.231

Hadst thou but shook thy head, or made a pause, . . .
Deep shame had struck me dumb.

There are many touches of nature in this conference of *John* with *Hubert*. A man engaged in wickedness would keep the profit to himself, and transfer the guilt to his accomplice. These reproaches vented against *Hubert* are not the words of art or policy, but the eruptions of a mind swelling with consciousness of a crime, and desirous of discharging its misery on another.

This account of the timidity of guilt is drawn *ab ipsis recessibus mentis*, from an intimate knowledge of mankind, particularly that line in which he says, that *to have bid him tell his tale* in *express words*, would have *struck him dumb*; nothing is more certain, than that bad men use all the arts of fallacy upon themselves, palliate their actions to their own minds by gentle terms, and hide themselves from their own detection in ambiguities and subterfuges.

The tragedy of *King John*, though not written with the utmost power of *Shakespeare*, is varied with a very pleasing interchange of incidents and characters. The Lady's grief is very affecting, and the character of the *Bastard* contains that mixture of greatness and lenity which this authour delighted to exhibit.

There is extant another play of *King John*, published with *Shakespeare*'s name, so different from this, and I think from all his other works, that there is reason to think his name was prefixed only to recommend it to sale. No man writes upon the same subject twice, without concurring in many places with himself.

KING RICHARD II
1.3.227

Shorten my days thou canst with sullen sorrow,
And pluck nights from me, but not lend a morrow;

It is matter of very melancholy consideration, that all human advantages confer more power of doing evil than good.

2.1.21

Report of fashions in proud Italy,

Our authour, who gives to all nations the customs of *England*, and to all ages the manners of his own; has charged the times of *Richard* with a folly not perhaps known then, but very frequent in *Shakespeare*'s time, and much lamented by the wisest and best of our ancestors.

3.2.56

The breath of worldly men cannot depose
The Deputy elected by the Lord.

Here is the doctrine of indefeasible right expressed in the strongest terms, but our poet did not learn it in the reign of King *James*, to which it is now the practice of all writers, whose opinions are regulated by fashion or interest, to impute the original of every tenet which they have been taught to think false or foolish.

3.2.93

Mine ear is open, and my heart prepar'd.

It seems to be the design of the poet to raise *Richard* to esteem in his fall, and consequently to interest the reader in his favour. He gives him only passive fortitude, the virtue of a confessor rather than of a king. In his prosperity we saw him imperious and oppressive, but in his distress he is wise, patient, and pious.

3.2.153

And that small model of the barren earth,
Which serves as paste and cover to our bones.

A metaphor, not of the most sublime kind, taken from a *pie*.

3.2.207

By heav'n, I'll hate him everlastingly,
That bids me be of comfort any more.

This sentiment is drawn from nature. Nothing is more offensive to a mind convinced that his distress is without a remedy, and preparing to submit quietly to irresistible calamity, than these petty and conjectured comforts which unskilful officiousness thinks it virtue to administer.

3.3.155

Or I'll be buried in the King's high way,
Some way of common Trade, where Subjects' feet
May hourly trample on their Sovereign's head.

Shakespeare is very apt to deviate from the *pathetick* to the *ridiculous*. Had the speech of *Richard* ended at this line it had exhibited the natural language of submissive misery, conforming its intention to the present fortune, and calmly ending its purposes in death.

4.1.40

My rapier's point.

Shakespeare deserts the manners of the age in which his drama is placed very often, without necessity or advantage. The edge of a sword had served his purpose as well as the *point of a rapier*, and he had then escaped the impropriety of giving the *English* nobles a weapon which was not seen in *England* till two centuries afterwards.

4.1.125

And shall the figure of God's Majesty,
His Captain, Steward, Deputy elect,——

Here is another proof that our authour did not learn in King *James*'s court his elevated notions of the right of kings. I know not any flatterer of the *Stuarts* who has expressed this doctrine in much stronger terms. It must be observed that the Poet intends from the beginning to the end to exhibit this bishop as brave, pious, and venerable.

4.1.322 . . .

The children yet unborn,
Shall feel this day as sharp to them as thorn.

This pathetick denunciation shews that *Shakespeare* intended to impress his auditors with dislike of the deposal of *Richard*.

5.1.46

For why? the senseless brands will sympathize.

The poet should have ended this speech with the foregoing line, and have spared his childish prattle about the fire.

This play is extracted from the Chronicle of *Hollingshead*, in which many passages may be found which *Shakespeare* has, with very little alteration, transplanted into his scenes; particularly a speech of the bishop of *Carlisle* in defence of King *Richard*'s unalienable right, and immunity from human jurisdiction.

Johnson, who, in his *Catiline* and *Sejanus*, has inserted many speeches from the *Roman* historians, was, perhaps, induced to that practice by the example of *Shakespeare*, who had condescended sometimes to copy more ignoble writers. But *Shakespeare* had more of his own than *Johnson*, and, if he sometimes was willing to spare his labour, shewed by what he performed at other times, that his extracts were made by choice or idleness rather than necessity.

This play is one of those which *Shakespeare* has apparently revised; but as success in works of invention is not always proportionate to labour, it is not finished at last with the happy force of some other of his tragedies, nor can be said much to affect the passions, or enlarge the understanding.

THE FIRST PART OF KING HENRY IV

Shakespeare has apparently designed a regular connection of these dramatick histories from *Richard the second* to *Henry the fifth*. King *Henry*, at the end of *Richard* the second, declares his purpose to visit the Holy Land, which he resumes in this speech. The complaint made by king *Henry* in the last act of *Richard* the second, of the wildness of his son, prepares the reader for the frolicks which are here to be recounted, and the characters which are now to be exhibited.

1.1.5–6

——*To be commenc'd in stronds afar remote.*
No more the thirsty entrance of this soil——

We may suppose a verse or two lost between these two lines. This is a cheap way of palliating an editor's inability; but I believe such omissions are more frequent in *Shakespeare* than is commonly imagined.

1.1.19

As far as to the sepulchre of Christ.

The lawfulness and justice of the *holy wars* have been much disputed; but perhaps there is a principle on which the question may be easily determined. If it be part of the religion of the Mahometans, to extirpate by the sword all other religions, it is, by the law of self defence, lawful for men of every other religion, and for Christians among others, to make war upon Mahometans, simply as Mahometans, as men obliged by their own principles to make war upon Christians, and only lying in wait till opportunity shall promise them success.

1.2.217

I know you all, and will a while uphold
The unyok'd humour of your idleness.——

This speech is very artfully introduced to keep the Prince from appearing vile in the opinion of the audience; it prepares them for his future reformation, and, what is yet more valuable, exhibits a natural picture of a great mind offering excuses to itself, and palliating those follies which it can neither justify nor forsake.

1.3.201

By heav'n, methinks, it were an easy leap,
To pluck bright honour from the pale-fac'd Moon.

So that we see, tho' the expression be sublime and daring, yet the thought is the natural movement of an heroic mind. *Euripides* at least thought so, when he put the very same sentiment, in the same words, into the mouth of *Eteocles*—*I will not, madam, disguise my thoughts; I could scale heaven, I could descend to the very entrails of the earth, if so be that by that price I could obtain a kingdom.*—WARBURTON.

Though I am very far from condemning this speech with *Gildon* and *Theobald* as *absolute madness*, yet I cannot find in it that profundity of reflection and beauty of allegory which the learned commentator has endeavoured to display. This sally of *Hotspur* may be, I think, soberly and rationally vindicated as the violent eruption of a mind inflated with ambition and fired with resentment; as the boastful clamour of a man able to do much, and eager to do more; as the hasty motion of turbulent desire; as the dark expression of indetermined thoughts. The passage from *Euripides* is surely not allegorical, yet it is produced, and properly, as parallel.

2.1.96

We have the receipt of Fern-seed, we walk invisible.

Fern is one of those plants which have their seed on the back of the leaf so small as to escape the sight. Those who perceived that *fern* was propagated by semination and yet could never see the seed, were much at a loss for a solution of the difficulty; and as wonder always endeavours to augment itself, they ascribed to *Fern-seed* many strange properties, some of which the rustick virgins have not yet forgotten or exploded.

2.4.41

Enter Francis *the drawer.*

This scene, helped by the distraction of the drawer, and grimaces of the prince, may entertain upon the stage, but afford not much delight to the reader. The authour has judiciously made it short.

2.4.394

You may buy land now as cheap as stinking mackerel.

In former times the prosperity of the nation was known by the value of land as now by the price of stocks. Before *Henry* the seventh made it safe to serve the king regnant, it was the practice at every revolution for the conqueror to confiscate the estates of those that opposed, and perhaps of those who did not assist him. Those, therefore, that foresaw a change of government, and thought their estates in danger, were desirous to sell them in haste for something that might be carried away.

562

2.4.442

Though the camomile, the more it is trodden on, the faster it grows.

This whole speech is supremely comick. The simile of camomile used to illustrate a contrary effect, brings to my remembrance an observation of a later writer of some merit, whom the desire of being witty has betrayed into a like thought. Meaning to enforce with great vehemence the mad temerity of young soldiers, he remarks, that *though* Bedlam *be in the road to* Hogsden, *it is out of the way to promotion.*

2.4.549

Go, hide thee behind the arras,

The bulk of *Falstaff* made him not the fittest to be concealed behind the hangings, but every poet sacrifices something to the scenery; if *Falstaff* had not been hidden he could not have been found asleep, nor had his pockets searched.

3.1.27

Diseased Nature oftentimes breaks forth
In strange eruptions.

The poet has here taken, from the perverseness and contrariousness of *Hotspur*'s temper, an opportunity of raising his character, by a very rational and philosophical confutation of superstitious errour.

3.1.96

Methinks, my moiety, north from Burton here,
In quantity equals not one of yours.

Hotspur is here just such a divider as the *Irishman* who made *three halves*: Therefore, for the honour of *Shakespeare*, I will suppose, with the *Oxford Editor*, that he wrote *portion.*—WARB.

I will not suppose it.

3.3.30

Thou art the Knight of the burning lamp.

This is a natural picture. Every man who feels in himself the pain of deformity, however, like this merry knight, he may affect to make sport with it among those whom it is his interest to please, is ready to revenge any hint of contempt upon one whom he can use with freedom.

4.1.97

All furnisht, all in arms,
All plum'd like Estridges, that with the wind
Baited like Eagles.

I read,

> *All furnish'd, all in arms,*
> *All plum'd like Estridges that* wing *the wind*
> *Baited like Eagles.*

This gives a strong image. They were not only plum'd like Estridges, but their plumes fluttered like those of an Estridge on the wing mounting against the wind. A more lively representation of young men ardent for enterprize perhaps no writer has ever given.

4.2.31

Younger sons to younger brothers.

Raleigh, in his discourse on *war*, uses this very expression for men of desperate fortune and wild adventure. Which borrowed it from the other I know not, but I think the play was printed before the discourse.

5.3.59

If Percy *be alive, I'll pierce him;*

To *pierce a vessel* is to *tap* it. *Falstaff* takes up his bottle which the Prince had tossed at his head, and being about to animate himself with a draught, cries if *Percy be alive I'll pierce him*, and so draws the cork. I do not propose this with much confidence.

THE SECOND PART OF KING HENRY IV
Induction

This speech of *Rumour* is not inelegant or unpoetical, but is wholly useless, since we are told nothing which the first scene does not clearly and naturally discover. The only end of such prologues is to inform the audience of some facts previous to the action, of which they can have no knowledge from the persons of the drama.

1.1.159

The rude scene may end,
And darkness be the burier of the dead.

The conclusion of this noble speech is extremely striking. There is no need to suppose it exactly philosophical, *darkness* in poetry may be absence of eyes as well as privation of light. Yet we may remark, that by an ancient opinion it has been held, that if the human race, for whom the world was made, were extirpated, the whole system of sublunary nature would cease.

1.2.166

The young Prince hath mis-led me. I am the fellow with the great belly, and he my dog.

I do not understand this joke. Dogs lead the blind, but why does a dog lead the fat?

1.2.206

Is not your voice broken? your wind short? your chin double? your wit single?

We call a man *single-witted* who attains but one species of knowledge. This sense I know not how to apply to *Falstaff*, and rather think that the *Chief Justice* hints at a calamity always incident to a gray-haired wit, whose misfortune is, that his merriment is unfashionable. His allusions are to forgotten facts; his illustrations are drawn from notions obscured by time; his *wit* is therefore *single*, such as none has any part in but himself.

2.2.189

Put on two leather jerkins and aprons, and wait upon him at his table, as drawers.

This was a plot very unlikely to succeed where the *Prince* and the drawers were all known, but it produces merriment, which our authour found more useful than probability.

4.2.122

Guard these traitors to the block of death.

It cannot but raise some indignation to find this horrible violation of faith passed over thus slightly by the poet, without any note of censure or detestation.

4.3.93

This same sober-blooded boy doth not love me, nor a man cannot make him laugh.

Falstaff speaks here like a veteran in life. The young prince did not love him, and he despaired to gain his affection, for he could not make him laugh. Men only become friends by community of pleasures. He who cannot be softened into gayety cannot easily be melted into kindness.

4.5.129

England shall double gild his treble Guilt.

Evidently the nonsense of some foolish Player. . . . —WARBURTON.

I know not why this commentator should speak with so much confidence what he cannot know, or determine so positively what so capricious a writer as our poet might either deliberately or wantonly produce. This line is indeed such as disgraces a few that precede and follow it, but it suits well enough with the *daggers hid in thought, and whetted on the flinty hearts*; and the answer which the prince makes, and which is applauded for wisdom, is not of a strain much higher than this ejected line.

4.5.211

To lead out many to the Holy Land;

This journey to the Holy Land, of which the king very frequently revives the mention, had two motives, religion and policy. He durst not wear the ill-gotten crown without expiation, but in the act of expiation he contrives to make his wickedness successful.

4.5.219

How I came by the Crown, O God, forgive!
And grant it may with thee in true peace live.

This is a true picture of a mind divided between heaven and earth. He prays for the prosperity of guilt while he deprecates its punishment.

5.1.90

Four terms or two actions.

There is something humorous in making a spendthrift compute time by the operation of an action for debt.

5.5.67

I banish thee, on pain of death.

Mr. *Rowe* observes, that many readers lament to see *Falstaff* so hardly used by his old friend. But if it be considered that the fat knight has never uttered one sentiment of generosity, and with all his power of exciting mirth, has nothing in him that can be esteemed, no great pain will be suffered from the reflection that he is compelled to live honestly, and maintained by the king, with a promise of advancement when he shall deserve it.

I think the poet more blameable for *Poins*, who is always represented as joining some virtues with his vices, and is therefore treated by the prince with apparent distinction, yet he does nothing in the time of action, and though after the bustle is over he is again a favourite, at last vanishes without notice. *Shakespeare* certainly lost him by heedlessness, in the multiplicity of his characters, the variety of his action, and his eagerness to end the play.

5.5.97

Go, carry Sir John Falstaff *to the* Fleet.

I do not see why *Falstaff* is carried to the Fleet. We have never lost sight of him since his dismission from the king; he has committed no new fault, and therefore incurred no punishment; but the different agitations of fear, anger, and surprise in him and his company, make a good scene to the eye; and our authour, who wanted them no longer on the stage, was glad to find this method of sweeping them away.

I fancy every reader, when he ends this play, cries out with *Desdemona, O most lame and impotent conclusion!* As this play was not, to our knowledge, divided into acts by the authour, I could be content to conclude it with the death of *Henry* the fourth.

In that Jerusalem shall Harry *dye.*

These scenes which now make the fifth act of *Henry* the fourth, might then be the first of *Henry* the fifth; but the truth is, that they do unite very commodiously to either play. When these plays were represented, I believe they ended as they are now ended in the books; but *Shakespeare* seems to have designed that the whole series of action from the beginning of *Richard* the second, to the end of *Henry* the fifth, should be considered by the reader as one work, upon one plan, only broken into parts by the necessity of exhibition.

None of *Shakespeare*'s plays are more read than the first and second parts of *Henry* the fourth. Perhaps no authour has ever in

567

two plays afforded so much delight. The great events are interesting, for the fate of kingdoms depends upon them; the slighter occurrences are diverting, and, except one or two, sufficiently probable; the incidents are multiplied with wonderful fertility of invention, and the characters diversified with the utmost nicety of discernment, and the profoundest skill in the nature of man.

The prince, who is the hero both of the comick and tragick part, is a young man of great abilities and violent passions, whose sentiments are right, though his actions are wrong; whose virtues are obscured by negligence, and whose understanding is dissipated by levity. In his idle hours he is rather loose than wicked, and when the occasion forces out his latent qualities, he is great without effort, and brave without tumult. The trifler is roused into a hero, and the hero again reposes in the trifler. This character is great, original, and just.

Piercy is a rugged soldier, cholerick, and quarrelsome, and has only the soldier's virtues, generosity and courage.

But *Falstaff* unimitated, unimitable *Falstaff*, how shall I describe thee? Thou compound of sense and vice; of sense which may be admired but not esteemed, of vice which may be despised, but hardly detested. *Falstaff* is a character loaded with faults, and with those faults which naturally produce contempt. He is a thief, and a glutton, a coward, and a boaster, always ready to cheat the weak, and prey upon the poor; to terrify the timorous and insult the defenceless. At once obsequious and malignant, he satirises in their absence those whom he lives by flattering. He is familiar with the prince only as an agent of vice, but of this familiarity he is so proud as not only to be supercilious and haughty with common men, but to think his interest of importance to the duke of *Lancaster*. Yet the man thus corrupt, thus despicable, makes himself necessary to the prince that despises him, by the most pleasing of all qualities, perpetual gaiety, by an unfailing power of exciting laughter, which is the more freely indulged, as his wit is not of the splendid or ambitious kind, but consists in easy escapes and sallies of levity, which make sport but raise no envy. It must be observed that he is stained with no enormous or sanguinary crimes, so that his licentiousness is not so offensive but that it may be borne for his mirth.

The moral to be drawn from this representation is, that no man is more dangerous than he that with a will to corrupt, hath the power to please; and that neither wit nor honesty ought to think themselves safe with such a companion when they see *Henry* seduced by *Falstaff*.

KING HENRY V

Prol. 18
Imaginary forces.

Imaginary for *imaginative*, or your powers of fancy. Active and passive words are by this authour frequently confounded.

Prol. 25
And make imaginary puissance.

This passage shews that *Shakespeare* was fully sensible of the absurdity of shewing battles on the theatre, which indeed is never done but tragedy becomes farce. Nothing can be represented to the eye but by something like it, and *within a wooden O* nothing very like a battle can be exhibited.

1.1.38
Hear him but reason in divinity, &c.

Why these lines should be divided [by *Warburton*] from the rest of the speech and applied to king *James*, I am not able to conceive; nor why an opportunity should be so eagerly snatched to treat with contempt that part of his character which was least contemptible. King *James*'s theological knowledge was not inconsiderable. To preside at disputations is not very suitable to a king, but to understand the questions is surely laudable. The poet, if he had *James* in his thoughts, was no skilful encomiast; for the mention of *Harry*'s skill in war, forced upon the remembrance of his audience the great deficiency of their present king; who yet with all his faults, and many faults he had, was such that Sir *Robert Cotton* says, *he would be content that* England *should never have a better, provided that it should never have a worse*.

1.1.47
When he speaks,
The air, a charter'd libertine, is still.

This line is exquisitely beautiful.

2.2.126

Oh, how hast thou with jealousy infected
The sweetness of affiance?

Shakespeare urges this aggravation of the guilt of treachery with great judgment. One of the worst consequences of breach of trust is the diminution of that confidence which makes the happiness of life, and the dissemination of suspicion, which is the poison of society.

2.2.165

My fault, but not my body, pardon, Sovereign.

One of the conspirators against Queen *Elizabeth*, I think *Parry*, concludes his letter to her with these words, a culpa, *but not* a pœna; *absolve me most dear Lady.* This letter was much read at that time, and the authour doubtless copied it.

2.3.26

Cold as any stone.

Such is the end of *Falstaff*, from whom *Shakespeare* had promised us in his epilogue to *Henry* IV. that we should receive more entertainment. It happened to *Shakespeare* as to other writers, to have his imagination crowded with a tumultuary confusion of images, which, while they were yet unsorted and unexamined, seemed sufficient to furnish a long train of incidents, and a new variety of merriment, but which, when he was to produce them to view, shrunk suddenly from him, or could not be accommodated to his general design. That he once designed to have brought *Falstaff* on the scene again, we know from himself; but whether he could contrive no train of adventures suitable to his character, or could match him with no companions likely to quicken his humour, or could open no new vein of pleasantry, and was afraid to continue the same strain lest it should not find the same reception, he has here for ever discarded him, and made haste to dispatch him, perhaps for the same reason for which *Addison* killed Sir *Roger*, that no other hand might attempt to exhibit him.

Let meaner authours learn from this example, that it is dangerous to sell the bear which is yet not hunted, to promise to the publick what they have not written.

This disappointment probably inclined Queen *Elizabeth* to

command the poet to produce him once again, and to shew him in love or courtship. This was indeed a new source of humour, and produced a new play from the former characters.

I forgot to note in the proper place, and therefore note here, that *Falstaff*'s courtship, or *The Merry Wives of* Windsor, should be read between *Henry* IV. and *Henry* V.

2.3.79

It were to be wished that the poor merriment of this dialogue had not been purchased with so much profaneness.

3.4

Alice, tu as esté en Angleterre.

The scene is indeed mean enough, when it is read, but the grimaces of two *French* women, and the odd accent with which they uttered the *English*, made it divert upon the stage. It may be observed, that there is in it not only the *French* language, but the *French* spirit. *Alice* compliments the princess upon her knowledge of four words, and tells her that she pronounces like the *English* themselves. The princess suspects no deficiency in her instructress, nor the instructress in herself. Throughout the whole scene there may be found *French* servility, and *French* vanity.

3.5.40

Charles Delabreth, high constable of France, &c.

Milton somewhere bids the *English* take notice how their names are mispelt by foreigners, and seems to think that we may lawfully treat foreign names in return with the same neglect. This privilege seems to be exercised in this catalogue of *French* names, which, since the sense of the authour is not affected, I have left it as I found it.

3.5.50

Rush on his host, as doth the melted snow
Upon the vallies; whose low vassal seat
The Alps *doth spit and void his rheum upon.*

The poet has here defeated himself by passing too soon from one image to another. To bid the *French* rush upon the *English* as the torrents formed from melted snow stream from the *Alps*, was at once vehement and proper, but its force is destroyed by the grossness of the thought in the next line.

3.6.112

His nose is executed, and his fire's out.

This is the last time that any sport can be made with the red face of *Bardolph*, which, to confess the truth, seems to have taken more hold on *Shakespeare*'s imagination than on any other. The conception is very cold to the solitary reader, though it may be somewhat invigorated by the exhibition on the stage. This poet is always more careful about the present than the future, about his audience than his readers.

3.6.131

Now speak we on our cue.

In our turn. This phrase the authour learned among players, and has imparted it to kings.

4. Chor. 2

The poring dark
Fills the wide vessel of the universe.

. . . we are not to think *Shakespear* so ignorant as to imagine it was night over the whole globe at once.—WARBURTON.

There is a better proof that *Shakespeare* knew the order of night and day in *Macbeth*.

> *Now o'er one half the* world
> *Nature seems dead.*

But there was no great need of any justification. The *universe*, in its original sense, no more means this globe singly than the circuit of the horizon; but, however large in its philosophical sense, it may be poetically used for as much of the world as falls under observation. Let me remark further, that ignorance cannot be certainly inferred from inaccuracy. Knowledge is not always present.

4.1.247

Upon the King! &c.

There is something very striking and solemn in this soliloquy, into which the king breaks immediately as soon as he is left alone. Something like this, on less occasions, every breast has felt. Reflection and seriousness rush upon the mind upon the separation of a gay company, and especially after forced and unwilling merriment.

4.3.24

By Jove, *I am not covetous of gold.*

The king prays like a christian, and swears like a heathen.

4.3.50

They'll remember, with advantages,
What feats they did that day.

Old men, notwithstanding the natural forgetfulness of age, shall remember *their feats of this day,* and remember to tell them *with advantage.* Age is commonly boastful, and inclined to magnify past acts and past times.

4.3.57

Crispin Crispian *shall ne'er go by,*
From this day to the ending of the world,
But we in it shall be remembered.

It may be observed that we are apt to promise to ourselves a more lasting memory than the changing state of human things admits. This prediction is not verified; the feast of *Crispin* passes by without any mention of *Agincourt.* Late events obliterate the former: the civil wars have left in this nation scarcely any tradition of more ancient history.

4.3.104

Mark then abounding valour in our English.

That the allusion is, as Mr. *Theobald* thinks, *exceedingly beautiful,* I am afraid few readers will discover. The *valour* of a putrid body, that destroys by the stench, is one of the thoughts that do no great honour to the poet. Perhaps from this putrid valour *Dryden* might borrow the posthumous empire of Don *Sebastian,* who was to reign wheresoever his atoms should be scattered.

4.7.50

The fat Knight with the great belly-doublet.

This is the last time that *Falstaff* can make sport. The poet was loath to part with him, and has continued his memory as long as he could.

5.1.94

Exit Pistol.

The comick scenes of the history of *Henry* the fourth and fifth are now at an end, and all the comick personages are now dismissed. *Falstaff* and Mrs. *Quickly* are dead; *Nym* and *Bardolph* are hanged; *Gadshill* was lost immediately after the robbery; *Poins* and *Peto* have vanished since, one knows not how; and *Pistol* is now beaten into obscurity. I believe every reader regrets their departure.

5.2.125

I'faith, Kate, *thou wouldst find me such a plain King*, &c.

I know not why *Shakespeare* now gives the king nearly such a character as he made him formerly ridicule in *Percy*. This military grossness and unskilfulness in all the softer arts, does not suit very well with the gaieties of his youth, with the general knowledge ascribed to him at his accession, or with the contemptuous message sent him by the *Dauphin*, who represents him as fitter for the ball room than the field, and tells him that he is not *to revel into dutchies*, or win provinces *with a nimble galliard*. The truth is, that the poet's matter failed him in the fifth act, and he was glad to fill it up with whatever he could get; and not even *Shakespeare* can write well without a proper subject. It is a vain endeavour for the most skilful hand to cultivate barrenness, or to paint upon vacuity.

5.2.307

We have here but a mean dialogue for princes; the merriment is very gross, and the sentiments are very worthless.

This play has many scenes of high dignity, and many of easy merriment. The character of the King is well supported, except in his courtship, where he has neither the vivacity of *Hal*, nor the grandeur of *Henry*. The humour of *Pistol* is very happily continued; his character has perhaps been the model of all the bullies that have yet appeared on the *English* stage.

The lines given to the chorus have many admirers; but the truth is, that in them a little may be praised, and much must be forgiven; nor can it be easily discovered why the intelligence given by the chorus is more necessary in this play than in many others where it is omitted. The great defect of this play is the emptiness and narrowness of the last act, which a very little diligence might have easily avoided.

THE FIRST PART OF KING HENRY VI
3.3.85

Done like a Frenchman: *turn, and turn again!*

The inconstancy of the *French* was always the subject of satire. I have read a dissertation written to prove that the index of the wind upon our steeples was made in form of a cock, to ridicule the *French* for their frequent changes.

4.5.1

Enter *Talbot* and his son.

For what reason this scene is written in rhyme I cannot guess. If *Shakespeare* had not in other plays mingled his rhymes and blank verses in the same manner, I should have suspected that this dialogue had been a part of some other poem which was never finished, and that being loath to throw his labour away, he inserted it here.

4.7.1

The return of rhyme where young *Talbot* is again mentioned and in no other place, strengthens the suspicion, that these verses were originally part of some other work, and were copied here only to save the trouble of composing new.

5.3.6

Monarch of the North.

The North was always supposed to be the particular habitation of bad spirits. *Milton* therefore assembles the rebel angels in the North.

5.3.62

As plays the sun upon the glassy streams, &c

This comparison, made between things which seem sufficiently unlike, is intended to express the softness and delicacy of Lady *Margaret*'s beauty, which delighted, but did not dazzle; which was bright, but gave no pain by its lustre.

Of this play there is no copy earlier than that of the folio in 1623, though the two succeeding parts are extant in two editions in quarto. That the second and third parts were published without the first may be admitted as no weak proof that the copies were surreptitiously obtained, and that the printers of that time gave the publick those plays not such as the authour designed, but such as they could get them. That this play was written before the two others is indubitably collected from the series of events; that it was written and played before *Henry* the fifth is apparent, because in the epilogue there is mention made of this play and not of the other parts.

> Henry *the sixth in swaddling bands crown'd king,*
> *Whose state so many had i' th' managing*
> *That they lost* France, *and made all* England *rue,*
> *Which oft our stage hath shewn.*

France is lost in this play. The two following contain, as the old title imports, the contention of the houses of *York* and *Lancaster*.

THE SECOND PART OF KING HENRY VI

It is apparent that this play begins where the former ends, and continues the series of transactions, of which it presupposes the first part already known. This is a sufficient proof that the second and third parts were not written without dependence on the first, though they were printed as containing a complete period of history.

2.1.3

> *The wind was very high,*
> *And, ten to one, old* Joan *had not gone out.*

I am told by a gentleman better acquainted with falconry than myself, that the meaning, however expressed, is, that, the wind being high, it was ten to one that the old hawk had flown quite away; a trick which hawks often play their masters in windy weather.

2.4.110

> *I long to see my prison.*

This impatience of a high spirit is very natural. It is not so dreadful to be imprisoned, as it is desirable in a state of disgrace to be sheltered from the scorn of gazers.

3.1.210

And as the Butcher takes away the Calf,
And binds the wretch, and beats it when it strays.

I am . . . inclined to believe that in this passage, as in many, there is a confusion of ideas, and that the poet had at once before him a butcher carrying a calf bound, and a butcher driving a calf to the slaughter, and beating him when he did not keep the path. Part of the line was suggested by one image and part by another, so that *strive* is the best word, but *stray* is the right.

3.2.161

Oft have I seen a timely-parted ghost,
Of ashy semblance, meager, pale, and bloodless.

All that is true of the *body* of a dead man is here said by *Warwick* of the soul. I would read,

Oft have I seen a timely-parted coarse,

But of two common words how or why was one changed for the other? I believe the transcriber thought that the epithet *timely-parted* could not be used of the body, but that, as in *Hamlet* there is mention of *peace-parted souls,* so here *timely-parted* must have the same substantive. He removed one imaginary difficulty and made many real. If the soul is parted from the body, the body is likewise parted from the soul.

I cannot but stop a moment to observe that this horrible description is scarcely the work of any pen but *Shakespeare*'s.

3.2.310

Would curses kill, as doth the mandrake's groan.

The fabulous accounts of the plant called a *mandrake* give it an inferior degree of animal life, and relate, that when it is torn from the ground, it groans, and that this groan being certainly fatal to him that is offering such unwelcome violence, the practice of those who gather mandrakes is to tie one end of a string to the plant, and the other to a dog, upon which the fatal groan discharges its malignity.

3.2.333

You bad me ban, and will you bid me leave?

This inconsistency is very common in real life. Those who are vexed to impatience are angry to see others less disturbed than themselves, but when others begin to rave, they immediately see in them, what they could not find in themselves, the deformity and folly of useless rage.

3.3

This is one of the scenes which have been applauded by the criticks, and which will continue to be admired when prejudice shall cease, and bigotry give way to impartial examination. These are beauties that rise out of nature and of truth; the superficial reader cannot miss them, the profound can image nothing beyond them.

4.1.1

The gaudy, blabbing, and remorseful day.

The epithet *blabbing* applied to the day by a man about to commit murder, is exquisitely beautiful. Guilt is afraid of light, considers darkness as a natural shelter, and makes night the confidante of those actions which cannot be trusted to the *tell-tale day*.

4.1.3

> *the jades*
> *That drag the tragick melancholy night,*
> *Who with their drowsy, slow, and flagging wings,*
> *Clip dead mens' graves;——*

The *wings* of the *jades* that drag night appears an unnatural image, till it is remembered that the chariot of the night is supposed, by *Shakespeare*, to be drawn by dragons.

4.2.37

For our enemies shall fall before us,

He alludes to his name *Cade*, from *cado*, Lat. *to fall*. He has too much learning for his character.

4.2.77

There shall be no money;

To mend the world by banishing money is an old contrivance of those who did not consider that the quarrels and mischiefs which arise from money, as the sign or ticket of riches, must, if money were to cease, arise immediately from riches themselves, and could never be at an end till every man was contented with his own share of the goods of life.

4.7.54

Thou ought'st not to let thy horse wear a cloak.

This is a reproach truly characteristical. Nothing gives so much offence to the lower ranks of mankind as the sight of superfluities merely ostentatious.

4.10.85

So wish I, I might thrust thy soul to hell.

Not to dwell upon the wickedness of this horrid wish, with which *Iden* debases his character, this whole speech is wild and confused. To draw a man *by the heels, headlong,* is somewhat difficult; nor can I discover how *the dunghill would be his grave* if *his trunk* were left *to be fed upon by crows.* These I conceive not to be the faults of corruption but of negligence, and therefore do not attempt correction.

THE THIRD PART OF KING HENRY VI

This play is only divided from the former for the convenience of exhibition; for the series of action is continued without interruption, nor are any two scenes of any play more closely connected than the first scene of this play with the last of the former.

1.1.236

What is it but to make thy Sepulchre.

The Queen's reproach is founded on a position long received among politicians, that the loss of a King's power is soon followed by loss of life.

1.2.22

An oath is of no moment, being not took
Before a true and lawful magistrate.

The obligation of an oath is here eluded by very despicable sophistry. A lawful magistrate alone has the power to exact an oath, but the oath derives no part of its force from the magistrate. The plea against the obligation of an oath obliging to maintain an usurper, taken from the unlawfulness of the oath itself in the fore-going play, was rational and just.

1.2.49

The Queen, with all the northern Earls and Lords,
Intend here to besiege you in your castle.

I know not whether the authour intended any moral instruction, but he that reads this has a striking admonition against that precipitancy by which men often use unlawful means to do that which a little delay would put honestly in their power. Had *York* staid but a few moments he had saved his cause from the strain of perjury.

2.1.130

Our soldiers, like the night-owl's lazy flight,
Or like a lazy thrasher with a flail,
Fell gently down.

This image is not very congruous to the subject, nor was it necessary to the comparison, which is happily enough compleated by the thresher.

2.5.21

O God! methinks it were a happy life
To be no better than a homely swain.

This speech is mournful and soft, exquisitely suited to the character of the king, and makes a pleasing interchange, by affording, amidst the tumult and horrour of the battle, an unexpected glimpse of rural innocence and pastoral tranquillity.

3.1.17

Thy balm washt off.

This is an image very frequent in the works of *Shakespeare*. So again in this Scene, *I was anointed King*. It is common in these Plays to find the same images, whether jocular or serious, frequently recurring.

3.2.161

Unlick'd bear-whelp.

It was an opinion which, in spite of its absurdity, prevailed long, that the bear brings forth only shapeless lumps of animated flesh, which she licks into the form of bears. It is now well known that the whelps of a bear are produced in the same state with those of other creatures.

3.2.166

> *To o'er-bear such*
> *As are of better person than myself.*

Richard speaks here the language of nature. Whoever is stigmatised with deformity has a constant source of envy in his mind, and would counterballance by some other superiority these advantages which they feel themselves to want. *Bacon* remarks that the deformed are commonly daring, and it is almost proverbially observed that they are ill-natured. The truth is, that the deformed, like all other men, are displeased with inferiority, and endeavour to gain ground by good or bad means, as they are virtuous or corrupt.

4.1.42

> *'Tis better using* France, *than trusting* France.
> *Let us be back'd with God, and with the seas.*

This has been the advice of every man who in any age understood and favoured the interest of *England*.

4.6.70

> *This pretty lad will prove our country's bliss.*

He was afterwards *Henry* VII. A man who put an end to the civil war of the two houses, but not otherwise remarkable for virtue. *Shakespeare* knew his trade. *Henry* VII. was Grandfather to Queen *Elizabeth*, and the King from whom *James* inherited.

5.5.51

> *Oh* Ned, *sweet* Ned!

The condition of this warlike queen would move compassion could it be forgotten that she gave *York,* to wipe his eyes in his captivity, a handkerchief stained with his young child's blood.

The three parts of *Henry* VI. are suspected, by Mr. *Theobald*, of being supposititious, and are declared, by Dr. *Warburton*, to be *certainly not Shakespeare's*. Mr. *Theobald's* suspicion arises from

T

some obsolete words; but the phraseology is like the rest of our authour's stile, and single words, of which however I do not observe more than two, can conclude little.

Dr. *Warburton* gives no reason, but I suppose him to judge upon deeper principles and more comprehensive views, and to draw his opinion from the general effect and spirit of the composition, which he thinks inferior to the other historical plays.

From mere inferiority nothing can be inferred; in the productions of wit there will be inequality. Sometimes judgment will err, and sometimes the matter itself will defeat the artist. Of every authour's works one will be the best, and one will be the worst. The colours are not equally pleasing, nor the attitudes equally graceful, in all the pictures of *Titian* or *Reynolds*.

Dissimilitude of stile and heterogeneousness of sentiment, may sufficiently show that a work does not really belong to the reputed authour. But in these plays no such marks of spuriousness are found. The diction, the versification, and the figures, are *Shakespeare*'s. These plays, considered, without regard to characters and incidents, merely as narratives in verse, are more happily conceived and more accurately finished than those of king *John*, *Richard* II. or the tragick scenes of *Henry* IV. and V. If we take these plays from *Shakespeare*, to whom shall they be given? What authour of that age had the same easiness of expression and fluency of numbers?

Having considered the evidence given by the plays themselves, and found it in their favour, let us now enquire what corroboration can be gained from other testimony. They are ascribed to *Shakespeare* by the first editors, whose attestation may be received in questions of fact, however unskilfully they superintended their edition. They seem to be declared genuine by the voice of *Shakespeare* himself, who refers to the second play in his epilogue to *Henry* V. and apparently connects the first act of *Richard* III. with the last of the third part of *Henry* VI. If it be objected that the plays were popular, and therefore he alluded to them as well known; it may be answered, with equal probability, that the natural passions of a poet would have disposed him to separate his own works from those of an inferior hand. And indeed if an authour's own testimony is to be overthrown by speculative criticism, no man can be any longer secure of literary reputation.

Of these three plays I think the second the best. The truth is, that they have not sufficient variety of action, for the incidents are too often of the same kind; yet many of the characters are well discriminated. King *Henry*, and his queen, king *Edward*, the duke of *Gloucester*, and the earl of *Warwick*, are very strongly and distinctly painted.

The old copies of the two latter parts of *Henry* VI. and of *Henry* V. are so apparently imperfect and mutilated, that there is no reason for supposing them the first draughts of *Shakespeare*. I am inclined to believe them copies taken by some auditor who wrote down, during the representation, what the time would permit, then perhaps filled up some of his omissions at a second or third hearing, and when he had by this method formed something like a play, sent it to the printer.

KING RICHARD III

1.1.28

And therefore, since I cannot prove a lover.

Shakespeare very diligently inculcates, that the wickedness of *Richard* proceeded from his deformity, from the envy that rose at the comparison of his own person with others, and which incited him to disturb the pleasures that he could not partake.

1.1.108

Whatsoe'er you will employ me in,
Were it to call King Edward's *widow sister,*
I will perform it.

This is a very covert and subtle manner of insinuating treason. The natural expression would have been, *were it to call King* Edward's wife *sister*. I will solicit for you though it should be at the expence of so much degradation and constraint, as to own the lowborn wife of King *Edward* for a sister. But by slipping as it were casually *widow* into the place of *wife*, he tempts *Clarence* with an oblique proposal to kill the king.

1.2.180

I did kill King Henry;
But 'twas thy beauty that provoked me.

Shakespeare countenances the observation, that no woman can ever be offended with the mention of her beauty.

1.3.228
——rooting hog!

She calls him *hog* as an appellation more contemptuous than *bear*, as he is elsewhere termed from his ensigns armorial. There is no such heap of allusion as [*Warburton*] imagines.

1.3.242
Bottled spider.

A *spider* is called bottled, because, like other insects, he has a middle slender and a belly protuberant. *Richard*'s form and venom make her liken him to a spider.

2.1.102
Have I a tongue to doom my brother's death.

This lamentation is very tender and pathetick. The recollection of the good qualities of the dead is very natural, and no less naturally does the king endeavour to communicate the crime to others.

5.3.177
Give me another horse:——

There is in this, as in many of our authour's speeches of passion, something very trifling, and something very striking. *Richard*'s debate, whether he should quarrel with himself, is too long continued, but the subsequent exaggeration of his crimes is truly tragical.

This is one of the most celebrated of our authour's performances; yet I know not whether it has not happened to him as to others, to be praised most when praise is not most deserved. That this play has scenes noble in themselves, and very well contrived to strike in the exhibition, cannot be denied. But some parts are trifling, others shocking, and some improbable.

KING HENRY VIII
1.1.15
Till this time Pomp was single, but now marry'd
To one above itself.

Dr. *Warburton* has here discovered more beauty than the authour intended, who meant only to say in a noisy periphrase, that *pomp was encreased on this occasion to more than twice as much as it had ever been before.* Pomp is no more married to the *English* than to the *French* king, for to neither is any preference given by the speaker. Pomp is only married to pomp, but the new pomp is greater than the old.

1.1.122
A beggar's book
Out-worths a noble's blood.

That is, the literary qualifications of a bookish beggar are more prized than the high descent of hereditary greatness. This is a contemptuous exclamation very naturally put into the mouth of one of the antient, unlettered, martial nobility.

1.2.1
My life itself, and the best heart of it,
Thanks you for this great care.

The expression is monstrous. The heart is supposed the seat of life: But, as if he had many lives, and to each of them, a heart, he says, *his best heart.* A way of speaking that would have become a cat rather than a King.—WARBURTON.

This expression is not more monstrous than many others. Heart is not here taken for the great organ of circulation and life, but, in a common and popular sense, for the most valuable or precious part. Our authour, in *Hamlet*, mentions, the *heart of heart.* Exhausted and effete ground is said by the farmer to be *out of heart.* The hard and inner part of the oak is called *heart of oak.*

1.2.34
Compell'd by hunger
And lack of other means.

Means does not signify methods of livelihood, for that was said immediately before—*unfit for other life*; but it signifies, *necessaries*—*compelled*, says the speaker, *for want of bread and other necessaries.* But the poet using, for the thing, [*want of bread*] the effect of it, [*hunger*] the passage is become doubly obscure; first, by using a term in a licentious sense, and then by putting it to a vicious construction. The not apprehending that this is one of the distinguishing peculiarities in *Shakespear's* stile, has been the occasion of so much ridiculous correction of him.— WARBURTON.

I have inserted this note rather because it seems to have been the writer's favourite, than because it is of much value. It explains what no reader has found difficult, and, I think, explains it wrong.

4.2.

Enter *Catherine* Dowager, sick, led between *Griffith* her gentleman usher, and *Patience* her woman.

This scene is above any other part of *Shakespeare*'s tragedies, and perhaps above any scene of any other poet, tender and pathetick, without gods, or furies, or poisons, or precipices, without the help of romantick circumstances, without improbable sallies of poetical lamentation, and without any throes of tumultuous misery.

5.3.10

——we are all men
In our own natures frail, and capable
Of frailty,——

This sentence I think needed no commentary. The meaning, and the plain meaning, is, *we are men frail by nature, and therefore liable to acts of frailty*, to deviations from the right. I wish every commentator, before he suffers his confidence to kindle, would repeat,

——We are all men
In our own natures frail, and capable
Of frailty; few are angels.

5.5.40

Nor shall this peace sleep with her.——

These lines, to the interruption by the King, seem to have been inserted at some revisal of the play after the accession of King *James*. If the passage, included in crotchets, be left out, the speech of *Cranmer* proceeds in a regular tenour of prediction and continuity of sentiments; but by the interposition of the new lines, he first celebrates *Elizabeth*'s successor, and then wishes he did not know that she was to die; first rejoices at the consequence, and then laments the cause. Our authour was at once politick and idle; he resolved to flatter *James*, but neglected to reduce the whole speech to propriety, or perhaps intended that the lines inserted should be spoken in the action, and omitted in the publication, if any publication ever was in his thoughts. Mr. *Theobald* has made the same observation.

The play of *Henry* the eighth is one of those which still keeps possession of the stage, by the splendour of its pageantry. The coronation about forty years ago drew the people together in multitudes for a great part of the winter. Yet pomp is not the only merit of this play. The meek sorrows and virtuous distress of *Catherine* have furnished some scenes which may be justly numbered among the greatest efforts of tragedy. But the genius of *Shakespeare* comes in and goes out with *Catherine*. Every other part may be easily conceived, and easily written.

Though it is very difficult to decide whether short pieces be genuine or spurious, yet I cannot restrain myself from expressing my suspicion that neither the prologue nor epilogue to this play is the work *of Shakespeare; non vultus, non color*. It appears to me very likely that they were supplied by the friendship or officious-ness of *Johnson*, whose manner they will be perhaps found exactly to resemble. There is yet another supposition possible: the pro-logue and epilogue may have been written after *Shakespeare*'s departure from the stage, upon some accidental revisal of the play, and there will then be reason for imagining that the writer, whoever he was, intended no great kindness to him, this play being recommended by a subtle and covert censure of his other works. There is in *Shakespeare* so much of *fool and fight*,

—— the fellow
In a long motley coat, guarded with yellow,

appears so often in his drama, that I think it not very likely that he would have animadverted so severely on himself. All this, however, must be received as very dubious, since we know not the exact date of this or the other plays, and cannot tell how our authour might have changed his practice or opinions.

The historical Dramas are now concluded, of which the two parts of *Henry* the Fourth, and *Henry* the Fifth, are among the happiest of our authour's compositions; and King *John*, *Richard* the Third, and *Henry* the Eighth, deservedly stand in the second class. Those whose curiosity would refer the historical scenes to their original, may consult *Hollingshead*, and sometimes *Hall*: from *Hollingshead Shakespeare* has often inserted whole speeches with no more alteration than was necessary to the numbers of his verse. To transcribe them into the margin was unnecessary, because the original is easily examined, and they are seldom less perspicuous in the poet than in the historian.

To play histories, or to exhibit a succession of events by action and dialogue, was a common entertainment among our rude ancestors upon great festivities. The parish clerks once performed at *Clerkenwell* a play which lasted three days, containing, *The History of the World.*

KING LEAR

1.1.149

Think'st thou, that duty shall have dread to speak,——

I have given this passage according to the old folio, from which the modern editions have silently departed, for the sake of better numbers, with a degree of insincerity, which, if not sometimes detected and censured, must impair the credit of antient books. One of the editors, and perhaps only one, knew how much mischief may be done by such clandestine alterations.

The quarto agrees with the folio, except for that *reserve thy state,* it gives, *reverse thy doom,* and has *stoops* instead of *falls to folly.*

The meaning of *answer my life my judgment* is, *Let my life be answerable for my judgment,* or *I will stake my life on my opinion.*

The reading which, without any right, has possessed all the modern copies is this,

> —— to plainness Honour
> *Is bound, when Majesty to folly falls.*
> *Reserve thy state; with better judgment check*
> *This hideous rashness; with my life I answer,*
> *Thy youngest daughter,* &c.

I am inclined to think that *reverse thy doom* was *Shakespeare*'s first reading, as more apposite to the present occasion, and that he changed it afterwards to *reserve thy state,* which conduces more to the progress of the action.

1.1.174

Which nor our nature, nor our place can bear,
Our potency made good.

Lear, who is characterized as hot, heady and violent, is, with very just observation of life, made to entangle himself with vows, upon any sudden provocation to vow revenge, and then to plead the obligation of a vow in defence of implacability.

1.2.128

This is the excellent foppery of the world, &c.

In *Shakespear's* best plays, besides the vices that arise from the subject, there is generally some peculiar prevailing folly, principally ridiculed, that runs thro' the whole piece. Thus, in the *Tempest,* the lying disposition of travellers, and in *As you like it,* the fantastick humour of courtiers, is exposed and satirised with infinite pleasantry. In like manner, in his play of *Lear,* the dotages of judicial astrology are severely ridiculed. I fancy, was the date of its first performance well considered, it would be found that something or other happened at that time which gave a more than ordinary run to this deceit, as these words seem to intimate, *I am thinking, brother, of a prediction I read this other day, what should follow these eclipses.* However this be, an impious cheat, which had so little foundation in nature or reason, so detestable an original, and such fatal consequences on the manners of the people, who were at that time strangely besotted with it, certainly deserved the severest lash of satire. It was a fundamental in this noble science, that whatever seeds of good dispositions the infant unborn might be endowed with, either from nature, or traductively from its parents, yet if, at the time of its birth, the delivery was by any casualty so accelerated or retarded, as to fall in with the predominancy of a malignant constellation, that momentary influence would entirely change its nature, and bias it to all the contrary ill qualities. So wretched and monstrous an opinion did it set out with. But the *Italians,* to whom we owe this, as well as most other unnatural crimes and follies of these latter ages, fomented its original impiety to the most detestable height of extravagance. *Petrus Aponensis,* an *Italian* physician of the XIIIth century, assures us that those prayers which are made to God when the moon is in conjunction with *Jupiter* in the Dragon's tail, are infallibly heard. The great *Milton* with a just indignation of this impiety, hath, in his *Paradise Regained,* satirized it in a very beautiful manner, by putting these reveries into the mouth of the Devil. Nor could the licentious *Rabelais* himself forbear to ridicule this impious dotage, which he does with exquisite address and humour, where, in the fable which he so agreeably tells from Æsop, of the man who applied to Jupiter for the loss of his hatchet, he makes those, who, on the poor man's good success, had projected to trick *Jupiter* by the same petition, a kind of astrologick atheists, who ascribed this good fortune, that they imagined they were now all going to partake of, to the influence of some rare conjunction and configuration of the stars. *Hen, hen, disent ils—Et doncques, telle est au temps present la revolution des Cieulx, la constellation des Astres, & aspect des Planetes, que quiconque Coignée perdra, soubdain deviendra ainsi riche?*—Nou. Prol. du IV. Livre.

But to return to *Shakespear.* So blasphemous a delusion, therefore, it became the honesty of our poet to expose. But it was a tender point, and required managing. For this impious juggle had in his time a kind of religious reverence paid to it. It was therefore to be done obliquely; and the circumstances of the scene furnished him with as good an opportunity as he could wish. The persons in the drama are all pagans, so that as, in compliance to custom, his good characters were not to speak ill of judicial Astrology, they could on account of their religion give no reputation to it. But in order to expose it the more, he, with great judgment, makes these pagans Fatalists; as appears by these words of *Lear.*

> *By all the operations of the orbs,*
> *From whom we do exist and cease to be.*

For the doctrine of fate is the true foundation of judicial Astrology. Having thus discredited it by the very commendations given to it, he was in no danger of having his direct satire against it mistaken, by its being put (as he was obliged, both in paying regard to custom, and in following nature) into the mouth of the villain and atheist, especially when he has added such force of reason to his ridicule, in the words referred to in the beginning of the note.

4.1.70

> *Let the superfluous and lust-dieted man,*
> *That slaves your ordinance.*

The language of *Shakespeare* is very licentious, and his words have often meanings remote from the proper and original use. To *slave* or *beslave* another is to *treat* him *with terms of indignity*; in a kindred sense, to *slave the ordinance* may be, *to* slight *or* ridicule *it.*

4.5.22

> *Let me unseal the letter.*

I know not well why *Shakespeare* gives the Steward, who is a mere factor of wickedness, so much fidelity. He now refuses the letter, and afterwards, when he is dying, thinks only how it may be safely delivered.

4.6.11

How fearful
And dizzy 'tis, to cast one's eyes so low!

This description has been much admired since the time of *Addison*, who has remarked, with a poor attempt at pleasantry, that *he who can read it without being giddy has a very good head, or a very bad one.* The description is certainly not mean, but I am far from thinking it wrought to the utmost excellence of poetry. He that looks from a precipice finds himself assailed by one great and dreadful image of irresistible destruction. But this overwhelming idea is dissipated and enfeebled from the instant that the mind can restore itself to the observation of particulars, and diffuse its attention to distinct objects. The enumeration of the choughs and crows, the samphire-man and the fishers, counteracts the great effect of the prospect, as it peoples the desert of intermediate vacuity, and stops the mind in the rapidity of its descent through emptiness and horrour.

4.6.80

Bear free and patient thoughts.

To be melancholy is to have the mind *chained down* to one painful idea, there is therefore great propriety in exhorting *Glo'ster* to *free thoughts*, to an emancipation of his soul from grief and despair.

5.3.166

Let's exchange charity.

Our authour by negligence gives his heathens the sentiments and practices of christianity. In *Hamlet* there is the same solemn act of final reconciliation, but with exact propriety, for the personages are Christians.

Exchange forgiveness with me, noble Hamlet, &c.

The Tragedy of *Lear* is deservedly celebrated among the dramas of *Shakespeare*. There is perhaps no play which keeps the attention so strongly fixed; which so much agitates our passions and interests our curiosity. The artful involutions of distinct interests, the striking opposition of contrary characters, the sudden changes of fortune, and the quick succession of events, fill the mind with a perpetual tumult of indignation, pity, and hope. There is no scene which does not contribute to the aggravation of the distress or conduct of the action, and scarce a line which does not conduce to the progress of the scene. So powerful is the current of the poet's imagination, that the mind, which once ventures within it, is hurried irresistibly along.

On the seeming improbability of *Lear*'s conduct it may be observed, that he is represented according to histories at that time vulgarly received as true. And perhaps if we turn our thoughts upon the barbarity and ignorance of the age to which this story is referred, it will appear not so unlikely as while we estimate *Lear*'s manners by our own. Such preference of one daughter to another, or resignation of dominion on such conditions, would be yet credible, if told of a petty prince of *Guinea* or *Madagascar*. *Shakespeare*, indeed, by the mention of his Earls and Dukes, has given us the idea of times more civilized, and of life regulated by softer manners; and the truth is, that though he so nicely discriminates, and so minutely describes the characters of men, he commonly neglects and confounds the characters of ages, by mingling customs ancient and modern, *English* and foreign.

My learned friend Mr. *Warton*, who has in the *Adventurer* very minutely criticised this play, remarks, that the instances of cruelty are too savage and shocking, and that the intervention of *Edmund* destroys the simplicity of the story. These objections may, I think, be answered, by repeating, that the cruelty of the daughters is an historical fact, to which the poet has added little, having only drawn it into a series by dialogue and action. But I am not able to apologise with equal plausibility for the extrusion of *Gloucester*'s eyes, which seems an act too horrid to be endured in dramatick exhibition, and such as must always compel the mind to relieve its distress by incredulity. Yet let it be remembered that our authour well knew what would please the audience for which he wrote.

The injury done by *Edmund* to the simplicity of the action is abundantly recompensed by the addition of variety, by the art with which he is made to co-operate with the chief design, and the opportunity which he gives the poet of combining perfidy with perfidy, and connecting the wicked son with the wicked daughters, to impress this important moral, that villany is never at a stop, that crimes lead to crimes, and at last terminate in ruin.

But though this moral be incidentally enforced, *Shakespeare* has suffered the virtue of *Cordelia* to perish in a just cause, contrary to the natural ideas of justice, to the hope of the reader, and, what is yet more strange, to the faith of chronicles. Yet this conduct is justified by the Spectator, who blames *Tate* for giving *Cordelia* success and happiness in his alteration, and declares, that, in his opinion, *the tragedy has lost half its beauty. Dennis* has remarked, whether justly or not, that, to secure the favourable reception of *Cato, the town was poisoned with much false and abominable criticism,* and that endeavours had been used to discredit and decry poetical justice. A play in which the wicked prosper, and the virtuous miscarry, may doubtless be good, because it is a just representation of the common events of human life: but since all reasonable beings naturally love justice, I cannot easily be persuaded, that the observation of justice makes a play worse; or, that if other excellencies are equal, the audience will not always rise better pleased from the final triumph of persecuted virtue.

In the present case the publick has decided. *Cordelia*, from the time of *Tate*, has always retired with victory and felicity. And, if my sensations could add any thing to the general suffrage, I might relate, that I was many years ago so shocked by *Cordelia*'s death, that I know not whether I ever endured to read again the last scenes of the play till I undertook to revise them as an editor.

There is another controversy among the criticks concerning this play. It is disputed whether the predominant image in *Lear*'s disordered mind be the loss of his kingdom or the cruelty of his daughters. Mr. *Murphy*, a very judicious critick, has evinced by induction of particular passages, that the cruelty of his daughters is the primary source of his distress, and that the loss of royalty affects him only as a secondary and subordinate evil; He observes with great justness, that *Lear* would move our compassion but little, did we not rather consider the injured father than the degraded king.

The story of this play, except the episode of *Edmund*, which is derived, I think, from *Sidney*, is taken originally from *Geoffry* of *Monmouth*, whom *Hollingshead* generally copied; but perhaps immediately from an old historical ballad. . . . My reason for believing that the play was posteriour to the ballad rather than the ballad to the play, is, that the ballad has nothing of *Shakespeare*'s nocturnal tempest, which is too striking to have been omitted, and

593

that it follows the chronicle; it has the rudiments of the play, but none of its amplifications: it first hinted *Lear*'s madness, but did not array it in circumstances. The writer of the ballad added something to the history, which is a proof that he would have added more, if more had occurred to his mind, and more must have occurred if he had seen *Shakespeare*.

TIMON OF ATHENS

1.1.21

Our Poesy is as a Gum,——

This speech of the poet is very obscure. He seems to boast the copiousness and facility of his vein, by declaring that verses drop from a poet as gums from odoriferous trees, and that his flame kindles itself without the violence necessary to elicite sparkles from the flint. What follows next? that it, *like a current, flies each bound it chafes.* This may mean, that it expands itself notwithstanding all obstructions: but the images in the comparison are so ill sorted, and the effect so obscurely expressed, that I cannot but think something omitted that connected the last sentence with the former. It is well known that the players often shorten speeches to quicken the representation; and it may be suspected, that they sometimes performed their amputations with more haste than judgment.

1.1.107

'Tis not enough to help the feeble up,
But to support him after.

This thought is better expressed by Dr. *Madden* in his elegy on Archbishop *Boulter.*

——He thought it mean
Only to help the poor to beg again.

4.2

Enter Flavius.

Nothing contributes more to the exaltation of *Timon*'s character than the zeal and fidelity of his servants. Nothing but real virtue can be honoured by domesticks; nothing but impartial kindness can gain affection from dependants.

4.3.193

I cannot concur [with *Warburton*] to censure *Theobald* as a *critick* very *unhappy*. He was weak, but he was cautious: finding but little power in his mind, he rarely ventured far under its conduct. This timidity hindered him from daring conjectures, and sometimes hindered him happily.

4.3.252

Hadst thou, like us. . . .

There is in this speech a sullen haughtiness, and malignant dignity, suitable at once to the lord and the manhater. The impatience with which he bears to have his luxury reproached by one that never had luxury within his reach, is natural and graceful.

There is in a letter written by the earl of *Essex*, just before his execution, to another nobleman, a passage somewhat resembling this, with which I believe every reader will be pleased, though it is so serious and solemn that it can scarcely be inserted without irreverence.

"God grant your lordship may quickly feel the comfort I now enjoy in my unfeigned conversion, but that you may never feel the torments I have suffered for my long delaying it. *I had none but deceivers to call upon me, to whom I said, if my ambition could have entered into their narrow breasts, they would not have been so humble; or if my delights had been once tasted by them, they would not have been so precise. But your lordship hath one to call upon you, that knoweth what it is you now enjoy; and what the greatest fruit and end is of all contentment that this world can afford.* Think therefore, dear earl, that I have staked and buoyed all the ways of pleasure unto you, and left them as sea-marks for you to keep the channel of religious virtue. For shut your eyes never so long, they must be open at the last, and then you must say with me, *there is no peace to the ungodly.*"

4.3.275

If thou hadst not been born the worst of men,
Thou hadst been knave and flatterer.

Dryden has quoted two verses of *Virgil* to shew how well he could have written satires. *Shakespeare* has here given a specimen of the same power by a line bitter beyond all bitterness, in which *Timon* tells *Apemantus*, that he had not virtue enough for the vices which he condemns.

5.3.6

I cannot read.

There is something elaborately unskilful in the contrivance of sending a soldier, who cannot read, to take the epitaph in wax, only that it may close the play by being read with more solemnity in the last scene.

The play of *Timon* is a domestick Tragedy, and therefore strongly fastens on the attention of the reader. In the plan there is not much art, but the incidents are natural, and the characters various and exact. The catastrophe affords a very powerful warning against that ostentatious liberality, which scatters bounty, but confers no benefits, and buys flattery, but not friendship.

In this Tragedy are many passages perplexed, obscure, and probably corrupt, which I have endeavoured to rectify or explain with due diligence; but having only one copy, cannot promise myself that my endeavours will be much applauded.

TITUS ANDRONICUS

All the editors and criticks agree with Mr. *Theobald* in supposing this play spurious. I see no reason for differing from them; for the colour of the stile is wholly different from that of the other plays, and there is an attempt at regular versification, and artificial closes, not always inelegant, yet seldom pleasing. The barbarity of the spectacles, and the general massacre which are here exhibited, can scarcely be conceived tolerable to any audience; yet we are told by *Johnson*, that they were not only born but praised. That *Shakespeare* wrote any part, though *Theobald* declares it *incontestable*, I see no reason for believing.

The chronology of this play does not prove it not to be *Shakespeare*'s. If it had been written twenty-five years, in 1614, it might have been written when *Shakespeare* was twenty-five years old. When he left *Warwickshire* I know not, but at the age of twenty-five it was rather too late to fly for deer-stealing.

Ravenscroft, who, in the reign of *Charles* II. revised this play, and restored it to the stage, tells us in his preface, from a theatrical tradition I suppose, which in his time might be of sufficient authority, that this play was touched in different parts by *Shakespeare*, but written by some other poet. I do not find *Shakespeare*'s touches very discernible.

MACBETH

1.1

Enter three Witches.

In order to make a true estimate of the abilities and merit of a writer, it is always necessary to examine the genius of his age, and the opinions of his contemporaries. A poet who should now make the whole action of his tragedy depend upon enchantment, and produce the chief events by the assistance of supernatural agents, would be censured as trangressing the bounds of probability, be banished from the Theatre to the nursery, and condemned to write fairy tales instead of tragedies; but a survey of the notions that prevailed at the time when this play was written, will prove that *Shakespeare* was in no danger of such censures, since he only turned the system that was then universally admitted to his advantage, and was far from overburthening the credulity of his audience.

The reality of witchcraft or enchantment, which, though not strictly the same, are confounded in this play, has in all ages and countries been credited by the common people, and in most by the learned themselves. These phantoms have indeed appeared more frequently, in proportion as the darkness of ignorance has been more gross; but it cannot be shown, that the brightest gleams of knowledge have at any time been sufficient to drive them out of the world. The time in which this kind of credulity was at its height, seems to have been that of the holy war, in which the christians imputed all their defeats to enchantments or diabolical opposition, as they ascribed their success to the assistance of their military saints; and the learned Dr. *Warburton* appears to believe (*Suppl. to the Introduction to Don* Quixote) that the first accounts of enchantments were brought into this part of the world by those who returned from their eastern expeditions. But there is always some distance between the birth and maturity of folly as of wickedness: this opinion had long existed, though perhaps the application of it had in no foregoing age been so frequent, nor the reception so general. *Olympiodorus*, in *Photius*'s extracts, tells us of one *Libanius*, who practised this kind of military magic, and having promised χωρὶς ὁπλιτῶν κατὰ βαρβάρων ἐνεργεῖν, *to perform great things against the barbarians without soldiers*, was, at the instances of the Emperess *Placidia*, put to Death, when he was about to have given proofs of his abilities. The Emperess shewed some kindness in her anger by cutting him off at a time so convenient for his reputation.

But a more remarkable proof of the antiquity of this notion may be found in St. *Chrysostom*'s book *de Sacerdotio*, which exhibits a scene of enchantments not exceeded by any romance of the middle age: he supposes a spectator overlooking a field of battle attended by one that points out all the various objects of horror, the engines of destruction, and the arts of slaughter. Δείκνυτο δὲ ἔτι παρὰ τοῖς ἐναντίοις καὶ πετομένους ἵππους διά τινος μαγγανείας, καὶ ὁπλίτας δι' ἀέρος φερομένους, καὶ πᾶσαν γοητείας δύναμιν καὶ ἰδέαν. *Let him then proceed to show him in the opposite armies horses flying by enchantment, armed men transported through the air, and every power and form of magic.* Whether St. *Chrysostom* believed that such performances were really to be seen in a day of battle, or only endeavoured to enliven his description, by adopting the notions of the vulgar, it is equally certain, that such notions were in his time received, and that therefore they were not imported from the *Saracens* in a later age; the wars with the *Saracens* however gave occasion to their propagation, not only as bigotry naturally discovers prodigies, but as the scene of action was removed to a great distance.

The reformation did not immediately arrive at its meridian, and tho' day was gradually encreasing upon us, the goblins of witchcraft still continued to hover in the twilight. In the time of Queen *Elizabeth* was the remarkable trial of the witches of *Warbois*, whose conviction is still commemorated in an annual sermon at *Huntingdon*. But in the reign of King *James*, in which this tragedy was written, many circumstances concurred to propagate and confirm this opinion. The King, who was much celebrated for his knowledge, had, before his arrival in *England*, not only examined in person a woman accused of witchcraft, but had given a very formal account of the practices and illusions of evil spirits, the compacts of witches, the ceremonies used by them, the manner of detecting them, and the justice of punishing them, in his Dialogues of *Dæmonologie*, written in the *Scottish* dialect, and published at *Edinburgh*. This book was, soon after his accession, reprinted at *London*, and as the ready way to gain King *James*'s favour was to flatter his speculations, the system of *Dæmonologie* was immediately adopted by all who desired either to gain preferment or not to lose it. Thus the doctrine of witchcraft was very powerfully inculcated; and as the greatest part of mankind have no other reason for their opinions than that they are in fashion, it cannot be doubted but this persuasion made a rapid progress, since vanity and credulity co-operated in its favour. The infection soon reached the parliament, who, in the first year of King *James*, made a law by which it was enacted, chap. xii. That "if any person shall use any invocation or conjuration of any evil or wicked spirit; 2. or shall consult, covenant with, entertain, employ, feed or reward any evil or cursed spirit to or for any intent or purpose; 3. or take up any dead man, woman or child out of the grave,—or the skin, bone, or any part of the dead person, to be employed or used in any manner of witchcraft, sorcery, charm, or enchantment; 4. or shall use, practise or exercise any sort of witchcraft, sorcery, charm, or enchantment; 5. whereby any person shall be destroyed, killed, wasted, consumed, pined, or lamed in any part of the body; 6. That every such person being convicted shall suffer death." This law was repealed in our own time.

Thus, in the time of *Shakespeare*, was the doctrine of witchcraft at once established by law and by the fashion, and it became not only unpolite, but criminal, to doubt it; and as prodigies are always seen in proportion as they are expected, witches were every day discovered, and multiplied so fast in some places, that bishop *Hall* mentions a village in *Lancashire*, where their number was greater than that of the houses. The jesuits and sectaries took advantage of this universal error, and endeavoured to promote the interest of their parties by pretended cures of persons afflicted by evil spirits; but they were detected and exposed by the clergy of the established church.

Upon this general infatuation *Shakespeare* might be easily allowed to found a play, especially since he has followed with great exactness such histories as were then thought true; nor can it be doubted that the scenes of enchantment, however they may now be ridiculed, were both by himself and his audience thought awful and affecting.

1.7.28

The arguments by which lady *Macbeth* persuades her husband to commit the murder, afford a proof of *Shakespeare*'s knowledge of human nature. She urges the excellence and dignity of courage, a glittering idea which has dazzled mankind from age to age, and animated sometimes the housebreaker, and sometimes the conqueror; but this sophism *Macbeth* has for ever destroyed by distinguishing true from false fortitude, in a line and a half; of which it may also be said, that they ought to bestow immortality on the author, though all his other productions had been lost.

> *I dare do all that may become a man,*
> *Who dares do more, is none.*

This topic, which has always been employed with too much success, is used in this scene with peculiar propriety, to a soldier by a woman. Courage is the distinguishing virtue of a soldier, and the reproach of cowardice cannot be borne by any man from a woman, without great impatience.

She then urges the oaths by which he had bound himself to murder *Duncan*, another art of sophistry by which men have sometimes deluded their consciences, and persuaded themselves that what would be criminal in others is virtuous in them; this argument *Shakespeare*, whose plan obliged him to make *Macbeth* yield, has not confuted, though he might easily have shown that a former obligation could not be vacated by a latter: that obligations laid on us by a higher power, could not be overruled by obligations which we lay upon ourselves.

2.1.49

> *Now o'er one half the world*
> *Nature seems dead.*

That is, *over our hemisphere all action and motion seem to have ceased*. This image, which is perhaps the most striking that poetry can produce, has been adopted by *Dryden* in his *Conquest of* Mexico.

> *All things are hush'd as Nature's self lay dead,*
> *The mountains seem to nod their drowsy head;*
> *The little birds in dreams their songs repeat,*
> *And sleeping flow'rs beneath the night dews sweat.*
> *Even lust and envy sleep!*

These lines, though so well known, I have transcribed, that the contrast between them and this passage of *Shakespeare* may be more accurately observed.

Night is described by two great poets, but one describes a night of quiet, the other of perturbation. In the night of *Dryden*, all the disturbers of the world are laid asleep; in that of *Shakespeare*, nothing but sorcery, lust and murder, is awake. He that reads *Dryden*, finds himself lull'd with serenity, and disposed to solitude and contemplation. He that peruses *Shakespeare*, looks round alarmed, and starts to find himself alone. One is the night of a lover, the other, of a murderer.

2.3.117

> *Here, lay* Duncan;
> *His silver skin laced with his golden blood,*
> *And his gash'd stabs look'd like a breach in nature*
> *For Ruin's wasteful entrance;*——

Mr. *Pope* has endeavoured to improve one of these lines by substituting *goary blood* for *golden blood*; but it may easily be admitted that he who could on such an occasion talk of *lacing the silver skin*, would *lace it* with *golden blood*. No amendment can be made to this line, of which every word is equally faulty, but by a general blot.

It is not improbable, that *Shakespeare* put these forced and unnatural metaphors into the mouth of *Macbeth* as a mark of artifice and dissimulation, to show the difference between the studied language of hypocrisy, and the natural outcries of sudden passion. This whole speech so considered, is a remarkable instance of judgment, as it consists entirely of antithesis and metaphor.

3.1.68

> *mine eternal jewel*
> *Giv'n to the common enemy of man,*

It is always an entertainment to an inquisitive reader, to trace a sentiment to its original source, and therefore though the term *enemy of man*, applied to the devil, is in itself natural and obvious, yet some may be pleased with being informed, that *Shakespeare* probably borrowed it from the first lines of the destruction of *Troy*, a book which he is known to have read.

That this remark may not appear too trivial, I shall take occasion from it to point out a beautiful passage of *Milton* evidently copied from a book of no greater authority, in describing the gates of hell. Book 2. v. 879. he says,

—— *On a sudden open fly,*
With impetuous recoil and jarring sound,
Th' infernal doors, and on their hinges grate
Harsh thunder.

In the history of *Don Bellianis*, when one of the knights approaches, as I remember, the castle of *Brandezar*, the gates are said to open *grating harsh thunder upon their brasen hinges.*

4.1

As this is the chief scene of inchantment in the play, it is proper in this place to observe, with how much judgment *Shakespeare* has selected all the Circumstances of his infernal ceremonies, and how exactly he has conformed to common opinions and traditions.

Thrice the brinded cat hath mew'd.

The usual form in which familiar spirits are reported to converse with witches, is that of a cat. A witch, who was tried about half a century before the time of *Shakespeare*, had a cat named *Rutterkin*, as the spirit of one of those witches was *Grimalkin*; and when any mischief was to be done she used to bid *Rutterkin go and fly*, but once when she would have sent *Rutterkin* to torment a daughter of the countess of *Rutland*, instead of *going* or *flying*, he only cried *mew*, from whence she discovered that the lady was out of his power, the power of witches not being universal, but limited, as *Shakespeare* has taken care to inculcate.

Though his bark cannot be lost,
Yet it shall be tempest tost.

The common afflictions which the malice of witches produced were melancholy, fits, and loss of flesh, which are threatned by one of *Shakespeare*'s witches.

Weary sev'n-nights, nine times nine,
Shall he dwindle, peak and pine.

It was likewise their practice to destroy the cattle of their neighbours, and the farmers have to this day many ceremonies to secure their cows and other cattle from witchcraft; but they seem to have been most suspected of malice against swine. *Shakespeare* has accordingly made one of his witches declare that she has been *killing swine*, and Dr. *Harsenet* observes, that about that time, *a sow could not be ill of the measles, nor a girl of the sullens, but some old woman was charged with witchcraft.*

> *Toad, that under the cold stone,*
> *Days and nights has, thirty-one,*
> *Swelter'd venom sleeping got;*
> *Boil thou first i'th' charmed pot.*

Toads have likewise long lain under the reproach of being by some means accessary to witchcraft, for which reason *Shakespeare*, in the first scene of this play, calls one of the spirits *Padocke* or *Toad*, and now takes care to put a toad first into the pot. When *Vaninus* was seized at *Tholouse*, there was found at his lodgings *ingens Bufo vitro inclusus, a great Toad shut in a Vial*, upon which those that prosecuted him *Veneficium ex probrabant, charged him*, I suppose, *with witchcraft.*

> *Fillet of a fenny snake,*
> *In the cauldron boil and bake;*
> *Eye of newt, and toe of frog;—*
> *For a charm, &c.*

The propriety of these ingredients may be known by consulting the books *de Viribus Animalium* and *de Mirabilibus Mundi*, ascribed to *Albertus Magnus*, in which the reader, who has time and credulity, may discover wonderful secrets.

> *Finger of birth-strangled babe,*
> *Ditch-deliver'd by a drab;——*

It has been already mentioned in the law against witches, that they are supposed to take up dead bodies to use in enchantments, which was confessed by the woman whom King *James* examined, and who had of a dead body that was divided in one of their assemblies, two fingers for her share. It is observable that *Shakespeare*, on this great occasion, which involves the fate of a king, multiplies all the circumstances of horror. The babe, whose finger is used, must be strangled in its birth; the grease must not only be human, but must have dropped from a gibbet, the gibbet of a murderer; and even the sow, whose blood is used, must have offended nature by devouring her own farrow. These are touches of judgment and genius.

> *And now about the cauldron sing——*
> *Black spirits and white,*
> *Blue spirits and grey,*
> *Mingle, mingle, mingle,*
> *You that mingle may.*

And in a former part,

> ——*weyward sisters, hand in hand,*——
> *Thus do go about, about,*
> *Thrice to thine, and thrice to mine,*
> *And thrice again to make up nine!*

These two passages I have brought together, because they both seem subject to the objection of too much levity for the solemnity of enchantment, and may both be shown, by one quotation from *Camden*'s account of *Ireland*, to be founded upon a practice really observed by the uncivilised natives of that country. "When any one gets a fall, *says the informer of* Camden, he starts up, and *turning three times to the right* digs a hole in the earth; for they imagine that there is a spirit in the ground, and if he falls sick in two or three days, they send one of their women that is skilled in that way to the place, where she says, I call thee from the east, west, north and south, from the groves, the woods, the rivers, and the fens, from the *fairies red, black, white.*" There was likewise a book written before the time of *Shakespeare*, describing, amongst other properties, the *colours* of spirits.

Many other circumstances might be particularised, in which *Shakespeare* has shown his judgment and his knowledge.

5.3.8
English *Epicures.*

The reproach of epicurism, on which Mr. *Theobald* has bestowed a note, is nothing more than a natural invective uttered by an inhabitant of a barren country, against those who have more opportunities of luxury.

This play is deservedly celebrated for the propriety of its fictions, and solemnity, grandeur, and variety of its action; but it has no nice discriminations of character, the events are too great to admit the influence of particular dispositions, and the course of the action necessarily determines the conduct of the agents.

The danger of ambition is well described; and I know not whether it may not be said in defence of some parts which now seem improbable, that, in *Shakespeare*'s time, it was necessary to warn credulity against vain and illusive predictions.

The passions are directed to their true end. Lady *Macbeth* is merely detested; and though the courage of *Macbeth* preserves some esteem, yet every reader rejoices at his fall.

CORIOLANUS

3.3.127

Have the power still
To banish your Defenders, 'till at length,
Your ignorance, which finds not, 'till it feels, &c.

Still retain the power of banishing your defenders, 'till your undiscerning folly, which can foresee no consequences, leave none in the city but yourselves, who are always labouring your own destruction.

It is remarkable, that, among the political maxims of the speculative *Harrington*, there is one which he might have borrowed from this speech. *The people*, says he, *cannot see, but they can feel.* It is not much to the honour of the people, that they have the same character of stupidity from their enemy and their friend. Such was the power of our authour's mind, that he looked through life in all its relations private and civil.

4.1.7

Fortune's blows,
When most struck home, being gentle wounded, craves
A noble cunning.

The sense is, When fortune strikes her hardest blows, to be wounded, and yet continue calm, requires a generous policy. He calls this calmness *cunning*, because it is the effect of reflection and philosophy. Perhaps the first emotions of nature are nearly uniform, and one man differs from another in the power of endurance, as he is better regulated by precept and instruction.

They bore as heroes, but they felt as man.

The Tragedy of *Coriolanus* is one of the most amusing of our authour's performances. The old man's merriment in *Menenius*; the lofty lady's dignity in *Volumnia*; the bridal modesty in *Virgilia*; the patrician and military haughtiness in *Coriolanus*; the plebeian malignity, and tribunitian insolence in *Brutus* and *Sicinius*, make a very pleasing and interesting variety: and the various revolutions of the hero's fortune fill the mind with anxious curiosity. There is, perhaps, too much bustle in the first act, and too little in the last.

JULIUS CAESAR

Of this tragedy many particular passages deserve regard, and the contention and reconcilement of *Brutus* and *Cassius* is universally celebrated; but I have never been strongly agitated in perusing it, and think it somewhat cold and unaffecting, compared with some other of *Shakespeare*'s plays; his adherence to the real story, and to *Roman* manners, seems to have impeded the natural vigour of his genius.

ANTONY AND CLEOPATRA

3.13.127

O that I were
Upon the hill of Basan, *to out-roar*
The horned herd.

It is not without pity and indignation that the reader of this great Poet meets so often with this low jest, which is too much a favourite to be left out of either mirth or fury.

4.9.15

Throw my heart
Against the flint and hardness of my fault,

The pathetick of *Shakespeare* too often ends in the ridiculous. It is painful to find the gloomy dignity of this noble scene destroyed by the intrusion of a conceit so far-fetched and unaffecting.

This Play keeps curiosity always busy, and the passions always interested. The continual hurry of the action, the variety of incidents, and the quick succession of one personage to another, call the mind forward without intermission from the first Act to the last. But the power of delighting is derived principally from the frequent changes of the scene; for, except the feminine arts, some of which are too low, which distinguish *Cleopatra*, no character is very strongly discriminated. *Upton,* who did not easily miss what he desired to find, has discovered that the language of *Antony* is, with great skill and learning, made pompous and superb, according to his real practice. But I think his diction not distinguishable from that of others: the most tumid speech in the Play is that which *Cæsar* makes to *Octavia*.

The events, of which the principal are described according to history, are produced without any art of connection or care of disposition.

CYMBELINE

1.5.18

QUEEN. *I will try the forces*
Of these thy compounds on such creatures as
We count not worth the hanging, but none human, . . .
CORNELIUS. *Your Highness*
Shall from this practice but make hard your heart;

There is in this passage nothing that much requires a note, yet I cannot forbear to push it forward into observation. The thought would probably have been more amplified, had our authour lived to be shocked with such experiments as have been published in later times, by a race of men that have practised tortures without pity, and related them without shame, and are yet suffered to erect their heads among human beings.

Cape saxa manu, cape robora, pastor.

2.4.118

The contract you pretend with that base wretch . . .
. . . it is no contract, none.

Here *Shakespeare* has not preserved, with his common nicety, the uniformity of character. The speech of *Cloten* is rough and harsh, but certainly not the talk of one,

> *Who can't take two from twenty, for his heart,*
> *And leave eighteen.*

His argument is just and well enforced, and its prevalence is allowed throughout all civil nations: As for rudeness, he seems not to be much undermatched.

3.3.35

What should we speak of
When we are old as you?

This dread of an old age, unsupplied with matter for discourse and meditation, is a sentiment natural and noble. No state can be more destitute than that of him who, when the delights of sense forsake him, has no pleasures of the mind.

3.3.101

I stole these babes;

Shakespeare seems to intend *Belarius* for a good character, yet he makes him forget the injury which he has done to the young princes, whom he has robbed of a kingdom only to rob their father of heirs.

The latter part of this soliloquy is very inartificial, there being no particular reason why *Belarius* should now tell to himself what he could not know better by telling it.

4.2.105

the snatches in his voice,
And burst of speaking, were as his; I'm absolute
'Twas very Cloten.

This is one of our authour's strokes of observation. An abrupt and tumultuous utterance very frequently accompanies a confused and cloudy understanding.

5.1.1

Yea, bloody cloth, &c.

This is a soliloquy of nature, uttered when the effervescence of a mind agitated and perturbed spontaneously and inadvertently discharges itself in words. The speech, throughout all its tenour, if the last conceit be excepted, seems to issue warm from the heart. He first condemns his own violence; then tries to disburden himself, by imputing part of the crime to *Pisanio*; he next sooths his mind to an artificial and momentary tranquillity, by trying to think that he has been only an instrument of the gods for the happiness of *Imogen.* He is now grown reasonable enough to determine, that having done so much evil he will do no more; that he will not fight against the country which he has already injured; but as life is not longer supportable, he will die in a just cause, and die with the obscurity of a man who does not think himself worthy to be remembered.

5.4.26

great Powers,
If you will take this audit, take this life,
And cancel those cold bonds.

This equivocal use of *bonds* is another instance of our authour's infelicity in pathetick speeches.

This Play has many just sentiments, some natural dialogues, and some pleasing scenes, but they are obtained at the expence of much incongruity.

To remark the folly of the fiction, the absurdity of the conduct, the confusion of the names and manners of different times, and the impossibility of the events in any system of life, were to waste criticism upon unresisting imbecillity, upon faults too evident for detection, and too gross for aggravation.

TROILUS AND CRESSIDA

5.1.23

cold palsies.

This catalogue of loathsome maladies ends in the folio at *cold palsies*. This passage, as it stands, is in the quarto; the retrenchment was in my opinion judicious.

It may be remarked, though it proves nothing, that, of the few alterations made by *Milton* in the second edition of his wonderful poem, one was, an enlargement of the enumeration of diseases.

5.3.23

It is the purpose that makes strong the vow.

The mad Prophetess speaks here with all the coolness and judgment of a skilful casuist. *The essence of a lawful vow, is a lawful purpose, and the vow of which the end is wrong must not be regarded as cogent.*

This Play is more correctly written than most of *Shakespeare*'s compositions, but it is not one of those in which either the extent of his views or elevation of his fancy is fully displayed. As the story abounded with materials, he has exerted little invention; but he has diversified his characters with great variety, and preserved them with great exactness. His vicious characters sometimes disgust, but cannot corrupt, for both *Cressida* and *Pandarus* are detested and contemned. The comick characters seem to have been the favourites of the writer, they are of the superficial kind, and exhibit more of manners than nature, but they are copiously filled and powerfully impressed.

Shakespeare has in his story followed for the greater part the old book of *Caxton,* which was then very popular; but the character of *Thersites,* of which it makes no mention, is a proof that this play was written after *Chapman* had published his version of *Homer.*

ROMEO AND JULIET
1.1.182

Why then, O brawling love ! O loving hate ! &c.

Of these lines neither the sense nor occasion is very evident. He is not yet in love with an enemy, and to love one and hate another is no such uncommon state, as can deserve all this toil of ιntithesis.

1.2.25

Earth-treading stars that made dark HEAVEN'S *light.*

This nonsense should be reformed thus,

Earth-treading stars that make dark EVEN *light.* . . .
WARBURTON

But why nonsense? Is anything more commonly said, than that beauties eclipse the sun? Has not *Pope* the thought and the word?

Sol through white curtains shot a tim'rous ray,
And ope'd those eyes that must eclipse *the day.*

Both the old and the new reading are philosophical nonsense, but they are both, and both equally poetical sense.

1.2.16

Such comfort as do lusty young men feel,
When well-apparel'd April *on the heel*
Of limping Winter treads,

To say, and to say in pompous words, that a *young man shall feel* as much in an assembly of beauties, *as young men feel in the month of April,* is surely to waste sound upon a very poor sentiment. I read,

Such comfort as do lusty yeomen *feel.*

You shall feel from the sight and conversation of these ladies, such hopes of happiness and such pleasure, as the farmer receives from the spring, when the plenty of the year begins, and the prospect of the harvest fills him with delight.

1.5.32

good cousin Capulet.

This cousin *Capulet* is *unkle* in the paper of invitation, but as *Capulet* is described as old, *cousin* is probably the right word in both places. I know not how *Capulet* and his lady might agree, their ages were very disproportionate; he has been past masking for thirty years, and her age, as she tells Juliet, is but eight and twenty.

2. *Prol.*

The use of this chorus is not easily discovered, it conduces nothing to the progress of the play, but relates what is already known, or what the next scenes will shew; and relates it without adding the improvement of any moral sentiment.

2.6.15

Too swift arrives as tardy as too slow.

He that travels too fast is as long before he comes to the end of his journey, as he that travels slow. Precipitation produces mishap.

3.1.2

The day is hot.

It is observed that in *Italy* almost all assassinations are committed during the heat of summer.

3.1.182

Affection makes him false.

The charge of falshood on *Bentivolio*, though produced at hazard, is very just. The authour, who seems to intend the character of *Bentivolio* as good, meant perhaps to shew, how the best minds, in a state of faction and discord, are detorted to criminal partiality.

3.5.84

And, yet, no Man like he doth grieve my heart.

Juliet's equivocations are rather too artful for a mind disturbed by the loss of a new lover.

611

4.3.2

leave me to myself to-night;
For I have need of many Orisons. . . .

Juliet plays most of her pranks under the appearance of religion :
perhaps *Shakespeare* meant to punish her hypocrisy.

5.1.3

My bosom's Lord sits lightly on his throne, . . .

These three lines are very gay and pleasing. But why does
Shakespeare give *Romeo* this involuntary cheerfulness just before
the extremity of unhappiness? Perhaps to shew the vanity of
trusting to those uncertain and casual exaltations or depressions,
which many consider as certain foretokens of good and evil.

5.3.229

I will be brief. . . .

It is much to be lamented that the Poet did not conclude the
dialogue with the action, and avoid a narrative of events which
the audience already knew.

This play is one of the most pleasing of our Author's performances. The scenes are busy and various, the incidents numerous
and important, the catastrophe irresistibly affecting, and the process of the action carried on with such probability, at least with
such congruity to popular opinions, as tragedy requires.

Here is one of the few attempts of *Shakespeare* to exhibit the
conversation of gentlemen, to represent the airy sprightliness of
juvenile elegance. Mr. *Dryden* mentions a tradition, which might
easily reach his time, of a declaration made by *Shakespeare*, that
he was obliged to kill Mercutio *in the third act, lest he should have been
killed by him*. Yet he thinks him *no such formidable person, but that
he might have lived through the play, and died in his bed*, without
danger to a poet. *Dryden* well knew, had he been in quest of truth,
that, in a pointed sentence, more regard is commonly had to the
words than the thought, and that it is very seldom to be rigorously
understood. *Mercutio's* wit, gaiety and courage, will always procure him friends that wish him a longer life; but his death is not
precipitated, he has lived out the time allotted him in the construction of the play; nor do I doubt the ability of *Shakespeare* to

have continued his existence, though some of his sallies are perhaps out of the reach of *Dryden*; whose genius was not very fertile of merriment, nor ductile to humour, but acute, argumentative, comprehensive, and sublime.

The Nurse is one of the characters in which the Authour delighted: he has, with great subtilty of distinction, drawn her at once loquacious and secret, obsequious and insolent, trusty and dishonest.

His comick scenes are happily wrought, but his pathetick strains are always polluted with some unexpected depravations. His persons, however distressed, *have a conceit left them in their misery, a miserable conceit.*

HAMLET

1.1.153

Whether in sea or fire, . . .

According to the pneumatology of that time, every element was inhabited by its peculiar order of spirits, who had dispositions different, according to their various places of abode. The meaning therefore is, that all *spirits extravagant*, wandering out of their element, whether aerial spirits visiting earth, or earthly spirits ranging the air, return to their station, to their proper limits in which they are *confined*.

2.1.114

It is as proper to our age
To cast beyond ourselves in our opinions,
As it is common for the younger sort
To lack discretion.

This is not the remark of a weak man. The vice of age is too much suspicion. Men long accustomed to the wiles of life *cast* commonly *beyond themselves*, let their cunning go further than reason can attend it. This is always the fault of a little mind, made artful by long commerce with the world.

2.2

[*Warburton's*] account of the character of *Polonius*, though it sufficiently reconciles the seeming inconsistency of so much wisdom with so much folly, does not perhaps correspond exactly to the ideas of our authour. The commentator makes the character of *Polonius*, a character only of manners, discriminated by properties superficial, accidental, and acquired. The poet intended a nobler delineation of a mixed character of manners and of nature. *Polonius* is a man bred in courts, exercised in business, stored with observation, confident of his knowledge, proud of his eloquence, and declining into dotage. His mode of oratory is truly represented as designed to ridicule the practice of those times, of prefaces that made no introduction, and of method that embarrassed rather than explained. This part of his character is accidental, the rest is natural. Such a man is positive and confident, because he knows that his mind was once strong, and knows not that it is become weak. Such a man excels in general principles, but fails in the particular application. He is knowing in retrospect, and ignorant in foresight. While he depends upon his memory, and can draw from his repositories of knowledge, he utters weighty sentences, and gives useful counsel; but as the mind in its enfeebled state cannot be kept long busy and intent, the old man is subject to sudden dereliction of his faculties, he loses the order of his ideas, and entangles himself in his own thoughts, till he recovers the leading principle, and falls again into his former train. This idea of dotage encroaching upon wisdom, will solve all the phænomena of the character of *Polonius*.

3.1.56

To be, or not to be? . . .

Of this celebrated soliloquy, which bursting from a man distracted with contrariety of desires, and overwhelmed with the magnitude of his own purposes, is connected rather in the speaker's mind, than on his tongue, I shall endeavour to discover the train, and to shew how one sentiment produces another.

Hamlet, knowing himself injured in the most enormous and atrocious degree, and seeing no means of redress, but such as must expose him to the extremity of hazard, meditates on his situation in this manner: *Before I can form any rational scheme of action under this pressure of distress*, it is necessary to decide, whether, *after our present state, we are* to be or not to be. That is the question, which, as it shall be answered, will determine, *whether 'tis nobler*, and more suitable to the dignity of reason, *to suffer the outrages of fortune* patiently, or to take arms against *them,* and by opposing end them, *though perhaps* with the loss of life. If *to die,* were *to sleep, no more, and by a sleep to end* the miseries of our nature, such a sleep were *devoutly to be wished;* but if *to sleep* in death, be *to dream,* to retain our powers of sensibility, we must *pause* to consider, *in that sleep of death what dreams may come.* This consideration *makes calamity* so long endured; *for who would bear* the vexations of life, which might be ended *by a bare bodkin,* but that he is afraid of something in unknown futurity? This fear it is that gives efficacy to conscience, which, by turning the mind upon *this regard,* chills the ardour of *resolution,* checks the vigour of *enterprise,* and makes the *current* of desire stagnate in inactivity.

We may suppose that he would have applied these general observations to his own case, but that he discovered *Ophelia.*

3.1.77

To groan and sweat . . .

All the old copies have, *to* grunt *and* sweat. It is undoubtedly the true reading, but can scarcely be born by modern ears.

3.1.89

Nymph, in thy orisons, . . .

This is a touch of nature. *Hamlet,* at the sight of *Ophelia,* does not immediately recollect, that he is to personate madness, but makes her an address grave and solemn, such as the foregoing meditation excited in his thoughts.

3.2.137

I know not why our editors should, with such implacable anger, persecute our predecessors. Οἱ νεκροὶ μὴ δάκνουσιν, the dead it is true can make no resistance, they may be attacked with great security; but since they can neither feel nor mend, the safety of mauling them seems greater than the pleasure; nor perhaps would it much misbeseem us to remember, amidst our triumphs over the *nonsensical* and the *senseless,* that we likewise are men; that *debemur morti*, and as *Swift* observed to *Burnet*, shall soon be among the dead ourselves.

3.3.94

That his soul may be as damn'd and black
As hell, whereto it goes.

This speech, in which *Hamlet*, represented as a virtuous character, is not content with taking blood for blood, but contrives damnation for the man that he would punish, is too horrible to be read or to be uttered.

4.5.84

In hugger mugger to inter him.

All the modern editions that I have consulted give it,

In private *to inter him;*——

That the words now replaced are better, I do not undertake to prove; it is sufficient that they are *Shakespeare*'s: If phraseology is to be changed as words grow uncouth by disuse, or gross by vulgarity, the history of every language will be lost; we shall no longer have the words of any authour; and, as these alterations will be often unskilfully made, we shall in time have very little of his meaning.

4.7.20

Would, like the spring that turneth wood to stone,
Convert his gyves to graces.

This simile is neither very seasonable in the deep interest of this conversation, nor very accurately applied. If the *spring* had changed base metals to gold, the thought had been more proper.

5.1.85

This might be the pate of a politician, which this ass o'er-offices.

In the quarto, for *over-offices* is, *over-reaches*, which agrees better with the sentence: I believe both the words were *Shakespeare*'s. An authour in revising his work, when his original ideas have faded from his mind, and new observations have produced new sentiments, easily introduces images which have been more newly impressed upon him, without observing their want of congruity to the general texture of his original design.

5.2.6

Rashly,
(And prais'd be rashness for it)

Hamlet, delivering an account of his escape, begins with saying, That he *rashly*——and then is carried into a reflection upon the weakness of human wisdom. I rashly——praised be rashness for it—*Let us* not think these events casual, but *let us know*, that is, *take notice and remember*, that we sometimes succeed by *indiscretion*, when we *fail* by *deep plots*, and infer the perpetual superintendence and *agency* of the *Divinity*. The observation is just, and will be allowed by every human being who shall reflect on the course of his own life.

5.2.41

As Peace should still her wheaten garland wear,
And stand a COMMA *'tween their amities;*

The expression of our authour is, like many of his phrases, sufficiently constrained and affected, but it is not incapable of explanation. The *Comma* is the note of *connection* and continuity of sentences; the *Period* is the note of *abruption* and disjunction. *Shakespeare* had it perhaps in his mind to write, That unless *England* complied with the mandate, *war should put a* period *to their amity*; he altered his mode of diction, and thought that, in an opposite sense, he might put, That *Peace should stand a* Comma *between their amities*. This is not an easy style; but is it not the style of *Shakespeare*?

5.2.237

Give me your pardon, Sir. I've done you wrong;

I wish *Hamlet* had made some other defence; it is unsuitable to the character of a good or a brave man, to shelter himself in falsehood.

If the dramas of *Shakespeare* were to be characterised, each by the particular excellence which distinguishes it from the rest, we must allow to the tragedy of *Hamlet* the praise of variety. The incidents are so numerous, that the argument of the play would make a long tale. The scenes are interchangeably diversified with merriment and solemnity; with merriment that includes judicious and instructive observations, and solemnity, not strained by poetical violence above the natural sentiments of man. New characters appear from time to time in continual succession, exhibiting various forms of life and particular modes of conversation. The pretended madness of *Hamlet* causes much mirth, the mournful distraction of *Ophelia* fills the heart with tenderness, and every personage produces the effect intended, from the apparition that in the first act chills the blood with horror, to the fop in the last, that exposes affectation to just contempt.

The conduct is perhaps not wholly secure against objections. The action is indeed for the most part in continual progression, but there are some scenes which neither forward nor retard it. Of the feigned madness of *Hamlet* there appears no adequate cause, for he does nothing which he might not have done with the reputation of sanity. He plays the madman most, when he treats *Ophelia* with so much rudeness, which seems to be useless and wanton cruelty.

Hamlet is, through the whole play, rather an instrument than an agent. After he has, by the stratagem of the play, convicted the King, he makes no attempt to punish him, and his death is at last effected by an incident which *Hamlet* has no part in producing.

The catastrophe is not very happily produced; the exchange of weapons is rather an expedient of necessity, than a stroke of art. A scheme might easily have been formed, to kill *Hamlet* with the dagger, and *Laertes* with the bowl.

The poet is accused of having shewn little regard to poetical justice, and may be charged with equal neglect of poetical probability. The apparition left the regions of the dead to little purpose; the revenge which he demands is not obtained but by the death of him that was required to take it; and the gratification which would arise from the destruction of an usurper and a murderer, is abated by the untimely death of *Ophelia*, the young, the beautiful, the harmless, and the pious.

OTHELLO

1.3.134

I spoke of most disastrous chances,
Of moving accidents by flood and field;

Whoever ridicules this account of the progress of love, shews his ignorance, not only of history, but of nature and manners. It is no wonder that, in any age, or in any nation, a lady, recluse, timorous, and delicate, should desire to hear of events and scenes which she could never see, and should admire the man who had endured dangers, and performed actions, which, however great, were yet magnified by her timidity.

2.1.305

The thought whereof
Doth, like a poisonous mineral, gnaw my inwards.

This is philosophical. Mineral poisons kill by corrosion.

3.3.90

Excellent Wretch!

The meaning of the word *wretch*, is not generally understood. It is now, in some parts of *England*, a term of the softest and fondest tenderness. It expresses the utmost degree of amiableness, joined with an idea, which perhaps all tenderness includes, of feebleness, softness, and want of protection. *Othello*, considering *Desdemona* as excelling in beauty and virtue, soft and timorous by her sex, and by her situation absolutely in his power, calls her, *Excellent Wretch*. It may be expressed,

Dear, harmless, helpless Excellence.

3.3.206

She did deceive her father, marrying you.

This and the following argument of *Iago* ought to be deeply impressed on every reader. Deceit and falsehood, whatever conveniences they may for a time promise or produce, are, in the sum of life, obstacles to happiness. Those who profit by the cheat, distrust the deceiver, and the act by which kindness was sought, puts an end to confidence.

The same objection may be made with a lower degree of strength against the imprudent generosity of disproportionate marriages. When the first heat of passion is over, it is easily succeeded by suspicion, that the same violence of inclination which caused one irregularity, may stimulate to another; and those who have shewn, that their passions are too powerful for their prudence, will, with very slight appearances against them, be censured, as not very likely to restrain them by their virtue.

3.4.103

'Tis not a year, or two, shews us a man.

From this line it may be conjectured, that the authour intended the action of this play to be considered as longer than is marked by any note of time. Since their arrival at *Cyprus*, to which they were hurried on their wedding-night, the fable seems to have been in one continual progress, nor can I see any vacuity into which a *year or two*, or even a month or two, could be put. On the night of *Othello*'s arrival, a feast was proclaimed; at that feast *Cassio* was degraded, and immediately applies to *Desdemona* to get him restored. *Iago* indeed advises *Othello* to hold him off a while, but there is no reason to think, that he has been held off long. A little longer interval would increase the probability of the story, though it might violate the rules of the drama.

4.1.40

Nature would not invest herself in such shadowing passion without some instruction.

There has always prevailed in the world an opinion, that when any great calamity happens at a distance, notice is given of it to the sufferer by some dejection or perturbation of mind, of which he discovers no external cause. This is ascribed to that general communication of one part of the universe with another, which is called sympathy and antipathy; or to the secret monition, *instruction*, and influence of a superior Being, which superintends the order of Nature and of life. *Othello* says, *Nature could not invest herself in such shadowing passion, without* instruction. *It is not words that shakes me thus.* This passion which spreads its clouds over me is the effect of some agency more than the operation of words; it is one of those notices which men have of unseen calamities.

5.2.21

This Sorrow's heavenly;
It strikes, where it doth love.

I wish these two lines could be honestly ejected. It is the fate of *Shakespeare* to counteract his own pathos.

5.2.63 . . .

Oh perjur'd woman! thou dost stone my heart,
And mak'st me call, what I intend to do,
A murder, which I thought a sacrifice.

This line is difficult. *Thou hast hardened my heart, and makest me*
kill thee with the rage of a *murderer*, when *I thought to have sacrificed*
thee to justice with the calmness of a priest striking a victim. . . .

I am glad that I have ended my revisal of this dreadful scene. It
is not to be endured.

The beauties of this play impress themselves so strongly upon
the attention of the reader, that they can draw no aid from critical
illustration. The fiery openness of *Othello*, magnanimous, artless,
and credulous, boundless in his confidence, ardent in his affection,
inflexible in his resolution, and obdurate in his revenge; the cool
malignity of *Iago*, silent in his resentment, subtle in his designs,
and studious at once of his interest and his vengeance; the soft
simplicity of *Desdemona*, confident of merit, and conscious of
innocence, her artless perseverance in her suit, and her slowness to
suspect that she can be suspected, are such proofs of *Shakespeare's*
skill in human nature, as, I suppose, it is vain to seek in any
modern writer. The gradual progress which *Iago* makes in the
Moor's conviction, and the circumstances which he employs to inflame him, are so artfully natural, that, though it will perhaps not
be said of him as he says of himself, that he is *a man not easily
jealous*, yet we cannot but pity him when at last we find him
perplexed in the extreme.

There is always danger lest wickedness conjoined with abilities
should steal upon esteem, though it misses of approbation; but the
character of *Iago* is so conducted, that he is from the first scene to
the last hated and despised.

Even the inferiour characters of this play would be very conspicuous in any other piece, not only for their justness but their
strength. *Cassio* is brave, benevolent, and honest, ruined only by
his want of stubbornness to resist an insidious invitation. *Roderigo's*
suspicious credulity, and impatient submission to the cheats
which he sees practised upon him, and which by persuasion he
suffers to be repeated, exhibit a strong picture of a weak mind
betrayed by unlawful desires, to a false friend; and the virtue of

Æmilia is such as we often find, worn loosely, but not cast off, easy to commit small crimes, but quickened and alarmed at atrocious villanies.

The Scenes from the beginning to the end are busy, varied by happy interchanges, and regularly promoting the progression of the story; and the narrative in the end, though it tells but what is known already, yet is necessary to produce the death of *Othello*.

Had the scene opened in *Cyprus,* and the preceding incidents been occasionally related, there had been little wanting to a drama of the most exact and scrupulous regularity.

THE BRAVERY OF
THE ENGLISH
COMMON SOLDIERS

The Bravery of the English Common Soldiers appeared first in the third edition of *The Idler*, London, 1767. The copy here used is that in the Bodleian Library, Oxford—2699. f. 225–6. The essay is at the end of the second volume, pp. 325–30.

THE
BRAVERY
OF THE
ENGLISH COMMON SOLDIERS

BY those who have compared the military genius of the *English* with that of the *French* nation, it is remarked, that *the French officers will always lead, if the soldiers will follow*; and that *the English soldiers will always follow, if their officers will lead.*

In all pointed sentences some degree of accuracy must be sacrificed to conciseness; and, in this comparison, our officers seem to lose what our soldiers gain. I know not any reason, for supposing that the *English* officers are less willing than the *French* to lead; but it is, I think, universally allowed, that the *English* soldiers are more willing to follow. Our nation may boast, beyond any other people in the world, of a kind of epidemick bravery, diffused equally through all its ranks. We can shew a peasantry of heroes, and fill our armies with clowns, whose courage may vie with that of their general.

There may be some pleasure in tracing the causes of this plebeian magnanimity. The qualities which commonly make an army formidable, are long habits of regularity, great exactness of discipline, and great confidence in the commander. Regularity may, in time, produce a kind of mechanical obedience to signals and commands, like that which the perverse *Cartesians* impute to animals; discipline may impress such an awe upon the mind, that any danger shall be less dreaded than the danger of punishment; and confidence in the wisdom or fortune of the general, may induce the soldiers to follow him blindly to the most dangerous enterprize.

What may be done by discipline and regularity, may be seen in the troops of the *Russian* empress, and *Prussian* monarch. We find that they may be broken without confusion, and repulsed without flight.

But the *English* troops have none of these requisites, in any eminent degree. Regularity is by no means part of their character: they are rarely exercised, and therefore shew very little dexterity in their evolutions as bodies of men, or in the manual use of their weapons as individuals; they neither are thought by others, nor by themselves, more active or exact than their enemies, and therefore derive none of their courage from such imaginary superiority.

The manner in which they are dispersed in quarters over the country during times of peace, naturally produces laxity of discipline: they are very little in sight of their officers; and, when they are not engaged in the slight duty of the guard, are suffered to live every man his own way.

The equality of *English* privileges, the impartiality of our laws, the freedom of our tenures, and the prosperity of our trade, dispose us very little to reverence of superiors. It is not to any great esteem of the officers that the *English* soldier is indebted for his spirit in the hour of battle; for perhaps it does not often happen that he thinks much better of his leader than of himself. The *French* count, who has lately published the *Art of War*, remarks how much soldiers are animated, when they see all their dangers shared by those who were born to be their masters, and whom they consider as beings of a different rank. The *Englishman* despises such motives of courage: he was born without a master; and looks not on any man, however dignified by lace or titles, as deriving from nature any claims to his respect, or inheriting any qualities superior to his own.

There are some, perhaps, who would imagine that every *Englishman* fights better than the subjects of absolute governments, because he has more to defend. But what has the *English* more than the *French* soldier? Property they are both commonly without. Liberty is, to the lowest rank of every nation, little more than the choice of working or starving; and this choice is, I suppose, equally allowed in every country. The *English* soldier seldom has his head very full of the constitution; nor has there been, for more than a century, any war that put the property or liberty of a single *Englishman* in danger.

Whence then is the courage of the *English* vulgar? It proceeds, in my opinion, from that dissolution of dependance which obliges every man to regard his own character. While every man is fed by his own hands, he has no need of any servile arts: he may always have wages for his labour; and is no less necessary to his employer, than his employer is to him. While he looks for no protection from others, he is naturally roused to be his own protector; and having nothing to abate his esteem of himself, he consequently aspires to the esteem of others. Thus every man that crowds our streets is a man of honour, disdainful of obligation, impatient of reproach, and desirous of extending his reputation among those of his own rank; and as courage is in most frequent use, the fame of courage is most eagerly pursued. From this neglect of subordination I do not deny that some inconveniences may from time to time proceed: the power of the law does not always sufficiently supply the want of reverence, or maintain the proper distinction between different ranks: but good and evil will grow up in this world together; and they who complain, in peace, of the insolence of the populace, must remember, that their insolence in peace is bravery in war.

PROLOGUE TO
THE GOOD NATUR'D MAN

Johnson's prologue to Oliver Goldsmith's *The Good Natur'd Man* was spoken at the first production of the play on January 29, 1768. The text here provided is from the British Museum's first edition (1768) of the play (11777. d. 44.). Ten versions are listed and collated in Nichol Smith's and McAdam's *The Poems of Samuel Johnson*.

PROLOGUE

TO

THE GOOD NATUR'D MAN

A COMEDY

SPOKEN BY MR. BENSLEY

PREST by the load of life, the weary mind
Surveys the general toil of human kind;
With cool submission joins the labouring train,
And social sorrow, loses half it's pain:
Our anxious Bard, without complaint, may share
This bustling season's epidemic care.
Like Cæsar's pilot, dignified by fate,
Tost in one common storm with all the great;
Distrest alike, the statesman and the wit,
When one a borough courts, and one the pit.
The busy candidates for power and fame,
Have hopes, and fears, and wishes, just the same;
Disabled both to combat, or to fly,
Must hear all taunts, and hear without reply.
Uncheck'd on both, loud rabbles vent their rage,
As mongrels bay the lion in a cage.
Th' offended burgess hoards his angry tale,
For that blest year when all that vote may rail;
Their schemes of spite the poet's foes dismiss,
Till that glad night, when all that hate may hiss.
This day the powder'd curls and golden coat,
Says swelling Crispin begg'd a cobler's vote.
This night, our wit, the pert apprentice cries,
Lies at my feet, I hiss him, and he dies.

PROLOGUE

The great, 'tis true, can charm th' electing tribe;
The bard may supplicate, but cannot bribe.
Yet judg'd by those, whose voices ne'er were sold,
He feels no want of ill persuading gold;
But confident of praise, if praise be due,
Trusts without fear, to merit and to you.

SELECTIONS FROM
THE FALSE ALARM

The False Alarm was first published in 1770. The text of these selections has been taken from the British Museum copy of the first edition (E. 2225(2).).

THE FALSE ALARM

ONE of the chief advantages derived by the present generation from the improvement and diffusion of Philosophy, is deliverance from unnecessary terrours, and exemption from false alarms. The unusual appearances, whether regular or accidental, which once spread consternation over ages of ignorance, are now the recreations of inquisitive security. The sun is no more lamented when it is eclipsed, than when it sets; and meteors play their coruscations without prognostick or prediction.

The advancement of political knowledge may be expected to produce in time the like effects. Causeless discontent and seditious violence will grow less frequent, and less formidable, as the science of Government is better ascertained by a diligent study of the theory of Man.

It is not indeed to be expected, that physical and political truth should meet with equal acceptance, or gain ground upon the world with equal facility. The notions of the naturalist find mankind in a state of neutrality, or at worst have nothing to encounter but prejudice and vanity; prejudice without malignity, and vanity without interest. But the politician's improvements are opposed by every passion that can exclude conviction or suppress it; by ambition, by avarice, by hope, and by terrour, by public faction, and private animosity.

It is evident, whatever be the cause, that this nation, with all its renown for speculation and for learning, have yet made little proficiency in civil wisdom. We are still so much unacquainted with our own state, and so unskilful in the pursuit of happiness, that we shudder without danger, and complain without grievances, and suffer our quiet to be disturbed, and our commerce to be interrupted, by an opposition to the government, raised only by interest, and supported only by clamour, which yet has so far prevailed upon ignorance and timidity, that many favour it as reasonable, and many dread it as powerful.

What is urged by those who have been so industrious to spread suspicion, and incite fury from one end of the kingdom to the other, may be known by perusing the papers which have been at once presented as petitions to the King, and exhibited in print as remonstrances to the people. It may therefore not be improper to lay before the public the reflections of a man who cannot favour the opposition, for he thinks it wicked, and cannot fear it, for he thinks it weak.

The grievance which has produced all this tempest of outrage, the oppression in which all other oppressions are included, the invasion which has left us no property, the alarm that suffers no patriot to sleep in quiet, is comprised in a vote of the House of Commons, by which the freeholders of Middlesex are deprived of a Briton's birth-right, representation in parliament.

They have indeed received the usual writ of election, but that writ, alas! was malicious mockery; they were insulted with the form, but denied the reality, for there was one man excepted from their choice.

> *Non de vi, neque cæde, nec veneno,*
> *Sed lis est mihi de tribus capellis.*

The character of the man thus fatally excepted, I have no purpose to delineate. Lampoon itself would disdain to speak ill of him of whom no man speaks well. It is sufficient that he is expelled the House of Commons, and confined in jail as being legally convicted of sedition and impiety.

That this man cannot be appointed one of the guardians and counsellors of the church and state, is a grievance not to be endured. Every lover of liberty stands doubtful of the fate of posterity, because the chief county in England cannot take its representative from a jail.

Whence Middlesex should obtain the right of being denominated the chief county, cannot easily be discovered; it is indeed the county where the chief city happens to stand, but how that city treated the favourite of Middlesex, is not yet forgotten. The county, as distinguished from the city, has no claim to particular consideration.

That a man was in jail for sedition and impiety, would, I believe, have been within memory a sufficient reason why he should not come out of jail a legislator. This reason, notwithstanding the mutability of fashion, happens still to operate on the House of Commons. Their notions, however strange, may be justified by a common observation, that few are mended by imprisonment, and that. he whose crimes have made confinement necessary, seldom makes any other use of his enlargement, than to do with greater cunning what he did before with less.

The progress of a petition is well known. An ejected placeman goes down to his county or his borough, tells his friends of his inability to serve them, and his constituents of the corruption of the government. His friends readily understand that he who can get nothing, will have nothing to give. They agree to proclaim a meeting, meat and drink are plentifully provided, a crowd is easily brought together, and those who think that they know the reason of their meeting, undertake to tell those who know it not. Ale and clamour unite their powers, the crowd, condensed and heated, begins to ferment with the leven of sedition. All see a thousand evils, though they cannot show them, and grow impatient for a remedy, though they know not what.

A speech is then made by the Cicero of the day, he says much, and suppresses more, and credit is equally given to what he tells, and what he conceals. The petition is read and universally approved. Those who are sober enough to write add their names, and the rest would sign it if they could.

Every man goes home and tells his neighbour of the glories of the day; how he was consulted and what he advised; how he was invited into the great room, where his lordship called him by his name; how he was caressed by Sir Francis, Sir Joseph, or Sir George; how he eat turtle and venison, and drank unanimity to the three brothers.

The poor loiterer, whose shop had confined him, or whose wife had locked him up, hears the tale of luxury with envy, and at last enquires what was their petition. Of the petition nothing is remembered by the narrator, but that it spoke much of fears and apprehensions, and something very alarming, and then he is sure it is against the government; the other is convinced that it must be right, and wishes he had been there, for he loves wine and venison, and is resolved as long as he lives to be against the government.

The petition is then handed from town to town, and from house to house, and wherever it comes the inhabitants flock together, that they may see that which must be sent to the King. Names are easily collected. One man signs because he hates the papists; another because he has vowed destruction to the turnpikes; one because it will vex the parson; another because he owes his landlord nothing; one because he is rich; another because he is poor; one to shew that he is not afraid, and another to shew that he can write.

The passage, however, is not always smooth. Those who collect contributions to sedition sometimes apply to a man of higher rank and more enlightened mind, who instead of lending them his name, calmly reproves them for being seducers of the people.

You who are here, says he, complaining of venality, are yourselves the agents of those, who having estimated themselves at too high a price, are only angry that they are not bought. You are appealing from the parliament to the rabble, and inviting those, who scarcely, in the most common affairs, distinguish right from wrong, to judge of a question complicated with law written and unwritten, with the general principles of government, and the particular customs of the House of Commons; you are shewing them a grievance, so distant that they cannot see it, and so light that they cannot feel it; for how, but by unnecessary intelligence and artificial provocation, should the farmers and shopkeepers of Yorkshire and Cumberland know or care how Middlesex is represented. Instead of wandering thus round the county to exasperate the rage of party, and darken the suspicions of ignorance, it is the duty of men like you, who have leisure for enquiry, to lead back the people to their honest labour; to tell them, that submission is the duty of the ignorant, and content the virtue of the poor; that they have no skill in the art of government, nor any interest in the dissentions of the great; and when you meet with any, as some there are, whose understandings are capable of conviction, it will become you to allay this foaming ebullition, by shewing them that they have as much happiness as the condition of life will easily receive, and that a government, of which an erroneous or unjust representation of Middlesex is the greatest crime that interest can discover, or malice can upbraid, is government approaching nearer to perfection, than any that experience has known, or history related.

The drudges of sedition wish to change their ground, they hear him with sullen silence, feel conviction without repentance, and are confounded but not abashed; they go forward to another door, and find a kinder reception from a man enraged against the government, because he has just been paying the tax upon his windows.

FALKLAND'S ISLANDS

Three copies of the first (1771) edition of *Thoughts on the Late Transactions respecting Falkland's Islands*—one of the first issue, two of the second (revised) issue—are in the British Museum (8154. d. 10.; 8154. bbb. 8.; C. 38. f. 44(2).). All have been consulted and compared in the preparation of these selections.

SELECTIONS FROM
THOUGHTS
On The LATE TRANSACTIONS
RESPECTING
FALKLAND'S ISLANDS

To proportion the eagerness of contest to its importance seems too hard a task for human wisdom. The pride of wit has kept ages busy in the discussion of useless questions, and the pride of power has destroyed armies to gain or to keep unprofitable possessions.

Not many years have passed since the cruelties of war were filling the world with terror and with sorrow; rage was at last appeased, or strength was exhausted, and to the harassed nations peace was restored, with its pleasures and its benefits. Of this state all felt the happiness, and all implored the continuance; but what continuance of happiness can be expected, when the whole system of European empire can be in danger of a new concussion, by a contention for a few spots of earth, which, in the deserts of the ocean, had almost escaped human notice, and which, if they had not happened to make a sea-mark, had perhaps never had a name.

Fortune often delights to dignify what nature has neglected, and that renown which cannot be claimed by intrinsick excellence or greatness, is sometimes derived from unexpected accidents. The Rubicon was ennobled by the passage of Cæsar, and the time is now come when Falkland's Islands demand their historian. But the writer to whom this employment shall be assigned, will have few opportunities of descriptive splendor, or narrative elegance. Of other countries it is told how often they have changed their government; these islands have hitherto changed only their name. Of heroes to conquer, or legislators to civilize, here has been no appearance; nothing has happened to them but that they have been sometimes seen by wandering navigators, who passed by them in search of better habitations.

. . . . .

As war is the last of remedies, *cuncta prius tentanda*, all lawful expedients must be used to avoid it. As war is the extremity of evil, it is surely the duty of those whose station intrusts them with the care of nations, to avert it from their charge. There are diseases of animal nature which nothing but amputation can remove; so there may, by the depravation of human passions, be sometimes a gangrene in collective life for which fire and the sword are the necessary remedies; but in what can skill or caution be better shewn than preventing such dreadful operations, while there is yet room for gentler methods?

It is wonderful with what coolness and indifference the greater part of mankind see war commenced. Those that hear of it at a distance, or read of it in books, but have never presented its evils to their minds, consider it as little more than a splendid game; a proclamation, an army, a battle, and a triumph. Some indeed must perish in the most successful field, but they die upon the bed of honour, *resign their lives amidst the joys of conquest, and, filled with England's glory, smile in death.*

The life of a modern soldier is ill represented by heroick fiction. War has means of destruction more formidable than the cannon and the sword. Of the thousands and ten thousands that perished in our late contests with France and Spain, a very small part ever felt the stroke of an enemy; the rest languished in tents and ships, amidst damps and putrefaction; pale, torpid, spiritless, and helpless; gasping and groaning unpitied among men made obdurate by long continuance of hopeless misery, and whelmed in pits, or heaved into the ocean, without notice and without remembrance. By incommodious encampments and unwholesome stations, where courage is useless, and enterprise impracticable, fleets are silently dispeopled, and armies sluggishly melted away.

Thus is a people gradually exhausted, for the most part with little effect. The wars of civilized nations make very slow changes in the system of empire. The publick perceives scarcely any alteration but an increase of debt; and the few individuals who are benefited, are not supposed to have the clearest right to their advantages. If he that shared the danger enjoyed the profit; if he that bled in the battle grew rich by the victory, he might shew his gains without envy. But at the conclusion of a ten years war, how are we recompensed for the death of multitudes and the expence of millions, but by contemplating the sudden glories of paymasters and agents, contractors and commissaries, whose equipages shine like meteors, and whose palaces rise like exhalations.

These are the men who, without virtue, labour, or hazard, are growing rich as their country is impoverished; they rejoice when obstinacy or ambition adds another year to slaughter and devastation; and laugh from their desks at bravery and science, while they are adding figure to figure, and cipher to cipher, hoping for a new contract from a new armament, and computing the profits of a siege or tempest.

Those who suffer their minds to dwell on these considerations will think it no great crime in the ministry that they have not snatched with eagerness the first opportunity of rushing into the field, when they were able to obtain by quiet negotiation all the real good that victory could have brought us.

.   .   .   .   .

An unsuccessful war would undoubtedly have had the effect which the enemies of the Ministry so earnestly desire; for who could have sustained the disgrace of folly ending in misfortune? But had wanton invasion undeservedly prospered, had Falkland's Island been yielded unconditionally with every right prior and posterior; though the rabble might have shouted, and the windows have blazed, yet those who know the value of life, and the uncertainty of publick credit, would have murmured, perhaps unheard, at the increase of our debt, and the loss of our people.

This thirst of blood, however the visible promoters of sedition may think it convenient to shrink from the accusation, is loudly avowed by Junius, the writer to whom his party owes much of its pride, and some of its popularity. Of Junius it cannot be said, as of Ulysses, that he scatters ambiguous expressions among the vulgar; for he cries *havock* without reserve, and endeavours to let slip the dogs of foreign or of civil war, ignorant whither they are going, and careless what may be their prey.

Junius has sometimes made his satire felt, but let not injudicious admiration mistake the venom of the shaft for the vigour of the bow. He has sometimes sported with lucky malice; but to him that knows his company, it is not hard to be sarcastick in a mask. While he walks like Jack the Giant-killer in a coat of darkness, he may do much mischief with little strength. Novelty captivates the superficial and thoughtless; vehemence delights the discontented and turbulent. He that contradicts acknowledged truth will always have an audience; he that vilifies established authority will always find abettors.

Junius burst into notice with a blaze of impudence which has rarely glared upon the world before, and drew the rabble after him as a monster makes a show. When he had once provided for his safety by impenetrable secrecy, he had nothing to combat but truth and justice, enemies whom he knows to be feeble in the dark. Being then at liberty to indulge himself in all the immunities of invisibility; out of the reach of danger, he has been bold; out of the reach of shame, he has been confident. As a rhetorician, he has had the art of persuading when he seconded desire; as a reasoner, he has convinced those who had no doubt before; as a moralist, he has taught that virtue may disgrace; and as a patriot, he has gratified the mean by insults on the high. Finding sedition ascendant, he has been able to advance it; finding the nation combustible, he has been able to inflame it. Let us abstract from his wit the vivacity of insolence, and withdraw from his efficacy the sympathetick favour of Plebeian malignity; I do not say that we shall leave him nothing; the cause that I defend scorns the help of falsehood; but if we leave him only his merit, what will be his praise?

It is not by his liveliness of imagery, his pungency of periods, or his fertility of allusion, that he detains the cits of London, and the boors of Middlesex. Of stile and sentiment they take no cognizance. They admire him for virtues like their own, for contempt of order, and violence of outrage, for rage of defamation and audacity of falsehood. The Supporters of the Bill of Rights feel no niceties of composition, nor dexterities of sophistry; their faculties are better proportioned to the bawl of Bellas, or barbarity of Beckford; but they are told that Junius is on their side, and they are therefore sure that Junius is infallible. Those who know not whither he would lead them, resolve to follow him; and those who cannot find his meaning, hope he means rebellion.

Junius is an unusual phænomenon on which some have gazed with wonder and some with terrour, but wonder and terrour are transitory passions. He will soon be more closely viewed or more attentively examined, and what folly has taken for a comet that from its flaming hair shook pestilence and war, enquiry will find to be only a meteor formed by the vapours of putrefying democracy, and kindled into flame by the effervescence of interest struggling with conviction; which after having plunged its followers in a bog, will leave us enquiring why we regard it.

Yet though I cannot think the stile of Junius secure from criticism, though his expressions are often trite, and his periods feeble, I should never have stationed him where he has placed himself, had I not rated him by his morals rather than his faculties. What, says Pope, must be the priest, where the monkey is a God? What must be the drudge of a party of which the heads are Wilkes and Crosby, Sawbridge and Townshend?

Junius knows his own meaning and can therefore tell it. He is an enemy to the ministry, he sees them growing hourly stronger. He knows that a war at once unjust and unsuccessful would have certainly displaced them, and is therefore, in his zeal for his country, angry that war was not unjustly made, and unsuccessfully conducted.

ΓΝΩΘΙ ΣΕΑΥΤΟΝ

The text of this poem is derived from the 1787 edition of Johnson's works (vol. 2, pp. 389–91). Two corrections have been made from a manuscript version, whence Nichol Smith and McAdam derive their text.

ΓΝΩΘΙ ΣΕΑΥΤΟΝ

Post Lexicon Anglicanum auctum et emendatum.

LEXICON ad finem longo luctamine tandem
Scaliger ut duxit, tenuis pertæsus opellæ,
Vile indignatus studium, nugasque molestas,
Ingemit exosus, scribendaque lexica mandat
Damnatis, pœnam pro pœnis omnibus unam.

   Ille quidem recte, sublimis, doctus et acer,
Quem decuit majora sequi, majoribus aptum,
Qui veterum modo facta ducum, modo carmina vatum,
Gesserat et quicquid virtus, sapientia quicquid,
Dixerat, imperiique vices, cœlique meatus,
Ingentemque animo seculorum volverat orbem.

   Fallimur exemplis; temere sibi turba scholarum
Ima tuas credit permitti Scaliger iras.
Quisque suum nôrit modulum; tibi, prime virorum
Ut studiis sperem, aut ausim par esse querelis,
Non mihi sorte datum; lenti seu sanguinis obsint
Frigora, seu nimium longo jacuisse veterno,
Sivi mihi mentem dederit natura minorem.

   Te sterili functum cura, vocumque salebris
Tuto eluctatum spatiis sapientia dia
Excipit æthereis, ars omnis plaudit amica,
Linguarumque omni terra discordia concors
Multiplici reducem circumsonat ore magistrum.

   Me, pensi immunis cum jam mihi reddor, inertis
Desidiæ sors dura manet, graviorque labore
Tristis et atra quies, et tardæ tædia vitæ.
Nascuntur curis curæ, vexatque dolorum
Importuna cohors, vacuæ mala somnia mentis.
Nunc clamosa juvant nocturnæ gaudia mensæ,
Nunc loca sola placent; frustra te, Somne, recumbens
Alme voco, impatiens noctis metuensque diei.

ΓΝΩΘΙ ΣΕΑΥΤΟΝ

Omnia percurro trepidus, circum omnia lustro,
Si qua usquam pateat melioris semita vitæ,
Nec quid agam invenio, meditatus grandia, cogor
Notior ipse mihi fieri, incultumque fateri
Pectus, et ingenium vano se robore jactans.
Ingenium nisi materiem doctrina ministrat,
Cessat inops rerum, ut torpet, si marmoris absit
Copia, Phidiaci fæcunda potentia cœli.
Quicquid agam, quocunque ferar, conatibus obstat
Res angusta domi, et macræ penuria mentis.

  Non rationis opes animus, nunc parta recensens
Conspicit aggestas, et se miratur in illis,
Nec sibi de gaza præsens quod postulat usus
Summus adesse jubet celsa dominator ab arce;
Non, operum serie seriem dum computat ævi,
Præteritis fruitur, lætos aut sumit honores
Ipse sui judex, actæ bene munera vitæ;
Sed sua regna videns, loca nocte silentia late
Horret, ubi vanæ species, umbræque fugaces,
Et rerum volitant raræ per inane figuræ.

  Quid faciam? tenebrisne pigram damnare senectam
Restat? an accingar studiis gravioribus audax?
Aut, hoc si nimium est, tandem nova lexica poscam?

SKIA

AND

ODE DE SKIA INSULA

The poem, *Skia*, was first printed in Boswell's *Journal of a Tour to the Hebrides*, 1785, whence this text is derived. A version in *The Gentleman's Magazine*, February, 1786, p. 156, col. 1, has also been consulted. Differences between the two texts are of punctuation only. Both err in giving the word *recedunt* in the last line.

Ode de Skia Insula, which was addressed to Mrs. Thrale, was also first printed in 1785, in Boswell's *Journal*. The present text is taken from *Thraliana* (Oxford, 1941) p. 215, which reproduces the transcript of Johnson's manuscript as originally sent to Mrs. Thrale.

SKIA

Ponti profundis clausa recessibus,
Strepens procellis, rupibus obsita,
Quam grata defesso virentem
Skia sinum nebulosa pandis.

His cura credo sedibus exulat;
His blanda certe pax habitat locis:
Non ira, non mœror quietis
Insidias meditatur horis.

At non cavata rupe latescere,
Menti nec ægræ montibus aviis
Prodest vagari, nec frementes
E scopulo numerare fluctus.

Humana virtus non sibi sufficit,
Datur nec æquum cuique animum sibi
Parare posse, ut Stoicorum
Secta crepet nimis alta fallax.

Exæstuantis pectoris impetum,
Rex summe, solus tu regis arbiter;
Mentisque, te tollente, surgunt,
Te recidunt moderante fluctus.

ODE DE SKIA INSULA

PERMEO terras, ubi nuda rupes
Saxeas miscet nebulis ruinas,
Torva ubi rident steriles coloni
                Rura labores.

Pervagor gentes, hominum ferorum
Vita ubi nullo decorata cultu
Squalet informis, tugurique fumis
                Fœda latescit.

Inter erroris salebrosa longi,
Inter ignotæ strepitus loquelæ,
Quot modis mecum, quid agat, requiro,
                Thralia dulcis.

Seu viri curas, pia nupta, mulcet,
Seu fovet mater sobolem benigna,
Sive cum libris novitate pascit
                Sedula mentem;

Sit memor nostri, fideique merces
Stet fides constans, meritoque blandum
Thraliæ discant resonare nomen
                Littora Sciæ.

A JOURNEY
TO THE
WESTERN ISLANDS
OF
SCOTLAND

Johnson's *Western Islands* was first published anonymously in 1775. The present text is taken from the British Museum copy (287. f. 15.) of this edition and one kindly lent to me by Messrs McLeish of Little Russell Street, London. The text of the second edition, of 1785 (B.M.: 579. g. 36.), has been consulted throughout.

Up to p. 719 (of this edition) *Raasay* is (in the first edition) spelt *Raasay*; on and after p. 736, it is spelt *Raasa*. It has here been corrected to *Raasay* throughout. *Iona*, which in the first edition is sometimes *Jona*, is here always printed *Iona*. Inaccuracies of dating have been left uncorrected.

A JOURNEY

TO THE

WESTERN ISLANDS

OF SCOTLAND

I HAD desired to visit the *Hebrides*, or Western Islands of Scotland, so long, that I scarcely remember how the wish was originally excited; and was in the Autumn of the year 1773 induced to undertake the journey, by finding in Mr. Boswell a companion, whose acuteness would help my inquiry, and whose gaiety of conversation and civility of manners are sufficient to counteract the inconveniencies of travel, in countries less hospitable than we have passed.

On the eighteenth of August we left Edinburgh, a city too well known to admit description, and directed our course northward, along the eastern coast of Scotland, accompanied the first day by another gentleman, who could stay with us only long enough to shew us how much we lost at separation.

As we crossed the *Frith* of *Forth*, our curiosity was attracted by *Inch Keith*, a small island, which neither of my companions had ever visited, though, lying within their view, it had all their lives solicited their notice. Here, by climbing with some difficulty over shattered crags, we made the first experiment of unfrequented coasts. Inch Keith is nothing more than a rock covered with a thin layer of earth, not wholly bare of grass, and very fertile of thistles. A small herd of cows grazes annually upon it in the summer. It seems never to have afforded to man or beast a permanent habitation.

We found only the ruins of a small fort, not so injured by time but that it might easily be restored to its former state. It seems never to have been intended as a place of strength, nor was built to endure a siege, but merely to afford cover to a few soldiers, who perhaps had the charge of a battery, or were stationed to give signals of approaching danger. There is therefore no provision of water within the walls, though the spring is so near, that it might have been easily enclosed. One of the stones had this inscription: "Maria Reg. 1564." It has probably been neglected from the time that the whole island had the same king.

We left this little island with our thoughts employed awhile on the different appearance that it would have made, if it had been placed at the same distance from London, with the same facility of approach; with what emulation of price a few rocky acres would have been purchased, and with what expensive industry they would have been cultivated and adorned.

When we landed, we found our chaise ready, and passed through *Kinghorn*, *Kirkaldy*, and *Cowpar*, places not unlike the small or straggling market-towns in those parts of *England* where commerce and manufactures have not yet produced opulence.

Though we were yet in the most populous part of Scotland, and at so small a distance from the capital, we met few passengers.

The roads are neither rough nor dirty; and it affords a southern stranger a new kind of pleasure to travel so commodiously without the interruption of toll-gates. Where the bottom is rocky, as it seems commonly to be in Scotland, a smooth way is made indeed with great labour, but it never wants repairs; and in those parts where adventitious materials are necessary, the ground once consolidated is rarely broken; for the inland commerce is not great, nor are heavy commodities often transported otherwise than by water. The carriages in common use are small carts, drawn each by one little horse; and a man seems to derive some degree of dignity and importance from the reputation of possessing a two-horse cart.

ST. ANDREWS

At an hour somewhat late we came to St. Andrews, a city once archiepiscopal; where that university still subsists in which philosophy was formerly taught by Buchanan, whose name has as fair a claim to immortality as can be conferred by modern latinity, and perhaps a fairer than the instability of vernacular languages admits.

We found, that by the interposition of some invisible friend, lodgings had been provided for us at the house of one of the professors, whose easy civility quickly made us forget that we were strangers; and in the whole time of our stay we were gratified by every mode of kindness, and entertained with all the elegance of lettered hospitality.

In the morning we rose to perambulate a city, which only history shows to have once flourished, and surveyed the ruins of ancient magnificence, of which even the ruins cannot long be visible, unless some care be taken to preserve them; and where is the pleasure of preserving such mournful memorials? They have been till very lately so much neglected, that every man carried away the stones who fancied that he wanted them.

The cathedral, of which the foundations may be still traced, and a small part of the wall is standing, appears to have been a spacious and majestick building, not unsuitable to the primacy of the kingdom. Of the architecture, the poor remains can hardly exhibit, even to an artist, a sufficient specimen. It was demolished, as is well known, in the tumult and violence of Knox's reformation.

Not far from the cathedral, on the margin of the water, stands a fragment of the castle, in which the archbishop anciently resided. It was never very large, and was built with more attention to security than pleasure. Cardinal Beatoun is said to have had workmen employed in improving its fortifications at the time when he was murdered by the ruffians of reformation, in the manner of which Knox has given what he himself calls a merry narrative.

The change of religion in Scotland, eager and vehement as it was, raised an epidemical enthusiasm, compounded of sullen scrupulousness and warlike ferocity, which, in a people whom idleness resigned to their own thoughts, and who, conversing only with each other, suffered no dilution of their zeal from the gradual influx of new opinions, was long transmitted in its full strength from the old to the young, but by trade and intercourse with England, is now visibly abating, and giving way too fast to that laxity of practice and indifference of opinion, in which men, not sufficiently instructed to find the middle point, too easily shelter themselves from rigour and constraint.

The city of St. Andrews, when it had lost its archiepiscopal pre-eminence, gradually decayed: One of its streets is now lost; and in those that remain, there is the silence and solitude of inactive indigence and gloomy depopulation.

The university, within a few years, consisted of three colleges, but is now reduced to two; the college of St. Leonard being lately dissolved by the sale of its buildings and the appropriation of its revenues to the professors of the two others. The chapel of the alienated college is yet standing, a fabrick not inelegant of external structure; but I was always, by some civil excuse, hindred from entering it. A decent attempt, as I was since told, has been made to convert it into a kind of green-house, by planting its area with shrubs. This new method of gardening is unsuccessful; the plants do not hitherto prosper. To what use it will next be put I have no pleasure in conjecturing. It is something that its present state is at least not ostentatiously displayed. Where there is yet shame, there may in time be virtue.

The dissolution of St. Leonard's college was doubtless necessary; but of that necessity there is reason to complain. It is surely not without just reproach, that a nation, of which the commerce is hourly extending, and the wealth encreasing, denies any participation of its prosperity to its literary societies; and while its merchants or its nobles are raising palaces, suffers its universities to moulder into dust.

Of the two colleges yet standing, one is by the institution of its founder appropriated to Divinity. It is said to be capable of containing fifty students; but more than one must occupy a chamber. The library, which is of late erection, is not very spacious, but elegant and luminous.

The doctor, by whom it was shewn, hoped to irritate or subdue my English vanity by telling me, that we had no such repository of books in England.

Saint Andrews seems to be a place eminently adapted to study and education, being situated in a populous, yet a cheap country, and exposing the minds and manners of young men neither to the levity and dissoluteness of a capital city, nor to the gross luxury of a town of commerce, places naturally unpropitious to learning; in one the desire of knowledge easily gives way to the love of pleasure, and in the other, is in danger of yielding to the love of money.

The students however are represented as at this time not exceeding a hundred. Perhaps it may be some obstruction to their increase that there is no episcopal chapel in the place. I saw no reason for imputing their paucity to the present professors; nor can the expence of an academical education be very reasonably objected. A student of the highest class may keep his annual session, or as the English call it, his term, which lasts seven months, for about fifteen pounds, and one of lower rank for less than ten; in which board, lodging, and instruction are all included.

The chief magistrate resident in the university, answering to our vice-chancellor, and to the *rector magnificus* on the continent, had commonly the title of Lord Rector; but being addressed only as *Mr. Rector* in an inauguratory speech by the present chancellor, he has fallen from his former dignity of style. Lordship was very liberally annexed by our ancestors to any station or character of dignity: They said, the *Lord General*, and *Lord Ambassador*; so we still say, *my Lord*, to the judge upon the circuit, and yet retain in our Liturgy *the Lords of the Council*.

In walking among the ruins of religious buildings, we came to two vaults over which had formerly stood the house of the sub-prior. One of the vaults was inhabited by an old woman, who claimed the right of abode there, as the widow of a man whose ancestors had possessed the same gloomy mansion for no less than four generations. The right, however it began, was considered as established by legal prescription, and the old woman lives undisturbed. She thinks however that she has a claim to something more than sufferance; for as her husband's name was Bruce, she is allied to royalty, and told Mr. Boswell that when there were persons of quality in the place, she was distinguished by some notice; that indeed she is now neglected, but she spins a thread, has the company of her cat, and is troublesome to nobody.

Having now seen whatever this ancient city offered to our curiosity, we left it with good wishes, having reason to be highly pleased with the attention that was paid us. But whoever surveys the world must see many things that give him pain. The kindness of the professors did not contribute to abate the uneasy remembrance of an university declining, a college alienated, and a church profaned and hastening to the ground.

St. Andrews indeed has formerly suffered more atrocious ravages and more extensive destruction, but recent evils affect with greater force. We were reconciled to the sight of archiepiscopal ruins. The distance of a calamity from the present time seems to preclude the mind from contact or sympathy. Events long past are barely known; they are not considered. We read with as little emotion the violence of Knox and his followers, as the irruptions of Alaric and the Goths. Had the university been destroyed two centuries ago, we should have not regretted it; but to see it pining in decay and struggling for life, fills the mind with mournful images and ineffectual wishes.

ABERBROTHICK

As we knew sorrow and wishes to be vain, it was now our business to mind our way. The roads of Scotland afford little diversion to the traveller, who seldom sees himself either encountered or overtaken, and who has nothing to contemplate but grounds that have no visible boundaries, or are separated by walls of loose stone. From the bank of the Tweed to St. Andrews I had never seen a single tree, which I did not believe to have grown up far within the present century. Now and then about a gentleman's house stands a small plantation, which in Scotch is called a *policy*, but of these there are few, and those few all very young. The variety of sun and shade is here utterly unknown. There is no tree for either shelter or timber. The oak and the thorn is equally a stranger, and the whole country is extended in uniform nakedness, except that in the road between *Kirkaldy* and *Cowpar*, I passed for a few yards between two hedges. A tree might be a show in Scotland as a horse in Venice. At St. Andrews Mr. Boswell found only one, and recommended it to my notice; I told him that it was rough and low, or looked as if I thought so. This, said he, is nothing to another a few miles off. I was still less delighted to hear that another tree was not to be seen nearer. Nay, said a gentleman that stood by, I know but of this and that tree in the county.

The Lowlands of Scotland had once undoubtedly an equal portion of woods with other countries. Forests are every where gradually diminished, as architecture and cultivation prevail by the increase of people and the introduction of arts. But I believe few regions have been denuded like this, where many centuries must have passed in waste without the least thought of future supply. Davies observes in his account of Ireland, that no Irishman had ever planted an orchard. For that negligence some excuse might be drawn from an unsettled state of life, and the instability of property; but in Scotland possession has long been secure, and inheritance regular, yet it may be doubted whether before the Union any Lowlander between Edinburgh and England had ever set a tree.

Of this improvidence no other account can be given than that it probably began in times of tumult, and continued because it had begun. Established custom is not easily broken, till some great event shakes the whole system of things, and life seems to recommence upon new principles. That before the Union the Scots had little trade and little money, is no valid apology; for plantation is the least expensive of all methods of improvement. To drop a seed into the ground can cost nothing, and the trouble is not great of protecting the young plant, till it is out of danger; though it must be allowed to have some difficulty in places like these, where they have neither wood for palisades, nor thorns for hedges.

Our way was over the Firth of Tay, where, though the water was not wide, we paid four shillings for ferrying the chaise. In Scotland the necessaries of life are easily procured, but superfluities and elegancies are of the same price at least as in England, and therefore may be considered as much dearer.

We stopped a while at Dundee, where I remember nothing remarkable, and mounting our chaise again, came about the close of the day to Aberbrothick.

The monastery of Aberbrothick is of great renown in the history of Scotland. Its ruins afford ample testimony of its ancient magnificence: Its extent might, I suppose, easily be found by following the walls among the grass and weeds, and its height is known by some parts yet standing. The arch of one of the gates is entire, and of another only so far dilapidated as to diversify the appearance. A square apartment of great loftiness is yet standing; its use I could not conjecture, as its elevation was very disproportionate to its area. Two corner towers, particularly attracted our attention. Mr. Boswell, whose inquisitiveness is seconded by great activity, scrambled in at a high window, but found the stairs within broken, and could not reach the top. Of the other tower we were told that the inhabitants sometimes climbed it, but we did not immediately discern the entrance, and as the night was gathering upon us, thought proper to desist. Men skilled in architecture might do what we did not attempt: They might probably form an exact ground-plot of this venerable edifice. They may from some parts yet standing conjecture its general form, and perhaps by comparing it with other buildings of the same kind and the same age, attain an idea very near to truth. I should scarcely have regretted my journey, had it afforded nothing more than the sight of Aberbrothick.

663

MONTROSE

Leaving these fragments of magnificence, we travelled on to Montrose, which we surveyed in the morning, and found it well built, airy, and clean. The town house is a handsome fabrick with a portico. We then went to view the English chapel, and found a small church, clean to a degree unknown in any other part of Scotland, with commodious galleries, and what was yet less expected, with an organ.

At our inn we did not find a reception such as we thought proportionate to the commercial opulence of the place; but Mr. Boswell desired me to observe that the innkeeper was an Englishman, and I then defended him as well as I could.

When I had proceeded thus far, I had opportunities of observing what I had never heard, that there are many beggars in Scotland. In Edinburgh the proportion is, I think, not less than in London, and in the smaller places it is far greater than in English towns of the same extent. It must, however, be allowed, that they are not importunate, nor clamorous. They solicit silently, or very modestly, and therefore though their behaviour may strike with more force the heart of a stranger, they are certainly in danger of missing the attention of their countrymen. Novelty has always some power, an unaccustomed mode of begging excites an unaccustomed degree of pity. But the force of novelty is by its own nature soon at an end; the efficacy of outcry and perseverance is permanent and certain.

The road from Montrose exhibited a continuation of the same appearances. The country is still naked, the hedges are of stone, and the fields so generally plowed, that it is hard to imagine where grass is found for the horses that till them. The harvest, which was almost ripe, appeared very plentiful.

Early in the afternoon Mr. Boswell observed that we were at no great distance from the house of lord Monboddo. The magnetism of his conversation easily drew us out of our way, and the entertainment which we received would have been a sufficient recompence for a much greater deviation.

The roads beyond Edinburgh, as they are less frequented, must be expected to grow gradually rougher; but they were hitherto by no means incommodious. We travelled on with the gentle pace of a Scotch driver, who having no rivals in expedition, neither gives himself nor his horses unnecessary trouble. We did not affect the impatience we did not feel, but were satisfied with the company of each other as well riding in the chaise, as sitting at an inn. The night and the day are equally solitary and equally safe; for where there are so few travellers, why should there be robbers.

ABERDEEN

We came somewhat late to Aberdeen, and found the inn so full, that we had some difficulty in obtaining admission, till Mr. Boswell made himself known: His name overpowered all objection, and we found a very good house and civil treatment.

I received the next day a very kind letter from Sir Alexander Gordon, whom I had formerly known in London, and after a cessation of all intercourse for near twenty years found here professor of physic in the King's College. Such unexpected renewals of acquaintance may be numbered among the most pleasing incidents of life.

The knowledge of one professor soon procured me the notice of the rest, and I did not want any token of regard, being conducted wherever there was any thing which I desired to see, and entertained at once with the novelty of the place, and the kindness of communication.

To write of the cities of our own island with the solemnity of geographical description, as if we had been cast upon a newly discovered coast, has the appearance of a very frivolous ostentation; yet as Scotland is little known to the greater part of those who may read these observations, it is not superfluous to relate, that under the name of Aberdeen are comprised two towns standing about a mile distant from each other, but governed, I think, by the same magistrates.

Old Aberdeen is the ancient episcopal city, in which are still to be seen the remains of the cathedral. It has the appearance of a town in decay, being built in times when commerce was yet unstudied, with very little attention to the commodities of the harbour.

New Aberdeen has all the bustle of prosperous trade, and all the shew of increasing opulence. It is built by the water-side. The houses are large and lofty, and the streets spacious and clean. They build almost wholly with the granite used in the new pavement of the streets of London, which is well known not to want hardness, yet they shape it easily. It is beautiful and must be very lasting.

What particular parts of commerce are chiefly exercised by the merchants of Aberdeen, I have not inquired. The manufacture which forces itself upon a stranger's eye is that of knit-stockings, on which the women of the lower class are visibly employed.

In each of these towns there is a college, or in stricter language, an university; for in both there are professors of the same parts of learning, and the colleges hold their sessions and confer degrees separately, with total independence of one on the other.

In old Aberdeen stands the King's College, of which the first president was *Hector Boece*, or *Boethius*, who may be justly reverenced as one of the revivers of elegant learning. When he studied at Paris, he was acquainted with *Erasmus*, who afterwards gave him a public testimony of his esteem, by inscribing to him a catalogue of his works. The stile of Boethius, though, perhaps, not always rigorously pure, is formed with great diligence upon ancient models, and wholly uninfected with monastic barbarity. His history is written with elegance and vigour, but his fabulousness and credulity are justly blamed. His fabulousness, if he was the author of the fictions, is a fault for which no apology can be made; but his credulity may be excused in an age, when all men were credulous. Learning was then rising on the world; but ages so long accustomed to darkness, were too much dazzled with its light to see any thing distinctly. The first race of scholars, in the fifteenth century, and some time after, were, for the most part, learning to speak, rather than to think, and were therefore more studious of elegance than of truth. The contemporaries of Boethius thought it sufficient to know what the ancients had delivered. The examination of tenets and of facts was reserved for another generation.

Boethius, as president of the university, enjoyed a revenue of forty Scottish marks, about two pounds four shillings and sixpence of sterling money. In the present age of trade and taxes, it is difficult even for the imagination so to raise the value of money, or so to diminish the demands of life, as to suppose four and forty shillings a year, an honourable stipend; yet it was probably equal, not only to the needs, but to the rank of Boethius. The wealth of England was undoubtedly to that of Scotland more than five to one, and it is known that Henry the eighth, among whose faults avarice was never reckoned, granted to Roger Ascham, as a reward of his learning, a pension of ten pounds a year.

The other, called the Marischal College, is in the new town. The

666

hall is large and well lighted. One of its ornaments is the picture of Arthur Johnston, who was principal of the college, and who holds among the Latin poets of Scotland the next place to the elegant Buchanan.

In the library I was shewn some curiosities; a Hebrew manuscript of exquisite penmanship, and a Latin translation of Aristotle's Politicks by *Leonardus Aretinus*, written in the Roman character with nicety and beauty, which, as the art of printing has made them no longer necessary, are not now to be found. This was one of the latest performances of the transcribers, for Aretinus died but about twenty years before typography was invented. This version has been printed, and may be found in libraries, but is little read; for the same books have been since translated both by *Victorius* and *Lambinus*, who lived in an age more cultivated, but perhaps owed in part to *Aretinus* that they were able to excel him. Much is due to those who first broke the way to knowledge, and left only to their successors the task of smoothing it.

In both these colleges the methods of instruction are nearly the same; the lectures differing only by the accidental difference of diligence, or ability in the professors. The students wear scarlet gowns and the professors black, which is, I believe, the academical dress in all the *Scottish* universities, except that of Edinburgh, where the scholars are not distinguished by any particular habit. In the King's College there is kept a public table, but the scholars of the Marischal College are boarded in the town. The expence of living is here, according to the information that I could obtain, somewhat more than at St. Andrews.

The course of education is extended to four years, at the end of which those who take a degree, who are not many, become masters of arts, and whoever is a master may, if he pleases, immediately become a doctor. The title of doctor, however, was for a considerable time bestowed only on physicians. The advocates are examined and approved by their own body; the ministers were not ambitious of titles, or were afraid of being censured for ambition; and the doctorate in every faculty was commonly given or sold into other countries. The ministers are now reconciled to distinction, and as it must always happen that some will excel others, have thought graduation a proper testimony of uncommon abilities or acquisitions.

The indiscriminate collation of degrees has justly taken away that respect which they originally claimed as stamps, by which the literary value of men so distinguished was authoritatively denoted. That academical honours, or any others should be conferred with exact proportion to merit, is more than human judgment or human integrity have given reason to expect. Perhaps degrees in universities cannot be better adjusted by any general rule than by the length of time passed in the public profession of learning. An English or Irish doctorate cannot be obtained by a very young man, and it is reasonable to suppose, what is likewise by experience commonly found true, that he who is by age qualified to be a doctor, has in so much time gained learning sufficient not to disgrace the title, or wit sufficient not to desire it.

The Scotch universities hold but one term or session in the year. That of St. Andrews continues eight months, that of Aberdeen only five, from the first of November to the first of April.

In Aberdeen there is an English chapel, in which the congregation was numerous and splendid. The form of public worship used by the church of England is in Scotland legally practised in licensed chapels served by clergymen of English or Irish ordination, and by tacit connivance quietly permitted in separate congregations supplied with ministers by the successors of the bishops who were deprived at the Revolution.

We came to Aberdeen on Saturday August 21. On Monday we were invited into the town-hall, where I had the freedom of the city given me by the Lord Provost. The honour conferred had all the decorations that politeness could add, and what I am afraid I should not have had to say of any city south of the Tweed, I found no petty officer bowing for a fee.

The parchment containing the record of admission is, with the seal appending, fastened to a riband and worn for one day by the new citizen in his hat.

By a lady who saw us at the chapel, the Earl of Errol was informed of our arrival, and we had the honour of an invitation to his seat, called Slanes Castle, as I am told, improperly, from the castle of that name, which once stood at a place not far distant.

The road beyond Aberdeen grew more stony, and continued equally naked of all vegetable decoration. We travelled over a tract of ground near the sea, which, not long ago, suffered a very uncommon, and unexpected calamity. The sand of the shore was raised by a tempest in such quantities, and carried to such a distance, that an estate was overwhelmed and lost. Such and so hopeless was the barrenness superinduced, that the owner, when he was required to pay the usual tax, desired rather to resign the ground.

SLANES CASTLE. THE BULLER OF BUCHAN

We came in the afternoon to *Slanes Castle*, built upon the margin of the sea, so that the walls of one of the towers seem only a continuation of a perpendicular rock, the foot of which is beaten by the waves. To walk round the house seemed impracticable. From the windows the eye wanders over the sea that separates Scotland from Norway, and when the winds beat with violence must enjoy all the terrifick grandeur of the tempestuous ocean. I would not for my amusement wish for a storm; but as storms, whether wished or not, will sometimes happen, I may say, without violation of humanity, that I should willingly look out upon them from Slanes Castle.

When we were about to take our leave, our departure was prohibited by the countess till we should have seen two places upon the coast, which she rightly considered as worthy of curiosity, *Dun Buy*, and the *Buller of Buchan*, to which Mr. Boyd very kindly conducted us.

Dun Buy, which in Erse is said to signify the *Yellow Rock*, is a double protuberance of stone, open to the main sea on one side, and parted from the land by a very narrow channel on the other. It has its name and its colour from the dung of innumerable sea-fowls, which in the Spring chuse this place as convenient for incubation, and have their eggs and their young taken in great abundance. One of the birds that frequent this rock has, as we were told, its body not larger than a duck's, and yet lays eggs as large as those of a goose. This bird is by the inhabitants named a *Coot*. That which is called *Coot* in England, is here a *Cooter*.

Upon these rocks there was nothing that could long detain attention, and we soon turned our eyes to the *Buller*, or *Bouilloir* of *Buchan*, which no man can see with indifference, who has either sense of danger or delight in rarity. It is a rock perpendicularly tubulated, united on one side with a high shore, and on the other rising steep to a great height, above the main sea. The top is open, from which may be seen a dark gulf of water which flows into the cavity, through a breach made in the lower part of the inclosing rock. It has the appearance of a vast well bordered with a wall. The edge of the Buller is not wide, and to those that walk round, appears very narrow. He that ventures to look downward sees, that if his foot should slip, he must fall from his dreadful elevation upon stones on one side, or into the water on the other. We however went round, and were glad when the circuit was completed.

When we came down to the sea, we saw some boats, and rowers, and resolved to explore the Buller at the bottom. We entered the arch, which the water had made, and found ourselves in a place, which, though we could not think ourselves in danger, we could scarcely survey without some recoil of the mind. The bason in which we floated was nearly circular, perhaps thirty yards in diameter. We were enclosed by a natural wall, rising steep on every side to a height which produced the idea of insurmountable confinement. The interception of all lateral light caused a dismal gloom. Round us was a perpendicular rock, above us the distant sky, and below an unknown profundity of water. If I had any malice against a walking spirit, instead of laying him in the Red-sea, I would condemn him to reside in the Buller of Buchan.

But terrour without danger is only one of the sports of fancy, a voluntary agitation of the mind that is permitted no longer than it pleases. We were soon at leisure to examine the place with minute inspection, and found many cavities which, as the watermen told us, went backward to a depth which they had never explored. Their extent we had not time to try; they are said to serve different purposes. Ladies come hither sometimes in the summer with collations, and smugglers make them storehouses for clandestine merchandise. It is hardly to be doubted but the pirates of ancient times often used them as magazines of arms, or repositories of plunder.

To the little vessels used by the northern rowers, the Buller may have served as a shelter from storms, and perhaps as a retreat from enemies; the entrance might have been stopped, or guarded with little difficulty, and though the vessels that were stationed within would have been battered with stones showered on them from above, yet the crews would have lain safe in the caverns.

Next morning we continued our journey, pleased with our reception at Slanes Castle, of which we had now leisure to recount the grandeur and the elegance; for our way afforded us few topics of conversation. The ground was neither uncultivated nor unfruitful;

but it was still all arable. Of flocks or herds there was no appearance. I had now travelled two hundred miles in Scotland, and seen only one tree not younger than myself.

BAMFF

We dined this day at the house of Mr. Frazer of *Streichton*, who shewed us in his grounds some stones yet standing of a druidical circle, and what I began to think more worthy of notice, some forest trees of full growth.

At night we came to Bamff, where I remember nothing that particularly claimed my attention. The ancient towns of Scotland have generally an appearance unusual to Englishmen. The houses, whether great or small, are for the most part built of stones. Their ends are now and then next the streets, and the entrance into them is very often by a flight of steps, which reaches up to the second story. The floor which is level with the ground being entered only by stairs descending within the house.

The art of joining squares of glass with lead is little used in Scotland, and in some places is totally forgotten. The frames of their windows are all of wood. They are more frugal of their glass than the English, and will often, in houses not otherwise mean, compose a square of two pieces, not joining like cracked glass, but with one edge laid perhaps half an inch over the other. Their windows do not move upon hinges, but are pushed up and drawn down in grooves, yet they are seldom accommodated with weights and pulleys. He that would have his window open must hold it with his hand, unless what may be sometimes found among good contrivers, there be a nail which he may stick into a hole, to keep it from falling.

What cannot be done without some uncommon trouble or particular expedient, will not often be done at all. The incommodiousness of the Scotch windows keeps them very closely shut. The necessity of ventilating human habitations has not yet been found by our northern neighbours; and even in houses well built and elegantly furnished, a stranger may be sometimes forgiven, if he allows himself to wish for fresher air.

These diminutive observations seem to take away something from the dignity of writing, and therefore are never communicated but with hesitation, and a little fear of abasement and contempt. But it must be remembered, that life consists not of a series of illustrious actions, or elegant enjoyments; the greater part of our time passes in compliance with necessities, in the performance of daily duties, in the removal of small inconveniencies, in the procurement of petty pleasures; and we are well or ill at ease, as the main stream of life glides on smoothly, or is ruffled by small obstacles and frequent interruption. The true state of every nation is the state of common life. The manners of a people are not to be found in the schools of learning, or the palaces of greatness, where the national character is obscured or obliterated by travel or instruction, by philosophy or vanity; nor is public happiness to be estimated by the assemblies of the gay, or the banquets of the rich. The great mass of nations is neither rich nor gay: they whose aggregate constitutes the people, are found in the streets, and the villages, in the shops and farms; and from them collectively considered, must the measure of general prosperity be taken. As they approach to delicacy a nation is refined, as their conveniencies are multiplied, a nation, at least a commercial nation, must be denominated wealthy.

ELGIN

Finding nothing to detain us at Bamff, we set out in the morning, and having breakfasted at Cullen, about noon came to *Elgin*, where in the inn, that we supposed the best, a dinner was set before us, which we could not eat. This was the first time, and except one, the last, that I found any reason to complain of a Scotish table; and such disappointments, I suppose, must be expected in every country, where there is no great frequency of travellers.

The ruins of the cathedral of Elgin afforded us another proof of the waste of reformation. There is enough yet remaining to shew, that it was once magnificent. Its whole plot is easily traced. On the north side of the choir, the chapter-house, which is roofed with an arch of stone, remains entire; and on the south side, another mass of building, which we could not enter, is preserved by the care of the family of Gordon; but the body of the church is a mass of fragments.

A paper was here put into our hands, which deduced from sufficient authorities the history of this venerable ruin. The church of Elgin had, in the intestine tumults of the barbarous ages, been laid waste by the irruption of a highland chief, whom the bishop had offended; but it was gradually restored to the state, of which the traces may be now discerned, and was at last not destroyed by the

672

tumultuous violence of Knox, but more shamefully suffered to dilapidate by deliberate robbery and frigid indifference. There is still extant, in the books of the council, an order, of which I cannot remember the date, but which was doubtless issued after the Reformation, directing that the lead, which covers the two cathedrals of Elgin and Aberdeen, shall be taken away, and converted into money for the support of the army. A Scotch army was in those times very cheaply kept; yet the lead of two churches must have born so small a proportion to any military expence, that it is hard not to believe the reason alleged to be merely popular, and the money intended for some private purse. The order however was obeyed; the two churches were stripped, and the lead was shipped to be sold in Holland. I hope every reader will rejoice that this cargo of sacrilege was lost at sea.

Let us not however make too much haste to despise our neighbours. Our own cathedrals are mouldering by unregarded dilapidation. It seems to be part of the despicable philosophy of the time to despise monuments of sacred magnificence, and we are in danger of doing that deliberately, which the Scots did not do but in the unsettled state of an imperfect constitution.

Those who had once uncovered the cathedrals never wished to cover them again; and being thus made useless, they were first neglected, and perhaps, as the stone was wanted, afterwards demolished.

Elgin seems a place of little trade, and thinly inhabited. The episcopal cities of Scotland, I believe, generally fell with their churches, though some of them have since recovered by a situation convenient for commerce. Thus *Glasgow*, though it has no longer an archbishop, has risen beyond its original state by the opulence of its traders; and *Aberdeen*, though its ancient stock had decayed, flourishes by a new shoot in another place.

In the chief street of Elgin, the houses jut over the lowest story, like the old buildings of timber in London, but with greater prominence; so that there is sometimes a walk for a considerable length under a cloister, or portico, which is now indeed frequently broken, because the new houses have another form, but seems to have been uniformly continued in the old city.

FORES. CALDER. FORT GEORGE

We went forwards the same day to Fores, the town to which Macbeth was travelling, when he met the weird sisters in his way. This to an Englishman is classic ground. Our imaginations were heated, and our thoughts recalled to their old amusements.

We had now a prelude to the Highlands. We began to leave fertility and culture behind us, and saw for a great length of road nothing but heath; yet at *Fochabars*, a seat belonging to the duke of Gordon, there is an orchard, which in *Scotland* I had never seen before, with some timber trees, and a plantation of oaks.

At Fores we found good accommodation, but nothing worthy of particular remark, and next morning entered upon the road, on which *Macbeth* heard the fatal prediction; but we travelled on not interrupted by promises of kingdoms, and came to *Nairn*, a royal burgh, which, if once it flourished, is now in a state of miserable decay; but I know not whether its chief annual magistrate has not still the title of Lord Provost.

At Nairn we may fix the verge of the Highlands; for here I first saw peat fires, and first heard the *Erse* language. We had no motive to stay longer than to breakfast, and went forward to the house of Mr. *Macaulay*, the minister who published an account of St. *Kilda*, and by his direction visited Calder Castle, from which *Macbeth* drew his second title. It has been formerly a place of strength. The draw-bridge is still to be seen, but the moat is now dry. The tower is very ancient: Its walls are of great thickness, arched on the top with stone, and surrounded with battlements. The rest of the house is later, though far from modern.

We were favoured by a gentleman, who lives in the castle, with a letter to one of the officers at Fort George, which being the most regular fortification in the island, well deserves the notice of a traveller, who has never travelled before. We went thither next day, found a very kind reception, were led round the works by a gentleman, who explained the use of every part, and entertained by Sir *Eyre Coote*, the governour, with such elegance of conversation as left us no attention to the delicacies of his table.

Of Fort George I shall not attempt to give any account. I cannot delineate it scientifically, and a loose and popular description is of use only when the imagination is to be amused. There was every where an appearance of the utmost neatness and regularity. But my suffrage is of little value, because this and Fort *Augustus* are the only garrisons that I ever saw.

We did not regret the time spent at the fort, though in consequence of our delay we came somewhat late to *Inverness*, the town which may properly be called the capital of the Highlands. Hither the inhabitants of the inland parts come to be supplied with what they cannot make for themselves: Hither the young nymphs of the mountains and valleys are sent for education, and as far as my observation has reached, are not sent in vain.

INVERNESS

Inverness was the last place which had a regular communication by high roads with the southern counties. All the ways beyond it have, I believe, been made by the soldiers in this century. At *Inverness* therefore *Cromwell*, when he subdued *Scotland*, stationed a garrison, as at the boundary of the Highlands. The soldiers seem to have incorporated afterwards with the inhabitants, and to have peopled the place with an English race; for the language of this town has been long considered as peculiarly elegant.

Here is a castle, called the castle of Macbeth, the walls of which are yet standing. It was no very capacious edifice, but stands upon a rock so high and steep, that I think it was once not accessible, but by the help of ladders, or a bridge. Over against it, on another hill, was a fort built by *Cromwell*, now totally demolished; for no faction of Scotland loved the name of *Cromwell*, or had any desire to continue his memory.

Yet what the Romans did to other nations, was in a great degree done by Cromwell to the Scots; he civilized them by conquest, and introduced by useful violence the arts of peace. I was told at *Aberdeen* that the people learned from Cromwell's soldiers to make shoes and to plant kail.

How they lived without kail, it is not easy to guess: They cultivate hardly any other plant for common tables, and when they had not kail they probably had nothing. The numbers that go barefoot are still sufficient to shew that shoes may be spared: They are not yet considered as necessaries of life; for tall boys, not otherwise meanly dressed, run without them in the streets and in the islands; the sons of gentlemen pass several of their first years with naked feet.

I know not whether it be not peculiar to the Scots to have

attained the liberal, without the manual arts, to have excelled in ornamental knowledge, and to have wanted not only the elegancies, but the conveniencies of common life. Literature soon after its revival found its way to *Scotland*, and from the middle of the sixteenth century, almost to the middle of the seventeenth, the politer studies were very diligently pursued. The Latin poetry of *Deliciæ Poëtarum Scotorum* would have done honour to any nation, at least till the publication of *May's Supplement* the English had very little to oppose.

Yet men thus ingenious and inquisitive were content to live in total ignorance of the trades by which human wants are supplied, and to supply them by the grossest means. Till the Union made them acquainted with English manners, the culture of their lands was unskilful, and their domestick life unformed; their tables were coarse as the feasts of Eskimeaux, and their houses filthy as the cottages of Hottentots.

Since they have known that their condition was capable of improvement, their progress in useful knowledge has been rapid and uniform. What remains to be done they will quickly do, and then wonder, like me, why that which was so necessary and so easy was so long delayed. But they must be for ever content to owe to the English that elegance and culture, which, if they had been vigilant and active, perhaps the English might have owed to them.

Here the appearance of life began to alter. I had seen a few women with plaids at *Aberdeen*; but at *Inverness* the Highland manners are common. There is I think a kirk, in which only the Erse language is used. There is likewise an English chapel, but meanly built, where on Sunday we saw a very decent congregation.

We were now to bid farewel to the luxury of travelling, and to enter a country upon which perhaps no wheel has ever rolled. We could indeed have used our post-chaise one day longer, along the military road to Fort *Augustus*, but we could have hired no horses beyond Inverness, and we were not so sparing of ourselves, as to lead them, merely that we might have one day longer the indulgence of a carriage.

At Inverness therefore we procured three horses for ourselves and a servant, and one more for our baggage, which was no very heavy load. We found in the course of our journey the convenience of having disencumbered ourselves, by laying aside whatever we could spare; for it is not to be imagined without experience, how in

climbing crags, and treading bogs, and winding through narrow
and obstructed passages, a little bulk will hinder, and a little
weight will burthen; or how often a man that has pleased himself at
home with his own resolution, will, in the hour of darkness and
fatigue, be content to leave behind him every thing but himself.

LOUGH NESS

We took two Highlanders to run beside us, partly to shew us the
way, and partly to take back from the sea-side the horses, of which
they were the owners. One of them was a man of great liveliness
and activity, of whom his companion said, that he would tire any
horse in Inverness. Both of them were civil and ready-handed.
Civility seems part of the national character of Highlanders. Every
chieftain is a monarch, and politeness, the natural product of royal
government, is diffused from the laird through the whole clan.
But they are not commonly dexterous: their narrowness of life
confines them to a few operations, and they are accustomed to
endure little wants more than to remove them.

We mounted our steeds on the thirteenth of August, and
directed our guides to conduct us to Fort Augustus. It is built at
the head of Lough Ness, of which *Inverness* stands at the outlet.
The way between them has been cut by the soldiers, and the greater
part of it runs along a rock, levelled with great labour and exactness, near the water-side.

Most of this day's journey was very pleasant. The day, though
bright, was not hot; and the appearance of the country, if I had not
seen the Peak, would have been wholly new. We went upon a surface so hard and level, that we had little care to hold the bridle, and
were therefore at full leisure for contemplation. On the left were
high and steep rocks shaded with birch, the hardy native of the
North, and covered with fern or heath. On the right the limpid
waters of *Lough Ness* were beating their bank, and waving their
surface by a gentle agitation. Beyond them were rocks sometimes
covered with verdure, and sometimes towering in horrid nakedness.
Now and then we espied a little corn-field, which served to impress
more strongly the general barrenness.

Lough Ness is about twenty-four miles long, and from one mile
to two miles broad. It is remarkable that *Boethius*, in his description of Scotland, gives it twelve miles of breadth. When historians
or geographers exhibit false accounts of places far distant, they

may be forgiven, because they can tell but what they are told; and that their accounts exceed the truth may be justly supposed, because most men exaggerate to others, if not to themselves: but *Boethius* lived at no great distance; if he never saw the lake, he must have been very incurious, and if he had seen it, his veracity yielded to very slight temptations.

Lough Ness, though not twelve miles broad, is a very remarkable diffusion of water without islands. It fills a large hollow between two ridges of high rocks, being supplied partly by the torrents which fall into it on either side, and partly, as is supposed, by springs at the bottom. Its water is remarkably clear and pleasant, and is imagined by the natives to be medicinal. We were told, that it is in some places a hundred and forty fathom deep, a profundity scarcely credible, and which probably those that relate it have never sounded. Its fish are salmon, trout, and pike.

It was said at fort *Augustus*, that *Lough Ness* is open in the hardest winters, though a lake not far from it is covered with ice. In discussing these exceptions from the course of nature, the first question is, whether the fact be justly stated. That which is strange is delightful, and a pleasing error is not willingly detected. Accuracy of narration is not very common, and there are so few rigidly philosophical, as not to represent as perpetual, what is only frequent, or as constant, what is really casual. If it be true that *Lough Ness* never freezes, it is either sheltered by its high banks from the cold blasts, and exposed only to those winds which have more power to agitate than congeal; or it is kept in perpetual motion by the rush of streams from the rocks that inclose it. Its profundity though it should be such as is represented can have little part in this exemption; for though deep wells are not frozen, because their water is secluded from the external air, yet where a wide surface is exposed to the full influence of a freezing atmosphere, I know not why the depth should keep it open. Natural philosophy is now one of the favourite studies of the Scottish nation, and *Lough Ness* well deserves to be diligently examined.

The road on which we travelled, and which was itself a source of entertainment, is made along the rock, in the direction of the lough, sometimes by breaking off protuberances, and sometimes by cutting the great mass of stone to a considerable depth. The fragments are piled in a loose wall on either side, with apertures left at very short spaces, to give a passage to the wintry currents. Part of it is bordered with low trees, from which our guides gathered nuts, and would have had the appearance of an English lane, except that an English lane is almost always dirty. It has been made with great labour, but has this advantage, that it cannot, without equal labour, be broken up.

Within our sight there were goats feeding or playing. The mountains have red deer, but they came not within view; and if what is said of their vigilance and subtlety be true, they have some claim to that palm of wisdom, which the eastern philosopher, whom Alexander interrogated, gave to those beasts which live furthest from men.

Near the way, by the water side, we espied a cottage. This was the first Highland Hut that I had seen; and as our business was with life and manners, we were willing to visit it. To enter a habitation without leave, seems to be not considered here as rudeness or intrusion. The old laws of hospitality still give this licence to a stranger.

A hut is constructed with loose stones, ranged for the most part with some tendency to circularity. It must be placed where the wind cannot act upon it with violence, because it has no cement; and where the water will run easily away, because it has no floor but the naked ground. The wall, which is commonly about six feet high, declines from the perpendicular a little inward. Such rafters as can be procured are then raised for a roof, and covered with heath, which makes a strong and warm thatch, kept from flying off by ropes of twisted heath, of which the ends, reaching from the center of the thatch to the top of the wall, are held firm by the weight of a large stone. No light is admitted but at the entrance, and through a hole in the thatch, which gives vent to the smoke. This hole is not directly over the fire, lest the rain should extinguish it; and the smoke therefore naturally fills the place before it escapes. Such is the general structure of the houses in which one of the nations of this opulent and powerful island has been hitherto content to live. Huts however are not more uniform than palaces; and this which we were inspecting was very far from one of the meanest, for it was divided into several apartments; and its inhabitants possessed such property as a pastoral poet might exalt into riches.

When we entered, we found an old woman boiling goats-flesh in a kettle. She spoke little English, but we had interpreters at hand;

679

and she was willing enough to display her whole system of economy. She has five children, of which none are yet gone from her. The eldest, a boy of thirteen, and her husband, who is eighty years old, were at work in the wood. Her two next sons were gone to *Inverness* to buy *meal*, by which oatmeal is always meant. Meal she considered as expensive food, and told us, that in Spring, when the goats gave milk, the children could live without it. She is mistress of sixty goats, and I saw many kids in an enclosure at the end of her house. She had also some poultry. By the lake we saw a potatoe-garden, and a small spot of ground on which stood four shucks, containing each twelve sheaves of barley. She has all this from the labour of their own hands, and for what is necessary to be bought, her kids and her chickens are sent to market.

With the true pastoral hospitality, she asked us to sit down and drink whisky. She is religious, and though the kirk is four miles off, probably eight English miles, she goes thither every Sunday. We gave her a shilling, and she begged snuff; for snuff is the luxury of a Highland cottage.

Soon afterwards we came to the *General's Hut,* so called because it was the temporary abode of Wade, while he superintended the works upon the road. It is now a house of entertainment for passengers, and we found it not ill stocked with provisions.

FALL OF FIERS

Towards evening we crossed, by a bridge, the river which makes the celebrated fall of Fiers. The country at the bridge strikes the imagination with all the gloom and grandeur of Siberian solitude. The way makes a flexure, and the mountains, covered with trees, rise at once on the left hand and in the front. We desired our guides to show us the fall, and dismounting, clambered over very rugged crags, till I began to wish that our curiosity might have been gratified with less trouble and danger. We came at last to a place where we could overlook the river, and saw a channel torn, as it seems, through black piles of stone, by which the stream is obstructed and broken, till it comes to a very steep descent, of such dreadful depth, that we were naturally inclined to turn aside our eyes.

But we visited the place at an unseasonable time, and found it divested of its dignity and terror. Nature never gives every thing at once. A long continuance of dry weather, which made the rest of the way easy and delightful, deprived us of the pleasure expected from the fall of Fiers. The river having now no water but what the springs supply, showed us only a swift current, clear and shallow, fretting over the asperities of the rocky bottom, and we were left to exercise our thoughts, by endeavouring to conceive the effect of a thousand streams poured from the mountains into one channel, struggling for expansion in a narrow passage, exasperated by rocks rising in their way, and at last discharging all their violence of waters by a sudden fall through the horrid chasm.

The way now grew less easy, descending by an uneven declivity, but without either dirt or danger. We did not arrive at Fort Augustus till it was late. Mr. *Boswell*, who, between his father's merit and his own, is sure of reception wherever he comes, sent a servant before to beg admission and entertainment for that night. Mr. Trapaud, the governor, treated us with that courtesy which is so closely connected with the military character. He came out to meet us beyond the gates, and apologized that, at so late an hour, the rules of a garrison suffered him to give us entrance only at the postern.

FORT AUGUSTUS

In the morning we viewed the fort, which is much less than that of St. *George*, and is said to be commanded by the neighbouring hills. It was not long ago taken by the Highlanders. But its situation seems well chosen for pleasure, if not for strength; it stands at the head of the lake, and, by a sloop of sixty tuns, is supplied from Inverness with great convenience.

We were now to cross the Highlands towards the western coast, and to content ourselves with such accommodations, as a way so little frequented could afford. The journey was not formidable, for it was but of two days, very unequally divided, because the only house, where we could be entertained, was not farther off than a third of the way. We soon came to a high hill, which we mounted by a military road, cut in traverses, so that as we went upon a higher stage, we saw the baggage following us below in a contrary direction. To make this way, the rock has been hewn to a level with labour that might have broken the perseverance of a Roman legion.

The country is totally denuded of its wood, but the stumps both of oaks and firs, which are still found, shew that it has been once a forest of large timber. I do not remember that we saw any animals, but we were told that, in the mountains, there are stags, roebucks, goats and rabbits.

We did not perceive that this tract was possessed by human beings, except that once we saw a corn field, in which a lady was walking with some gentlemen. Their house was certainly at no great distance, but so situated that we could not descry it.

Passing on through the dreariness of solitude, we found a party of soldiers from the fort, working on the road, under the superintendence of a serjeant. We told them how kindly we had been treated at the garrison, and as we were enjoying the benefit of their labours, begged leave to show our gratitude by a small present.

ANOCH

Early in the afternoon we came to Anoch, a village in *Glenmollison* of three huts, one of which is distinguished by a chimney. Here we were to dine and lodge, and were conducted through the first room, that had the chimney, into another lighted by a small glass window. The landlord attended us with great civility, and told us what he could give us to eat and drink. I found some books on a shelf, among which were a volume or more of Prideaux's Connection.

This I mentioned as something unexpected, and perceived that I did not please him. I praised the propriety of his language, and was answered that I need not wonder, for he had learned it by grammar.

By subsequent opportunities of observation, I found that my host's diction had nothing peculiar. Those Highlanders that can speak English, commonly speak it well, with few of the words, and little of the tone by which a Scotchman is distinguished. Their language seems to have been learned in the army or the navy, or by some communication with those who could give them good examples of accent and pronunciation. By their Lowland neighbours they would not willingly be taught; for they have long considered them as a mean and degenerate race. These prejudices are wearing fast away; but so much of them still remains, that when I asked a very learned minister in the islands, which they considered as their most savage clans: *"Those*, said he, *that live next the Lowlands."*

As we came hither early in the day, we had time sufficient to survey the place. The house was built like other huts of loose stones, but the part in which we dined and slept was lined with turf and wattled with twigs, which kept the earth from falling. Near it was a garden of turnips and a field of potatoes. It stands in a glen, or valley, pleasantly watered by a winding river. But this country, however it may delight the gazer or amuse the naturalist, is of no great advantage to its owners. Our landlord told us of a gentleman, who possesses lands, eighteen Scotch miles in length, and three in breadth; a space containing at least a hundred square English miles. He has raised his rents, to the danger of depopulating his farms, and he fells his timber, and by exerting every art of augmentation, has obtained an yearly revenue of four hundred pounds, which for a hundred square miles is three halfpence an acre.

Some time after dinner we were surprised by the entrance of a young woman, not inelegant either in mien or dress, who asked us whether we would have tea. We found that she was the daughter of our host, and desired her to make it. Her conversation, like her appearance, was gentle and pleasing. We knew that the girls of the Highlands are all gentlewomen, and treated her with great respect, which she received as customary and due, and was neither elated by it, nor confused, but repaid my civilities without embarrassment, and told me how much I honoured her country by coming to survey it.

She had been at *Inverness* to gain the common female qualifications, and had, like her father, the English pronunciation. I presented her with a book, which I happened to have about me, and should not be pleased to think that she forgets me.

In the evening the soldiers, whom we had passed on the road, came to spend at our inn the little money that we had given them. They had the true military impatience of coin in their pockets, and had marched at least six miles to find the first place where liquor could be bought. Having never been before in a place so wild and unfrequented, I was glad of their arrival, because I knew that we had made them friends, and to gain still more of their good will, we went to them, where they were carousing in the barn, and added something to our former gift. All that we gave was not much, but it detained them in the barn, either merry or quarrelling, the whole night, and in the morning they went back to their work, with great indignation at the bad qualities of whisky.

We had gained so much the favour of our host, that, when we left his house in the morning, he walked by us a great way, and entertained us with conversation both on his own condition, and that of the country. His life seemed to be merely pastoral, except that he differed from some of the ancient Nomades in having a settled dwelling. His wealth consists of one hundred sheep, as many goats, twelve milk-cows, and twenty-eight beeves ready for the drover.

From him we first heard of the general dissatisfaction, which is now driving the Highlanders into the other hemisphere; and when I asked him whether they would stay at home, if they were well treated, he answered with indignation, that no man willingly left his native country. Of the farm, which he himself occupied, the rent had, in twenty-five years, been advanced from five to twenty pounds, which he found himself so little able to pay, that he would be glad to try his fortune in some other place. Yet he owned the reasonableness of raising the Highland rents in a certain degree, and declared himself willing to pay ten pounds for the ground which he had formerly had for five.

Our host having amused us for a time, resigned us to our guides. The journey of this day was long, not that the distance was great, but that the way was difficult. We were now in the bosom of the Highlands, with full leisure to contemplate the appearance and properties of mountainous regions, such as have been, in many countries, the last shelters of national distress, and are every where the scenes of adventures, stratagems, surprises and escapes.

Mountainous countries are not passed but with difficulty, not merely from the labour of climbing; for to climb is not always necessary: but because that which is not mountain is commonly bog, through which the way must be picked with caution. Where there are hills, there is much rain, and the torrents pouring down into the intermediate spaces, seldom find so ready an outlet, as not to stagnate, till they have broken the texture of the ground.

Of the hills, which our journey offered to the view on either side, we did not take the height, nor did we see any that astonished us with their loftiness. Towards the summit of one, there was a white spot, which I should have called a naked rock, but the guides, who had better eyes, and were acquainted with the phænomena of the country, declared it to be snow. It had already lasted to the end of August, and was likely to maintain its contest with the sun, till it should be reinforced by winter.

The height of mountains philosophically considered is properly computed from the surface of the next sea; but as it affects the eye or imagination of the passenger, as it makes either a spectacle or an obstruction, it must be reckoned from the place where the rise begins to make a considerable angle with the plain. In extensive continents the land may, by gradual elevation, attain great height, without any other appearance than that of a plane gently inclined, and if a hill placed upon such raised ground be described, as having its altitude equal to the whole space above the sea, the representation will be fallacious.

These mountains may be properly enough measured from the inland base; for it is not much above the sea. As we advanced at evening towards the western coast, I did not observe the declivity to be greater than is necessary for the discharge of the inland waters.

We passed many rivers and rivulets, which commonly ran with a clear shallow stream over a hard pebbly bottom. These channels, which seem so much wider than the water that they convey would naturally require, are formed by the violence of wintry floods, produced by the accumulation of innumerable streams that fall in rainy weather from the hills, and bursting away with resistless impetuosity, make themselves a passage proportionate to their mass.

Such capricious and temporary waters cannot be expected to produce many fish. The rapidity of the wintry deluge sweeps them away, and the scantiness of the summer stream would hardly sustain them above the ground. This is the reason why in fording the northern rivers, no fishes are seen, as in England, wandering in the water.

Of the hills many may be called with Homer's Ida *abundant in springs*, but few can deserve the epithet which he bestows upon Pelion by *waving their leaves*. They exhibit very little variety; being almost wholly covered with dark heath, and even that seems to be checked in its growth. What is not heath is nakedness, a little deversified by now and then a stream rushing down the steep. An eye accustomed to flowery pastures and waving harvests is astonished and repelled by this wide extent of hopeless sterility. The appearance is that of matter incapable of form or usefulness, dismissed by nature from her care, and disinherited of her favours, left in its original elemental state, or quickened only with one sullen power of useless vegetation.

It will very readily occur, that this uniformity of barrenness can afford very little amusement to the traveller; that it is easy to sit at home and conceive rocks and heath, and waterfalls; and that these journeys are useless labours, which neither impregnate the imagination, nor enlarge the understanding. It is true that of far the greater part of things, we must content ourselves with such knowledge as description may exhibit, or analogy supply; but it is true likewise, that these ideas are always incomplete, and that at least, till we have compared them with realities, we do not know them to be just. As we see more, we become possessed of more certainties, and consequently gain more principles of reasoning, and found a wider basis of analogy.

Regions mountainous and wild, thinly inhabited, and little cultivated, make a great part of the earth, and he that has never seen them, must live unacquainted with much of the face of nature, and with one of the great scenes of human existence.

As the day advanced towards noon, we entered a narrow valley not very flowery, but sufficiently verdant. Our guides told us, that the horses could not travel all day without rest or meat, and intreated us to stop here, because no grass would be found in any other place. The request was reasonable and the argument cogent. We therefore willingly dismounted and diverted ourselves as the place gave us opportunity.

I sat down on a bank, such as a writer of Romance might have delighted to feign. I had indeed no trees to whisper over my head, but a clear rivulet streamed at my feet. The day was calm, the air soft, and all was rudeness, silence, and solitude. Before me, and on either side, were high hills, which by hindering the eye from ranging, forced the mind to find entertainment for itself. Whether I spent the hour well I know not; for here I first conceived the thought of this narration.

We were in this place at ease and by choice, and had no evils to suffer or to fear; yet the imaginations excited by the view of an unknown and untravelled wilderness are not such as arise in the artificial solitude of parks and gardens, a flattering notion of self-sufficiency, a placid indulgence of voluntary delusions, a secure expansion of the fancy, or a cool concentration of the mental powers. The phantoms which haunt a desert are want, and misery, and danger; the evils of dereliction rush upon the thoughts; man is made unwillingly acquainted with his own weakness, and meditation shews him only how little he can sustain, and how little he can perform. There were no traces of inhabitants, except perhaps a rude pile of clods called a summer hut, in which a herdsman had rested in the favourable seasons. Whoever had been in the place where I then sat, unprovided with provisions and ignorant of the country, might, at least before the roads were made, have wandered among the rocks, till he had perished with hardship, before he could have found either food or shelter. Yet what are these hillocks to the ridges of Taurus, or these spots of wildness to the desarts of America?

It was not long before we were invited to mount, and continued our journey along the side of a lough, kept full by many streams, which with more or less rapidity and noise, crossed the road from the hills on the other hand. These currents, in their diminished state, after several dry months, afford, to one who has always lived in level countries, an unusual and delightful spectacle; but in the rainy season, such as every winter may be expected to bring, must precipitate an impetuous and tremendous flood. I suppose the way by which we went, is at that time impassable.

GLENSHEALS

The lough at last ended in a river broad and shallow like the rest, but that it may be passed when it is deeper, there is a bridge over it. Beyond it is a valley called *Glensheals*, inhabited by the clan of Macrae. Here we found a village called *Auknasheals*, consisting of many huts, perhaps twenty, built all of *dry-stone*, that is, stones piled up without mortar.

We had, by the direction of the officers at Fort *Augustus*, taken bread for ourselves, and tobacco for those Highlanders who might show us any kindness. We were now at a place where we could obtain milk, but must have wanted bread if we had not brought it. The people of this valley did not appear to know any English, and our guides now became doubly necessary as interpreters. A woman, whose hut was distinguished by greater spaciousness and better architecture, brought out some pails of milk. The villagers gathered about us in considerable numbers, I believe without any evil intention, but with a very savage wildness of aspect and manner. When our meal was over, Mr. *Boswell* sliced the bread, and divided it amongst them, as he supposed them never to have tasted a wheaten loaf before. He then gave them little pieces of twisted tobacco, and among the children we distributed a small handful of halfpence, which they received with great eagerness. Yet I have been since told, that the people of that valley are not indigent; and

687

when we mentioned them afterwards as needy and pitiable, a Highland lady let us know, that we might spare our commiseration; for the dame whose milk we drank had probably more than a dozen milk-cows. She seemed unwilling to take any price, but being pressed to make a demand, at last named a shilling. Honesty is not greater where elegance is less. One of the by-standers, as we were told afterwards, advised her to ask more, but she said a shilling was enough. We gave her half a crown, and I hope got some credit by our behaviour; for the company said, if our interpreters did not flatter us, that they had not seen such a day since the old laird of Macleod passed through their country.

The Macraes, as we heard afterwards in the Hebrides, were originally an indigent and subordinate clan, and having no farms nor stock, were in great numbers servants to the Maclellans, who, in the war of Charles the First, took arms at the call of the heroic *Montrose*, and were, in one of his battles, almost all destroyed. The women that were left at home, being thus deprived of their husbands, like the Scythian ladies of old, married their servants, and the Macraes became a considerable race.

THE HIGHLANDS

As we continued our journey, we were at leisure to extend our speculations, and to investigate the reason of those peculiarities by which such rugged regions as these before us are generally distinguished.

Mountainous countries commonly contain the original, at least the oldest race of inhabitants, for they are not easily conquered, because they must be entered by narrow ways, exposed to every power of mischief from those that occupy the heights; and every new ridge is a new fortress, where the defendants have again the same advantages. If the assailants either force the strait, or storm the summit, they gain only so much ground; their enemies are fled to take possession of the next rock, and the pursuers stand at gaze, knowing neither where the ways of escape wind among the steeps, nor where the bog has firmness to sustain them: besides that, mountaineers have an agility in climbing and descending distinct from strength or courage, and attainable only by use.

If the war be not soon concluded, the invaders are dislodged by hunger; for in those anxious and toilsome marches, provisions cannot easily be carried, and are never to be found. The wealth of mountains is cattle, which, while the men stand in the passes, the women drive away. Such lands at last cannot repay the expence of conquest, and therefore perhaps have not been so often invaded by the mere ambition of dominion; as by resentment of robberies and insults, or the desire of enjoying in security the more fruitful provinces.

As mountaineers are long before they are conquered, they are likewise long before they are civilized. Men are softened by intercourse mutually profitable, and instructed by comparing their own notions with those of others. Thus Cæsar found the maritime parts of Britain made less barbarous by their commerce with the Gauls. Into a barren and rough tract no stranger is brought either by the hope of gain or of pleasure. The inhabitants having neither commodities for sale, nor money for purchase, seldom visit more polished places, or if they do visit them, seldom return.

It sometimes happens that by conquest, intermixture, or gradual refinement, the cultivated parts of a country change their language. The mountaineers then become a distinct nation, cut off by dissimilitude of speech from conversation with their neighbours. Thus in Biscay, the original Cantabrian, and in Dalecarlia, the old Swedish still subsists. Thus Wales and the Highlands speak the tongue of the first inhabitants of Britain, while the other parts have received first the Saxon, and in some degree afterwards the French, and then formed a third language between them.

That the primitive manners are continued where the primitive language is spoken, no nation will desire me to suppose, for the manners of mountaineers are commonly savage, but they are rather produced by their situation than derived from their ancestors.

Such seems to be the disposition of man, that whatever makes a distinction produces rivalry. England, before other causes of enmity were found, was disturbed for some centuries by the contests of the northern and southern counties; so that at Oxford, the peace of study could for a long time be preserved only by chusing annually one of the Proctors from each side of the Trent. A tract intersected by many ridges of mountains, naturally divides its inhabitants into petty nations, which are made by a thousand causes enemies to each other. Each will exalt its own chiefs, each will boast the valour of its men, or the beauty of its women, and every claim of superiority irritates competition; injuries will sometimes be done, and be more injuriously defended; retaliation will sometimes be attempted, and the debt exacted with too much interest.

In the Highlands it was a law, that if a robber was sheltered from justice, any man of the same clan might be taken in his place. This was a kind of irregular justice, which, though necessary in savage times, could hardly fail to end in a feud, and a feud once kindled among an idle people, with no variety of pursuits to divert their thoughts, burnt on for ages either sullenly glowing in secret mischief, or openly blazing into publick violence. Of the effects of this violent judicature, there are not wanting memorials. The cave is now to be seen to which one of the Campbells, who had injured the Macdonalds, retired with a body of his own clan. The Macdonalds required the offender, and being refused, made a fire at the mouth of the cave, by which he and his adherents were suffocated together.

Mountaineers are warlike, because by their feuds and competitions they consider themselves as surrounded with enemies, and are always prepared to repel incursions, or to make them. Like the Greeks in their unpolished state, described by Thucydides, the Highlanders, till lately, went always armed, and carried their weapons to visits, and to church.

Mountaineers are thievish, because they are poor, and having neither manufactures nor commerce, can grow richer only by robbery. They regularly plunder their neighbours, for their neighbours are commonly their enemies; and having lost that reverence for property, by which the order of civil life is preserved, soon consider all as enemies, whom they do not reckon as friends, and think themselves licensed to invade whatever they are not obliged to protect.

By a strict administration of the laws, since the laws have been introduced into the Highlands, this disposition to thievery is very much represt. Thirty years ago no herd had ever been conducted through the mountains, without paying tribute in the night, to some of the clans; but cattle are now driven, and passengers travel without danger, fear, or molestation.

Among a warlike people, the quality of highest esteem is personal courage, and with the ostentatious display of courage are closely connected promptitude of offence and quickness of resentment. The Highlanders, before they were disarmed, were so addicted to quarrels, that the boys used to follow any publick procession or ceremony, however festive, or however solemn, in expectation of the battle, which was sure to happen before the company dispersed.

Mountainous regions are sometimes so remote from the seat of government, and so difficult of access, that they are very little under the influence of the sovereign, or within the reach of national justice. Law is nothing without power; and the sentence of a distant court could not be easily executed, nor perhaps very safely promulgated, among men ignorantly proud and habitually violent, unconnected with the general system, and accustomed to reverence only their own lords. It has therefore been necessary to erect many particular jurisdictions, and commit the punishment of crimes, and the decision of right to the proprietors of the country who could enforce their own decrees. It immediately appears that such judges will be often ignorant, and often partial; but in the immaturity of political establishments no better expedient could be found. As government advances towards perfection, provincial judicature is perhaps in every empire gradually abolished.

Those who had thus the dispensation of law, were by consequence themselves lawless. Their vassals had no shelter from outrages and oppressions; but were condemned to endure, without resistance, the caprices of wantonness, and the rage of cruelty.

In the Highlands, some great lords had an hereditary jurisdiction over counties; and some chieftains over their own lands; till the final conquest of the Highlands afforded an opportunity of crushing all the local courts, and of extending the general benefits of equal law to the low and the high, in the deepest recesses and obscurest corners.

While the chiefs had this resemblance of royalty, they had little inclination to appeal, on any question, to superior judicatures. A claim of lands between two powerful lairds was decided like a contest for dominion between sovereign powers. They drew their forces into the field, and right attended on the strongest. This was, in ruder times, the common practice, which the kings of Scotland could seldom control.

Even so lately as in the last years of King William, a battle was fought at *Mull Roy*, on a plain a few miles to the south of *Inverness*, between the clans of *Mackintosh* and *Macdonald* of *Keppoch*. *Col. Macdonald*, the head of a small clan, refused to pay the dues demanded from him by *Mackintosh*, as his superior lord. They dis-

691

dained the interposition of judges and laws, and calling each his followers to maintain the dignity of the clan, fought a formal battle, in which several considerable men fell on the side of *Mackintosh*, without a complete victory to either. This is said to have been the last open war made between the clans by their own authority.

The Highland lords made treaties, and formed alliances, of which some traces may still be found, and some consequences still remain as lasting evidences of petty regality. The terms of one of these confederacies were, that each should support the other in the right, or in the wrong, except against the king.

The inhabitants of mountains form distinct races, and are careful to preserve their genealogies. Men in a small district necessarily mingle blood by intermarriages, and combine at last into one family, with a common interest in the honour and disgrace of every individual. Then begins that union of affections, and co-operation of endeavours, that constitute a clan. They who consider themselves as ennobled by their family, will think highly of their progenitors, and they who through successive generations live always together in the same place, will preserve local stories and hereditary prejudices. Thus every Highlander can talk of his ancestors, and recount the outrages which they suffered from the wicked inhabitants of the next valley.

Such are the effects of habitation among mountains, and such were the qualities of the Highlanders, while their rocks secluded them from the rest of mankind, and kept them an unaltered and discriminated race. They are now losing their distinction, and hastening to mingle with the general community.

GLENELG

We left *Auknasheals* and the *Macraes* in the afternoon, and in the evening came to *Ratiken*, a high hill on which a road is cut, but so steep and narrow, that it is very difficult. There is now a design of making another way round the bottom. Upon one of the precipices, my horse, weary with the steepness of the rise, staggered a little, and I called in haste to the Highlander to hold him. This was the only moment of my journey, in which I thought myself endangered.

Having surmounted the hill at last, we were told that at *Glenelg*, on the sea-side, we should come to a house of lime and slate and glass. This image of magnificence raised our expectation. At last we came to our inn weary and peevish, and began to inquire for meat and beds.

Of the provisions the negative catalogue was very copious. Here was no meat, no milk, no bread, no eggs, no wine. We did not express much satisfaction. Here however we were to stay. Whisky we might have, and I believe at last they caught a fowl and killed it. We had some bread, and with that we prepared ourselves to be contented, when we had a very eminent proof of Highland hospitality. Along some miles of the way, in the evening, a gentleman's servant had kept us company on foot with very little notice on our part. He left us near *Glenelg*, and we thought on him no more till he came to us again, in about two hours, with a present from his master of rum and sugar. The man had mentioned his company, and the gentleman, whose name, I think, is *Gordon*, well knowing the penury of the place, had this attention to two men, whose names perhaps he had not heard, by whom his kindness was not likely to be ever repaid, and who could be recommended to him only by their necessities.

We were now to examine our lodging. Out of one of the beds, on which we were to repose, started up, at our entrance, a man black as a Cyclops from the forge. Other circumstances of no elegant recital concurred to disgust us. We had been frighted by a lady at Edinburgh, with discouraging representations of Highland lodgings. Sleep, however, was necessary. Our Highlanders had at last found some hay, with which the inn could not supply them. I directed them to bring a bundle into the room, and slept upon it in my riding coat. Mr. Boswell being more delicate, laid himself sheets with hay over and under him, and lay in linen like a gentleman.

SKY. ARMIDEL

In the morning, September the twentieth, we found ourselves on the edge of the sea. Having procured a boat, we dismissed our Highlanders, whom I would recommend to the service of any future travellers, and were ferried over to the isle of Sky. We landed at *Armidel*, where we were met on the sands by Sir Alexander Macdonald, who was at that time there with his lady, preparing to leave the island and reside at Edinburgh.

Armidel is a neat house, built where the *Macdonalds* had once a seat, which was burnt in the commotions that followed the Revolution. The walled orchard, which belonged to the former house, still remains. It is well shaded by tall ash trees, of a species, as Mr. Janes the fossilist informed me, uncommonly valuable. This plantation is very properly mentioned by Dr. *Campbell*, in his new account of the state of *Britain*, and deserves attention; because it proves that the present nakedness of the *Hebrides* is not wholly the fault of Nature.

As we sat at Sir Alexander's table, we were entertained, according to the ancient usage of the North, with the melody of the bagpipe. Every thing in those countries has its history. As the bagpiper was playing, an elderly Gentleman informed us, that in some remote time, the *Macdonalds* of Glengary having been injured, or offended by the inhabitants of *Culloden*, and resolving to have justice or vengeance, came to *Culloden* on a Sunday, where finding their enemies at worship, they shut them up in the church, which they set on fire; and this, said he, is the tune that the piper played while they were burning.

Narrations like this, however uncertain, deserve the notice of a traveller, because they are the only records of a nation that has no historians, and afford the most genuine representation of the life and character of the ancient Highlanders.

Under the denomination of *Highlander* are comprehended in Scotland all that now speak the Erse language, or retain the primitive manners, whether they live among the mountains or in the islands; and in that sense I use the name, when there is not some apparent reason for making a distinction.

In *Sky* I first observed the use of Brogues, a kind of artless shoes, stitched with thongs so loosely, that though they defend the foot from stones, they do not exclude water. Brogues were formerly made of raw hides, with the hair inwards, and such are perhaps still used in rude and remote parts; but they are said not to last above two days. Where life is somewhat improved, they are now made of leather tanned with oak bark, as in other places, or with the bark of birch, or roots of tormentil, a substance recommended in defect of bark, about forty years ago, to the Irish tanners, by one to whom the parliament of that kingdom voted a reward. The leather of *Sky* is not completely penetrated by vegetable matter, and therefore cannot be very durable.

My inquiries about brogues, gave me an early specimen of Highland information. One day I was told, that to make brogues was a domestick art, which every man practised for himself, and that a pair of brogues was the work of an hour. I supposed that the husband made brogues as the wife made an apron, till next day it was told me, that a brogue-maker was a trade, and that a pair would cost half a crown. It will easily occur that these representations may both be true, and that, in some places, men may buy them, and in others, make them for themselves; but I had both the accounts in the same house within two days.

Many of my subsequent inquiries upon more interesting topicks ended in the like uncertainty. He that travels in the Highlands may easily saturate his soul with intelligence, if he will acquiesce in the first account. The Highlander gives to every question an answer so prompt and peremptory, that skepticism itself is dared into silence, and the mind sinks before the bold reporter in unresisting credulity; but, if a second question be ventured, it breaks the enchantment; for it is immediately discovered, that what was told so confidently was told at hazard, and that such fearlessness of assertion was either the sport of negligence, or the refuge of ignorance.

If individuals are thus at variance with themselves, it can be no wonder that the accounts of different men are contradictory. The traditions of an ignorant and savage people have been for ages negligently heard, and unskilfully related. Distant events must have been mingled together, and the actions of one man given to another. These, however, are deficiencies in story, for which no man is now to be censured. It were enough, if what there is yet opportunity of examining were accurately inspected, and justly represented; but such is the laxity of Highland conversation, that the inquirer is kept in continual suspense, and by a kind of intellectual retrogradation, knows less as he hears more.

In the islands the plaid is rarely worn. The law by which the Highlanders have been obliged to change the form of their dress, has, in all the places that we have visited, been universally obeyed. I have seen only one gentleman completely clothed in the ancient habit, and by him it was worn only occasionally and wantonly. The common people do not think themselves under any legal necessity of having coats; for they say that the law against plaids was made by Lord Hardwicke, and was in force only for his life: but the same poverty that made it then difficult for them to change their clothing, hinders them now from changing it again.

The fillibeg, or lower garment, is still very common, and the bonnet almost universal; but their attire is such as produces, in a sufficient degree, the effect intended by the law, of abolishing the dissimilitude of appearance between the Highlanders and the other inhabitants of Britain; and, if dress be supposed to have much influence, facilitates their coalition with their fellow-subjects.

What we have long used we naturally like, and therefore the Highlanders were unwilling to lay aside their plaid, which yet to an unprejudiced spectator must appear an incommodious and cumbersome dress; for hanging loose upon the body, it must flutter in a quick motion, or require one of the hands to keep it close. The Romans always laid aside the gown when they had any thing to do. It was a dress so unsuitable to war, that the same word which signified a gown signified peace. The chief use of a plaid seems to be this, that they could commodiously wrap themselves in it, when they were obliged to sleep without a better cover.

In our passage from *Scotland* to *Sky*, we were wet for the first time with a shower. This was the beginning of the Highland winter, after which we were told that a succession of three dry days was not to be expected for many months. The winter of the *Hebrides* consists of little more than rain and wind. As they are surrounded by an ocean never frozen, the blasts that come to them over the water are too much softened to have the power of congelation. The salt loughs, or inlets of the sea, which shoot very far into the island, never have any ice upon them, and the pools of fresh water will never bear the walker. The snow that sometimes falls, is soon dissolved by the air, or the rain.

This is not the description of a cruel climate, yet the dark months are here a time of great distress; because the summer can do little more than feed itself, and winter comes with its cold and its scarcity upon families very slenderly provided.

CORIATACHAN IN SKY

The third or fourth day after our arrival at *Armidel*, brought us an invitation to the isle of *Raasay*, which lies east of *Sky*. It is incredible how soon the account of any event is propagated in these narrow countries by the love of talk, which much leisure produces, and the relief given to the mind in the penury of insular conversation by a new topick. The arrival of strangers at a place so rarely visited, excites rumour, and quickens curiosity. I know not whether we touched at any corner, where Fame had not already prepared us a reception.

To gain a commodious passage to *Raasay*, it was necessary to pass over a large part of *Sky*. We were furnished therefore with horses and a guide. In the Islands there are no roads, nor any marks by which a stranger may find his way. The horseman has always at his side a native of the place, who, by pursuing game, or tending cattle, or being often employed in messages or conduct, has learned where the ridge of the hill has breadth sufficient to allow a horse and his rider a passage, and where the moss or bog is hard enough to bear them. The bogs are avoided as toilsome at least, if not unsafe, and therefore the journey is made generally from precipice to precipice; from which if the eye ventures to look down, it sees below a gloomy cavity, whence the rush of water is sometimes heard.

But there seems to be in all this more alarm than danger. The Highlander walks carefully before, and the horse, accustomed to the ground, follows him with little deviation. Sometimes the hill is too steep for the horseman to keep his seat, and sometimes the moss is too tremulous to bear the double weight of horse and man. The rider then dismounts, and all shift as they can.

Journeys made in this manner are rather tedious than long. A very few miles require several hours. From *Armidel* we came at night to *Coriatachan*, a house very pleasantly situated between two brooks, with one of the highest hills of the island behind it. It is the residence of Mr. *Mackinnon*, by whom we were treated with very liberal hospitality, among a more numerous and elegant company than it could have been supposed easy to collect.

The hill behind the house we did not climb. The weather was rough, and the height and steepness discouraged us. We were told that there is a cairne upon it. A cairne is a heap of stones thrown upon the grave of one eminent for dignity of birth, or splendour of atchievements. It is said that by digging, an urn is always found under these cairnes: they must therefore have been thus piled by a people whose custom was to burn the dead. To pile stones is, I believe, a northern custom, and to burn the body was the Roman practice; nor do I know when it was that these two acts of sepulture were united.

The weather was next day too violent for the continuation of our journey; but we had no reason to complain of the interruption.

We saw in every place, what we chiefly desired to know, the manners of the people. We had company, and, if we had chosen retirement, we might have had books.

I never was in any house of the Islands, where I did not find books in more languages than one, if I staid long enough to want them, except one from which the family was removed. Literature is not neglected by the higher rank of the Hebridians.

It need not, I suppose, be mentioned, that in countries so little frequented as the Islands, there are no houses where travellers are entertained for money. He that wanders about these wilds, either procures recommendations to those whose habitations lie near his way, or, when night and weariness come upon him, takes the chance of general hospitality. If he finds only a cottage, he can expect little more than shelter; for the cottagers have little more for themselves: but if his good fortune brings him to the residence of a gentleman, he will be glad of a storm to prolong his stay. There is, however, one inn by the sea-side at Sconsor, in Sky, where the post-office is kept.

At the tables where a stranger is received, neither plenty nor delicacy is wanting. A tract of land so thinly inhabited, must have much wild-fowl; and I scarcely remember to have seen a dinner without them. The moorgame is every where to be had. That the sea abounds with fish, needs not be told, for it supplies a great part of Europe. The isle of *Sky* has stags and roebucks, but no hares. They sell very numerous droves of oxen yearly to England, and therefore cannot be supposed to want beef at home. Sheep and goats are in great numbers, and they have the common domestick fowls.

But as here is nothing to be bought, every family must kill its own meat, and roast part of it somewhat sooner than Apicius would prescribe. Every kind of flesh is undoubtedly excelled by the variety and emulation of English markets; but that which is not best may be yet very far from bad, and he that shall complain of his fare in the *Hebrides*, has improved his delicacy more than his manhood.

Their fowls are not like those plumped for sale by the poulterers of London, but they are as good as other places commonly afford, except that the geese, by feeding in the sea, have universally a fishy rankness.

These geese seem to be of a middle race, between the wild and domestick kinds. They are so tame as to own a home, and so wild as sometimes to fly quite away.

Their native bread is made of oats, or barley. Of oatmeal they spread very thin cakes, coarse and hard, to which unaccustomed palates are not easily reconciled. The barley cakes are thicker and softer; I began to eat them without unwillingness; the blackness of their colour raises some dislike, but the taste is not disagreeable. In most houses there is wheat flower, with which we were sure to be treated, if we staid long enough to have it kneaded and baked. As neither yeast nor leaven are used among them, their bread of every kind is unfermented. They make only cakes, and never mould a loaf.

A man of the Hebrides, for of the women's diet I can give no account, as soon as he appears in the morning, swallows a glass of whisky; yet they are not a drunken race, at least I never was present at much intemperance; but no man is so abstemious as to refuse the morning dram, which they call a *skalk*.

The word *whisky* signifies water, and is applied by way of eminence to *strong water*, or distilled liquor. The spirit drunk in the North is drawn from barley. I never tasted it, except once for experiment at the inn in *Inverary*, when I thought it preferable to any *English* malt brandy. It was strong, but not pungent, and was free from the empyreumatick taste or smell. What was the process I had no opportunity of inquiring, nor do I wish to improve the art of making poison pleasant.

Not long after the dram, may be expected the breakfast, a meal in which the Scots, whether of the lowlands or mountains, must be confessed to excel us. The tea and coffee are accompanied not only with butter, but with honey, conserves, and marmalades. If an epicure could remove by a wish, in quest of sensual gratifications, wherever he had supped he would breakfast in Scotland.

In the islands however, they do what I found it not very easy to endure. They pollute the tea-table by plates piled with large slices of cheshire cheese, which mingles its less grateful odours with the fragrance of the tea.

Where many questions are to be asked, some will be omitted. I forgot to inquire how they were supplied with so much exotic luxury. Perhaps the French may bring them wine for wool, and the Dutch give them tea and coffee at the fishing season, in exchange for fresh provision. Their trade is unconstrained; they pay no customs; for there is no officer to demand them, whatever therefore is made dear only by impost, is obtained here at an easy rate.

A dinner in the Western Islands differs very little from a dinner in *England*, except that in the place of tarts, there are always set different preparations of milk. This part of their diet will admit some improvement. Though they have milk, and eggs, and sugar, few of them know how to compound them in a custard. Their gardens afford them no great variety, but they have always some vegetables on the table. Potatoes at least are never wanting, which, though they have not known them long, are now one of the principal parts of their food. They are not of the mealy, but the viscous kind.

Their more elaborate cookery, or made dishes, an Englishman at the first taste is not likely to approve, but the culinary compositions of every country are often such as become grateful to other nations only by degrees; though I have read a French author, who, in the elation of his heart, says, that French cookery pleases all foreigners, but foreign cookery never satisfies a Frenchman.

Their suppers are, like their dinners, various and plentiful. The table is always covered with elegant linen. Their plates for common use are often of that kind of manufacture which is called cream coloured, or queen's ware. They use silver on all occasions where it is common in *England*, nor did I ever find a spoon of horn, but in one house.

The knives are not often either very bright, or very sharp. They are indeed instruments of which the Highlanders have not been long acquainted with the general use. They were not regularly laid on the table, before the prohibition of arms, and the change of dress. Thirty years ago the Highlander wore his knife as a companion to his dirk or dagger, and when the company sat down to meat, the men who had knives, cut the flesh into small pieces for the women, who with their fingers conveyed it to their mouths.

There was perhaps never any change of national manners so quick, so great, and so general, as that which has operated in the Highlands, by the last conquest, and the subsequent laws. We came thither too late to see what we expected, a people of peculiar appearance, and a system of antiquated life. The clans retain little now of their original character, their ferocity of temper is softened, their military ardour is extinguished, their dignity of independence is depressed, their contempt of government subdued, and their

700

reverence for their chiefs abated. Of what they had before the late conquest of their country, there remain only their language and their poverty. Their language is attacked on every side. Schools are erected, in which *English* only is taught, and there were lately some who thought it reasonable to refuse them a version of the holy scriptures, that they might have. no monument of their mother-tongue.

That their poverty is gradually abated, cannot be mentioned among the unpleasing consequences of subjection. They are now acquainted with money, and the possibility of gain will by degrees make them industrious. Such is the effect of the late regulations, that a longer journey than to the Highlands must be taken by him whose curiosity pants for savage virtues and barbarous grandeur.

RAASAY

At the first intermission of the stormy weather we were informed, that the boat, which was to convey us to *Raasay*, attended us on the coast. We had from this time our intelligence facilitated, and our conversation enlarged, by the company of Mr. Macqueen, minister of a parish in *Sky*, whose knowledge and politeness give him a title equally to kindness and respect, and who, from this time, never forsook us till we were preparing to leave Sky, and the adjacent places.

The boat was under the direction of Mr. *Malcolm Macleod*, a gentleman of *Raasay*. The water was calm, and the rowers were vigorous; so that our passage was quick and pleasant. When we came near the island, we saw the laird's house, a neat modern fabrick, and found Mr. *Macleod*, the proprietor of the Island, with many gentlemen, expecting us on the beach. We had, as at all other places, some difficulty in landing. The craggs were irregularly broken, and a false step would have been very mischievous.

It seemed that the rocks might, with no great labour, have been hewn almost into a regular flight of steps; and as there are no other landing places, I considered this rugged ascent as the consequence of a form of life inured to hardships, and therefore not studious of nice accommodations. But I know not whether, for many ages, it was not considered as a part of military policy, to keep the country not easily accessible. The rocks are natural fortifications, and an enemy climbing with difficulty, was easily destroyed by those who stood high above him.

Our reception exceeded our expectations. We found nothing but civility, elegance, and plenty. After the usual refreshments, and the usual conversation, the evening came upon us. The carpet was then rolled off the floor; the musician was called, and the whole company was invited to dance, nor did ever fairies trip with greater alacrity. The general air of festivity, which predominated in this place, so far remote from all those regions which the mind has been used to contemplate as the mansions of pleasure, struck the imagination with a delightful surprise, analogous to that which is felt at an unexpected emersion from darkness into light.

When it was time to sup, the dance ceased, and six and thirty persons sat down to two tables in the same room. After supper the ladies sung *Erse* songs, to which I listened as an *English* audience to an *Italian* opera, delighted with the sound of words which I did not understand.

I inquired the subjects of the songs, and was told of one, that it was a love song, and of another, that it was a farewell composed by one of the Islanders that was going, in this epidemical fury of emigration, to seek his fortune in *America*. What sentiments would rise, on such an occasion, in the heart of one who had not been taught to lament by precedent, I should gladly have known; but the lady, by whom I sat, thought herself not equal to the work of translating.

Mr. *Macleod* is the proprietor of the islands of *Raasay*, *Rona*, and *Fladda*, and possesses an extensive district in *Sky*. The estate has not, during four hundred years, gained or lost a single acre.

One of the old Highland alliances has continued for two hundred years, and is still subsisting between *Macleod* of *Raasay* and *Macdonald* of *Sky*, in consequence of which, the survivor always inherits the arms of the deceased; a natural memorial of military friendship. At the death of the late Sir *James Macdonald*, his sword was delivered to the present laird of *Raasay*.

The family of *Raasay* consists of the laird, the lady, three sons, and ten daughters. For the sons there is a tutor in the house, and the lady is said to be very skilful and diligent in the education of her girls. More gentleness of manners, or a more pleasing appearance of domestick society, is not found in the most polished countries.

Raasay is the only inhabited island in Mr. *Macleod's* possession. *Rona* and *Fladda* afford only pasture for cattle, of which one hundred and sixty winter in *Rona*, under the superintendence of a solitary herdsman.

The length of *Raasay* is, by computation, fifteen miles, and the breadth two. These countries have never been measured, and the computation by miles is negligent and arbitrary. We observed in travelling, that the nominal and real distance of places had very little relation to each other. *Raasay* probably contains near a hundred square miles. It affords not much ground, notwithstanding its extent, either for tillage, or pasture; for it is rough, rocky, and barren. The cattle often perish by falling from the precipices. It is like the other islands, I think, generally naked of shade, but it is naked by neglect; for the laird has an orchard, and very large forest trees grow about his house. Like other hilly countries it has many rivulets. One of the brooks turns a corn-mill, and at least one produces trouts.

In the streams or fresh lakes of the Islands, I have never heard of any other fish than trouts and eels. The trouts, which I have seen, are not large; the colour of their flesh is tinged as in *England*. Of their eels I can give no account, having never tasted them; for I believe they are not considered as wholesome food.

It is not very easy to fix the principles upon which mankind have agreed to eat some animals, and reject others; and as the principle is not evident, it is not uniform. That which is selected as delicate in one country, is by its neighbours abhorred as loathsome. The Neapolitans lately refused to eat potatoes in a famine. An Englishman is not easily persuaded to dine on snails with an Italian, on frogs with a Frenchman, or on horse-flesh with a Tartar. The vulgar inhabitants of *Sky*, I know not whether of the other islands, have not only eels, but pork and bacon in abhorrence, and accordingly I never saw a hog in the *Hebrides*, except one at *Dunvegan*.

Raasay has wild fowl in abundance, but neither deer, hares, nor rabbits. Why it has them not, might be asked, but that of such questions there is no end. Why does any nation want what it might have? Why are not spices transplanted to *America*? Why does tea continue to be brought from China? Life improves but by slow degrees, and much in every place is yet to do. Attempts have been made to raise roebucks in *Raasay*, but without effect. The young ones it is extremely difficult to rear, and the old can very seldom be taken alive.

Hares and rabbits might be more easily obtained. That they have

703

few or none of either in *Sky*, they impute to the ravage of the foxes, and have therefore set, for some years past, a price upon their heads, which, as the number was diminished, has been gradually raised, from three shillings and sixpence to a guinea, a sum so great in this part of the world, that, in a short time, *Sky* may be as free from foxes, as *England* from wolves. The fund for these rewards is a tax of sixpence in the pound, imposed by the farmers on themselves, and said to be paid with great willingness.

The beasts of prey in the Islands are foxes, otters, and weasels. The foxes are bigger than those of *England*; but the otters exceed ours in a far greater proportion. I saw one at *Armidel*, of a size much beyond that which I supposed them ever to attain; and Mr. *Maclean*, the heir of *Col*, a man of middle stature, informed me that he once shot an otter, of which the tail reached the ground, when he held up the head to a level with his own. I expected the otter to have a foot particularly formed for the art of swimming; but upon examination, I did not find it differing much from that of a spaniel. As he preys in the sea, he does little visible mischief, and is killed only for his fur. White otters are sometimes seen.

In *Raasay* they might have hares and rabbits, for they have no foxes. Some depredations, such as were never made before, have caused a suspicion that a fox has been lately landed in the island by spite or wantonness. This imaginary stranger has never yet been seen, and therefore, perhaps, the mischief was done by some other animal. It is not likely that a creature so ungentle, whose head could have been sold in *Sky* for a guinea, should be kept alive only to gratify the malice of sending him to prey upon a neighbour: and the passage from *Sky* is wider than a fox would venture to swim, unless he were chased by dogs into the sea, and perhaps than his strength would enable him to cross. How beasts of prey came into any islands is not easy to guess. In cold countries they take advantage of hard winters, and travel over the ice: but this is a very scanty solution; for they are found where they have no discoverable means of coming.

The corn of this island is but little. I saw the harvest of a small field. The women reaped the corn, and the men bound up the sheaves. The strokes of the sickle were timed by the modulation of the harvest song, in which all their voices were united. They accompany in the Highlands every action, which can be done in equal time, with an appropriate strain, which has, they say, not much meaning; but its effects are regularity and cheerfulness. The ancient proceleusmatick song, by which the rowers of galleys were animated, may be supposed to have been of this kind. There is now an *oar-song* used by the *Hebridians*.

The ground of *Raasay* seems fitter for cattle than for corn, and of black cattle I suppose the number is very great. The Laird himself keeps a herd of four hundred, one hundred of which are annually sold. Of an extensive domain, which he holds in his own hands, he considers the sale of cattle as repaying him the rent, and supports the plenty of a very liberal table with the remaining product.

Raasay is supposed to have been very long inhabited. On one side it of they show caves, into which the rude nations of the first ages retreated from the weather. These dreary vaults might have had other uses. There is still a cavity near the house called the *oar-cave*, in which the seamen, after one of these piratical expeditions, which in rougher times were very frequent, used, as tradition tells, to hide their oars. This hollow was near the sea, that nothing so necessary might be far to be fetched; and it was secret, that enemies, if they landed, could find nothing. Yet it is not very evident of what use it was to hide their oars from those, who, if they were masters of the coast, could take away their boats.

A proof much stronger of the distance at which the first possessors of this island lived from the present time, is afforded by the stone heads of arrows which are very frequently picked up. The people call them *Elf-bolts*, and believe that the fairies shoot them at the cattle. They nearly resemble those which Mr. *Banks* has lately brought from the savage countries in the Pacifick Ocean, and must have been made by a nation to which the use of metals was unknown.

The number of this little community has never been counted by its ruler, nor have I obtained any positive account, consistent with the result of political computation. Not many years ago, the late Laird led out one hundred men upon a military expedition. The sixth part of a people is supposed capable of bearing arms: *Raasay* had therefore six hundred inhabitants. But because it is not likely, that every man able to serve in the field would follow the summons, or that the chief would leave his lands totally defenceless, or take away all the hands qualified for labour, let it be supposed, that half as many might be permitted to stay at home. The whole number will then be nine hundred, or nine to a square mile; a degree of populousness greater than those tracts of desolation can often show. They are content with their country, and faithful to their chiefs, and yet uninfected with the fever of migration.

Near the house, at *Raasay*, is a chapel unroofed and ruinous, which has long been used only as a place of burial. About the churches, in the Islands, are small squares enclosed with stone, which belong to particular families, as repositories for the dead. At *Raasay* there is one, I think, for the proprietor, and one for some collateral house.

It is told by *Martin*, that at the death of the Lady of the Island, it has been here the custom to erect a cross. This we found not to be true. The stones that stand about the chapel at a small distance, some of which perhaps have crosses cut upon them, are believed to have been not funeral monuments, but the ancient boundaries of the sanctuary or consecrated ground.

Martin was a man not illiterate: he was an inhabitant of *Sky*, and therefore was within reach of intelligence, and with no great difficulty might have visited the places which he undertakes to describe; yet with all his opportunities, he has often suffered himself to be deceived. He lived in the last century, when the chiefs of the clans had lost little of their original influence. The mountains were yet unpenetrated, no inlet was opened to foreign novelties, and the feudal institutions operated upon life with their full force. He might therefore have displayed a series of subordination and a form of government, which, in more luminous and improved regions, have been long forgotten, and have delighted his readers with many uncouth customs that are now disused, and wild opinions that prevail no longer. But he probably had not knowledge of the world sufficient to qualify him for judging what would deserve or gain the attention of mankind. The mode of life which was familiar to himself, he did not suppose unknown to others, nor imagined that he could give pleasure by telling that of which it was, in his little country, impossible to be ignorant.

What he has neglected cannot now be performed. In nations, where there is hardly the use of letters, what is once out of sight is lost for ever. They think but little, and of their few thoughts, none are wasted on the past, in which they are neither interested by fear nor hope. Their only registers are stated observances and practical representations. For this reason an age of ignorance is an age of ceremony. Pageants, and processions, and commemorations, gradually shrink away, as better methods come into use of recording events, and preserving rights.

It is not only in *Raasay* that the chapel is unroofed and useless; through the few islands which we visited, we neither saw nor heard of any house of prayer, except in *Sky*, that was not in ruins. The malignant influence of *Calvinism* has blasted ceremony and decency together; and if the remembrance of papal superstition is obliterated, the monuments of papal piety are likewise effaced.

It has been, for many years, popular to talk of the lazy devotion of the Romish clergy; over the sleepy laziness of men that erected churches, we may indulge our superiority with a new triumph, by comparing it with the fervid activity of those who suffer them to fall.

Of the destruction of churches, the decay of religion must in time be the consequence; for while the publick acts of the ministry are now performed in houses, a very small number can be present; and as the greater part of the Islanders make no use of books, all must necessarily live in total ignorance who want the opportunity of vocal instruction.

From these remains of ancient sanctity, which are every where to be found, it has been conjectured, that, for the last two centuries, the inhabitants of the Islands have decreased in number. This argument, which supposes that the churches have been suffered to fall, only because they were no longer necessary, would have some force, if the houses of worship still remaining were sufficient for the people. But since they have now no churches at all, these venerable fragments do not prove the people of former times to have been more numerous, but to have been more devout. If the inhabitants were doubled with their present principles, it appears not that any provision for publick worship would be made. Where the religion of a country enforces consecrated buildings, the number of those buildings may be supposed to afford some indication, however uncertain, of the populousness of the place; but where by a change of manners a nation is contented to live without them, their decay implies no diminution of inhabitants.

Some of these dilapidations are said to be found in islands now uninhabited; but I doubt whether we can thence infer that they were ever peopled. The religion of the middle age, is well known to have placed too much hope in lonely austerities. Voluntary solitude was the great art of propitiation, by which crimes were effaced, and conscience was appeased; it is therefore not unlikely, that oratories were often built in places where retirement was sure to have no disturbance.

Raasay has little that can detain a traveller, except the Laird and his family; but their power wants no auxiliaries. Such a seat of hospitality, amidst the winds and waters, fills the imagination with a delightful contrariety of images. Without is the rough ocean and the rocky land, the beating billows and the howling storm; within is plenty and elegance, beauty and gaiety, the song and the dance. In *Raasay*, if I could have found an Ulysses, I had fancied a *Phœacia*.

DUNVEGAN

At *Raasay*, by good fortune, *Macleod*, so the chief of the clan is called, was paying a visit, and by him we were invited to his seat at *Dunvegan*. *Raasay* has a stout boat, built in *Norway*, in which, with six oars, he conveyed us back to *Sky*. We landed at *Port Re*, so called, because *James* the Fifth of *Scotland*, who had curiosity to visit the islands, came into it. The port is made by an inlet of the sea, deep and narrow, where a ship lay waiting to dispeople *Sky*, by carrying the natives away to *America*.

In coasting *Sky*, we passed by the cavern in which it was the custom, as *Martin* relates, to catch birds in the night, by making a fire at the entrance. This practice is disused; for the birds, as is known often to happen, have changed their haunts.

Here we dined at a publick house, I believe the only inn of the island, and having mounted our horses, travelled in the manner already described, till we came to *Kingsborough*, a place distinguished by that name, because the king lodged here when he landed at *Port Re*. We were entertained with the usual hospitality by Mr. *Macdonald* and his lady, *Flora Macdonald*, a name that will be mentioned in history, and if courage and fidelity be virtues, mentioned with honour. She is a woman of middle stature, soft features, gentle manners, and elegant presence.

In the morning we sent our horses round a promontory to meet us, and spared ourselves part of the day's fatigue, by crossing an arm of the sea. We had at last some difficulty in coming to *Dunvegan*; for our way led over an extensive moor, where every step was to be taken with caution, and we were often obliged to alight, because the ground could not be trusted. In travelling this watery flat, I perceived that it had a visible declivity, and might without much expense or difficulty be drained. But difficulty and expence are relative terms, which have different meanings in different places.

To *Dunvegan* we came, very willing to be at rest, and found our fatigue amply recompensed by our reception. Lady *Macleod*, who had lived many years in *England*, was newly come hither with her son and four daughters, who knew all the arts of southern elegance, and all the modes of English economy. Here therefore we settled, and did not spoil the present hour with thoughts of departure.

Dunvegan is a rocky prominence, that juts out into a bay, on the west side of *Sky*. The house, which is the principal seat of *Macleod*, is partly old and partly modern; it is built upon the rock, and looks upon the water. It forms two sides of a small square: on the third side is the skeleton of a castle of unknown antiquity, supposed to have been a *Norwegian* fortress, when the *Danes* were masters of the islands. It is so nearly entire, that it might have easily been made habitable, were there not an ominous tradition in the family, that the owner shall not long outlive the reparation. The grand-father of the present Laird, in defiance of prediction, began the work, but desisted in a little time, and applied his money to worse uses.

As the inhabitants of the *Hebrides* lived, for many ages, in continual expectation of hostilities, the chief of every clan resided in a fortress. This house was accessible only from the water, till the last possessor opened an entrance by stairs upon the land.

They had formerly reason to be afraid, not only of declared wars and authorized invaders, or of roving pirates, which, in the northern seas, must have been very common; but of inroads and insults from rival clans, who, in the plenitude of feudal independence, asked no leave of their Sovereign to make war on one another. Sky has been ravaged by a feud between the two mighty powers of *Macdonald* and *Macleod*. *Macdonald* having married a *Macleod*, upon some discontent dismissed her, perhaps because she had brought him no children. Before the reign of *James* the Fifth, a Highland Laird made a trial of his wife for a certain time, and if she did not please him, he was then at liberty to send her away. This however must always have offended, and *Macleod* resenting the injury, whatever were its circumstances, declared, that the wedding had been solemnized without a bonfire, but that the

z   709

separation should be better illuminated; and raising a little army, set fire to the territories of *Macdonald*, who returned the visit, and prevailed.

Another story may show the disorderly state of insular neighbourhood. The inhabitants of the Isle of *Egg*, meeting a boat manned by *Macleods*, tied the crew hand and foot, and set them a-drift. *Macleod* landed upon *Egg*, and demanded the offenders; but the inhabitants refusing to surrender them, retreated to a cavern, into which they thought their enemies unlikely to follow them. *Macleod* choked them with smoke, and left them lying dead by families as they stood.

Here the violence of the weather confined us for some time, not at all to our discontent or inconvenience. We would indeed very willingly have visited the Islands, which might be seen from the house scattered in the sea, and I was particularly desirous to have viewed *Isay*; but the storms did not permit us to launch a boat, and we were condemned to listen in idleness to the wind, except when we were better engaged by listening to the ladies.

We had here more wind than waves, and suffered the severity of a tempest, without enjoying its magnificence. The sea being broken by the multitude of islands, does not roar with so much noise, nor beat the storm with such foamy violence, as I have remarked on the coast of *Sussex*. Though, while I was in the *Hebrides*, the wind was extremely turbulent, I never saw very high billows.

The country about *Dunvegan* is rough and barren. There are no trees, except in the orchard, which is a low sheltered spot surrounded with a wall.

When this house was intended to sustain a siege, a well was made in the court, by boring the rock downwards, till water was found, which though so near to the sea, I have not heard mentioned as brackish, though it has some hardness, or other qualities, which make it less fit for use; and the family is now better supplied from a stream, which runs by the rock, from two pleasing water-falls.

Here we saw some traces of former manners, and heard some standing traditions. In the house is kept an ox's horn, hollowed so as to hold perhaps two quarts, which the heir of *Macleod* was expected to swallow at one draught, as a test of his manhood, before he was permitted to bear arms, or could claim a seat among the men. It is held that the return of the Laird to *Dunvegan*, after any considerable absence, produces a plentiful capture of herrings; and that, if any woman crosses the water to the opposite Island, the herrings will desert the coast. *Boetius* tells the same of some other place. This tradition is not uniform. Some hold that no woman may pass, and others that none may pass but a *Macleod*.

Among other guests, which the hospitality of *Dunvegan* brought to the table, a visit was paid by the Laird and Lady of a small island south of *Sky*, of which the proper name is *Muack*, which signifies swine. It is commonly called *Muck*, which the proprietor not liking, has endeavoured, without effect, to change to *Monk*. It is usual to call gentlemen in *Scotland* by the name of their possessions, as *Raasay, Bernera, Loch Buy*, a practice necessary in countries inhabited by clans, where all that live in the same territory have one name, and must be therefore discriminated by some addition. This gentleman, whose name, I think, is *Maclean*, should be regularly called *Muck*; but the appellation, which he thinks too coarse for his Island, he would like still less for himself, and he is therefore addressed by the title of, *Isle of Muck*.

This little Island, however it be named, is of considerable value. It is two *English* miles long, and three quarters of a mile broad, and consequently contains only nine hundred and sixty *English* acres. It is chiefly arable. Half of this little dominion the Laird retains in his own hand, and on the other half, live one hundred and sixty persons, who pay their rent by exported corn. What rent they pay, we were not told, and could not decently inquire. The proportion of the people to the land is such, as the most fertile countries do not commonly maintain.

The Laird having all his people under his immediate view, seems to be very attentive to their happiness. The devastation of the small-pox, when it visits places where it comes seldom, is well known. He has disarmed it of its terrour at *Muack*, by inoculating eighty of his people. The expence was two shillings and sixpence a head. Many trades they cannot have among them, but upon occasion, he fetches a smith from the Isle of *Egg*, and has a tailor from the main land, six times a year. This Island well deserved to be seen, but the Laird's absence left us no opportunity.

Every inhabited Island has its appendant and subordinate islets. *Muck*, however small, has yet others smaller about it, one of which has only ground sufficient to afford pasture for three wethers.

At *Dunvegan* I had tasted lotus, and was in danger of forgetting that I was ever to depart, till Mr. Boswell sagely reproached me with my sluggishness and softness. I had no very forcible defence to make; and we agreed to pursue our journey. *Macleod* accompanied us to *Ulinish*, where we were entertained by the sheriff of the Island.

ULINISH

Mr. *Macqueen* travelled with us, and directed our attention to all that was worthy of observation. With him we went to see an ancient building, called a dun or borough. It was a circular enclosure, about forty-two feet in diameter, walled round with loose stones, perhaps to the height of nine feet. The walls are very thick, diminishing a little towards the top, and though in these countries stone is not brought far, must have been raised with much labour. Within the great circle were several smaller rounds of wall, which formed distinct apartments. Its date, and its use are unknown. Some suppose it the original seat of the chiefs of the *Macleods*. Mr. *Macqueen* thought it a *Danish* fort.

The entrance is covered with flat stones, and is narrow, because it was necessary that the stones which lie over it should reach from one wall to the other; yet, strait as the passage is, they seem heavier than could have been placed where they now lie, by the naked strength of as many men as might stand about them. They were probably raised by putting long pieces of wood under them, to which the action of a long line of lifters might be applied. Savages, in all countries, have patience proportionate to their unskilfulness, and are content to attain their end by very tedious methods.

If it was ever roofed, it might once have been a dwelling, but as there is no provision for water, it could not have been a fortress. In *Sky*, as in every other place, there is an ambition of exalting whatever has survived memory, to some important use, and referring it to very remote ages. I am inclined to suspect, that in lawless times, when the inhabitants of every mountain stole the cattle of their neighbour, these inclosures were used to secure the herds and flocks in the night. When they were driven within the wall, they might be easily watched, and defended as long as could be needful; for the robbers durst not wait till the injured clan should find them in the morning.

The interiour inclosures, if the whole building were once a house, were the chambers of the chief inhabitants. If it was a place of security for cattle, they were probably the shelters of the keepers.

From the *Dun* we were conducted to another place of security, a cave carried a great way under ground, which had been discovered by digging after a fox. These caves, of which many have been found, and many probably remain concealed, are formed, I believe, commonly by taking advantage of a hollow, where banks or rocks rise on either side. If no such place can be found, the ground must be cut away. The walls are made by piling stones against the earth, on either side. It is then roofed by larger stones laid across the cavern, which therefore cannot be wide. Over the roof, turfs were placed, and grass was suffered to grow; and the mouth was concealed by bushes, or some other cover.

These caves were represented to us as the cabins of the first rude inhabitants, of which, however, I am by no means persuaded. This was so low, that no man could stand upright in it. By their construction they are all so narrow, that two can never pass along them together, and being subterraneous, they must be always damp. They are not the work of an age much ruder than the present; for they are formed with as much art as the construction of a common hut requires. I imagine them to have been places only of occasional use, in which the Islander, upon a sudden alarm, hid his utensils or his cloaths, and perhaps sometimes his wife and children.

This cave we entered, but could not proceed the whole length, and went away without knowing how far it was carried. For this omission we shall be blamed, as we perhaps have blamed other travellers; but the day was rainy, and the ground was damp. We had with us neither spades nor pickaxes, and if love of ease surmounted our desire of knowledge, the offence has not the invidiousness of singularity.

Edifices, either standing or ruined, are the chief records of an illiterate nation. In some part of this journey, at no great distance from our way, stood a shattered fortress, of which the learned minister, to whose communication we are much indebted, gave us an account.

Those, said he, are the walls of a place of refuge, built in the time of James the Sixth, by Hugh Macdonald, who was next heir to the dignity and fortune of his chief. Hugh, being so near his wish, was impatient of delay; and had art and influence sufficient to engage several gentlemen in a plot against the Laird's life. Something must be stipulated on both sides; for they would not dip their hands in blood merely for Hugh's advancement. The compact was formally written, signed by the conspirators, and placed in the hands of one Macleod.

It happened that Macleod had sold some cattle to a drover, who, not having ready money, gave him a bond for payment. The debt was discharged, and the bond redemanded; which Macleod, who could not read, intending to put into his hands, gave him the conspiracy. The drover, when he had read the paper, delivered it privately to Macdonald; who, being thus informed of his danger, called his friends together, and provided for his safety. He made a publick feast, and inviting Hugh Macdonald and his confederates, placed each of them at the table between two men of known fidelity. The compact of conspiracy was then shewn, and every man confronted with his own name. Macdonald acted with great moderation. He upbraided Hugh, both with disloyalty and ingratitude; but told the rest, that he considered them as men deluded and misinformed. Hugh was sworn to fidelity, and dismissed with his companions; but he was not generous enough to be reclaimed by lenity; and finding no longer any countenance among the gentlemen, endeavoured to execute the same design by meaner hands. In this practice he was detected, taken to Macdonald's castle, and imprisoned in the dungeon. When he was hungry, they let down a plentiful meal of salted meat; and when, after his repast, he called for drink, conveyed to him a covered cup, which, when he lifted the lid, he found empty. From that time they visited him no more, but left him to perish in solitude and darkness.

We were then told of a cavern by the sea-side, remarkable for the powerful reverberation of sounds. After dinner we took a boat, to explore this curious cavity. The boatmen, who seemed to be of a rank above that of common drudges, inquired who the strangers were, and being told we came one from *Scotland*, and the other from *England*, asked if the *Englishman* could recount a long genealogy. What answer was given them, the conversation being in *Erse*, I was not much inclined to examine.

They expected no good event of the voyage; for one of them declared that he heard the cry of an *English* ghost. This omen I was not told till after our return, and therefore cannot claim the dignity of despising it.

The sea was smooth. We never left the shore, and came without any disaster to the cavern, which we found rugged and misshapen, about one hundred and eighty feet long, thirty wide in the broadest part, and in the loftiest, as we guessed, about thirty high. It was now dry, but at high water the sea rises in it near six feet. Here I saw what I had never seen before, limpets and mussels in their natural state. But, as a new testimony to the veracity of common fame, here was no echo to be heard.

We then walked through a natural arch in the rock, which might have pleased us by its novelty, had the stones, which encumbered our feet, given us leisure to consider it. We were shown the gummy seed of the kelp, that fastens itself to a stone, from which it grows into a strong stalk.

In our return, we found a little boy upon the point of a rock, catching with his angle a supper for the family. We rowed up to him, and borrowed his rod, with which Mr. *Boswell* caught a cuddy.

The cuddy is a fish of which I know not the philosophical name. It is not much bigger than a gudgeon, but it is of great use in these Islands, as it affords the lower people both food, and oil for their lamps. Cuddies are so abundant, at some times of the year, that they are caught like whitebait in the Thames, only by dipping a basket and drawing it back.

If it were always practicable to fish, these Islands could never be in much danger from famine; but unhappily in the winter, when other provision fails, the seas are commonly too rough for nets, or boats.

TALISKER IN SKY

From *Ulinish*, our next stage was to *Talisker*, the house of colonel *Macleod*, an officer in the *Dutch* service, who, in this time of universal peace, has for several years been permitted to be absent from his regiment. Having been bred to physick, he is consequently a scholar, and his lady, by accompanying him in his different places of residence, is become skilful in several languages. *Talisker* is the place beyond all that I have seen, from which the gay and the jovial seem utterly excluded; and where the hermit might expect to grow old in meditation, without possibility of disturbance or interruption. It is situated very near the sea, but upon a coast where no vessel lands but when it is driven by a tempest on the rocks. Towards the land are lofty hills streaming with waterfalls. The garden is sheltered by firs or pines, which grow there so prosperously, that some, which the present inhabitant planted, are very high and thick.

At this place we very happily met with Mr. *Donald Maclean*, a young gentleman, the eldest son of the Laird of *Col*, heir to a very great extent of land, and so desirous of improving his inheritance, that he spent a considerable time among the farmers of *Hertfordshire*, and *Hampshire*, to learn their practice. He worked with his own hands at the principal operations of agriculture, that he might not deceive himself by a false opinion of skill, which, if he should find it deficient at home, he had no means of completing. If the world has agreed to praise the travels and manual labours of the Czar of *Muscovy*, let *Col* have his share of the like applause, in the proportion of his dominions to the empire of *Russia*.

This young gentleman was sporting in the mountains of *Sky*, and when he was weary with following his game, repaired for lodging to *Talisker*. At night he missed one of his dogs, and when he went to seek him in the morning, found two eagles feeding on his carcass.

Col, for he must be named by his possessions, hearing that our intention was to visit *Iona*, offered to conduct us to his chief, Sir *Allan Maclean*, who lived in the isle of *Inch Kenneth*, and would readily find us a convenient passage. From this time was formed an acquaintance, which being begun by kindness, was accidentally continued by constraint; we derived much pleasure from it, and I hope have given him no reason to repent it.

The weather was now almost one continued storm, and we were to snatch some happy intermission to be conveyed to *Mull*, the third Island of the *Hebrides*, lying about a degree south of *Sky*, whence we might easily find our way to *Inch Kenneth*, where Sir *Allan Maclean* resided, and afterward to *Jona*.

For this purpose, the most commodious station that we could take was *Armidel*, which Sir *Alexander Macdonald* had now left to a gentleman, who lived there as his factor or steward.

In our way to *Armidel* was Coriatachan, where we had already been, and to which therefore we were very willing to return. We staid however so long at *Talisker*, that a great part of our journey was performed in the gloom of the evening. In travelling even thus almost without light thro' naked solitude, when there is a guide whose conduct may be trusted, a mind not naturally too much disposed to fear, may preserve some degree of cheerfulness; but what must be the solicitude of him who should be wandering, among the craggs and hollows, benighted, ignorant, and alone?

The fictions of the *Gothick* romances were not so remote from

716

credibility as they are now thought. In the full prevalence of the feudal institution, when violence desolated the world, and every baron lived in a fortress, forests and castles were regularly succeeded by each other, and the adventurer might very suddenly pass from the gloom of woods, or the ruggedness of moors, to seats of plenty, gaiety, and magnificence. Whatever is imaged in the wildest tale, if giants, dragons, and enchantment be excepted, would be felt by him, who, wandering in the mountains without a guide, or upon the sea without a pilot, should be carried amidst his terror and uncertainty, to the hospitality and elegance of *Raasay* or *Dunvegan*.

To Coriatachan at last we came, and found ourselves welcomed as before. Here we staid two days, and made such inquiries as curiosity suggested. The house was filled with company, among whom Mr. *Macpherson* and his sister distinguished themselves by their politeness and accomplishments. By him we were invited to *Ostig*, a house not far from *Armidel*, where we might easily hear of a boat, when the weather would suffer us to leave the Island.

OSTIG IN SKY

At *Ostig*, of which Mr. *Macpherson* is minister, we were entertained for some days, then removed to *Armidel*, where we finished our observations on the island of Sky.

As this Island lies in the fifty-seventh degree, the air cannot be supposed to have much warmth. The long continuance of the sun above the horizon, does indeed sometimes produce great heat in northern latitudes; but this can only happen in sheltered places, where the atmosphere is to a certain degree stagnant, and the same mass of air continues to receive for many hours the rays of the sun, and the vapours of the earth. *Sky* lies open on the west and north to a vast extent of ocean, and is cooled in the summer by a perpetual ventilation, but by the same blasts is kept warm in winter. Their weather is not pleasing. Half the year is deluged with rain. From the autumnal to the vernal equinox, a dry day is hardly known, except when the showers are suspended by a tempest. Under such skies can be expected no great exuberance of vegetation. Their winter overtakes their summer, and their harvest lies upon the ground drenched with rain. The autumn struggles hard to produce some of our early fruits. I gathered gooseberries in September; but they were small, and the husk was thick.

717

The winter is seldom such as puts a full stop to the growth of plants, or reduces the cattle to live wholly on the surplusage of the summer. In the year Seventy-one they had a severe season, remembered by the name of the Black Spring, from which the island has not yet recovered. The snow lay long upon the ground, a calamity hardly known before. Part of their cattle died for want, part were unseasonably sold to buy sustenance for the owners; and, what I have not read or heard of before, the kine that survived were so emaciated and dispirited, that they did not require the male at the usual time. Many of the roebucks perished.

The soil, as in other countries, has its diversities. In some parts there is only a thin layer of earth spread upon a rock, which bears nothing but short brown heath, and perhaps is not generally capable of any better product. There are many bogs or mosses of greater or less extent, where the soil cannot be supposed to want depth, though it is too wet for the plow. But we did not observe in these any aquatick plants. The vallies and the mountains are alike darkened with heath. Some grass, however, grows here and there, and some happier spots of earth are capable of tillage.

Their agriculture is laborious, and perhaps rather feeble than unskilful. Their chief manure is sea-weed, which, when they lay it to rot upon the field, gives them a better crop than those of the Highlands. They heap sea shells upon the dunghill, which in time moulder into a fertilising substance. When they find a vein of earth where they cannot use it, they dig it up, and add it to the mould of a more commodious place.

Their corn grounds often lie in such intricacies among the craggs, that there is no room for the action of a team and plow. The soil is then turned up by manual labour, with an instrument called a crooked spade, of a form and weight which to me appeared very incommodious, and would perhaps be soon improved in a country where workmen could be easily found and easily paid. It has a narrow blade of iron fixed to a long and heavy piece of wood, which must have, about a foot and a half above the iron, a knee or flexure with the angle downwards. When the farmer encounters a stone which is the great impediment of his operations, he drives the blade under it, and bringing the knee or angle to the ground, has in the long handle a very forcible lever.

According to the different mode of tillage, farms are distinguished into *long land* and *short land*. Long land is that which

718

affords room for a plow, and short land is turned up by the spade.

The grain which they commit to the furrows thus tediously formed, is either oats or barley. They do not sow barley without very copious manure, and then they expect from it ten for one, an increase equal to that of better countries; but the culture is so operose that they content themselves commonly with oats; and who can relate without compassion, that after all their diligence they are to expect only a triple increase? It is in vain to hope for plenty, when a third part of the harvest must be reserved for seed.

When their grain is arrived at the state which they must consider as ripeness, they do not cut, but pull the barley: to the oats they apply the sickle. Wheel carriages they have none, but make a frame of timber, which is drawn by one horse with the two points behind pressing on the ground. On this they sometimes drag home their sheaves, but often convey them home in a kind of open panier, or frame of sticks upon the horse's back.

Of that which is obtained with so much difficulty, nothing surely ought to be wasted; yet their method of clearing their oats from the husk is by parching them in the straw. Thus with the genuine improvidence of savages, they destroy that fodder for want of which their cattle may perish. From this practice they have two petty conveniences. They dry the grain so that it is easily reduced to meal, and they escape the theft of the thresher. The taste contracted from the fire by the oats, as by every other scorched substance, use must long ago have made grateful. The oats that are not parched must be dried in a kiln.

The barns of *Sky* I never saw. That which *Macleod* of *Raasay* had erected near his house was so contrived, because the harvest is seldom brought home dry, as by perpetual perflation to prevent the mow from heating.

Of their gardens I can judge only from their tables. I did not observe that the common greens were wanting, and suppose, that by choosing an advantageous exposition, they can raise all the more hardy esculent plants. Of vegetable fragrance or beauty they are not yet studious. Few vows are made to Flora in the *Hebrides*.

They gather a little hay, but the grass is mown late; and is so often almost dry and again very wet, before it is housed, that it becomes a collection of withered stalks without taste or fragrance;

it must be eaten by cattle that have nothing else, but by most English farmers would be thrown away.

In the Islands I have not heard that any subterraneous treasures have been discovered, though where there are mountains, there are commonly minerals. One of the rocks in *Col* has a black vein, imagined to consist of the ore of lead; but it was never yet opened or essayed. In *Sky* a black mass was accidentally picked up, and brought into the house of the owner of the land, who found himself strongly inclined to think it a coal, but unhappily it did not burn in the chimney. Common ores would be here of no great value; for what requires to be separated by fire, must, if it were found, be carried away in its mineral state, here being no fewel for the smelting-house or forge. Perhaps by diligent search in this world of stone, some valuable species of marble might be discovered. But neither philosophical curiosity, nor commercial industry, have yet fixed their abode here, where the importunity of immediate want supplied but for the day, and craving on the morrow, has left little room for excursive knowledge or the pleasing fancies of distant profit.

They have lately found a manufacture considerably lucrative. Their rocks abound with kelp, a sea-plant, of which the ashes are melted into glass. They burn kelp in great quantities, and then send it away in ships, which come regularly to purchase them. This new source of riches has raised the rents of many maritime farms; but the tenants pay, like all other tenants, the additional rent with great unwillingness; because they consider the profits of the kelp as the mere product of personal labour, to which the landlord contributes nothing. However, as any man may be said to give, what he gives the power of gaining, he has certainly as much right to profit from the price of kelp as of any thing else found or raised upon his ground.

This new trade has excited a long and eager litigation between *Macdonald* and *Macleod*, for a ledge of rocks, which, till the value of kelp was known, neither of them desired the reputation of possessing.

The cattle of *Sky* are not so small as is commonly believed. Since they have sent their beeves in great numbers to southern marts, they have probably taken more care of their breed. At stated times the annual growth of cattle is driven to a fair, by a general drover, and with the money, which he returns to the farmer, the rents are paid.

The price regularly expected, is from two to three pounds a head: there was once one sold for five pounds. They go from the Islands very lean, and are not offered to the butcher, till they have been long fatted in *English* pastures.

Of their black cattle, some are without horns, called by the Scots *humble* cows, as we call a bee an *humble* bee, that wants a sting. Whether this difference be specifick, or accidental, though we inquired with great diligence, we could not be informed. We are not very sure that the bull is ever without horns, though we have been told, that such bulls there are. What is produced by putting a horned and unhorned male and female together, no man has ever tried, that thought the result worthy of observation.

Their horses are, like their cows, of a moderate size. I had no difficulty to mount myself commodiously by the favour of the gentlemen. I heard of very little cows in *Barra*, and very little horses in *Rum*, where perhaps no care is taken to prevent that diminution of size, which must always happen, where the greater and the less copulate promiscuously, and the young animal is restrained from growth by penury of sustenance.

The goat is the general inhabitant of the earth, complying with every difference of climate, and of soil. The goats of the *Hebrides* are like others: nor did I hear any thing of their sheep, to be particularly remarked.

In the penury of these malignant regions, nothing is left that can be converted to food. The goats and the sheep are milked like the cows. A single meal of a goat is a quart, and of a sheep a pint. Such at least was the account, which I could extract from those of whom I am not sure that they ever had inquired.

The milk of goats is much thinner than that of cows, and that or sheep is much thicker. Sheeps milk is never eaten before it is boiled: as it is thick, it must be very liberal of curd, and the people of St. *Kilda* form it into small cheeses.

The stags of the mountains are less than those of our parks, or forests, perhaps not bigger than our fallow deer. Their flesh has no rankness, nor is inferiour in flavour to our common venison. The roebuck I neither saw nor tasted. These are not countries for a regular chase. The deer are not driven with horns and hounds. A sportsman, with his gun in his hand, watches the animal, and when he has wounded him, traces him by the blood.

They have a race of brinded greyhounds, larger and stronger

than those with which we course hares, and those are the only dogs used by them for the chase.

Man is by the use of fire-arms made so much an overmatch for other animals, that in all countries, where they are in use, the wild part of the creation sensibly diminishes. There will probably not be long, either stags or roebucks in the Islands. All the beasts of chase would have been lost long ago in countries well inhabited, had they not been preserved by laws for the pleasure of the rich.

There are in *Sky* neither rats nor mice, but the weasel is so frequent, that he is heard in houses rattling behind chests or beds, as rats in *England*. They probably owe to his predominance that they have no other vermin; for since the great rat took possession of this part of the world, scarce a ship can touch at any port, but some of his race are left behind. They have within these few years began to infest the isle of *Col*, where being left by some trading vessel, they have increased for want of weasels to oppose them.

The inhabitants of *Sky*, and of the other Islands, which I have seen, are commonly of the middle stature, with fewer among them very tall or very short, than are seen in *England*, or perhaps, as their numbers are small, the chances of any deviation from the common measure are necessarily few. The tallest men that I saw are among those of higher rank. In regions of barrenness and scarcity, the human race is hindered in its growth by the same causes as other animals.

The ladies have as much beauty here as in other places, but bloom and softness are not to be expected among the lower classes, whose faces are exposed to the rudeness of the climate, and whose features are sometimes contracted by want, and sometimes hardened by the blasts. Supreme beauty is seldom found in cottages or work-shops, even where no real hardships are suffered. To expand the human face to its full perfection, it seems necessary that the mind should co-operate by placidness of content, or consciousness of superiority.

Their strength is proportionate to their size, but they are accustomed to run upon rough ground, and therefore can with great agility skip over the bog, or clamber the mountain. For a campaign in the wastes of *America*, soldiers better qualified could not have been found. Having little work to do, they are not willing, nor perhaps able to endure a long continuance of manual labour, and are therefore considered as habitually idle.

Having never been supplied with those accommodations, which life extensively diversified with trades affords, they supply their wants by very insufficient shifts, and endure many inconveniences, which a little attention would easily relieve. I have seen a horse carrying home the harvest on a crate. Under his tail was a stick for a crupper, held at the two ends by twists of straw. Hemp will grow in their islands, and therefore ropes may be had. If they wanted hemp, they might make better cordage of rushes, or perhaps of nettles, than of straw.

Their method of life neither secures them perpetual health, nor exposes them to any particular diseases. There are physicians in the Islands, who, I believe, all practise chirurgery, and all compound their own medicines.

It is generally supposed, that life is longer in places where there are few opportunities of luxury; but I found no instance here of extraordinary longevity. A cottager grows old over his oaten cakes, like a citizen at a turtle feast. He is indeed seldom incommoded by corpulence. Poverty preserves him from sinking under the burden of himself, but he escapes no other injury of time. Instances of long life are often related, which those who hear them are more willing to credit than examine. To be told that any man has attained a hundred years, gives hope and comfort to him who stands trembling on the brink of his own climacterick.

Length of life is distributed impartially to very different modes of life in very different climates; and the mountains have no greater examples of age and health than the low lands, where I was introduced to two ladies of high quality; one of whom, in her ninety-fourth year, presided at her table with the full exercise of all her powers; and the other has attained her eighty-fourth, without any diminution of her vivacity, and with little reason to accuse time of depredations on her beauty.

In the Islands, as in most other places, the inhabitants are of different rank, and one does not encroach here upon another. Where there is no commerce nor manufacture, he that is born poor can scarcely become rich; and if none are able to buy estates, he that is born to land cannot annihilate his family by selling it. This was once the state of these countries. Perhaps there is no example, till within a century and half, of any family whose estate was alienated otherwise than by violence or forfeiture. Since money has been brought amongst them, they have found, like others, the art of spending more than they receive; and I saw with grief the chief of a very ancient clan, whose Island was condemned by law to be sold for the satisfaction of his creditors.

The name of highest dignity is Laird, of which there are in the extensive isle of *Sky* only three, *Macdonald*, *Macleod*, and *Mackinnon*. The Laird is the original owner of the land, whose natural power must be very great, where no man lives but by agriculture; and where the produce of the land is not conveyed through the labyrinths of traffick, but passes directly from the hand that gathers it to the mouth that eats it. The Laird has all those in his power that live upon his farms. Kings can, for the most part, only exalt or degrade. The Laird at pleasure can feed or starve, can give bread, or withold it. This inherent power was yet strengthened by the kindness of consanguinity, and the reverence of patriarchal authority. The Laird was the father of the Clan, and his tenants commonly bore his name. And to these principles of original command was added, for many ages, an exclusive right of legal jurisdiction.

This multifarious, and extensive obligation operated with force scarcely credible. Every duty, moral or political, was absorbed in affection and adherence to the Chief. Not many years have passed since the clans knew no law but the Laird's will. He told them to whom they should be friends or enemies, what King they should obey, and what religion they should profess.

When the Scots first rose in arms against the succession of the house of *Hanover*, *Lovat*, the Chief of the Frasers, was in exile for a rape. The Frasers were very numerous, and very zealous against the government. A pardon was sent to *Lovat*. He came to the *English* camp, and the clan immediately deserted to him.

Next in dignity to the Laird is the Tacksman; a large taker or lease-holder of land, of which he keeps part, as a domain, in his own hand, and lets part to under tenants. The Tacksman is necessarily a man capable of securing to the Laird the whole rent, and is commonly a collateral relation. These *tacks*, or subordinate possessions, were long considered as hereditary, and the occupant was distinguished by the name of the place at which he resided. He held a middle station, by which the highest and the lowest orders were connected. He paid rent and reverence to the Laird, and received them from the tenants. This tenure still subsists, with its original operation, but not with the primitive stability. Since the islanders, no longer content to live, have learned the desire of growing rich, an ancient dependent is in danger of giving way to a higher bidder, at the expence of domestick dignity and hereditary power. The stranger, whose money buys him preference, considers himself as paying for all that he has, and is indifferent about the Laird's honour or safety. The commodiousness of money is indeed great; but there are some advantages which money cannot buy, and which therefore no wise man will by the love of money be tempted to forego.

I have found in the hither parts of *Scotland*, men not defective in judgment or general experience, who consider the Tacksman as a useless burden of the ground, as a drone who lives upon the product of an estate, without the right of property, or the merit of labour, and who impoverishes at once the landlord and the tenant. The land, say they, is let to the Tacksman at six-pence an acre, and by him to the tenant at ten-pence. Let the owner be the immediate landlord to all the tenants; if he sets the ground at eight-pence, he will increase his revenue by a fourth part, and the tenant's burden will be diminished by a fifth.

Those who pursue this train of reasoning, seem not sufficiently to inquire whither it will lead them, nor to know that it will equally show the propriety of suppressing all wholesale trade, of shutting up the shops of every man who sells what he does not make, and of extruding all whose agency and profit intervene between the manufacturer and the consumer. They may, by stretching their understandings a little wider, comprehend, that all those who by undertaking large quantities of manufacture, and affording employment to many labourers, make themselves considered as benefactors to the publick, have only been robbing their workmen with one hand, and their customers with the other. If Crowley had sold only what he could make, and all his smiths had wrought their own iron with their own hammers, he would have lived on less, and they would have sold their work for more. The salaries of superintendents and clerks would have been partly saved, and partly shared, and nails been sometimes cheaper by a farthing in a hundred. But then if the smith could not have found an immediate purchaser, he must have deserted his anvil; if there had by accident at any time been more sellers than buyers, the workmen must have reduced their profit to nothing, by underselling one another; and as no great stock could have been in any hand, no sudden demand of large quantities could have been answered, and the builder must have stood still till the nailer could supply him.

According to these schemes, universal plenty is to begin and end in universal misery. Hope and emulation will be utterly extinguished; and as all must obey the call of immediate necessity, nothing that requires extensive views, or provides for distant consequences, will ever be performed.

To the southern inhabitants of Scotland, the state of the mountains and the islands is equally unknown with that of *Borneo* or *Sumatra*: Of both they have only heard a little, and guess the rest. They are strangers to the language and the manners, to the advantages and wants of the people, whose life they would model, and whose evils they would remedy.

Nothing is less difficult than to procure one convenience by the forfeiture of another. A soldier may expedite his march by throwing away his arms. To banish the Tacksman is easy, to make a country plentiful by diminishing the people, is an expeditious mode of husbandry; but that abundance, which there is nobody to enjoy, contributes little to human happiness.

As the mind must govern the hands, so in every society the man of intelligence must direct the man of labour. If the Tacksmen be taken away, the Hebrides must in their present state be given up to grossness and ignorance; the tenant, for want of instruction, will be unskilful, and for want of admonition, will be negligent. The Laird in these wide estates, which often consist of islands remote from one another, cannot extend his personal influence to all his tenants; and the steward having no dignity annexed to his character, can have little authority among men taught to pay reverence only to birth, and who regard the Tacksman as their hereditary superior; nor can the steward have equal zeal for the prosperity of an estate profitable only to the Laird, with the Tacksman, who has the Laird's income involved in his own.

The only gentlemen in the Islands are the Lairds, the Tacksmen, and the Ministers, who frequently improve their livings by becoming farmers. If the Tacksmen be banished, who will be left to impart knowledge, or impress civility? The Laird must always be at a distance from the greater part of his lands; and if he resides at all upon them, must drag his days in solitude, having no longer either a friend or a companion; he will therefore depart to some more comfortable residence, and leave the tenants to the wisdom and mercy of a factor.

Of tenants there are different orders, as they have greater or less stock. Land is sometimes leased to a small fellowship, who live in a cluster of huts, called a Tenants Town, and are bound jointly and separately for the payment of their rent. These, I believe, employ in the care of their cattle, and the labour of tillage, a kind of tenants yet lower; who having a hut, with grass for a certain number of cows and sheep, pay their rent by a stipulated quantity of labour.

The condition of domestick servants, or the price of occasional labour, I do not know with certainty. I was told that the maids have sheep, and are allowed to spin for their own clothing; perhaps they have no pecuniary wages, or none but in very wealthy families. The state of life, which has hitherto been purely pastoral, begins now to be a little variegated with commerce; but novelties enter by degrees, and till one mode has fully prevailed over the other, no settled notion can be formed.

Such is the system of insular subordination, which, having little variety, cannot afford much delight in the view, nor long detain the mind in contemplation. The inhabitants were for a long time perhaps not unhappy; but their content was a muddy mixture of pride and ignorance, an indifference for pleasures which they did not know, a blind veneration for their chiefs, and a strong conviction of their own importance.

Their pride has been crushed by the heavy hand of a vindictive conqueror, whose severities have been followed by laws, which, though they cannot be called cruel, have produced much discontent, because they operate upon the surface of life, and make every eye bear witness to subjection. To be compelled to a new dress has always been found painful.

Their Chiefs being now deprived of their jurisdiction, have already lost much of their influence; and as they gradually degenerate from patriarchal rulers to rapacious landlords, they will divest themselves of the little that remains.

That dignity which they derived from an opinion of their military importance, the law, which disarmed them, has abated. An old gentleman, delighting himself with the recollection of better days, related, that forty years ago, a Chieftain walked out attended by ten or twelve followers, with their arms rattling. That animating rabble has now ceased. The Chief has lost his formidable retinue;

and the Highlander walks his heath unarmed and defenceless, with the peaceable submission of a French peasant or English cottager.

Their ignorance grows every day less, but their knowledge is yet of little other use than to shew them their wants. They are now in the period of education, and feel the uneasiness of discipline, without yet perceiving the benefit of instruction.

The last law, by which the Highlanders are deprived of their arms, has operated with efficacy beyond expectation. Of former statutes made with the same design, the execution had been feeble, and the effect inconsiderable. Concealment was undoubtedly practised, and perhaps often with connivance. There was tenderness, or partiality, on one side, and obstinacy on the other. But the law, which followed the victory of Culloden, found the whole nation dejected and intimidated; informations were given without danger, and without fear, and the arms were collected with such rigour, that every house was despoiled of its defence.

To disarm part of the Highlands, could give no reasonable occasion of complaint. Every government must be allowed the power of taking away the weapon that is lifted against it. But the loyal clans murmured, with some appearance of justice, that after having defended the King, they were forbidden for the future to defend themselves; and that the sword should be forfeited, which had been legally employed. Their case is undoubtedly hard, but in political regulations, good cannot be complete, it can only be predominant.

Whether by disarming a people thus broken into several tribes, and thus remote from the seat of power, more good than evil has been produced, may deserve inquiry. The supreme power in every community has the right of debarring every individual, and every subordinate society from self-defence, only because the supreme power is able to defend them; and therefore where the governor cannot act, he must trust the subject to act for himself. These Islands might be wasted with fire and sword before their sovereign would know their distress. A gang of robbers, such as has been lately found confederating themselves in the Highlands, might lay a wide region under contribution. The crew of a petty privateer might land on the largest and most wealthy of the Islands, and riot without control in cruelty and waste. It was observed by one of the Chiefs of Sky, that fifty armed men might, without resistance, ravage the country. Laws that place the subjects in such a state, contravene the first principles of the compact of authority: they exact obedience, and yield no protection.

It affords a generous and manly pleasure to conceive a little nation gathering its fruits and tending its herds with fearless confidence, though it lies open on every side to invasion, where, in contempt of walls and trenches, every man sleeps securely with his sword beside him; where all on the first approach of hostility came together at the call to battle, as at a summons to a festal show; and committing their cattle to the care of those whom age or nature has disabled, engage the enemy with that competition for hazard and for glory, which operate in men that fight under the eye of those, whose dislike or kindness they have always considered as the greatest evil or the greatest good.

This was, in the beginning of the present century, the state of the Highlands. Every man was a soldier, who partook of national confidence, and interested himself in national honour. To lose this spirit, is to lose what no small advantage will compensate.

It may likewise deserve to be inquired, whether a great nation ought to be totally commercial? whether amidst the uncertainty of human affairs, too much attention to one mode of happiness may not endanger others? whether the pride of riches must not sometimes have recourse to the protection of courage? and whether, if it be necessary to preserve in some part of the empire the military spirit, it can subsist more commodiously in any place, than in remote and unprofitable provinces, where it can commonly do little harm, and whence it may be called forth at any sudden exigence?

It must however be confessed, that a man, who places honour only in successful violence, is a very troublesome and pernicious animal in time of peace; and that the martial character cannot prevail in a whole people, but by the diminution of all other virtues. He that is accustomed to resolve all right into conquest, will have very little tenderness or equity. All the friendship in such a life can be only a confederacy of invasion, or alliance of defence. The strong must flourish by force, and the weak subsist by stratagem.

Till the Highlanders lost their ferocity, with their arms, they suffered from each other all that malignity could dictate, or precipitance could act. Every provocation was revenged with blood, and no man that ventured into a numerous company, by whatever occasion brought together, was sure of returning without a wound.

If they are now exposed to foreign hostilities, they may talk of the danger, but can seldom feel it. If they are no longer martial, they are no longer quarrelsome. Misery is caused for the most part, not by a heavy crush of disaster, but by the corrosion of less visible evils, which canker enjoyment, and undermine security. The visit of an invader is necessarily rare, but domestick animosities allow no cessation.

The abolition of the local jurisdictions, which had for so many ages been exercised by the chiefs, has likewise its evil and its good. The feudal constitution naturally diffused itself into long ramifications of subordinate authority. To this general temper of the government was added the peculiar form of the country, broken by mountains into many subdivisions scarcely accessible but to the natives, and guarded by passes, or perplexed with intricacies, through which national justice could not find its way.

The power of deciding controversies, and of punishing offences, as some such power there must always be, was intrusted to the Lairds of the country, to those whom the people considered as their natural judges. It cannot be supposed that a rugged proprietor of the rocks, unprincipled and unenlightened, was a nice resolver of entangled claims, or very exact in proportioning punishment to offences. But the more he indulged his own will, the more he held his vassals in dependance. Prudence and innocence, without the favour of the Chief, conferred no security; and crimes involved no danger, when the judge was resolute to acquit.

When the chiefs were men of knowledge and virtue, the convenience of a domestick judicature was great. No long journies were necessary, nor artificial delays could be practised; the character, the alliances, and interests of the litigants were known to the court, and all false pretences were easily detected. The sentence, when it was past, could not be evaded; the power of the Laird superseded formalities, and justice could not be defeated by interest or stratagem.

I doubt not but that since the regular judges have made their circuits through the whole country, right has been every where more wisely and more equally distributed; the complaint is, that litigation is grown troublesome, and that the magistrates are too few, and therefore often too remote for general convenience.

Many of the smaller Islands have no legal officer within them. I once asked, If a crime should be committed, by what authority the offender could be seized? and was told, that the Laird would exert his right; a right which he must now usurp, but which surely necessity must vindicate, and which is therefore yet exercised in lower degrees, by some of the proprietors, when legal processes cannot be obtained.

In all greater questions, however, there is now happily an end to all fear or hope from malice or from favour. The roads are secure in those places through which, forty years ago, no traveller could pass without a convoy. All trials of right by the sword are forgotten, and the mean are in as little danger from the powerful as in other places. No scheme of policy has, in any country, yet brought the rich and poor on equal terms into courts of judicature. Perhaps experience, improving on experience, may in time effect it.

Those who have long enjoyed dignity and power, ought not to lose it without some equivalent. There was paid to the Chiefs by the publick, in exchange for their privileges, perhaps a sum greater than most of them had ever possessed, which excited a thirst for riches, of which it showed them the use. When the power of birth and station ceases, no hope remains but from the prevalence of money. Power and wealth supply the place of each other. Power confers the ability of gratifying our desire without the consent of others. Wealth enables us to obtain the consent of others to our gratification. Power, simply considered, whatever it confers on one, must take from another. Wealth enables its owner to give to others, by taking only from himself. Power pleases the violent and proud: wealth delights the placid and the timorous. Youth therefore flies at power, and age grovels after riches.

The Chiefs, divested of their prerogatives, necessarily turned their thoughts to the improvement of their revenues, and expect more rent, as they have less homage. The tenant, who is far from perceiving that his condition is made better in the same proportion, as that of his landlord is made worse, does not immediately see why his industry is to be taxed more heavily than before. He refuses to pay the demand, and is ejected; the ground is then let to a stranger, who perhaps brings a larger stock, but who, taking the land at its full price, treats with the Laird upon equal terms, and considers him not as a Chief, but as a trafficker in land. Thus the estate perhaps is improved, but the clan is broken.

It seems to be the general opinion, that the rents have been raised with too much eagerness. Some regard must be paid to prejudice. Those who have hitherto paid but little, will not suddenly be persuaded to pay much, though they can afford it. As ground is gradually improved, and the value of money decreases, the rent may be raised without any diminution of the farmer's profits: yet it is necessary in these countries, where the ejection of a tenant is a greater evil, than in more populous places, to consider not merely what the land will produce, but with what ability the inhabitant can cultivate it. A certain stock can allow but a certain payment; for if the land be doubled, and the stock remains the same, the tenant becomes no richer. The proprietors of the Highlands might perhaps often increase their income, by subdividing the farms, and allotting to every occupier only so many acres as he can profitably employ, but that they want people.

There seems now, whatever be the cause, to be through a great part of the Highlands a general discontent. That adherence, which was lately professed by every man to the chief of his name, has now little prevalence; and he that cannot live as he desires at home, listens to the tale of fortunate islands, and happy regions, where every man may have land of his own, and eat the product of his labour without a superior.

Those who have obtained grants of American lands, have, as is well known, invited settlers from all quarters of the globe; and among other places, where oppression might produce a wish for new habitations, their emissaries would not fail to try their persuasions in the Isles of Scotland, where at the time when the clans were newly disunited from their Chiefs, and exasperated by unprecedented exactions, it is no wonder that they prevailed.

Whether the mischiefs of emigration were immediately perceived, may be justly questioned. They who went first, were probably such as could best be spared; but the accounts sent by the earliest adventurers, whether true or false, inclined many to follow them; and whole neighbourhoods formed parties for removal; so that departure from their native country is no longer exile. He that goes thus accompanied, carries with him all that makes life pleasant. He sits down in a better climate, surrounded by his kindred and his friends: they carry with them their language, their opinions, their popular songs, and hereditary merriment: they change nothing but the place of their abode; and of that change they perceive the benefit.

This is the real effect of emigration, if those that go away together settle on the same spot, and preserve their ancient union. But some relate that these adventurous visitants of unknown regions, after a voyage passed in dreams of plenty and felicity, are dispersed at last upon a Sylvan wilderness, where their first years must be spent in toil, to clear the ground which is afterwards to be tilled, and that the whole effect of their undertaking is only more fatigue and equal scarcity.

Both accounts may be suspected. Those who are gone will endeavour by every art to draw others after them; for as their numbers are greater, they will provide better for themselves. When *Nova Scotia* was first peopled, I remember a letter, published under the character of a New Planter, who related how much the climate put him in mind of Italy. Such intelligence the *Hebridians* probably receive from their transmarine correspondents. But with equal temptations of interest, and perhaps with no greater niceness of veracity, the owners of the Islands spread stories of American hardships to keep their people content at home.

Some method to stop this epidemick desire of wandering, which spreads its contagion from valley to valley, deserves to be sought with great diligence. In more fruitful countries, the removal of one only makes room for the succession of another: but in the *Hebrides*, the loss of an inhabitant leaves a lasting vacuity; for nobody born in any other parts of the world will choose this country for his residence; and an Island once depopulated will remain a desert, as long as the present facility of travel gives every one, who is discontented and unsettled, the choice of his abode.

Let it be inquired, whether the first intention of those who are fluttering on the wing, and collecting a flock that they may take their flight, be to attain good, or to avoid evil. If they are dissatisfied with that part of the globe, which their birth has allotted them, and resolve not to live without the pleasures of happier climates; if they long for bright suns, and calm skies, and flowery fields, and fragrant gardens, I know not by what eloquence they can be persuaded, or by what offers they can be hired to stay.

But if they are driven from their native country by positive evils, and disgusted by ill-treatment, real or imaginary, it were fit to remove their grievances, and quiet their resentment; since, if they have been hitherto undutiful subjects, they will not much mend their principles by American conversation.

To allure them into the army, it was thought proper to indulge them in the continuance of their national dress. If this concession could have any effect, it might easily be made. That dissimilitude of appearance, which was supposed to keep them distinct from the rest of the nation, might disincline them from coalescing with the *Pensylvanians*, or people of *Connecticut*. If the restitution of their arms will reconcile them to their country, let them have again those weapons, which will not be more mischievous at home than in the Colonies. That they may not fly from the increase of rent, I know not whether the general good does not require that the land-lords be, for a time, restrained in their demands, and kept quiet by pensions proportionate to their loss.

To hinder insurrection, by driving away the people, and to govern peaceably, by having no subjects, is an expedient that argues no great profundity of politicks. To soften the obdurate, to convince the mistaken, to mollify the resentful, are worthy of a statesman; but it affords a legislator like self-applause to consider, that where there was formerly an insurrection, there is now a wilderness.

It has been a question often agitated without solution, why those northern regions are now so thinly peopled, which formerly over-whelmed with their armies the Roman empire. The question sup-poses what I believe is not true, that they had once more inhabi-tants than they could maintain, and overflowed only because they were full.

This is to estimate the manners of all countries and ages by our own. Migration, while the state of life was unsettled, and there was little communication of intelligence between distant places, was among the wilder nations of Europe, capricious and casual. An adventurous projector heard of a fertile coast unoccupied, and led out a colony; a chief of renown for bravery, called the young men together, and led them out to try what fortune would present. When Cæsar was in *Gaul*, he found the Helvetians preparing to go they knew not whither, and put a stop to their motions. They settled again in their own country, where they were so far from wanting room, that they had accumulated three years provision for their march.

The religion of the North was military; if they could not find enemies, it was their duty to make them: they travelled in quest of danger, and willingly took the chance of Empire or Death. If their troops were numerous, the countries from which they were collected are of vast extent, and without much exuberance of people great armies may be raised where every man is a soldier. But their true numbers were never known. Those who were conquered by them are their historians, and shame may have excited them to say, that they were overwhelmed with multitudes. To count is a modern practice, the ancient method was to guess; and when numbers are guessed they are always magnified.

Thus England has for several years been filled with the atchievements of seventy thousand Highlanders employed in *America*. I have heard from an English officer, not much inclined to favour them, that their behaviour deserved a very high degree of military praise; but their number has been much exaggerated. One of the ministers told me, that seventy thousand men could not have been found in all the Highlands, and that more than twelve thousand never took the field. Those that went to the American war, went to destruction. Of the old Highland regiment, consisting of twelve hundred, only seventy-six survived to see their country again.

The Gothick swarms have at least been multiplied with equal liberality. That they bore no great proportion to the inhabitants, in whose countries they settled, is plain from the paucity of northern words now found in the provincial languages. Their country was not deserted for want of room, because it was covered with forests of vast extent; and the first effect of plenitude of inhabitants is the destruction of wood. As the Europeans spread over *America*, the lands are gradually laid naked.

I would not be understood to say, that necessity had never any part in their expeditions. A nation, whose agriculture is scanty or unskilful, may be driven out by famine. A nation of hunters may have exhausted their game. I only affirm that the northern regions were not, when their irruptions subdued the Romans, overpeopled with regard to their real extent of territory, and power of fertility. In a country fully inhabited, however afterward laid waste, evident marks will remain of its former populousness. But of *Scandinavia* and *Germany*, nothing is known but that as we trace their state upwards into antiquity, their woods were greater, and their cultivated ground was less.

That causes very different from want of room may produce a general disposition to seek another country is apparent from the present conduct of the Highlanders, who are in some places ready to threaten a total secession. The numbers which have already gone, though like other numbers they may be magnified, are very great, and such as if they had gone together and agreed upon any certain settlement, might have founded an independent government in the depths of the western continent. Nor are they only the lowest and most indigent; many men of considerable wealth have taken with them their train of labourers and dependants; and if they continue the feudal scheme of polity, may establish new clans in the other hemisphere.

That the immediate motives of their desertion must be imputed to their landlords, may be reasonably concluded, because some Lairds of more prudence and less rapacity have kept their vassals undiminished. From *Raasay* only one man had been seduced, and at *Col* there was no wish to go away.

The traveller who comes hither from more opulent countries, to speculate upon the remains of pastoral life, will not much wonder that a common Highlander has no strong adherence to his native soil; for of animal enjoyments, or of physical good, he leaves nothing that he may not find again wheresoever he may be thrown.

The habitations of men in the *Hebrides* may be distinguished into huts and houses. By a *house*, I mean a building with one story over another; by a *hut*, a dwelling with only one floor. The Laird, who formerly lived in a castle, now lives in a house; sometimes sufficiently neat, but seldom very spacious or splendid. The Tacksmen and the Ministers have commonly houses. Wherever there is a house, the stranger finds a welcome, and to the other evils of exterminating Tacksmen may be added the unavoidable cessation of hospitality, or the devolution of too heavy a burden on the Ministers.

Of the houses little can be said. They are small, and by the necessity of accumulating stores, where there are so few opportunities of purchase, the rooms are very heterogeneously filled. With want of cleanliness it were ingratitude to reproach them. The servants having been bred upon the naked earth, think every floor clean, and the quick succession of guests, perhaps not always over-elegant, does not allow much time for adjusting their apartments.

Huts are of many gradations; from murky dens, to commodious dwellings.

The wall of a common hut is always built without mortar, by a skilful adaptation of loose stones. Sometimes perhaps a double wall of stones is raised, and the intermediate space filled with earth. The air is thus completely excluded. Some walls are, I think, formed of turfs, held together by a wattle, or texture of twigs. Of the meanest huts, the first room is lighted by the entrance, and the second by the smoke-hole. The fire is usually made in the middle. But there are huts, or dwellings, of only one story, inhabited by gentlemen, which have walls cemented with mortar, glass windows, and boarded floors. Of these all have chimneys, and some chimneys have grates.

The house and the furniture are not always nicely suited. We were driven once, by missing a passage, to the hut of a gentleman, where, after a very liberal supper, when I was conducted to my chamber, I found an elegant bed of Indian cotton, spread with fine sheets. The accommodation was flattering; I undressed myself, and felt my feet in the mire. The bed stood upon the bare earth, which a long course of rain had softened to a puddle.

In pastoral countries the condition of the lowest rank of people is sufficiently wretched. Among manufacturers, men that have no property may have art and industry, which make them necessary, and therefore valuable. But where flocks and corn are the only wealth, there are always more hands than work, and of that work there is little in which skill and dexterity can be much distinguished. He therefore who is born poor never can be rich. The son merely occupies the place of the father, and life knows nothing of progression or advancement.

The petty tenants, and labouring peasants, live in miserable cabins, which afford them little more than shelter from the storms. The Boor of *Norway* is said to make all his own utensils. In the *Hebrides*, whatever might be their ingenuity, the want of wood leaves them no materials. They are probably content with such accommodations as stones of different forms and sizes can afford them.

Their food is not better than their lodging. They seldom taste the flesh of land animals; for here are no markets. What each man eats is from his own stock. The great effect of money is to break property into small parts. In towns, he that has a shilling may have a piece of meat; but where there is no commerce, no man can eat mutton but by killing a sheep.

Fish in fair weather they need not want; but, I believe, man never lives long on fish, but by constraint; he will rather feed upon roots and berries.

The only fewel of the Islands is peat. Their wood is all consumed, and coal they have not yet found. Peat is dug out of the marshes, from the depth of one foot to that of six. That is accounted the best which is nearest the surface. It appears to be a mass of black earth held together by vegetable fibres. I know not whether the earth be bituminous, or whether the fibres be not the only combustible part; which, by heating the interposed earth red hot, make a burning mass. The heat is not very strong or lasting. The ashes are yellowish, and in a large quantity. When they dig peat, they cut it into square pieces, and pile it up to dry beside the house. In some places it has an offensive smell. It is like wood charked for the smith. The common method of making peat fires, is by heaping it on the hearth; but it burns well in grates, and in the best houses is so used.

The common opinion is, that peat grows again where it has been cut; which, as it seems to be chiefly a vegetable substance, is not unlikely to be true, whether known or not to those who relate it.

There are water mills in *Sky* and *Raasay*; but where they are too far distant, the house-wives grind their oats with a quern, or hand-mill, which consists of two stones, about a foot and a half in diameter, the lower is a little convex, to which the concavity of the upper must be fitted. In the middle of the upper stone is a round hole, and on one side is a long handle. The grinder sheds the corn gradually into the hole with one hand, and works the handle round with the other. The corn slides down the convexity of the lower stone, and by the motion of the upper is ground in its passage. These stones are found in *Lochabar*.

The Islands afford few pleasures, except to the hardy sportsman, who can tread the moor and climb the mountain. The distance of one family from another, in a country where travelling has so much difficulty, makes frequent intercourse impracticable. Visits last several days, and are commonly paid by water; yet I never saw a boat furnished with benches, or made commodious by any addition to the first fabrick. Conveniencies are not missed where they never were enjoyed.

The solace which the bagpipe can give, they have long enjoyed; but among other changes, which the last Revolution introduced, the use of the bagpipe begins to be forgotten. Some of the chief families still entertain a piper, whose office was anciently hereditary. *Macrimmon* was piper to *Macleod*, and *Rankin* to *Maclean* of *Col.*

The tunes of the bagpipe are traditional. There has been in *Sky*, beyond all time of memory, a college of pipers, under the direction of *Macrimmon*, which is not quite extinct. There was another in *Mull*, superintended by *Rankin*, which expired about sixteen years ago. To these colleges, while the pipe retained its honour, the students of musick repaired for education. I have had my dinner exhilarated by the bagpipe, at *Armidale*, at *Dunvegan*, and in *Col.*

The general conversation of the Islanders has nothing particular. I did not meet with the inquisitiveness of which I have read, and suspect the judgment to have been rashly made. A stranger of curiosity comes into a place where a stranger is seldom seen: he importunes the people with questions, of which they cannot guess the motive, and gazes with surprise on things which they, having had them always before their eyes, do not suspect of any thing wonderful. He appears to them like some being of another world, and then thinks it peculiar that they take their turn to inquire whence he comes, and whither he is going.

The Islands were long unfurnished with instruction for youth, and none but the sons of gentlemen could have any literature. There are now parochial schools, to which the lord of every manor pays a certain stipend. Here the children are taught to read; but by the rule of their institution, they teach only *English*, so that the natives read a language which they may never use or understand. If a parish, which often happens, contains several Islands, the school being but in one, cannot assist the rest. This is the state of *Col*, which, however, is more enlightened than some other places; for the deficiency is supplied by a young gentleman, who, for his own improvement, travels every year on foot over the Highlands to the session at Aberdeen; and at his return, during the vacation, teaches to read and write in his native Island.

In *Sky* there are two grammar schools, where boarders are taken to be regularly educated. The price of board is from three pounds, to four pounds ten shillings a year, and that of instruction is half a crown a quarter. But the scholars are birds of passage, who live at school only in the summer; for in winter provisions cannot be made for any considerable number in one place. This periodical dispersion impresses strongly the scarcity of these countries.

Having heard of no boarding-school for ladies nearer than *Inver-*

739

ness, I suppose their education is generally domestick. The elder daughters of the higher families are sent into the world, and may contribute by their acquisitions to the improvement of the rest.

Women must here study to be either pleasing or useful. Their deficiencies are seldom supplied by very liberal fortunes. A hundred pounds is a portion beyond the hope of any but the Laird's daughter. They do not indeed often give money with their daughters; the question is, How many cows a young lady will bring her husband. A rich maiden has from ten to forty; but two cows are a decent fortune for one who pretends to no distinction.

The religion of the Islands is that of the Kirk of *Scotland*. The gentlemen with whom I conversed are all inclined to the *English* liturgy; but they are obliged to maintain the established Minister, and the country is too poor to afford payment to another, who must live wholly on the contribution of his audience.

They therefore all attend the worship of the Kirk, as often as a visit from their Minister, or the practicability of travelling, gives them opportunity; nor have they any reason to complain of insufficient pastors; for I saw not one in the Islands, whom I had reason to think either deficient in learning, or irregular in life; but found several with whom I could not converse without wishing, as my respect increased, that they had not been Presbyterians.

The ancient rigour of puritanism is now very much relaxed, though all are not yet equally enlightened. I sometimes met with prejudices sufficiently malignant, but they were prejudices of ignorance. The Ministers in the Islands had attained such knowledge as may justly be admired in men, who have no motive to study, but generous curiosity, or, what is still better, desire of usefulness; with such politeness as so narrow a circle of converse could not have supplied, but to minds naturally disposed to elegance.

Reason and truth will prevail at last. The most learned of the Scottish Doctors would now gladly admit a form of prayer, if the people would endure it. The zeal or rage of congregations has its different degrees. In some parishes the Lord's Prayer is suffered: in others it is still rejected as a form; and he that should make it part of his supplication would be suspected of heretical pravity.

The principle upon which extemporary prayer was originally introduced, is no longer admitted. The Minister formerly, in the effusion of his prayer, expected immediate, and perhaps perceptible inspiration, and therefore thought it his duty not to think before what he should say. It is now universally confessed, that men pray as they speak on other occasions, according to the general measure of their abilities and attainments. Whatever each may think of a form prescribed by another, he cannot but believe that he can himself compose by study and meditation a better prayer than will rise in his mind at a sudden call; and if he has any hope of supernatural help, why may he not as well receive it when he writes as when he speaks?

In the variety of mental powers, some must perform extemporary prayer with much imperfection; and in the eagerness and rashness of contradictory opinions, if publick liturgy be left to the private judgment of every Minister, the congregation may often be offended or misled.

There is in Scotland, as among ourselves, a restless suspicion of popish machinations, and a clamour of numerous converts to the Romish religion. The report is, I believe, in both parts of the Island equally false. The Romish religion is professed only in *Egg* and *Canna*, two small islands, into which the Reformation never made its way. If any missionaries are busy in the Highlands, their zeal entitles them to respect, even from those who cannot think favourably of their doctrine.

The political tenets of the Islanders I was not curious to investigate, and they were not eager to obtrude. Their conversation is decent and inoffensive. They disdain to drink for their principles, and there is no disaffection at their tables. I never heard a health offered by a Highlander that might not have circulated with propriety within the precincts of the King's palace.

Legal government has yet something of novelty to which they cannot perfectly conform. The ancient spirit, that appealed only to the sword, is yet among them. The tenant of *Scalpa*, an island belonging to Macdonald, took no care to bring his rent; when the landlord talked of exacting payment, he declared his resolution to keep his ground, and drive all intruders from the Island, and continued to feed his cattle as on his own land, till it became necessary for the Sheriff to dislodge him by violence.

The various kinds of superstition which prevailed here, as in all other regions of ignorance, are by the diligence of the Ministers almost extirpated.

Of *Browny*, mentioned by Martin, nothing has been heard for many years. *Browny* was a sturdy Fairy; who, if he was fed, and kindly treated, would, as they said, do a great deal of work. They now pay him no wages, and are content to labour for themselves.

In *Troda*, within these three-and-thirty years, milk was put every Saturday for *Greogach*, or *the Old Man with the Long Beard*. Whether *Greogach* was courted as kind, or dreaded as terrible, whether they meant, by giving him the milk, to obtain good, or avert evil, I was not informed. The Minister is now living by whom the practice was abolished.

They have still among them a great number of charms for the cure of different diseases; they are all invocations, perhaps transmitted to them from the times of popery, which increasing knowledge will bring into disuse.

They have opinions, which cannot be ranked with superstition, because they regard only natural effects. They expect better crops of grain, by sowing their seed in the moon's increase. The moon has great influence in vulgar philosophy. In my memory it was a precept annually given in one of the *English* Almanacks, *to kill hogs when the moon was increasing, and the bacon would prove the better in boiling*.

We should have had little claim to the praise of curiosity, if we had not endeavoured with particular attention to examine the question of the *Second Sight*. Of an opinion received for centuries by a whole nation, and supposed to be confirmed through its whole descent, by a series of successive facts, it is desirable that the truth should be established, or the fallacy detected.

The *Second Sight* is an impression made either by the mind upon the eye, or by the eye upon the mind, by which things distant or future are perceived, and seen as if they were present. A man on a journey far from home falls from his horse, another, who is perhaps at work about the house, sees him bleeding on the ground, commonly with a landscape of the place where the accident befalls him. Another seer, driving home his cattle, or wandering in idleness, or musing in the sunshine, is suddenly surprised by the appearance of a bridal ceremony, or funeral procession, and counts the mourners or attendants, of whom, if he knows them, he relates the names, if he knows them not, he can describe the dresses. Things distant are seen at the instant when they happen. Of things future I know not that there is any rule for determining the time between the Sight and the event.

This receptive faculty, for power it cannot be called, is neither voluntary nor constant. The appearances have no dependence upon choice: they cannot be summoned, detained, or recalled. The impression is sudden, and the effect often painful.

By the term *Second Sight*, seems to be meant a mode of seeing, superadded to that which Nature generally bestows. In the *Earse* it is called *Taisch*; which signifies likewise a spectre, or a vision. I know not, nor is it likely that the Highlanders ever examined, whether by *Taisch*, used for *Second Sight*, they mean the power of seeing, or the thing seen.

I do not find it to be true, as it is reported, that to the *Second Sight* nothing is presented but phantoms of evil. Good seems to have the same proportion in those visionary scenes, as it obtains in real life: almost all remarkable events have evil for their basis; and are either miseries incurred, or miseries escaped. Our sense is so much stronger of what we suffer, than of what we enjoy, that the ideas of pain predominate in almost every mind. What is recollection but a revival of vexations, or history but a record of wars, treasons, and calamities? Death, which is considered as the greatest evil, happens to all. The greatest good, be it what it will, is the lot but of a part.

That they should often see death is to be expected; because death is an event frequent and important. But they see likewise more pleasing incidents. A gentleman told me, that when he had once gone far from his own Island, one of his labouring servants predicted his return, and described the livery of his attendant, which he had never worn at home; and which had been, without any previous design, occasionally given him.

Our desire of information was keen, and our inquiry frequent. Mr. Boswell's frankness and gaiety made every body communicative; and we heard many tales of these airy shows, with more or less evidence and distinctness.

It is the common talk of the Lowland *Scots*, that the notion of the *Second Sight* is wearing away with other superstitions; and that its reality is no longer supposed, but by the grossest people. How far its prevalence ever extended, or what ground it has lost, I know not. The Islanders of all degrees, whether of rank or understanding, universally admit it, except the Ministers, who universally deny it, and are suspected to deny it, in consequence of a system, against conviction. One of them honestly told me, that he came to *Sky* with a resolution not to believe it.

Strong reasons for incredulity will readily occur. This faculty of seeing things out of sight is local, and commonly useless. It is a breach of the common order of things, without any visible reason or perceptible benefit. It is ascribed only to a people very little enlightened; and among them, for the most part, to the mean and the ignorant.

To the confidence of these objections it may be replied, that by presuming to determine what is fit, and what is beneficial, they presuppose more knowledge of the universal system than man has attained; and therefore depend upon principles too complicated and extensive for our comprehension; and that there can be no security in the consequence, when the premises are not understood; that the *Second Sight* is only wonderful because it is rare, for, considered in itself, it involves no more difficulty than dreams, or perhaps than the regular exercise of the cogitative faculty; that a general opinion of communicative impulses, or visionary representations, has prevailed in all ages and all nations; that particular instances have been given, with such evidence, as neither *Bacon* nor *Bayle* has been able to resist; that sudden impressions, which the event has verified, have been felt by more than own or publish them; that the *Second Sight* of the *Hebrides* implies only the local frequency of a power, which is nowhere totally unknown; and that where we are unable to decide by antecedent reason, we must be content to yield to the force of testimony.

By pretension to *Second Sight*, no profit was ever sought or gained. It is an involuntary affection, in which neither hope nor fear are known to have any part. Those who profess to feel it, do not boast of it as a privilege, nor are considered by others as advantageously distinguished. They have no temptation to feign; and their hearers have no motive to encourage the imposture.

To talk with any of these seers is not easy. There is one living in *Sky*, with whom we would have gladly conversed; but he was very gross and ignorant, and knew no *English*. The proportion in these countries of the poor to the rich is such, that if we suppose the quality to be accidental, it can very rarely happen to a man of education; and yet on such men it has sometimes fallen. There is now a Second Sighted gentleman in the Highlands, who complains of the terrors to which he is exposed.

The foresight of the Seers is not always prescience: they are impressed with images, of which the event only shews them the meaning. They tell what they have seen to others, who are at that time not more knowing than themselves, but may become at last very adequate witnesses, by comparing the narrative with its verification.

To collect sufficient testimonies for the satisfaction of the publick, or of ourselves, would have required more time than we could bestow. There is, against it, the seeming analogy of things confusedly seen, and little understood; and for it, the indistinct cry of national persuasion, which may be perhaps resolved at last into prejudice and tradition. I never could advance my curiosity to conviction; but came away at last only willing to believe.

As there subsists no longer in the Islands much of that peculiar and discriminative form of life, of which the idea had delighted our imagination, we were willing to listen to such accounts of past times as would be given us. But we soon found what memorials were to be expected from an illiterate people, whose whole time is a series of distress; where every morning is labouring with expedients for the evening; and where all mental pains or pleasure arose from the dread of winter, the expectation of spring, the caprices of their Chiefs, and the motions of the neighbouring clans; where there was neither shame from ignorance, nor pride in knowledge; neither curiosity to inquire, nor vanity to communicate.

The Chiefs indeed were exempt from urgent penury, and daily difficulties; and in their houses were preserved what accounts remained of past ages. But the Chiefs were sometimes ignorant and careless, and sometimes kept busy by turbulence and contention; and one generation of ignorance effaces the whole series of unwritten history. Books are faithful repositories, which may be a while neglected or forgotten; but when they are opened again, will again impart their instruction: memory, once interrupted, is not to be recalled. Written learning is a fixed luminary, which, after the cloud that had hidden it has past away, is again bright in its proper station. Tradition is but a meteor, which, if once it falls, cannot be rekindled.

It seems to be universally supposed, that much of the local history was preserved by the Bards, of whom one is said to have been retained by every great family. After these Bards were some of my first inquiries; and I received such answers as, for a while, made me please myself with my increase of knowledge; for I had not then learned how to estimate the narration of a Highlander.

They said that a great family had a *Bard* and a *Senachi*, who were the poet and historian of the house; and an old gentleman told me that he remembered one of each. Here was a dawn of intelligence. Of men that had lived within memory, some certain knowledge might be attained. Though the office had ceased, its effects might continue; the poems might be found, though there was no poet.

Another conversation indeed informed me, that the same man was both Bard and Senachi. This variation discouraged me; but as the practice might be different in different times, or at the same time in different families, there was yet no reason for supposing that I must necessarily sit down in total ignorance.

Soon after I was told by a gentleman, who is generally acknowledged the greatest master of *Hebridian* antiquities, that there had indeed once been both Bards and Senachies; and that *Senachi* signified *the man of talk*, or of conversation; but that neither Bard nor Senachi had existed for some centuries. I have no reason to suppose it exactly known at what time the custom ceased, nor did it probably cease in all houses at once. But whenever the practice of recitation was disused, the works, whether poetical or historical, perished with the authors; for in those times nothing had been written in the *Earse* language.

Whether the *Man of talk* was a historian, whose office was to tell truth, or a story-teller, like those which were in the last century, and perhaps are now among the Irish, whose trade was only to amuse, it now would be vain to inquire.

Most of the domestick offices were, I believe, hereditary; and probably the laureat of a clan was always the son of the last laureat. The history of the race could no otherwise be communicated, or retained; but what genius could be expected in a poet by inheritance?

The nation was wholly illiterate. Neither bards nor Senachies could write or read; but if they were ignorant, there was no danger of detection; they were believed by those whose vanity they flattered.

The recital of genealogies, which has been considered as very efficacious to the preservation of a true series of ancestry, was anciently made, when the heir of the family came to manly age. This practice has never subsisted within time of memory, nor was much credit due to such rehearsers, who might obtrude fictitious pedigrees, either to please their masters, or to hide the deficiency of their own memories.

Where the Chiefs of the Highlands have found the histories of their descent is difficult to tell; for no *Earse* genealogy was ever written. In general this only is evident, that the principal house of a clan must be very ancient, and that those must have lived long in a place, of whom it is not known when they came thither.

Thus hopeless are all attempts to find any traces of Highland learning. Nor are their primitive customs and ancient manner of life otherwise than very faintly and uncertainly remembered by the present race.

The peculiarities which strike the native of a commercial country, proceeded in a great measure from the want of money. To the servants and dependents that were not domesticks, and if an estimate be made from the capacity of any of their old houses which I have seen, their domesticks could have been but few, were appropriated certain portions of land for their support. *Macdonald* has a piece of ground yet, called the Bards or Senachies field. When a beef was killed for the house, particular parts were claimed as fees by the several officers, or workmen. What was the right of each I have not learned. The head belonged to the smith, and the udder of a cow to the piper: the weaver had likewise his particular part; and so many pieces followed these prescriptive claims, that the Laird's was at last but little.

The payment of rent in kind has been so long disused in England, that it is totally forgotten. It was practised very lately in the *Hebrides*, and probably still continues, not only at St. *Kilda*, where money is not yet known, but in others of the smaller and remoter Islands. It were perhaps to be desired, that no change in this particular should have been made. When the Laird could only eat the produce of his lands, he was under the necessity of residing upon them; and when the tenant could not convert his stock into more portable riches, he could never be tempted away from his farm, from the only place where he could be wealthy. Money confounds subordination, by overpowering the distinctions of rank and birth, and weakens authority by supplying power of resistance, or expedients for escape. The feudal system is formed for a nation employed in agriculture, and has never long kept its hold where gold and silver have become common.

Their arms were anciently the *Glaymore*, or great two-handed sword, and afterwards the two-edged sword and target, or buckler, which was sustained on the left arm. In the midst of the target, which was made of wood, covered with leather, and studded with nails, a slender lance, about two feet long, was sometimes fixed; it was heavy and cumberous, and accordingly has for some time past been gradually laid aside. Very few targets were at Culloden. The dirk, or broad dagger, I am afraid, was of more use in private quarrels than in battles. The Lochaber-ax is only a slight alteration of the old *English* bill.

After all that has been said of the force and terrour of the Highland sword, I could not find that the art of defence was any part of common education. The gentlemen were perhaps sometimes skilful gladiators, but the common men had no other powers than those of violence and courage. Yet it is well known, that the onset of the Highlanders was very formidable. As an army cannot consist of philosophers, a panick is easily excited by any unwonted mode of annoyance. New dangers are naturally magnified; and men accustomed only to exchange bullets at a distance, and rather to hear their enemies than see them, are discouraged and amazed when they find themselves encountered hand to hand, and catch the gleam of steel flashing in their faces.

The Highland weapons gave opportunity for many exertions of personal courage, and sometimes for single combats in the field; like those which occur so frequently in fabulous wars. At Falkirk, a gentleman now living, was, I suppose after the retreat of the King's troops, engaged at a distance from the rest with an Irish dragoon. They were both skilful swordsmen, and the contest was not easily decided: the dragoon at last had the advantage, and the Highlander called for quarter; but quarter was refused him, and the fight continued till he was reduced to defend himself upon his knee. At that instant one of the Macleods came to his rescue; who, as it is said, offered quarter to the dragoon, but he thought himself obliged to reject what he had before refused, and, as battle gives little time to deliberate, was immediately killed.

Funerals were formerly solemnized by calling multitudes together, and entertaining them at a great expence. This emulation of useless cost has been for some time discouraged, and at last in the Isle of *Sky* is almost suppressed.

Of the Earse language, as I understand nothing, I cannot say more than I have been told. It is the rude speech of a barbarous people, who had few thoughts to express, and were content, as they conceived grossly, to be grossly understood. After what has been lately talked of Highland Bards, and Highland genius, many will startle when they are told, that the *Earse* never was a written language; that there is not in the world an Earse manuscript a hundred years old; and that the sounds of the Highlanders were never expressed by letters, till some little books of piety were translated, and a metrical version of the Psalms was made by the synod of *Argyle*. Whoever therefore now writes in this language, spells according to his own perception of the sound, and his own idea of the power of the letters. The *Welsh* and the *Irish* are cultivated tongues. The Welsh, two hundred years ago, insulted their *English* neighbours for the instability of their Orthography; while the *Earse* merely floated in the breath of the people, and could therefore receive little improvement.

When a language begins to teem with books, it is tending to refinement; as those who undertake to teach others must have undergone some labour in improving themselves, they set a proportionate value on their own thoughts, and wish to enforce them by efficacious expressions; speech becomes embodied and permanent; different modes and phrases are compared, and the best obtains an establishment. By degrees one age improves upon another. Exactness is first obtained, and afterwards elegance. But diction, merely vocal, is always in its childhood. As no man leaves his eloquence behind him, the new generations have all to learn. There may possibly be books without a polished language, but there can be no polished language without books.

That the Bards could not read more than the rest of their countrymen, it is reasonable to suppose; because, if they had read, they could probably have written; and how high their compositions may reasonably be rated, an inquirer may best judge by considering what stores of imagery, what principles of ratiocination, what comprehension of knowledge, and what delicacy of elocution he has known any man attain who cannot read. The state of the Bards was yet more hopeless. He that cannot read, may now converse with those that can; but the Bard was a barbarian among barbarians, who, knowing nothing himself, lived with others that knew no more.

There has lately been in the Islands one of these illiterate poets, who hearing the Bible read at church, is said to have turned the sacred history into verse. I heard part of a dialogue, composed by him, translated by a young lady in *Mull*, and thought it had more

749

meaning than I expected from a man totally uneducated; but he had some opportunities of knowledge; he lived among a learned people. After all that has been done for the instruction of the Highlanders, the antipathy between their language and literature still continues; and no man that has learned only *Earse* is, at this time, able to read.

The *Earse* has many dialects, and the words used in some Islands are not always known in others. In literate nations, though the pronunciation, and sometimes the words of common speech, may differ, as now in *England*, compared with the South of *Scotland*, yet there is a written diction, which pervades all dialects, and is understood in every province. But where the whole language is colloquial, he that has only one part, never gets the rest, as he cannot get it but by change of residence.

In an unwritten speech, nothing that is not very short is transmitted from one generation to another. Few have opportunities of hearing a long composition often enough to learn it, or have inclination to repeat it so often as is necessary to retain it; and what is once forgotten is lost for ever. I believe there cannot be recovered, in the whole *Earse* language, five hundred lines of which there is any evidence to prove them a hundred years old. Yet I hear that the father of Ossian boasts of two chests more of ancient poetry, which he suppresses, because they are too good for the *English*.

He that goes into the Highlands with a mind naturally acquiescent, and a credulity eager for wonders, may come back with an opinion very different from mine; for the inhabitants knowing the ignorance of all strangers in their language and antiquities, perhaps are not very scrupulous adherents to truth; yet I do not say that they deliberately speak studied falsehood, or have a settled purpose to deceive. They have inquired and considered little, and do not always feel their own ignorance. They are not much accustomed to be interrogated by others; and seem never to have thought upon interrogating themselves; so that if they do not know what they tell to be true, they likewise do not distinctly perceive it to be false.

Mr. Boswell was very diligent in his inquiries; and the result of his investigations was, that the answer to the second question was commonly such as nullified the answer to the first.

We were a while told, that they had an old translation of the scriptures; and told it till it would appear obstinacy to inquire again. Yet by continued accumulation of questions we found, that the translation meant, if any meaning there were, was nothing else than the *Irish* Bible.

We heard of manuscripts that were, or that had been in the hands of somebody's father, or grandfather; but at last we had no reason to believe they were other than Irish. Martin mentions Irish, but never any Earse manuscripts, to be found in the Islands in his time.

I suppose my opinion of the poems of Ossian is already discovered. I believe they never existed in any other form than that which we have seen. The editor, or author, never could shew the original; nor can it be shewn by any other; to revenge reasonable incredulity, by refusing evidence, is a degree of insolence, with which the world is not yet acquainted; and stubborn audacity is the last refuge of guilt. It would be easy to shew it if he had it; but whence could it be had? It is too long to be remembered, and the language formerly had nothing written. He has doubtless inserted names that circulate in popular stories, and may have translated some wandering ballads, if any can be found; and the names, and some of the images being recollected, make an inaccurate auditor imagine, by the help of Caledonian bigotry, that he has formerly heard the whole.

I asked a very learned Minister in Sky, who had used all arts to make me believe the genuineness of the book, whether at last he believed it himself? but he would not answer. He wished me to be deceived, for the honour of his country; but would not directly and formally deceive me. Yet has this man's testimony been publickly produced, as of one that held Fingal to be the work of Ossian.

It is said, that some men of integrity profess to have heard parts of it, but they all heard them when they were boys; and it was never said that any of them could recite six lines. They remember names, and perhaps some proverbial sentiments; and having no distinct ideas, coin a resemblance without an original. The persuasion of the Scots, however, is far from universal; and in a question so capable of proof, why should doubt be suffered to continue? The editor has been heard to say, that part of the poem was received by him, in the Saxon character. He has then found, by some peculiar fortune, an unwritten language, written in a character which the natives probably never beheld.

I have yet supposed no imposture but in the publisher, yet I am far from certainty, that some translations have not been lately made, that may now be obtruded as parts of the original work. Credulity on one part is a strong temptation to deceit on the other, especially to deceit of which no personal injury is the consequence, and which flatters the author with his own ingenuity. The Scots have something to plead for their easy reception of an improbable fiction: they are seduced by their fondness for their supposed ancestors. A Scotchman must be a very sturdy moralist, who does not love *Scotland* better than truth: he will always love it better than inquiry; and if falsehood flatters his vanity, will not be very diligent to detect it. Neither ought the *English* to be much influenced by *Scotch* authority; for of the past and present state of the whole *Earse* nation, the Lowlanders are at least as ignorant as ourselves. To be ignorant is painful; but it is dangerous to quiet our uneasiness by the delusive opiate of hasty persuasion.

But this is the age in which those who could not read, have been supposed to write; in which the giants of antiquated romance have been exhibited as realities. If we know little of the ancient Highlanders, let us not fill the vacuity with *Ossian*. If we have not searched the *Magellanick* regions, let us however forbear to people them with *Patagons*.

Having waited some days at *Armidel*, we were flattered at last with a wind that promised to convey us to *Mull*. We went on board a boat that was taking in kelp, and left the Isle of *Sky* behind us. We were doomed to experience, like others, the danger of trusting to the wind, which blew against us, in a short time, with such violence, that we, being no seasoned sailors, were willing to call it a tempest. I was sea-sick, and lay down. Mr. *Boswell* kept the deck. The master knew not well whither to go; and our difficulties might perhaps have filled a very pathetick page, had not Mr. *Maclean* of *Col*, who, with every other qualification which insular life requires, is a very active and skilful mariner, piloted us safe into his own harbour.

COL

In the morning we found ourselves under the Isle of *Col*, where we landed; and passed the first day and night with captain *Maclean*, a gentleman who has lived some time in the *East Indies*; but having dethroned no Nabob, is not too rich to settle in his own country.

Next day the wind was fair, and we might have had an easy passage to *Mull*; but having, contrarily to our own intention, landed upon a new Island, we would not leave it wholly unexamined. We therefore suffered the vessel to depart without us, and trusted the skies for another wind.

Mr. *Maclean* of *Col*, having a very numerous family, has, for some time past, resided at *Aberdeen*, that he may superintend their education, and leaves the young gentleman, our friend, to govern his dominions, with the full power of a Highland Chief. By the absence of the Laird's family, our entertainment was made more difficult, because the house was in a great degree disfurnished; but young Col's kindness and activity supplied all defects, and procured us more than sufficient accommodation.

Here I first mounted a little Highland steed; and if there had been many spectators, should have been somewhat ashamed of my figure in the march. The horses of the Islands, as of other barren countries, are very low: they are indeed musculous and strong, beyond what their size gives reason for expecting; but a bulky man upon one of their backs makes a very disproportionate appearance.

From the habitation of captain *Maclean*, we went to *Grissipol*, but called by the way on Mr. *Hector Maclean*, the Minister of *Col*, whom we found in a hut, that is, a house of only one floor, but with windows and chimney, and not inelegantly furnished. Mr. *Maclean* has the reputation of great learning: he is seventy-seven years old, but not infirm, with a look of venerable dignity, excelling what I remember in any other man.

His conversation was not unsuitable to his appearance. I lost some of his goodwill, by treating a heretical writer with more regard than, in his opinion, a heretick could deserve. I honoured his orthodoxy, and did much censure his asperity. A man who has settled his opinions, does not love to have the tranquillity of his conviction disturbed; and at seventy-seven it is time to be in earnest.

Mention was made of the *Earse* translation of the New Testament, which has been lately published, and of which the learned Mr. Macqueen of Sky spoke with commendation; but Mr. Maclean said he did not use it, because he could make the text more intelligible to his auditors by an extemporary version. From this I in-

ferred, that the language of the translation was not the language of
the isle of *Col*.

He has no publick edifice for the exercise of his ministry; and can
officiate to no greater number, than a room can contain; and the
room of a hut is not very large. This is all the opportunity of
worship that is now granted to the inhabitants of the Island, some
of whom must travel thither perhaps ten miles. Two chapels were
erected by their ancestors, of which I saw the skeletons, which now
stand faithful witnesses of the triumph of Reformation.

The want of churches is not the only impediment to piety; there
is likewise a want of Ministers. A parish often contains more Islands
than one; and each Island can have the Minister only in its own
turn. At *Raasay* they had, I think, a right to service only every
third Sunday. All the provision made by the present ecclesiastical
constitution, for the inhabitants of about a hundred square miles,
is a prayer and sermon in a little room, once in three weeks: and
even this parsimonious distribution is at the mercy of the weather;
and in those Islands where the Minister does not reside, it is impossible to tell how many weeks or months may pass without any
publick exercise of religion.

GRISSIPOL IN COL

After a short conversation with Mr. *Maclean*, we went on to
Grissipol, a house and farm tenanted by Mr. *Macsweyn*, where I
saw more of the ancient life of a Highlander than I had yet found.
Mrs. *Macsweyn* could speak no *English*, and had never seen any
other places than the Islands of *Sky*, *Mull*, and *Col*: but she was
hospitable and good-humoured, and spread her table with sufficient liberality. We found tea here, as in every other place, but
our spoons were of horn.

The house of Grissipol stands by a brook very clear and quick;
which is, I suppose, one of the most copious streams in the Island.
This place was the scene of an action, much celebrated in the traditional history of *Col*, but which probably no two relaters will tell
alike.

Some time, in the obscure ages, *Macneil* of *Barra* married the
lady *Maclean*, who had the Isle of *Col* for her jointure. Whether
Macneil detained *Col*, when the widow was dead, or whether she
lived so long as to make her heirs impatient, is perhaps not now
known. The younger son, called *John Gerves*, or *John the Giant*, a

man of great strength, who was then in *Ireland*, either for safety, or for education, dreamed of recovering his inheritance; and getting some adventurers together, which, in those unsettled times, was not hard to do, invaded *Col*. He was driven away, but was not discouraged, and collecting new followers, in three years came again with fifty men. In his way he stopped at *Artorinish* in *Morvern*, where his uncle was prisoner to *Macleod*, and was then with his enemies in a tent. *Maclean* took with him only one servant, whom he ordered to stay at the outside; and where he should see the tent pressed outwards, to strike with his dirk; it being the intention of *Maclean*, as any man provoked him, to lay hands upon him, and push him back. He entered the tent alone, with his *Lochabar-axe* in his hand, and struck such terror into the whole assembly, that they dismissed his uncle.

When he landed at *Col*, he saw the sentinel, who kept watch towards the sea, running off to *Grissipol*, to give *Macneil*, who was there with a hundred and twenty men, an account of the invasion. He told *Macgill*, one of his followers, that if he intercepted that dangerous intelligence, by catching the courier, he would give him certain lands in *Mull*. Upon his promise, *Macgill* pursued the messenger, and either killed, or stopped him; and his posterity, till very lately, held the lands in *Mull*.

The alarm being thus prevented, he came unexpectedly upon *Macneil*. Chiefs were in those days never wholly unprovided for an enemy. A fight ensued, in which one of their followers is said to have given an extraordinary proof of activity, by bounding backwards over the brook of *Grissipol*. *Macneil* being killed, and many of his clan destroyed, *Maclean* took possession of the Island, which the *Macneils* attempted to conquer by another invasion, but were defeated and repulsed.

Maclean, in his turn, invaded the estate of the *Macneils*, took the castle of Brecacig, and conquered the isle of *Barra*, which he held for seven years, and then restored it to the heirs.

CASTLE OF COL

From *Grissipol*, Mr. *Maclean* conducted us to his father's seat; a neat new house, erected near the old castle, I think, by the last proprietor. Here we were allowed to take our station, and lived very commodiously, while we waited for moderate weather and a fair wind, which we did not so soon obtain, but we had time to get some information of the present state of *Col*, partly by inquiry, and partly by occasional excursions.

Col is computed to be thirteen miles in length, and three in breadth. Both the ends are the property of the Duke of *Argyle*, but the middle belongs to *Maclean*, who is called *Col*, as the only Laird.

Col is not properly rocky; it is rather one continued rock, of a surface much diversified with protuberances, and covered with a thin layer of earth, which is often broken, and discovers the stone. Such a soil is not for plants that strike deep roots; and perhaps in the whole Island nothing has ever yet grown to the height of a table. The uncultivated parts are clothed with heath, among which industry has interspersed spots of grass and corn; but no attempt has been made to raise a tree. Young *Col*, who has a very laudable desire of improving his patrimony, purposes some time to plant an orchard; which, if it be sheltered by a wall, may perhaps succeed. He has introduced the culture of turnips, of which he has a field, where the whole work was performed by his own hand. His intention is to provide food for his cattle in the winter. This innovation was considered by Mr. *Macsweyn* as the idle project of a young head, heated with *English* fancies; but he has now found that turnips will really grow, and that hungry sheep and cows will really eat them.

By such acquisitions as these, the *Hebrides* may in time rise above their annual distress. Wherever heath will grow, there is reason to think something better may draw nourishment; and by trying the production of other places, plants will be found suitable to every soil.

Col has many lochs, some of which have trouts and eels, and others have never yet been stocked; another proof of the negligence of the Islanders, who might take fish in the inland waters, when they cannot go to sea.

Their quadrupeds are horses, cows, sheep, and goats. They have neither deer, hares, nor rabbits. They have no vermin, except rats, which have been lately brought thither by sea, as to other places; and are free from serpents, frogs, and toads.

The harvest in *Col*, and in *Lewis*, is ripe sooner than in *Sky*; and the winter in *Col* is never cold, but very tempestuous. I know not that I ever heard the wind so loud in any other place; and Mr. *Boswell* observed, that its noise was all its own, for there were no trees to increase it.

Noise is not the worst effect of the tempests; for they have thrown the sand from the shore over a considerable part of the land; and it is said still to encroach and destroy more and more pasture; but I am not of opinion, that by any surveys or land-marks, its limits have been ever fixed, or its progression ascertained. If one man has confidence enough to say, that it advances, nobody can bring any proof to support him in denying it. The reason why it is not spread to a greater extent, seems to be, that the wind and rain come almost together, and that it is made close and heavy by the wet before the storms can put it in motion. So thick is the bed, and so small the particles, that if a traveller should be caught by a sudden gust in dry weather, he would find it very difficult to escape with life.

For natural curiosities, I was shown only two great masses of stone, which lie loose upon the ground; one on the top of a hill, and the other at a small distance from the bottom. They certainly were never put into their present places by human strength or skill; and though an earthquake might have broken off the lower stone, and rolled it into the valley, no account can be given of the other, which lies on the hill, unless, which I forgot to examine, there be still near it some higher rock, from which it might be torn. All nations have a tradition, that their earliest ancestors were giants, and these stones are said to have been thrown up and down by a giant and his mistress. There are so many more important things, of which human knowledge can give no account, that it may be forgiven us, if we speculate no longer on two stones in *Col*.

This Island is very populous. About nine-and-twenty years ago, the fencible men of *Col* were reckoned one hundred and forty, which is the sixth of eight hundred and forty; and probably some contrived to be left out of the list. The Minister told us, that a few years ago the inhabitants were eight hundred, between the ages of seven and of seventy. Round numbers are seldom exact. But in this case the authority is good, and the errour likely to be little. If to the eight hundred be added what the laws of computation require, they will be increased to at least a thousand; and if the dimensions of the country have been accurately related, every mile maintains more than twenty-five.

This proportion of habitation is greater than the appearance of the country seems to admit; for wherever the eye wanders, it sees much waste and little cultivation. I am more inclined to extend the land, of which no measure has ever been taken, than to diminish the people, who have been really numbered. Let it be supposed, that a computed mile contains a mile and a half, as was commonly found true in the mensuration of the *English* roads, and we shall then allot nearly twelve to a mile, which agrees much better with ocular observation.

Here, as in *Sky* and other Islands, are the Laird, the Tacksmen, and the under tenants.

Mr. *Maclean*, the Laird, has very extensive possessions, being proprietor, not only of far the greater part of *Col*, but of the extensive Island of *Rum*, and a very considerable territory in *Mull*.

Rum is one of the larger Islands, almost square, and therefore of great capacity in proportion to its sides. By the usual method of estimating computed extent, it may contain more than a hundred and twenty square miles.

It originally belonged to *Clanronald*, and was purchased by *Col*; who, in some dispute about the bargain, made *Clanronald* prisoner, and kept him nine months in confinement. Its owner represents it as mountainous, rugged, and barren. In the hills there are red deer. The horses are very small, but of a breed eminent for beauty. *Col*, not long ago, bought one of them from a tenant; who told him, that as he was of a shape uncommonly elegant, he could not sell him but at a high price; and that whoever had him should pay a guinea and a half.

There are said to be in *Barra* a race of horses yet smaller, of which the highest is not above thirty-six inches.

The rent of *Rum* is not great. Mr. *Maclean* declared, that he should be very rich, if he could set his land at two-pence halfpenny an acre. The inhabitants are fifty-eight families, who continued Papists for some time after the Laird became a Protestant. Their adherence to their old religion was strengthened by the countenance of the Laird's sister, a zealous Romanist, till one Sunday, as they were going to mass under the conduct of their patroness, *Maclean* met them on the way, gave one of them a blow on the head with a *yellow stick*, I suppose a cane, for which the *Earse* had no name, and drove them to the kirk, from which they have never since departed. Since the use of this method of conversion, the inhabitants of *Egg* and *Canna*, who continue Papists, call the Protestantism of *Rum*, the religion of the *Yellow Stick*.

The only Popish Islands are *Egg* and *Canna*. *Egg* is the principal

Island of a parish, in which, though he has no congregation, the Protestant Minister resides. I have heard of nothing curious in it, but the cave in which a former generation of the Islanders were smothered by *Macleod*.

If we had travelled with more leisure, it had not been fit to have neglected the Popish Islands. Popery is favourable to ceremony; and among ignorant nations, ceremony is the only preservative of tradition. Since protestantism was extended to the savage parts of Scotland, it has perhaps been one of the chief labours of the Ministers to abolish stated observances, because they continued the remembrance of the former religion. We therefore who came to hear old traditions, and see antiquated manners, should probably have found them amongst the Papists.

Canna, the other Popish Island, belongs to *Clanronald*. It is said not to comprise more than twelve miles of land, and yet maintains as many inhabitants as *Rum*.

We were at *Col* under the protection of the young Laird, without any of the distresses, which Mr. *Pennant*, in a fit of simple credulity, seems to think almost worthy of an elegy by Ossian. Wherever we roved, we were pleased to see the reverence with which his subjects regarded him. He did not endeavour to dazzle them by any magnificence of dress: his only distinction was a feather in his bonnet; but as soon as he appeared, they forsook their work and clustered about him: he took them by the hand, and they seemed mutually delighted. He has the proper disposition of a Chieftain, and seems desirous to continue the customs of his house. The bagpiper played regularly, when dinner was served, whose person and dress made a good appearance; and he brought no disgrace upon the family of *Rankin*, which has long supplied the Lairds of *Col* with hereditary musick.

The Tacksmen of *Col* seem to live with less dignity and convenience than those of *Sky*; where they had good houses, and tables not only plentiful, but delicate. In *Col* only two houses pay the window tax; for only two have six windows, which, I suppose, are the Laird's and Mr. *Macsweyn*'s.

The rents have, till within seven years, been paid in kind, but the tenants finding that cattle and corn varied in their price, desired for the future to give their landlord money; which, not having yet arrived at the philosophy of commerce, they consider as being every year of the same value.

We were told of a particular mode of undertenure. The Tacksman admits some of his inferiour neighbours to the cultivation of his grounds, on condition that performing all the work, and giving a third part of the seed, they shall keep a certain number of cows, sheep, and goats, and reap a third part of the harvest. Thus by less than the tillage of two acres they pay the rent of one.

There are tenants below the rank of Tacksmen, that have got smaller tenants under them; for in every place, where money is not the general equivalent, there must be some whose labour is immediately paid by daily food.

A country that has no money, is by no means convenient for beggars, both because such countries are commonly poor, and because charity requires some trouble and some thought. A penny is easily given upon the first impulse of compassion, or impatience of importunity; but few will deliberately search their cupboards or their granaries to find out something to give. A penny is likewise easily spent; but victuals, if they are unprepared, require house-room, and fire, and utensils, which the beggar knows not where to find.

Yet beggars there sometimes are, who wander from Island to Island. We had, in our passage to *Mull*, the company of a woman and her child, who had exhausted the charity of *Col*. The arrival of a beggar on an Island is accounted a sinistrous event. Every body considers that he shall have the less for what he gives away. Their alms, I believe, is generally oatmeal.

Near to *Col* is another Island called *Tireye*, eminent for its fertility. Though it has but half the extent of *Rum*, it is so well peopled, that there have appeared, not long ago, nine hundred and fourteen at a funeral. The plenty of this Island enticed beggars to it, who seemed so burdensome to the inhabitants, that a formal compact was drawn up, by which they obliged themselves to grant no more relief to casual wanderers, because they had among them an indigent woman of high birth, whom they considered as entitled to all that they could spare. I have read the stipulation, which was indited with juridical formality, but was never made valid by regular subscription.

If the inhabitants of *Col* have nothing to give, it is not that they are oppressed by their landlord: their leases seem to be very profitable. One farmer, who pays only seven pounds a year, has maintained seven daughters and three sons, of whom the eldest is educated at *Aberdeen* for the ministry; and now, at every vacation, opens a school in *Col*.

Life is here, in some respects, improved beyond the condition of some other Islands. In *Sky* what is wanted can only be bought, as the arrival of some wandering pedlar may afford an opportunity; but in *Col* there is a standing shop, and in *Mull* there are two. A shop in the Islands, as in other places of little frequentation, is a repository of every thing requisite for common use. Mr. *Boswell*'s journal was filled, and he bought some paper in *Col*. To a man that ranges the streets of *London*, where he is tempted to contrive wants for the pleasure of supplying them, a shop affords no image worthy of attention; but in an Island, it turns the balance of existence between good and evil. To live in perpetual want of little things, is a state not indeed of torture, but of constant vexation. I have in *Sky* had some difficulty to find ink for a letter; and if a woman breaks her needle, the work is at a stop.

As it is, the Islanders are obliged to content themselves with succedaneous means for many common purposes. I have seen the chief man of a very wide district riding with a halter for a bridle, and governing his hobby with a wooden curb.

The people of *Col*, however, do not want dexterity to supply some of their necessities. Several arts which make trades, and demand apprenticeships in great cities, are here the practices of daily economy. In every house candles are made, both moulded and dipped. Their wicks are small shreds of linen cloth. They all know how to extract from the Cuddy, oil for their lamps. They all tan skins, and make brogues.

As we travelled through *Sky*, we saw many cottages, but they very frequently stood single on the naked ground. In *Col*, where the hills opened a place convenient for habitation, we found a petty village, of which every hut had a little garden adjoining; thus they made an appearance of social commerce and mutual offices, and of some attention to convenience and future supply. There is not in the *Western Islands* any collection of buildings that can make pretensions to be called a town, except in the Isle of *Lewis*, which I have not seen.

If *Lewis* is distinguished by a town, *Col* has also something peculiar. The young Laird has attempted what no Islander perhaps ever thought on. He has begun a road capable of a wheel-carriage. He has carried it about a mile, and will continue it by annual elongation from his house to the harbour.

Of taxes here is no reason for complaining; they are paid by a very easy composition. The *malt-tax* for *Col* is twenty shillings. Whisky is very plentiful: there are several stills in the Island, and more is made than the inhabitants consume.

The great business of insular policy is now to keep the people in their own country. As the world has been let in upon them, they have heard of happier climates, and less arbitrary government; and if they are disgusted, have emissaries among them ready to offer them land and houses, as a reward for deserting their Chief and clan. Many have departed both from the main of *Scotland*, and from the Islands; and all that go may be considered as subjects lost to the *British* crown; for a nation scattered in the boundless regions of *America* resembles rays diverging from a focus. All the rays remain, but the heat is gone. Their power consisted in their concentration: when they are dispersed, they have no effect.

It may be thought that they are happier by the change; but they are not happy as a nation, for they are a nation no longer. As they contribute not to the prosperity of any community, they must want that security, that dignity, that happiness, whatever it be, which a prosperous community throws back upon individuals.

The inhabitants of *Col* have not yet learned to be weary of their heath and rocks, but attend their agriculture and their dairies, without listening to American seducements.

There are some however who think that this emigration has raised terrour disproportionate to its real evil; and that it is only a new mode of doing what was always done. The Highlands, they say, never maintained their natural inhabitants; but the people, when they found themselves too numerous, instead of extending cultivation, provided for themselves by a more compendious method, and sought better fortune in other countries. They did not indeed go away in collective bodies, but withdrew invisibly, a few at a time; but the whole number of fugitives was not less, and the difference between other times and this, is only the same as between evaporation and effusion.

This is plausible, but I am afraid it is not true. Those who went before, if they were not sensibly missed, as the argument supposes, must have gone either in less number, or in a manner less detrimental, than at present; because formerly there was no complaint.

Those who then left the country were generally the idle dependants on overburdened families, or men who had no property; and therefore carried away only themselves. In the present eagerness of emigration, families, and almost communities, go away together. Those who were considered as prosperous and wealthy sell their stock and carry away the money. Once none went away but the useless and poor; in some parts there is now reason to fear, that none will stay but those who are too poor to remove themselves, and too useless to be removed at the cost of others.

Of antiquity there is not more knowledge in *Col* than in other places; but every where something may be gleaned.

How ladies were portioned, when there was no money, it would be difficult for an *Englishman* to guess. In 1649, *Maclean* of *Dronart* in *Mull* married his sister *Fingala* to *Maclean* of *Coll*, with a hundred and eighty kine; and stipulated, that if she became a widow, her jointure should be three hundred and sixty. I suppose some proportionate tract of land was appropriated to their pasturage.

The disposition to pompous and expensive funerals which has at one time or other prevailed in most parts of the civilized world, is not yet suppressed in the Islands, though some of the ancient solemnities are worn away, and singers are no longer hired to attend the procession. Nineteen years ago, at the burial of the Laird of *Col*, were killed thirty cows, and about fifty sheep. The number of the cows is positively told, and we must suppose other victuals in like proportion.

Mr. *Maclean* informed us of an odd game, of which he did not tell the original, but which may perhaps be used in other places, where the reason of it is not yet forgot. At New-year's eve, in the hall or castle of the Laird, where, at festal seasons, there may be supposed a very numerous company, one man dresses himself in a cow's hide, upon which other men beat with sticks. He runs with all this noise round the house, which all the company quits in a counterfeited fright: the door is then shut. At New-year's eve there is no great pleasure to be had out of doors in the *Hebrides*. They are sure soon to recover from their terrour enough to solicit for re-admission; which, for the honour of poetry, is not to be obtained but by repeating a verse, with which those that are knowing and provident take care to be furnished.

Very near the house of *Maclean* stands the castle of *Col*, which was the mansion of the Laird, till the house was built. It is built upon a rock, as Mr. *Boswell* remarked, that it might not be mined. It is very strong, and having been not long uninhabited, is yet in repair. On the wall was, not long ago, a stone with an inscription, importing, that *if any man of the clan of Maclonich shall appear before this castle, though he come at midnight, with a man's head in his hand, he shall there find safety and protection against all but the King.*

This is an old Highland treaty made upon a very memorable occasion. *Maclean*, the son of *John Gerves*, who recovered *Col*, and conquered *Barra*, had obtained, it is said, from *James* the Second, a grant of the lands of *Lochiel*, forfeited, I suppose, by some offence against the state.

Forfeited estates were not in those days quietly resigned; *Maclean*, therefore, went with an armed force to seize his new possessions, and, I know not for what reason, took his wife with him. The *Camerons* rose in defence of their Chief, and a battle was fought at the head of *Loch Ness*, near the place where *Fort Augustus* now stands, in which *Lochiel* obtained the victory, and *Maclean*, with his followers, was defeated and destroyed.

The lady fell into the hands of the conquerors, and being found pregnant was placed in the custody of *Maclonich*, one of a tribe or family branched from *Cameron*, with orders, if she brought a boy, to destroy him, if a girl, to spare her.

Maclonich's wife, who was with child likewise, had a girl about the same time at which lady *Maclean* brought a boy, and *Maclonich* with more generosity to his captive, than fidelity to his trust, contrived that the children should be changed.

Maclean being thus preserved from death, in time recovered his original patrimony; and in gratitude to his friend, made his castle a place of refuge to any of the clan that should think himself in danger; and as a proof of reciprocal confidence, *Maclean* took upon himself and his posterity the care of educating the heir of *Maclonich*.

This story, like all other traditions of the Highlands, is variously related, but though some circumstances are uncertain, the principal fact is true. *Maclean* undoubtedly owed his preservation to *Maclonich*; for the treaty between the two families has been strictly observed: it did not sink into disuse and oblivion, but continued in its full force while the chieftains retained their power. I have read a demand of protection, made not more than thirty-seven years ago, for one of the *Maclonichs*, named *Ewen Cameron*, who had been accessary to the death of *Macmartin*, and had been banished by

Lochiel, his lord, for a certain term; at the expiration of which he returned married from *France*, but the *Macmartins*, not satisfied with the punishment, when he attempted to settle, still threatened him with vengeance. He therefore asked, and obtained, shelter in the Isle of *Col*.

The power of protection subsists no longer, but what the law permits is yet continued, and *Maclean* of *Col* now educates the heir of *Maclonich*.

There still remains in the Islands, though it is passing fast away, the custom of fosterage. A Laird, a man of wealth and eminence, sends his child, either male or female, to a tacksman, or tenant, to be fostered. It is not always his own tenant, but some distant friend that obtains this honour; for an honour such a trust is very reasonably thought. The terms of fosterage seem to vary in different islands. In *Mull*, the father sends with his child a certain number of cows, to which the same number is added by the fosterer. The father appropriates a proportionable extent of ground, without rent, for their pasturage. If every cow brings a calf, half belongs to the fosterer, and half to the child; but if there be only one calf between two cows, it is the child's, and when the child returns to the parents, it is accompanied by all the cows given, both by the father and by the fosterer, with half of the increase of the stock by propagation. These beasts are considered as a portion, and called *Macalive* cattle, of which the father has the produce, but is supposed not to have the full property, but to owe the same number to the child, as a portion to the daughter, or a stock for the son.

Children continue with the fosterer perhaps six years, and cannot, where this is the practice, be considered as burdensome. The fosterer, if he gives four cows, receives likewise four, and has, while the child continues with him, grass for eight without rent, with half the calves, and all the milk, for which he pays only four cows when he dismisses his *Dalt*, for that is the name for a foster child.

Fosterage is, I believe, sometimes performed upon more liberal terms. Our friend, the young Laird of *Col*, was fostered by *Macsweyn* of *Grissipol*. *Macsweyn* then lived a tenant to Sir *James Macdonald* in the Isle of *Sky*; and therefore *Col*, whether he sent him cattle or not, could grant him no land. The *Dalt*, however, at his return, brought back a considerable number of *Macalive cattle*, and of the friendship so formed there have been good effects.

When *Macdonald* raised his rents, *Macsweyn* was, like other tenants, discontented, and, resigning his farm, removed from *Sky* to *Col*, and was established at *Grissipol*.

These observations we made by favour of the contrary wind that drove us to *Col*, an Island not often visited; for there is not much to amuse curiosity, or to attract avarice.

The ground has been hitherto, I believe, used chiefly for pasturage. In a district, such as the eye can command, there is a general herdsman, who knows all the cattle of the neighbourhood, and whose station is upon a hill, from which he surveys the lower grounds; and if one man's cattle invade another's grass, drives them back to their own borders. But other means of profit begin to be found; kelp is gathered and burnt, and sloops are loaded with the concreted ashes. Cultivation is likely to be improved by the skill and encouragement of the present heir, and the inhabitants of those obscure vallies will partake of the general progress of life.

The rents of the parts which belong to the Duke of Argyle, have been raised from fifty-five to one hundred and five pounds, whether from the land or the sea I cannot tell. The bounties of the sea have lately been so great, that a farm in *Southuist* has risen in ten years from a rent of thirty pounds to one hundred and eighty.

He who lives in *Col*, and finds himself condemned to solitary meals, and incommunicable reflection, will find the usefulness of that middle order of Tacksmen, which some who applaud their own wisdom are wishing to destroy. Without intelligence man is not social, he is only gregarious; and little intelligence will there be, where all are constrained to daily labour, and every mind must wait upon the hand.

After naving listened for some days to the tempest, and wandered about the Island till our curiosity was satisfied, we began to think about our departure. To leave *Col* in October was not very easy. We however found a sloop which lay on the coast to carry kelp; and for a price which we thought levied upon our necessities, the master agreed to carry us to *Mull*, whence we might readily pass back to *Scotland*.

MULL

As we were to catch the first favourable breath, we spent the night not very elegantly, nor pleasantly in the vessel, and were landed next day at *Tobor Morar*, a port in *Mull*, which appears to an unexperienced eye formed for the security of ships; for its mouth is closed by a small island, which admits them through narrow channels into a bason sufficiently capacious. They are indeed safe from the sea, but there is a hollow between the mountains, through which the wind issues from the land with very mischievous violence.

There was no danger while we were there, and we found several other vessels at anchor; so that the port had a very commercial appearance.

The young Laird of *Col*, who had determined not to let us lose his company, while there was any difficulty remaining, came over with us. His influence soon appeared; for he procured us horses, and conducted us to the house of Doctor *Maclean*, where we found very kind entertainment, and very pleasing conversation. Miss *Maclean*, who was born, and had been bred at *Glasgow*, having removed with her father to *Mull*, added to other qualifications, a great knowledge of the *Earse* language, which she had not learned in her childhood, but gained by study, and was the only interpreter of *Earse* poetry that I could ever find.

The Isle of *Mull* is perhaps in extent the third of the *Hebrides*. It is not broken by waters, nor shot into promontories, but is a solid and compact mass, of breadth nearly equal to its length. Of the dimensions of the larger Islands, there is no knowledge approaching to exactness. I am willing to estimate it as containing about three hundred square miles.

Mull had suffered like *Sky* by the black winter of seventy-one, in which, contrary to all experience, a continued frost detained the snow eight weeks upon the ground. Against a calamity never known, no provision had been made, and the people could only pine in helpless misery. One tenant was mentioned, whose cattle perished to the value of three hundred pounds; a loss which probably more than the life of man is necessary to repair. In countries like these, the descriptions of famine become intelligible. Where by vigorous and artful cultivation of a soil naturally fertile, there is commonly a superfluous growth both of grain and grass; where the fields are crowded with cattle; and where every hand is able to attract wealth from a distance, by making something that promotes ease, or gratifies vanity, a dear year produces only a comparative want, which is rather seen than felt, and which terminates commonly in no worse effect, than that of condemning the lower orders of the community to sacrifice a little luxury to convenience, or at most a little convenience to necessity.

But where the climate is unkind, and the ground penurious, so that the most fruitful years produce only enough to maintain themselves; where life unimproved, and unadorned, fades into something little more than naked existence, and every one is busy for himself, without any arts by which the pleasure of others may be increased; if to the daily burden of distress any additional weight be added, nothing remains but to despair and die. In *Mull* the disappointment of a harvest, or a murrain among the cattle, cuts off the regular provision; and they who have no manufactures can purchase no part of the superfluities of other countries. The consequence of a bad season is here not scarcity, but emptiness; and they whose plenty was barely a supply of natural and present need, when that slender stock fails, must perish with hunger.

All travel has its advantages. If the passenger visits better countries, he may learn to improve his own, and if fortune carries him to worse, he may learn to enjoy it.

Mr. *Boswell's* curiosity strongly impelled him to survey *Jona*, or *Icolmkil*, which was to the early ages the great school of Theology, and is supposed to have been the place of sepulture for the ancient kings. I, though less eager, did not oppose him.

That we might perform this expedition, it was necessary to traverse a great part of *Mull*. We passed a day at Dr. *Maclean's*, and could have been well contented to stay longer. But *Col* provided us horses, and we pursued our journey. This was a day of inconvenience, for the country is very rough, and my horse was but little. We travelled many hours through a tract, black and barren, in which, however, there were the reliques of humanity; for we found a ruined chapel in our way.

It is natural, in traversing this gloom of desolation, to inquire, whether something may not be done to give nature a more cheerful face, and whether those hills and moors that afford heath cannot with a little care and labour bear something better? The first thought that occurs is to cover them with trees, for that in many of these naked regions trees will grow, is evident, because stumps and roots are yet remaining; and the speculatist hastily proceeds to censure that negligence and laziness that has omitted for so long a time so easy an improvement.

To drop seeds into the ground, and attend their growth, requires little labour and no skill. He who remembers that all the woods, by which the wants of man have been supplied from the Deluge till now, were self-sown, will not easily be persuaded to think all the art and preparation necessary, which the Georgick writers prescribe to planters. Trees certainly have covered the earth with very little culture. They wave their tops among the rocks of *Norway*, and might thrive as well in the Highlands and *Hebrides*.

But there is a frightful interval between the seed and timber. He that calculates the growth of trees, has the unwelcome remembrance of the shortness of life driven hard upon him. He knows that he is doing what will never benefit himself; and when he rejoices to see the stem rise, is disposed to repine that another shall cut it down.

Plantation is naturally the employment of a mind unburdened with care, and vacant to futurity, saturated with present good, and at leisure to derive gratification from the prospect of posterity. He that pines with hunger, is in little care how others shall be fed. The poor man is seldom studious to make his grandson rich. It may be soon discovered, why in a place, which hardly supplies the cravings of necessity, there has been little attention to the delights of fancy, and why distant convenience is unregarded, where the thoughts are turned with incessant solicitude upon every possibility of immediate advantage.

Neither is it quite so easy to raise large woods, as may be conceived. Trees intended to produce timber must be sown where they are to grow; and ground sown with trees must be kept useless for a long time, inclosed at an expence from which many will be discouraged by the remoteness of the profit, and watched with that attention, which, in places where it is most needed, will neither be given nor bought. That it cannot be plowed is evident; and if cattle be suffered to graze upon it, they will devour the plants as fast as they rise. Even in coarser countries, where herds and flocks are not fed, not only the deer and the wild goats will browse upon them, but the hare and rabbit will nibble them. It is therefore reasonable to believe, what I do not remember any naturalist to have remarked, that there was a time when the world was very thinly inhabited by beasts, as well as men, and that the woods had leisure to rise high before animals had bred numbers sufficient to intercept them.

Sir *James Macdonald*, in part of the wastes of his territory, set or sowed trees, to the number, as I have been told, of several millions, expecting, doubtless, that they would grow up into future navies and cities; but for want of inclosure, and of that care which is always necessary, and will hardly ever be taken, all his cost and labour have been lost, and the ground is likely to continue an useless heath.

Having not any experience of a journey in *Mull*, we had no doubt of reaching the sea by day-light, and therefore had not left Dr. *Maclean*'s very early. We travelled diligently enough, but found the country, for road there was none, very difficult to pass. We were always struggling with some obstruction or other, and our vexation was not balanced by any gratification of the eye or mind. We were now long enough acquainted with hills and heath to have lost the emotion that they once raised, whether pleasing or painful, and had our mind employed only on our own fatigue. We were however sure, under *Col's* protection, of escaping all real evils. There was no house in *Mull* to which he could not introduce us. He had intended to lodge us, for that night, with a gentleman that lived upon the coast, but discovered on the way, that he then lay in bed without hope of life.

We resolved not to embarrass a family, in a time of so much sorrow, if any other expedient could be found; and as the Island of *Ulva* was over-against us, it was determined that we should pass the strait and have recourse to the Laird, who, like the other gentlemen of the Islands, was known to *Col*. We expected to find a ferry-boat, but when at last we came to the water, the boat was gone.

We were now again at a stop. It was the sixteenth of *October*, a time when it is not convenient to sleep in the *Hebrides* without a cover, and there was no house within our reach, but that which we had already declined.

ULVA

While we stood deliberating, we were happily espied from an *Irish* ship, that lay at anchor in the strait. The master saw that we wanted a passage, and with great civility sent us his boat, which quickly conveyed us to *Ulva*, where we were very liberally entertained by Mr. *Macquarry*.

To *Ulva* we came in the dark, and left it before noon the next day. A very exact description therefore will not be expected. We were told, that it is an Island of no great extent, rough and barren, inhabited by the *Macquarrys*; a clan not powerful nor numerous, but of antiquity, which most other families are content to reverence. The name is supposed to be a depravation of some other; for the *Earse* language does not afford it any etymology. *Macquarry* is proprietor both of *Ulva* and some adjacent Islands, among which is *Staffa*, so lately raised to renown by Mr. *Banks*.

When the Islanders were reproached with their ignorance, or insensibility of the wonders of *Staffa*, they had not much to reply. They had indeed considered it little, because they had always seen it; and none but philosophers, nor they always, are struck with wonder, otherwise than by novelty. How would it surprise an unenlightened ploughman, to hear a company of sober men, inquiring by what power the hand tosses a stone, or why the stone, when it is tossed, falls to the ground!

Of the ancestors of *Macquarry*, who thus lie hid in his unfrequented Island, I have found memorials in all places where they could be expected.

Inquiring after the reliques of former manners, I found that in *Ulva*, and, I think, no where else, is continued the payment of the *Mercheta Mulierum*; a fine in old times due to the Laird at the marriage of a virgin. The original of this claim, as of our tenure of *Borough English*, is variously delivered. It is pleasant to find ancient customs in old families. This payment, like others, was, for want of money, made anciently in the produce of the land. *Macquarry* was used to demand a sheep, for which he now takes a crown, by that inattention to the uncertain proportion between the value and the denomination of money, which has brought much disorder into *Europe*. A sheep has always the same power of supplying human wants, but a crown will bring at one time more, at another less.

Ulva was not neglected by the piety of ancient times: it has still to show what was once a church.

INCH KENNETH

In the morning we went again into the boat, and were landed on *Inch Kenneth*, an Island about a mile long, and perhaps half a mile broad, remarkable for pleasantness and fertility. It is verdant and grassy, and fit both for pasture and tillage; but it has no trees. Its only inhabitants were Sir *Allan Maclean*, and two young ladies, his daughters, with their servants.

771

Romance does not often exhibit a scene that strikes the imagination more than this little desert in these depths of Western obscurity, occupied not by a gross herdsman, or amphibious fisherman, but by a gentleman and two ladies, of high birth, polished manners, and elegant conversation, who, in a habitation raised not very far above the ground, but furnished with unexpected neatness and convenience, practised all the kindness of hospitality, and refinement of courtesy.

Sir *Allan* is the Chieftain of the great clan of *Maclean*, which is said to claim the second place among the Highland families, yielding only to *Macdonald*. Though by the misconduct of his ancestors, most of the extensive territory, which would have descended to him, has been alienated, he still retains much of the dignity and authority of his birth. When soldiers were lately wanting for the *American* war, application was made to Sir *Allan*, and he nominated a hundred men for the service, who obeyed the summons, and bore arms under his command.

He had then, for some time, resided with the young ladies in *Inch Kenneth*, where he lives not only with plenty, but with elegance, having conveyed to his cottage a collection of books, and what else is necessary to make his hours pleasant.

When we landed, we were met by Sir *Allan* and the Ladies, accompanied by Miss *Macquarry*, who had passed some time with them, and now returned to *Ulva* with her father.

We all walked together to the mansion, where we found one cottage for Sir *Allan*, and I think two more for the domesticks and the offices. We entered, and wanted little that palaces afford. Our room was neatly floored, and well lighted; and our dinner, which was dressed in one of the other huts, was plentiful and delicate.

In the afternoon Sir *Allan* reminded us, that the day was Sunday, which he never suffered to pass without some religious distinction, and invited us to partake in his acts of domestick worship; which I hope neither Mr. *Boswell* nor myself will be suspected of a disposition to refuse. The elder of the Ladies read the *English* service.

Inch Kenneth was once a seminary of ecclesiasticks, subordinate, I suppose, to *Icolmkill*. Sir *Allan* had a mind to trace the foundation of the college, but neither I nor Mr. *Boswell*, who *bends* a keener *eye on vacancy*, were able to perceive them.

Our attention, however, was sufficiently engaged by a venerable chapel, which stands yet entire, except that the roof is gone. It is about sixty feet in length, and thirty in breadth. On one side of the altar is a bas relief of the blessed Virgin, and by it lies a little bell; which, though cracked, and without a clapper, has remained there for ages, guarded only by the venerableness of the place. The ground round the chapel is covered with grave-stones of Chiefs and ladies; and still continues to be a place of sepulture.

Inch Kenneth is a proper prelude to *Icolmkill*. It was not without some mournful emotion that we contemplated the ruins of religious structures, and the monuments of the dead.

On the next day we took a more distinct view of the place, and went with the boat to see oysters in the bed, out of which the boatmen forced up as many as were wanted. Even *Inch Kenneth* has a subordinate Island, named *Sandiland*, I suppose, in contempt, where we landed, and found a rock, with a surface of perhaps four acres, of which one is naked stone, another spread with sand and shells, some of which I picked up for their glossy beauty, and two covered with a little earth and grass, on which Sir *Allan* has a few sheep. I doubt not but when there was a college at *Inch Kenneth*, there was a hermitage upon *Sandiland*.

Having wandered over those extensive plains, we committed ourselves again to the winds and waters; and after a voyage of about ten minutes, in which we met with nothing very observable, were again safe upon dry ground.

We told Sir *Allan* our desire of visiting *Icolmkill*, and entreated him to give us his protection, and his company. He thought proper to hesitate a little, but the Ladies hinted, that as they knew he would not finally refuse, he would do better if he preserved the grace of ready compliance. He took their advice, and promised to carry us on the morrow in his boat.

We passed the remaining part of the day in such amusements as were in our power. Sir *Allan* related the *American* campaign, and at evening one of the Ladies played on her harpsichord, while *Col* and Mr. *Boswell* danced a *Scottish* reel with the other.

We could have been easily persuaded to a longer stay upon *Inch Kenneth*, but life will not be all passed in delight. The session at *Edinburgh* was approaching, from which Mr. *Boswell* could not be absent.

In the morning our boat was ready: it was high and strong. Sir *Allan* victualled it for the day, and provided able rowers. We now parted from the young Laird of *Col*, who had treated us with so much kindness, and concluded his favours by consigning us to Sir *Allan*. Here we had the last embrace of this amiable man, who, while these pages were preparing to attest his virtues, perished in the passage between *Ulva* and *Inch Kenneth*.

Sir *Allan*, to whom the whole region was well known, told us of a very remarkable cave, to which he would show us the way. We had been disappointed already by one cave, and were not much elevated by the expectation of another.

It was yet better to see it, and we stopped at some rocks on the coast of *Mull*. The mouth is fortified by vast fragments of stone, over which we made our way, neither very nimbly, nor very securely. The place, however, well repaid our trouble. The bottom, as far as the flood rushes in, was encumbered with large pebbles, but as we advanced was spread over with smooth sand. The breadth is about forty-five feet: the roof rises in an arch, almost regular, to a height which we could not measure; but I think it about thirty feet.

This part of our curiosity was nearly frustrated; for though we went to see a cave, and knew that caves are dark, we forgot to carry tapers, and did not discover our omission till we were wakened by our wants. Sir *Allan* then sent one of the boatmen into the country, who soon returned with one little candle. We were thus enabled to go forward, but could not venture far. Having passed inward from the sea to a great depth, we found on the right hand a narrow passage, perhaps not more than six feet wide, obstructed by great stones, over which we climbed, and came into a second cave, in breadth twenty-five feet. The air in this apartment was very warm, but not oppressive, nor loaded with vapours. Our light showed no tokens of a feculent or corrupted atmosphere. Here was a square stone, called, as we are told, *Fingal's Table*.

If we had been provided with torches, we should have proceeded in our search, though we had already gone as far as any former adventurer, except some who are reported never to have returned; and, measuring our way back, we found it more than a hundred and sixty yards, the eleventh part of a mile.

Our measures were not critically exact, having been made with a walking pole, such as it is convenient to carry in these rocky countries, of which I guessed the length by standing against it. In this there could be no great errour, nor do I much doubt but the Highlander, whom we employed, reported the number right. More nicety however is better, and no man should travel unprovided with instruments for taking heights and distances.

There is yet another cause of errour not always easily surmounted, though more dangerous to the veracity of itinerary narratives, than imperfect mensuration. An observer deeply impressed by any remarkable spectacle, does not suppose, that the traces will soon vanish from his mind, and having commonly no great convenience for writing, defers the description to a time of more leisure, and better accommodation.

He who has not made the experiment, or who is not accustomed to require rigorous accuracy from himself, will scarcely believe how much a few hours take from certainty of knowledge, and distinctness of imagery; how the succession of objects will be broken, how separate parts will be confused, and how many particular features and discriminations will be compressed and conglobated into one gross and general idea.

To this dilatory notation must be imputed the false relations of travellers, where there is no imaginable motive to deceive. They trusted to memory, what cannot be trusted safely but to the eye, and told by guess what a few hours before they had known with certainty. Thus it was that *Wheeler* and *Spen* described with irreconcilable contrariety things which they surveyed together, and which both undoubtedly designed to show as they saw them.

When we had satisfied our curiosity in the cave, so far as our penury of light permitted us, we clambered again to our boats, and proceeded along the coast of *Mull* to a headland, called *Atun*, remarkable for the columnar form of the rocks, which rise in a series of pilasters, with a degree of regularity, which Sir *Allan* thinks not less worthy of curiosity than the shore of *Staffa*.

Not long after we came to another range of black rocks, which had the appearance of broken pilasters, set one behind another to a great depth. This place was chosen by Sir *Allan* for our dinner. We were easily accommodated with seats, for the stones were of all heights, and refreshed ourselves and our boatmen, who could have no other rest till we were at *Icolmkill*.

The evening was now approaching, and we were yet at a considerable distance from the end of our expedition. We could therefore stop no more to make remarks in the way, but set forward with some degree of eagerness. The day soon failed us, and the moon presented a very solemn and pleasing scene. The sky was clear, so that the eye commanded a wide circle: the sea was neither still nor turbulent: the wind neither silent nor loud. We were never far from one coast or another, on which, if the weather had become violent, we could have found shelter, and therefore contemplated at ease the region through which we glided in the tranquillity of the night, and saw now a rock and now an island grow gradually conspicuous and gradually obscure. I committed the fault which I have just been censuring, in neglecting, as we passed, to note the series of this placid navigation.

We were very near an Island, called *Nun's Island*, perhaps from an ancient convent. Here is said to have been dug the stone which was used in the buildings of *Icolmkill*. Whether it is now inhabited we could not stay to inquire.

At last we came to *Icolmkill*, but found no convenience for landing. Our boat could not be forced very near the dry ground, and our Highlanders carried us over the water.

We were now treading that illustrious Island, which was once the luminary of the *Caledonian* regions, whence savage clans and roving barbarians derived the benefits of knowledge, and the blessings of religion. To abstract the mind from all local emotion would be impossible, if it were endeavoured, and would be foolish, if it were possible. Whatever withdraws us from the power of our senses; whatever makes the past, the distant, or the future predominate over the present, advances us in the dignity of thinking beings. Far from me and from my friends, be such frigid philosophy as may conduct us indifferent and unmoved over any ground which has been dignified by wisdom, bravery, or virtue. That man is little to be envied, whose patriotism would not gain force upon the plain of *Marathon*, or whose piety would not grow warmer among the ruins of *Iona*.

We came too late to visit monuments: some care was necessary for ourselves. Whatever was in the Island, Sir *Allan* could demand, for the inhabitants were *Macleans*; but having little they could not give us much. He went to the headman of the Island, whom Fame, but Fame delights in amplifying, represents as worth no less than fifty pounds. He was perhaps proud enough of his guests, but ill prepared for our entertainment; however, he soon produced more provision than men not luxurious require. Our lodging was next to be provided. We found a barn well stocked with hay, and made our beds as soft as we could.

In the morning we rose and surveyed the place. The churches of the two convents are both standing, though unroofed. They were built of unhewn stone, but solid, and not inelegant. I brought away rude measures of the buildings, such as I cannot much trust myself, inaccurately taken, and obscurely noted. Mr. *Pennant's* delineations, which are doubtless exact, have made my unskilful description less necessary.

The episcopal church consists of two parts, separated by the belfry, and built at different times. The original church had, like others, the altar at one end, and tower at the other; but as it grew too small, another building of equal dimension was added, and the tower then was necessarily in the middle.

That these edifices are of different ages seems evident. The arch of the first church is *Roman*, being part of a circle; that of the additional building is pointed, and therefore *Gothick*, or *Saracenical*; the tower is firm, and wants only to be floored and covered.

Of the chambers or cells belonging to the monks, there are some walls remaining, but nothing approaching to a complete apartment.

The bottom of the church is so incumbered with mud and rubbish, that we could make no discoveries of curious inscriptions, and what there are have been already published. The place is said to be known where the black stones lie concealed, on which the old Highland Chiefs, when they made contracts and alliances, used to take the oath, which was considered as more sacred than any other obligation, and which could not be violated without the blackest infamy. In those days of violence and rapine, it was of great importance to impress upon savage minds the sanctity of an oath, by some particular and extraordinary circumstances. They would not have recourse to the black stones, upon small or common occasions, and when they had established their faith by this tremendous sanction, inconstancy and treachery were no longer feared.

The chapel of the nunnery is now used by the inhabitants as a kind of general cow-house, and the bottom is consequently too miry for examination. Some of the stones which covered the later abbesses have inscriptions, which might yet be read, if the chapel were cleansed. The roof of this, as of all the other buildings, is totally destroyed, not only because timber quickly decays when it is neglected, but because in an island utterly destitute of wood, it was wanted for use, and was consequently the first plunder of needy rapacity.

The chancel of the nuns' chapel is covered with an arch of stone, to which time has done no injury; and a small apartment communicating with the choir, on the north side, like the chapter-house in cathedrals, roofed with stone in the same manner, is likewise entire.

In one of the churches was a marble altar, which the superstition of the inhabitants has destroyed. Their opinion was, that a fragment of this stone was a defence against shipwrecks, fire, and miscarriages. In one corner of the church the bason for holy water is yet unbroken.

The cemetery of the nunnery was, till very lately, regarded with such reverence, that only women were buried in it. These reliques of veneration always produce some mournful pleasure. I could have forgiven a great injury more easily than the violation of this imaginary sanctity.

South of the chapel stand the walls of a large room, which was probably the hall, or refectory of the nunnery. This apartment is capable of repair. Of the rest of the convent there are only fragments.

Besides the two principal churches, there are, I think, five chapels yet standing, and three more remembered. There are also crosses, of which two bear the names of St. *John* and St. *Matthew*.

A large space of ground about these consecrated edifices is covered with grave-stones, few of which have any inscription. He that surveys it, attended by an insular antiquary, may be told where the Kings of many nations are buried, and if he loves to sooth his imagination with the thoughts that naturally rise in places where the great and the powerful lie mingled with the dust, let him listen in submissive silence; for if he asks any questions, his delight is at an end.

Iona has long enjoyed, without any very credible attestation, the honour of being reputed the cemetery of the *Scottish* kings. It is not unlikely that, when the opinion of local sanctity was prevalent, the Chieftains of the Isles, and perhaps some of the *Norwegian* or *Irish* princes were reposited in this venerable enclosure. But by whom the subterraneous vaults are peopled is now utterly unknown. The graves are very numerous, and some of them undoubtedly contain the remains of men, who did not expect to be so soon forgotten.

Not far from this awful ground, may be traced the garden of the monastery: the fishponds are yet discernible, and the aqueduct, which supplied them, is still in use.

There remains a broken building, which is called the Bishop's house, I know not by what authority. It was once the residence of some man above the common rank, for it has two stories and a chimney. We were shewn a chimney at the other end, which was only a nich, without perforation, but so much does antiquarian credulity, or patriotick vanity prevail, that it was not much more safe to trust the eye of our instructor than the memory.

There is in the Island one house more, and only one, that has a chimney: we entered it, and found it neither wanting repair nor inhabitants; but to the farmers, who now possess it, the chimney is of no great value; for their fire was made on the floor, in the middle of the room, and notwithstanding the dignity of their mansion, they rejoiced, like their neighbours, in the comforts of smoke.

It is observed, that ecclesiastical colleges are always in the most pleasant and fruitful places. While the world allowed the monks their choice, it is surely no dishonour that they chose well. This Island is remarkably fruitful. The village near the churches is said to contain seventy families, which, at five in a family, is more than a hundred inhabitants to a mile. There are perhaps other villages; yet both corn and cattle are annually exported.

But the fruitfulness of *Iona* is now its whole prosperity. The inhabitants are remarkably gross, and remarkably neglected: I know not if they are visited by any Minister. The Island, which was once the metropolis of learning and piety, has now no school for education, nor temple for worship, only two inhabitants that can speak *English*, and not one that can write or read.

The people are of the clan of *Maclean*; and though Sir *Allan* had not been in the place for many years, he was received with all the reverence due to their Chieftain. One of them being sharply reprehended by him, for not sending him some rum, declared after his departure, in Mr. *Boswell*'s presence, that he had no design of disappointing him, *for*, said he, *I would cut my bones for him; and if he had sent his dog for it, he should have had it.*

When we were to depart, our boat was left by the ebb at a great distance from the water, but no sooner did we wish it afloat, than the islanders gathered round it, and, by the union of many hands, pushed it down the beach; every man who could contribute his help seemed to think himself happy in the opportunity of being, for a moment, useful to his Chief.

We now left those illustrious ruins, by which Mr. *Boswell* was much affected, nor would I willingly be thought to have looked upon them without some emotion. Perhaps, in the revolutions of the world, *Iona* may be sometime again the instructress of the Western Regions.

It was no long voyage to *Mull*, where, under Sir *Allan's* protection, we landed in the evening, and were entertained for the night by Mr. *Maclean*, a Minister that lives upon the coast, whose elegance of conversation, and strength of judgment, would make him conspicuous in places of greater celebrity. Next day we dined with Dr. *Maclean*, another physician, and then travelled on to the house of a very powerful Laird, *Maclean* of *Lochbuy*; for in this country every man's name is *Maclean*.

Where races are thus numerous, and thus combined, none but the Chief of a clan is addressed by his name. The Laird of *Dunvegan* is called *Macleod*, but other gentlemen of the same family are denominated by the places where they reside, as *Raasay*, or *Talisker*. The distinction of the meaner people is made by their Christian names. In consequence of this practice, the late Laird of *Macfarlane*, an eminent genealogist, considered himself as disrespectfully treated, if the common addition was applied to him. Mr. *Macfarlane*, said he, may with equal propriety be said to many; but I, and I only, am *Macfarlane*.

Our afternoon journey was through a country of such gloomy desolation, that Mr. *Boswell* thought no part of the Highlands equally terrifick, yet we came without any difficulty, at evening, to *Lochbuy*, where we found a true Highland Laird, rough and haughty, and tenacious of his dignity: who, hearing my name, inquired whether I was of the *Johnstons* of *Glencroe*, or of *Ardnamurchan*.

Lochbuy has, like the other insular Chieftains, quitted the castle that sheltered his ancestors, and lives near it, in a mansion not very spacious or splendid. I have seen no houses in the Islands much to be envied for convenience or magnificence, yet they bear testimony to the progress of arts and civility, as they show that rapine and surprise are no longer dreaded, and are much more commodious than the ancient fortresses.

780

The castles of the *Hebrides,* many of which are standing, and many ruined, were always built upon points of land, on the margin of the sea. For the choice of this situation there must have been some general reason, which the change of manners has left in obscurity. They were of no use in the days of piracy, as defences of the coast; for it was equally accessible in other places. Had they been sea-marks or light-houses, they would have been of more use to the invader than the natives, who could want no such directions on their own waters: for a watch-tower, a cottage on a hill would have been better, as it would have commanded a wider view.

If they be considered merely as places of retreat, the situation seems not well chosen; for the Laird of an Island is safest from foreign enemies in the center: on the coast he might be more suddenly surprised than in the inland parts; and the invaders, if their enterprise miscarried, might more easily retreat. Some convenience, however, whatever it was, their position on the shore afforded; for uniformity of practice seldom continues long without good reason.

A castle in the Islands is only a single tower of three or four stories, of which the walls are sometimes eight or nine feet thick, with narrow windows, and close winding stairs of stone. The top rises in a cone, or pyramid of stone, encompassed by battlements. The intermediate floors are sometimes frames of timber, as in common houses, and sometimes arches of stone, or alternately stone and timber; so that there was very little danger from fire. In the center of every floor, from top to bottom, is the chief room, of no great extent, round which there are narrow cavities, or recesses, formed by small vacuities, or by a double wall. I know not whether there be ever more than one fire-place. They had not capacity to contain many people, or much provision; but their enemies could seldom stay to blockade them; for if they failed in their first attack, their next care was to escape.

The walls were always too strong to be shaken by such desultory hostilities; the windows were too narrow to be entered, and the battlements too high to be scaled. The only danger was at the gates, over which the wall was built with a square cavity, not unlike a chimney, continued to the top. Through this hollow the defendants let fall stones upon those who attempted to break the gate, and poured down water, perhaps scalding water, if the attack was made with fire. The castle of *Lochbuy* was secured by double doors, of which the outer was an iron grate.

In every castle is a well and a dungeon. The use of the well is evident. The dungeon is a deep subterraneous cavity, walled on the sides, and arched on the top, into which the descent is through a narrow door, by a ladder or a rope, so that it seems impossible to escape, when the rope or ladder is drawn up. The dungeon was, I suppose, in war, a prison for such captives as were treated with severity, and, in peace, for such delinquents as had committed crimes within the Laird's jurisdiction; for the mansions of many Lairds were, till the late privation of their privileges, the halls of justice to their own tenants.

As these fortifications were the productions of mere necessity, they are built only for safety, with little regard to convenience, and with none to elegance or pleasure. It was sufficient for a Laird of the *Hebrides*, if he had a strong house, in which he could hide his wife and children from the next clan. That they are not large nor splendid is no wonder. It is not easy to find how they were raised, such as they are, by men who had no money, in countries where the labourers and artificers could scarcely be fed. The buildings in different parts of the Islands shew their degrees of wealth and power. I believe that for all the castles which I have seen beyond the *Tweed*, the ruins yet remaining of some one of these which the *English* built in *Wales*, would supply materials.

These castles afford another evidence that the fictions of romantick chivalry had for their basis the real manners of the feudal times, when every Lord of a seignory lived in his hold lawless and unaccountable, with all the licentiousness and insolence of uncontested superiority and unprincipled power. The traveller, whoever he might be, coming to the fortified habitation of a Chieftain, would, probably, have been interrogated from the battlements, admitted with caution at the gate, introduced to a petty Monarch, fierce with habitual hostility, and vigilant with ignorant suspicion; who, according to his general temper, or accidental humour, would have seated a stranger as his guest at the table, or as a spy confined him in the dungeon.

Lochbuy means the *Yellow Lake*, which is the name given to an inlet of the sea, upon which the castle of Mr. *Maclean* stands. The reason of the appellation we did not learn.

We were now to leave the *Hebrides*, where we had spent some weeks with sufficient amusement, and where we had amplified our thoughts with new scenes of nature, and new modes of life. More time would have given us a more distinct view, but it was necessary that Mr. *Boswell* should return before the courts of justice were opened; and it was not proper to live too long upon hospitality, however liberally imparted.

Of these Islands it must be confessed, that they have not many allurements, but to the mere lover of naked nature. The inhabitants are thin, provisions are scarce, and desolation and penury give little pleasure.

The people collectively considered are not few, though their numbers are small in proportion to the space which they occupy. *Mull* is said to contain six thousand, and *Sky* fifteen thousand. Of the computation respecting *Mull*, I can give no account; but when I doubted the truth of the numbers attributed to *Sky*, one of the Ministers exhibited such facts as conquered my incredulity.

Of the proportion, which the product of any region bears to the people, an estimate is commonly made according to the pecuniary price of the necessaries of life; a principle of judgment which is never certain, because it supposes what is far from truth, that the value of money is always the same, and so measures an unknown quantity by an uncertain standard. It is competent enough when the markets of the same country, at different times, and those times not too distant, are to be compared; but of very little use for the purpose of making one nation acquainted with the state of another. Provisions, though plentiful, are sold in places of great pecuniary opulence for nominal prices, to which, however scarce, where gold and silver are yet scarcer, they can never be raised.

In the *Western Islands* there is so little internal commerce, that hardly any thing has a known or settled rate. The price of things brought in, or carried out, is to be considered as that of a foreign market; and even this there is some difficulty in discovering, because their denominations of quantity are different from ours; and when there is ignorance on both sides, no appeal can be made to a common measure.

This, however, is not the only impediment. The *Scots*, with a vigilance of jealousy which never goes to sleep, always suspect that an *Englishman* despises them for their poverty, and to convince him that they are not less rich than their neighbours, are sure to tell him a price higher than the true. When *Lesley*, two hundred years ago, related so punctiliously, that a hundred hen eggs, new laid, were sold in the islands for a peny, he supposed that no inference could possibly follow, but that eggs were in great abundance. Posterity has since grown wiser; and having learned, that nominal and real value may differ, they now tell no such stories, lest the foreigner should happen to collect, not that eggs are many, but that pence are few.

Money and wealth have by the use of commercial language been so long confounded, that they are commonly supposed to be the same; and this prejudice has spread so widely in *Scotland*, that I know not whether I found man or woman, whom I interrogated concerning payments of money, that could surmount the illiberal desire of deceiving me, by representing every thing as dearer than it is.

From *Lochbuy* we rode a very few miles to the side of *Mull*, which faces *Scotland*, where, having taken leave of our kind protector, Sir *Allan*, we embarked in a boat, in which the seat provided for our accommodation was a heap of rough brushwood; and on the twenty-second of *October* reposed at a tolerable inn on the main land.

On the next day we began our journey southwards. The weather was tempestuous. For half the day the ground was rough, and our horses were still small. Had they required much restraint, we might have been reduced to difficulties; for I think we had amongst us but one bridle. We fed the poor animals liberally, and they performed their journey well. In the latter part of the day, we came to a firm and smooth road, made by the soldiers, on which we travelled with great security, busied with contemplating the scene about us. The night came on while we had yet a great part of the way to go, though not so dark, but that we could discern the cataracts which poured down the hills, on one side, and fell into one general channel that ran with great violence on the other. The wind was loud, the rain was heavy, and the whistling of the blast, the fall of the shower, the rush of the cataracts, and the roar of the torrent, made a nobler chorus of the rough musick of nature than it had ever been my chance to hear before. The streams, which ran cross the way from the hills to the main current, were so frequent, that after a while I began to count them; and, in ten miles, reckoned fifty-five, probably missing some, and having let some pass

784

before they forced themselves upon my notice. At last we came to *Inverary*, where we found an inn, not only commodious, but magnificent.

The difficulties of peregrination were now at an end. Mr. *Boswell* had the honour of being known to the Duke of *Argyle*, by whom we were very kindly entertained at his splendid seat, and supplied with conveniences for surveying his spacious park and rising forests.

After two days stay at *Inverary* we proceeded *Southward* over *Glencroe*, a black and dreary region, now made easily passable by a military road, which rises from either end of the *glen* by an acclivity not dangerously steep, but sufficiently laborious. In the middle, at the top of the hill, is a seat with this inscription, *Rest, and be thankful*. Stones were placed to mark the distances, which the inhabitants have taken away, resolved, they said, *to have no new miles*.

In this rainy season the hills streamed with waterfalls, which, crossing the way, formed currents on the other side, that ran in contrary directions as they fell to the north or south of the summit. Being, by the favour of the Duke, well mounted, I went up and down the hill with great convenience.

From *Glencroe* we passed through a pleasant country to the banks of *Loch Lomond*, and were received at the house of Sir *James Colquhoun*, who is owner of almost all the thirty islands of the Loch, which we went in a boat next morning to survey. The heaviness of the rain shortened our voyage, but we landed on one island planted with yew, and stocked with deer, and on another containing perhaps not more than half an acre, remarkable for the ruins of an old castle, on which the osprey builds her annual nest. Had *Loch Lomond* been in a happier climate, it would have been the boast of wealth and vanity to own one of the little spots which it incloses, and to have employed upon it all the arts of embellishment. But as it is, the islets, which court the gazer at a distance, disgust him at his approach, when he finds instead of soft lawns and shady thickets, nothing more than uncultivated ruggedness.

Where the Loch discharges itself into a river, called the *Leven*, we passed a night with Mr. *Smollet*, a relation of Doctor *Smollet*, to whose memory he has raised an obelisk on the bank near the house in which he was born. The civility and respect which we found at every place, it is ungrateful to omit, and tedious to repeat. Here we were met by a post-chaise, that conveyed us to *Glasgow*.

To describe a city so much frequented as *Glasgow*, is unnecessary. The prosperity of its commerce appears by the greatness of many private houses, and a general appearance of wealth. It is the only episcopal city whose cathedral was left standing in the rage of Reformation. It is now divided into many separate places of worship, which, taken all together, compose a great pile, that had been some centuries in building, but was never finished; for the change of religion intercepted its progress, before the cross isle was added, which seems essential to a *Gothick* cathedral.

The college has not had a sufficient share of the increasing magnificence of the place. The session was begun; for it commences on the tenth of *October*, and continues to the tenth of *June*, but the students appeared not numerous, being, I suppose, not yet returned from their several homes. The division of the academical year into one session, and one recess, seems to me better accommodated to the present state of life, than that variegation of time by terms and vacations derived from distant centuries, in which it was probably convenient, and still continued in the *English* universities. So many solid months as the *Scotch* scheme of education joins together, allow and encourage a plan for each part of the year; but with us, he that has settled himself to study in the college is soon tempted into the country, and he that has adjusted his life in the country, is summoned back to his college.

Yet when I have allowed to the universities of *Scotland* a more rational distribution of time, I have given them, so far as my inquiries have informed me, all that they can claim. The students, for the most part, go thither boys, and depart before they are men; they carry with them little fundamental knowledge, and therefore the superstructure cannot be lofty. The grammar schools are not generally well supplied; for the character of a school-master being there less honourable than in *England*, is seldom accepted by men who are capable to adorn it, and where the school has been deficient, the college can effect little.

Men bred in the universities of *Scotland* cannot be expected to be often decorated with the splendours of ornamental erudition, but they obtain a mediocrity of knowledge, between learning and ignorance, not inadequate to the purposes of common life, which is, I believe, very widely diffused among them, and which countenanced in general by a national combination so invidious, that their friends cannot defend it, and actuated in particulars by a spirit of enterprise, so vigorous, that their enemies are constrained to praise it, enables them to find, or to make their way to employment, riches, and distinction.

From *Glasgow* we directed our course to *Auchinleck*, an estate devolved, through a long series of ancestors, to Mr. *Boswell*'s father, the present possessor. In our way we found several places remarkable enough in themselves, but already described by those who viewed them at more leisure, or with much more skill; and stopped two days at Mr. *Campbell*'s, a gentleman married to Mr. *Boswell*'s sister.

Auchinleck, which signifies a *stony field*, seems not now to have any particular claim to its denomination. It is a district generally level, and sufficiently fertile, but like all the *Western* side of *Scotland*, incommoded by very frequent rain. It was, with the rest of the country, generally naked, till the present possessor finding, by the growth of some stately trees near his old castle, that the ground was favourable enough to timber, adorned it very diligently with annual plantations.

Lord *Auchinleck*, who is one of the Judges of *Scotland*, and therefore not wholly at leisure for domestick business or pleasure, has yet found time to make improvements in his patrimony. He has built a house of hewn stone, very stately, and durable, and has advanced the value of his lands with great tenderness to his tenants.

I was, however, less delighted with the elegance of the modern mansion, than with the sullen dignity of the old castle. I clambered with Mr. *Boswell* among the ruins, which afford striking images of ancient life. It is, like other castles, built upon a point of rock, and was, I believe, anciently surrounded with a moat. There is another rock near it, to which the draw-bridge, when it was let down, is said to have reached. Here, in the ages of tumult and rapine, the Laird was surprised and killed by the neighbouring Chief, who perhaps might have extinguished the family, had he not in a few days been seized and hanged, together with his sons, by *Douglas*, who came with his forces to the relief of *Auchinleck*.

At no great distance from the house runs a pleasing brook, by a red rock, out of which has been hewn a very agreeable and commodious summer-house, at less expence, as Lord *Auchinleck* told me, than would have been required to build a room of the same dimensions. The rock seems to have no more dampness than any other wall. Such opportunities of variety it is judicious not to neglect.

We now returned to *Edinburgh*, where I passed some days with men of learning, whose names want no advancement from my commemoration, or with women of elegance, which perhaps disclaims a pedant's praise.

The conversation of the *Scots* grows every day less unpleasing to the *English*; their peculiarities wear fast away; their dialect is likely to become in half a century provincial and rustick, even to themselves. The great, the learned, the ambitious, and the vain, all cultivate the *English* phrase, and the *English* pronunciation, and in splendid companies *Scotch* is not much heard, except now and then from an old Lady.

There is one subject of philosophical curiosity to be found in *Edinburgh*, which no other city has to shew; a college of the deaf and dumb, who are taught to speak, to read, to write, and to practice arithmetick, by a gentleman, whose name is *Braidwood*. The number which attends him is, I think, about twelve, which he brings together into a little school, and instructs according to their several degrees of proficiency.

I do not mean to mention the instruction of the deaf as new. Having been first practised upon the son of a constable of *Spain*, it was afterwards cultivated with much emulation in *England*, by *Wallis* and *Holder*, and was lately professed by Mr. *Baker*, who once flattered me with hopes of seeing his method published. How far any former teachers have succeeded, it is not easy to know; the improvement of Mr. *Braidwood*'s pupils is wonderful. They not only speak, write, and understand what is written, but if he that speaks looks towards them, and modifies his organs by distinct and full utterance, they know so well what is spoken, that it is an expression scarcely figurative to say, they hear with the eye. That any have attained to the power mentioned by *Burnet*, of feeling sounds, by laying a hand on the speaker's mouth, I know not; but I have seen so much, that I can believe more; a single word, or a short sentence, I think, may possibly be so distinguished.

It will readily be supposed by those that consider this subject, that Mr. *Braidwood*'s scholars spell accurately. Orthography is vitiated among such as learn first to speak, and then to write, by imperfect notions of the relation between letters and vocal utterance; but to those students every character is of equal importance;

for letters are to them not symbols of names, but of things; when they write they do not represent a sound, but delineate a form.

This school I visited, and found some of the scholars waiting for their master, whom they are said to receive at his entrance with smiling countenances and sparkling eyes, delighted with the hope of new ideas. One of the young Ladies had her slate before her, on which I wrote a question consisting of three figures, to be multiplied by two figures. She looked upon it, and quivering her fingers in a manner which I thought very pretty, but of which I knew not whether it was art or play, multiplied the sum regularly in two lines, observing the decimal place; but did not add the two lines together, probably disdaining so easy an operation. I pointed at the place where the sum total should stand, and she noted it with such expedition as seemed to shew that she had it only to write.

It was pleasing to see one of the most desperate of human calamities capable of so much help: whatever enlarges hope, will exalt courage; after having seen the deaf taught arithmetick, who would be afraid to cultivate the *Hebrides*?

Such are the things which this journey has given me an opportunity of seeing, and such are the reflections which that sight has raised. Having passed my time almost wholly in cities, I may have been surprised by modes of life and appearances of nature, that are familiar to men of wider survey and more varied conversation. Novelty and ignorance must always be reciprocal, and I cannot but be conscious that my thoughts on national manners, are the thoughts of one who has seen but little.

SELECTIONS FROM
LIVES OF THE POETS

Johnson's *Lives of the Poets* appeared, from 1779 to 1781, as *Prefaces, Biographical and Critical, to the Works of the English Poets*. The two British Museum examples of the ten volumes of this edition (11601. c. 1–10. and 1162. e. 6–15.) have been used for the preparation of the present text.

Johnson's own corrected proof of a portion of the life of Dryden, now in the British Museum (C. 28. e. 10.), has been consulted, as also have the British Museum copies of the second (1781) edition (673. f. 20–23.) and third (1783) edition (1066. g. 20–3.).

LIVES of the POETS

ABRAHAM COWLEY

ABRAHAM COWLEY was born in the year one thousand six hundred and eighteen. His father was a grocer, whose condition Dr. Sprat conceals under the general appellation of a citizen; and, what would probably not have been less carefully suppressed, the omission of his name in the register of St. Dunstan's parish, gives reason to suspect that his father was a sectary. Whoever he was, he died before the birth of his son, and consequently left him to the care of his mother; whom Wood represents as struggling earnestly to procure him a literary education, and who, as she lived to the age of eighty, had her solicitude rewarded by seeing her son eminent, and, I hope, by seeing him fortunate, and partaking his prosperity. We know at least, from Sprat's account, that he always acknowledged her care, and justly paid the dues of filial gratitude.

In the window of his mother's apartment lay Spenser's Fairy Queen; in which he very early took delight to read, till, by feeling the charms of verse, he became, as he relates, irrecoverably a Poet. Such are the accidents, which, sometimes remembered, and perhaps sometimes forgotten, produce that particular designation of mind, and propensity for some certain science or employment, which is commonly called Genius. The true Genius is a mind of large general powers, accidentally determined to some particular direction. The great Painter of the present age had the first fondness for his art excited by the perusal of Richardson's treatise.

By his mother's solicitation he was admitted into Westminster-school, where he was soon distinguished. He was wont, says Sprat, to relate, "That he had this defect in his memory at that time, that his teachers never could bring it to retain the ordinary rules of grammar."

This is an instance of the natural desire of man to propagate a wonder. It is surely very difficult to tell any thing as it was heard, when Sprat could not refrain from amplifying a commodious incident, though the book to which he prefixed his narrative contained its confutation. A memory admitting some things, and rejecting others, an intellectual digestion that concocted the pulp of learning, but refused the husks, had the appearance of an instinctive elegance, of a particular provision made by Nature for literary politeness. But in the author's own honest relation, the marvel vanishes: he was, he says, such "an enemy to all constraint, that his master never could prevail on him to learn the rules without book." He does not tell that he could not learn the rules, but that being able to perform his exercises without them, and being an "enemy to constraint," he spared himself the labour.

In the year 1647, his "Mistress" was published; for he imagined, as he declared in his preface to a subsequent edition, that "poets are scarce thought freemen of their company without paying some duties, or obliging themselves to be true to Love."

This obligation to amorous ditties owes, I believe, its original to the fame of Petrarch, who, in an age rude and uncultivated, by his tuneful homage to his Laura, refined the manners of the lettered world, and filled Europe with love and poetry. But the basis of all excellence is truth: he that professes love ought to feel its power. Petrarch was a real lover, and Laura doubtless deserved his tenderness. Of Cowley, we are told by Barnes, who had means enough of information, that, whatever he may talk of his own inflammability, and the variety of characters by which his heart was divided, he in reality was in love but once, and then never had resolution to tell his passion.

This consideration cannot but abate, in some measure, the reader's esteem for the work and the author. To love excellence, is natural; it is natural likewise for the lover to solicit reciprocal regard by an elaborate display of his own qualifications. The desire of pleasing has in different men produced actions of heroism, and effusions of wit; but it seems as reasonable to appear the champion as the poet of an "airy nothing," and to quarrel as to write for what Cowley might have learned from his master Pindar to call the "dream of a shadow."

It is surely not difficult, in the solitude of a college, or in the bustle of the world, to find useful studies and serious employment.

No man needs to be so burthened with life as to squander it in voluntary dreams of fictitious occurrences. The man that sits down to suppose himself charged with treason or peculation, and heats his mind to an elaborate purgation of his character from crimes which he was never within the possibility of committing, differs only by the infrequency of his folly from him who praises beauty which he never saw, complains of jealousy which he never felt; supposes himself sometimes invited, and sometimes forsaken; fatigues his fancy, and ransacks his memory, for images which may exhibit the gaiety of hope, or the gloominess of despair, and dresses his imaginary Chloris or Phyllis sometimes in flowers fading as her beauty, and sometimes in gems lasting as her virtues.

This year [1656] he published his poems, with a preface, in which he seems to have inserted something, suppressed in subsequent editions, which was interpreted to denote some relaxation of his loyalty. In this preface he declares, that "his desire had been for some days past, and did still very vehemently continue, to retire himself to some of the American plantations, and to forsake this world for ever."

From the obloquy which the appearance of submission to the usurpers brought upon him, his biographer has been very diligent to clear him, and indeed it does not seem to have lessened his reputation. His wish for retirement we can easily believe to be undissembled; a man harassed in one kingdom, and persecuted in another, who, after a course of business that employed all his days and half his nights in cyphering and decyphering, comes to his own country and steps into a prison, will be willing enough to retire to some place of quiet, and of safety. Yet let neither our reverence for a genius, nor our pity for a sufferer, dispose us to forget that, if his activity was virtue, his retreat was cowardice.

He then took upon himself the character of Physician, still, according to Sprat, with intention "to dissemble the main design of his coming over," and, as Mr. Wood relates, "complying with the men then in power (which was much taken notice of by the royal party) he obtained an order to be created Doctor of Physick, which being done to his mind (whereby he gained the ill-will of some of his friends), he went into France again, having made a copy of verses on Oliver's death."

This is no favourable representation, yet even in this not much

795

wrong can be discovered. How far he complied with the men in power, is to be enquired before he can be blamed. It is not said that he told them any secrets, or assisted them by intelligence, or any other act. If he only promised to be quiet, that they in whose hands he was might free him from confinement, he did what no law of society prohibits.

The man whose miscarriage in a just cause has put him in the power of his enemy may, without any violation of his integrity, regain his liberty, or preserve his life by a promise of neutrality: for the stipulation gives the enemy nothing which he had not before; the neutrality of a captive may be always secured by his imprisonment or death. He that is at the disposal of another, may not promise to aid him in any injurious act, because no power can compel active obedience. He may engage to do nothing, but not to do ill.

.   .   .   .   .

At the same time were produced from the same university, the two great Poets, Cowley and Milton, of dissimilar genius, of opposite principles; but concurring in the cultivation of Latin poetry, in which the English, till their works and May's poem appeared, seemed unable to contest the palm with any other of the lettered nations.

If the Latin performances of Cowley and Milton be compared, for May I hold to be superior to both, the advantage seems to lie on the side of Cowley. Milton is generally content to express the thoughts of the ancients in their language; Cowley, without much loss of purity or elegance, accommodates the diction of Rome to his own conceptions.

.   .   .   .   .

"Cutter of Coleman-street"

Mr. Dryden, who went with Mr. Sprat to the first exhibition, related to Mr. Dennis, "that when they told Cowley how little favour had been shewn him, he received the news of his ill success, not with so much firmness as might have been expected from so great a man."

What firmness they expected, or what weakness Cowley discovered, cannot be known. He that misses his end will never be as much pleased as he that attains it, even when he can impute no part of his failure to himself; and when the end is to please the multitude, no man perhaps has a right, in things admitting of gradation and comparison, to throw the whole blame upon his judges, and totally to exclude diffidence and shame by a haughty consciousness of his own excellence.

For the rejection of this play, it is difficult now to find the reason: it certainly has, in a very great degree, the power of fixing attention and exciting merriment.

．　　　　　．　　　　　．

His vehement desire of retirement now came again upon him. "Not finding," says the morose Wood, "that preferment conferred upon him which he expected, while others for their money carried away most places, he retired discontented into Surrey."

"He was now," says the courtly Sprat, "weary of the vexations and formalities of an active condition. He had been perplexed with a long compliance to foreign manners. He was satiated with the arts of a court; which sort of life, though his virtue made it innocent to him, yet nothing could make it quiet. Those were the reasons that moved him to follow the violent inclination of his own mind, which, in the greatest throng of his former business, had still called upon him, and represented to him the true delights of solitary studies, of temperate pleasures, and a moderate revenue below the malice and flatteries of fortune."

So differently are things seen, and so differently are they shown; but actions are visible, though motives are secret. Cowley certainly retired; first to Barn-elms, and afterwards to Chertsey, in Surrey. He seems, however, to have lost part of his dread of the *hum of men*. He thought himself now safe enough from intrusion, without the defence of mountains and oceans; and instead of seeking shelter in America, wisely went only so far from the bustle of life as that he might easily find his way back, when solitude should grow tedious.

．　　　　．　　　　．　　　　．　　　　．

Cowley, like other poets who have written with narrow views, and instead of tracing intellectual pleasure to its natural sources in the mind of man, paid their court to temporary prejudices, has been at one time too much praised, and too much neglected at another.

Wit, like all other things subject by their nature to the choice of man, has its changes and fashions, and at different times takes different forms. About the beginning of the seventeenth century appeared a race of writers that may be termed the metaphysical poets; of whom, in a criticism on the works of Cowley, the last of the race, it is not improper to give some account.

The metaphysical poets were men of learning, and to shew their learning was their whole endeavour; but, unluckily resolving to shew it in rhyme, instead of writing poetry, they only wrote verses, and very often such verses as stood the trial of the finger better than of the ear; for the modulation was so imperfect, that they were only found to be verses by counting the syllables.

If the father of criticism has rightly denominated poetry τέχνη μιμητικὴ, *an imitative art*, these writers will, without great wrong, lose their right to the name of poets; for they cannot be said to have imitated any thing; they neither copied nature nor life; neither painted the forms of matter, nor represented the operations of intellect.

Those however who deny them to be poets, allow them to be wits. Dryden confesses of himself and his contemporaries, that they fall below Donne in wit, but maintains that they surpass him in poetry.

If Wit be well described by Pope, as being "that which has been often thought, but was never before so well expressed," they certainly never attained, nor ever sought it; for they endeavoured to be singular in their thoughts, and were careless of their diction. But Pope's account of wit is undoubtedly erroneous: he depresses it below its natural dignity, and reduces it from strength of thought to happiness of language.

If by a more noble and more adequate conception that be considered as Wit, which is at once natural and new, that which, though not obvious, is, upon its first production, acknowledged to be just; if it be that, which he that never found it, wonders how he missed; to wit of this kind the metaphysical poets have seldom risen. Their thoughts are often new, but seldom natural; they are not obvious, but neither are they just; and the reader, far from wondering that he missed them, wonders more frequently by what perverseness of industry they were ever found.

But Wit, abstracted from its effects upon the hearer, may be more rigorously and philosophically considered as a kind of *discordia concors*; a combination of dissimilar images, or discovery of occult resemblances in things apparently unlike. Of wit, thus defined, they have more than enough. The most heterogeneous ideas are yoked by violence together; nature and art are ransacked for illustrations, comparisons, and allusions; their learning instructs, and their subtilty surprises; but the reader commonly thinks his improvement dearly bought, and though he sometimes admires is seldom pleased.

From this account of their compositions it will be readily inferred, that they were not successful in representing or moving the affections. As they were wholly employed on something unexpected and surprising, they had no regard to that uniformity of sentiment which enables us to conceive and to excite the pains and the pleasure of other minds: they never enquired what, on any occasion, they should have said or done; but wrote rather as beholders than partakers of human nature; as Beings looking upon good and evil, impassive and at leisure; as Epicurean deities making remarks on the actions of men, and the vicissitudes of life, without interest and without emotion. Their courtship was void of fondness, and their lamentation of sorrow. Their wish was only to say what they hoped had been never said before.

Nor was the sublime more within their reach than the pathetick; for they never attempted that comprehension and expanse of thought which at once fills the whole mind, and of which the first effect is sudden astonishment, and the second rational admiration. Sublimity is produced by aggregation, and littleness by dispersion. Great thoughts are always general, and consist in positions not limited by exceptions, and in descriptions not descending to minuteness. It is with great propriety that Subtlety, which in its original import means exility of particles, is taken in its metaphorical meaning for nicety of distinction. Those writers who lay on the watch for novelty could have little hope of greatness; for great things cannot have escaped former observation. Their attempts were always analytick; they broke every image into fragments; and could no more represent, by their slender conceits and laboured particularities, the prospects of nature, or the scenes of life, than he, who dissects a sun-beam with a prism, can exhibit the wide effulgence of a summer noon.

What they wanted however of the sublime, they endeavoured to supply by hyperbole; their amplification had no limits; they left not only reason but fancy behind them; and produced combinations of confused magnificence, that not only could not be credited, but could not be imagined.

Yet great labour, directed by great abilities, is never wholly lost: if they frequently threw away their wit upon false conceits, they likewise sometimes struck out unexpected truth: if their conceits were far-fetched, they were often worth the carriage. To write on their plan, it was at least necessary to read and think. No man cold be born a metaphysical poet, nor assume the dignity of a writer, by descriptions copied from descriptions, by imitations borrowed from imitations, by traditional imagery, and hereditary similies, by readiness of rhyme, and volubility of syllables.

In perusing the works of this race of authours, the mind is exercised either by recollection or inquiry; either something already learned is to be retrieved, or something new is to be examined. If their greatness seldom elevates, their acuteness often surprises; if the imagination is not always gratified, at least the powers of reflection and comparison are employed; and in the mass of materials which ingenious absurdity has thrown together, genuine wit and useful knowledge may be sometimes found, buried perhaps in grossness of expression, but useful to those who know their value; and such as, when they are expanded to perspicuity, and polished to elegance, may give lustre to works which have more propriety, though less copiousness of sentiment.

This kind of writing, which was, I believe, borrowed from Marino and his followers, had been recommended by the example of Donne, a man of very extensive and various knowledge, and by Jonson, whose manner resembled that of Donne more in the ruggedness of his lines than in the cast of his sentiments.

When their reputation was high, they had undoubtedly more imitators, than time has left behind. Their immediate successors, of whom any remembrance can be said to remain, were Suckling, Waller, Denham, Cowley, Cleveland, and Milton. Denham and Waller sought another way to fame, by improving the harmony of our numbers. Milton tried the metaphysick stile only in his lines upon Hobson the Carrier. Cowley adopted it, and excelled his predecessors, having as much sentiment, and more musick. Suckling neither improved versification, nor abounded in conceits. The fashionable stile remained chiefly with Cowley; Suckling could not reach it, and Milton disdained it.

Critical Remarks are not easily understood without examples; and I have therefore collected instances of the modes of writing by which this species of poets, for poets they were called by themselves and their admirers, was eminently distinguished.

As the authors of this race were perhaps more desirous of being admired than understood, they sometimes drew their conceits from

recesses of learning not very much frequented by common readers
of poetry. Thus Cowley on *Knowledge*:

> The sacred tree midst the fair orchard grew;
>   The phœnix Truth did on it rest,
>   And built his perfum'd nest,
> That right Porphyrian tree which did true Logick shew.
>   Each leaf did learned notions give,
>   And th' apples were demonstrative:
> So clear their colour and divine,
> The very shade they cast did other lights outshine.

On Anacreon continuing a lover in his old age:

> Love was with thy life entwin'd,
> Close as heat with fire is join'd,
> A powerful brand prescrib'd the date
> Of thine, like Meleager's fate.
> Th' antiperistasis of age
> More enflam'd thy amorous rage.

In the following verses we have an allusion to a Rabbinical
opinion concerning Manna:

> Variety I ask not: give me one
> To live perpetually upon.
> The person Love does to us fit,
> Like manna, has the taste of all in it.

Thus *Donne* shews his medicinal knowledge in some encomiastick
verses:

> In every thing there naturally grows
> A Balsamum to keep it fresh and new,
>   If 'twere not injur'd by extrinsique blows;
> Your youth and beauty are this balm in you.
>   But, you of learning and religion,
> And virtue and such ingredients, have made
>   A mithridate, whose operation
> Keeps off, or cures what can be done or said.

Though the following lines of Donne, on the last night of the
year, have something in them too scholastick, they are not inelegant:

> This twilight of two years, not past nor next,
>   Some emblem is of me, or I of this,
> Who meteor-like, of stuff and form perplext,
>   Whose what and where, in disputation is,
>   If I should call me any thing, should miss.

I sum the years and me, and find me not
  Debtor to th' old, nor creditor to th' new,
That cannot say, my thanks I have forgot,
  Nor trust I this with hopes; and yet scarce true
  This bravery is, since these times shew'd me you.
DONNE.

Yet more abstruse and profound is *Donne's* reflection upon Man as a Microcosm:

If men be worlds, there is in every one
Something to answer in some proportion
All the world's riches: and in good men, this
Virtue, our form's form, and our soul's soul is.

Of thoughts so far-fetched, as to be not only unexpected, but unnatural, all their books are full.

To a Lady, who wrote poesies for rings.

They, who above do various circles find,
Say, like a ring th' æquator heaven does bind.
When heaven shall be adorn'd by thee,
(Which then more heav'n than 'tis, will be)
'Tis thou must write the poesy there,
For it wanteth one as yet,
Tho' the sun pass through 't twice a year,
The sun, which is esteem'd the god of Wit.
COWLEY.

The difficulties which have been raised about identity in philosophy, are by Cowley with still more perplexity applied to Love:

Five years ago (says story) I lov'd you,
For which you call me most inconstant now;
Pardon me, madam, you mistake the man;
For I am not the same that I was then;
No flesh is now the same 'twas then in me,
And that my mind is chang'd yourself may see.

The same thoughts to retain still, and intents
Were more inconstant far; for accidents
Must of all things most strangely inconstant prove,
If from one subject they t' another move:
My members then, the father members were
From whence these take their birth, which now are here.
If then this body love what th' other did,
'Twere incest, which by nature is forbid.

802

The love of different women is, in geographical poetry, compared
to travel through different countries:

> Hast thou not found, each woman's breast
> (The lands where thou hast travelled)
> Either by savages possest,
>   Or wild, and uninhabited ?
>   What joy could'st take, or what repose
> In countries so uncivilis'd as those ?
> Lust, the scorching dog-star, here
>   Rages with immoderate heat;
> Whilst Pride, the rugged Northern Bear,
>   In others makes the cold too great.
> And where these are temp'rate known,
> The soil's all barren sand, or rocky stone.

COWLEY.

A lover, burnt up by his affection, is compared to Egypt:

> The fate of Egypt I sustain,
> And never feel the dew of rain,
> From clouds which in the head appear;
>   But all my too much moisture owe,
>   To overflowings of the heart below.   COWLEY.

The lover supposes his lady acquainted with the ancient laws of
augury and rites of sacrifice:

> And yet this death of mine, I fear,
> Will ominous to her appear:
>   When sound in every other part,
> Her sacrifice is found without an heart.
>   For the last tempest of my death
> Shall sigh out that too, with my breath.

That the chaos was harmonised has been recited of old; but
whence the different sounds arose, remained for a modern to
discover:

> Th' ungovern'd parts no correspondence knew,
> An artless war from thwarting motions grew;
> Till they to number and fixt rules were brought.
> Water and air he for the tenor chose,
> Earth made the Base, the Treble flame arose.

COWLEY.

The tears of lovers are always of great poetical account; but
Donne has extended them into worlds. If the lines are not easily
understood, they may be read again.

> On a round ball
> A workman, that hath copies by, can lay
> An Europe, Afric, and an Asia,
> And quickly make that, which was nothing, all.

803

> So doth each tear,
> Which thee doth wear,
> A globe, yea world, by that impression grow,
> Till thy tears mixt with mine do overflow
> This world, by waters sent from thee my heaven
> dissolved so.

On reading the following lines the reader may perhaps cry out—
Confusion worse confounded.

> Here lies a she sun, and a he moon there,
> She gives the best light to his sphere,
> Or each is both, and all, and so
> They unto one another nothing owe.　　　Donne.

Who but Donne would have thought that a good man is a telescope?

> Tho' God be our true glass, thro' which we see
> All, since the being of all things is he,
> Yet are the trunks, which do to us derive
> Things, in proportion fit, by perspective
> Deeds of good men; for by their living here,
> Virtues, indeed remote, seem to be near.

Who would imagine it possible that in a very few lines so many remote ideas could be brought together:

> Since 'tis my doom, Love's undershrieve,
> Why this reprieve?
> Why doth my She Advowson fly
> Incumbency?
> To sell thyself dost thou intend
> By candle's end,
> And hold the contrast thus in doubt,
> Life's taper out?
> Think but how soon the market fails,
> Your sex lives faster than the males;
> As if to measure age's span,
> The sober Julian were th' account of man,
> Whilst you live by the fleet Gregorian.　　　Cleveland.

Of enormous and disgusting hyperboles, these may be examples:

> By every wind, that comes this way,
> Send me at least a sigh or two,
> Such and so many I'll repay
> As shall themselves make winds to get to you.
> 　　　　　　　　　　　　　Cowley.

> In tears I'll waste these eyes
> By love so vainly fed;
> So lust of old the Deluge punished.　　　Cowley.

All arm'd in brass, the richest dress of war,
(A dismal glorious sight), he shone afar.
The sun himself started with sudden fright,
To see his beams return so dismal bright.　COWLEY.

An universal consternation:

His bloody eyes he hurls round, his sharp paws
Tear up the ground; then runs he wild about,
Lashing his angry tail and roaring out.
Beasts creep into their dens, and tremble there;
Trees, tho' no wind is stirring, shake with fear;
Silence and horrour fill the place around:
Echo itself dares scarce repeat the sound.　COWLEY.

Their fictions were often violent and unnatural.

Of his Mistress bathing:

The fish around her crouded, as they do
To the false light that treach'rous fishers shew,
And all with as much ease might taken be,
　　As she at first took me:
　　For ne'er did light so clear
　　Among the waves appear,
Tho' ev'ry night the sun himself set there.

COWLEY.

The poetical effect of a Lover's name upon glass:

My name engrav'd herein,
Doth contribute my firmness to this glass;
　Which, ever since that charm, hath been
As hard, as that which grav'd it, was.　DONNE.

Their conceits were sometimes slight and trifling:

On an inconstant woman.

He enjoys thy calmy sunshine now,
　And no breath stirring hears,
In the clear heaven of thy brow,
　No smallest cloud appears.
　He sees thee gentle, fair and gay,
And trusts the faithless April of thy May.

COWLEY.

Upon a paper written with the juice of lemon, and read by the
fire:

Nothing yet in thee is seen,
But when a genial heat warms thee within,
A new-born wood of various lines there grows;
　Here buds an L, and there a B,
　Here sprouts a V, and there a T,
And all the flourishing letters stand in rows.　COWLEY.

As they sought only for novelty, they did not much enquire whether their allusions were to things high or low, elegant or gross; whether they compared the little to the great, or the great to the little.

Physick and Chirurgery for a Lover.

Gently, ah gently, madam, touch
 The wound, which you yourself have made;
That pain must needs be very much,
 Which makes me of your hand afraid.
Cordials of pity give me now,
For I too weak for purgings grow.   COWLEY.

The World and a Clock.

Mahol, th' inferior world's fantastic face,
Thro' all the turns of matter's maze did trace;
Great Nature's well-set clock in pieces took;
On all the springs and smallest wheels did look
Of life and motion; and with equal art
Made up again the whole of every part.   COWLEY.

A coal-pit has not often found its poet; but that it may not want its due honour, Cleveland has paralleled it with the Sun:

The mod'rate value of our guiltless ore,
Makes no man atheist, nor no woman whore:
Yet why should hallow'd vestals sacred shrine
Deserve more honour than a flaming mine?
These pregnant wombs of heat would fitter be
Than a few embers for a deity.
Had he our pits, the Persian would admire
No sun, but warm's devotion at our fire:
He'd leave the trotting whipster, and prefer
Our profound Vulcan 'bove that waggoner.
For wants he heat? or light? or would have store?
Or both? 'tis here: and what can suns give more?
Nay, what's the sun, but in a different name,
A coal-pit rampant, or a mine on flame!
Then let this truth reciprocally run,
The sun's heaven's coalery, and coals our sun.

Death, a Voyage:

              No family
E'er rigg'd a soul for heaven's discovery,
With whom more venturers might boldly dare
Venture their stakes, with him in joy to share.   DONNE.

Their thoughts and expressions were sometimes grossly absurd, and such as no figures or licence can reconcile to the understanding.

A Lover neither dead nor alive:

Then down I laid my head,
Down on cold earth; and for a while was dead,
And my freed soul to a strange somewhere fled:
    Ah sottish soul, said I,
    When back to its cage again I saw it fly:
    Fool to resume her broken chain!
    And row her galley here again!
    Fool, to that body to return
Where it condemn'd and destin'd is to burn!
    Once dead, how can it be,
Death should a thing so pleasant seem to thee,
That thou should'st come to live it o'er again in me?

COWLEY.

A Lover's heart, a hand grenado.

Wo to her stubborn heart, if once mine come
    Into the self-same room,
    'Twill tear and blow up all within,
Like a grenado shot into a magazin.
Then shall love keep the ashes, and torn parts,
    Of both our broken hearts:
    Shall out of both one new one make;
From her's th' alloy; from mine, the metal take.

COWLEY.

The poetical Propagation of Light.

The Prince's favour is diffus'd o'er all,
From which all fortunes, names and natures fall;
Then from those wombs of stars, the Bride's bright eyes,
At every glance, a constellation flies,
And sowes the court with stars, and doth prevent
In light and power, the all-ey'd firmament;
First her eye kindles other ladies' eyes,
Then from their beams their jewels lustres rise;
And from their jewels torches do take fire,
And all is warmth, and light, and good desire.   DONNE.

They were in very little care to clothe their notions with elegance of dress, and therefore miss the notice and the praise which are often gained by those, who think less, but are more diligent to adorn their thoughts.

That a mistress beloved is fairer in idea than in reality, is by Cowley thus expressed:

Thou in my fancy dost much higher stand,
Than women can be plac'd by Nature's hand;
And I must needs, I'm sure, a loser be,
To change thee, as thou'rt there, for very thee.

That prayer and labour should co-operate, are thus taught by Donne:

> In none but us, are such mixt engines found,
> As hands of double office: for the ground
> We till with them; and them to heav'n we raise;
> Who prayerless labours, or without this, prays,
> Doth but one half, that's none.

By the same author, a common topick, the danger of procrastination, is thus illustrated :

> ——That which I should have begun
> In my youth's morning, now late must be done;
> And I, as giddy travellers must do,
> Which stray or sleep all day, and having lost
> Light and strength, dark and tir'd must then ride post.

All that Man has to do is to live and die; the sum of humanity is comprehended by Donne in the following lines:

> Think in how poor a prison thou didst lie,
> After, enabled but to suck and cry.
> Think, when 'twas grown to most, 'twas a poor inn,
> A province pack'd up in two yards of skin,
> And that usurp'd, or threaten'd with a rage
> Of sicknesses, or their true mother, age.
> But think that death hath now enfranchis'd thee;
> Thou hast thy expansion now, and liberty;
> Think, that a rusty piece discharg'd is flown
> In pieces, and the bullet is his own,
> And freely flies: this to thy soul allow,
> Think thy shell broke, think thy soul hatch'd but now.

They were sometimes indelicate and disgusting. Cowley thus apostrophises beauty:

> ——Thou tyrant, which leav'st no man free!
> Thou subtle thief, from whom nought safe can be!
> Thou murth'rer, which hast kill'd, and devil, which would'st damn me.

Thus he addresses his Mistress:

> Thou, who in many a propriety,
> So truly art the sun to me,
> Add one more likeness, which I'm sure you can,
> And let me and my sun beget a man.

Thus he represents the meditations of a Lover:

> Tho' in thy thoughts scarce any tracts have been
>   So much as of original sin,
> Such charms thy beauty wears as might
> Desires in dying confest saints excite.

> Thou with strange adultery
> Dost in each breast a brothel keep;
> Awake, all men do lust for thee,
> And some enjoy thee when they sleep.

The true taste of Tears.

> Hither with crystal vials, lovers, come,
> And take my tears, which are love's wine,
> And try your mistress' tears at home,
> For all are false, that taste not just like mine.
>
> DONNE.

This is yet more indelicate:

> As the sweet sweat of roses in a still,
> As that which from chaf'd musk-cat's pores doth trill,
> As the almighty balm of th' early East,
> Such as the sweet drops of my mistress' breast.
> And on her neck her skin such lustre sets,
> They seem no sweat drops, but pearl coronets:
> Rank sweaty froth thy mistress' brow defiles.
>
> DONNE.

Their expressions sometimes raise horror, when they intend perhaps to be pathetic:

> As men in hell are from diseases free,
> So from all other ills am I,
> Free from their known formality:
> But all pains eminently lie in thee.   COWLEY.

They were not always strictly curious, whether the opinions from which they drew their illustrations were true; it was enough that they were popular. Bacon remarks, that some falsehoods are continued by tradition, because they supply commodious allusions.

> It gave a piteous groan, and so it broke;
> In vain it something would have spoke:
> The love within too strong for 't was,
> Like poison put into a Venice-glass.   COWLEY.

In forming descriptions they looked out not for images, but for conceits. Night has been a common subject, which poets have contended to adorn. Dryden's Night is well known; Donne's is as follows:

> Thou seest me here at midnight, now all rest:
> Time's dead low-water; when all minds divest
> To-morrow's business, when the labourers have
> Such rest in bed, that their last church-yard grave,
> Subject to change, will scarce be a type of this,
> Now when the client, whose last hearing is

> To-morrow, sleeps; when the condemned man,
> Who when he opes his eyes, must shut them then
> Again by death, altho' sad watch he keep,
> Doth practise dying by a little sleep,
> Thou at this midnight seest me.

It must be however confessed of these writers, that if they are upon common subjects often unnecessarily and unpoetically subtle; yet where scholastick speculation can be properly admitted, their copiousness and acuteness may justly be admired. What Cowley has written upon Hope, shews an unequalled fertility of invention:

> Hope, whose weak being ruin'd is,
>   Alike if it succeed, and if it miss;
> Whom good or ill does equally confound,
> And both the horns of Fate's dilemma wound.
>   Vain shadow, which dost vanquish quite,
>   Both at full moon and perfect night!
>   The stars have not a possibility
>   Of blessing thee;
> If things then from their end we happy call,
> 'Tis Hope is the most hopeless thing of all.
>
> Hope, thou bold taster of delight,
>   Who, whilst thou should'st but taste, devour'st it quite!
> Thou bring'st us an estate, yet leav'st us poor,
> By clogging it with legacies before!
>   The joys which we entire should wed,
>   Come deflow'r'd virgins to our bed;
> Good fortunes without gain imported be,
>   Such mighty custom's paid to thee:
> For joy, like wine, kept close does better taste;
> If it take air before, its spirits waste.

To the following comparison of a man that travels, and his wife that stays at home, with a pair of compasses, it may be doubted whether absurdity or ingenuity has the better claim.

> Our two souls therefore, which are one,
>   Tho' I must go, endure not yet
> A breach, but an expansion,
>   Like gold to airy thinness beat.
>
> If they be two, they are two so
>   As stiff twin-compasses are two,
> Thy soul the fixt foot, make no show
>   To move, but doth, if th' other do.

And tho' it in the centre sit,
  Yet when the other far doth roam,
It leans, and hearkens after it,
  And grows erect, as that comes home.

Such wilt thou be to me, who must
  Like th' other foot, obliquely run.
Thy firmness makes my circle just,
  And makes me end, where I begun.   DONNE.

In all these examples it is apparent, that whatever is improper or vitious, is produced by a voluntary deviation from nature in pursuit of something new and strange; and that the writers fail to give delight, by their desire of exciting admiration.

.   .   .   .   .

In his poem on the death of Hervey, there is much praise, but little passion, a very just and ample delineation of such virtues as a studious privacy admits, and such intellectual excellence as a mind not yet called forth to action can display. He knew how to distinguish, and how to commend the qualities of his companion; but when he wishes to make us weep, he forgets to weep himself, and diverts his sorrow by imagining how his crown of bays if he had it, would *crackle* in the *fire*. It is the odd fate of this thought to be worse for being true. The bay-leaf crackles remarkably as it burns; as therefore this property was not assigned it by chance, the mind must be thought sufficiently at ease that could attend to such minuteness of physiology. But the power of Cowley is not to move the affections, but to exercise the understanding.

The *Chronicle* is a composition unrivalled and alone: such gaiety of fancy, such facility of expression, such varied similitude, such a succession of images, and such a dance of words, it is vain to expect except from Cowley. His strength always appears in his agility; his volatility is not the flutter of a light but the bound of an elastick mind. His levity never leaves his learning behind it; the moralist, the politician, and the critick, mingle their influence even in this airy frolick of genius. To such a performance Suckling could have brought the gaiety, but not the knowledge; Dryden could have supplied the knowledge, but not the gaiety.

.   .   .   .

To the Miscellanies succeed the *Anacreontiques*, or paraphrastical translations of some little poems, which pass, however justly, under the name of Anacreon. Of those songs dedicated to festivity and gaiety, in which even the morality is voluptuous, and which teach nothing but the enjoyment of the present day, he has given rather a pleasing than a faithful representation, having retained their spriteliness, but lost their simplicity. The Anacreon of Cowley, like the Homer of Pope, has admitted the decoration of some modern graces, by which he is undoubtedly made more amiable to common readers, and perhaps, if they would honestly declare their own perceptions, to far the greater part of those whom courtesy and ignorance are content to stile the Learned.

These little pieces will be found more finishèd in their kind than any other of Cowley's works. The diction shews nothing of the mould of time, and the sentiments are at no great distance from our present habitudes of thought. Real mirth must be always natural, and nature is uniform. Men have been wise in very different modes; but they have always laughed the same way.

Levity of thought naturally produced familiarity of language, and the familiar part of language continues long the same: the dialogue of comedy, when it is transcribed from popular manners and real life, is read from age to age with equal pleasure. The artifice of inversion by which the established order of words is changed, or of innovation, by which new words or new meanings of words are introduced, is practised not by those who talk to be understood, but by those who write to be admired.

The Anacreontiques therefore of Cowley give now all the pleasure which they ever gave. If he was formed by nature for one kind of writing more than for another, his power seems to have been greatest in the familiar and the festive.

The next class of his poems is called *The Mistress*, of which it is not necessary to select any particular pieces for praise or censure. They have all the same beauties and faults, and nearly in the same proportion. They are written with exuberance of wit, and with copiousness of learning; and it is truly asserted by Sprat, that the plentitude of the writer's knowledge flows in upon his page, so that the reader is commonly surprised into some improvement. But, considered as the verses of a lover, no man that has ever loved will much commend them. They are neither courtly nor pathetick, have neither gallantry nor fondness. His praises are too far-sought, and too hyperbolical, either to express love, or to excite it: every stanza is crouded with darts and flames, with wounds and death, with mingled souls, and with broken hearts.

The principal artifice by which *The Mistress* is filled with conceits is very copiously displayed by Addison. Love is by Cowley, as by other poets, expressed metaphorically by flame and fire; and that which is true of real fire is said of love, or figurative fire, the same word in the same sentence retaining both significations. Thus, "observing the cold regard of his mistress's eyes, and at the same time their power of producing love in him, he considers them as burning-glasses made of ice. Finding himself able to live in the greatest extremities of love, he concludes the torrid zone to be habitable. Upon the dying of a tree, on which he had cut his loves, he observes, that his flames had burnt up and withered the tree."

These conceits Addison calls mixed wit; that is, wit which consists of thoughts true in one sense of the expression, and false in the other. Addison's representation is sufficiently indulgent. That confusion of images may entertain for a moment; but being unnatural, it soon grows wearisome. Cowley delighted in it, as much as if he had invented it; but, not to mention the ancients, he might have found it full-blown in modern Italy. Thus Sannazaro;

> Aspice quam variis distringar Vesbia curis,
> Uror, & heu! nostro manat ab igne liquor;
> Sum Nilus, sumque Aetna simul; restringite flammas
> O lacrimae, aut lacrimas ebibe flamma meas.

One of the severe theologians of that time censured him as having published *a book of profane and lascivious Verses*. From the charge of profaneness, the constant tenour of his life, which seems to have been eminently virtuous, and the general tendency of his opinions, which discover no irreverence of religion, must defend him; but that the accusation of lasciviousness is unjust, the perusal of his works will sufficiently evince.

Cowley's *Mistress* has no power of seduction; "she plays round the head, but comes not at the heart." Her beauty and absence, her kindness and cruelty, her disdain and inconstancy, produce no correspondence of emotion. His poetical account of the virtues of plants, and colours of flowers, is not perused with more sluggish frigidity. The compositions are such as might have been written for penance by a hermit, or for hire by a philosophical rhymer who had only heard of another sex; for they turn the mind only on the writer, whom, without thinking on a woman but as the subject for

a task, we sometimes esteem as learned, and sometimes despise
as trifling, always admire as ingenious, and always condemn as unnatural.

.   .   .   .   .

The fault of Cowley, and perhaps of all the writers of the metaphysical race, is that of pursuing his thoughts to their last ramifications, by which he loses the grandeur of generality; for of the
greatest things the parts are little; what is little can be but pretty,
and by claiming dignity becomes ridiculous. Thus all the power of
description is destroyed by a scrupulous enumeration; and the
force of metaphors is lost, when the mind by the mention of particulars is turned more upon the original than the secondary sense,
more upon that from which the illustration is drawn than that to
which it is applied.

Of this we have a very eminent example in the ode intituled *The
Muse*, who goes to *take the air* in an intellectual chariot, to which
he harnesses Fancy and Judgement, Wit and Eloquence, Memory
and Invention: how he distinguished Wit from Fancy, or how
Memory could properly contribute to Motion, he has not explained:
we are however content to suppose that he could have justified his
own fiction, and wish to see the Muse begin her career; but there is
yet more to be done.

> Let the postilion Nature mount, and let
> The coachman Art be set;
> And let the airy footmen, running all beside,
> Make a long row of goodly pride;
> Figures, conceits, raptures, and sentences,
> In a well-worded dress,
> And innocent loves, and pleasant truths, and useful lies,
> In all their gaudy liveries.

Every mind is now disgusted with this cumber of magnificence;
yet I cannot refuse myself the four next lines:

> Mount, glorious queen, thy travelling throne,
>   And bid it to put on;
>   For long though cheerful is the way,
> And life alas allows but one ill winter's day.

In the same ode, celebrating the power of the Muse, he gives her
prescience, or, in poetical language, the foresight of events hatch-
ing in futurity; but having once an egg in his mind, he cannot forbear to shew us that he knows what an egg contains:

> Thou into the close nests of time do'st peep,
>   And there with piercing eye
> Through the firm shell and the thick white dost spy
>   Years to come a-forming lie,
> Close in their sacred fecundine asleep.

.   .   .   .   .

To the disproportion and incongruity of Cowley's sentiments must be added the uncertainty and looseness of his measures. He takes the liberty of using in any place a verse of any length, from two syllables to twelve. The verses of Pindar have, as he observes, very little harmony to a modern ear; yet by examining the syllables we perceive them to be regular, and have reason enough for supposing that the ancient audiences were delighted with the sound. The imitator ought therefore to have adopted what he found, and to have added what was wanting; to have preserved a constant return of the same numbers, and to have supplied smoothness of transition and continuity of thought.

It is urged by Dr. Sprat, that the *irregularity of numbers is the very thing* which makes *that kind of poesy fit for all manner of subjects*. But he should have remembered, that what is fit for every thing can fit nothing well. The great pleasure of verse arises from the known measure of the lines, and uniform structure of the stanzas, by which the voice is regulated, and the memory relieved.

If the Pindarick stile be, what Cowley thinks it, *the highest and noblest kind of writing in verse*, it can be adapted only to high and noble subjects; and it will not be easy to reconcile the poet with the critick, or to conceive how that can be the highest kind of writing in verse, which, according to Sprat, *is chiefly to be preferred for its near affinity to prose*.

This lax and lawless versification so much concealed the deficiencies of the barren, and flattered the laziness of the idle, that it immediately overspread our books of poetry; all the boys and girls caught the pleasing fashion, and they that could do nothing else could write like Pindar. The rights of antiquity were invaded, and disorder tried to break into the Latin: a poem on the Sheldonian Theatre, in which all kinds of verse are shaken together, is unhappily inserted in the *Musæ Anglicanæ*. Pindarism prevailed above half a century; but at last died gradually away, and other imitations supply its place.

815

The Pindarique Odes have so long enjoyed the highest degree of poetical reputation, that I am not willing to dismiss them with unabated censure; and surely though the mode of their composition be erroneous, yet many parts deserve at least that admiration which is due to great comprehension of knowledge, and great fertility of fancy. The thoughts are often new, and often striking; but the greatness of one part is disgraced by the littleness of another, and total negligence of language gives the noblest conceptions the appearance of a fabrick august in the plan, but mean in the materials. Yet surely those verses are not without a just claim to praise; of which it may be said with truth, that no man but Cowley could have written them.

"Davideis"

Sacred History has been always read with submissive reverence, and an imagination over-awed and controlled. We have been accustomed to acquiesce in the nakedness and simplicity of the authentick narrative, and to repose on its veracity with such humble confidence, as suppresses curiosity. We go with the historian as he goes, and stop with him when he stops. All amplification is frivolous and vain; all addition to that which is already sufficient for the purposes of religion, seems not only useless, but in some degree profane.

Such events as were produced by the visible interposition of Divine Power are above the power of human genius to dignify. The miracle of Creation, however it may teem with images, is best described with little diffusion of language: *He spake the word, and they were made.*

To the subject, thus originally indisposed to the reception of poetical embellishments, the writer brought little that could reconcile impatience, or attract curiosity. Nothing can be more disgusting than a narrative spangled with conceits, and conceits are all that the Davideis supplies.

One of the great sources of poetical delight is description, or the power of presenting pictures to the mind. Cowley gives inferences instead of images, and shews not what may be supposed to have been seen, but what thoughts the sight might have suggested.

The dress of Gabriel deserves attention:

> He took for skin a cloud most soft and bright,
> That e'er the midday sun pierc'd thro' with light,
> Upon his cheeks a lively blush he spread,
> Wash'd from the morning beauties deepest red,
> An harmless flatt'ring meteor shone for hair,
> And fell adown his shoulders with loose care;
> He cuts out a silk mantle from the skies,
> Where the most spritely azure pleas'd the eyes;
> This he with starry vapours sprinkles all,
> Took in their prime ere they grow ripe and fall;
> Of a new rainbow, ere it fret or fade,
> The choicest piece cut out, a scarfe is made.

This is a just specimen of Cowley's imagery: what might in general expressions be great and forcible, he weakens and makes ridiculous by branching it into small parts. That Gabriel was invested with the softest or brightest colours of the sky, we might have been told, and dismissed to improve the idea in our different proportions of conception; but Cowley could not let us go till he had related where Gabriel got first his skin, and then his mantle, then his lace, and then his scarfe, and related it in the terms of the mercer and taylor.

.   .   .   .   .

In the general review of Cowley's poetry it will be found, that he wrote with abundant fertility, but negligent or unskilful selection; with much thought, but with little imagery; that he is never pathetick, and rarely sublime, but always either ingenious or learned, either acute or profound.

It is said by Denham in his elegy,

> To him no author was unknown;
> Yet what he writ was all his own.

This wide position requires less limitation, when it is affirmed of Cowley, than perhaps of any other poet—He read much, and yet borrowed little.

His character of writing was indeed not his own: he unhappily adopted that which was predominant. He saw a certain way to present praise, and not sufficiently enquiring by what means the ancients have continued to delight through all the changes of human manners, he contented himself with a deciduous laurel, of which the verdure in its spring was bright and gay, but which time has been continually stealing from his brows.

817

He was in his own time considered as of unrivalled excellence. Clarendon represents him as having taken a flight beyond all that went before him; and Milton is said to have declared, that the three greatest English poets were Spenser, Shakespeare, and Cowley.

His manner he had in common with others; but his sentiments were his own. Upon every subject he thought for himself; and such was his copiousness of knowledge, that something at once remote and applicable rushed into his mind; yet it is not likely that he always rejected a commodious idea merely because another had used it: his known wealth was so great, that he might have borrowed without loss of credit.

.   .   .   .   .

His diction was in his own time censured as negligent. He seems not to have known, or not to have considered, that words being arbitrary must owe their power to association, and have the influence, and that only, which custom has given them. Language is the dress of thought; and as the noblest mien, or most graceful action, would be degraded and obscured by a garb appropriated to the gross employments of rusticks or mechanicks, so the most heroick sentiments will lose their efficacy, and the most splendid ideas drop their magnificence, if they are conveyed by words used commonly upon low and trivial occasions, debased by vulgar mouths, and contaminated by inelegant applications.

Truth indeed is always truth, and reason is always reason; they have an intrinsick and unalterable value, and constitute that intellectual gold which defies destruction: but gold may be so concealed in baser matter that only a chymist can recover it, sense may be so hidden in unrefined and plebeian words that none but philosophers can distinguish it; and both may be so buried in impurities, as not to pay the cost of their extraction.

The diction being the vehicle of the thoughts, first presents itself to the intellectual eye; and if the first appearance offends, a further knowledge is not often sought. Whatever professes to benefit by pleasing, must please at once. The pleasures of reason imply something sudden and unexpected; that which elevates must always surprise. What is perceived by slow degrees may gratify us with the consciousness of improvement, but will never strike with the sense of pleasure.

Of all this, Cowley appears to have been without knowledge, or without care. He makes no selection of words, nor seeks any neatness of phrase: he has no elegancies either lucky or elaborate; as his endeavours were rather to impress sentences upon the understanding than images on the fancy, he has few epithets, and those scattered without peculiar propriety or nice adaptation. It seems to follow from the necessity of the subject, rather than the care of the writer, that the diction of his heroick poem is less familiar than that of his slightest writings. He has given not the same numbers, but the same diction to the gentle Anacreon and the tempestuous Pindar.

His versification seems to have had very little of his care; and if what he thinks be true, that his numbers are unmusical only when they are ill read, the art of reading them is at present lost; for they are commonly harsh to modern ears. He has indeed many noble lines, such as the feeble care of Waller never could produce. The bulk of his thoughts sometimes swelled his verse to unexpected and inevitable grandeur; but his excellence of this kind is merely fortuitous: he sinks willingly down to his general carelessness, and avoids with very little care either meanness or asperity.

. . . . .

After so much criticism on his Poems, the Essays which accompany them must not be forgotten. What is said by Sprat of his conversation, that no man could draw from it any suspicion of his excellence in poetry, may be applied to these compositions. No author ever kept his verse and his prose at a greater distance from each other. His thoughts are natural, and his stile has a smooth and placid equability, which has never yet obtained its due commendation. Nothing is far-sought, or hard-laboured; but all is easy without feebleness, and familiar without grossness.

JOHN DENHAM

DENHAM is deservedly considered as one of the fathers of English poetry. "Denham and Waller," says Prior, "improved our versification, and Dryden perfected it." He has given specimens of various composition, descriptive, ludicrous, didactick, and sublime.

He appears to have had, in common with almost all mankind, the ambition of being upon proper occasions *a merry fellow*, and in common with most of them to have been by nature, or by early habits, debarred from it. Nothing is less exhilarating than the ludicrousness of Denham. He does not fail for want of efforts: he is familiar, he is gross; but he is never merry, unless the "Speech

against peace in the close Committee" be excepted. For grave burlesque, however, his imitation of Davenant shews him to have been
well qualified.

His poem on the death of Cowley was his last, and, among his
shorter works, his best performance: the numbers are musical, and
the thoughts are just.

COOPER'S HILL is the work that confers upon him the rank and
dignity of an original author. He seems to have been, at least
among us, the author of a species of composition that may be denominated local poetry, of which the fundamental subject is some
particular landschape, to be poetically described, with the addition
of such embellishments as may be supplied by historical retrospection, or incidental meditation.

To trace a new scheme of poetry has in itself a very high claim to
praise, and its praise is yet more when it is apparently copied by
Garth and Pope; after whose names little will be gained by an
enumeration of smaller poets, that have left scarce a corner of the
island undignified by rhime, or blank verse.

COOPER'S HILL, if it be maliciously inspected, will not be found
without its faults. The digressions are too long, the morality too
frequent, and the sentiments sometimes such as will not bear a
rigorous enquiry.

The four verses, which, since Dryden has commended them, almost
every writer for a century past has imitated, are generally known:

> "O could I flow like thee, and make thy stream
> My great example, as it is my theme!
> Tho' deep, yet clear; tho' gentle, yet not dull;
> Strong without rage, without o'erflowing full."

The lines are in themselves not perfect; for most of the words,
thus artfully opposed, are to be understood simply on one side of
the comparison, and metaphorically on the other; and if there be
any language which does not express intellectual operations by
material images, into that language they cannot be translated. But
so much meaning is comprised in so few words; the particulars of
resemblance are so perspicaciously collected, and every mode of excellence separated from its adjacent fault by so nice a line of limitation; the different parts of the sentence are so accurately adjusted;
and the flow of the last couplet is so smooth and sweet, that the
passage, however celebrated, has not been praised above its merit.

It has beauty peculiar to itself, and must be numbered among those felicities which cannot be produced at will by wit and labour, but must arise unexpectedly in some hour propitious to poetry.

JOHN MILTON

HE now hired a lodging at the house of one Russel, a taylor in St. Bride's Church-yard, and undertook the education of John and Edward Phillips, his sister's sons. Finding his rooms too little, he took a house and garden in Aldersgate-street, which was not then so much out of the world as it is now; and chose his dwelling at the upper end of a passage, that he might avoid the noise of the street. Here he received more boys, to be boarded and instructed.

Let not our veneration for Milton forbid us to look with some degree of merriment on great promises and small performance, on the man who hastens home, because his countrymen are contending for their liberty, and, when he reaches the scene of action, vapours away his patriotism in a private boarding-school. This is the period of his life from which all his biographers seem inclined to shrink. They are unwilling that Milton should be degraded to a school-master; but since it cannot be denied that he taught boys, one finds out that he taught for nothing, and another that his motive was only zeal for the propagation of learning and virtue; and all tell what they do not know to be true, only to excuse an act which no wise man will consider as in itself disgraceful. His father was alive; his allowance was not ample, and he supplied its deficiencies by an honest and useful employment.

It is told, that in the art of education he performed wonders; and a formidable list is given of the authors, Greek and Latin, that were read in Aldersgate-street, by youth between ten and fifteen or sixteen years of age. Those who tell or receive these stories, should consider that nobody can be taught faster than he can learn. The speed of the best horseman must be limited by the power of his horse. Every man, that has ever undertaken to instruct others, can tell what slow advances he has been able to make, and how much patience it requires to recall vagrant inattention, to stimulate sluggish indifference, and to rectify absurd misapprehension.

The purpose of Milton, as it seems, was to teach something more solid than the common literature of schools, by reading those authors that treat of physical subjects; such as the Georgick, and astronomical treatises of the ancients. This was a scheme of improvement which seems to have busied many literary projectors of that age. Cowley, who had more means than Milton of knowing what was wanting to the embellishments of life, formed the same plan of education in his imaginary College.

But the truth is, that the knowledge of external nature, and of the sciences which that knowledge requires or includes, is not the great or the frequent business of the human mind. Whether we provide for action or conversation, whether we wish to be useful or pleasing, the first requisite is the religious and moral knowledge of right and wrong; the next is an acquaintance with the history of mankind, and with those examples which may be said to embody truth, and prove by events the reasonableness of opinions. Prudence and justice are virtues, and excellencies, of all times, and of all places; we are perpetually moralists, but we are geometricians only by chance. Our intercourse with intellectual nature is necessary; our speculations upon matter are voluntary, and at leisure. Physical knowledge is of such rare emergence, that one man may know another half his life without being able to estimate his skill in hydrostaticks or astronomy; but his moral and prudential character immediately appears.

Those authors, therefore, are to be read at schools that supply most axioms of prudence, most principles of moral truth, and most materials for conversation; and these purposes are best served by poets, orators, and historians.

Let me not be censured for this digression as pedantick or paradoxical; for if I have Milton against me, I have Socrates on my side. It was his labour to turn philosophy from the study of nature to speculations upon life, but the innovators whom I oppose are turning off attention from life to nature. They seem to think, that we are placed here to watch the growth of plants, or the motions of the stars. Socrates was rather of opinion, that what we had to learn was, how to do good, and avoid evil.

"Οττι τοι ἐν μεγάροισι κακόν τ' ἀγαθόν τε τέτυκται.

Of institutions we may judge by their effects. From this wonder-working academy, I do not know that there ever proceeded any man very eminent for knowledge: its only genuine product, I believe, is a small History of Poetry, written in Latin by his nephew, of which perhaps none of my readers has ever heard.

·   ·   ·   ·

He that changes his party by his humour, is not more virtuous than he that changes it by his interest; he loves himself rather than truth.

.   .   .   .   .

He published about the same time [1644] his *Areopagitica, a Speech of Mr.* John Milton *for the liberty of unlicensed Printing.* The danger of such unbounded liberty, and the danger of bounding it, have produced a problem in the science of Government, which human understanding seems hitherto unable to solve. If nothing may be published but what civil authority shall have previously approved, power must always be the standard of truth; if every dreamer of innovations may propagate his projects, there can be no settlement; if every murmurer at government may diffuse discontent, there can be no peace; and if every sceptick in theology may teach his follies, there can be no religion. The remedy against these evils is to punish the authors; for it is yet allowed that every society may punish, though not prevent, the publication of opinions, which that society shall think pernicious: but this punishment, though it may crush the author, promotes the book; and it seems not more reasonable to leave the right of printing unrestrained, because writers may be afterwards censured, than it would be to sleep with doors unbolted, because by our laws we can hang a thief.

.   .   .   .   .

He had taken a larger house in Barbican for the reception of scholars; but the numerous relations of his wife, to whom he generously granted refuge for a while, occupied his rooms. In time, however, they went away; and the "house again," says Philips, "now looked like a house of the Muses only, though the accession of scholars was not great. Possibly his having proceeded so far in the education of youth, may have been the occasion of his adversaries calling him pedagogue and school-master; whereas it is well known he never set up for a publick school, to teach all the young fry of a parish; but only was willing to impart his learning and knowledge to relations, and the sons of gentlemen who were his intimate friends; and that neither his writings nor his way of teaching ever savoured in the least of pedantry."

Thus laboriously does his nephew extenuate what cannot be denied, and what might be confessed without disgrace. Milton was not a man who could become mean by a mean employment. This, however, his warmest friends seem not to have found; they therefore shift and palliate. He did not sell literature to all comers at an open shop; he was a chamber-milliner, and measured his commodities only to his friends.

Philips, evidently impatient of viewing him in this state of degradation, tells us that it was not long continued; and, to raise his character again, has a mind to invest him with military splendour: "He is much mistaken," he says, "if there was not about this time a design of making him an adjutant-general in Sir William Waller's army. But the new-modelling of the army proved an obstruction to the design." An event cannot be set at a much greater distance than by having been only *designed, about some time*, if a man *be not much mistaken*. Milton shall be a pedagogue no longer; for, if Philips be not much mistaken, somebody at some time designed him for a soldier.

. . . . .

No man forgets his original trade: the rights of nations, and of kings, sink into questions of grammar, if grammarians discuss them.

. . . . .

Cromwel had now dismissed the parliament by the authority of which he had destroyed monarchy, and commenced monarch himself, under the title of protector, but with kingly and more than kingly power. That his authority was lawful, never was pretended; he himself founded his right only in necessity; but Milton, having now tasted the honey of publick employment, would not return to hunger and philosophy, but, continuing to exercise his office under a manifest usurpation, betrayed to his power that liberty which he had defended. Nothing can be more just than that rebellion should end in slavery; that he, who had justified the murder of his king, for some acts which to him seemed unlawful, should now sell his services, and his flatteries, to a tyrant, of whom it was evident that he could do nothing lawful.

. . . . .

This dependance of the soul upon the seasons, those temporary and periodical ebbs and flows of intellect, may, I suppose, justly be derided as the fumes of vain imagination. *Sapiens dominabitur astris*. The author that thinks himself weather-bound will find, with a little help from hellebore, that he is only idle or exhausted. But while this notion has possession of the head, it produces the inability which it supposes. Our powers owe much of their energy to our hopes; *possunt quia posse videntur*. When success seems attainable, diligence is enforced; but when it is admitted that the faculties are suppressed by a cross wind, or a cloudy sky, the day is given up without resistance; for who can contend with the course of Nature? From such prepossessions Milton seems not to have been free.

. . . . .

"Paradise Lost"

At what particular times of his life the parts of his work were written, cannot often be known. The beginning of the third book shews that he had lost his sight; and the Introduction to the seventh, that the return of the king had clouded him with discountenance; and that he was offended by the licentious festivity of the Restoration. There are no other internal notes of time. Milton, being now cleared from all effects of his disloyalty, had nothing required from him but the common duty of living in quiet, to be rewarded with the common right of protection: but this, which, when he sculked from the approach of his king, was perhaps more than he hoped, seems not to have satisfied him; for no sooner is he safe, than he finds himself in danger, *fallen on evil days and evil tongues, and with darkness and with danger compass'd round.* This darkness, had his eyes been better employed, had undoubtedly deserved compassion; but to add the mention of danger was ungrateful and unjust. He was fallen indeed on *evil days*; the time was come in which regicides could no longer boast their wickedness. But of *evil tongues* for Milton to complain, required impudence at least equal to his other powers; Milton, whose warmest advocates must allow, that he never spared any asperity of reproach or brutality of insolence.

But the charge itself seems to be false; for it would be hard to recollect any reproach cast upon him, either serious or ludicrous, through the whole remaining part of his life. He persued his studies, or his amusements, without persecution, molestation, or insult. Such is the reverence paid to great abilities, however misused: they who contemplated in Milton the scholar and the wit, were contented to forget the reviler of his king.

. . . . .

The slow sale and tardy reputation of this poem, have been always mentioned as evidences of neglected merit, and of the uncertainty of literary fame; and enquiries have been made, and conjecture offered, about the causes of its long obscurity and late reception. But has the case been truly stated? Have not lamentation and wonder been lavished on an evil that was never felt?

That in the reigns of Charles and James the *Paradise Lost* received no publick acclamations is readily confessed. Wit and literature were on the side of the Court: and who that solicited favour or fashion would venture to praise the defender of the regicides? All that he himself could think his due, from *evil tongues* in *evil days*, was that reverential silence which was generously preserved. But it cannot be inferred that his poem was not read, or not, however unwillingly, admired.

The sale, if it be considered, will justify the publick. Those who have no power to judge of past times but by their own, should always doubt their conclusions. The sale of books was not in Milton's age what it is in the present. To read was not then a general amusement; neither traders, nor often gentlemen, thought themselves disgraced by ignorance. The women had not then aspired to literature, nor was every house supplied with a closet of books. Those indeed, who professed learning, were not less learned than at any other time; but of that middle race of students who read for pleasure or accomplishment, and who buy the numerous products of modern typography, the number was then comparatively small. To prove the paucity of readers, it may be sufficient to remark, that the nation had been satisfied, from 1623 to 1664, that is, forty-one years, with only two editions of the works of Shakespeare, which probably did not together make one thousand copies.

The sale of thirteen hundred copies in two years, in opposition to so much recent enmity, and to a style of versification new to all and disgusting to many, was an uncommon example of the prevalence of genius. The demand did not immediately encrease; for many more readers than were supplied at first the nation did not afford. Only three thousand were sold in eleven years; for it forced its way without assistance: its admirers did not dare to publish their opinion; and the opportunities now given of attracting notice by advertisements were then very few; for the means of proclaiming the publication of new books have been produced by that general literature which now pervades the nation through all its ranks.

But the reputation and price of the copy still advanced, till the

Revolution put an end to the secrecy of love, and *Paradise Lost* broke into open view with sufficient security of kind reception.

Fancy can hardly forbear to conjecture with what temper Milton surveyed the silent progress of his work, and marked his reputation stealing its way in a kind of subterraneous current through fear and silence. I cannot but conceive him calm and confident, little disappointed, not at all dejected, relying on his own merit with steady consciousness, and waiting, without impatience, the vicissitudes of opinion, and the impartiality of a future generation.

.   .   .   .   .

Milton has the reputation of having been in his youth eminently beautiful, so as to have been called the Lady of his college. His hair, which was of a light brown, parted at the foretop, and hung down upon his shoulders, according to the picture which he has given of Adam. He was, however, not of the heroick stature, but rather below the middle size, according to Mr. Richardson, who mentions him as having narrowly escaped from being *short and thick*. He was vigorous and active, and delighted in the exercise of the sword, in which he is related to have been eminently skilful. His weapon was, I believe, not the rapier, but the backsword, of which he recommends the use in his book on Education.

His eyes are said never to have been bright; but, if he was a dexterous fencer, they must have been once quick.

His domestick habits, so far as they are known, were those of a severe student. He drank little strong drink of any kind, and fed without delicacy of choice or excess in quantity. In his youth he studied late at night; but afterwards changed his hours, and rested in bed from nine to four in the Summer, and five in the Winter. The course of his day was best known after he was blind. When he first rose he heard a chapter in the Hebrew Bible, and then studied till twelve; then took some exercise for an hour; then dined; then plaid on the organ, and sung, or heard another sing; then studied to six; then entertained his visiters, till eight; then supped, and, after a pipe of tobacco and a glass of water, went to bed.

So is his life described; but this even tenour appears attainable only in Colleges. He that lives in the world will sometimes have the succession of his practice broken and confused. Visiters, of whom Milton is represented to have had great numbers, will come and stay unseasonably; business, of which every man has some, must be done when others will do it.

When he did not care to rise early, he had something read to him by his bedside; perhaps at this time his daughters were employed. He composed much in the morning, and dictated in the day, sitting obliquely in an elbow-chair, with his leg thrown over the arm.

. . . . .

His theological opinions are said to have been first calvinistical; and afterwards, perhaps when he began to hate the Presbyterians, to have tended towards Arminianism. In the mixed questions of theology and government, he never thinks that he can recede far enough from popery, or prelacy; but what Baudius says of Erasmus seems applicable to him, *magis habuit quod fugeret, quam quod sequeretur.* He had determined rather what to condemn than what to approve. He has not associated himself with any denomination of Protestants: we know rather what he was not, than what he was. He was not of the church of Rome; he was not of the church of England.

To be of no church is dangerous. Religion, of which the rewards are distant, and which is animated only by Faith and Hope, will glide by degrees out of the mind, unless it be invigorated and re-impressed by external ordinances, by stated calls to worship, and the salutary influence of example. Milton, who appears to have had full conviction of the truth of Christianity, and to have regarded the Holy Scriptures with the profoundest veneration, to have been untainted by an heretical peculiarity of opinion, and to have lived in a confirmed belief of the immediate and occasional agency of Providence, yet grew old without any visible worship. In the distribution of his hours, there was no hour of prayer, either solitary, or with his household; omitting publick prayers, he omitted all.

Of this omission the reason has been sought, upon a supposition which ought never to be made, that men live with their own approbation, and justify their conduct to themselves. Prayer certainly was not thought superfluous by him, who represents our first parents as praying acceptably in the state of innocence, and efficaciously after their fall. That he lived without prayer can hardly be affirmed; his studies and meditations were an habitual prayer. The neglect of it in his family was probably a fault for which he condemned himself, and which he intended to correct, but that death, as too often happens, intercepted his reformation.

His political notions were those of an acrimonious and surly republican, for which it is not known that he gave any better reason than that *a popular government was the most frugal; for the trappings of a monarchy would set up an ordinary commonwealth.* It is surely very shallow policy, that supposes money to be the chief good; and even this, without considering that the support and expence of a Court is, for the most part, only a particular kind of traffick, by which money is circulated, without any national impoverishment.

Milton's republicanism was, I am afraid, founded in an envious hatred of greatness, and a sullen desire of independence; in petulance, impatient of controul, and pride disdainful of superiority. He hated monarchs in the state, and prelates in the church; for he hated all whom he was required to obey. It is to be suspected that his predominant desire was to destroy rather than establish, and that he felt not so much the love of liberty as repugnance to authority.

It has been observed, that they who most loudly clamour for liberty do not most liberally grant it. What we know of Milton's character, in domestick relations, is, that he was severe and arbitrary. His family consisted of women; and there appears in his books something like a Turkish contempt of females, as subordinate and inferiour beings. That his own daughters might not break the ranks, he suffered them to be depressed by a mean and penurious education. He thought woman made only for obedience, and man only for rebellion.

. . . . .

In the examination of Milton's poetical works, I shall pay so much regard to time as to begin with his juvenile productions. . . . The English poems, though they make no promises of *Paradise Lost*, have this evidence of genius, that they have a cast original and unborrowed. But their peculiarity is not excellence: if they differ from verses of others, they differ for the worse; for they are too often distinguished by repulsive harshness; the combinations of words are new, but they are not pleasing; the rhymes and epithets seem to be laboriously sought, and violently applied.

That in the early part of his life he wrote with much care appears from his manuscripts, happily preserved at Cambridge, in which many of his smaller works are found as they were first written, with the subsequent corrections. Such reliques shew how excellence is acquired; what we hope ever to do with ease, we may learn first to do with diligence.

Those who admire the beauties of this great poet, sometimes

force their own judgement into false approbation of his little pieces, and prevail upon themselves to think that admirable which is only singular. All that short compositions can commonly attain is neatness and elegance. Milton never learned the art of doing little things with grace; he overlooked the milder excellence of suavity and softness; he was a *Lion* that had no skill *in dandling the Kid*.

One of the poems on which much praise has been bestowed is *Lycidas*; of which the diction is harsh, the rhymes uncertain, and the numbers unpleasing. What beauty there is, we must therefore seek in the sentiments and images.

It is not to be considered as the effusion of real passion; for passion runs not after remote allusions and obscure opinions. Passion plucks no berries from the myrtle and ivy, nor calls upon Arethuse and Mincius, nor tells of rough *satyrs* and *fauns with cloven heel*. Where there is leisure for fiction there is little grief.

In this poem there is no nature, for there is no truth; there is no art, for there is nothing new. Its form is that of a pastoral, easy, vulgar, and therefore disgusting: whatever images it can supply, are long ago exhausted; and its inherent improbability always forces dissatisfaction on the mind. When Cowley tells of Hervey that they studied together, it is easy to suppose how much he must miss the companion of his labours, and the partner of his discoveries; but what image of tenderness can be excited by these lines?

> We drove a field, and both together heard
> What time the grey fly winds her sultry horn,
> Batt'ning our flocks with the fresh dews of night.

We know that they never drove a field, and that they had no flocks to batten; and though it be allowed that the representation may be allegorical, the true meaning is so uncertain and remote, that it is never sought, because it cannot be known when it is found.

Among the flocks, and copses, and flowers, appear the heathen deities; Jove and Phœbus, Neptune and Æolus, with a long train of mythological imagery, such as a College easily supplies. Nothing can less display knowledge, or less exercise invention, than to tell how a shepherd has lost his companion, and must now feed his flocks alone, without any judge of his skill in piping; and how one god asks another god what is become of Lycidas, and how neither god can tell. He who thus grieves will excite no sympathy; he who thus praises will confer no honour.

This poem has yet a grosser fault. With these trifling fictions are mingled the most awful and sacred truths, such as ought never to be polluted with such irreverend combinations. The shepherd likewise is now a feeder of sheep, and afterwards an ecclesiastical pastor, a superintendent of a Christian flock. Such equivocations are always unskilful, but here they are indecent, and at least approach to impiety, of which, however, I believe the writer not to have been conscious.

Such is the power of reputation justly acquired, that its blaze drives away the eye from nice examination. Surely no man could have fancied that he read *Lycidas* with pleasure, had he not known its author.

Of the two pieces, *L'Allegro* and *Il Penseroso*, I believe opinion is uniform; every man that reads them, reads them with pleasure. The author's design is not, what Theobald has remarked, merely to shew how objects derive their colours from the mind, by representing the operation of the same things upon the gay and the melancholy temper, or upon the same man as he is differently disposed; but rather how, among the successive variety of appearances, every disposition of mind takes hold on those by which it may be gratified.

The *chearful* man hears the lark in the morning; the *pensive* man hears the nightingale in the evening. The *chearful* man sees the cock strut, and hears the horn and hounds echo in the wood; then walks *not unseen* to observe the glory of the rising sun, or listen to the singing milk-maid, and view the labours of the plowman and the mower; then casts his eyes about him over scenes of smiling plenty, and looks up to the distant tower, the residence of some fair inhabitant; thus he pursues rural gaiety through a day of labour or of play, and delights himself at night with the fanciful narratives of superstitious ignorance.

The *pensive* man, at one time, walks *unseen* to muse at midnight; and at another hears the sullen curfew. If the weather drives him home, he sits in a room lighted only by *glowing embers*; or by a lonely lamp outwatches the North Star, to discover the habitation of separate souls, and varies the shades of meditation, by contemplating the magnificent or pathetick scenes of tragick and epic poetry. When the morning comes, a morning gloomy with rain and wind, he walks into the dark trackless woods, falls asleep by some murmuring water, and with melancholy enthusiasm expects some dream of prognostication, or some musick plaid by aerial performers.

Both Mirth and Melancholy are solitary, silent inhabitants of the breast that neither receive nor transmit communication; no mention is therefore made of a philosophical friend, or a pleasant companion. Seriousness does not arise from any participation of calamity, nor gaiety from the pleasures of the bottle.

The man of *chearfulness*, having exhausted the country, tries what *towered cities* will afford, and mingles with scenes of splendor, gay assemblies, and nuptial festivities; but he mingles a mere spectator, as when the learned comedies of Jonson, or the wild dramas of Shakespeare, are exhibited, he attends the theatre.

The *pensive* man never loses himself in crowds, but walks the cloister, or frequents the cathedral. Milton probably had not yet forsaken the Church.

Both his characters delight in musick; but he seems to think that chearful notes would have obtained from Pluto a compleat dismission of Eurydice, of whom solemn sounds only procured a conditional release.

For the old age of Chearfulness he makes no provision; but Melancholy he conducts with great dignity to the close of life.

Through these two poems the images are properly selected, and nicely distinguished; but the colours of the diction seem not sufficiently discriminated. His Chearfulness is without levity, and his Pensiveness without asperity. I know not whether the characters are kept sufficiently apart. No mirth can, indeed, be found in his melancholy; but I am afraid that I always meet some melancholy in his mirth. They are two noble efforts of imagination.

The greatest of his juvenile performances is the *Mask of Comus*; in which may very plainly be discovered the dawn or twilight of *Paradise Lost*. Milton appears to have formed very early that system of diction, and mode of verse, which his maturer judgement approved, and from which he never endeavoured nor desired to deviate.

Nor does *Comus* afford only a specimen of his language; it exhibits likewise his power of description, and his vigour of sentiment, employed in the praise and defence of virtue. A work more truly poetical is rarely found; allusions, images, and descriptive epithets, embellish almost every period with lavish decoration. As a series of lines, therefore, it may be considered as worthy of all the admiration with which the votaries have received it.

As a drama it is deficient. The action is not probable. A Masque, in those parts where supernatural intervention is admitted, must indeed be given up to all the freaks of imagination; but, so far as the action is merely human, it ought to be reasonable, which can hardly be said of the conduct of the two brothers; who, when their sister sinks with fatigue in a pathless wilderness, wander both away together in search of berries too far to find their way back, and leave a helpless lady to all the sadness and danger of solitude. This however is a defect over-balanced by its convenience.

What deserves more reprehension is, that the prologue spoken in the wild wood by the attendant Spirit is addressed to the audience; a mode of communication so contrary to the nature of dramatick representation, that no precedents can support it.

The discourse of the Spirit is too long: an objection that may be made to almost all the following speeches: they have not the spriteliness of a dialogue animated by reciprocal contention, but seem rather declamations deliberately composed, and formally repeated, on a moral question. The auditor therefore listens as to a lecture, without passion, without anxiety.

The song of Comus has airiness and jollity; but, what may recommend Milton's morals as well as his poetry, the invitations to pleasure are so general, that they excite no distinct images of corrupt enjoyment, and take no dangerous hold on the fancy.

The following soliloquies of Comus and the Lady are elegant, but tedious. The song must owe much to the voice, if it ever can delight. At last the brothers enter, with too much tranquillity; and when they have feared lest their sister should be in danger, and hoped that she is not in danger, the Elder makes a speech in praise of chastity, and the Younger finds how fine it is to be a philosopher.

Then descends the Spirit in form of a shepherd; and the brother, instead of being in haste to ask his help, praises his singing, and enquires his business in that place. It is remarkable, that at this interview the brother is taken with a short fit of rhyming. The Spirit relates that the Lady is in the power of Comus; the brother moralises again; and the Spirit makes a long narration, of no use because it is false, and therefore unsuitable to a good Being.

In all these parts the language is poetical, and the sentiments are generous; but there is something wanting to allure attention.

The dispute between the Lady and Comus is the most animated and affecting scene of the drama, and wants nothing but a brisker reciprocation of objections and replies to invite attention, and detain it.

The songs are vigorous, and full of imagery; but they are harsh in their diction, and not very musical in their numbers.

Throughout the whole, the figures are too bold, and the language too luxuriant for dialogue. It is a drama in the epic stile, inelegantly splendid, and tediously instructive.

The *Sonnets* were written in different parts of Milton's life, upon different occasions. They deserve not any particular criticism; for of the best it can only be said, that they are not bad; and perhaps only the eighth and the twenty-first are truly entitled to this slender commendation. The fabrick of a sonnet, however adapted to the Italian language, has never succeeded in ours, which, having greater variety of termination, requires the rhymes to be often changed.

Those little pieces may be dispatched without much anxiety; a greater work calls for greater care. I am now to examine *Paradise Lost*; a poem, which, considered with respect to design, may claim the first place, and with respect to performance the second among the productions of the human mind.

By the general consent of criticks, the first praise of genius is due to the writer of an epick poem, as it requires an assemblage of all the powers which are singly sufficient for other compositions. Poetry is the art of uniting pleasure with truth, by calling imagination to the help of reason. Epick poetry undertakes to teach the most important truths by the most pleasing precepts, and therefore relates some great event in the most affecting manner. History must supply the writer with the rudiments of narration, which he must improve and exalt by a nobler art, animate by dramatick energy, and diversify by retrospection and anticipation; morality must teach him the exact bounds, and different shades, of vice and virtue: from policy, and the practice of life, he has to learn the discriminations of character, and the tendency of the passions, either single or combined; and physiology must supply him with illustrations and images. To put these materials to poetical use, is required an imagination capable of painting nature, and realizing fiction. Nor is he yet a poet till he has attained the whole extension of his language, distinguished all the delicacies of phrase, and all the colours of words, and learned to adjust their different sounds to all the varieties of metrical modulation.

Bossu is of opinion that the poet's first work is to find a *moral*, which his fable is afterwards to illustrate and establish. This seems to have been the process only of Milton; the moral of other poems is incidental and consequent; in Milton's only it is essential and intrinsick. His purpose was the most useful and the most arduous; *to vindicate the ways of God to man*; to shew the reasonableness of religion, and the necessity of obedience to the Divine Law.

To convey this moral there must be a *fable*, a narration artfully constructed, so as to excite curiosity, and surprise expectation. In this part of his work, Milton must be confessed to have equalled every other poet. He has involved in his account of the Fall of Man the events which preceded, and those that were to follow it: he has interwoven the whole system of theology with such propriety, that every part appears to be necessary; and scarcely any recital is wished shorter for the sake of quickening the progress of the main action.

The subject of an epick poem is naturally an event of great importance. That of Milton is not the destruction of a city, the conduct of a colony, or the foundation of an empire. His subject is the fate of worlds, the revolutions of heaven and of earth; rebellion against the Supreme King, raised by the highest order of created beings; the overthrow of their host, and the punishment of their crime; the creation of a new race of reasonable creatures; their original happiness and innocence, their forfeiture of immortality, and their restoration to hope and peace.

Great events can be hastened or retarded only by persons of elevated dignity. Before the greatness displayed in Milton's poem, all other greatness shrinks away. The weakest of his agents are the highest and noblest of human beings, the original parents of mankind; with whose actions the elements consented; on whose rectitude, or deviation of will, depended the state of terrestrial nature, and the condition of all the future inhabitants of the globe.

Of the other agents in the poem, the chief are such as it is irreverence to name on slight occasions. The rest are lower powers;

—— of which the least could wield
Those elements, and arm him with the force
Of all their regions;

powers, which only the controul of Omnipotence restrains from laying creation waste, and filling the vast expanse of space with ruin and confusion. To display the motives and actions of beings thus superiour, so far as human reason can examine them, or human imagination represent them, is the task which this mighty poet has undertaken and performed.

To the compleatness or *integrity* of the design nothing can be objected; it has distinctly and clearly what Aristotle requires, a beginning, a middle, and an end. There is perhaps no poem, of the same length, from which so little can be taken without apparent mutilation. Here are no funeral games, nor is there any long description of a shield. The short digressions at the beginning of the third, seventh, and ninth books, might doubtless be spared; but superfluities so beautiful, who would take away? or who does not wish that the author of the *Iliad* had gratified succeeding ages with a little knowledge of himself? Perhaps no passages are more frequently or more attentively read than those extrinsick paragraphs; and, since the end of poetry is pleasure, that cannot be unpoetical with which all are pleased.

The thoughts which are occasionally called forth in the progress, are such as could only be produced by an imagination in the highest degree fervid and active, to which materials were supplied by incessant study and unlimited curiosity. The heat of Milton's mind might be said to sublimate his learning, to throw off into his work the spirit of science, unmingled with its grosser parts.

He had considered creation in its whole extent, and his descriptions are therefore learned. He had accustomed his imagination to unrestrained indulgence, and his conceptions therefore were extensive. The characteristick quality of his poem is sublimity. He sometimes descends to the elegant, but his element is the great. He can occasionally invest himself with grace; but his natural port is gigantick loftiness. He can please when pleasure is required; but it is his peculiar power to astonish.

He seems to have been well acquainted with his own genius, and to know what it was that Nature had bestowed upon him more bountifully than upon others; the power of displaying the vast, illuminating the splendid, enforcing the awful, darkening the gloomy, and aggravating the dreadful: he therefore chose a subject on which too much could not be said, on which he might tire his fancy without the censure of extravagance.

The appearances of nature, and the occurrences of life, did not satiate his appetite of greatness. To paint things as they are, requires a minute attention, and employs the memory rather than the fancy. Milton's delight was to sport in the wide regions of possibility; reality was a scene too narrow for his mind. He sent his faculties out upon discovery, into worlds where only imagination can travel, and delighted to form new modes of existence, and furnish sentiment and action to superior beings, to trace the counsels of hell, or accompany the choirs of heaven.

But he could not be always in other worlds: he must sometimes revisit earth, and tell of things visible and known. When he cannot raise wonder by the sublimity of his mind, he gives delight by its fertility.

Whatever be his subject, he never fails to fill the imagination. But his images and descriptions of the scenes or operations of Nature do not seem to be always copied from original form, nor to have the freshness, raciness, and energy of immediate observation. He saw Nature, as Dryden expresses it, *through the spectacles of books*; and on most occasions calls learning to his assistance. The garden of Eden brings to his mind the vale of *Enna*, where Proserpine was gathering flowers. Satan makes his way through fighting elements, like *Argo* between the *Cyanean* rocks, or *Ulysses* between the two *Sicilian* whirlpools, when he shunned *Charybdis* on the *larboard*. The mythological allusions have been justly censured, as not being always used with notice of their vanity; but they contribute variety to the narration, and produce an alternate exercise of the memory and the fancy.

His similies are less numerous, and more various, than those of his predecessors. But he does not confine himself within the limits of rigorous comparison: his great excellence is amplitude, and he expands the adventitious image beyond the dimensions which the occasion required. Thus, comparing the shield of Satan to the orb of the Moon, he crowds the imagination with the discovery of the telescope, and all the wonders which the telescope discovers.

.   .   .   .   .

The plan of *Paradise Lost* has this inconvenience, that it comprises neither human actions nor human manners. The man and woman who act and suffer, are in a state which no other man or woman can ever know. The reader finds no transaction in which he can be engaged; beholds no condition in which he can by any effort of imagination place himself; he has, therefore, little natural curiosity or sympathy.

We all, indeed, feel the effects of Adam's disobedience; we all sin like Adam, and like him must all bewail our offences; we have restless and insidious enemies in the fallen angels, and in the blessed spirits we have guardians and friends; in the Redemption of mankind we hope to be included; in the description of heaven and hell we are surely interested, as we are all to reside hereafter either in the regions of horror or of bliss.

But these truths are too important to be new; they have been taught to our infancy; they have mingled with our solitary thoughts and familiar conversation, and are habitually interwoven with the whole texture of life. Being therefore not new, they raise no unaccustomed emotion in the mind; what we knew before we cannot learn; what is not unexpected cannot surprise.

Of the ideas suggested by these awful scenes, from some we recede with reverence, except when stated hours require their association; and from others we shrink with horror, or admit them only as salutary inflictions, as counterpoises to our interests and passions. Such images rather obstruct the career of fancy than incite it.

Pleasure and terrour are indeed the genuine sources of poetry; but poetical pleasure must be such as human imagination can at least conceive, and poetical terrour such as human strength and fortitude may combat. The good and evil of Eternity are too ponderous for the wings of wit; the mind sinks under them in passive helplessness, content with calm belief and humble adoration.

Known truths, however, may take a different appearance, and be conveyed to the mind by a new train of intermediate images. This Milton has undertaken, and performed with pregnancy and vigour of mind peculiar to himself. Whoever considers the few radical positions which the Scriptures afforded him, will wonder by what energetick operation he expanded them to such extent, and ramified them to so much variety, restrained as he was by religious reverence from licentiousness of fiction.

Here is a full display of the united force of study and genius; of a great accumulation of materials, with judgement to digest, and fancy to combine them: Milton was able to select from nature, or from story, from ancient fable, or from modern science, whatever could illustrate or adorn his thoughts. An accumulation of knowledge impregnated his mind, fermented by study, and sublimed by imagination.

It has been therefore said, without an indecent hyperbole, by one of his encomiasts, that in reading *Paradise Lost* we read a book of universal knowledge.

But original deficience cannot be supplied. The want of human interest is always felt. *Paradise Lost* is one of the books which the reader admires and lays down, and forgets to take up again. Its perusal is a duty rather than a pleasure. We read Milton for instruction, retire harrassed and overburdened, and look elsewhere for recreation; we desert our master, and seek for companions.

. . . . .

Dryden remarks, that Milton has some flats among his elevations. This is only to say that all the parts are not equal. In every work one part must be for the sake of others; a palace must have passages; a poem must have transitions. It is no more to be required that wit should always be blazing, than that the sun should always stand at noon. In a great work there is a vicissitude of luminous and opaque parts, as there is in the world a succession of day and night. Milton, when he has expatiated in the sky, may be allowed sometimes to revisit earth; for what other author ever soared so high, or sustained his flight so long?

. . . . .

Of *Paradise Regained*, the general judgement seems now to be right, that it is in many parts elegant, and every-where instructive. It was not to be supposed that the writer of *Paradise Lost* could ever write without great effusions of fancy, and exalted precepts of wisdom. The basis of *Paradise Regained* is narrow; a dialogue without action can never please like an union of the narrative and dramatick powers. Had this poem been written not by Milton, but by some imitator, it would have claimed and received universal praise.

If *Paradise Regained* has been too much depreciated, *Samson Agonistes* has in requital been too much admired. It could only be by long prejudice, and the bigotry of learning, that Milton could prefer the ancient tragedies, with their encumbrance of a chorus, to the exhibitions of the French and English stages; and it is only by a blind confidence in the reputation of Milton, that a drama can be praised in which the intermediate parts have neither cause nor consequence, neither hasten nor retard the catastrophe.

In this tragedy are however many particular beauties, many just sentiments and striking lines; but it wants that power of attracting the attention which a well-connected plan produces.

Milton would not have excelled in dramatick writing; he knew human nature only in the gross, and had never studied the shades of character, nor the combinations of concurring, or the perplexity of contending passions. He had read much, and knew what books could teach; but had mingled little in the world, and was deficient in the knowledge which experience must confer.

Through all his greater works there prevails an uniform peculiarity of *Diction*, a mode and cast of expression which bears little resemblance to that of any former writer, and which is so far removed from common use, that an unlearned reader, when he first opens his book, finds himself surprised by a new language.

This novelty has been, by those who can find nothing wrong in Milton, imputed to his laborious endeavours after words suitable to the grandeur of his ideas. *Our language*, says Addison, *sunk under him*. But the truth is, that, both in prose and verse, he had formed his stile by a perverse and pedantick principle. He was desirous to use English words with a foreign idiom. This in all his prose is discovered and condemned; for there judgement operates freely, neither softened by the beauty nor awed by the dignity of his thoughts; but such is the power of his poetry, that his call is obeyed without resistance, the reader feels himself in captivity to a higher and a nobler mind, and criticism sinks in admiration.

Milton's stile was not modified by his subject: what is shown with greater extent in *Paradise Lost*, may be found in *Comus*. One source of his peculiarity was his familiarity with the Tuscan poets: the disposition of his words is, I think, frequently Italian; perhaps sometimes combined with other tongues. Of him, at last, may be said what Jonson says of Spenser, that *he wrote no language*, but has formed what *Butler* calls a *Babylonish Dialect*, in itself harsh and barbarous, but made by exalted genius, and extensive learning, the vehicle of so much instruction and so much pleasure, that, like other lovers, we find grace in its deformity.

Whatever be the faults of his diction, he cannot want the praise of copiousness and variety: he was master of his language in its full extent; and has selected the melodious words with such diligence, that from his book alone the Art of English Poetry might be learned.

.   .   .   .   .

Rhyme, he says, and says truly, *is no necessary adjunct of true poetry.* But perhaps, of poetry as a mental operation, metre or musick is no necessary adjunct: it is however by the musick of metre that poetry has been discriminated in all languages; and in languages melodiously constructed, by a due proportion of long and short syllables, metre is sufficient. But one language cannot communicate its rules to another: where metre is scanty and imperfect, some help is necessary. The musick of the English heroick line strikes the ear so faintly that it is easily lost, unless all the syllables of every line co-operate together: this co-operation can be only obtained by the preservation of every verse unmingled with another, as a distinct system of sounds; and this distinctness is obtained and preserved by the artifice of rhyme. The variety of pauses, so much boasted by the lovers of blank verse, changes the measures of an English poet to the periods of a declaimer; and there are only a few skilful and happy readers of Milton, who enable their audience to perceive where the lines end or begin. *Blank verse*, said an ingenious critick, *seems to be verse only to the eye.*

Poetry may subsist without rhyme, but English poetry will not often please; nor can rhyme ever be safely spared but where the subject is able to support itself. Blank verse makes some approach to that which is called the *lapidary stile*; has neither the easiness of prose, nor the melody of numbers, and therefore tires by long continuance. Of the Italian writers without rhyme, whom Milton alleges as precedents, not one is popular; what reason could urge in its defence, has been confuted by the ear.

But, whatever be the advantage of rhyme, I cannot prevail on myself to wish that Milton had been a rhymer; for I cannot wish his work to be other than it is; yet, like other heroes, he is to be admired rather than imitated. He that thinks himself capable of astonishing, may write blank verse; but those that hope only to please, must condescend to rhyme.

The highest praise of genius is original invention. Milton cannot be said to have contrived the structure of an epick poem, and therefore must yield to that vigour and amplitude of mind to which all generations must be indebted for the art of poetical narration, for the texture of the fable, the variation of incidents, the interposition of dialogue, and all the stratagems that surprise and enchain attention. But, of all the borrowers from Homer, Milton is perhaps the least indebted. He was naturally a thinker for himself, confident of his own abilities, and disdainful of help or hindrance: he did not refuse admission to the thoughts or images of his predecessors, but he did not seek them. From his contemporaries he neither courted nor received support; there is in his writings nothing by which the pride of other authors might be gratified, or favour gained; no exchange of praise, nor solicitation of support. His great works were performed under discountenance, and in blindness, but difficulties vanished at his touch; he was born for whatever is arduous, and his work is not the greatest of heroick poems, only because it is not the first.

SAMUEL BUTLER

THE poem of Hudibras is one of those compositions of which a nation may justly boast; as the images which it exhibits are domestick, the sentiments unborrowed and unexpected, and the strain of diction original and peculiar. We must not, however, suffer the pride which we assume as the countrymen of Butler to make any encroachment upon justice, nor appropriate those honours which others have a right to share. The poem of Hudibras is not wholly English; the original idea is to be found in the history of Don Quixote; a book to which a mind of the greatest powers may be indebted without disgrace.

Cervantes shews a man, who, having, by the incessant perusal of incredible tales, subjected his understanding to his imagination, and familiarised his mind by pertinacious meditation to trains of incredible events and scenes of impossible existence, goes out in the pride of knighthood, to redress wrongs, and defend virgins, to rescue captive princesses, and tumble usurpers from their thrones; attended by a squire, whose cunning, too low for the suspicion of a generous mind, enables him often to cheat his master.

The hero of Butler is a Presbyterian Justice, who, in the confidence of legal authority, and the rage of zealous ignorance, ranges the country to repress superstition and correct abuses, accompanied by an Independant clerk, disputatious and obstinate, with whom he often debates, but never conquers him.

Cervantes had so much kindness for Don Quixote, that, however he embarrasses him with absurd distresses, he gives him so much sense and virtue as may preserve our esteem: wherever he is, or whatever he does, he is made by matchless dexterity commonly ridiculous, but never contemptible.

But for poor Hudibras, his poet had no tenderness: he chuses not that any pity should be shewn or respect paid him: he gives him up at once to laughter and contempt, without any quality that can dignify or protect him.

In forming the character of Hudibras, and describing his person and habiliments, the author seems to labour with a tumultuous confusion of dissimilar ideas. He had read the history of the mock knights errant; he knew the notions and manners of a presbyterian magistrate, and tried to unite the absurdities of both, however distant, in one personage. Thus he gives him that pedantick ostentation of knowledge which has no relation to chivalry, and loads him with martial encumbrances that can add nothing to his civil dignity. He sends him out a *colonelling*, and yet never brings him within sight of war.

If Hudibras be considered as the representative of the Presbyterians, it is not easy to say why his weapons should be represented as ridiculous or useless; for, whatever judgement might be passed upon their knowledge or their arguments, experience had sufficiently shown that their swords were not to be despised.

.   .   .   .   .

The great source of pleasure is variety. Uniformity must tire at last, though it be uniformity of excellence. We love to expect; and, when expectation is disappointed or gratified, we want to be again expecting. For this impatience of the present, whoever would please, must make provision. The skilful writer *irritat, mulcet*, makes a due distribution of the still and animated parts. It is for want of this artful intertexture, and those necessary changes, that the whole of a book may be tedious, though all the parts are praised.

If inexhaustible wit could give perpetual pleasure, no eye would ever leave half-read the work of Butler; for what poet has ever brought so many remote images so happily together? It is scarcely possible to peruse a page without finding some association of images that was never found before. By the first paragraph the reader is amused, by the next he is delighted, and by a few more strained to astonishment; but astonishment is a toilsome pleasure: he is soon weary of wondering, and longs to be diverted.

Omnia vult belle Matho dicere, dic aliquando
Et bene, dic neutrum, dic aliquando male.

Imagination is useless without knowledge: nature gives in vain the power of combination, unless study and observation supply materials to be combined. Butler's treasures of knowledge appear proportioned to his expence: whatever topick employs his mind, he shews himself qualified to expand and illustrate it with all the accessories that books can furnish: he is found not only to have travelled the beaten road, but the bye-paths of literature; not only to have taken general surveys, but to have examined particulars with minute inspection.

If the French boast the learning of Rabelais, we need not be afraid of confronting them with Butler.

But the most valuable parts of his performance are those which retired study and native wit cannot supply. He that merely makes a book from books may be useful, but can scarcely be great. Butler had not suffered life to glide beside him unseen or unobserved. He had watched with great diligence the operations of human nature, and traced the effects of opinion, humour, interest, and passion. From such remarks proceeded that great number of sententious distichs which have passed into conversation, and are added as proverbial axioms to the general stock of practical knowledge.

. . . . .

But human works are not easily found without a perishable part. Of the ancient poets every reader feels the mythology tedious and oppressive. Of Hudibras the manners, being founded on opinions, are temporary and local, and therefore become every day less intelligible and less striking. What Cicero says of philosophy is true likewise of wit and humour, that "time effaces the fictions of opinion, and confirms the determinations of Nature." Such manners as depend upon standing relations and general passions are co-extended with the race of man; but those modifications of life, and peculiarities of practice, which are the progeny of error and perverseness, or at best of some accidental influence or transient persuasion, must perish with their parents.

Much therefore of that humour which transported the last century with merriment is lost to us, who do not know the sour solemnity, the sullen superstition, the gloomy moroseness, and the stubborn scruples of the ancient Puritans; or, if we know them, derive our information only from books, or from tradition, have never had them before our eyes, and cannot but by recollection and study understand the lines in which they are satirised. Our grandfathers knew the picture from the life; we judge of the life by contemplating the picture.

It is scarcely possible, in the regularity and composure of the present time, to image the tumult of absurdity, and clamour of contradiction, that perplexed doctrine, and disturbed both publick and private quiet, in that age, when subordination was broken, and awe was hissed away; when any unsettled innovator who could hatch a half-formed notion produced it to the publick; when every man might become a preacher, and almost every preacher could collect a congregation.

The wisdom of the nation is very reasonably supposed to reside in the parliament. What can be concluded of the lower classes of the people, when in one of the parliaments summoned by Cromwell it was seriously proposed, that all the records in the Tower should be burnt, that all memory of things past should be effaced, and that the whole system of life should commence anew?

We have never been witnesses of animosities excited by the use of minced pies and plumb porridge; nor seen with what abhorrence those who could eat them at all other times of the year would shrink from them in December. An old Puritan, who was alive in my childhood, being at one of the feasts of the church invited by a neighbour to partake his cheer, told him, that, if he would treat him at an alehouse with beer, brewed for all times and seasons, he should accept his kindness, but would have none of his superstitious meats or drinks.

. . . . .

Nor, even though another Butler should arise, would another Hudibras obtain the same regard. Burlesque consists in a disproportion between the stile and the sentiments, or between the adventitious sentiments and the fundamental subject. It therefore, like all bodies compounded of heterogeneous parts, contains in it a principle of corruption. All disproportion is unnatural, and from what is unnatural we can derive only the pleasure which novelty produces. We admire it awhile as a strange thing; but, when it is no longer strange, we perceive its deformity. It is a kind of artifice, which by frequent repetition detects itself; and the reader, learning in time what he is to expect, lays down his book, as the spectator turns away from a second exhibition of those tricks, of which the only use is to shew that they can be played.

ROSCOMMON

He now busied his mind with literary projects, and formed the plan of a society for refining our language, and fixing its standard; *in imitation*, says Fenton, *of those learned and polite societies with which he had been acquainted abroad.* In this design his friend Dryden is said to have assisted him.

The same design, it is well known, was revived by Dr. Swift in the ministry of Oxford; but it has never since been publickly mentioned, though at that time great expectations were formed by some at least of its establishment and its effects. Such a society might, perhaps, without much difficulty be collected; but that it would produce what is expected from it, may be doubted.

The Italian academy seems to have obtained its end. The language was refined, and so fixed that it has changed but little. The French academy thought that they refined their language, and doubtless thought rightly; but the event has not shewn that they fixed it; for the French of the present time is very different from that of the last century.

In this country an academy could be expected to do but little. If an academician's place were profitable, it would be given by interest; if attendance were gratuitous, it would be rarely paid, and no man would endure the least disgust. Unanimity is impossible, and debate would separate the assembly.

But suppose the philological decree made and promulgated, what would be its authority? In absolute governments, there is sometimes a general reverence paid to all that has the sanction of power, and the countenance of greatness. How little this is the state of our country needs not to be told. We live in an age in which it is a kind of publick sport to refuse all respect that cannot be enforced. The edicts of an English academy would probably be read by many, only that they might be sure to disobey them.

That our language is in perpetual danger of corruption cannot be denied; but what prevention can be found? The present manners of the nation would deride authority, and therefore nothing is left but that every writer should criticise himself.

EDMUND WALLER

WHEN he had lost all hopes of Sacharissa, he looked round him for an easier conquest, and gained a lady of the family of Bresse, or Breaux. The time of his marriage is not exactly known. It has not been discovered that his wife was won by his poetry; nor is any thing told of her, but that she brought him many children. He doubtless praised many whom he would have been afraid to marry; and perhaps married one whom he would have been ashamed to praise. Many qualities contribute to domestick happiness, upon which poetry has no colours to bestow; and many airs and sallies may delight imagination, which he who flatters them never can approve. There are charms made only for distant admiration. No spectacle is nobler than a blaze.

         .   .   .

Cromwell, now protector, received Waller, as his kinsman, to familiar conversation. Waller, as he used to relate, found him sufficiently versed in ancient history; and when any of his enthusiastick friends came to advise or consult him, could sometimes over-hear him discoursing in the cant of the times: but, when he returned, he would say, "Cousin Waller, I must talk to these men in their own way"; and resumed the common stile of conversation.

He repaid the Protector for his favours (1654), by the famous panegyrick, which has been always considered as the first of his poetical productions. His choice of encomiastick topicks is very judicious; for he considers Cromwel in his exaltation, without en-quiring how he attained it; there is consequently no mention of the rebel or the regicide. All the former part of his hero's life is veiled with shades, and nothing is brought to view but the chief, the governor, the defender of England's honour, and the enlarger of her dominion. The act of violence by which he obtained the su-preme power is lightly treated, and decently justified. It was cer-tainly to be desired that the detestable band should be dissolved, which had destroyed the church, murdered the king, and filled the nation with tumult and oppression; yet Cromwel had not the right of dissolving them, for all that he had before done, could be justi-fied only by supposing them invested with lawful authority. But combinations of wickedness would overwhelm the world by the ad-vantage which licentious principles afford, did not those who have long practised perfidy, grow faithless to each other.

Shorter Poems

Of these petty compositions, neither the beauties nor the faults deserve much attention. The amorous verses have this to recommend them, that they are less hyperbolical than those of some other poets. Waller is not always at the last gasp; he does not die of a frown, nor live upon a smile. There is however too much love, and too many trifles. Little things are made too important; and the Empire of Beauty is represented as exerting its influence further than can be allowed by the multiplicity of human passions, and the variety of human wants. Such books therefore may be considered as shewing the world under a false appearance, and so far as they obtain credit from the young and unexperienced, as misleading expectation, and misguiding practice.

.   .   .   .   .

It has been the frequent lamentation of good men, that verse has been too little applied to the purposes of worship, and many attempts have been made to animate devotion by pious poetry; that they have very seldom attained their end is sufficiently known, and it may not be improper to enquire why they have miscarried.

Let no pious ear be offended if I advance, in opposition to many authorities, that poetical devotion cannot often please. The doctrines of religion may indeed be defended in a didactick poem; and he who has the happy power of arguing in verse, will not lose it because his subject is sacred. A poet may describe the beauty and the grandeur of Nature, the flowers of the Spring, and the harvests of Autumn, the vicissitudes of the Tide, and the revolutions of the Sky, and praise the Maker for his works in lines which no reader shall lay aside. The subject of the disputation is not piety, but the motives to piety; that of the description is not God, but the works of God.

Contemplative piety, or the intercourse between God and the human soul, cannot be poetical. Man admitted to implore the mercy of his Creator, and plead the merits of his Redeemer, is already in a higher state than poetry can confer.

The essence of poetry is invention; such invention as, by producing something unexpected, surprises and delights. The topicks of devotion are few, and being few are universally known; but few as they are, they can be made no more; they can receive no grace from novelty of sentiment, and very little from novelty of expression.

Poetry pleases by exhibiting an idea more grateful to the mind than things themselves afford. This effect proceeds from the display of those parts of nature which attract, and the concealment of those which repel the imagination: but religion must be shewn as it is; suppression and addition equally corrupt it; and such as it is, it is known already.

From poetry the reader justly expects, and from good poetry always obtains, the enlargement of his comprehension and elevation of his fancy; but this is rarely to be hoped by Christians from metrical devotion. Whatever is great, desireable, or tremendous, is comprised in the name of the Supreme Being. Omnipotence cannot be exalted; Infinity cannot be amplified; Perfection cannot be improved.

The employments of pious meditation are Faith, Thanksgiving, Repentance, and Supplication. Faith, invariably uniform, cannot be invested by fancy with decorations. Thanksgiving, the most joyful of all holy effusions, yet addressed to a Being without passions, is confined to a few modes, and is to be felt rather than expressed. Repentance, trembling in the presence of the Judge, is not at leisure for cadences and epithets. Supplication of man to man may diffuse itself through many topicks of persuasion; but supplication to God can only cry for mercy.

Of sentiments purely religious, it will be found that the most simple expression is the most sublime. Poetry loses its lustre and its power, because it is applied to the decoration of something more excellent than itself. All that verse can do is to help the memory, and delight the ear, and for these purposes it may be very useful; but it supplies nothing to the mind. The ideas of Christian Theology are too simple for eloquence, too sacred for fiction, and too majestick for ornament; to recommend them by tropes and figures, is to magnify by a concave mirror the sidereal hemisphere.

JOHN POMFRET

OF Mr. John Pomfret nothing is known but from a slight and confused account prefixed to his poems by a nameless friend; who relates, that he was the son of the Rev. Mr. Pomfret, rector of Luton in Bedfordshire; that he was bred at Cambridge, entered into orders, and was rector of Malden in Bedfordshire, and might have risen in the Church; but that, when he applied to Dr. Compton, bishop of London, for institution to a living of considerable value, to which he had been presented, he found a troublesome obstruction raised by a malicious interpretation of some passage in his *Choice*; from which it was inferred, that he considered happiness as more likely to be found in the company of a mistress than of a wife.

This reproach was easily obliterated: for it had happened to Pomfret as to almost all other men who plan schemes of life; he had departed from his purpose, and was then married.

The malice of his enemies had however a very fatal consequence: the delay constrained his attendance in London, where he caught the small-pox, and died in 1703, in the thirty-sixth year of his age.

He published his poems in 1699; and has been always the favourite of that class of readers, who, without vanity or criticism, seek only their own amusement.

His *Choice* exhibits a system of life adapted to common notions, and equal to common expectations; such a state as affords plenty and tranquillity, without exclusion of intellectual pleasures. Perhaps no composition in our language has been oftener perused than Pomfret's *Choice*.

In his other poems there is an easy volubility; the pleasure of smooth metre is afforded to the ear, and the mind is not oppressed with ponderous or entangled with intricate sentiment. He pleases many, and he who pleases many must have merit.

GEORGE STEPNEY

IT is reported that the juvenile compositions of Stepney *made grey authors blush*. I know not whether his poems will appear such wonders to the present age. One cannot always easily find the reason for which the world has sometimes conspired to squander praise. It is not very unlikely that he wrote very early as well as he ever wrote; and the performances of youth have many favourers, because the authors yet lay no claim to publick honours, and are therefore not considered as rivals by the distributors of fame.

JOHN PHILIPS

PHILIPS has been always praised, without contradiction, as a man modest, blameless, and pious; who bore a narrow fortune without discontent, and tedious and painful maladies without impatience; beloved by those that knew him, but not ambitious to be known.

He was probably not formed for a wide circle. His conversation is commended for its innocent gaiety, which seems to have flowed only among his intimates; for I have been told, that he was in company silent and barren, and employed only upon the pleasures of his pipe. His addiction to tobacco is mentioned by one of his biographers, who remarks that in all his writings, except *Blenheim*, he has found an opportunity of celebrating the fragrant fume. In common life he was probably one of those who please by not offending, and whose person was loved because his writings were admired. He died honoured and lamented, before any part of his reputation had withered, and before his patron St. John had disgraced him.

His works are few. The *Splendid Shilling* has the uncommon merit of an original design, unless it may be thought precluded by the ancient *Centos*. To degrade the sounding words and stately construction of Milton, by an application to the lowest and most trivial things, gratifies the mind with a momentary triumph over that grandeur which hitherto held its captives in admiration; the words and things are presented with a new appearance, and novelty is always grateful where it gives no pain.

But the merit of such performances begins and ends with the first author. He that should again adapt Milton's phrase to the gross incidents of common life, and even adapt it with more art, which would not be difficult, must yet expect but a small part of the praise which Philips has obtained; he can only hope to be considered as the repeater of a jest.

He imitates Milton's numbers indeed, but imitates them very injudiciously. Deformity is easily copied; and whatever there is in Milton which the reader wishes away, all that is obsolete, peculiar, or licentious, is accumulated with great care by Philips. Milton's verse was harmonious, in proportion to the general state of our metre in Milton's age; and, if he had written after the improvements made by Dryden, it is reasonable to believe that he would have admitted a more pleasing modulation of numbers into his work; but Philips sits down with a resolution to make no more musick than he found; to want all that his master wanted, though he is very far from having what his master had. Those asperities, therefore, that are venerable in the *Paradise Lost*, are contemptible in the *Blenheim*.

JOHN DRYDEN

Secret Love, or the Maiden Queen, is a tragi-comedy. In the preface
he discusses a curious question, whether a poet can judge well of
his own productions: and determines very justly, that, of the plan
and disposition, and all that can be reduced to principles of science
the author may depend upon his own opinion; but that, in those
parts where fancy predominates, self-love may easily deceive. He
might have observed, that what is good only because it pleases,
cannot be pronounced good till it has been found to please.

. . . . .

The Tempest is an alteration of Shakespeare's play, made by
Dryden in conjunction with Davenant. . . . The effect produced by
the conjunction of these two powerful minds was, that to Shakespeare's monster Caliban is added a sister-monster Sicorax; and a
woman, who, in the original play, had never seen a man, is in this
brought acquainted with a man that had never seen a woman.

. . . . .

The two parts of the *Conquest of Granada* are written with a
seeming determination to glut the publick with dramatick wonders; to exhibit in its highest elevation a theatrical meteor of incredible love and impossible valour, and to leave no room for a
wilder flight to the extravagance of posterity. All the rays of romantick heat, whether amorous or warlike, glow in Almanzor by a
kind of concentration. He is above all laws; he is exempt from all
restraints; he ranges the world at will, and governs wherever he
appears. He fights without enquiring the cause, and loves in spite
of the obligations of justice, of rejection by his mistress, and of prohibition from the dead. Yet the scenes are, for the most part, delightful; they exhibit a kind of illustrious depravity, and majestick
madness: such as, if it is sometimes despised, is often reverenced,
and in which the ridiculous is mingled with the astonishing.

. . . . .

All for Love, or the World well lost, a tragedy founded upon the
story of Antony and Cleopatra, he tells us, *is the only play which he
wrote for himself*; the rest were given to the people. It is by universal consent accounted the work in which he has admitted the fewest
improprieties of style or character; but it has one fault equal to
many, though rather moral than critical, that, by admitting the
romantick omnipotence of Love, he has recommended as laudable

852

and worthy of imitation that conduct which, through all ages, the good have censured as vitious, and the bad despised as foolish.

. . . .

In 1681, Dryden became yet more conspicuous by uniting politicks with poetry, in the memorable satire called *Absalom and Achitophel*, written against the faction which, by lord Shaftesbury's incitement, set the duke of Monmouth at its head.

Of this poem, in which personal satire was applied to the support of publick principles, and in which therefore every mind was interested, the reception was eager, and the sale so large, that my father, an old bookseller, told me, he had not known it equalled but by *Sacheverel's* trial.

The reason of this general perusal Addison has attempted to derive from the delight which the mind feels in the investigation of secrets; and thinks that curiosity to decypher the names procured readers to the poem. There is no need to enquire why those verses were read, which, to all the attractions of wit, elegance, and harmony, added the co-operation of all the factious passions, and filled every mind with triumph or resentment.

It could not be supposed that all the provocation given by Dryden would be endured without resistance or reply. Both his person and his party were exposed in their turns to the shafts of satire, which, though neither so well pointed nor perhaps so well aimed, undoubtedly drew blood.

One of these poems is called *Dryden's Satire on his Muse*; ascribed, though, as Pope says, falsely, to *Somers*, who was afterwards Chancellor. The poem, whose soever it was, has much virulence, and some spriteliness. The writer tells all the ill that he can collect, both of Dryden and his friends.

The poem of *Absalom and Achitophel* had two answers, now both forgotten; one called *Azaria and Hushai*; the other, *Absalom senior*. Of these hostile compositions, Dryden apparently imputes *Absalom senior* to *Settle*, by quoting in his verses against him the second line. *Azaria and Hushai* was, as *Wood* says, imputed to him, though it is somewhat unlikely that he should write twice on the same occasion. This is a difficulty which I cannot remove, for want of a minuter knowledge of poetical transactions.

The same year he published the *Medal*, of which the subject is a medal struck on lord Shaftesbury's escape from a prosecution, by the *ignoramus* of a grand jury of Londoners.

In both poems he maintains the same principles, and saw them both attacked by the same antagonist. Elkanah Settle, who had answered *Absalom*, appeared with equal courage in opposition to the *Medal*, and published an answer called *The Medal reversed*, with so much success in both encounters, that he left the palm doubtful, and divided the suffrages of the nation. Such are the revolutions of fame, or such is the prevalence of fashion, that the man whose works have not yet been thought to deserve the care of collecting them; who died forgotten in an hospital; and whose latter years were spent in contriving shows for fairs, and carrying an elegy or epithalamium, of which the beginning and end were occasionally varied, but the intermediate parts were always the same, to every house where there was a funeral or a wedding; might, with truth, have had inscribed upon his stone,

Here lies the Rival and Antagonist of Dryden.

Settle was, for this rebellion, severely chastised by Dryden under the name of *Doeg*, in the second part of *Absalom and Achitophel*, and was perhaps for his factious audacity made the city poet, whose annual office was to describe the glories of the Mayor's day. Of these bards he was the last, and seems not much to have deserved even this degree of regard, if it was paid to his political opinions; for he afterwards wrote a panegyrick on the virtues of judge Jefferies, and what more could have been done by the meanest zealot for prerogative?

Soon after the accession of king James, when the design of re-conciling the nation to the church of Rome became apparent, and the religion of the court gave the only efficacious title to its favours, Dryden declared himself a convert to popery. This at any other time might have passed with little censure. Sir *Kenelm Digby* embraced popery; the two *Rainholds* reciprocally converted one another; and *Chillingworth* himself was a while so entangled in the wilds of controversy, as to retire for quiet to an infallible church. If men of argument and study can find such diffi-culties, or such motives, as may either unite them to the church of Rome, or detain them in uncertainty, there can be no wonder that a man, who perhaps never enquired why he was a protestant, should by an artful and experienced disputant be made a papist, overborne by the sudden violence of new and unexpected arguments, or deceived by a representation which shews only the doubts on one part, and only the evidence on the other.

That conversion will always be suspected that apparently concurs with interest. He that never finds his error till it hinders his progress towards wealth or honour, will not be thought to love Truth only for herself. Yet it may easily happen that information may come at a commodious time; and as truth and interest are not by any fatal necessity at variance, that one may by accident introduce the other. When opinions are struggling into popularity, the arguments by which they are opposed or defended become more known; and he that changes his profession would perhaps have changed it before, with the like opportunities of instruction. This was then the state of popery; every artifice was used to shew it in its fairest form; and it must be owned to be a religion of external appearance sufficiently attractive.

It is natural to hope that a comprehensive is likewise an elevated soul, and that whoever is wise is also honest. I am willing to believe that Dryden, having employed his mind, active as it was, upon different studies, and filled it, capacious as it was, with other materials, came unprovided to the controversy, and wanted rather skill to discover the right than virtue to maintain it. But enquiries into the heart are not for man; we must now leave him to his Judge.

. . . . .

There are men whose powers operate only at leisure and in retirement, and whose intellectual vigour deserts them in conversation; whom merriment confuses, and objection disconcerts; whose bashfulness restrains their exertion, and suffers them not to speak till the time of speaking is past; or whose attention to their own character makes them unwilling to utter at hazard what has not been considered, and cannot be recalled.

Of Dryden's sluggishness in conversation it is vain to search or to guess the cause. He certainly wanted neither sentiments nor language; his intellectual treasures were great, though they were locked up from his own use. *His thoughts, when he wrote, flowed in upon him so fast, that his only care was which to chuse, and which to reject.* Such rapidity of composition naturally promises a flow of talk, yet we must be content to believe what an enemy says of him, when he likewise says it of himself.

. . . . .

Of the mind that can trade in corruption, and can deliberately pollute itself with ideal wickedness for the sake of spreading the contagion in society, I wish not to conceal or excuse the depravity. —Such degradation of the dignity of genius, such abuse of superlative abilities, cannot be contemplated but with grief and indignation. What consolation can be had, Dryden has afforded, by living to repent, and to testify his repentance.

Of dramatick immorality he did not want examples among his predecessors, or companions among his contemporaries; but in the meanness and servility of hyperbolical adulation, I know not whether, since the days in which the Roman emperors were deified, he has been ever equalled, except by Afra Behn in an address to Eleanor Gwyn. When once he has undertaken the task of praise, he no longer retains shame in himself, nor supposes it in his patron. As many odoriferous bodies are observed to diffuse perfumes from year to year, without sensible diminution of bulk or weight, he appears never to have impoverished his mint of flattery by his expences, however lavish. He had all the forms of excellence, intellectual and moral, combined in his mind, with endless variation; and when he had scattered on the hero of the day the golden shower of wit and virtue, he had ready for him, whom he wished to court on the morrow, new wit and virtue with another stamp. Of this kind of meanness he never seems to decline the practice, or lament the necessity: he considers the great as entitled to encomiastick homage, and brings praise rather as a tribute than a gift, more delighted with the fertility of his invention than mortified by the prostitution of his judgement. It is indeed not certain, that on these occasions his judgement much rebelled against his interest. There are minds which easily sink into submission, that look on grandeur with undistinguishing reverence, and discover no defect where there is elevation of rank and affluence of riches.

.   .   .   .   .

Dryden may be properly considered as the father of English criticism, as the writer who first taught us to determine upon principles the merit of composition. Of our former poets, the greatest dramatist wrote without rules, conducted through life and nature by a genius that rarely misled, and rarely deserted him. Of the rest, those who knew the laws of propriety had neglected to teach them.

Two *Arts of English Poetry* were written in the days of Elizabeth by Webb and Puttenham, from which something might be learned, and a few hints had been given by Jonson and Cowley; but Dryden's *Essay on Dramatick Poetry* was the first regular treatise on the art of writing.

He who, having formed his opinions in the present age of English literature, turns back to peruse this dialogue, will not perhaps find much increase of knowledge, or much novelty of instruction; but he is to remember that critical principles were then in the hands of a few, who had gathered them partly from the Ancients, and partly from the Italians and French. The structure of dramatick poems was not then generally understood. Audiences applauded by instinct, and poets perhaps often pleased by chance.

A writer who obtains his full purpose loses himself in his own lustre. Of an opinion which is no longer doubted, the evidence ceases to be examined. Of an art universally practised, the first teacher is forgotten. Learning once made popular is no longer learning; it has the appearance of something which we have bestowed upon ourselves, as the dew appears to rise from the field which it refreshes.

To judge rightly of an author, we must transport ourselves to his time, and examine what were the wants of his contemporaries, and what were his means of supplying them. That which is easy at one time was difficult at another. Dryden at least imported his science, and gave his country what it wanted before; or rather, he imported only the materials, and manufactured them by his own skill.

The dialogue on the Drama was one of his first essays of criticism, written when he was yet a timorous candidate for reputation, and therefore laboured with that diligence which he might allow himself somewhat to remit, when his name gave sanction to his positions, and his awe of the public was abated, partly by custom, and partly by success. It will not be easy to find, in all the opulence of our language, a treatise so artfully variegated with successive representations of opposite probabilities, so enlivened with imagery, so brightened with illustrations. His portraits of the English dramatists are wrought with great spirit and diligence. The account of Shakespeare may stand as a perpetual model of encomiastick criticism; exact without minuteness, and lofty without exaggeration. The praise lavished by Longinus, on the attestation of the heroes of Marathon, by Demosthenes, fades away before it. In a few lines is exhibited a character, so extensive in its comprehension, and so curious in its limitations, that nothing can be added, diminished, or reformed; nor can the editors and admirers of Shakespeare, in all their emulation of reverence, boast of much more than of having diffused and paraphrased this epitome of excellence, of having changed Dryden's gold for baser metal, of lower value though of greater bulk.

In this, and in all his other essays on the same subject, the criticism of Dryden is the criticism of a poet; not a dull collection of theorems, nor a rude detection of faults, which perhaps the censor was not able to have committed; but a gay and vigorous dissertation, where delight is mingled with instruction, and where the author proves his right of judgement, by his power of performance.

The different manner and effect with which critical knowledge may be conveyed, was perhaps never more clearly exemplified than in the performances of Rymer and Dryden. It was said of a dispute between two mathematicians, 'malim cum Scaligero errare, quam cum Clavio recte sapere'; that *it was more eligible to go wrong with one than right with the other*. A tendency of the same kind every mind must feel at the perusal of Dryden's prefaces and Rymer's discourses. With Dryden we are wandering in quest of Truth; whom we find, if we find her at all, drest in the graces of elegance; and if we miss her, the labour of the pursuit rewards itself; we are led only through fragrance and flowers: Rymer, without taking a nearer, takes a rougher way; every step is to be made through thorns and brambles; and Truth, if we meet her, appears repulsive by her mien, and ungraceful by her habit. Dryden's criticism has the majesty of a queen; Rymer's has the ferocity of a tyrant.

As he had studied with great diligence the art of poetry, and enlarged or rectified his notions, by experience perpetually increasing, he had his mind stored with principles and observations; he poured out his knowledge with great liberality, and seldom published any work without a critical dissertation, by which he encreased the book and the price, with little labour to himself; for of labour, notwithstanding the multiplicity of his productions, there is sufficient reason to suspect that he was not a lover. To write *con amore*, with fondness for the employment, with perpetual touches and retouches, with unwillingness to take leave of his own idea, and an unwearied pursuit of unattainable perfection, was, I think, no part of his character.

Criticism, either didactick or defensive, occupies almost all his prose, except those pages which he has devoted to his patrons; but none of his prefaces were ever thought tedious. They have not the formality of a settled style, in which the first half of the sentence betrays the other. The clauses are never balanced, nor the periods modelled; every word seems to drop by chance, though it falls into its proper place. Nothing is cold or languid; the whole is airy, animated, and vigorous; what is little, is gay; what is great, is splendid. He may be thought to mention himself too frequently; but while he forces himself upon our esteem, we cannot refuse him to stand high in his own. Every thing is excused by the play of images and the spriteliness of expression. Though all is easy, nothing is feeble; though all seems careless, there is nothing harsh; and though, since his earlier works, more than a century has passed, they have nothing yet uncouth or obsolete.

He who writes much, will not easily escape a manner, such a recurrence of particular modes as may be easily noted. Dryden is always *another and the same,* he does not exhibit a second time the same elegancies in the same form, nor appears to have any art other than that of expressing with clearness what he thinks with vigour. His stile could not easily be imitated, either seriously or ludicrously, for being always equable and always varied, it has no prominent or discriminative characters. The beauty who is totally free from disproportion of parts and features cannot be ridiculed by an overcharged resemblance.

From his prose however, Dryden derives only his accidental and secondary praise; the veneration with which his name is pronounced by every cultivator of English Literature, is paid to him as he refined the language, improved the sentiments, and tuned the numbers of English Poetry.

After about half a century of forced thoughts, and rugged metre, some advances towards nature and harmony had been already made by Waller and Denham; they had shewn that long discourses in rhyme grew more pleasing when they were broken into couplets, and that verse consisted not only in the number but the arrangement of syllables.

But though they did much, who can deny that they left much to do? Their works were not many, nor were their minds of very ample comprehension. More examples of more modes of composition were necessary for the establishment of regularity, and the introduction of propriety in word and thought.

Every language of a learned nation necessarily divides itself into diction scholastick and popular, grave and familiar, elegant and gross; and from a nice distinction of these different parts, arises a great part of the beauty of stile. But if we except a few minds, the favourites of nature, to whom their own original rectitude was in the place of rules, this delicacy of selection was little known to our authors; our speech lay before them in a heap of confusion, and every man took for every purpose what chance might offer him.

There was therefore before the time of Dryden no poetical diction, no system of words at once refined from the grossness of domestick use, and free from the harshness of terms appropriated to particular arts. Words too familiar, or too remote, defeat the purpose of a poet. From those sounds which we hear on small or on coarse occasions, we do not easily receive strong impressions, or delightful images, and words to which we are nearly strangers, whenever they occur, draw that attention on themselves which they should convey to things.

Those happy combinations of words which distinguish poetry from prose, had been rarely attempted; we had few elegancies or flowers of speech, the roses had not yet been plucked from the bramble, or different colours had not been joined to enliven one another.

It may be doubted whether Waller and Denham could have over-born the prejudices which had long prevailed, and which even then were sheltered by the protection of Cowley. The new versification, as it was called, may be considered as owing its establishment to Dryden; from whose time it is apparent that English poetry has had no tendency to relapse to its former savageness.

.   .   .   .   .

In an occasional performance no height of excellence can be expected from any mind, however fertile in itself, and however stored with acquisitions. He whose work is general and arbitrary, has the choice of his matter, and takes that which his inclination and his studies have best qualified him to display and decorate. He is at liberty to delay his publication, till he has satisfied his friends and himself; till he has reformed his first thoughts by subsequent examination; and polished away those faults which the precipitance of ardent composition is likely to leave behind it. Virgil is related to have poured out a great number of lines in the morning, and to have passed the day in reducing them to fewer.

The occasional poet is circumscribed by the narrowness of his subject. Whatever can happen to man has happened so often, that little remains for fancy or invention. We have been all born; we have most of us been married; and so many have died before us, that our deaths can supply but few materials for a poet. In the fate of princes the publick has an interest; and what happens to them of good or evil, the poets have always considered as business for the Muse. But after so many inauguratory gratulations, nuptial hymns, and funeral dirges, he must be highly favoured by nature, or by fortune, who says any thing not said before. Even war and conquest, however splendid, suggest no new images; the triumphal chariot of a victorious monarch can be decked only with those ornaments that have graced his predecessors.

Not only matter but time is wanting. The poem must not be delayed till the occasion is forgotten. The lucky moments of animated imagination cannot be attended; elegancies and illustrations cannot be multiplied by gradual accumulation; the composition must be dispatched while conversation is yet busy, and admiration fresh; and haste is to be made, lest some other event should lay hold upon mankind.

"Annus Mirabilis"

His description of the Fire is painted by resolute meditation, out of a mind better formed to reason than to feel. The conflagration of a city, with all its tumults of concomitant distress, is one of the most dreadful spectacles which this world can offer to human eyes; yet it seems to raise little emotion in the breast of the poet; he watches the flame coolly from street to street, with now a reflection, and now a simile, till at last he meets the king, for whom he makes a speech, rather tedious in a time so busy; and then follows again the progress of the fire.

Absalom and Achitophel is a work so well known, that particular criticism is superfluous. If it be considered as a poem political and controversial, it will be found to comprise all the excellencies of which the subject is susceptible; acrimony of censure, elegance of praise, artful delineation of characters, variety and vigour of sentiment, happy turns of language and pleasing harmony of numbers; and all these raised to such a height as can scarcely be found in any other English composition.

It is not, however, without faults; some lines are inelegant or **im-**

proper, and too many are irreligiously licentious. The original structure of the poem was defective; allegories drawn to great length will always break; Charles could not run continually parallel with David.

The subject had likewise another inconvenience: it admitted little imagery or description, and a long poem of mere sentiments easily becomes tedious; though all the parts are forcible, and every line kindles new rapture, the reader, if not relieved by the interposition of something that sooths the fancy, grows weary of admiration, and defers the rest.

As an approach to historical truth was necessary, the action and catastrophe were not in the poet's power; there is therefore an unpleasing disproportion between the beginning and the end. We are alarmed by a faction formed out of many sects various in their principles, but agreeing in their purpose of mischief, formidable for their numbers and strong by their supports, while the king's friends are few and weak. The chiefs on either part are set forth to view; but when expectation is at the height, the king makes a speech, and

> Henceforth a series of new times began.

Who can forbear to think of an enchanted castle, with a wide moat and lofty battlements, walls of marble, and gates of brass, which vanishes at once into air, when the destined knight blows his horn before it?

. . . . .

Not long afterwards he undertook, perhaps the most arduous work of its kind, a translation of Virgil, for which he had shewn how well he was qualified by his version of the Pollio, and two episodes, one of Nisus and Euryalus, the other of Mezentius and Lausus.

In the comparison of Homer and Virgil, the discriminative excellence of Homer is elevation and comprehension of thought, and that of Virgil is grace and splendor of diction. The beauties of Homer are therefore difficult to be lost, and those of Virgil difficult to be retained. The massy trunk of sentiment is safe by its solidity, but the blossoms of elocution easily drop away. The author, having the choice of his own images, selects those which he can best adorn: the translator must, at all hazards, follow his original, and express thoughts which perhaps he would not have chosen. When to this primary difficulty is added the inconvenience of a language so much inferior in harmony to the Latin, it cannot be expected that they who read the Georgick and the Eneid should be much delighted with any version.

All these obstacles Dryden saw, and all these he determined to encounter. The expectation of his work was undoubtedly great; the nation considered its honour as interested in the event. One gave him the different editions of his author, and another helped him in the subordinate parts. The arguments of the several books were given him by Addison.

The hopes of the publick were not disappointed. He produced, says Pope, *the most noble and spirited translation that I know in any language*. It certainly excelled whatever had appeared in English, and appears to have satisfied his friends, and, for the most part, to have silenced his enemies. Milbourne, indeed, a clergyman, attacked it; but his outrages seem to be the ebullitions of a mind agitated by stronger resentment than bad poetry can excite, and previously resolved not to be pleased.

When admiration had subsided, the translation was more coolly examined, and found, like all others, to be sometimes erroneous, and sometimes licentious. Those who could find faults, thought they could avoid them; and Dr. Brady attempted in blank verse a translation of the Eneid, which, when dragged into the world, did not live long enough to cry. I have never seen it; but that such a version there is, or has been, perhaps some old catalogue informed me.

With not much better success, Trapp, when his Tragedy and his Prelections had given him reputation, attempted another blank version of the Eneid; to which, notwithstanding the slight regard with which it was treated, he had afterwards perseverance enough to add the Eclogues and Georgicks. His book may continue its existence as long as it is the clandestine refuge of schoolboys.

Since the English ear has been accustomed to the mellifluence of Pope's numbers, and the diction of poetry has become more splendid, new attempts have been made to translate Virgil; and all his works have been attempted by men better qualified to contend with Dryden. I will not engage myself in an invidious comparison, by opposing one passage to another; a work of which there would be no end, and which might be often offensive without use.

It is not by comparing line with line that the merit of great works is to be estimated, but by their general effects and ultimate result. It is easy to note a weak line, and write one more vigorous in its place; to find a happiness of expression in the original, and transplant it by force into the version: but what is given to the parts, may be subducted from the whole, and the reader may be weary, though the critick may commend. Works of imagination excel by their allurement and delight; by their power of attracting and detaining the attention. That book is good in vain, which the reader throws away. He only is the master, who keeps the mind in pleasing captivity; whose pages are perused with eagerness, and in hope of new pleasure are perused again; and whose conclusion is perceived with an eye of sorrow, such as the traveller casts upon departing day.

By his proportion of this predomination I will consent that Dryden should be tried; of this, which, in opposition to reason, makes Ariosto the darling and the pride of Italy; of this, which, in defiance of criticism, continues Shakespeare the sovereign of the drama.

One composition must, however, be distinguished. The ode for *St. Cecilia's* Day, perhaps the last effort of his poetry, has been always considered as exhibiting the highest flight of fancy, and the exactest nicety of art. This is allowed to stand without a rival. If indeed there is any excellence beyond it, in some other of Dryden's works that excellence must be found. Compared with the Ode on *Killigrew*, it may be pronounced perhaps superiour in the whole; but without any single part, equal to the first stanza of the other.

It is said to have cost Dryden a fortnight's labour; but it does not want its negligences: some of the lines are without correspondent rhymes; a defect, which I never detected but after an acquaintance of many years, and which the enthusiasm of the writer might hinder him from perceiving.

His last stanza has less emotion than the former; but it is not less elegant in the diction. The conclusion is vitious; the musick of *Timotheus*, which *raised a monarch to the skies*, had only a metaphorical power; that of *Cecilia*, which *drew an angel down*, had a real effect: the crown therefore could not reasonably be divided.

In a general survey of Dryden's labours, he appears to have had a mind very comprehensive by nature, and much enriched with acquired knowledge. His compositions are the effects of a vigorous genius operating upon large materials.

The power that predominated in his intellectual operations was rather strong reason than quick sensibility. Upon all occasions that were presented, he studied rather than felt, and produced sentiments not such as Nature enforces, but meditation supplies. With the simple and elemental passions, as they spring separate in the mind, he seems not much acquainted; and seldom describes them but as they are complicated by the various relations of society, and confused in the tumults and agitations of life.

What he says of Love may contribute to the explanation of his character:

> Love various minds does variously inspire;
> It stirs in gentle bosoms gentle fire,
> Like that of incense on the altar laid;
> But raging flames tempestuous souls invade;
> A fire which every windy passion blows,
> With pride it mounts, or with revenge it glows.

Dryden's was not one of the *gentle bosoms*: Love, as it subsists in itself, with no tendency but to the person loved, and wishing only for correspondent kindness; such love as shuts out all other interest; the love of the Golden Age, was too soft and subtle to put his faculties in motion. He hardly conceived it but in its turbulent effervescence with some other desires; when it was inflamed by rivalry, or obstructed by difficulties; when it invigorated ambition, or exasperated revenge.

He is therefore, with all his variety of excellence, not often pathetick; and had so little sensibility of the power of effusions purely natural, that he did not esteem them in others. Simplicity gave him no pleasure; and for the first part of his life he looked on *Otway* with contempt, though at last, indeed very late, he confessed that in his play *there* was *Nature, which is the chief beauty*.

We do not always know our own motives. I am not certain whether it was not rather the difficulty which he found in exhibiting the genuine operations of the heart, than a servile submission to an injudicious audience, that filled his plays with false magnificence. It was necessary to fix attention; and the mind can be captivated only by recollection, or by curiosity; by reviving former thoughts, or impressing new: sentences were readier at his call than images; he could more easily fill the ear with some splendid novelty, than awaken those ideas that slumber in the heart.

The favourite exercise of his mind was ratiocination; and, that argument might not be too soon at an end, he delighted to talk of liberty and necessity, destiny and contingence; these he discusses in the language of the school with so much profundity, that the terms which he uses are seldom understood. It is indeed learning, but learning out of place.

When once he had engaged himself in disputation, thoughts flowed in on either side: he was now no longer at a loss; he had always argument at command: *verbaque provisam rem*—give him matter for his verse, and he finds without difficulty verse for his matter.

In Comedy, for which he professes himself not naturally qualified, the mirth which he excites will perhaps not be found so much to arise from any original humour, or peculiarity of character nicely distinguished and diligently pursued, as from incidents and circumstances, artifices and surprizes; from jests of action rather than of sentiment. What he had of humorous or passionate, he seems to have had not from nature, but from other poets; if not always as a plagiary, at least as an imitator.

Next to argument, his delight was in wild and daring sallies of sentiment, in the irregular and excentrick violence of wit. He delighted to tread upon the brink of meaning, where light and darkness begin to mingle; to approach the precipice of absurdity, and hover over the abyss of unideal vacancy. This inclination sometimes produced nonsense, which he knew; as,

> Move swiftly, sun, and fly a lover's pace,
> Leave weeks and months behind thee in thy race.
> > Amariel flies
> To guard thee from the demons of the air;
> My flaming sword above them to display,
> All keen, and ground upon the edge of day.

And sometimes it issued in absurdities, of which perhaps he was not conscious:

> Then we upon our orb's last verge shall go,
> And see the ocean leaning on the sky;
> From thence our rolling neighbours we shall know,
> And on the lunar world securely pry.

These lines have no meaning; but may we not say, in imitation of Cowley on another book,

> 'Tis so like *sense* 'twill serve the turn as well?

He had a vanity unworthy of his abilities; to shew, as may be suspected, the rank of the company with whom he lived, by the use of French words, which had then crept into conversation; such as *fraicheur* for *coolness*, *fougue* for *turbulence*, and a few more, none of which the language has incorporated or retained. They continue only where they stood first, perpetual warnings to future innovators.

These are his faults of affectation; his faults of negligence are beyond recital. Such is the unevenness of his compositions, that ten lines are seldom found together without something of which the reader is ashamed. Dryden was no rigid judge of his own pages; he seldom struggled after supreme excellence, but snatched in haste what was within his reach, and when he could content others was himself contented. He did not keep present to his mind an idea of pure perfection; nor compare his works, such as they were, with what they might be made. He knew to whom he should be opposed. He had more musick than Waller, more vigour than Denham, and more nature than Cowley; and from his contemporaries he was in no danger. Standing therefore in the highest place, he had no care to rise by contending with himself; but while there was no name above his own, was willing to enjoy fame on the easiest terms.

He was no lover of labour. What he thought sufficient, he did not stop to make better; and allowed himself to leave many parts unfinished, in confidence that the good lines would overbalance the bad. What he had once written, he dismissed from his thoughts; and, I believe, there is no example to be found of any correction or improvement made by him after publication. The hastiness of his productions might be the effect of necessity; but his subsequent neglect could hardly have any other cause than impatience of study.

What can be said of his versification, will be little more than a dilatation of the praise given it by Pope.

> Waller was smooth; but Dryden taught to join ⎤
> The varying verse, the full-resounding line, ⎬
> The long majestick march, and energy divine. ⎦

Some improvements had been already made in English numbers; but the full force of our language was not yet felt; the verse that was smooth was commonly feeble. If Cowley had sometimes a finished line, he had it by chance. Dryden knew how to chuse the flowing and the sonorous words; to vary the pauses, and adjust the accents; to diversify the cadence, and yet preserve the smoothness of his metre.

. . . .

Of Dryden's works it was said by Pope, that *he could select from them better specimens of every mode of poetry than any other English writer could supply*. Perhaps no nation ever produced a writer that enriched his language with such variety of models. To him we owe the improvement, perhaps the completion of our metre, the refinement of our language, and much of the correctness of our sentiments. By him we were taught *sapere & fari*, to think naturally and express forcibly. He taught us that it was possible to reason in rhyme. He shewed us the true bounds of a translator's liberty. What was said of Rome, adorned by Augustus, may be applied by an easy metaphor to English poetry embellished by Dryden, *lateritiam invenit, marmoream reliquit*, he found it brick, and he left it marble.

GILBERT WALMSLEY AND DAVID GARRICK

OF Gilbert Walmsley, thus presented to my mind, let me indulge myself in the remembrance. I knew him very early; he was one of the first friends that literature procured me, and I hope that at least my gratitude made me worthy of his notice.

He was of an advanced age, and I was only not a boy; yet he never received my notions with contempt. He was a Whig, with all the virulence and malevolence of his party; yet difference of opinion did not keep us apart. I honoured him, and he endured me.

He had mingled with the gay world, without exemption from its vices or its follies, but had never neglected the cultivation of his mind; his belief of Revelation was unshaken; his learning preserved his principles; he grew first regular, and then pious.

His studies had been so various, that I am not able to name a man of equal knowledge. His acquaintance with books was great; and what he did not immediately know, he could at least tell where to find. Such was his amplitude of learning, and such his copiousness of communication, that it may be doubted whether a day now passes in which I have not some advantage from his friendship.

At this man's table I enjoyed many chearful and instructive

hours, with companions such as are not often found; with one who has lengthened, and one who has gladdened life; with Dr. James, whose skill in physick will be long remembered; and with David Garrick, whom I hoped to have gratified with this character of our common friend: but what are the hopes of man! I am disappointed by that stroke of death, which has eclipsed the gaiety of nations, and impoverished the publick stock of harmless pleasure.

THOMAS SPRAT

Burnet is not very favourable to his memory; but he and Burnet were old rivals. On some publick occasion they both preached before the house of commons. There prevailed in those days an indecent custom: when the preacher touched any favourite topick in a manner that delighted his audience, their approbation was expressed by a loud *hum*, continued in proportion to their zeal or pleasure. When Burnet preached, part of his congregation *hummed* so loudly and so long, that he sat down to enjoy it, and rubbed his face with his handkerchief. When Sprat preached, he likewise was honoured with the like animating *hum*; but he stretched out his hand to the congregation, and cried, "Peace, peace, I pray you, peace."

This I was told in my youth by an old man, who had been no careless observer of the passages of those times.

Burnet's sermon, says Salmon, was remarkable for sedition, and Sprat's for loyalty. Burnet had the thanks of the house; Sprat had no thanks, but a good living from the king; which, he said, was of as much value as the thanks of the Commons.

The works of Sprat, besides his few poems, are, The History of the Royal Society, the Life of Cowley, The Answer to Sorbiere, The History of the Ryehouse Plot; the Relation of his own Examination, and a volume of Sermons. I have heard it observed, with great justness, that every book is of a different kind, and that each has its distinct and characteristical excellence.

My business is only with his poems. He considered Cowley as a model; and supposed that as he was imitated, perfection was approached. Nothing therefore but Pindarick liberty was to be expected. There is in his few productions no want of such conceits as he thought excellent; and of those our judgement may be settled by the first that appears in his praise of Cromwell, where he says that Cromwell's *fame, like man, will grow white as it grows old.*

HALIFAX

Of him, who from a poet became a patron of poets, it will be readily believed that the works would not miss of celebration. Addison began to praise him early, and was followed or accompanied by other poets; perhaps by almost all, except by Swift and Pope; who forbore to flatter him in his life, and after his death spoke of him, Swift with slight censure, and Pope in the character Bufo with acrimonious contempt.

He was, as Pope says, *fed with dedications*; for Tickell affirms that no dedicator was unrewarded. To charge all unmerited praise with the guilt of flattery, and to suppose that the encomiast always knows and feels the falsehood of his assertions, is surely to discover great ignorance of human nature and human life. In determinations depending not on rules, but on experience and comparison, judgement is always in some degree subject to affection. Very near to admiration is the wish to admire.

Every man willingly gives value to the praise which he receives, and considers the sentence passed in his favour as the sentence of discernment. We admire in a friend that understanding that selected us for confidence; we admire more, in a patron, that judgement which, instead of scattering bounty indiscriminately, directed it to us; and those performances which gratitude forbids us to blame, affection will easily dispose us to exalt.

To these prejudices, hardly culpable, interest adds a power always operating, though not always, because not willingly, perceived. The modesty of praise wears gradually away; and perhaps the pride of patronage may be in time so increased, that modest praise will no longer please.

Many a blandishment was practised upon Halifax, which he would never have known, had he had no other attractions than those of his poetry, of which a short time has withered the beauties. It would now be esteemed no honour, by a contributor to the monthly bundles of verses, to be told, that, in strains either familiar or solemn, he sings like Montague.

THOMAS PARNELL

The Life of Dr. Parnell is a task which I should very willingly decline, since it has been lately written by Goldsmith, a man of such variety of powers, and such felicity of performance, that he always seemed to do best that which he was doing; a man who had the art of being minute without tediousness, and general without confusion; whose language was copious without exuberance, exact without constraint, and easy without weakness.

What such an author has told, who would tell again? I have made an abstract from his larger narrative; and shall have this gratification from my attempt, that it gives me an opportunity of paying due tribute to the memory of a departed genius.

Τὸ γὰρ γέρας ἐστὶ θανόντων.

.   .   .   .   .

The general character of Parnell is not great extent of comprehension, or fertility of mind. Of the little that appears still less is his own. His praise must be derived from the easy sweetness of his diction: in his verses there is *more happiness than pains*; he is spritely without effort, and always delights though he never ravishes; every thing is proper, yet every thing seems casual. If there is some appearance of elaboration in the *Hermit*, the narrative, as it is less airy, is less pleasing. Of his other compositions it is impossible to say whether they are the productions of Nature, so excellent as not to want the help of Art, or of Art so refined as to resemble Nature.

This criticism relates only to the pieces published by Pope. Of the large appendages which I find in this edition, I can only say that I know not whence they came, nor have ever enquired whither they are going. They stand upon the faith of the compilers.

NICHOLAS ROWE

FEW characters can bear the microscopick scrutiny of wit quickened by anger; and perhaps the best advice to authors would be, that they should keep out of the way of one another.

JOSEPH ADDISON

AT the school of the Chartreux, to which he was removed either from that of Salisbury or Lichfield, he pursued his juvenile studies under the care of Dr. Ellis, and contracted that intimacy with Sir Richard Steele, which their joint labours have so effectually recorded.

Of this memorable friendship the greater praise must be given to Steele. It is not hard to love those from whom nothing can be feared, and Addison never considered Steele as a rival; but Steele lived, as he confesses, under an habitual subjection to the predominating genius of Addison, whom he always mentioned with reverence, and treated with obsequiousness.

Addison, who knew his own dignity, could not always forbear to shew it, by playing a little upon his admirer; but he was in no danger of retort: his jests were endured without resistance or resentment.

But the sneer of jocularity was not the worst. Steele, whose imprudence of generosity, or vanity of profusion, kept him always incurably necessitous, upon some pressing exigence, in an evil hour, borrowed an hundred pounds of his friend, probably without much purpose of repayment; but Addison, who seems to have had other notions of a hundred pounds, grew impatient of delay, and reclaimed his loan by an execution. Steele felt with great sensibility the obduracy of his creditor; but with emotions of sorrow rather than of anger.

·   ·   ·   ·

When the marquis of Wharton was appointed lord lieutenant of Ireland, Addison attended him as his secretary; and was made keeper of the records in Birmingham's Tower, with a salary of three hundred pounds a year. The office was little more than nominal, and the salary was augmented for his accommodation.

Interest and faction allow little to the operation of particular dispositions, or private opinions. Two men of personal characters more opposite than those of Wharton and Addison could not easily be brought together. Wharton was impious, profligate, and shameless, without regard, or appearance of regard, to right and wrong: whatever is contrary to this, may be said of Addison; but as agents of a party they were connected, and how they adjusted their other sentiments we cannot know.

·   ·   ·   ·   ·

To teach the minuter decencies and inferior duties, to regulate the practice of daily conversation, to correct those depravities which are rather ridiculous than criminal, and remove those grievances which, if they produce no lasting calamities, impress hourly vexation, was first attempted by *Casa* in his book of *Manners*, and *Castiglione* in his *Courtier*, two books yet celebrated in Italy for purity and elegance, and which, if they are now less read, are neglected only because they have effected that reformation which their authors intended, and their precepts now are no longer wanted. Their usefulness to the age in which they were written, is sufficiently attested by the translations which almost all the nations of Europe were in haste to obtain.

This species of instruction was continued, and perhaps advanced, by the French; among whom *La Bruyere's* Manners of the Age, though, as Boileau remarked, it is written without connection, certainly deserves great praise, for liveliness of description and justness of observation.

Before the Tatler and Spectator, if the writers for the theatre are excepted, England had no masters of common life. No writers had yet undertaken to reform either the savageness of neglect, or the impertinence of civility; to teach when to speak, or to be silent; how to refuse, or how to comply. We wanted not books to teach us our more important duties, and to settle opinions in philosophy or politicks; but an *Arbiter elegantiarum*, a judge of propriety, was yet wanting, who should survey the track of daily conversation, and free it from thorns and prickles, which teaze the passer, though they do not wound him.

For this purpose nothing is so proper as the frequent publication of short papers, which we read not as study but amusement. If the subject be slight, the treatise likewise is short. The busy may find time, and the idle may find patience.

This mode of conveying cheap and easy knowledge began among us in the Civil War, when it was much the interest of either party to raise and fix the prejudices of the people. At that time appeared Mercurius Aulicus, Mercurius Rusticus, and Mercurius Civicus. It is said that when any title grew popular, it was stolen by the antagonist, who by this stratagem conveyed his notions to those who would not have received him had he not worn the appearance of a friend. The tumult of those unhappy days left scarcely any man leisure to treasure up occasional compositions; and so much were they neglected, that a complete collection is no where to be found.

These Mercuries were succeeded by L'Estrange's Observator, and that by Lesley's Rehearsal, and perhaps by others; but hitherto nothing had been conveyed to the people, in this commodious manner, but controversy relating to the Church or State; of which they taught many to talk, whom they could not teach to judge.

It has been suggested that the Royal Society was instituted soon after the Restoration, to divert the attention of the people from public discontent. The Tatler and Spectator had the same tendency: they were published at a time when two parties, loud, restless, and violent, each with plausible declarations, and each perhaps without any distinct termination of its views, were agitating the nation; to minds heated with political contest, they supplied cooler and more inoffensive reflections; and it is said by Addison, in a subsequent work, that they had a perceptible influence upon the conversation of that time, and taught the frolick and the gay to unite merriment with decency; an effect which they can never wholly lose, while they continue to be among the first books by which both sexes are initiated in the elegancies of knowledge.

This year * he married the countess dowager of Warwick, whom he had solicited by a very long and anxious courtship, perhaps with behaviour not very unlike that of Sir Roger to his disdainful widow; and who, I am afraid, diverted herself often by playing with his passion. He is said to have first known her by becoming tutor to her son. "He formed," said Tonson, "the design of getting that lady, from the time when he was first recommended into the family." In what part of his life he obtained the recommendation, or how long, and in what manner he lived in the family, I know not. His advances at first were certainly timorous, but grew bolder as his reputation and influence increased; till at last the lady was persuaded to marry him, on terms much like those on which a Turkish princess is espoused, to whom the Sultan is reported to pronounce, "Daughter, I give thee this man for thy slave." The marriage, if uncontradicted report can be credited, made no addition to his happiness; it neither found them nor made them equal. She always remembered her own rank, and thought herself entitled to treat with very little ceremony the tutor of her son. Rowe's ballad of the *Despairing Shepherd* is said to have been written, either before or after marriage, upon this memorable pair; and it is certain that Addison has left behind him no encouragement for ambitious love.

The abundance of his own mind left him little need of adventitious sentiments; his wit always could suggest what the occasion

* August 2, 1716.

874

demanded. He had read with critical eyes the important volume of human life, and knew the heart of man from the depths of stratagem to the surface of affectation.

. . . .

Of the course of Addison's familiar day, before his marriage, Pope has given a detail. He had in the house with him Budgell, and perhaps Philips. His chief companions were Steele, Budgell, Philips, Carey, Davenant, and colonel Brett. With one or other of these he always breakfasted. He studied all morning; then dined at a tavern, and went afterwards to Button's.

Button had been a servant in the countess of Warwick's family, who, under the patronage of Addison, kept a coffee-house on the south-side of Russel-street, about two doors from Covent-garden. Here it was that the wits of that time used to assemble. It is said, that when Addison had suffered any vexation from the countess, he withdrew the company from Button's house.

From the coffee-house he went again to a tavern, where he often sat late, and drank too much wine. In the bottle, discontent seeks for comfort, cowardice for courage, and bashfulness for confidence. It is not unlikely that Addison was first seduced to excess by the manumission which he obtained from the servile timidity of his sober hours. He that feels oppression from the presence of those to whom he knows himself superior, will desire to set loose his powers of conversation; and who, that ever asked succour from Bacchus, was able to preserve himself from being enslaved by his auxiliary?

Among those friends it was that Addison displayed the elegance of his colloquial accomplishments, which may easily be supposed such as Pope represents them. The remark of Mandeville, who, when he had passed an evening in his company, declared that he was a parson in a tye-wig, can detract little from his character; he was always reserved to strangers, and was not incited to uncommon freedom by a character like that of Mandeville.

From any minute knowledge of his familiar manners, the intervention of sixty years has now debarred us. Steele once promised Congreve and the publick a complete description of his character; but the promises of authors are like the vows of lovers. Steele thought no more on his design, or thought on it with anxiety that at last disgusted him, and left his friend in the hands of Tickell.

His works will supply some information. It appears from his

various pictures of the world, that, with all his bashfulness, he had conversed with many distinct classes of men, had surveyed their ways with very diligent observation, and marked with great acuteness the effects of different modes of life. He was a man in whose presence nothing reprehensible was out of danger; quick in discerning whatever was wrong or ridiculous, and not unwilling to expose it. *There are,* says Steele, *in his writings many oblique strokes upon some of the wittiest men of the age.* His delight was more to excite merriment than detestation, and he detects follies rather than crimes.

If any judgement be made, from his books, of his moral character, nothing will be found but purity and excellence. Knowledge of mankind indeed, less extensive than that of Addison, will shew that to write and to live are very different. Many who praise virtue, do no more than praise it. Yet it is reasonable to believe that Addison's professions and practice were at no great variance, since, amidst that storm of faction in which most of his life was passed, though his station made him conspicuous, and his activity made him formidable, the character given him by his friends was never contradicted by his enemies: of those with whom interest or opinion united him, he had not only the esteem but the kindness; and of others, whom the violence of opposition drove against him, though he might lose the love, he retained the reverence.

It is justly observed by Tickell, that he employed wit on the side of virtue and religion. He not only made the proper use of wit himself, but taught it to others; and from his time it has been generally subservient to the cause of reason and of truth. He has dissipated the prejudice that had long connected gaiety with vice, and easiness of manners with laxity of principles. He has restored virtue to its dignity, and taught innocence not to be ashamed. This is an elevation of literary character, *above all Greek, above all Roman fame.* No greater felicity can genius attain than that of having purified intellectual pleasure, separated mirth from indecency, and wit from licentiousness; of having taught a succession of writers to bring elegance and gaiety to the aid of goodness; and, if I may use expressions yet more awful, of having *turned many to righteousness.*

. . . .

His poetry is first to be considered; of which it must be confessed that it has not often those felicities of diction which give lustre to sentiments, or that vigour of sentiment that animates diction:

there is little of ardour, vehemence, or transport; there is very rarely the awfulness of grandeur, and not very often the splendour of elegance. He thinks justly; but he thinks faintly. This is his general character, to which doubtless many single passages will furnish exceptions.

Yet if he seldom reaches supreme excellence, he rarely sinks into dulness, and is still more rarely entangled in absurdity. He did not trust his powers enough to be negligent. There is in most of his compositions a calmness and equability, deliberate and cautious, sometimes with little that delights, but seldom with any thing that offends.

No passage in the Campaign has been more often mentioned than the simile of the Angel, which is said in the Tatler to be *one of the noblest thoughts that ever entered into the heart of man,* and is therefore worthy of attentive consideration. Let it be first enquired whether it be at last a simile. A poetical simile is the discovery of likeness between two actions, in their general nature dissimilar, or of causes terminating by different operations in some resemblance of effect. But the mention of another like consequence from a like cause, or of a like performance by a like agency, is not a simile, but an exemplification. It is not a simile to say that the Thames waters fields, as the Po waters fields; or that as Hecla vomits flames in Iceland, so Ætna vomits flames in Sicily. When Horace says of Pindar, that he pours his violence and rapidity of verse, as a river swoln with rain rushes from the mountain; or of himself, that his genius wanders in quest of poetical decorations, as the bee wanders to collect honey, he, in either case, produces a simile; the mind is impressed with the resemblance of things generally unlike, as unlike as intellect and body. But if Pindar had been described as writing with the copiousness and grandeur of Homer, or Horace had told that he reviewed and finished his own poetry with the same care as Isocrates polished his orations, instead of similitude he would have exhibited almost identity; he would have given the same portraits with different names. In this poem, when the English are represented as gaining a fortified pass, by repetition of attack and perseverance of resolution; their obstinacy of courage, and vigour of onset, is well illustrated by the sea that breaks, with incessant battery, the dikes of Holland. This is a simile; but when Addison, having celebrated the beauty of Marlborough's person, tells us that *Achilles thus was form'd with every grace,* here is no simile, but a mere exemplification. A simile may be compared to lines converging at a point, and is more excellent as the lines approach from greater distance: an exemplification may be considered as two parallel lines which run on together without approximation, never far separated, and never joined.

Marlborough is so like the angel in the poem, that the action of both is almost the same, and performed by both in the same manner. Marlborough *teaches the battle to rage*; the angel *directs the storm*: Marlborough is *unmoved in peaceful thought*; the angel is *calm and serene*: Marlborough stands *unmoved amidst the shock of hosts*; the angel rides *calm in the whirlwind.* The lines on Marlborough are just and noble; but the simile gives almost the same images a second time.

But perhaps this thought, though hardly a simile, was remote from vulgar conceptions, and required great labour of research, or dexterity of application. Of this, Dr. Madden, a name which Ireland ought to honour, once gave me his opinion. *If I had set,* said he, *ten school-boys to write on the battle of* Blenheim, *and eight had brought me the Angel, I should not have been surprised.*

. . . . .

The tragedy of Cato, which, contrarily to the rule observed in selecting the works of other poets, has by the weight of its character forced its way into this collection, is unquestionably the noblest production of Addison's genius. Of a work so much read, it is difficult to say any thing new. About things on which the publick thinks long, it commonly attains to think right; and of Cato it has been not unjustly determined, that it is rather a poem in dialogue than a drama, rather a succession of just sentiments in elegant language than a representation of natural affections, or of any state probable or possible in human life. Nothing here *excites or asswages emotion*; here is *no magical power of raising phantastick terror or wild anxiety.* The events are expected without solicitude, and are remembered without joy or sorrow. Of the agents we have no care: we consider not what they are doing, or what they are suffering; we wish only to know what they have to say. Cato is a being above our solicitude; a man of whom the gods take care, and whom we leave to their care with heedless confidence. To the rest neither gods nor men can have much attention; for there is not one amongst them that strongly attracts either affection or esteem.

But they are made the vehicles of such sentiments and such expression, that there is scarcely a scene in the play which the reader does not wish to impress upon his memory.

.   .   .   .

Addison is now to be considered as a critick; a name which the present generation is scarcely willing to allow him. His criticism is condemned as tentative or experimental, rather than scientifick, and he is considered as deciding by taste rather than by principles.

It is not uncommon for those who have grown wise by the labour of others, to add a little of their own, and overlook their masters. Addison is now despised by some who perhaps would never have seen his defects, but by the lights which he afforded them. That he always wrote as he would think it necessary to write now, cannot be affirmed; his instructions were such as the character of his readers made proper. That general knowledge which now circulates in common talk was in his time rarely to be found. Men not professing learning were not ashamed of ignorance; and in the female world any acquaintance with books was distinguished only to be censured. His purpose was to infuse literary curiosity, by gentle and unsuspected conveyance, into the gay, the idle, and the wealthy; he therefore presented knowledge in the most alluring form, not lofty and austere, but accessible and familiar. When he shewed them their defects, he shewed them likewise that they might be easily supplied. His attempt succeeded; enquiry was awakened, and comprehension expanded. An emulation of intellectual elegance was excited, and from his time to our own life has been gradually exalted, and conversation purified and enlarged.

Dryden had, not many years before, scattered criticism over his Prefaces with very little parsimony; but, though he sometimes condescended to be somewhat familiar, his manner was in general too scholastick for those who had yet their rudiments to learn, and found it not easy to understand their master. His observations were framed rather for those that were learning to write, than for those that read only to talk.

An instructor like Addison was now wanting, whose remarks being superficial, might be easily understood, and being just, might prepare the mind for more attainments. Had he presented *Paradise Lost* to the publick with all the pomp of system and severity of science, he would perhaps have been admired, and the book still have been neglected; but by the blandishments of gentleness and facility, he has made Milton an universal favourite, with whom readers of every class think it necessary to be pleased.

He descended now and then to lower disquisitions, and by a serious display of the beauties of *Chevy Chase* exposed himself to the ridicule of Wagstaff, who bestowed a like pompous character on *Tom Thumb*; and to the contempt of Dennis, who, considering the fundamental position of his criticism, that *Chevy Chase* pleases, and ought to please, because it is natural, observes, "that there is a way of deviating from nature, by bombast or tumour, which soars above nature, and enlarges images beyond their real bulk; by affectation, which forsakes nature in quest of something unsuitable; and by imbecillity, which degrades nature by faintness and diminution, by obscuring images, and weakening effects." In *Chevy Chace* there is not much of either bombast or affectation; but there is chill and lifeless imbecillity. The story cannot possibly be told in a manner that shall make less impression on the mind.

. . . . .

As a describer of life and manners, he must be allowed to stand perhaps the first of the first rank. His humour, which, as Steele observes, is peculiar to himself, is so happily diffused as to give the grace of novelty to domestick scenes and daily occurrences. He never *outsteps the modesty of nature*, nor raises merriment or wonder by the violation of truth. His figures neither divert by distortion, nor amaze by aggravation. He copies life with so much fidelity, that he can be hardly said to invent; yet his exhibitions have an air so much original, that it is difficult to suppose them not merely the product of imagination.

As a teacher of wisdom he may be confidently followed. His religion has nothing in it enthusiastick or superstitious: he appears neither weakly credulous nor wantonly sceptical; his morality is neither dangerously lax, nor impracticably rigid. All the enchantment of fancy and all the cogency of argument are employed to recommend to the reader his real interest, the care of pleasing the Author of his being. Truth is shewn sometimes as the phantom of a vision, sometimes appears half-veiled in an allegory; sometimes attracts regard in the robes of fancy, and sometimes steps forth in the confidence of reason. She wears a thousand dresses, and in all is pleasing.

Mille habet ornatus, mille decenter habet.

880

His prose is the model of the middle stile; on grave subjects not formal, on light occasions not grovelling; pure without scrupulosity, and exact without apparent elaboration; always equable, and always easy, without glowing words or pointed sentences. Addison never deviates from his track to snatch a grace; he seeks no ambitious ornaments, and tries no hazardous innovations. His page is always luminous, but never blazes in unexpected splendour.

It seems to have been his principal endeavour to avoid all harshness and severity of diction; he is therefore sometimes verbose in his transitions and connections, and sometimes descends too much to the language of conversation; yet if his language had been less idiomatical, it might have lost somewhat of its genuine Anglicism. What he attempted, he performed; he is never feeble, and he did not wish to be energetick; he is never rapid, and he never stagnates. His sentences have neither studied amplitude, nor affected brevity: his periods, though not diligently rounded, are voluble and easy. Whoever wishes to attain an English stile, familiar but not coarse, and elegant but not ostentatious, must give his days and nights to the volumes of Addison.

MATTHEW PRIOR

EVERY thing has its day. Through the reigns of William and Anne no prosperous event passed undignified by poetry. In the last war, when France was disgraced and overpowered in every quarter of the globe, when Spain coming to her assistance only shared her calamities, and the name of an Englishman was reverenced through Europe, no poet was heard amidst the general acclamation; the fame of our counsellors and heroes was intrusted to the Gazetteer.

.   .   .   .   .

Solomon is the work to which he entrusted the protection of his name, and which he expected succeeding ages to regard with veneration. His affection was natural; it had undoubtedly been written with great labour, and who is willing to think that he has been labouring in vain? He had infused into it much knowledge and much thought; had often polished it to elegance, often dignified it with splendour, and sometimes heightened it to sublimity: he perceived in it many excellencies, and did not discover that it wanted that without which all others are of small avail, the power of engaging attention and alluring curiosity.

Tediousness is the most fatal of all faults; negligences or errors are single and local, but tediousness pervades the whole; other faults are censured and forgotten, but the power of tediousness propagates itself. He that is weary the first hour, is more weary the second; as bodies forced into motion, contrary to their tendency, pass more and more slowly through every successive interval of space.

Unhappily this pernicious failure is that which an author is least able to discover. We are seldom tiresome to ourselves; and the act of composition fills and delights the mind with change of language and succession of images; every couplet when produced is new, and novelty is the great source of pleasure. Perhaps no man ever thought a line superfluous when he first wrote it, or contracted his work till his ebullitions of invention had subsided. If he should controul his desire of immediate renown, and keep his work *nine years* unpublished, he will be still the author, and still in danger of deceiving himself; and if he consults his friends, he will probably find men who have more kindness than judgement, or more fear to offend than desire to instruct.

The tediousness of this poem proceeds not from the uniformity of the subject, for it is sufficiently diversified, but from the continued tenour of the narration; in which Solomon relates the successive vicissitudes of his own mind, without the intervention of any other speaker, or the mention of any other agent, unless it be Abra; and the reader is only to learn what he thought, and to be told that he thought wrong. The event of every experiment is foreseen, and therefore the process is not much regarded.

Yet the work is far from deserving to be neglected. He that shall peruse it will be able to mark many passages, to which he may recur for instruction or delight; many from which the poet may learn to write, and the philosopher to reason.

．　　　　．　　　　．　　　　．　　　　．

His numbers are such as mere diligence may attain; they seldom offend the ear, and seldom sooth it; they commonly want airiness, lightness, and facility; what is smooth, is not soft. His verses always roll, but they seldom flow.

A survey of the life and writings of Prior may exemplify a sentence which he doubtless understood well, when he read Horace at his uncle's; *the vessel long retains the scent which it first receives*. In his private relaxation he revived the tavern, and in his amorous pedantry he exhibited the college. But on higher occasions, and nobler subjects, when habit was overpowered by the necessity of reflection, he wanted not wisdom as a statesman, nor elegance as a poet.

WILLIAM CONGREVE

CONGREVE has merit of the highest kind; he is an original writer, who borrowed neither the models of his plot, nor the manner of his dialogue. Of his plays I cannot speak distinctly; for since I inspected them many years have passed; but what remains upon my memory is, that his characters are commonly fictitious and artificial, with very little of nature, and not much of life. He formed a peculiar idea of comick excellence, which he supposed to consist in gay remarks and unexpected answers; but that which he endeavoured, he seldom failed of performing. His scenes exhibit not much of humour, imagery, or passion: his personages are a kind of intellectual gladiators; every sentence is to ward or strike; the contest of smartness is never intermitted; his wit is a meteor playing to and fro with alternate coruscations. His comedies have therefore, in some degree, the operation of tragedies; they surprise rather than divert, and raise admiration oftener than merriment. But they are the works of a mind replete with images, and quick in combination.

Of his miscellaneous poetry, which this collection has admitted, I cannot say any thing very favourable. The powers of Congreve seem to desert him when he leaves the stage, as Antæus was no longer strong than he could touch the ground. It cannot be observed without wonder, that a mind so vigorous and fertile in dramatick compositions should on any other occasion discover nothing but impotence and poverty. He has in these little pieces neither elevation of fancy, selection of language, nor skill in versification: yet if I were required to select from the whole mass of English poetry the most poetical paragraph, I know not what I could prefer to an exclamation in *The Mourning Bride*:

ALMERIA

It was a fancy'd noise; for all is hush'd.

LEONORA

It bore the accent of a human voice.

ALMERIA

It was thy fear, or else some transient wind
Whistling thro' hollows of this vaulted isle:
We'll listen——

LEONORA

Hark!

ALMERIA

No, all is hush'd, and still as death.—'Tis dreadful!
How reverend is the face of this tall pile;
Whose ancient pillars rear their marble heads,
To bear aloft its arch'd and pond'rous roof,
By its own weight made stedfast and immoveable,
Looking tranquillity! It strikes an awe
And terror on my aching sight; the tombs
And monumental caves of death look cold,
And shoot a chilness to my trembling heart.
Give me thy hand, and let me hear thy voice;
Nay, quickly speak to me, and let me hear
Thy voice—my own affrights me with its echoes.

He who reads those lines enjoys for a moment the powers of a poet; he feels what he remembers to have felt before, but he feels it with great increase of sensibility; he recognizes a familiar image, but meets it again amplified and expanded, embellished with beauty, and enlarged with majesty.

RICHARD BLACKMORE

CORRECTION seldom effects more than the suppression of faults: a happy line, or a single elegance, may perhaps be added; but of a large work the general character must always remain; the original constitution can be very little helped by local remedies; inherent and radical dulness will never be much invigorated by extrinsick animation.

.   .   .   .

He was not yet deterred from heroick poetry; there was another monarch of this island, for he did not fetch his heroes from foreign countries, whom he considered as worthy of the Epick Muse, and he dignified Alfred (1723) with twelve books. But the opinion of the nation was now settled; a hero introduced by Blackmore was not likely to find either respect or kindness; *Alfred* took his place by *Eliza* in silence and darkness: benevolence was ashamed to favour, and malice was weary of insulting. Of his four Epick Poems the first had such reputation and popularity as enraged the criticks;

884

the second was at least known enough to be ridiculed; the two last had neither friends nor enemies.

Contempt is a kind of gangrene, which if it seizes one part of a character corrupts all the rest by degrees. Blackmore, being despised as a poet, was in time neglected as a physician; his practice, which was once invidiously great, forsook him in the latter part of his life; but being by nature, or by principle, averse from idleness, he employed his unwelcome leisure in writing books on physick, and teaching others to cure those whom he could himself cure no longer. I know not whether I can enumerate all the treatises by which he has endeavoured to diffuse the art of healing; for there is scarcely any distemper, of dreadful name, which he has not taught his reader how to oppose. He has written on the small-pox, with a vehement invective against inoculation; on consumptions, the spleen, the gout, the rheumatism, the king's-evil, the dropsy, the jaundice, the stone, the diabetes, and the plague.

JOHN GAY

"Beggar's Opera"

Of this performance, when it was printed, the reception was different, according to the different opinions of its readers. Swift commended it for the excellence of its morality, as a piece that *placed all kinds of vice in the strongest and most odious light*; but others, and among them Dr. Herring, afterwards archbishop of Canterbury, censured it as giving encouragement not only to vice but to crimes, by making a highwayman the hero, and dismissing him at last unpunished. It has been even said, that after the exhibition of the *Beggar's Opera* the gangs of robbers were evidently multiplied.

Both these decisions are surely exaggerated. The play, like many others, was plainly written only to divert, without any moral purpose, and is therefore not likely to do good; nor can it be conceived, without more speculation than life requires or admits, to be productive of much evil. Highwaymen and housebreakers seldom frequent the playhouse, or mingle in any elegant diversion; nor is it possible for any one to imagine that he may rob with safety, because he sees Macheath reprieved upon the stage.

.   .   .   .   .

As a poet, he cannot be rated very high. He was, as I once heard a female critick remark, *of a lower order*. He had not in any great degree the *mens divinior*, the dignity of genius. Much however must be allowed to the author of a new species of composition, though it be not of the highest kind. We owe to Gay the Ballad Opera; a mode of comedy which at first was supposed to delight only by its novelty, but has now by the experience of half a century been found so well accommodated to the disposition of a popular audience, that it is likely to keep long possession of the stage. Whether this new drama was the product of judgement or of luck, the praise of it must be given to the inventor; and there are many writers read with more reverence, to whom such merit of originality cannot be attributed.

A Pastoral of an hundred lines may be endured; but who will hear of sheep and goats, and myrtle bowers and purling rivulets, through five acts? Such scenes please Barbarians in the dawn of literature, and children in the dawn of life; but will be for the most part thrown away, as men grow wise, and nations grow learned.

WILLIAM SOMERVILE

OF Mr. Somervile's life I am not able to say any thing that can satisfy curiosity.

His great work is his *Chase*, which he undertook in his maturer age, when his ear was improved to the approbation of blank verse, of which however his two first lines give a bad specimen. To this poem praise cannot be totally denied. He is allowed by sportsmen to write with great intelligence of his subject, which is the first requisite to excellence; and though it is impossible to interest the common readers of verse in the dangers or pleasures of the chase, he has done all that transition and variety could easily effect; and has, with great propriety, enlarged his plan by the modes of hunting used in other countries.

With still less judgement did he chuse blank verse as the vehicle of *Rural Sports*. If blank verse be not tumid and gorgeous, it is crippled prose; and familiar images in laboured language have nothing to recommend them but absurd novelty, which wanting the attractions of Nature, cannot please long. One excellence of the *Splendid Shilling* is, that it is short. Disguise can gratify no longer than it deceives.

JONATHAN SWIFT

HE wrote the same year [1711] a *Letter to the October Club*, a number of Tory Gentlemen sent from the country to Parliament, who formed themselves into a club, to the number of about a hundred, and met to animate the zeal and raise the expectations of each other. They thought, with great reason, that the Ministers were losing opportunities; that sufficient use was not made of the general ardour of the nation; they called loudly for more changes, and stronger efforts; and demanded the punishment of part, and the dismission of the rest, of those whom they considered as publick robbers.

Their eagerness was not gratified by the Queen, or by Harley. The Queen was probably slow because she was afraid, and Harley was slow because he was doubtful; he was a Tory only by necessity, or for convenience; and when he had power in his hands, had no settled purpose for which he should employ it; forced to gratify to a certain degree the Tories who supported him, but unwilling to make his reconcilement to the Whigs utterly desperate, he corresponded at once with the two expectants of the Crown, and kept, as has been observed, the succession undetermined. Not knowing what to do, he did nothing; and with the fate of a double-dealer, at last he lost his power, but kept his enemies.

Swift seems to have concurred in opinion with the *October Club*; but it was not in his power to quicken the tardiness of Harley, whom he stimulated as much as he could, but with little effect. He that knows not whither to go, is in no haste to move. Harley, who was perhaps not quick by nature, became yet more slow by irresolution; and was content to hear that dilatoriness lamented as natural, which he applauded in himself as politick.

Without the Tories, however, nothing could be done; and as they were not to be gratified, they must be appeased; and the conduct of the Minister, if it could not be vindicated, was to be plausibly excused.

Swift now attained the zenith of his political importance: he published (1712) the *Conduct of the Allies*, ten days before the Parliament assembled. The purpose was to persuade the nation to a peace, and never had any writer more success. The people, who had been amused with bonfires and triumphal processions, and looked with idolatry on the General and his friends, who, as they

887

thought, had made England the arbitress of nations, were confounded between shame and rage, when they found that *mines had been exhausted, and millions destroyed*, to secure the Dutch or aggrandise the Emperor, without any advantage to ourselves; that we had been bribing our neighbours to fight their own quarrel; and that amongst our enemies we might number our allies.

That is now no longer doubted, of which the nation was then first informed, that the war was unnecessarily protracted to fill the pockets of Marlborough; and that it would have been continued without end, if he could have continued his annual plunder. But Swift, I suppose, did not yet know what he has since written, that a commission was drawn which would have appointed him General for life, had it not become ineffectual by the resolution of Lord Cowper, who refused the seal.

Whatever is received, say the schools, *is received in proportion to the recipient.* The power of a political treatise depends much upon the disposition of the people; the nation was then combustible, and a spark set it on fire. It is boasted, that between November and January eleven thousand were sold; a great number at that time, when we were not yet a nation of readers. To its propagation certainly no agency of power or influence was wanting. It furnished arguments for conversation, speeches for debate, and materials for parliamentary resolutions.

Yet, surely, whoever surveys this wonder-working pamphlet with cool perusal, will confess that its efficacy was supplied by the passions of its readers; that it operates by the mere weight of facts, with very little assistance from the hand that produced them.

Swift, being now the declared favourite and supposed confidant of the Tory Ministry, was treated by all that depended on the Court with the respect which dependents know how to pay. He soon began to feel part of the misery of greatness; he that could say he knew him, considered himself as having fortune in his power. Commissions, solicitations, remonstrances, crouded about him; he was expected to do every man's business, to procure employment for one, and to retain it for another. In assisting those who addressed him, he represents himself as sufficiently diligent; and desires to have others believe, what he probably believed himself, that by his interposition many Whigs of merit, and among them Addison and Congreve, were continued in their places. But every man of known influence has so many petitions which he cannot grant, that he must necessarily offend more than he gratifies, as the preference given to one affords all the rest a reason for complaint. *When I give away a place*, said Lewis XIV., *I make a hundred discontented, and one ungrateful.*

Much has been said of the equality and independence which he preserved in his conversation with the Ministers, of the frankness of his remonstrances, and the familiarity of his friendship. In accounts of this kind a few single incidents are set against the general tenour of behaviour. No man, however, can pay a more servile tribute to the Great, than by suffering his liberty in their presence to aggrandize him in his own esteem. Between different ranks of the community there is necessarily some distance: he who is called by his superior to pass the interval, may very properly accept the invitation; but petulance and obtrusion are rarely produced by magnanimity; nor have often any nobler cause than the pride of importance, and the malice of inferiority. He who knows himself necessary may set, while that necessity lasts, a high value upon himself; as, in a lower condition, a servant eminently skilful may be saucy; but he is saucy only because he is servile. Swift appears to have preserved the kindness of those that wanted him no longer; and therefore it must be allowed, that the childish freedom, to which he seems enough inclined, was overpowered by his better qualities.

In 1723 died Mrs. Van Homrigh, a woman made unhappy by her admiration of wit, and ignominiously distinguished by the name of *Vanessa*, whose conduct has been already sufficiently discussed, and whose history is too well known to be minutely repeated. She was a young woman fond of literature, whom *Decanus* the *Dean*, called *Cadenus* by transposition of the letters, took pleasure in directing and instructing; till, from being proud of his praise, she grew fond of his person. Swift was then about forty-seven, at an age when vanity is strongly excited by the amorous attention of a young woman. If it be said that Swift should have checked a passion which he never meant to gratify, recourse must be had to that extenuation which he so much despised, *men are but men*: perhaps however he did not at first know his own mind, and, as he represents himself, was undetermined. For his admission of her courtship, and his indulgence of her hopes after his marriage to Stella no other honest plea can be found, than that he delayed a disagreeable discovery from time to time, dreading the immediate burst of distress, and watching for a favourable moment. She thought herself neglected, and died of disappointment; having ordered by her will the poem to be published, in which *Cadenus* had proclaimed her excellence, and confessed his love.

.　　　　.　　　　.　　　　.　　　　.

The great acquisition of esteem and influence was made by the *Drapier's Letters* in 1724. One Wood of Wolverhampton in Staffordshire, a man enterprising and rapacious, had, as is said, by a present to the Dutchess of Munster, obtained a patent empowering him to coin one hundred and eighty thousand pounds of half-pence and farthings for the kingdom of Ireland, in which there was a very inconvenient and embarrassing scarcity of copper coin; so that it was possible to run in debt upon the credit of a piece of money. The cook or keeper of an alehouse could not refuse to supply a man that had silver in his hand, and the buyer would not leave his money without change.

The project was therefore plausible. The scarcity, which was already great, Wood took care to make greater, by agents who gathered up the old half-pence; and was about to turn his brass into gold, by pouring his treasures of his new mint upon Ireland, when Swift, finding that the metal was debased to an enormous degree, wrote Letters, under the name of *M. B. Drapier*, to shew the folly of receiving, and the mischief that must ensue, by giving gold and silver for coin worth perhaps not a third part of its nominal value.

The nation was alarmed; the new coin was universally refused: but the governors of Ireland considered resistance to the King's patent as highly criminal; and one Whitshed, then Chief Justice, who had tried the printer of the former pamphlet, and sent out the Jury nine times, till by clamour and menaces they were frighted into a special verdict, now presented the *Drapier*, but could not prevail on the Grand Jury to find the bill.

Lord Carteret and the Privy Council published a proclamation, offering three hundred pounds for discovering the author of the Fourth Letter. Swift had concealed himself from his printers, and trusted only his butler, who transcribed the paper. The man, immediately after the appearance of the proclamation, strolled from the house, and staid out all night and part of the next day. There was reason enough to fear that he had betrayed his master for the reward; but he came home, and the Dean ordered him to put off his livery, and leave the house; "for," says he, "I know that my life is in your power, and I will not bear, out of fear, either your insolence or negligence." The man excused his fault with great submission, and begged that he might be confined in the house while it was in his power to endanger his master; but the Dean resolutely turned him out, without taking further notice of him, till the term of information had expired, and then received him again. Soon afterwards he ordered him and the rest of the servants into his presence, without telling his intentions, and bade them take notice that their fellow-servant was no longer Robert the butler; but that his integrity had made him Mr. Blakeney, verger of St. Patrick's; an officer whose income was between thirty and forty pounds a year, but he still continued for some years to serve his old master as his butler.

Swift was known from this time by the appellation of *The Dean*. He was honoured by the populace as the champion, patron, and instructer of Ireland; and gained such power as, considered both in its extent and duration, scarcely any man has ever enjoyed without greater wealth or higher station.

He was from this important year the oracle of the traders, and the idol of the rabble, and by consequence was feared and courted by all to whom the kindness of the traders or the populace was necessary. The *Drapier* was a sign; the *Drapier* was a health; and which way soever the eye or the ear was turned, some tokens were found of the nation's gratitude to the *Drapier*.

The benefit was indeed great; he had rescued Ireland from a very oppressive and predatory invasion; and the popularity which he had gained he was diligent to keep, by appearing forward and zealous on every occasion where the publick interest was supposed to be involved. Nor did he much scruple to boast his influence; for when, upon some attempts to regulate the coin, Archbishop Boulter, then one of the Justices, accused him of exasperating the people, he exculpated himself by saying, "If I had lifted up my finger, they would have torn you to pieces."

. . . . . .

He returned to a home of sorrow: poor Stella was sinking into the grave, and, after a languishing decay of about two months, died in her forty-fourth year, on January 28, 1728. How much he wished her life, his papers tell us; nor can it be doubted that he

891

dreaded the death of her whom he loved most, aggravated by the consciousness that himself had hastened it.

Beauty and the power of pleasing, the greatest external advantages that woman can desire or possess, were fatal to the unfortunate Stella. The man whom she had the misfortune to love was, as Delany observes, fond of singularity, and desirous to make a mode of happiness for himself, out of the general course of things and order of Providence. From the time of her arrival in Ireland he seems resolved to keep her in his power, and therefore hindered a match sufficiently advantageous, by accumulating unreasonable demands, and prescribing conditions that could not be performed. While she was at her own disposal he did not consider his possession as secure; resentment, ambition, or caprice, might separate them; he was therefore resolved to make *assurance double sure*, and to appropriate her by a private marriage, to which he had annexed the expectation of all the pleasures of perfect friendship, without the uneasiness of conjugal restraint. But with this state poor Stella was not satisfied; she never was treated as a wife, and to the world she had the appearance of a mistress. She lived sullenly on, in hope that in time he would own and receive her; but the time did not come till the change of his manners and depravation of his mind made her tell him, when he offered to acknowledge her, that *it was too late*. She then gave up herself to sorrowful resentment, and died under the tyranny of him by whom she was in the highest degree loved and honoured.

What were her claims to this excentrick tenderness, by which the laws of Nature were violated to retain her, curiosity will enquire; but how shall it be gratified? Swift was a lover; his testimony may be suspected. Delany and the Irish saw with Swift's eyes, and therefore add little confirmation. That she was virtuous, beautiful, and elegant, in a very high degree, such admiration from such a lover makes it very probable; but she had not much literature, for she could not spell her own language; and of her wit, so loudly vaunted, the smart sayings which Swift himself has collected afford no splendid specimen.

The reader of Swift's *Letter to a Lady on her Marriage*, may be allowed to doubt whether his opinion of female excellence ought implicitly to be admitted; for if his general thoughts on women were such as he exhibits, a very little sense in a Lady would enrapture, and a very little virtue would astonish him. Stella's supremacy, therefore, was perhaps only local; she was great, because her associates were little.

In some Remarks lately published on the Life of Swift, this marriage is mentioned as fabulous, or doubtful; but, alas! poor Stella, as Dr. Madden told me, related her melancholy story to Dr. Sheridan, when he attended her as a clergyman to prepare her for death; and Delany tells it not with doubt, but only with regret. Swift never mentioned her without a sigh.

His asperity continually increasing, condemned him to solitude; and his resentment of solitude sharpened his asperity. He was not, however, totally deserted: some men of learning, and some women of elegance, often visited him; and he wrote from time to time either verse or prose; of his verses he willingly gave copies, and is supposed to have felt no discontent when he saw them printed. His favourite maxim was *vive la bagatelle*; he thought trifles a necessary part of life, and perhaps found them necessary to himself. It seems impossible to him to be idle, and his disorders made it difficult or dangerous to be long seriously studious, or laboriously diligent. The love of ease is always gaining upon age, and he had one temptation to petty amusements peculiar to himself; whatever he did, he was sure to hear applauded; and such was his predominance over all that approached, that all their applauses were probably sincere. He that is much flattered, soon learns to flatter himself: we are commonly taught our duty by fear or shame, and how can they act upon the man who hears nothing but his own praises?

When Swift is considered as an author, it is just to estimate his powers by their effects. In the reign of Queen Anne he turned the stream of popularity against the Whigs, and must be confessed to have dictated for a time the political opinions of the English nation. In the succeeding reign he delivered Ireland from plunder and oppression; and shewed that wit, confederated with truth, had such force as authority was unable to resist. He said truly of himself, that Ireland *was his debtor*. It was from the time when he first began to patronize the Irish, that they may date their riches and prosperity. He taught them first to know their own interest, their weight, and their strength, and gave them spirit to assert that equality with their fellow-subjects to which they have ever since been making vigorous advances, and to claim those rights which they have at last established. Nor can they be charged with ingratitude to their benefactor; for they reverenced him as a guardian, and obeyed him as a dictator.

In his works, he has given very different specimens both of sentiment and expression. His *Tale of a Tub* has little resemblance to his other pieces. It exhibits a vehemence and rapidity of mind, a copiousness of images, and vivacity of diction, such as he afterwards never possessed, or never exerted. It is of a mode so distinct and peculiar, that it must be considered by itself; what is true of that, is not true of any thing else which he has written.

In his other works is found an equable tenour of easy language, which rather trickles than flows. His delight was in simplicity. That he has in his works no metaphor, as has been said, is not true; but his few metaphors seem to be received rather by necessity than choice. He studied purity; and though perhaps all his structures are not exact, yet it is not often that solecisms can be found; and whoever depends on his authority may generally conclude himself safe. His sentences are never too much dilated or contracted; and it will not be easy to find any embarrassment in the complication of his clauses, any inconsequence in his connections, or abruptness in his transitions.

His stile was well suited to his thoughts, which are never subtilised by nice disquisitions, decorated by sparkling conceits, elevated by ambitious sentences, or variegated by far-sought learning. He pays no court to the passions; he excites neither surprize nor admiration; he always understands himself, and his reader always understands him: the peruser of Swift wants little previous knowledge: it will be sufficient that he is acquainted with common words and common things; he is neither required to mount elevations, nor to explore profundities; his passage is always on a level, along solid ground, without asperities, without obstruction.

This easy and safe conveyance of meaning it was Swift's desire to attain, and for having attained he certainly deserves praise, though perhaps not the highest praise. For purposes merely didactick, when something is to be told that was not known before, it is in the highest degree proper, but against that inattention by which known truths are suffered to lie neglected, it makes no provision; it instructs, but does not persuade.

By his political education he was associated with the Whigs; but he deserted them when they deserted their principles, yet without running into the contrary extreme; he continued throughout his life to retain the disposition which he assigns to the *Church-of-England Man*, of thinking commonly with the Whigs of the State, and with the Tories of the Church.

He was a churchman rationally zealous; he desired the prosperity and maintained the honour of the Clergy; of the Dissenters he did not wish to infringe the toleration, but he opposed their encroachments.

To his duty as Dean he was very observant. He managed the revenues of his church with exact œconomy; and it is said by Delany, that more money was, under his direction, laid out in repairs than had ever been in the same time since its first erection. Of his choir he was eminently careful; and, though he neither loved nor understood musick, took care that all the singers were well qualified, admitting none without the testimony of skilful judges.

In his church he restored the practice of weekly communion, and distributed the sacramental elements in the most solemn and devout manner with his own hand. He came to church every morning, preached commonly in his turn, and attended the evening anthem, that it might not be negligently performed.

He read the service *rather with a strong nervous voice than in a graceful manner; his voice was sharp and high-toned, rather than harmonious.*

He entered upon the clerical state with hope to excel in preaching; but complained, that, from the time of his political controversies, *he could only preach pamphlets*. This censure of himself, if judgement be made from those sermons which have been published, was unreasonably severe.

The suspicions of his irreligion proceeded in a great measure from his dread of hypocrisy; instead of wishing to seem better, he delighted in seeming worse than he was. He went in London to early prayers, lest he should be seen at church; he read prayers to his servants every morning with such dexterous secrecy, that Dr. Delany was six months in his house before he knew it. He was not only careful to hide the good which he did, but willingly incurred the suspicion of evil which he did not. He forgot what himself had formerly asserted, that hypocrisy is less mischievous than open impiety. Dr. Delany, with all his zeal for his honour, has justly condemned this part of his character.

The person of Swift had not many recommendations. He had a kind of muddy complexion, which, though he washed himself with

895

oriental scrupulosity, did not look clear. He had a countenance sour and severe, which he seldom softened by any appearance of gaiety. He stubbornly resisted any tendency to laughter.

To his domesticks he was naturally rough; and a man of a rigorous temper, with that vigilance of minute attention which his works discover, must have been a master that few could bear. That he was disposed to do his servants good, on important occasions, is no great mitigation; benefaction can be but rare, and tyrannick peevishness is perpetual. He did not spare the servants of others. Once, when he dined alone with the Earl of Orrery, he said, of one that waited in the room, *That man has, since we sat to the table, committed fifteen faults.* What the faults were, Lord Orrery, from whom I heard the story, had not been attentive enough to discover. My number may perhaps not be exact.

In his œconomy he practised a peculiar and offensive parsimony, without disguise or apology. The practice of saving being once necessary, became habitual, and grew first ridiculous, and at last detestable. But his avarice, though it might exclude pleasure, was never suffered to encroach upon his virtue. He was frugal by inclination, but liberal by principle; and if the purpose to which he destined his little accumulations be remembered, with his distribution of occasional charity, it will perhaps appear that he only liked one mode of expence better than another, and saved only that he might have something to give. He did not grow rich by injuring his successors, but left both Laracor and the Deanery more valuable than he found them.—With all this talk of his covetousness and generosity, it should be remembered that he was never rich. The revenue of his Deanery was not much more than seven hundred a year.

His beneficence was not graced with tenderness or civility; he relieved without pity, and assisted without kindness, so that those who were fed by him could hardly love him.

He made a rule to himself to give but one piece at a time, and therefore always stored his pocket with coins of different value.

Whatever he did, he seemed willing to do in a manner peculiar to himself, without sufficiently considering that singularity, as it implies a contempt of the general practice, is a kind of defiance which justly provokes the hostility of ridicule; he therefore who indulges peculiar habits is worse than others, if he be not better.

In the intercourse of familiar life, he indulged his disposition to petulance and sarcasm, and thought himself injured if the licentiousness of his raillery, the freedom of his censures, or the petulance of his frolicks, was resented or repressed. He predominated over his companions with very high ascendency, and probably would bear none over whom he could not predominate. To give him advice was, in the stile of his friend Delany, *to venture to speak to him*. This customary superiority soon grew too delicate for truth; and Swift, with all his penetration, allowed himself to be delighted with low flattery.

On all common occasions, he habitually affects a stile of arrogance, and dictates rather than persuades. This authoritative and magisterial language he expected to be received as his peculiar mode of jocularity; but he apparently flattered his own arrogance by an assumed predomination, in which he was ironical only to the resentful, and to the submissive sufficiently serious.

He told stories with great felicity, and delighted in doing what he knew himself to do well. He was therefore captivated by the respectful silence of a steady listener, and told the same tales too often.

He did not, however, claim the right of talking alone; for it was his rule, when he had spoken a minute, to give room by a pause for any other speaker. Of time, on all occasions, he was an exact computer, and knew the minutes required to every common operation.

It may be justly supposed that there was in his conversation, what appears so frequently in his Letters, an affectation of familiarity with the Great, an ambition of momentary equality sought and enjoyed by the neglect of those ceremonies which custom has established as the barriers between one order of society and another. This transgression of regularity was by himself and his admirers termed greatness of soul. But a great mind disdains to hold any thing by courtesy, and therefore never usurps what a lawful claimant may take away. He that encroaches on another's dignity, puts himself in his power; he is either repelled with helpless indignity, or endured by clemency and condescension.

Of Swift's general habits of thinking if his Letters can be supposed to afford any evidence, he was not a man to be either loved or envied. He seems to have wasted life in discontent, by the rage of neglected pride, and the languishment of unsatisfied desire. He is querulous and fastidious, arrogant and malignant; he scarcely speaks of himself but with indignant lamentations, or of others but with insolent superiority when he is gay, and with angry contempt when he is gloomy. From the Letters that pass between him and Pope it might be inferred that they, with Arbuthnot and Gay, had engrossed all the understanding and virtue of mankind, that their merits filled the world; or that there was no hope of more. They shew the age involved in darkness, and shade the picture with sullen emulation.

When the Queen's death drove him into Ireland, he might be allowed to regret for a time the interception of his views, the extinction of his hopes, and his ejection from gay scenes, important employment, and splendid friendships; but when time had enabled reason to prevail over vexation, the complaints, which at first were natural, became ridiculous because they were useless. But querulousness was now grown habitual, and he cried out when he probably had ceased to feel. His reiterated wailings persuaded Bolingbroke that he was really willing to quit his deanery for an English parish; and Bolingbroke procured an exchange, which was rejected, and Swift still retained the pleasure of complaining.

The greatest difficulty that occurs, in analysing his character, is to discover by what depravity of intellect he took delight in revolving ideas, from which almost every other mind shrinks with disgust. The ideas of pleasure, even when criminal, may solicite the imagination; but what has disease, deformity, and filth, upon which the thoughts can be allured to dwell? Delany is willing to think that Swift's mind was not much tainted with this gross corruption before his long visit to Pope. He does not consider how he degrades his hero, by making him at fifty-nine the pupil of turpitude, and liable to the malignant influence of an ascendant mind. But the truth is, that Gulliver had described his *Yahoos* before the visit, and he that had formed those images had nothing filthy to learn.

ALEXANDER POPE

ALMOST every poem, consisting of precepts, is so far arbitrary and immethodical, that many of the paragraphs may change places with no apparent inconvenience; for of two or more positions, depending upon some remote and general principle, there is seldom any cogent reason why one should precede the other. But for the order in which they stand, whatever it be, a little ingenuity may easily give a reason. *It is possible*, says Hooker, *that by long circum-*

duction, from any one truth all truth may be inferred. Of all homogeneous truths at least, of all truths respecting the same general end, in whatever series they may be produced, a concatenation by intermediate ideas may be formed, such as, when it is once shewn, shall appear natural; but if this order be reversed, another mode of connection equally specious may be found or made. Aristotle is praised for naming Fortitude first of the cardinal virtues, as that without which no other virtue can steadily be practised; but he might, with equal propriety, have placed Prudence and Justice before it, since without Prudence Fortitude is mad; without Justice, it is mischievous.

As the end of method is perspicuity, that series is sufficiently regular that avoids obscurity; and where there is no obscurity it will not be difficult to discover method.

It is reasonable to infer, from his Letters, that the verses on the *Unfortunate Lady* were written about the time when his *Essay* was published. The Lady's name and adventures I have sought with fruitless enquiry.

I can therefore tell no more than I have learned from Mr. Ruffhead, who writes with the confidence of one who could trust his information. She was a woman of eminent rank and large fortune, the ward of an unkle, who, having given her a proper education, expected like other guardians that she should make at least an equal match, and such he proposed to her, but found it rejected in favour of a young gentleman of inferior condition.

Having discovered the correspondence between the two lovers, and finding the young lady determined to abide by her own choice, he supposed that separation might do what can rarely be done by arguments, and sent her into a foreign country, where she was obliged to converse only with those from whom her unkle had nothing to fear.

Her lover took care to repeat his vows; but his letters were intercepted and carried to her guardian, who directed her to be watched with still greater vigilance; till of this restraint she grew so impatient, that she bribed a woman-servant to procure her a sword, which she directed to her heart.

From this account, given with evident intention to raise the Lady's character, it does not appear that she had any claim to praise, nor much to compassion. She seems to have been impatient, violent, and ungovernable. Her unkle's power could not have lasted long; the hour of liberty and choice would have come in time. But her desires were too hot for delay, and she liked self-murder better than suspense.

Nor is it discovered that the unkle, whoever he was, is with much justice delivered to posterity as a *false Guardian*; he seems to have done only that for which a guardian is appointed; he endeavoured to direct his niece till she should be able to direct herself. Poetry has not often been worse employed than in dignifying the amorous fury of a raving girl.

. . . . .

The *Rape of the Lock* stands forward, in the classes of literature, as the most exquisite example of ludicrous poetry. Berkley congratulated him upon the display of powers more truly poetical than he had shewn before; with elegance of description and justness of precepts, he had now exhibited boundless fertility of invention.

He always considered the intertexture of the machinery with the action as his most successful exertion of poetical art. He indeed could never afterwards produce any thing of such unexampled excellence. Those performances, which strike with wonder, are combinations of skilful genius with happy casualty; and it is not likely that any felicity, like the discovery of a new race of preternatural agents, should happen twice to the same man.

. . . . .

When we find him translating fifty lines a day, it is natural to suppose that he would have brought his work to a more speedy conclusion. The *Iliad*, containing less than sixteen thousand verses, might have been despatched in less than three hundred and twenty days by fifty verses in a day. The notes, compiled with the assistance of his mercenaries, could not be supposed to require more time than the text. According to this calculation, the progress of Pope may seem to have been slow; but the distance is commonly very great between actual performances and speculative possibility. It is natural to suppose, that as much as has been done today may be done to-morrow; but on the morrow some difficulty emerges, or some external impediment obstructs. Indolence, interruption, business, and pleasure, all take their turns of retardation; and every long work is lengthened by a thousand causes that can, and ten thousand that cannot, be recounted. Perhaps no extensive

900

and multifarious performance was ever effected within the term originally fixed in the undertaker's mind. He that runs against Time, has an antagonist not subject to casualties.

A grotto is not often the wish or pleasure of an Englishman, who has more frequent need to solicit than exclude the sun; but Pope's excavation was requisite as an entrance to his garden, and, as some men try to be proud of their defects, he extracted an ornament from an inconvenience, and vanity produced a grotto where necessity enforced a passage. It may be frequently remarked of the studious and speculative, that they are proud of trifles, and that their amusements seem frivolous and childish; whether it be that men conscious of great reputation think themselves above the reach of censure, and safe in the admission of negligent indulgences, or that mankind expect from elevated genius an uniformity of greatness, and watch its degradation with malicious wonder; like him who having followed with his eye an eagle into the clouds, should lament that she ever descended to a perch.

The filial piety of Pope was in the highest degree amiable and exemplary; his parents had the happiness of living till he was at the summit of poetical reputation, till he was at ease in his fortune, and without a rival in his fame, and found no diminution of his respect or tenderness. Whatever was his pride, to them he was obedient; and whatever was his irritability, to them he was gentle. Life has, among its soothing and quiet comforts, few things better to give than such a son.

Pope's epistolary excellence had an open field; he had no English rival, living or dead. . . . It is indeed not easy to distinguish affectation from habit; he that has once studiously formed a style, rarely writes afterwards with complete ease. Pope may be said to write always with his reputation in his head; Swift perhaps like a man who remembered that he was writing to Pope; but Arbuthnot like one who lets thoughts drop from his pen as they rise into his mind.

About this time Warburton began to make his appearance in the first ranks of learning. He was a man of vigorous faculties, a mind fervid and vehement, supplied by incessant and unlimited enquiry, with wonderful extent and variety of knowledge, which yet had not oppressed his imagination, nor clouded his perspicacity. To every work he brought a memory full fraught with a fancy fertile of original combinations, and at once exerted the powers of the scholar, the reasoner, and the wit. But his knowledge was too multifarious to be always exact, and his pursuits were too eager to be always cautious. His abilities gave him an haughty confidence, which he disdained to conceal or mollify; and his impatience of opposition disposed him to treat his adversaries with such contemptuous superiority as made his readers commonly his enemies, and excited against him the wishes of some who favoured his cause. He seems to have adopted the Roman Emperor's determination, *oderint dum metuant*; he used no allurements of gentle language, but wished to compel rather than persuade.

His style is copious without selection, and forcible without neatness; he took the words that presented themselves: his diction is coarse and impure, and his sentences are unmeasured.

.   .   .   .   .

"The Use of Riches"

Into this poem some incidents are historically thrown, and some known characters are introduced, with others of which it is difficult to say how far they are real or fictitious; but the praise of *Kyrl*, the *Man of Ross*, deserves particular examination, who, after a long and pompous enumeration of his publick works and private charities, is said to have diffused all those blessings from *five hundred a year*. Wonders are willingly told, and willingly heard. The truth is, that *Kyrl* was a man of known integrity, and active benevolence, by whose solicitation the wealthy were persuaded to pay contributions to his charitable schemes; this influence he obtained by an example of liberality exerted to the utmost extent of his power, and was thus enabled to give more than he had. This account Mr. *Victor* received from the minister of the place, and I have preserved it, that the praise of a good man being made more credible, may be more solid. Narrations of romantick and impracticable virtue will be read with wonder, but that which is unattainable is recommended in vain; that good may be endeavoured, it must be shewn to be possible.

.   .   .   .   .

He afterwards (1734) inscribed to Lord Cobham his *Characters of Men*, written with close attention to the operations of the mind and modifications of life. In this poem he has endeavoured to establish and exemplify his favourite theory of the *Ruling Passion*, by which he means an original direction of desire to some particular object, an innate affection which gives all action a determinate and invariable tendency, and operates upon the whole system of life, either openly, or more secretly by the intervention of some accidental or subordinate propension.

Of any passion, thus innate and irresistible, the existence may reasonably be doubted. Human characters are by no means constant; men change by change of place, of fortune, of acquaintance; he who is at one time a lover of pleasure, is at another a lover of money. Those indeed who attain any excellence, commonly spend life in one pursuit; for excellence is not often gained upon easier terms. But to the particular species of excellence men are directed, not by an ascendant planet or predominating humour, but by the first book which they read, some early conversation which they heard, or some accident which excited ardour and emulation.

It must be at least allowed that this *ruling Passion*, antecedent to reason and observation, must have an object independent of human contrivance; for there can be no natural desire of artificial good. No man therefore can be born, in the strict acceptation, a lover of money; for he may be born where money does not exist; nor can he be born, in a moral sense, a lover of his country; for society, politically regulated, is a state contradistinguished from a state of nature; and any attention to that coalition of interests which makes the happiness of a country, is possible only to those whom enquiry and reflection have enabled to comprehend it.

This doctrine is in itself pernicious as well as false: its tendency is to produce the belief of a kind of moral predestination, or overruling principle which cannot be resisted; he that admits it, is prepared to comply with every desire that caprice or opportunity shall excite, and to flatter himself that he submits only to the lawful dominion of Nature, in obeying the resistless authority of his *ruling Passion*.

.   .   .   .   .

Arbuthnot was a man of great comprehension, skilful in his profession, versed in the sciences, acquainted with ancient literature, and able to animate his mass of knowledge by a bright and active imagination; a scholar with great brilliancy of wit; a wit, who, in the crowd of life, retained and discovered a noble ardour of religious zeal.

.   .   .   .   .

Letter from Cibber to Pope

The pamphlet was written with little power of thought or language, and, if suffered to remain without notice, would have been very soon forgotten. Pope had now been enough acquainted with human life to know, if his passion had not been too powerful for his understanding, that, from a contention like his with Cibber, the world seeks nothing but diversion, which is given at the expence of the higher character. When Cibber lampooned Pope, curiosity was excited; what Pope would say of Cibber nobody enquired, but in hope that Pope's asperity might betray his pain and lessen his dignity.

He should therefore have suffered the pamphlet to flutter and die, without confessing that it stung him. The dishonour of being shewn as Cibber's antagonist could never be compensated by the victory. Cibber had nothing to lose; when Pope had exhausted all his malignity upon him, he would rise in the esteem both of his friends and his enemies. Silence only could have made him despicable; the blow which did not appear to be felt, would have been struck in vain.

But Pope's irascibility prevailed, and he resolved to tell the whole English world that he was at war with Cibber; and to shew that he thought him no common adversary, he prepared no common vengeance; he published a new edition of the *Dunciad*, in which he degraded *Theobald* from his painful pre-eminence, and enthroned *Cibber* in his stead. Unhappily the two heroes were of opposite characters, and Pope was unwilling to lose what he had already written; he has therefore depraved his poem by giving to Cibber the old books, the cold pedantry and sluggish pertinacity of Theobald.

Pope was ignorant enough of his own interest to make another change, and introduced Osborne contending for the prize among the booksellers. Osborne was a man intirely destitute of shame, without sense of any disgrace but that of poverty. He told me, when he was doing that which raised Pope's resentment, that he should be put into the *Dunciad*; but he had the fate of *Cassandra*; I gave no credit to his prediction, till in time I saw it accomplished. The shafts of satire were directed equally in vain against Cibber and Osborne; being repelled by the impenetrable impudence of one, and deadened by the impassive dulness of the other. Pope confessed his own pain by his anger; but he gave no pain to those

who had provoked him. He was able to hurt none but himself; by
transferring the same ridicule from one to another, he destroyed its
efficacy; for by shewing that what he had said of one he was ready
to say of another, he reduced himself to the insignificance of his
own magpye, who from his cage calls cuckold at a venture.

Cibber, according to his engagement, repaid the *Dunciad* with
another pamphlet, which, Pope said, *would be as good as a dose of
hartshorn to him*; but his tongue and his heart were at variance. I
have heard Mr. Richardson relate, that he attended his father the
painter on a visit, when one of Cibber's pamphlets came into the
hands of Pope, who said, *These things are my diversion*. They sat by
him while he perused it, and saw his features writhen with anguish;
and young Richardson said to his father, when they returned, that
he hoped to be preserved from such diversion as had been that day
the lot of Pope.

.   .   .   .   .

While he was yet capable of amusement and conversation, as he
was one day sitting in the air with Lord Bolingbroke and Lord
Marchmont, he saw his favourite Martha Blount at the bottom of
the terrace, and asked Lord Bolingbroke to go and hand her up.
Bolingbroke, not liking his errand, crossed his legs, and sat still;
but Lord Marchmont, who was younger and less captious, waited
on the Lady; who, when he came to her, asked, *What, is he not
dead yet*? She is said to have neglected him, with shameful unkindness, in the latter time of his decay; yet, of the little which he had
to leave, she had a very great part. Their acquaintance begun early;
the life of each was pictured on the other's mind; their conversation therefore was endearing, for when they met, there was an immediate coalition of congenial notions. Perhaps he considered her
unwillingness to approach the chamber of sickness as female weakness, or human frailty; perhaps he was conscious to himself of
peevishness and impatience, or, though he was offended by her inattention, might yet consider her merit as overbalancing her fault;
and, if he had suffered his heart to be alienated from her, he could
have found nothing that might fill her place; he could have only
shrunk within himself; it was too late to transfer his confidence or
fondness.

In May 1744, his death was approaching; on the sixth, he was all
day delirious, which he mentioned four days afterwards as a sufficient humiliation of the vanity of man; he afterwards complained

of seeing things as through a curtain, and in false colours; and one day, in the presence of Dodsley, asked what arm it was that came out from the wall. He said, that his greatest inconvenience was inability to think.

Bolingbroke sometimes wept over him in this state of helpless decay; and being told by Spence, that Pope, at the intermission of his deliriousness, was always saying something kind either of his present or absent friends, and that his humanity seemed to have survived his understanding, answered, *It has so.* And added, *I never in my life knew a man that had so tender a heart for his particular friends, or a more general friendship for mankind.* At another time he said, *I have known Pope these thirty years, and value myself more in his friendship than* — his grief then suppressed his voice.

Pope expressed undoubting confidence of a future state. Being asked by his friend Mr. Hooke, a papist, whether he would not die like his father and mother, and whether a priest should not be called, he answered, *I do not think it essential, but it will be very right; and I thank you for putting me in mind of it.*

In the morning, after the priest had given him the last sacraments, he said, " There is nothing that is meritorious but virtue and friendship, and indeed friendship itself is only a part of virtue."

.   .   .   .   .

The person of Pope is well known not to have been formed by the nicest model. He has, in his account of the *Little Club*, compared himself to a spider, and is described as protuberant behind and before. He is said to have been beautiful in his infancy; but he was of a constitution originally feeble and weak; and as bodies of a tender frame are easily distorted, his deformity was probably in part the effect of his application. His stature was so low, that, to bring him to a level with common tables, it was necessary to raise his seat. But his face was not displeasing, and his eyes were animated and vivid.

By natural deformity, or accidental distortion, his vital functions were so much disordered, that his life was a *long disease.* His most frequent assailant was the headach, which he used to relieve by inhaling the steam of coffee, which he very frequently required.

Most of what can be told concerning his petty peculiarities was communicated by a female domestick of the Earl of Oxford, who knew him perhaps after the middle of life. He was then so weak as to stand in perpetual need of female attendance; extremely sensible of cold, so that he wore a kind of fur doublet, under a shirt of a very coarse warm linen with fine sleeves. When he rose, he was invested in boddice made of stiff canvas, being scarce able to hold himself erect till they were laced, and he then put on a flannel waistcoat. One side was contracted. His legs were so slender, that he enlarged their bulk with three pair of stockings, which were drawn on and off by the maid; for he was not able to dress or undress himself, and neither went to bed nor rose without help. His weakness made it very difficult for him to be clean.

His hair had fallen almost all away; and he used to dine sometimes with Lord Oxford, privately, in a velvet cap. His dress of ceremony was black, with a tye-wig, and a little sword.

The indulgence and accommodation which his sickness required, had taught him all the unpleasing and unsocial qualities of a valetudinary man. He expected that every thing should give way to his ease or humour, as a child, whose parents will not hear her cry, has an unresisted dominion in the nursery.

> *C'est que l'enfant toujours est homme,*
> *C'est que l'homme est toujours enfant.*

When he wanted to sleep, he *nodded in company*; and once slumbered at his own table, while the Prince of Wales was talking of poetry.

The reputation which his friendship gave, procured him many invitations; but he was a very troublesome inmate. He brought no servant, and had so many wants, that a numerous attendance was scarcely able to supply them. Wherever he was, he left no room for another, because he exacted the attention and employed the activity of the whole family. His errands were so frequent and frivolous, that the footmen in time avoided and neglected him; and the Earl of Oxford discharged some of the servants for their resolute refusal of his messages. The maids, when they had neglected their business, alleged that they had been employed by Mr. Pope. One of his constant demands was of coffee in the night, and to the woman that waited on him in his chamber he was very burthensome; but he was careful to recompense her want of sleep; and Lord Oxford's servant declared, that in a house where her business was to answer his call, she would not ask for wages.

He had another fault, easily incident to those who, suffering much pain, think themselves entitled to whatever pleasures they can snatch. He was too indulgent to his appetite; he loved meat highly seasoned and of strong taste; and, at the intervals of the table, amused himself with biscuits and dry conserves. If he sat down to a variety of dishes, he would oppress his stomach with repletion, and though he seemed angry when a dram was offered him, did not forbear to drink it. His friends, who knew the avenues to his heart, pampered him with presents of luxury, which he did not suffer to stand neglected. The death of great men is not always proportioned to the lustre of their lives. Hannibal, says Juvenal, did not perish by a javelin or a sword; the slaughters of Cannæ were revenged by a ring. The death of Pope was imputed by some of his friends to a silver saucepan, in which it was his delight to heat potted lampreys.

That he loved too well to eat, is certain; but that his sensuality shortened his life will not be hastily concluded, when it is remembered that a conformation so irregular lasted six and fifty years, notwithstanding such pertinacious diligence of study and meditation.

In all his intercourse with mankind, he had great delight in artifice, and endeavoured to attain all his purposes by indirect and unsuspected methods. *He hardly drank tea without a stratagem.* If, at the house of his friends, he wanted any accommodation, he was not willing to ask for it in plain terms, but would mention it remotely as something convenient; though, when it was procured, he soon made it appear for whose sake it had been recommended. Thus he teized Lord Orrery till he obtained a screen. He practised his arts on such small occasions, that Lady Bolingbroke used to say, in a French phrase, that *he plaid the politician about cabbages and turnips.* His unjustifiable impression of the *Patriot King*, as it can be imputed to no particular motive, must have proceeded from his general habit of secrecy and cunning; he caught an opportunity of a sly trick, and pleased himself with the thought of outwitting Bolingbroke.

In familiar or convivial conversation, it does not appear that he excelled. He may be said to have resembled Dryden, as being not one that was distinguished by vivacity in company. It is remarkable, that, so near his time, so much should be known of what he has written, and so little of what he has said: traditional memory retains no sallies of raillery, nor sentences of observation; nothing either pointed or solid, either wise or merry. One apophthegm only stands upon record. When an objection raised against his inscription for Shakspeare was defended by the authority of *Patrick*, he replied—*horresco referens*—that *he would allow the publisher of a Dictionary to know the meaning of a single word, but not of two words put together.*

. . . . .

Of this fortune, which as it arose from publick approbation was very honourably obtained, his imagination seems to have been too full: it would be hard to find a man, so well entitled to notice by his wit, that ever delighted so much in talking of his money. In his Letters, and in his Poems, his garden and his grotto, his quincunx and his vines, or some hints of his opulence, are always to be found. The great topick of his ridicule is poverty; the crimes with which he reproaches his antagonists are their debts, their habitation in the Mint, and their want of a dinner. He seems to be of an opinion not very uncommon in the world, that to want money is to want every thing.

Next to the pleasure of contemplating his possessions, seems to be that of enumerating the men of high rank with whom he was acquainted, and whose notice he loudly proclaims not to have been obtained by any practices of meanness or servility; a boast which was never denied to be true, and to which very few poets have ever aspired. Pope never set his genius to sale; he never flattered those whom he did not love, or praised those whom he did not esteem. Savage however remarked, that he began a little to relax his dignity when he wrote a distich for *his Highness's dog.*

His admiration of the Great seems to have increased in the advance of life. He passed over peers and statesmen to inscribe his *Iliad* to Congreve, with a magnanimity of which the praise had been compleat, had his friend's virtue been equal to his wit. Why he was chosen for so great an honour, it is not now possible to know; there is no trace in literary history of any particular intimacy between them. The name of Congreve appears in the Letters among those of his other friends, but without any observable distinction or consequence. To his latter works, however, he took care to annex names dignified with titles, but was not very happy in his choice; for, except Lord Bathurst, none of his noble friends were such as that a good man would wish to have his intimacy with them known to posterity: he can derive little honour from the notice of Cobham, Burlington, or Bolingbroke.

Of his social qualities, if an estimate be made from his Letters, an opinion too favourable cannot easily be formed; they exhibit a perpetual and unclouded effulgence of general benevolence, and particular fondness. There is nothing but liberality, gratitude, constancy, and tenderness. It has been so long said as to be commonly believed, that the true characters of men may be found in their Letters, and that he who writes to his friend lays his heart open before him. But the truth is, that such were simple friendships of the *Golden Age*, and are now the friendships only of children. Very few can boast of hearts which they dare lay open to themselves, and of which, by whatever accident exposed, they do not shun a distinct and continued view; and, certainly, what we hide from ourselves we do not shew to our friends. There is, indeed, no transaction which offers stronger temptations to fallacy and sophistication than epistolary intercourse. In the eagerness of conversation the first emotions of the mind often burst out, before they are considered; in the tumult of business, interest and passion have their genuine effect; but a friendly Letter is a calm and deliberate performance, in the cool of leisure, in the stillness of solitude, and surely no man sits down to depreciate by design his own character.

Friendship has no tendency to secure veracity; for by whom can a man so much wish to be thought better than he is, as by him whose kindness he desires to gain or keep? Even in writing to the world there is less constraint; the author is not confronted with his reader, and takes his chance of approbation among the different dispositions of mankind; but a Letter is addressed to a single mind, of which the prejudices and partialities are known; and must therefore please, if not by favouring them, by forbearing to oppose them.

To charge those favourable representations, which every man gives of himself, with the guilt of hypocritical falshood, would shew more severity than knowledge. The writer commonly believes himself. Almost every man's thoughts, while they are general, are right; and most hearts are pure, while temptation is away. It is easy to awaken generous sentiments in privacy; to despise death when there is no danger; to glow with benevolence when there is nothing to be given. While such ideas are formed they are felt, and self-love does not suspect the gleam of virtue to be the meteor of fancy.

If the Letters of Pope are considered merely as compositions, they seem to be premeditated and artificial. It is one thing to write because there is something which the mind wishes to discharge, and another, to solicit the imagination because ceremony or vanity requires something to be written. Pope confesses his early Letters to be vitiated with *affectation and ambition*: to know whether he disentangled himself from these perverters of epistolary integrity, his book and his life must be set in comparison.

One of his favourite topicks is contempt of his own poetry. For this, if it had been real, he would deserve no commendation, and in this he was certainly not sincere; for his high value of himself was sufficiently observed, and of what could he be proud but of his poetry? He writes, he says, when *he has just nothing else to do*; yet Swift complains that he was never at leisure for conversation, because he *had always some poetical scheme in his head*. It was punctually required that his writing-box should be set upon his bed before he rose; and Lord Oxford's domestick related, that, in the dreadful winter of Forty, she was called from her bed by him four times in one night, to supply him with paper, lest he should lose a thought.

He pretends insensibility to censure and criticism, though it was observed by all who knew him that every pamphlet disturbed his quiet, and that his extreme irritability laid him open to perpetual vexation; but he wished to despise his criticks, and therefore hoped that he did despise them.

As he happened to live in two reigns when the Court paid little attention to poetry, he nursed in his mind a foolish disesteem of Kings, and proclaims that *he never sees Courts*. Yet a little regard shewn him by the Prince of Wales melted his obduracy; and he had not much to say when he was asked by his Royal Highness, *how he could love a Prince while he disliked Kings*?

He very frequently professes contempt of the world, and represents himself as looking on mankind, sometimes with gay indifference, as on emmets of a hillock, below his serious attention; and sometimes with gloomy indignation, as on monsters more worthy of hatred than of pity. These were dispositions apparently counterfeited. How could he despise those whom he lived by pleasing, and on whose approbation his esteem of himself was superstructed? Why should he hate those to whose favour he owed his honour and his ease? Of things that terminate in human life, the world is the proper judge; to despise its sentence, if it were possible, is not just; and if it were just, is not possible. Pope was far enough from this unreasonable temper; he was sufficiently *a fool to Fame*, and his fault was that he pretended to neglect it. His levity and his sullenness were only in his Letters; he passed through common life, sometimes vexed, and sometimes pleased, with the natural emotions of common men.

His scorn of the Great is repeated too often to be real; no man thinks much of that which he despises; and as falsehood is always in danger of inconsistency, he makes it his boast at another time that he lives among them.

It is evident that his own importance swells often in his mind. He is afraid of writing, lest the clerks of the Post-office should know his secrets; he has many enemies; he considers himself as surrounded by universal jealousy; *after many deaths, and many dispersions, two or three of us*, says he, *may still be brought together, not to plot, but to divert ourselves, and the world too, if it pleases*; and they can live together, and *shew what friends wits may be, in spite of all the fools in the world*. All this while it was likely that the clerks did not know his hand; he certainly had no more enemies than a publick character like his inevitably excites, and with what degree of friendship the wits might live very few were so much fools as ever to enquire.

Some part of this pretended discontent he learned from Swift, and expresses it, I think, most frequently in his correspondence with him. Swift's resentment was unreasonable, but it was sincere; Pope's was the mere mimickry of his friend, a fictitious part which he began to play before it became him. When he was only twenty-five years old, he related that *a glut of study and retirement had thrown him on the world*, and that there was danger lest *a glut of the world should throw him back upon study and retirement*. To this Swift answered with great propriety, that Pope had not yet either acted or suffered enough in the world to have become weary of it. And, indeed, it must be some very powerful reason that can drive back to solitude him who has once enjoyed the pleasures of society.

In the Letters both of Swift and Pope there appears such narrowness of mind, as makes them insensible of any excellence that has not some affinity with their own, and confines their esteem and approbation to so small a number, that whoever should form his opinion of the age from their representation, would suppose them to have lived amidst ignorance and barbarity, unable to find among their contemporaries either virtue or intelligence, and persecuted by those that could not understand them.

When Pope murmurs at the world, when he professes contempt of fame, when he speaks of riches and poverty, of success and disappointment, with negligent indifference, he certainly does not express his habitual and settled sentiments, but either wilfully disguises his own character, or, what is more likely, invests himself with temporary qualities, and sallies out in the colours of the present moment. His hopes and fears, his joys and sorrows, acted strongly upon his mind; and if he differed from others, it was not by carelessness; he was irritable and resentful; his malignity to Philips, whom he had first made ridiculous, and then hated for being angry, continued too long. Of his vain desire to make Bentley contemptible, I never heard any adequate reason. He was sometimes wanton in his attacks; and, before Chandos, Lady Wortley, and Hill, was mean in his retreat.

The virtues which seem to have had most of his affection were liberality and fidelity of friendship, in which it does not appear that he was other than he describes himself. His fortune did not suffer his charity to be splendid and conspicuous; but he assisted Dodsley with a hundred pounds, that he might open a shop; and of the subscription of forty pounds a year that he raised for Savage, twenty were paid by himself. He was accused of loving money, but his love was eagerness to gain, not solicitude to keep it.

In the duties of friendship he was zealous and constant: his early maturity of mind commonly united him with men older than himself, and therefore, without attaining any considerable length of life, he saw many companions of his youth sink into the grave; but it does not appear that he lost a single friend by coldness or by injury; those who loved him once, continued their kindness. His ungrateful mention of Allen in his will, was the effect of his adherence to one whom he had known much longer, and whom he naturally loved with greater fondness. His violation of the trust reposed in him by Bolingbroke could have no motive inconsistent with the warmest affection; he either thought the action so near to indifferent that he forgot it, or so laudable that he expected his friend to approve it.

It was reported, with such confidence as almost to enforce belief, that in the papers intrusted to his executors was found a defamatory Life of Swift, which he had prepared as an instrument of vengeance to be used, if any provocation should be ever given. About this I enquired of the Earl of Marchmont, who assured me that no such piece was among his remains.

The religion in which he lived and died was that of the Church of Rome, to which in his correspondence with Racine he professes himself a sincere adherent. That he was not scrupulously pious in some part of his life, is known by many idle and indecent applications of sentences taken from the Scriptures; a mode of merriment which a good man dreads for its profaneness, and a witty man disdains for its easiness and vulgarity. But to whatever levities he has been betrayed, it does not appear that his principles were ever corrupted, or that he ever lost his belief of Revelation. The positions which he transmitted from Bolingbroke he seems not to have understood, and was pleased with an interpretation that made them orthodox.

A man of such exalted superiority, and so little moderation, would naturally have all his delinquences observed and aggravated: those who could not deny that he was excellent, would rejoice to find that he was not perfect.

Perhaps it may be imputed to the unwillingness with which the same man is allowed to possess many advantages, that his learning has been depreciated. He certainly was in his early life a man of great literary curiosity; and when he wrote his *Essay on Criticism* had, for his age, a very wide acquaintance with books. When he entered into the living world, it seems to have happened to him as to many others, that he was less attentive to dead masters; he studied in the academy of Paracelsus, and made the universe his favourite volume. He gathered his notions fresh from reality, not from the copies of authors, but the originals of Nature. Yet there is no reason to believe that literature ever lost his esteem; he always professed to love reading; and Dobson, who spent some time at his house translating his *Essay on Man*, when I asked him what learning he found him to possess, answered, *More than I expected.* His frequent references to history, his allusions to various kinds of knowledge, and his images selected from art and nature, with his observations on the operations of the mind and the modes of life, shew an intelligence perpetually on the wing, excursive, vigorous, and diligent, eager to pursue knowledge, and attentive to retain it.

From this curiosity arose the desire of travelling, to which he alludes in his verses to Jervas, and which, though he never found an opportunity to gratify it, did not leave him till his life declined.

Of his intellectual character, the constituent and fundamental principle was Good Sense, a prompt and intuitive perception of consonance and propriety. He saw immediately, of his own conceptions, what was to be chosen, and what to be rejected; and, in the works of others, what was to be shunned, and what was to be copied.

But good sense alone is a sedate and quiescent quality, which manages its possessions well, but does not increase them; it collects few materials for its own operations, and preserves safety, but never gains supremacy. Pope had likewise genius; a mind active, ambitious, and adventurous, always investigating, always aspiring; in its widest searches still longing to go forward, in its highest flights still wishing to be higher; always imagining something greater than it knows, always endeavouring more than it can do.

To assist these powers, he is said to have had great strength and exactness of memory. That which he had heard or read was not easily lost; and he had before him not only what his own meditation suggested, but what he had found in other writers that might be accommodated to his present purpose.

These benefits of nature he improved by incessant and unwearied diligence; he had recourse to every source of intelligence, and lost no opportunity of information; he consulted the living as well as the dead; he read his compositions to his friends, and was never content with mediocrity when excellence could be attained. He considered poetry as the business of his life, and however he might seem to lament his occupation, he followed it with constancy; to make verses was his first labour, and to mend them was his last.

From his attention to poetry he was never diverted. If conversation offered any thing that could be improved, he committed it to paper; if a thought, or perhaps an expression more happy than was common, rose to his mind, he was careful to write it; an independent distich was preserved for an opportunity of insertion, and some little fragments have been found containing lines, or parts of lines, to be wrought upon at some other time.

He was one of those few whose labour is their pleasure: he was never elevated to negligence, nor wearied to impatience; he never passed a fault unamended by indifference, nor quitted it by despair. He laboured his works first to gain reputation, and afterwards to keep it.

Of composition there are different methods. Some employ at once memory and invention, and, with little intermediate use of the pen, form and polish large masses by continued meditation, and write their productions only when, in their own opinion, they have completed them. It is related of Virgil, that his custom was to pour out a great number of verses in the morning, and pass the day in retrenching exuberances and correcting inaccuracies. The method of Pope, as may be collected from his translation, was to write his first thoughts in his first words, and gradually to amplify, decorate, rectify, and refine them.

With such faculties, and such dispositions, he excelled every other writer in *poetical prudence*; he wrote in such a manner as might expose him to few hazards. He used almost always the same fabrick of verse; and, indeed, by those few essays which he made of any other, he did not enlarge his reputation. Of this uniformity the certain consequence was readiness and dexterity. By perpetual practice, language had in his mind a systematical arrangement; having always the same use for words, he had words so selected and combined as to be ready at his call. This increase of facility he confessed himself to have perceived in the progress of his translation.

But what was yet of more importance, his effusions were always voluntary, and his subjects chosen by himself. His independence secured him from drudging at a task, and labouring upon a barren topick: he never exchanged praise for money, nor opened a shop of condolence or congratulation. His poems, therefore, were scarce ever temporary. He suffered coronations and royal marriages to pass without a song, and derived no opportunities from recent events, or popularity from the accidental disposition of his readers. He was never reduced to the necessity of soliciting the sun to shine upon a birth-day, of calling the Graces and Virtues to a wedding, or of saying what multitudes have said before him. When he could produce nothing new, he was at liberty to be silent.

His publications were for the same reason never hasty. He is said to have sent nothing to the press till it had lain two years under his inspection: it is at least certain, that he ventured nothing without nice examination. He suffered the tumult of imagination to subside, and the novelties of invention to grow familiar. He knew that the mind is always enamoured of its own productions, and did not trust his first fondness. He consulted his friends, and listened with great willingness to criticism; and, what was of more importance, he consulted himself, and let nothing pass against his own judgement.

He professed to have learned his poetry from Dryden, whom, whenever an opportunity was presented, he praised through his whole life with unvaried liberality; and perhaps his character may receive some illustration, if he be compared with his master.

Integrity of understanding and nicety of discernment were not allotted in a less proportion to Dryden than to Pope. The rectitude of Dryden's mind was sufficiently shewn by the dismission of his poetical prejudices, and the rejection of unnatural thoughts and rugged numbers. But Dryden never desired to apply all the judgement that he had. He wrote, and professed to write, merely for the people; and when he pleased others, he contented himself. He spent no time in struggles to rouse latent powers; he never attempted to make that better which was already good, nor often to mend what he must have known to be faulty. He wrote, as he tells us, with very little consideration; when occasion or necessity called upon him, he poured out what the present moment happened to supply, and, when once it had passed the press, ejected it from his mind; for when he had no pecuniary interest, he had no further solicitude.

Pope was not content to satisfy; he desired to excel, and therefore always endeavoured to do his best: he did not court the candour, but dared the judgement of his reader, and expecting no indulgence from others, he shewed none to himself. He examined lines and words with minute and punctilious observation, and retouched every part with indefatigable diligence, till he had left nothing to be forgiven.

For this reason he kept his pieces very long in his hands, while he considered and reconsidered them. The only poems which can be supposed to have been written with such regard to the times as might hasten their publication, were the two satires of *Thirty-eight*; of which Dodsley told me, that they were brought to him by the author, that they might be fairly copied. "Every line," said he, "was then written twice over; I gave him a clean transcript, which he sent some time afterwards to me for the press, with every line written twice over a second time."

His declaration, that his care for his works ceased at their publication, was not strictly true. His parental attention never abandoned them; what he found amiss in the first edition, he silently corrected in those that followed. He appears to have revised the

Iliad, and freed it from some of its imperfections; and the *Essay on Criticism* received many improvements after its first appearance. It will seldom be found that he altered without adding clearness, elegance, or vigour. Pope had perhaps the judgement of Dryden; but Dryden certainly wanted the diligence of Pope.

In acquired knowledge, the superiority must be allowed to Dryden, whose education was more scholastick, and who before he became an author had been allowed more time for study, with better means of information. His mind has a larger range, and he collects his images and illustrations from a more extensive circumference of science. Dryden knew more of man in his general nature, and Pope in his local manners. The notions of Dryden were formed by comprehensive speculation, and those of Pope by minute attention. There is more dignity in the knowledge of Dryden, and more certainty in that of Pope.

Poetry was not the sole praise of either; for both excelled likewise in prose; but Pope did not borrow his prose from his predecessor. The style of Dryden is capricious and varied, that of Pope is cautious and uniform; Dryden obeys the motions of his own mind, Pope constrains his mind to his own rules of composition. Dryden is sometimes vehement and rapid; Pope is always smooth, uniform, and gentle. Dryden's page is a natural field, rising into inequalities, and diversified by the varied exuberance of abundant vegetation; Pope's is a velvet lawn, shaven by the scythe, and levelled by the roller.

Of genius, that power which constitutes a poet; that quality without which judgement is cold and knowledge is inert; that energy which collects, combines, amplifies, and animates; the superiority must, with some hesitation, be allowed to Dryden. It is not to be inferred that of this poetical vigour Pope had only a little, because Dryden had more; for every other writer since Milton must give place to Pope; and even of Dryden it must be said, that if he has brighter paragraphs, he has not better poems. Dryden's performances were always hasty, either excited by some external occasion, or extorted by domestick necessity; he composed without consideration, and published without correction. What his mind could supply at call, or gather in one excursion, was all that he sought, and all that he gave. The dilatory caution of Pope enabled him to condense his sentiments, to multiply his images, and to accumulate all that study might produce, or chance might supply.

If the flights of Dryden therefore are higher, Pope continues longer on the wing. If of Dryden's fire the blaze is brighter, of Pope's the heat is more regular and constant. Dryden often surpasses expectation, and Pope never falls below it. Dryden is read with frequent astonishment, and Pope with perpetual delight.

This parallel will, I hope, when it is well considered, be found just; and if the reader should suspect me, as I suspect myself, of some partial fondness for the memory of Dryden, let him not too hastily condemn me; for meditation and enquiry may, perhaps, shew him the reasonableness of my determination.

One of his greatest though of his earliest works is the *Essay on Criticism*, which, if he had written nothing else, would have placed him among the first cricticks and the first poets, as it exhibits every mode of excellence that can embellish or dignify didactick composition, selection of matter, novelty of arrangement, justness of precept, splendour of illustration, and propriety of digression. I know not whether it be pleasing to consider that he produced this piece at twenty, and never afterwards excelled it: he that delights himself with observing that such powers may be so soon attained, cannot but grieve to think that life was ever after at a stand.

To mention the particular beauties of the Essay would be unprofitably tedious; but I cannot forbear to observe, that the comparison of a student's progress in the sciences with the journey of a traveller in the Alps, is perhaps the best that English poetry can shew. A simile, to be perfect, must both illustrate and ennoble the subject; must shew it to the understanding in a clearer view, and display it to the fancy with greater dignity; but either of these qualities may be sufficient to recommend it. In didactick poetry, of which the great purpose is instruction, a simile may be praised which illustrates, though it does not ennoble; in heroicks, that may be admitted which ennobles, though it does not illustrate. That it may be complete, it is required to exhibit, independently of its references, a pleasing image; for a simile is said to be a short episode. To this antiquity was so attentive, that circumstances were sometimes added, which, having no parallels, served only to fill the imagination, and produced what Perrault ludicrously called *comparisons with a long tail*. In their similies the greatest writers have sometimes failed; the ship-race, compared with the chariot-race, is neither illustrated nor aggrandised; land and water make all the difference: when Apollo, running after Daphne, is likened to a grey-hound chasing a hare, there is nothing gained; the ideas of pursuit and flight are too plain to be made plainer, and a god and the daughter of a god are not represented much to their advantage by a hare and dog. The simile of the Alps has no useless parts, yet affords a striking picture by itself; it makes the foregoing position better understood, and enables it to take faster hold on the attention; it assists the apprehension, and elevates the fancy.

Let me likewise dwell a little on the celebrated paragraph, in which it is directed that *the sound should seem an echo to the sense*; a precept which Pope is allowed to have observed beyond any other English poet.

This notion of representative metre, and the desire of discovering frequent adaptations of the sound to the sense, have produced, in my opinion, many wild conceits and imaginary beauties. All that can furnish this representation are the sounds of the words considered singly, and the time in which they are pronounced. Every language has some words framed to exhibit the noises which they express, as *thump, rattle, growl, hiss*. These however are but few, and the poet cannot make them more, nor can they be of any use but when sound is to be mentioned. The time of pronunciation was in the dactylick measures of the learned languages capable of considerable variety; but that variety could be accommodated only to motion or duration, and different degrees of motion were perhaps expressed by verses rapid or slow, with very little attention of the writer, when the image had full possession of his fancy; but our language having little flexibility, our verses can differ very little in their cadence. The fancied resemblances, I fear, arise sometimes merely from the ambiguity of words; there is supposed to be some relation between a *soft* line and *soft* couch, or between *hard* syllables and *hard* fortune.

Motion, however, may be in some sort exemplified; and yet it may be suspected that even in such resemblances the mind often governs the ear, and the sounds are estimated by their meaning. One of the most successful attempts has been to describe the labour of Sisyphus:

> With many a weary step, and many a groan,
> Up a high hill he heaves a huge round stone;
> The huge round stone, resulting with a bound,
> Thunders impetuous down, and smoaks along the ground.

Who does not perceive the stone to move slowly upward, and roll violently back? But set the same numbers to another sense;

> While many a merry tale, and many a song,
> Chear'd the rough road, we wish'd the rough road long.
> The rough road then, returning in a round,
> Mock'd our impatient steps, for all was fairy ground.

We have now surely lost much of the delay, and much of the rapidity.

But to shew how little the greatest master of numbers can fix the principles of representative harmony, it will be sufficient to remark that the poet, who tells us, that

> When Ajax strives—the words move slow.
> Not so when swift Camilla scours the plain,
> Flies o'er th' unbending corn, and skims along the main;

when he had enjoyed for about thirty years the praise of Camilla's lightness of foot, tried another experiment upon *sound* and *time*, and produced this memorable triplet:

> Waller was smooth; but Dryden taught to join
> The varying verse, the full resounding line,
> The long majestick march, and energy divine.

Here are the swiftness of the rapid race, and the march of slow-paced majesty, exhibited by the same poet in the same sequence of syllables, except that the exact prosodist will find the line of *swiftness* by one time longer than that of *tardiness*.

Beauties of this kind are commonly fancied; and when real, are technical and nugatory, not to be rejected, and not to be solicited.

To the praises which have been accumulated on *The Rape of the Lock* by readers of every class, from the critick to the waiting-maid, it is difficult to make any addition. Of that which is universally allowed to be the most attractive of all ludicrous compositions, let it rather be now enquired from what sources the power of pleasing is derived.

Dr. Warburton, who excelled in critical perspicacity, has remarked that the preternatural agents are very happily adapted to the purposes of the poem. The heathen deities can no longer gain attention: we should have turned away from a contest between Venus and Diana; the employment of allegorical persons always excites conviction of its own absurdity; they may produce effects, but cannot conduct actions; when the phantom is put in motion it dissolves; thus *Discord* may raise a mutiny, but *Discord* cannot conduct a march, nor besiege a town. Pope brought into view a new race of Beings, with powers and passions proportionate to their operation. The sylphs and gnomes act at the toilet and the tea-table; what more terrifick and more powerful phantoms perform on the stormy ocean, or the field of battle, they give their proper help, and do their proper mischief.

Pope is said, by an objector, not to have been the inventor of this petty nation; a charge which might with more justice have been brought against the author of the *Iliad*, who doubtless adopted the religious system of his country; for what is there but the names of his agents which Pope has not invented? Has he not assigned them characters and operations never heard of before? Has he not, at least, given them their first poetical existence? If this is not sufficient to denominate his work original, nothing original ever can be written.

In this work are exhibited, in a very high degree, the two most engaging powers of an author. New things are made familiar, and familiar things are made new. A race of aerial people, never heard of before, is presented to us in a manner so clear and easy, that the reader seeks for no further information, but immediately mingles with his new acquaintance, adopts their interests, and attends their pursuits, loves a sylph, and detests a gnome.

That familiar things are made new, every paragraph will prove. The subject of the poem is an event below the common incidents of common life; nothing real is introduced that is not seen so often as to be no longer regarded, yet the whole detail of a female-day is here brought before us invested with so much art of decoration, that, though nothing is disguised, every thing is striking, and we feel all the appetite of curiosity for that from which we have a thousand times turned fastidiously away.

The purpose of the Poet is, as he tells us, to laugh at *the little unguarded follies of the female sex*. It is therefore without justice that Dennis charges the *Rape of the Lock* with the want of a moral, and for that reason sets it below the *Lutrin*, which exposes the pride and discord of the clergy. Perhaps neither Pope nor Boileau has made the world much better than he found it; but if they had both succeeded, it were easy to tell who would have deserved most from publick gratitude. The freaks, and humours, and spleen, and vanity of women, as they embroil families in discord, and fill houses with disquiet, do more to obstruct the happiness of life in a year than the ambition of the clergy in many centuries. It has been well observed, that the misery of man proceeds not from any single crush of overwhelming evil, but from small vexations continually repeated.

． ． ． ．

The Epistle of *Eloise to Abelard* is one of the most happy productions of human wit: the subject is so judiciously chosen, that it would be difficult, in turning over the annals of the world, to find another which so many circumstances concur to recommend. We regularly interest ourselves most in the fortune of those who most deserve our notice. Abelard and Eloise were conspicuous in their days for eminence of merit. The heart naturally loves truth. The adventures and misfortunes of this illustrious pair are known from undisputed history. Their fate does not leave the mind in hopeless dejection; for they both found quiet and consolation in retirement and piety. So new and so affecting is their story, that it supersedes invention, and imagination ranges at full liberty without straggling into scenes of fable.

The story, thus skilfully adopted, has been diligently improved. Pope has left nothing behind him, which seems more the effect of studious perseverance and laborious revisal. Here is particularly observable the *curiosa felicitas*, a fruitful soil, and careful cultivation. Here is no crudeness of sense, nor asperity of language.

． ． ． ． ．

Translation of "The Iliad"

The chief help of Pope in this arduous undertaking was drawn from the versions of Dryden. Virgil had borrowed much of his imagery from Homer, and part of the debt was now paid by his translator. Pope searched the pages of Dryden for happy combinations of heroick diction; but it will not be denied that he added much to what he found. He cultivated our language with so much diligence and art, that he has left in his *Homer* a treasure of poetical elegances to posterity. His version may be said to have tuned the English tongue; for since its appearance no writer, however deficient in other powers, has wanted melody. Such a series of lines so elaborately corrected, and so sweetly modulated, took possession of the publick ear, the vulgar was enamoured of the poem, and the learned wondered at the translation.

But in the most general applause discordant voices will always be heard. It has been objected by some, who wish to be numbered among the sons of learning, that Pope's version of Homer is not Homerical; that it exhibits no resemblance of the original characteristick manner of the Father of Poetry, as it wants his awful simplicity, his artless grandeur, his unaffected majesty. This cannot be totally denied; but it must be remembered that *necessitas quod cogit defendit*; that may be lawfully done which cannot be forborn. Time and place will always enforce regard. In estimating this translation, consideration must be had of the nature of our language, the form of our metre, and, above all, of the change which two thousand years have made in the modes of life and the habits of thought. Virgil wrote in a language of the same general fabrick with that of Homer, in verses of the same measure, and in an age nearer to Homer's time by eighteen hundred years; yet he found, even then, the state of the world so much altered, and the demand for elegance so much increased, that mere nature would be endured no longer; and perhaps, in the multitude of borrowed passages, very few can be shewn which he has not embellished.

There is a time when nations emerging from barbarity, and falling into regular subordination, gain leisure to grow wise, and feel the shame of ignorance and the craving pain of unsatisfied curiosity. To this hunger of the mind plain sense is grateful; that which fills the void removes uneasiness, and to be free from pain for a while is pleasure; but repletion generates fastidiousness; a saturated intellect soon becomes luxurious, and knowledge finds no willing reception till it is recommended by artificial diction. Thus it will be found, as learning advances, that in all nations the first writers are simple, and that every age improves in elegance. One refinement always makes way for another, and what was expedient to Virgil was necessary to Pope.

I suppose many readers of the English *Iliad*, when they have been touched with some unexpected beauty of the lighter kind, have tried to enjoy it in the original, where, alas! it was not to be found. Homer doubtless owes to his translator many *Ovidian* graces not exactly suitable to his character; but to have added can be no great crime, if nothing be taken away. Elegance is surely to be desired, if it be not gained at the expence of dignity. A hero would wish to be loved, as well as to be reverenced.

To a thousand cavils one answer is sufficient; the purpose of a writer is to be read, and the criticism which would destroy the power of pleasing must be blown aside. Pope wrote for his own age and his own nation: he knew that it was necessary to colour the images and point the sentiments of his author; he therefore made him graceful, but lost him some of his sublimity.

The copious notes with which the version is accompanied, and by which it is recommended to many readers, though they were undoubtedly written to swell the volumes, ought not to pass without praise: commentaries which attract the reader by the pleasure of perusal have not often appeared; the notes of others are read to clear difficulties, those of Pope to vary entertainment.

It has however been objected, with sufficient reason, that there is in the commentary too much of unseasonable levity and affected gaiety; that too many appeals are made to the Ladies, and the ease which is so carefully preserved is sometimes the ease of a trifler. Every art has its terms, and every kind of instruction its proper style; the gravity of common criticks may be tedious, but is less despicable than childish merriment.

.　　　　.　　　　.　　　　.　　　　.

The *Essay on Man* was a work of great labour and long consideration, but certainly not the happiest of Pope's performances. The subject is perhaps not very proper for poetry, and the poet was not sufficiently master of his subject; metaphysical morality was to him a new study, he was proud of his acquisitions, and, supposing himself master of great secrets, was in haste to teach what he had not learned. Thus he tells us, in the first Epistle, that from the nature of the Supreme Being may be deduced an order of beings such as mankind, because Infinite Excellence can do only what is best. He finds out that *all the question is whether man be in a wrong place.* Surely if, according to the poet's Leibnitian reasoning, we may infer that man ought to be, only because he is, we may allow that his place is the right place, because he has it. Supreme Wisdom is not less infallible in disposing than in creating. But what is meant by *somewhere* and *place*, and *wrong place*, it had been vain to ask Pope, who probably had never asked himself.

Having exalted himself into the chair of wisdom, he tells us much that every man knows, and much that he does not know himself; that we see but little, and that the order of the universe is beyond our comprehension; an opinion not very uncommon; and that there is a chain of subordinate beings *from infinite to nothing*, of which himself and his readers are equally ignorant. But he gives us one comfort, which, without his help, he supposes unattainable, in the position *that though we are fools, yet God is wise.*

This Essay affords an egregious instance of the predominance of genius, the dazzling splendour of imagery, and the seductive powers of eloquence. Never was penury of knowledge and vulgarity of sentiment so happily disguised. The reader feels his mind full, though he learns nothing; and when he meets it in its new array, no longer knows the talk of his mother and his nurse. When these wonder-working sounds sink into sense, and the doctrine of the Essay disrobed of its ornaments, is left to the powers of its naked excellence, what shall we discover? That we are, in comparison with our Creator, very weak and ignorant; that we do not uphold the chain of existence, and that we could not make one another with more skill than we are made. We may learn yet more; that the arts of human life were copied from the instinctive operations of other animals; that if the world be made for man, it may be said that man was made for geese. To these profound principles of natural knowledge are added some moral instructions equally new; that self-interest, well understood, will produce social concord; that men are mutual gainers by mutual benefits; that evil is sometimes balanced by good; that human advantages are unstable and fallacious, of uncertain duration, and doubtful effects; that our true honour is not to have a great part, but to act it well; that virtue only is our own; and that happiness is always in our power.

Surely a man of no very comprehensive search may venture to say that he has heard all this before; but it was never till now recommended by such a blaze of embellishment, or such sweetness of melody. The vigorous contraction of some thoughts, the luxuriant amplification of others, the incidental illustrations, and sometimes the dignity, sometimes the softness of the verses, enchain philosophy, suspend criticism, and oppress judgement by overpowering pleasure.

This is true of many paragraphs; yet if I had undertaken to exemplify Pope's felicity of composition before a rigid critick, I should not select the *Essay on Man*; for it contains more lines unsuccessfully laboured, more harshness of diction, more thoughts imperfectly expressed, more levity without elegance, and more heaviness without strength, than will easily be found in all his other works.

Pope had, in proportions very nicely adjusted to each other, all the qualities that constitute genius. He had *Invention*, by which new trains of events are formed, and new scenes of imagery displayed, as in the *Rape of the Lock*; or extrinsick and adventitious embellishments and illustrations are connected with a known subject, as in the *Essay on Criticism*. He had *Imagination*, which strongly impresses on the writer's mind, and enables him to convey to the reader the various forms of nature, incidents of life, and energies of passion, as in his *Eloisa, Windsor Forest*, and the *Ethick Epistles*. He had *Judgement*, which selects from life or nature what the present purpose requires, and by separating the essence of things from its concomitants often makes the representation more powerful than the reality: and he had colours of language always before him, ready to decorate his matter with every grace of elegant expression, as when he accommodates his diction to the wonderful multiplicity of Homer's sentiments and descriptions.

Poetical expression includes sound as well as meaning; *Musick*, says Dryden, *is inarticulate poetry*; among the excellencies of Pope, therefore, must be mentioned the melody of his metre. By perusing the works of Dryden, he discovered the most perfect fabrick of English verse, and habituated himself to that only which he found the best; in consequence of which restraint his poetry has been censured as too uniformly musical, and as glutting the ear with unvaried sweetness. I suspect this objection to be the cant of those who judge by principles rather than perception; and who would even themselves have less pleasure in his works, if he had tried to relieve attention by studied discords, or affected to break his lines and vary his pauses.

.   .   .   .   .

It is remarked by Watts, that there is scarcely a happy combination of words, or a phrase poetically elegant in the English language, which Pope has not inserted into his version of Homer. How he obtained possession of so many beauties of speech, it were desirable to know. That he gleaned from authors, obscure as well as eminent, what he thought brilliant or useful, and preserved it all in a regular collection, is not unlikely. When, in his last years, Hall's *Satires* were shewn him, he wished that he had seen them sooner.

New sentiments and new images others may produce; but to attempt any further improvement of versification will be dangerous. Art and diligence have now done their best, and what shall be added will be the effort of tedious toil and needless curiosity.

After all this, it is surely superfluous to answer the question that has once been asked, Whether Pope was a poet? otherwise than by asking in return, If Pope be not a poet, where is poetry to be found? To circumscribe poetry by a definition will only shew the narrowness of the definer, though a definition which shall exclude Pope will not easily be made. Let us look round upon the present time, and back upon the past; let us enquire to whom the voice of mankind has decreed the wreath of poetry; let their productions be examined, and their claims stated, and the pretensions of Pope will be no more disputed. Had he given the world only his version, the name of poet must have been allowed him: if the writer of the *Iliad* were to class his successors, he would assign a very high place to his translator, without requiring any other evidence of Genius.

·　　　　·　　　　·　　　　·

On Mrs. CORBET,

who died of a Cancer in her Breast.

Here rests a woman, good without pretence,
Blest with plain reason, and with sober sense:
No conquests she, but o'er herself desir'd;
No arts essay'd, but not to be admir'd.
Passion and pride were to her soul unknown,
Convinc'd that Virtue only is our own.
So unaffected, so compos'd a mind,
So firm, yet soft, so strong, yet so refin'd,
Heaven, as its purest gold, by tortures try'd,
The saint sustain'd it, but the woman dy'd.

I have always considered this as the most valuable of all Pope's epitaphs; the subject of it is a character not discriminated by any shining or eminent peculiarities; yet that which really makes, though not the splendor, the felicity of life, and that which every wise man will choose for his final and lasting companion in the languor of age, in the quiet of privacy, when he departs weary and disgusted from the ostentatious, the volatile, and the vain. Of such a character, which the dull overlook, and the gay despise, it was fit that the value should be made known, and the dignity established. Domestic virtue, as it is exerted without great occasions, or conspicuous consequences, in an even unnoted tenor, required the genius of Pope to display it in such a manner as might attract regard, and enforce reverence. Who can forbear to lament that this amiable woman has no name in the verses?

If the particular lines of this inscription be examined, it will appear less faulty than the rest. There is scarce one line taken from common places, unless it be that in which *only Virtue* is said to be *our own*. I once heard a Lady of great beauty and elegance object to the fourth line, that it contained an unnatural and incredible panegyrick. Of this let the Ladies judge.

JAMES THOMSON

THE benevolence of Thomson was fervid, but not active; he would give, on all occasions, what assistance his purse would supply; but the offices of intervention or solicitation he could not conquer his sluggishness sufficiently to perform. The affairs of others, however, were not more neglected than his own. He had often felt the inconveniences of idleness, but he never cured it; and was so conscious of his own character, that he talked of writing an Eastern Tale of *The Man who Loved to be in Distress*.

As a writer he is entitled to one praise of the highest kind; his mode of thinking, and of expressing his thoughts, is original. His blank verse is no more the blank verse of Milton, or of any other poet, than the rhymes of Prior are the rhymes of Cowley. His numbers, his pauses, his diction, are of his own growth, without transcription, without imitation. He thinks in a peculiar train, and he thinks always as a man of genius; he looks round on Nature and on Life, with the eye which Nature bestows only on a poet; the eye that distinguishes, in every thing presented to its view, whatever there is on which imagination can delight to be detained, and with a mind that at once comprehends the vast, and attends to the minute. The reader of the *Seasons* wonders that he never saw before what Thomson shews him, and that he never yet has felt what Thomson impresses.

His is one of the works in which blank verse seems properly used; Thomson's wide expansion of general views, and his enumeration of circumstantial varieties, would have been obstructed and embarrassed by the frequent intersections of the sense, which are the necessary effects of rhyme.

His descriptions of extended scenes and general effects bring before us the whole magnificence of Nature, whether pleasing or dreadful. The gaiety of *Spring*, the splendour of *Summer*, the tranquillity of *Autumn*, and the horror of *Winter*, take in their turns possession of the mind. The poet leads us through the appearances of things as they are successively varied by the vicissitudes of the year, and imparts to us so much of his own enthusiasm, that our thoughts expand with his imagery, and kindle with his sentiments. Nor is the naturalist without his part in the entertainment; for he is assisted to recollect and to combine, to arrange his discoveries, and to amplify the sphere of his contemplation.

The great defect of the *Seasons* is want of method; but for this I know not that there was any remedy. Of many appearances subsisting all at once, no rule can be given why one should be mentioned before another; yet the memory wants the help of order, and the curiosity is not excited by suspense or expectation.

His diction is in the highest degree florid and luxuriant, such as may be said to be to his images and thoughts *both their lustre and their shade*; such as invests them with splendour, through which perhaps they are not always easily discerned. It is too exuberant, and sometimes may be charged with filling the ear more than the mind.

These Poems, with which I was acquainted at their first appearance, I have since found altered and enlarged by subsequent revisals, as the author supposed his judgement to grow more exact, and as books or conversation extended his knowledge and opened his prospects. They are, I think, improved in general; yet I know not whether they have not lost part of what Temple calls their *race*; a word which, applied to wines, in its primitive sense, means the flavour of the soil.

Liberty, when it first appeared, I tried to read, and soon desisted. I have never tried again, and therefore will not hazard either praise or censure.

The highest praise which he has received ought not to be supprest; it is said by Lord Lyttleton in the Prologue to his posthumous play, that his works contained

No line which, dying, he could wish to blot.

ISAAC WATTS

HE was one of the first authors that taught the Dissenters to court attention by the graces of language. Whatever they had among them before, whether of learning or acuteness, was commonly obscured and blunted by coarseness and inelegance of stile. He shewed them, that zeal and purity might be expressed and enforced by polished diction.

He continued to the end of his life the teacher of a congregation, and no reader of his works can doubt his fidelity or diligence. In the pulpit, though his low stature, which very little exceeded five feet, graced him with no advantages of appearance, yet the gravity and propriety of his utterance made his discourses very efficacious. I once mentioned the reputation which Mr. Foster had gained by his proper delivery to my friend Dr. Hawkesworth, who told me, that in the art of pronunciation he was far inferior to Dr. Watts.

Such was his flow of thoughts, and such his promptitude of language, that in the latter part of his life he did not precompose his cursory sermons; but having adjusted the heads, and sketched out some particulars, trusted for success to his extemporary powers.

He did not endeavour to assist his eloquence by any gesticulations; for, as no corporeal actions have any correspondence with theological truth, he did not see how they could enforce it.

At the conclusion of weighty sentences he gave time, by a short pause, for the proper impression.

To stated and publick instruction he added familiar visits and personal application, and was careful to improve the opportunities which conversation offered of diffusing and increasing the influence of religion.

By his natural temper he was quick of resentment; but, by his established and habitual practice, he was gentle, modest, and inoffensive. His tenderness appeared in his attention to children, and to the poor. To the poor, while he lived in the family of his friend, he allowed the third part of his annual revenue; and for children, he condescended to lay aside the scholar, the philosopher, and the wit, to write little poems of devotion, and systems of instruction, adapted to their wants and capacities, from the dawn of reason through its gradations of advance in the morning of life. Every man, acquainted with the common principles of human action, will look with veneration on the writer who is at one time combating Locke, and at another making a catechism for children in their fourth year. A voluntary descent from the dignity of science is perhaps the hardest lesson that humility can teach.

Few men have left behind such purity of character, or such monuments of laborious piety. He has provided instruction for all ages, from those who are lisping their first lessons, to the enlightened readers of Malbranche and Locke; he has left neither corporeal nor spiritual nature unexamined; he has taught the art of reasoning, and the science of the stars.

His character, therefore, must be formed from the multiplicity and diversity of his attainments rather than from any single performance; for it would not be safe to claim for him the highest rank in any single denomination of literary dignity; yet perhaps there was nothing in which he would not have excelled, if he had not divided his powers to different pursuits.

As a poet, had he been only a poet, he would probably have stood high among the authors with whom he is now associated. For his judgement was exact, and he noted beauties and faults with very nice discernment; his imagination, as the *Dacian Battle* proves, was vigorous and active, and the stores of knowledge were large by which his imagination was to be supplied. His ear was well-tuned, and his diction was elegant and copious. But his devotional poetry is, like that of others, unsatisfactory. The paucity of its topicks enforces perpetual repetition, and the sanctity of the matter rejects the ornaments of figurative diction. It is sufficient for Watts to have done better than others what no man has done well.

His poems on other subjects seldom rise higher than might be expected from the amusements of a Man of Letters, and have different degrees of value as they are more or less laboured, or as the occasion was more or less favourable to invention.

He writes too often without regular measures, and too often in blank verse; the rhymes are not always sufficiently correspondent. He is particularly unhappy in coining names expressive of characters. His lines are commonly smooth and easy, and his thoughts always religiously pure; but who is there that, to so much piety and innocence, does not wish for a greater measure of spriteliness and vigour? He is at least one of the few poets with whom youth and ignorance may be safely pleased; and happy will be that reader whose mind is disposed by his verses, or his prose, to imitate him in all but his non-conformity, to copy his benevolence to man, and his reverence to God.

WILLIAM COLLINS

ABOUT this time I fell into his company. His appearance was decent and manly; his knowledge considerable, his views extensive, his conversation elegant, and his disposition chearful. By degrees I gained his confidence; and one day was admitted to him when he was immured by a bailiff, that was prowling in the street. On this occasion recourse was had to the booksellers, who, on the credit of a translation of Aristotle's Poeticks, which he engaged to write with a large commentary, advanced as much money as enabled him to escape into the country. He shewed me the guineas safe in his hand. Soon afterwards his uncle, Mr. Martin, a lieutenant-colonel, left him about two thousand pounds; a sum which Collins could scarcely think exhaustible, and which he did not live to exhaust. The guineas were then repaid, and the translation neglected.

But man is not born for happiness. Collins, who, while he *studied to live,* felt no evil but poverty, no sooner *lived to study* than his life was assailed by more dreadful calamities, disease and insanity.

Having formerly written his character, while perhaps it was yet more distinctly impressed upon my memory, I shall insert it here.

"Mr. Collins was a man of extensive literature, and of vigorous faculties. He was acquainted not only with the learned tongues, but with the Italian, French, and Spanish languages. He had employed his mind chiefly upon works of fiction, and subjects of fancy; and by indulging some peculiar habits of thought, was eminently delighted with those flights of imagination which pass the bounds of nature, and to which the mind is reconciled only by a passive acquiescence in popular traditions. He loved fairies, genii, giants, and monsters; he delighted to rove through the meanders of inchantment, to gaze on the magnificence of golden palaces, to repose by the water-falls of Elysian gardens.

"This was however the character rather of his inclination than his genius; the grandeur of wildness, and the novelty of extravagance, were always desired by him, but were not always attained. Yet as diligence is never wholly lost; if his efforts sometimes caused harshness and obscurity, they likewise produced in happier moments sublimity and splendour. This idea which he had formed of excellence, led him to oriental fictions and allegorical imagery; and perhaps, while he was intent upon description, he did not sufficiently cultivate sentiment. His poems are the productions of a

2G

mind not deficient in fire, nor unfurnished with knowledge either of books or life, but somewhat obstructed in its progress by deviation in quest of mistaken beauties.

"His morals were pure, and his opinions pious: in a long continuance of poverty, and long habits of dissipation, it cannot be expected that any character should be exactly uniform. There is a degree of want by which the freedom of agency is almost destroyed; and long association with fortuitous companions will at last relax the strictness of truth, and abate the fervour of sincerity. That this man, wise and virtuous as he was, passed always unentangled through the snares of life, it would be prejudice and temerity to affirm; but it may be said that at least he preserved the source of action unpolluted, that his principles were never shaken, that his distinctions of right and wrong were never confounded, and that his faults had nothing of malignity or design, but proceeded from some unexpected pressure, or casual temptation.

"The latter part of his life cannot be remembered but with pity and sadness. He languished some years under that depression of mind which enchains the faculties without destroying them, and leaves reason the knowledge of right without the power of pursuing it. These clouds which he perceived gathering on his intellects, he endeavoured to disperse by travel, and passed into France; but found himself constrained to yield to his malady, and returned. He was for some time confined in a house of lunaticks, and afterwards retired to the care of his sister in Chichester, where death in 1756 came to his relief.

"After his return from France, the writer of this character paid him a visit at Islington, where he was waiting for his sister, whom he had directed to meet him: there was then nothing of disorder discernible in his mind by any but himself; but he had withdrawn from study, and travelled with no other book than an English Testament, such as children carry to the school: when his friend took it into his hand, out of curiosity to see what companion a Man of Letters had chosen, *I have but one book*, said Collins, *but that is the best*."

Such was the fate of Collins, with whom I once delighted to converse, and whom I yet remember with tenderness.

.   .   .   .   .

To what I have formerly said of his writings may be added, that his diction was often harsh, unskilfully laboured, and injudiciously selected. He affected the obsolete when it was not worthy of revival; and he puts his words out of the common order, seeming to think, with some later candidates for fame, that not to write prose is certainly to write poetry. His lines commonly are of slow motion, clogged and impeded with clusters of consonants. As men are often esteemed who cannot be loved, so the poetry of Collins may sometimes extort praise when it gives little pleasure.

WILLIAM SHENSTONE

Now began his delight in rural pleasures, and his ambition of rural elegance: he began from this time to point his prospects, to diversify his surface, to entangle his walks, and to wind his waters; which he did with such judgement and such fancy, as made his little domain the envy of the great, and the admiration of the skilful; a place to be visited by travellers, and copied by designers. Whether to plant a walk in undulating curves, and to place a bench at every turn where there is an object to catch the view; to make water run where it will be heard, and to stagnate where it will be seen; to leave intervals where the eye will be pleased, and to thicken the plantation where there is something to be hidden, demands any great powers of mind, I will not enquire; perhaps a sullen and surly speculator may think such performances rather the sport than the business of human reason. But it must be at least confessed, that to embellish the form of Nature is an innocent amusement; and some praise must be allowed by the most supercilious observer to him, who does best what such multitudes are contending to do well.

This praise was the praise of Shenstone; but, like all other modes of felicity, it was not enjoyed without its abatements. Lyttelton was his neighbour and his rival, whose empire, spacious and opulent, looked with disdain on the *petty State* that *appeared behind it.* For a while the inhabitants of Hagley affected to tell their acquaintance of the little fellow that was trying to make himself admired; but when by degrees the Leasowes forced themselves into notice, they took care to defeat the curiosity which they could not suppress, by conducting their visitants perversely to inconvenient points of view, and introducing them at the wrong end of a walk to detect a deception; injuries of which Shenstone would heavily complain. Where there is emulation there will be vanity, and where there is vanity there will be folly.

The pleasure of Shenstone was all in his eye; he valued what he valued merely for its looks; nothing raised his indignation more than to ask if there were any fishes in his water.

His house was mean, and he did not improve it; his care was of his grounds. When he came home from his walks he might find his floors flooded by a shower through a broken roof; but could spare no money for its reparation.

In time his expences brought clamours about him, that overpowered the lamb's bleat and the linnet's song; and his groves were haunted by beings very different from fawns and fairies. He spent his estate in adorning it, and his death was probably hastened by his anxieties. He was a lamp that spent its oil in blazing. It is said, that if he had lived a little longer he would have been assisted by a pension: such bounty could not have been ever more properly bestowed; but that it was ever asked is not certain; it is too certain that it never was enjoyed.

DAVID MALLET

Of David Mallet, having no written memorial, I am able to give no other account than such as is supplied by the unauthorised loquacity of common fame, and a very slight personal knowledge.

He was by his original one of the Macgregors, a clan that became, about sixty years ago, under the conduct of Robin Roy, so formidable and so infamous for violence and robbery, that the name was annulled by a legal abolition; and when they were all to denominate themselves anew, the father, I suppose, of this author called himself Malloch.

David Malloch was, by the penury of his parents, compelled to be *Janitor* of the High School at Edinburgh; a mean office, of which he did not afterwards delight to hear. But he surmounted the disadvantages of his birth and fortune; for when the duke of Montrose applied to the College of Edinburgh for a tutor to educate his sons, Malloch was recommended; and I never heard that he dishonoured his credentials.

When his pupils were sent to see the world, they were intrusted to his care; and having conducted them round the common circle of modish travels, he returned with them to London, where, by the influence of the family in which he resided, he naturally gained admission to many persons of the highest rank, and the highest character, to wits, nobles, and statesmen.

Of his works, I know not whether I can trace the series. His first production was *William and Margaret*; of which, though it contains nothing very striking or difficult, he has been envied the reputation; and plagiarism has been boldly charged, but never proved.

Not long afterwards he published the *Excursion* (1728); a desultory and capricious view of such scenes of Nature as his fancy led him, or his knowledge enabled him, to describe. It is not devoid of poetical spirit. Many of the images are striking, and many of the paragraphs are elegant. The cast of diction seems to be copied from Thomson, whose *Seasons* were then in their full blossom of reputation. He has Thomson's beauties and his faults.

His poem on *Verbal Criticism* (1733) was written to pay court to Pope, on a subject which he either did not understand or willingly misrepresented; and is little more than an improvement, or rather expansion, of a fragment which Pope printed in a Miscellany long before he engrafted it into a regular poem. There is in this piece more pertness than wit, and more confidence than knowledge. The versification is tolerable, nor can criticism allow it a higher praise.

His first tragedy was *Eurydice*, acted at Drury-Lane in 1731; of which I know not the reception nor the merit, but have heard it mentioned as a mean performance. He was not then too high to accept a Prologue and Epilogue from Aaron Hill, neither of which can be much commended.

Having cleared his tongue from his native pronunciation so as to be no longer distinguished as a Scot, he seems inclined to disencumber himself from all adherences of his original, and took upon him to change his name from Scotch *Malloch* to English *Mallet*, without any imaginable reason of preference which the eye or ear can discover. What other proofs he gave of disrespect to his native country I know not; but it was remarked of him, that he was the only Scot whom Scotchmen did not commend.

.   .   .   .   .

His stature was diminutive, but he was regularly formed; his appearance, till he grew corpulent, was agreeable, and he suffered it to want no recommendation that dress could give it. His conversation was elegant and easy. The rest of his character may, without injury to his memory, sink into silence.

MARK AKENSIDE

WHETHER, when he resolved not to be a dissenting minister, he ceased to be a Dissenter, I know not. He certainly retained an unnecessary and outrageous zeal for what he called and thought liberty; a zeal which sometimes disguises from the world, and not rarely from the mind which it possesses, an envious desire of plundering wealth or degrading greatness; and of which the immediate tendency is innovation and anarchy, an impetuous eagerness to subvert and confound, with very little care what shall be established.

Akenside was a young man, warm with every notion that by nature or accident had been connected with the sound of liberty, and by an excentricity which such dispositions do not easily avoid, a lover of contradiction, and no friend to any thing established. He adopted Shaftesbury's foolish assertion of the efficacy of ridicule for the discovery of truth. For this he was attacked by Warburton, and defended by Dyson: Warburton afterwards reprinted his remarks at the end of his dedication to the Freethinkers.

The result of all the arguments which have been produced in a long and eager discussion of this idle question, may easily be collected. If ridicule be applied to any position as the test of truth, it will then become a question whether such ridicule be just; and this can only be decided by the application of truth, as the test of ridicule. Two men, fearing, one a real and the other a fancied danger, will be for a while equally exposed to the inevitable consequences of cowardice, contemptuous censure, and ludicrous representation; and the true state of both cases must be known, before it can be decided whose terror is rational, and whose is ridiculous; who is to be pitied, and who to be despised.

Akenside is to be considered as a didactick and lyrick poet. His great work is the *Pleasures of Imagination*; a performance which, published, as it was, at the age of twenty-three, raised expectations which were not afterwards very amply satisfied. It has undoubtedly a just claim to very particular notice, as an example of great felicity of genius, and uncommon amplitude of acquisitions, of a young mind stored with images, and much exercised in combining and comparing them.

938

With the philosophical or religious tenets of the author I have nothing to do; my business is with his poetry. This subject is well-chosen, as it includes all images that can strike or please, and thus comprises every species of poetical delight. The only difficulty is in the choice of examples and illustrations, and it is not easy in such exuberance of matter to find the middle point between penury and satiety. The parts seem artificially disposed, with sufficient coherence, so as that they cannot change their places without injury to the general design.

His images are displayed with such luxuriance of expression, that they are hidden, like Butler's Moon, by a *Veil of Light*; they are forms fantastically lost under superfluity of dress. *Pars minima est ipsa Puella sui*. The words are multiplied till the sense is hardly perceived; attention deserts the mind, and settles in the ear. The reader wanders through the gay diffusion sometimes amazed, and sometimes delighted; but, after many turnings in the flowery labyrinth, comes out as he went in. He remarked little, and laid hold on nothing.

To his versification justice requires that praise should not be denied. In the general fabrication of his lines he is perhaps superior to any other writer of blank verse; his flow is smooth, and his pauses are musical; but the concatenation of his verses is commonly too long continued, and the full close does not recur with sufficient frequency. The sense is carried on through a long intertexture of complicated clauses, and as nothing is distinguished, nothing is remembered.

The exemption which blank verse affords from the necessity of closing the sense with the couplet, betrays luxuriant and active minds into such indulgence, that they pile image upon image, ornament upon ornament, and are not easily persuaded to close the sense at all. Blank verse will therefore, I fear, be too often found in description exuberant, in argument loquacious, and in narration tiresome.

His diction is certainly so far poetical as it is not prosaick, and so far valuable as it is not common. He is to be commended as having fewer artifices of disgust than most of his brethren of the blank song. He rarely either recalls old phrases or twists his metre into harsh inversions. The sense however of his words is strained; when *he views the* Ganges *from* Alpine *heights*; that is, from mountains like the Alps. And the pedant surely intrudes, but when was

939

blank verse without pedantry? when he tells how *Planets* absolve *the stated round of Time.*

. . . . .

His other poems are now to be considered; but a short consideration will dispatch them. It is not easy to guess why he addicted himself so diligently to lyrick poetry, having neither the ease and airiness of the lighter, nor the vehemence and elevation of the grander ode. When he lays his ill-fated hand upon his harp, his former powers seem to desert him; he has no longer his luxuriance of expression, nor variety of images. His thoughts are cold, and his words inelegant. Yet such was his love of lyricks, that, having written with great vigour and poignancy his *Epistle to Curio*, he transformed it afterwards into an ode disgraceful only to its author.

Of his odes nothing favourable can be said; the sentiments commonly want force, nature, or novelty; the diction is sometimes harsh and uncouth, the stanzas ill-constructed and unpleasant, and the rhymes dissonant, or unskilfully disposed, too distant from each other, or arranged with too little regard to established use, and therefore perplexing to the ear, which in a short composition has not time to grow familiar with an innovation.

To examine such compositions singly, cannot be required; they have doubtless brighter and darker parts: but when they are once found to be generally dull, all further labour may be spared; for to what use can the work be criticised that will not be read?

THOMAS GRAY

GRAY'S Poetry is now to be considered; and I hope not to be looked on as an enemy to his name, if I confess that I contemplate it with less pleasure than his life.

His ode on *Spring* has something poetical, both in the language and the thought; but the language is too luxuriant, and the thoughts have nothing new. There has of late arisen a practice of giving to adjectives, derived from substantives, the termination of participles; such as the *cultured* plain, the *dasied* bank; but I was sorry to see, in the lines of a scholar like Gray, the *honied* Spring. The morality is natural, but too stale; the conclusion is pretty.

The poem on the *Cat* was doubtless by its author considered as a trifle, but it is not a happy trifle. In the first stanza *the azure flowers* that *blow*, shew resolutely a rhyme is sometimes made when it cannot easily be found. *Selima*, the *Cat*, is called a nymph, with some violence both to language and sense; but there is good use made of it when it is done; for of the two lines,

> What female heart can gold despise?
> What cat's averse to fish?

the first relates merely to the nymph, and the second only to the cat. The sixth stanza contains a melancholy truth, that *a favourite has no friend*; but the last ends in a pointed sentence of no relation to the purpose; if *what glistered* had been *gold*, the cat would not have gone into the water; and, if she had, would not less have been drowned.

The *Prospect of Eaton College* suggests nothing to Gray, which every beholder does not equally think and feel. His supplication to father *Thames*, to tell him who drives the hoop or tosses the ball, is useless and puerile. Father *Thames* has no better means of knowing than himself. His epithet *buxom health* is not elegant; he seems not to understand the word. Gray thought his language more poetical as it was more remote from common use: finding in Dryden *honey redolent of Spring*, an expression that reaches the utmost limits of our language, Gray drove it a little more beyond common apprehension, by making *gales* to be *redolent of joy and youth*.

Of the *Ode on Adversity*, the hint was at first taken from *O Diva, gratum quæ regis Antium*; but Gray has excelled his original by the variety of his sentiments, and by their moral application. Of this piece, at once poetical and rational, I will not by slight objections violate the dignity.

My process has now brought me to the *wonderful Wonder of Wonders*, the two Sister Odes; by which, though either vulgar ignorance or common sense at first universally rejected them, many have been since persuaded to think themselves delighted. I am one of those that are willing to be pleased, and therefore would gladly find the meaning of the first stanza of *The Progress of Poetry*.

Gray seems in his rapture to confound the images of *spreading sound* and *running water*. A *stream of musick* may be allowed; but where does *Musick*, however *smooth and strong*, after having visited the *verdant vales, rowl down the steep amain*, so as that *rocks and nodding groves rebellow to the roar*? If this be said of *Musick*, it is nonsense; if it be said of *Water*, it is nothing to the purpose.

The second stanza, exhibiting Mars's car and Jove's eagle, is unworthy of further notice. Criticism disdains to chase a school-boy to his common places.

To the third it may likewise be objected, that it is drawn from Mythology, though such as may be more easily assimilated to real life. Idalia's *velvet-green* has something of cant. An epithet or metaphor drawn from Nature ennobles Art; an epithet or metaphor drawn from Art degrades Nature. Gray is too fond of words arbitrarily compounded. *Many-twinkling* was formerly censured as not analogical; we may say *many-spotted*, but scarcely *many-spotting*. This stanza, however, has something pleasing.

Of the second ternary of stanzas, the first endeavours to tell something, and would have told it, had it not been crossed by Hyperion: the second describes well enough the universal prevalence of Poetry; but I am afraid that the conclusion will not rise from the premises. The caverns of the North and the plains of Chili are not the residences of *Glory* and *generous Shame*. But that Poetry and Virtue go always together is an opinion so pleasing, that I can forgive him who resolves to think it true.

The third stanza sounds big with *Delphi*, and *Egean*, and *Ilissus*, and *Meander*, and *hallowed fountain* and *solemn sound*; but in all Gray's odes there is a kind of cumbrous splendor which we wish away. His position is at last false: in the time of Dante and Petrarch, from whom he derives our first school of Poetry, Italy was over-run by *tyrant power* and *coward vice*; nor was our state much better when we first borrowed the Italian arts.

Of the third ternary, the first gives a mythological birth of Shakespeare. What is said of that mighty genius is true; but it is not said happily: the real effects of his poetical power are put out of sight by the pomp of machinery. Where truth is sufficient to fill the mind, fiction is worse than useless; the counterfeit debases the genuine.

His account of Milton's blindness, if we suppose it caused by study in the formation of his poem, a supposition surely allowable, is poetically true, and happily imagined. But the *car* of Dryden, with his *two coursers*, has nothing in it peculiar; it is a car in which any other rider may be placed.

The Bard appears, at the first view, to be, as Algarotti and others have remarked, an imitation of the prophecy of Nereus. Algarotti thinks it superior to its original; and, if preference depends only on the imagery and animation of the two poems, his judgement is right. There is in *The Bard* more force, more thought, and more variety. But to copy is less than to invent, and the copy has been unhappily produced at a wrong time. The fiction of Horace was to the Romans credible; but its revival disgusts us with apparent and unconquerable falsehood. *Incredulus odi.*

To select a singular event, and swell it to a giant's bulk by fabulous appendages of spectres and predictions, has little difficulty, for he that forsakes the probable may always find the marvellous; and it has little use, we are affected only as we believe; we are improved only as we find something to be imitated or declined. I do not see that *The Bard* promotes any truth, moral or political.

His stanzas are too long, especially his epodes; the ode is finished before the ear has learned its measures, and consequently before it can receive pleasure from their consonance and recurrence.

Of the first stanza the abrupt beginning has been celebrated; but technical beauties can give praise only to the inventor. It is in the power of any man to rush abruptly upon his subject, that has read the ballad of *Johnny Armstrong.*

Is there ever a man in all Scotland—

The initial resemblances, or alliterations, *ruin, ruthless, helm nor hauberk,* are below the grandeur of a poem that endeavours at sublimity.

In the second stanza the *Bard* is well described; but in the third we have the puerilities of obsolete mythology. When we are told that *Cadwallo hush'd the stormy main,* and that *Modred* made *huge Plinlimmon bow his cloud-top'd head,* attention recoils from the repetition of a tale that, even when it was first heard, was heard with scorn.

The *weaving* of the *winding sheet* he borrowed, as he owns, from the northern Bards; but their texture, however, was very properly the work of female powers, as the art of spinning the thread of life in another mythology. Theft is always dangerous; Gray has made weavers of his slaughtered bards, by a fiction outrageous and incongruous. They are then called upon to *Weave the warp, and weave the woof,* perhaps with no great propriety; for it is by crossing the *woof* with the *warp* that men *weave* the *web* or piece; and the first line was dearly bought by the admission of its wretched correspondent, *Give ample room and verge enough.* He has, however, no other line as bad.

The third stanza of the second ternary is commended, I think, beyond its merit. The personification is indistinct. *Thirst* and

943

Hunger are not alike; and their features, to make the imagery perfect, should have been discriminated. We are told, in the same stanza, how *towers* are *fed*. But I will no longer look for particular faults; yet let it be observed that the ode might have been concluded with an action of better example; but suicide is always to be had, without expence of thought.

These odes are marked by glittering accumulations of ungraceful ornaments; they strike, rather than please; the images are magnified by affectation; the language is laboured into harshness. The mind of the writer seems to work with unnatural violence. *Double, double, toil and trouble.* He has a kind of strutting dignity, and is tall by walking on tiptoe. His art and his struggle are too visible, and there is too little appearance of ease and nature.

To say that he has no beauties, would be unjust: a man like him, of great learning and great industry, could not but produce something valuable. When he pleases least, it can only be said that a good design was ill directed.

His translations of Northern and Welsh Poetry deserve praise; the imagery is preserved, perhaps often improved; but the language is unlike the language of other poets.

In the character of his Elegy I rejoice to concur with the common reader; for by the common sense of readers uncorrupted with literary prejudices, after all the refinements of subtilty and the dogmatism of learning, must be finally decided all claim to poetical honours. The *Church-yard* abounds with images which find a mirrour in every mind, and with sentiments to which every bosom returns an echo. The four stanzas beginning *Yet even these bones*, are to me original: I have never seen the notions in any other place; yet he that reads them here, persuades himself that he has always felt them. Had Gray written often thus, it had been vain to blame, and useless to praise him.

GEORGE LYTTELTON

ABOUT this time Lyttelton published his *Dialogues of the Dead*, which were very eagerly read, though the production rather, as it seems, of leisure than of study, rather effusions than compositions. The names of his persons too often enable the reader to anticipate their conversation; and when they have met, they too often part without any conclusion. He has copied *Fenelon* more than *Fontenelle*.

When they were first published they were kindly commended by the *Critical Reviewers*; and poor Lyttelton, with humble gratitude, returned his acknowledgements in a note which I have read; acknowledgements either for flattery or justice.

When, in the latter part of the last reign, the inauspicious commencement of the war made the dissolution of the ministry unavoidable, Sir George Lyttelton, losing his employment, with the rest, was recompensed with a peerage; and rested from political turbulence in the House of Lords.

His last literary production was his *History of Henry the Second*, elaborated by the searches and deliberations of twenty years, and published with such anxiety as only vanity can dictate.

The story of this publication is remarkable. The whole work was printed twice over, a great part of it three times, and many sheets four or five times. The booksellers paid for the first impression; but the charges and repeated operations of the Press were at the expence of the author, whose ambitious accuracy is known to have cost him at least a thousand pounds. He began to print in 1755. Three volumes appeared in 1764, a second edition of them in 1767, a third edition in 1768, and the conclusion in 1771.

Andrew Reid, a man not without considerable abilities, and not unacquainted with letters or with life, undertook to persuade Lyttelton, as he had persuaded himself, that he was master of the secret of punctuation; and, as fear begets credulity, he was employed, I know not at what price, to point the pages of *Henry the Second*. The book was at last pointed and printed, and sent into the world. Lyttelton took money for his copy, of which, when he had paid the *Pointer*, he probably gave the rest away; for he was very liberal to the indigent.

When time brought the History to a third edition, Reid was either dead or discarded; and the superintendence of typography and punctuation was committed to a man originally a combmaker, but then known by the stile of Dr. Saunders. Something uncommon was probably expected, and something uncommon was at last done; for to the edition of Dr. Saunders is appended, what the world had hardly seen before, a list of errors of nineteen pages.

A SHORT SONG
OF CONGRATULATION

The text of this poem, first printed in Mrs. Piozzi's *Anecdotes*, in 1786, is taken from the manuscript in the Huntington Library, California, U.S.A. Many versions, with numerous variations, exist. It seems likely that the version which A. E. Housman knew was that which reads, in line 17,

> Wealth, my lad, was made to wander.

Note by G. M. Young

"Housman was staying one week-end with W. P. Ker in All Souls. After breakfast on Sunday they were standing in the garden together. W. P. K. waved to me to join them. As I came up, they were talking about Johnson's verses, and Housman said either 'That poem started the *Shropshire Lad*' or (more nearly, I think) 'That poem was in my mind when I was starting the *Shropshire Lad*'. That the verb was *start* I am quite sure, but my memory will not guarantee the context."

A SHORT

SONG OF CONGRATULATION

To Sir John Lade

Long-expected one and twenty
Ling'ring year at last is flown,
Pomp and Pleasure, Pride and Plenty
Great Sir John, are all your own.

Loosen'd from the Minor's tether,
Free to mortgage or to sell,
Wild as wind, and light as feather
Bid the slaves of thrift farewell.

Call the Bettys, Kates, and Jennys
Ev'ry name that laughs at Care,
Lavish of your Grandsire's guineas,
Show the Spirit of an heir.

All that prey on vice and folly
Joy to see their quarry fly,
Here the Gamester light and jolly
There the Lender grave and sly.

Wealth, Sir John, was made to wander
Let it wander as it will;
See the Jocky, see the Pander,
Bid them come, and take their fill.

When the bonny Blade carouses,
Pockets full, and Spirits high,
What are acres? What are houses?
Only dirt, or wet or dry

A SHORT SONG OF CONGRATULATION

If the Guardian or the Mother,
Tell the woes of wilful waste,
Scorn their counsel and their pother,
You can hang or drown at last.

LINES
WRITTEN IN RIDICULE

The first printed version of this parody of Thomas Warton is in Mrs. Piozzi's *Anecdotes*, 1786. This text is taken from that printed in *Thraliana* (1941), p. 209.

LINES

WRITTEN IN RIDICULE OF CERTAIN POEMS

PUBLISHED IN 1777

WHERESOE'ER I turn my View,
All is strange, yet nothing new;
Endless Labour all along,
Endless Labour to be wrong;
Phrase that Time has flung away,
Uncouth Words in Disarray:
Trickt in Antique Ruff and Bonnet,
Ode and Elegy and Sonnet.

ON THE DEATH OF
DR. ROBERT LEVET

Of the numerous versions of this poem, the first printed one, from *The Gentleman's Magazine*, August, 1783, p. 695, col. 1, has been chosen. The text has been checked with that of the *Works*, 1787 (vol. 2, pp. 365–6) and *Thraliana*, pp. 532–3.

ON THE DEATH OF

DR. ROBERT LEVET

Condemn'd to hope's delusive mine,
  As on we toil from day to day,
By sudden blasts, or slow decline,
  Our social comforts drop away.

Well tried through many a varying year,
  See LEVET to the grave descend;
Officious, innocent, sincere,
  Of ev'ry friendless name the friend.

Yet still he fills affection's eye,
  Obscurely wise, and coarsely kind;
Nor, letter'd arrogance, deny
  Thy praise to merit unrefin'd.

When fainting nature call'd for aid,
  And hov'ring death prepar'd the blow,
His vig'rous remedy display'd
  The power of art without the show.

In misery's darkest caverns known,
  His useful care was ever nigh,
Where hopeless anguish pour'd his groan,
  And lonely want retir'd to die.

No summons mock'd by chill delay,
  No petty gain disdain'd by pride,
The modest wants of ev'ry day
  The toil of ev'ry day supplied.

His virtues walk'd their narrow round,
    Nor made a pause, nor left a void;
And sure th' Eternal Master found
    The single talent well employ'd.

The busy day, the peaceful night,
    Unfelt, uncounted, glided by;
His frame was firm, his powers were bright,
    Tho' now his eightieth year was nigh.

Then with no throbbing fiery pain,
    No cold gradations of decay,
Death broke at once the vital chain,
    And forc'd his soul the nearest way.

IN RIVUM
A MOLA STOANA
LICHFELDIÆ
DIFFLUENTEM

The text of this poem is that of Johnson's *Works*, 1787, vol. 2, p. 389.

IN RIVUM
A MOLA STOANA
LICHFELDIÆ
DIFFLUENTEM

Errat adhuc vitreus per prata virentia rivus,
  Quo toties lavi membra tenella puer;
Hic delusa rudi frustrabar brachia motu,
  Dum docuit blanda voce natare pater.
Fecerunt rami latebras, tenebrisque diurnis
  Pendula secretas abdidit arbor aquas.
Nunc veteres duris periere securibus umbræ,
  Longinquisque oculis nuda lavacra patent.
Lympha tamen cursus agit indefessa perennis,
  Tectaque qua fluxit, nunc et aperta fluit.
Quid ferat externi velox, quid deterat ætas,
  Tu quoque securus res age, Nise, tuas.